THE CAMBRIDGE HISTORY OF RELIGIONS IN THE ANCIENT WORLD

VOLUME I

From the Bronze Age to the Hellenistic Age

The Cambridge History of Religions in the Ancient World provides a comprehensive and in-depth analysis of the religions of the ancient Near East and Mediterranean world. The fourteen essays in Volume I begin in the third millennium BCE with the Sumerians and extend to the fourth century BCE through the fall of the Achaemenid Persian empire and the demise of Alexander the Great. Its contributors, all acknowledged experts in their fields, analyze a wide spectrum of textual and material evidence. An introductory essay by the General Editor, Michele Renee Salzman, sets out the central questions, themes, and historical trends considered in Volumes I and II. Marvin A. Sweeney provides an introduction to the chapters of Volume I, as does William Adler for Volume II. The regional and historical orientations of the essays will enable readers to see how a religious tradition or movement assumed a distinctive local identity, even as they view its development within a comparative framework. Supplemented with maps, illustrations, and detailed indexes, the volumes are an excellent reference tool for scholars of the ancient Near East and Mediterranean world.

Michele Renee Salzman is University of California Presidential Chair (2009–2012) and Professor of History at the University of California, Riverside. She is the author of three books and numerous articles, including *On Roman Time: The Codex-Calendar of 354 and the Rhythms of Urban Life in Late Antiquity* (1990); *The Making of a Christian Aristocracy* (2002); and *The Letters of Symmachus: Book 1*, translation (with Michael Roberts), Introduction, and Commentary (2011). She is on the Editorial Board of the *American Journal of Archaeology* and has served on the Executive Committee of the American Academy in Rome.

Marvin A. Sweeney is Professor of Religion at the Claremont School of Theology. He is the author of nine volumes and numerous studies, including *1 and 2 Kings: A Commentary* (2007) and *Form and Intertextuality in Prophetic and Apocalyptic Literature* (2005). He is the Editor of *Hebrew Studies*, the founding Editor of the *Review of Biblical Literature*, Co-editor of the *Forms of the Old Testament Literature* commentary series, Mitarbeiter for the *De Gruyter International Encyclopedia of the Bible*, and CEO of 'Ancient Biblical Manuscript Center for Preservation and Research.

THE CAMBRIDGE HISTORY OF RELIGIONS IN THE ANCIENT WORLD

VOLUME I

FROM THE BRONZE AGE TO THE HELLENISTIC AGE

Edited by

Michele Renee Salzman
General Editor
University of California, Riverside

Marvin A. Sweeney
Claremont School of Theology

CAMBRIDGE
UNIVERSITY PRESS

University Printing House, Cambridge CB2 8BS, United Kingdom

One Liberty Plaza, 20th Floor, New York, NY 10006, USA

477 Williamstown Road, Port Melbourne, VIC 3207, Australia

314-321, 3rd Floor, Plot 3, Splendor Forum, Jasola District Centre, New Delhi - 110025, India

79 Anson Road, #06-04/06, Singapore 079906

Cambridge University Press is part of the University of Cambridge.

It furthers the University's mission by disseminating knowledge in the pursuit of
education, learning and research at the highest international levels of excellence.

www.cambridge.org
Information on this title: www.cambridge.org/9781108703130

© Cambridge University Press 2013

This publication is in copyright. Subject to statutory exception
and to the provisions of relevant collective licensing agreements,
no reproduction of any part may take place without the written
permission of Cambridge University Press.

First published 2013
First paperback edition 2018

A catalogue record for this publication is available from the British Library

Library of Congress Cataloging in Publication data
The Cambridge history of religions in the ancient world: from the Bronze
Age to the Hellenistic Age / [edited by] Michele Renee Salzman, Marvin A. Sweeney.
p. cm.
Includes bibliographical references and indexes.
ISBN 978-1-107-01999-7 (hardback set) –
ISBN 978-0-521-85830-4 (volume 1) – ISBN 978-0-521-85831-1 (volume 2)
1. Religions. 2. Civilization, Ancient. I. Salzman, Michele Renee,
1953– II. Sweeney, Marvin A. (Marvin Alan).
BL96.C363 2012
200.93–dc23 2011049012

ISBN 978-0-521-85830-4 Volume I Hardback
ISBN 978-0-521-85831-1 Volume II Hardback
ISBN 978-1-107-01999-7 Two-volume Hardback
ISBN 978-1-108-70313-0 Paperback

Cambridge University Press has no responsibility for the persistence or
accuracy of URLs for external or third-party internet websites referred to in
this publication, and does not guarantee that any content on such websites is,
or will remain, accurate or appropriate.

CONTENTS

List of Figures and Maps	*page* vii
List of Contributors	ix
List of Abbreviations	xi
Acknowledgments	xiii

Introduction to Volumes I and II	I
MICHELE RENEE SALZMAN, GENERAL EDITOR	
Introduction to Volume I	23
MARVIN A. SWEENEY, EDITOR	

Part I. Mesopotamia and the Near East

1.	Sumerian Religion	31
	GRAHAM CUNNINGHAM	
2.	Assyrian and Babylonian Religions	54
	TAMMI J. SCHNEIDER	
3.	Hittite Religion	84
	GARY BECKMAN	
4.	Zoroastrianism	102
	PRODS OKTOR SKJÆRVØ	
5.	Syro-Canaanite Religions	129
	DAVID P. WRIGHT	
6.	Israelite and Judean Religions	151
	MARVIN A. SWEENEY	

v

Part II. Egypt and North Africa

7. Egyptian Religion 177
DENISE M. DOXEY

8. Phoenician-Punic Religion 205
PHILIP C. SCHMITZ

Part III. Greece and the Eastern Mediterranean

9. Minoan Religion 237
NANNO MARINATOS

10. Mycenaean Religion 256
IAN RUTHERFORD

11. Archaic and Classical Greek Religion 280
EMILY KEARNS

Part IV. The Western Mediterranean and Europe

12. Etruscan Religion 309
NANCY T. DE GRUMMOND

13. Roman Religion through the Early Republic 336
JÖRG RÜPKE

14. Celtic Religion in Western and Central Europe 364
DOROTHY WATTS

Suggestions for Further Reading 387
General Index 393
Index of Citations 441
    Textual and Material Sources 441
    Scriptural Sources 448

FIGURES AND MAPS

FIGURES

1.	Uruk (Warka) vase	*page* 42
2.	Representation of Ra from the temple of Ramesses III, Medinet Habu, dynasty 20	180
3.	Osiris and king Amenhotep II from the tomb of Amenhotep II, Thebes, dynasty 18	182
4.	The sun-god in the form of the beetle, Khepri, from the White Chapel of Senwosret I, Thebes, dynasty 12	185
5.	Procession of the solar barque, from the temple of Ramesses III, Medinet Habu, dynasty 20	189
6.	Pylon of the temple of Ramesses III, Medinet Habu, dynasty 20, showing the king smiting foreign enemies	190
7.	Senwosret I and his *ka,* from the White Chapel of Senwosret I, Thebes, dynasty 12	196
8.	Step pyramid complex of Djoser at Saqqara, dynasty 3	199
9.	Mastaba complex of Senedjemib family, Giza, dynasty 5	200
10.	Punic priest officiating at altar	214
11.	Plaque inscribed with eleven lines in Punic	215
12.	King accompanied by griffin	243
13.	Divine palace. Ring from Poros, Crete	245
14.	Man shaking tree and woman dancing; scene of ecstatic divination. Ring from Vapheio, Peloponnese	245
15.	Wounded girl. Mural from Thera (Santorini)	248
16.	Woman leaning over a stone; scene of estatic divination. Ring from Hagia Triada, Crete	249
17.	Goddess and young god or king greeting each other under a solar sign. Ring from Thebes	251

viii *Figures and Maps*

18. Seated goddess receiving offerings from lion-creatures under sun and moon. Gold ring from Tiryns 251
19. God (?) in a boat attacking Leviathan-type sea monster. Ring impression from Knossos (slightly restored) 253
20. Sacrificial procession from Pitsa, near ancient Sikyon, ca.540–530 BCE 292
21. Plan and reconstruction of the Argive Heraion, a major extra-urban sanctuary built on a terraced slope 295
22. Libation at an altar. Attic red-figure oinochoe (wine jug) ca.480 BCE 300
23. Bronze model of a sheep's liver 312
24. Bronze Etruscan mirror with scene of Pava Tarchies reading a liver in the presence of Avl Tarchunus 313
25. Model of the city of Rome 338
26. Terracotta figures of Herakles (Hercules) and Athena from the Temple of Mater Matuta in the Forum Boarium 340

MAPS

1. Mesopotamia and Persia 55
2. Anatolia and Syria 85
3. Egypt and Canaan 130
4. Israel and Judah 152
5. The western Mediterranean 206
6. The Aegean 238
7. Etruscan Italy 311
8. Central Italy 312
9. Rome 337
10. Celtic Europe 365

CONTRIBUTORS

Gary Beckman is Professor of Hittite and Mesopotamian Studies at the University of Michigan and studies the reception and adaptation of Syro-Mesopotamian culture by the Hittites of ancient Anatolia. He is currently completing an edition of the tablets of the Epic of Gilgamesh recovered at the site of the Hittite capital, Hattusa.

Graham Cunningham is a Research Fellow at the University of Cambridge. He specializes in the cultural and linguistic history of the ancient Middle East and is the author of *Deliver Me from Evil: Mesopotamian Incantations 2500–1500 BC* (Pontifical Biblical Institute, 1997). He has also published on religious studies from a more interdisciplinary perspective as in *Religion and Magic: Approaches and Theories* (Edinburgh University Press, 1999).

Nancy T. de Grummond is the M. Lynette Thompson Distinguished Research Professor at Florida State University. She was named Charles Eliot Norton Lecturer for the Archaeological Institute of America for 2011–2012.

Denise M. Doxey is Curator, Ancient Egyptian, Nubian and Near Eastern Art at the Museum of Fine Arts, Boston. She is the co-curator of the recent exhibition *The Secrets of Tomb 10A: Egypt 2000 BC* and co-author of the accompanying catalog.

Emily Kearns is a Senior Research Fellow at St Hilda's College, University of Oxford. Her most recent book is *Ancient Greek Religion: A Sourcebook* (Wiley-Blackwell, 2010).

Nanno Marinatos is Professor of Classics at the University of Illinois at Chicago and author of *Minoan Religion* (1993) and *Minoan Kingship and the Solar Goddess* (2010).

Jörg Rüpke is Fellow for History of Religion at the Max Weber Centre of the University of Erfurt and co-director of the research team "Religious Individualisation in Historical Perspective." He has recently been appointed Honorary Professor of the University of Aarhus (Denmark).

Ian Rutherford is Professor of Classics at the University of Reading. He is the author of *Pindar's Paeans: A Reading of the Fragments with a Survey of the Genre* (Oxford, 2001) and a co-editor of *Seeing the Gods: Pilgrimage in Greco-Roman and Early Christian Antiquity* (Oxford, 2006) (with Jas Elsner) and *Anatolian Interfaces: Hittites, Greeks and Their Neighbours,* Proceedings of an International Conference on Cross-cultural Interaction, September 17–19, 2004, Emory University, Atlanta, Georgia (Oxbow Books, 2008) (with M. Bachvarova and B.-J. Collins).

Philip C. Schmitz is Professor of History at Eastern Michigan University. He specializes in Northwest Semitic epigraphy and is a member of the editorial advisory boards of *Carthage Studies* (Ghent) and *Studi Epigrafici e Linguistici sul Vicino Oriente Antico* (Verona). He was assistant editor of the *Anchor Bible Dictionary* and editor of the *Index to Book Reviews in Religion.*

Tammi J. Schneider is Professor of Religion in the School of Religion at Claremont Graduate University. Her most recent book is *An Introduction to Ancient Mesopotamian Religion* (Eerdmans, 2011).

Prods Oktor Skjærvø is Aga Khan Professor of Iranian at Harvard University. His most recent books are *The Spirit of Zoroastrianism,* containing translations of Zoroastrian texts (Yale University Press, 2012), and *Manikeiske skrifter,* translations with E. Thomassen (Bokklubben, 2011).

Dorothy Watts is an Honorary Research Consultant and a former Head of Classics and Ancient History at the University of Queensland. She is a Fellow of the Society of Antiquaries of London and a Fellow of the Australian College of Educators. Her most recent book is *Boudicca's Heirs: Women in Early Britain* (Routledge, 2005).

David P. Wright is Professor of Hebrew Bible and Ancient Near East at Brandeis University. His most recent book is *Inventing God's Law: How the Covenant Code of the Bible Used and Revised the Laws of Hammurabi* (Oxford, 2009).

ABBREVIATIONS

Agora	*The Athenian Agora: Results of the Excavations Conducted by the American School of Classical Studies in Athens* (Princeton, 1951–).
ANEP	J. B. Pritchard, *The Ancient Near East in Pictures* (Princeton, 1969).
ANET	J. B. Pritchard, *Ancient Near Eastern Texts Relating to the Old Testament* (Princeton, 1969).
CAT	M. Dietrich, O. Loretz, and J. Sanmartín, *The Cuneiform Alphabetic* Texts *from Ugarit, Ras Ibn Hani and Other Places* (Münster, 1995) (second edition of 1976 German edition).
CIS	*Corpus Inscriptionum Semiticarum* (Paris, 1881–1962).
CMS	F. Matz, H. Biesantz, and I. Pini, eds., *Corpus der minoischen und mykenischen Siegel* (Berlin, 1964–).
COS	W. W. Hallow and K. L. Younger, eds., *The Context of Scripture* (Leiden, 2003).
CTH	Emmanuel Laroche, *Catalogue des texts Hittites* (Études et commentaries 75; Paris: Klincksieck, 1971).
DCSL	*The Diachronic Corpus of Sumerian Literature* (http://etcsl.orinst.ox.ac.uk/).
DMG	M. Ventris and J. Chadwick, *Documents in Mycenaean Greek*, 2nd ed. (1973).
DMic	Francisco Aura Jorro, *Diccionario micénico*, 2 vols. (Madrid, 1985–1993).
ETCSL	*The Electronic Text Corpus of Sumerian Literature* (http://dcsl.orinst.ox.ac.uk/).
FGrH	Felix Jacoby (ed.), *Die Fragmente der griechischen Historiker*, 3 vols. (Berlin and Leiden, 1923–1958).
IG	*Inscriptiones Graecae* (Berlin, 1973–).

KAI	H. Donner and W. Röllig, *Kanaanäische und aramäische Inschriften* (Wiesbaden, 1966–1969).
ILLRP	*Inscriptiones Latinae Liberae Rei Publica*, ed. A. Degrassi, vol. 1, 2nd ed. (Florence, 1965), 2 (Rome, 1963).
KUB	Keilschrift-urkunden aus Boghazköi.
LSAM	F. Sokolowski, *Lois sacrées de l'Asie mineure* (1955).
LSCG	F. Sokolowski, *Lois sacrées des cités grecques* (1969).
LSS	F. Sokolowski, *Lois sacrées: supplement* (1962).
NGSL	E. Lupu, *Greek Sacred Law: A Collection of New Documents* (Leiden, 2005).
RIB	R. G. Collingwood and R. P. Wright, *The Roman Inscriptions of Britain* (Oxford, 1965).
Rix *ET*	Helmut Rix, *Etruskische Texte, Editio Minor*, 2 vols. (Tübingen, 1991).
Syll.	W. Dittenberger, *Sylloge inscriptionum Graecarum*, 3rd ed. (Leipzig, 1915–1924).
ThesCRA	*Thesaurus Caltus et Rituum Antiquorum*, 5 vols. (Oxford, 2005–2006).
TLE	Massimo Pallottino, ed., *Testimonia linguae Etruscae* (Florence, 1968).

ACKNOWLEDGMENTS

In a project as large as this one, there are numerous people and institutions whose support must be acknowledged. I appreciate the professionalism of the volume editors and contributors. At various stages in the realization of this project, external advisers have been critical. I want to thank David Frankfurter, James Rives, Francesca Rochberg, and Karen Torjesen for their advice on a wide variety of issues. I want to note here the support given to me by the Institute for Advanced Studies, Jerusalem, as a Visiting Scholar in spring 2010, where I benefited from its resources and the conversation of a group of sophisticated scholars in religion, most especially that of Oded Irshai and Brouria Ashkeloni. Ingrid De Haas has been an invaluable assistant in the preparation of Volume I and its index, and Matthew (Alex) Poulos and Ann Rives for Volume II. Throughout this project, Beatrice Rehl has been an inspiring editor; the volumes have benefited tremendously from her astute advice, and I appreciate her fine editorial instincts and intelligence in helping me to steer this project through the dangers of Scylla and Charybdis. Finally, I want to thank my husband, Steven Brint, and my children, Ben and Juliana, for their love and encouragement in all things.

Michele Renee Salzman

INTRODUCTION TO VOLUMES I AND II

MICHELE RENEE SALZMAN

DEFINING ANCIENT RELIGION

"Religion" is not a native term; it is a term created by scholars for their intellectual purposes and therefore is theirs to define. It is a second-order, generic concept that plays the same role in establishing a disciplinary horizon that a concept such as "language" plays in linguistics or "culture" plays in anthropology. There can be no disciplined study of religion without such a horizon.[1]

Any effort to define religion in the ancient Mediterranean world is constrained from the very outset by the absence of a single-word equivalent in the ancient languages. The English word "religion" does not convey the same meaning as the Latin word from which it is derived. *Religio* is "a supernatural feeling of constraint, usually having the force of a prohibition or impediment" or "a positive obligation or rule."[2] This latter sense is reflected in the importance attached to required ritual among the Romans, who generally associated it with active worship according to the rules. Christian authors were ambivalent about the suitability of the word to their own beliefs and practices. In the third century, the Christian apologist Lactantius continued to use the word *religio* to describe the tie between god and man.[3] But Augustine later found the word problematic because it could also refer to an obligation owed to another human or to a god or gods. Hence, Augustine wrote, using the term *religio* "does not secure against ambiguity when used in discussing the worship paid to God"; and so it was possible to employ this term only by abolishing

---

[1] Smith, "Religion, Religions, Religious," 193–4.
[2] *Oxford Latin Dictionary*, s.v. *religio 1. and b.*
[3] Lactantius, *Inst.* 4.28; Bremmer, "'Religion,' 'Ritual,' and the Opposition 'Sacred vs. Profane,'" 10.

one meaning of the word, namely, the observance of duties in human relationships.[4]

I mention Augustine's reflections on the problems of finding the right terminology to express his notion of his faith and rituals directed toward the one true Christian God, because his redefinition of *religio* has helped to shape modern usage. One standard contemporary dictionary, reminiscent of Augustine's understanding, defines religion as "the belief in and worship of a superhuman controlling power, especially a personal God or gods," or "a particular system of faith and worship."[5] As J. Rüpke has observed, even more inclusive descriptions of religion as "an active response by human beings to the call of the sacred," or as "an experience of the numinous," "merely ... substitute a less specific term, albeit quasi-Christian or para-Christian, for the Christian God."[6] Increasingly, historians have come to understand how modern notions of religion have been shaped by the European religious tradition and the efforts of theologians to find in the term "religion" a means by which they "could claim [Christianity] to be a special form of a much wider phenomenon."[7] As they have shown, the analytical category of religion was constructed by "relatively recent intra-Christian debates, Enlightenment intellectuals, and colonial encounters in the seventeenth and eighteenth centuries."[8]

Modern culturally constructed definitions of religion have also distorted earlier studies of ancient religion. For some time, there was a tendency to dismiss pre-Christian religions because they did not comport with a Protestant understanding of piety; this led to a tendency to view public cult worship as formulaic and to a devaluation of ritual.[9] Yet, as historians of religion have emphasized more recently, public cult and ritual figured prominently in the ancients' understanding of their own religiosity. In the first century BCE, for example, Roman elites used the term *religio* in talking about what we could call religion precisely in order to stress its "strong ritualistic aspect ... connected with active worship according to the rules."[10] Cotta, the representative of Academic philosophy in Cicero's *On the Nature*

---

[4] Aug. *Civ.* 10.1 includes a discussion of terminology, including his preference for the Greek word, *latreia*, meaning ritual and service to a deity (*ritu ac servitudine*), akin to *cultus* in Latin; see too Aug. *Pref.* to *Civ.* 6.

[5] *The New Oxford Dictionary of English*, s.v. *Religion*; and cf. *The American Heritage Dictionary*, s.v. *Religion*.

[6] Rüpke, *Religion of the Romans*, 5.

[7] Ibid., 6, aptly citing the work of J. Z. Smith, "Religion, Religions, Religious."

[8] See especially Smith, "Religion, Religions, Religious," 179–96; Asad, *Genealogies of Religion*, 27–54; and Nongbri, "Dislodging 'Embedded' Religion," 445.

[9] For a brilliant discussion of this, see Smith, *Drudgery Divine*.

[10] Bremmer, "'Religion,' 'Ritual,' and the Opposition 'Sacred vs. Profane,'" 10.

of the Gods, claimed that "the *religio* of the Roman people comprises ritual, auspices, and the third additional division consisting of all such prophetic warnings as the interpreters of the Sybil [*sic*] or the soothsayers have derived from portents and prodigies. … I hold that none of these *religiones* should ever be omitted" (3.2.4). The plural, *religiones* – literally "religions" but here more likely what we mean by religious practices – points to this ritualistic emphasis as a key component of the first-century Roman elite notion of "religion."[11]

In order to avoid preconceptions arising from definitional pitfalls, the contributors to these volumes have tried to analyze ancient religions on their own terms, in full cognizance of how these traditions diverge from modern definitions of religion. Most ancients, like our first-century-BCE Romans, saw nothing wrong with entertaining multiple "religions" or religious practices for multiple deities. In keeping with this wide variety of practices and gods, "religious" practitioners might include the sorts of people whom moderns might not consider particularly "religious," that is, diviners, augurs, soothsayers, and even the public officials who regularly also performed key public rites such as sacrifice.

Coexistence of such diverse rituals and deities was possible partly because ancient religions did not necessarily have their own systematic set of core beliefs and principles, with sacred texts, personnel, and rites. Rather, as J. Rives observed in reference to Roman religion, "it is almost impossible, apart from a few exceptions such as Judaism and Christianity, to identify any coherent or unified systems of religion at all."[12] Nor did all ancient religions possess the same "normative" religious components (i.e., sacred texts, sacred personnel, a moral code, a coherent systematic body of knowledge). Because the transmission of religious knowledge in the ancient world took place through various channels, it is all the more critical that modern scholars resist the tendency to elevate textually based religious traditions (or at least textual evidence) over other forms of religious expression. In certain ancient cultures, such as the Minoans on Crete, knowledge of the divine was realized through myths, but the sacred personnel – of which we are largely uninformed – seem entirely dependent on the palace and the king; in others, such as the empire of the Hittites, there are no extant theological tracts to trace the notion of the divine.[13]

---

[11] Ando, *The Matter of the Gods*, 5–8, on this passage; and cf. Ngombri, "Dislodging 'Embedded' Religion," 448–50.
[12] Rives, *Religion in the Roman Empire*, 5.
[13] For Minoan religion on Crete, see Marinatos, Chapter 9 in Volume I; for the Hittites, see Beckman, Chapter 3 in Volume I.

In contrast to the modern American ideal of the separation of church and state, ancient religions cannot be confined to a specific sphere of life; on the contrary, religion in the ancient world extended into "areas that nowadays are not identified as religious at all."[14] It has often been said that ancient religion was "embedded" in daily life in the ancient world, a reference to the ways in which religion was integrated into all areas of ancient society.[15] In Rome, for instance, senators could meet in any ritually inaugurated space or *templum*; but before they entered to vote on issues of the day, they were sure to burn some incense and pour some wine for the goddess Victory. Although the incorporation of religious rituals into political life is distinctive of Greek and Roman religions, it is also found in several others traditions, including Babylonian, Sumerian, Egyptian, and ancient Israelite/Judean religions.

The difficulties of studying ancient religions – with their diverse gods, rites, personnel, and beliefs across the Ancient Near East and Mediterranean regions – have caused some historians to question whether the ancients had anything at all comparable to a modern *category* of religion, so deeply embedded in Christianity as it has been and hence so different from ancient ideas about religion or religions.[16] But granted the absence of an ancient category comparable to the modern term "religion," modern scholars need not be bound by the words used by the cultures they study.[17] Rather, the contributors to these volumes have discerned in antiquity the components of what are nowadays taken to characterize religion.[18] In these essays and in the volumes as a whole, the editors and contributing scholars have taken the view that if scholars are explicit in how they define "religion" and its components, they can recognize religion even in very diverse and unevenly documented ancient societies. Our aim is not only to advance understanding of religion in the ancient world and in the cultures in which these religions thrived, but also to augment our understanding of the category "religion" as a cultural construction.[19]

---

[14] Rüpke, *Religion of the Romans*, 6; Beard, North, and Price, *Religions of Rome*, 1.43.
[15] Although Nongbri, "Dislodging 'Embedded' Religion," 440–60, argues with some reason that the trope of embedded religion can "produce the false impression that religion is a descriptive concept" rather than a constructed one, this does not negate the close integration of ancient religion as a constructed category in ancient society.
[16] See especially ibid.
[17] For this emic/etic distinction applied to ancient religion, see, for example, Bremmer, "'Religion,' 'Ritual,' and the Opposition 'Sacred vs. Profane,'" 12; and Rüpke, *Religion of the Romans*, 6. For a more generalized discussion, see McCutcheon, *The Insider/Outsider Problem*, 17.
[18] See, for example, Rüpke, *Religion of the Romans*, 6, on religion among the Romans in the Republic: "It [ancient religion] knew gods and their temples; it knew holy days and priests."
[19] This is in essence how I take J. Z. Smith to intend the categories of description and redescription to work; see Smith, *Drudgery Divine*.

APPROACHING ANCIENT RELIGION

The religions of the ancient Mediterranean each had their own trajectory, which unfolded in specific places and times. How adherents conceptualized and communicated with the divine varied considerably within individual religious traditions. The local variations and the unsystematic nature of ancient cult make it all the more important to examine ancient religions as they were expressed in particular places and time periods. In the third century CE, the Christian writer Tertullian attested to the local dimension of ancient religion: "Each province and city has its own god: Syria has Astarte, Arabia Dursares, Noricum Belenus, Africa Caelestis, Mauretania its own princes; the Egyptians even worship animals."[20]

The aspects of ancient religion analyzed in these essays – rituals, practices, and forms of divine knowledge – are based on a broad consensus among scholars of ancient religion about its most critical components. Byron Earhart's view of religion is a standard one, but it is worth including here for it lists these components succinctly: Religion comprises a "distinctive set of beliefs, symbols, rituals, doctrines, institutions and practices that enables the members of the tradition to establish, maintain, and celebrate a meaningful world. ... [And it] is a tradition that is handed down, moving through time and manifesting a continuous identity along with a tendency to change and be transformed."[21] This view of religion and its key components serves as a guidepost for scholars of diverse ancient religions.

In order to approach these diverse religions in a systematic way, however, contributors were asked to address the same set of topics concerning ancient religion in the ancient Near Eastern and Mediterranean regions (see below). Moreover, each author was asked to restrict his or her essay to a specific time period. The death of Alexander and the end of his empire was a turning point for many ancient societies, and hence it was used by the editors to divide the religious traditions between Volumes I and II. But because this date is not relevant to all religions, it was not strictly adhered to by all contributors. Local variation and diverging, independent scholarly opinions explain the chronological overlaps between the two volumes.

We see many advantages in this approach. Each chapter looks at ancient religion in its physical, social, political, and cultural context. In taking into account the influences of neighboring religions and peoples, authors have sought to re-create the reality of fluid interactions in antiquity. The essays are analytical, rather than merely descriptive of orthopraxy, mythology,

---

[20] Tertullian, *Apol.* 24.7.
[21] Earhart, ed., *Religious Traditions of the World*, 7.

or textual evidence. Each author has incorporated the most recent scholarship on relevant texts and material culture. Although the resulting volumes present a history of the religions of the Ancient Near East and Mediterranean worlds, they do not simply reflect recent trends in scholarship; they are intended to shape the future trajectory of that scholarship as well. Read together and in their diversity, we hope the ancient religions can be felt as well as analyzed. Ancient religion has recognizable components, but because it is radically different in so many ways from religion in the twenty-first century, it continues to intrigue.

As an organizational tool, the editors established seven topics that we considered important for arriving at a more synthetic understanding of ancient religion.

First, because the history of each religion (as above) has been excavated and reconstructed through the lens of past scholarship, we asked each author to consider how modern theories have shaped and sometimes distorted perceptions about specific religions and their origins. In Volume I, E. Kearns's essay, "Archaic and Classical Greek Religion," builds on and critiques earlier arguments about the importance of the *polis* or city-state for understanding Greek religion.[22] William van Andringa's essay, "Religions and Cities in Roman Gaul (First to Fourth Centuries CE)," in Volume II shows how the modern notion of "tolerance," a term tied to the history of modern states, is ill-suited to define religious phenomena associated with the ancient city. Historiography can be critical, as here, in enabling modern scholars to discern errors of earlier scholars in viewing ancient religions.

Second, each scholar was asked to consider the nature of ritual and its relation to conceptualizing divinity. Given the strong emphasis on orthopraxy in many ancient religions, this component is central to a wide range of cultures. However, the nature of the surviving evidence for ritual varies considerably across traditions. In the case of the ancient Israelite and Judean religions down through the age of Alexander, we can extract evidence for ritual only from texts; here we can see how these rituals relate to a notion of the divine through the perspective of the originators of these texts, as M. Sweeney has observed in his essay, "Israelite and Judean Religions," in Volume I. On the other hand, for other religions, such as that of the Hittites, only illustrations of ritual in material culture remain; there are no theological treatises or surveys of belief, a fact that forced G. Beckman to elucidate the meaning of Hittite rituals for conceptions of

---

[22] For more on the *polis*-religion model and its critics, see my discussion below.

divinity through a reconstruction of very diverse evidences in his chapter on Hittite religion in Volume I. Similarly, in Volume II, B. Shaw's discussion of the evidence for human sacrifice in Punic cult in North Africa depends mostly on material evidence.

Third, scholars were asked to consider the relationship of their religious tradition to the social and historical contexts within which that religious tradition developed, with specific reference to how public religion relates to political life and how private or domestic religion is integrated into social and cultural life. In his analysis of Sumerian religion in Volume I, G. Cunningham discusses how political change – the rise of the city-state in the middle of the third millennium BCE and the growth of regional state/empire in the later third and early second millennium BCE – reflected onto the divinities worshipped. Although the nature of the Sumerian evidence did not allow Cunningham to discuss private or domestic religion at length, other historians have been able to do so for their areas. L. Roller's contribution, for example, examines traditional religions in Greece and Asia Minor in Volume II and includes the phenomenon of private cult at the bequest of an individual donor to perpetuate the memory of a family member. One example was the case of a wife setting up cult honoring the Muses and the "heroes," a term used to designate cult rites in memory too of her deceased husband. Roller's essay extends our understanding of the cult of the dead as practiced by individual Greeks.

In considering their particular religious traditions, authors were asked to consider, fourth, the influence of other religions and cultures. In his chapter on ancient Israelite and Judean religions, Sweeney observed Near Eastern influences on the Northern Kingdom of Israel including the use of golden calves as typical mounts for YHWH and Canaanite influences including the use of uninscribed cultic pillars (*massetbot*), likely a symbol associated with the Canaanite god Baal that came to represent YHWH in Israelite sanctuaries such as Beth El (Genesis 28). Shared cultural patterns are relevant, though they also highlight the distinctive nature of ancient Israelite and Judean religions. Such shared cultural patterns can be seen in numerous traditions; N. Marinatos, for one, has elucidated the particular practices found in Minoan religion through comparison with Egypt and the Near East in her essay in Volume I. The Hellenistic influence on religions in the eastern Mediterranean, in Egypt and the Roman Near East, is discussed in Volume II by several authors (see, among others, F. Dunand, J. van der Horst, T. Kaizer, F. Trombley, and M. Stone).

Because religion was so often integrated into the social and political fabric of ancient societies, we asked contributors to consider, fifth, changing ideas of religious identity and community. Judaism, for example, appears quite distinct in diaspora communities, such as those of Asia Minor, Italy, and Egypt, as compared to Judaism in Palestine, and so required separate treatments in Volume II. D. Watts traces how the coming of the Romans affected Celtic religion in her essay in Volume I, and W. van Andringa also considers the impact of the Romans and urbanization on religion in Gaul in his essay in Volume II. In keeping with our interest in religious identity and community, we requested that contributors incorporate the role of women in ancient religion within their specific local context. This is a topic that has too often been overlooked in histories of ancient religion, in part because the surviving evidence so frequently highlights the religious roles of men. One instance of this interest is the referencing of women in Jewish communities in Italy along with their male relatives by G. Lacerenza in his contribution in Volume II. Similarly, D. Trout has incorporated the role of aristocratic women along with men in Christian circles in Italy in his study in Volume II.

Last, because of the very diverse nature of the evidence for many ancient religions, authors were asked to consider all sorts of evidence, including (where possible) key monuments and material culture. This last area takes on added import because for many ancient societies, religion was so much a part of daily life. D. Doxey, for one, analyzed Egyptian religion not based on any one written doctrine, but rather through a variety of material evidences – funerary spells, literary works, inscriptions, excavations of temples and tombs, images of gods and goddesses. In some regions, the material evidence is all we have; in others, texts predominate. But even where documentary texts survive – as for Manichaeism and Zoroastrianism in Iran and Armenia in the Parthian and Sasanian empires – authors were asked to incorporate material evidence to present a more balanced response to the topics noted above and to try, where possible, to extend analysis of religion beyond the kings and elites of their respective societies. This was not always possible. At the end of certain essays where these are particularly relevant, a list of key textual and material sources provides suggestions for further study; bibliography has been included for each essay.

The contributors naturally differed with respect to how much emphasis they gave to these topics. In addition to individual judgment, the vagaries of the surviving evidence required authors to privilege certain components and/or topics over others. At times, they have had to adopt innovative methodologies to address the diverse nature of ancient religion and/or the uneven evidence about it. Using textual and temple archaeological evidence, T. Schneider sees in the *enuma elish* text and the myth of Atrahasis

Introduction to Volumes I and II 9

evidence of the shared Assyrian and Babylonian notion that "humans were created so the gods did not have to work."[23] Another creative approach had to be adopted in order to comprehend the sparsely attested evidence for Syro-Canaanite religion. D. Wright uses analogy in his chapter to explain the Syro-Canaanite association of deities with natural phenomena; in this culture, he observes, deities, conceived as sentient but more powerful agents than humans, were thus responsible for events in the observable world (i.e., the cycle of the seasons, calamitous droughts or floods) on analogy with the ways humans act as agents in society.

These volumes present components of each ancient religious tradition within its specific place and time. As scholars of these religions discuss these topics, we believe these volumes can provide a more synthetic understanding of the ancient religious tradition under consideration.

Moreover, analysis of the same components and topics will allow for comparison across religious traditions. Indeed, in the midst of the diversity of rituals, practices, and conceptualizations of the divine in the essays in these volumes, there emerge certain shared concepts and categories of religion. Sacrifice is one such rite that has been considered central to ancient religion. Yet sacrifice entails a range of practices that varies across religions, holding contemporary ritual significance as well as mythical import, or even being transformed, as in Jewish and Christian traditions, to commemorate a symbolic historical moment.[24] Similarly, the Sumerian practice whereby a temple, the symbolic center of the city, takes on interrelated functions as the earthly residence of deities and as an administrative center for the city is another category of religious life that is found in numerous cities across the ancient world, from Mesopotamia to Greece and throughout the Mediterranean, East and West. Widespread, too, are such shared components of religion as divination, the veneration of ancestors, shamans, the assumption that the divine dwells in material objects, and the attribution of divine favor to political rulers.

Scholars have suggested that a partial explanation for such pervasive commonalities across ancient religions is the presence of shared conceptual

---

[23] Schneider, Chapter 2 in Volume I. Schneider denies the view of scholars, such as the influential A. Leo Oppenheim (*Ancient Mesopotamia*, 171), that we not consider Mesopotamian religion as a valid analytical category.

[24] The centrality of sacrifice in non-Christian traditions and even the value of "sacrifice" as an analytical category has been called into question; see McClymond, *Beyond Sacred Violence*, and Frankfurter, "Egyptian Religion and the Problem of the Category 'Sacrifice,'" 75–93. Certainly, variation in the ritual and in the objects of sacrifice as well as its significance exists across traditions, but the fact remains that animal or plant sacrifice was a pervasive ritual in all the ancient religions included in Volume I. In Volume II its metaphorical importance for Christian and Jewish religious traditions still makes sacrifice a key shared concept in the ancient religions included there.

and linguistic categories.[25] Those who were speakers of ancient Semitic languages – Old Akkadian, Assyro-Babylonian, Hebrew, Phoenician, Aramaic, Palaeo-Syrian – and those who were speakers of an Indo-European language – Italic, Celtic, Indo-Iranian, Hellenic, Anatolian – may have also shared a religious "knowledge" of divine powers, such as the names and categories or institutions in the area of cultural practices that we call religion.[26] The name of Anath in Egyptian texts in the late period, for instance, shows Israelite influence.[27] But, in discussing religion in the Roman Near East, T. Kaizer notes that the "jury is still out" as to the degree to which relevant phraseology in Semitic languages "was shared between different local and sub-regional communities."[28] How much weight we should grant these linguistic or cultural influences in explaining types of religious behavior varies by region, and in many areas it is contested. For the scholars in these volumes, of greater significance are the analysis and description of the particular religious pattern and what that pattern tells us about the culture and religious tradition in which it is found.

More relevant, and more often discussed in these volumes, are the similar sociopolitical systems that appear in relationship to rituals, practices, and conceptions of the divine. In the Near East and Mediterranean, the city-state (*polis*) alternated with the regional empire as the dominant socio-political institution. Indeed, Volume I begins in Mesopotamia with Sumerian religion because there, with the agricultural revolution, we find the emergence of the world's first cities and states.[29] But, as G. Cunningham noted, the Sumerians (as attested by the Sumerian king list) considered kingship an institution descended from heaven and passed from city-state to city-state; to the Sumerians, kingship was a divine gift to the city-state that in turn required devotion to the gods and goddesses of the city-state. Similarly, in its most fully developed form in the archaic and classical *poleis* in Greece and Rome, "the public cults of the city, shared in some sense by all who are

---

[25] Graf, "What Is Ancient Mediterranean Religion?" especially 4–5 and 11–12, raises this issue eloquently. This is not to deny the possibility that biological and cognitive approaches to religion might also be relevant to understanding religious commonalities; these commonalities are, however, not at odds with the social significance of local religious representations, nor are they the object of historical analysis in these volumes. For a defence of these two approaches to religion, see Martin, "Disenchanting," 36–44.

[26] Rüpke, *Religion of the Romans*, 3; Lipinski, *Semitic Languages*, 21–4. For a good overview of the Indo-European languages, see Fortson, *Indo-European Language and Culture*, 1–16.

[27] Frankfurter, private correspondence, 7 February 2010.

[28] Kaizer, Chapter 2 in Volume II.

[29] The "State and Urban Revolution," ca.3100 BCE, led to the adoption of the Sumerian city-state model by different language speakers who represent the three major ethnic groups in Mesopotamia, namely, the Sumerians, Semites, and Elamites. For a schematic but clear overview of these developments, see Nagle, *The Ancient World*, 1–53.

Introduction to Volumes I and II 11

citizens of it, occupied a central place in ancient religion. Those cults were controlled and presided over by priests drawn from the civic elite, which collectively also had authority over the entirety of religious action within the *polis* and by its citizens."[30] In Greece and Rome, as in Mesopotamia and in Phoenician-Punic sacrificial legislation, many scholars have interpreted ancient religious traditions based on what, in the Greco-Roman tradition, G. Woolf has called "the *polis*-religion model"; central to this approach is the homology of the sacred and the socio-political.[31] And because the *polis*-religion model of the archaic and classical *poleis* in Greece and Republican Rome spread though the Mediterranean in the Hellenistic and late Roman Republican periods, scholars have found additional reasons for religious similarities across broad regions. The development of regional empires – which often coexisted with city-states – also has been linked to ancient religion. The worship of the king in Hellenistic empires, for example, has long been considered as a model for the worship of the Roman emperor in Greece and Asia Minor as well as in the western Mediterranean in the first three centuries CE.[32]

Because religion in the ancient world often provided a sacred or mythic framework for sanctioning political ideology and institutions, understanding the relationship between religion and socio-political developments is one focus of the essays in these volumes. Scholars who have advanced a "*polis-religion model*" – meaning (as above) that the core of the Greco-Roman religious tradition is to be found in the public cults of the city, which must be understood as a religious as well as social community[33] – have argued that it is simplistic to consider ancient politicians as insincerely "manipulating" religion for political ends. A more nuanced appreciation of the interconnectivity of these areas of ancient society rejects such a view and sheds light on new religious developments. Viewed in this way, the cults created for the new Cleisthenic tribes and the new role for freedmen in the imperial cult in the western provinces of the Roman empire emerge as sincere expressions of religious as well as civic identity. The *polis*-religion model has thus enabled scholars to see beyond the modern western stress

[30] Woolf, "*Polis*-Religion and Its Alternatives," 41.
[31] Ibid., 42–5; Woolf discusses this term and the influence of the views of C. Sourvinou-Inwood, "What Is *Polis* Religion?" 295–322.
[32] For more on this observation, see Woolf, "*Polis*-Religion and Its Alternatives," 71–84; and Roller, Chapter 11 in Volume II.
[33] Rives, "Graeco-Roman Religion," 270. As Rives notes, the phrase "*polis* religion model" is not restricted only to Greek city-states, nor is it a single coherent model. Rather, it is used here as by Woolf and other scholars to summarize a set of current ideas about the nature of ancient religion and its relationship to the socio-political traditions of the ancient world.

on the private manifestations of religious commitment. Religious ritual in ancient societies such as Rome consisted in public or communal events, and those involved did not view this in a negative light. Even family and private cults can be interpreted as, in certain regards, representing "the state cult on a smaller scale."[34]

Although there were important ties between religious and socio-political institutions and patterns of behavior in the ancient world, it would nonetheless also be misleading to see ancient religion as homologous with them. The *polis*-religion model, and along with it, the focus on the public cults of the city-state or empire, have rightly been criticized for making this error. and hence overlooking the non-authorized, privately initiated areas of ancient religious tradition. Oracles and sanctuaries continued outside the range of city-state or ruler cult. So, too, domestic cults continued, alongside public civic expressions of religion; these were not merely reflections of the state cult.[35] In truth, a diverse pantheon of deities, practices, and rites outside of the sphere of the *polis*-state or the empire continued, showing by its very survival that religion and socio-political life were never identical.[36] Even within any one city, as was certainly the case in one as large as imperial Rome, the *polis*-religion model does not adequately address the complexities of ancient religious life in which the public cults were but one of many in the marketplace of religious options.[37]

More importantly, the *polis*-religion model does not easily explain how religious change came about. As G. Woolf has observed:

many public "innovations" seem in fact to be responses to changes in what might be termed the religious *koine* of the Mediterranean world. If the origins of religious innovation most often came from the world of "private religion," any account that marginalizes non-public cult is bound to be handicapped in accounting for change."[38]

The *polis*-religion model is certainly handicapped in explaining the continued popularity of traditional public cults in the fourth and fifth centuries when the state no longer supported them.[39] Nor does this model

---

[34] Beard and Crawford, *Rome in the Late Republic*, 30. For more on this topic, see van Andringa, Chapter 17, and Kulikowski, Chapter 19, both in Volume II.

[35] Woolf, "*Polis*-Religion and Its Alternatives," 71–84.

[36] For additional criticism of the *polis*-religion model, see Bendlin, "Peripheral Centres," 47–63.

[37] Rüpke, "Antike Grossstadtreligion," 13–30.

[38] Woolf, "*Polis*-Religion and Its Alternatives," 76.

[39] For an excellent overview of the criticism of the polis-religion model and its advances in scholarship, see Rives, "Graeco-Roman Religion," 268–76.

elucidate what some scholars have considered as key to investigating religious traditions, namely, the religious mentalities of the people under consideration.[40]

In considering the diversity of ancient religions, the central role of geography cannot be over-emphasized. In my view, what I would call the geography of religion is one master key to understanding religious multiplicity in the ancient world. Lacking our communications technology and interconnectivity, geography influenced religion in the ancient world far more than in the modern. One's religion was determined at first by place of birth, for religion was entangled with local political and social structures. Physical places, such as springs or mountaintops, were also intimately connected with myth and were seen as having immanent in them divine powers onto which cult was grafted. Such cult associations were not always movable. Many of these sacred places had religious status for centuries; veneration of the healing sanctuaries of Aesculapius at Epidauros and Pergamun was rooted in these places even apart from the cults of the city-state or empires that developed around them.

Veneration of the same sorts of sacred geography – trees, mountain tops, springs, rivers, caves – can lend a certain surface similarity to the worship found in the polytheistic religions of the ancient world. This does not mean, however, that similar geographical places always had similar sorts of cults, or that there was necessarily a "cultural or social *koine* characterized by common modes of relating to the divine."[41] Rather, I want to assert the more fundamental point that certain sorts of places in the Mediterranean and Near East accrued sacred significances that remained central to religious traditions for centuries, even if the religious practices and significances that developed at these places changed over time.

Geography, too, is key to understanding the interconnections of religious influence. Although, in Tertullian's terms, "each province and city has its own god," the same gods and goddesses were worshipped in more than one city or province. Gods and goddesses traveled along an interlocking complex of water and land-ways into the Near East and around the Mediterranean Sea. As P. Horden and N. Purcell argued in their important work *The Corrupting Sea*, the Mediterranean Sea with its "myriad micro ecologies" in which one could discern an "all too apparent fragmentation"

---

[40] See Kearns, Chapter 11 in Volume I.
[41] Woolf, "A Sea of Faith," 126.

14   *Michele Renee Salzman*

also had the potential to "unite the sea and its coastlands in a way far exceeding anything predictable of a continent."[42] The implications for religion are important:

the (Mediterranean) sea itself has been the medium of religious differentiation, as it is also the vehicle of religious change. On one hand, it has served to establish rival conceptual claims about the extent and limits of religious influence. ... On the other hand, it is the milieu in which the Orientalizing religious forms of the seventh century B.C., Diaspora Judaism and Pauline Christianity were disseminated. In religion, therefore, we see clearly instantiated the important paradox ... that the Mediterranean is both a zone of easy lateral transmission of ideas and practices and a barrier which promotes divisions between cultural systems.[43]

Horden and Purcell's study of the environmental and geographic linkages of the communities around the Mediterranean Sea reflects the late-twentieth/early-twenty-first century scholarly recognition of the importance of geography in enabling different cultures to be "exposed to a diversity of religions, both indigenous and imported."[44] Indeed, as gods moved with traders, soldiers, or priests, local religious traditions interacted with and altered the ways in which a deity and his or her cult came to be conceptualized and venerated. The Greeks, for example, called the Phrygian Mountain Mother Goddess of Pessinus "Mountain Mother" (*Meter Oreia*) and turned her epithet *kubileya* into a name, Cybele. But they worshiped her as a form of Rhea, the ancient mother of Zeus, with rites quite different from those used in Asia. In Italy the Romans called this goddess by her Latin name, Magna Mater, and worshipped her differently than did her contemporary Greek or Asian devotees.[45] The Roman historian Tacitus famously called this process *interpretatio*;[46] modern scholars refer to it as assimilation and transformation, and talk of a variety of "Great Mother religions" just as they speak of a range of "Christianities" and "Judaisms."

Since geography is so important to the study of ancient religion, the editors have made geography central both to the organization and to the approach of the essays in these volumes. Based on the recognition of the ways in which local geographic factors influenced religion, these essays disrupt traditional disciplinary barriers separating historians of the religions of the Near East and of the Mediterranean worlds. Even though

---

[42] Horden and Purcell, *The Corrupting Sea*, 24.
[43] Ibid., 408.
[44] Johnston, *Religions of the Ancient World*, "Introduction," X.
[45] For more on this deity see Roller, *In Search of God the Mother*, 1 ff.
[46] Tacitus, *Germania* 43.4. For an interesting discussion of *interpretatio*, see Ando, *The Matter of the Gods*, 43–58.

the separation between classics and theology was effectively established in universities in the late eighteenth and early nineteenth centuries, this division continues until today.[47] Because these disciplinary boundaries do not reflect ancient realities, however, they should not be reproduced in modern scholarship. Hence, these essays and their organization into religious traditions by distinct areas reflect the awareness of how thoroughly inhabitants of the Ancient Mediterranean and Near East were influenced by one another. The editors have thus sought contributors from a wide range of academic disciplines, including those who study the Judeo-Christian world religions of today in religious studies, theological, or history departments, along with those who reside in Classical, Near Eastern, or Semitic Language departments. Historians who are willing to cross these boundaries, and who are disposed, where possible, to take into account the influences of other religions on the religious tradition under consideration, can make real the interconnections between peoples.

Acknowledging that regional variations in ancient religions are the result of complex processes of transmission, adaptation, and assimilation has meant that the scholars of these essays do not simply describe particular cults or deities, or assume simple continuities of practice, though it is also true that for many religions simply defining and assessing origins and practices remain difficult tasks. Rather, each was asked to consider the interaction between place and peoples, indigenous or migratory, as phenomena that change over time. In doing so, they have constructed their own categories of analysis and used terms that do not necessarily reproduce the ancient society's "native" viewpoint. Granted, the Egyptians may have had no word for religion, for example. Even so, D. Doxey can isolate what she views as key components of Egyptian religion – rituals, practices, and conceptions of the divine. And she can address many of the topics outlined above to arrive at a synthetic view of Egyptian religion as deeply tied to the natural world while mediating "one's place in a hierarchy including the gods, the king, the family, peers, and dependents."[48]

No book is without its limitations, and the same is true of these volumes. The authors sought to incorporate a wide range of material for each religious tradition and to consider their specific religions and areas within broad chronological and geographic limits. Hence, the reader searching for a theoretical discussion of a specific ritual, such as sacrifice, may find suggestions where to look for such a discussion, but no extended treatment

---

[47] See, for example, Burkert, *The Orientalizing Revolution*, 1–8.
[48] Doxey, Chapter 7 in Volume I.

16   *Michele Renee Salzman*

in these pages. Moreover, although we encouraged the contributors to consider the influences of other religions and cultures on the tradition under
discussion, the degree to which this was possible or considered necessary
varied by scholarly choice.

SOME TERMS OF ANALYSIS

The importance of finding terms that can work across many diverse ancient
religious traditions has made us all the more aware of the terminology we
have adopted for these volumes. We have self-consciously tried to avoid
vocabulary that even implicitly claims that any one religious tradition was
more evolved than or superior to another.

Because Christian missionaries used the word "syncretism" to censure
the mixing of Christianity with native religious traditions in a colonial
enterprise, its historical associations and normative implications have
made it a problematic term for many scholars in the twenty-first century.[49] The history of the misapplication of and distortions implied by this
term has led many scholars to reject it entirely. Other scholars, aware of
its historical association, embrace its usage, while attempting to strip it
of its Christianizing sanctions.[50] Indeed, the reality implied by this word,
understood rather positively as a "creative, synthetic process by which
any idea, symbol or idiom is appropriated and embraced in a culture,"[51]
fuels the argument in support of some term to identify this phenomenon. Some scholars have proposed using the term "hybridity," derived
from post-colonial theory, to refer to the adaptation and assimilation of
either native or immigrant cultures or languages to the dominant culture
or language.[52] But this term does not always seem applicable. When, as
Horace observed, "captured Greece took captive its victor, Rome,"[53] the
dominant political culture of the Romans was overtaken by the more culturally sophisticated Hellenic one. In the essays in these volumes, the editors have advised against uncritical use of either of the terms "syncretism"
or "hybridity." We have favored instead descriptive and neutral, analytical
language, calling such phenomena as the Christian preservation of a tree
sacred to a Celtic god the incorporation or assimilation of one religious

---

[49] For further discussion of this term, see too van Andringa, Chapter 17, and Kaizer, Chapter 2, both
in Volume II.
[50] Stewart and Shaw, "Introduction: Problematizing Syncretism," 1–26.
[51] Frankfurter, "Syncretism and the Holy Man," 344.
[52] Graf, "What Is Ancient Mediterranean Religion?" 10.
[53] Horace, *Epistulae* 2.1.156–7: "Graecia capta Romam victricem captam subducit."

Introduction to Volumes I and II 17

tradition by another. Even if scholars use these terms with critical awareness, there are complicating implications.[54]

A term that has proven more intractable is the label "paganism" or "pagan." These words were most often used by late ancient Christians, leading some scholars to criticize their continued use as implying the "Christian view of the division in society."[55] Alternative terms for non-Christian, non-Jewish religionists in the ancient Mediterranean have not been entirely satisfactory. The word "polytheist," derived from the usage of anthropology, has been proposed as a more neutral alternative, focusing on the multiplicity of cults worshipped, "highly discontinuous with one another, highly dissimilar."[56] However, although polytheists were the majority, not all pagans were polytheists; a growing number of scholars see monotheistic tendencies among non-Christians and non-Jews in the early Roman Empire and have argued that some pagans were virtual monotheists, either on the basis of their philosophical studies or through their focus on a single deity as supreme, such as that of *Theos Hypsistos*.[57] So some pagans are, arguably, monotheists much as Jews were, insofar as they focused on one god even as many Jews, although directing their worship to their one supreme god, also thought that there were other lesser divinities.[58] When Christians call non-Christians polytheists, they are denigrating them just as if they were calling them "pagans"; in this way, too, they could turn the strong tradition of philosophic monotheism against non-Christians.[59] Substitution of the term "Hellene"[60] for paganism does not resolve the issue either. By the late Roman Empire, the word "Hellene" came to be used by Christian apologists and polemicists for non-Christians. When used as a general term to describe all non-Christian and native religious elements, however, it tends to give everything an Attic or intellectualizing patina that obscures the fact that the religions under consideration entailed also Roman, Egyptian, and native cults and rites.

Given the problems in finding alternative terminology, some scholars have fallen back on the term "pagan," using it to mean "upholders of the ancient or traditional religions" of the Mediterranean. P. Chuvin

---

[54] See note 50 above.
[55] O'Donnell, *Review*, 4.
[56] Ibid.; Fowden, *Empire to Commonwealth*, 119.
[57] Athanassiadi and Frede, *Pagan Monotheism*, 1–20; for *Theos Hypsistos*, see Mitchell, "The Cult of *Theos Hypsistos*," 81–148, and "Further Thoughts on the Cult of *Theos Hypsistos*," 167–208; van der Horst, Chapter 12 in Volume II.
[58] Fredriksen, *Review*, 532.
[59] North, "Pagans, Polytheists," 142.
[60] Trombley, *Hellenic Religion and Christianization*, 1–58.

has justified his use of this term by turning to the etymology of *pagani* or pagans as people of the place, town, or country who preserved their local customs, whereas the *alieni*, the people from elsewhere, were increasingly Christian. Thus, for Chuvin, paganism is the "religion of the homeland in its narrowest sense: the city and its outlying countryside, characterized by diversity of practices and beliefs."[61] For Chuvin, paganism was essentially homologous with the city-state, itself a problematic model.[62] But Chuvin's focus on contacts between native religious traditions and Christianity is undermined by Cameron, who argues for "pagan" as a fourth-century-CE idiom for the "outsider." The very history of its usage by Christians to make derogative remarks about non-Chrstians has made "pagan" a desirable term for certain scholars who want to highlight the historical associations of pagans and paganism.[63] Others propose using these terms, stripping them of any derogatory meaning.[64] Given the problems raised by this term, we have avoided using the labels "pagan" or "paganism." Rather, the authors in these volumes have focused on geographically specified, contextualized religious traditions or practices, rituals, and cults. Where these local trends become trans-local – as, for instance, in the cult of Isis in the Roman empire – we have so noted it. Such an approach undermines the view of ancient religions as unified or uniform, a notion conveyed by the term "paganism." Viewing ancient religions as geographically based religious traditions is in keeping with the geographical organization of these volumes.

ORGANIZATION OF THE VOLUMES: BEGINNINGS AND ENDINGS

Volume I begins in the middle of the third millennium BCE in Mesopotamia because, as noted above, in Sumer we have the first case of a religion that can be studied via texts as well as artifacts within a complex, urban society. The contributions conclude, chronologically, with the reign of Alexander (336–323 BCE). This is a relevant turning point for the history of many ancient religions because the ramifications of his conquests emerged most clearly in the Hellenistic age that followed the disintegration of his empire. The Hellenistic kingdoms helped to reshape the ancient world, its political, social, and religious horizons, even if, in the western Mediterranean, these events were only distantly and slowly perceived. Yet diverging local

---

[61] Chuvin, *A Chronicle*, 9.
[62] Chuvin, ibid., sees paganism as a "mosaic of established religions linked to the political order."
[63] Cameron, *The Last Pagans*, 14–32; North, "Pagans, Polytheists," 142.
[64] For a similar practice, see Bowersock, *Hellenism*, 6.

Introduction to Volumes I and II

and regional religious traditions explain why some contributors ended their essays in Volume I either earlier or later than this period, and some contributors in Volume II similarly felt the need to adjust the beginning and ending points to address their particular religious tradition.

The editors decided to begin Volume II with the Hellenistic age and extend the essays into the late Roman period. It makes sense to define a general end to the discussion with the demise of the last western Roman emperor, Romulus Augustulus (476 CE), an event that marked the new political and social reality of the Germanic kingdoms in the decades of the increasingly open assertion of Christian religious authority across the Mediterranean. The persistence of local religious traditions explains why some authors continued their essays into the next century. It was important, however, to continue the volume past the end of publicly financed polytheism in the late fourth century of the Roman Empire; traditional religions continued past this date, into the next centuries. Moreover, the fifth century saw important changes in the nature of Christianity and Judaism, in response to the Roman state's support for Christianity. In the late fourth and fifth centuries, too, we find non-Christians (polytheists, but especially Jews and Manichees) as well as Christian sects labeled heresies facing discrimination on religious grounds in new ways. The late-fifth-century ending date for Volume II has allowed the contributors to incorporate some of these changes in their essays. The volume had to stop before the rise of Islam, for that would have required substantial additions to Volume II that extend well beyond the fifth century.

The volumes are organized by region because, as noted above, geography plays such a central role in understanding ancient religions. As noted earlier, Volume I begins in Mesopotamia with Sumerian religion, the first case of a religion that can be studied via texts as well as artifacts within a complex, urban society. The volume proceeds in this same region to discuss religion in Old Babylonia/Assyria, the Iranian Plateau (Zoroastrianism), the Hittite Kingdom, Ancient Israel/Judea, and Syria and Canaan. The next section moves west to focus on religion in Egypt and North Africa among the Phoenicians and Carthaginians. Part III turns to the religions of the Eastern Mediterranean: Mycenaean religion in Greece, Minoan religion on Crete, and religion in Greece. The volume concludes in the western Mediterranean with traditional Roman religion in the early and middle Republic in Italy, Etruscan religion in Italy, and Celtic religion in Western Europe.

Volume II includes the same regions as in Volume I, although different religious traditions appear. It begins with Iran and the Ancient Near East, including traditional religions in these areas, as well as essays on Judaism in Palestine in the Hellenistic-Roman periods, and post–70 CE Judaism in Roman Judea and the Near East, ending with Christianity in Syria. Volume II then turns west to Egypt and North Africa to examine traditional religions in Egypt, Judaism in Egypt, and Christianity in Egypt, before looking at traditional Punic and Roman religions and Christianity in North Africa. Part III turns to Greece and Asia Minor: traditional religions in Greece and Asia Minor, Judaism in Asia Minor, and Christianity in Asia Minor. The final section is devoted to the western Mediterranean, where we have evidence for traditional religions in Rome and Italy, Judaism in Italy and the West, Christianity in Italy, traditional religions in Roman Gaul, and Christianity in Gaul; a final essay unites discussion of traditional religions along with Christianity in Roman Spain.

There are introductory essays to each volume by the volume editors, Professor Marvin Sweeney for Volume I and Professor William Adler for Volume II, that provide a framework within which to read the essays. At the end of each essay, bibliographies are included that contain all works cited and in some cases, additional materials as well.

BIBLIOGRAPHY

Ando, Clifford. *The Matter of the Gods: Religion and the Roman Empire.* The Transformation of the Classical Heritage 44 (Berkeley, 2008).

Asad, Talal. *Genealogies of Religion: Discipline and Reasons of Power in Christianity and Islam* (Baltimore, 1993).

Athanassiadi, Polymnia, and Michael Frede. *Pagan Monotheism in Late Antiquity* (Oxford, 1999).

Beard, Mary, and Michael H. Crawford. *Rome in the Late Republic* (Ithaca, 1985).

Beard, Mary, John North, and Simon Price. *Religions of Rome:* Volume I, *A History* (Cambridge, 1998).

Bendlin, Andreas. "Peripheral Centres – Central Peripheries: Religious Communication in the Roman Empire." In *Römische Reichsreligion und Provinzialreligion*, ed. Hubert Cancik and Jörg Rüpke (Tübingen, 1997): 35–68.

Bowersock, Glen W. *Hellenism in Late Antiquity* (Ann Arbor, 1990).

Bremmer, Jan A. "'Religion,' 'Ritual,' and the Opposition 'Sacred vs. Profane': Notes towards a Terminological 'Genealogy.'" In *Ansichten griechischer Rituale. Geburtstags-Symposium für Walter Burkert*, ed. Fritz Graf (Stuttgart, 1998): 9–32.

Burkert, Walter. *The Orientalizing Revolution: Near Eastern Influence on Greek Culture in the Early Archaic Age*, trans. Margaret Pinder (Cambridge, Mass., 1998).

Cameron, Alan. *The Last Pagans of Rome* (New York, 2011).

Chuvin, Pierre. *A Chronicle of the Last Pagans* (Cambridge, Mass., 1990).

Earhart, H. Byron, ed. *Religious Traditions of the World: A Journey through Africa, Mesoamerica, North America, Judaism, Christianism, Islam, Hinduism, Buddhism, China and Japan* (San Francisco, 1992).

Fortson, Benjamin W. IV. *Indo-European Language and Culture: An Introduction*, 2nd ed. (Oxford, 2010).

Fowden, Garth. *Empire to Commonwealth: Consequences of Monotheism in Late Antiquity.* (Princeton, 1993).

Frankfurter, David. "Syncretism and the Holy Man in Late Antique Egypt." *JECS* 11 (2003): 339–85.

"Egyptian Religion and the Problem of the Category 'Sacrifice.'" In *Animal Sacrifice in the Ancient World*, ed. J. Knust and Z. Varhelyi (Oxford, 2011): 75–93.

Fredriksen, Paula. *Review* of G. Clark *Christianity and Roman Society*, Cambridge, UK, 2005, *JECS* 13 (2005): 532.

Graf, Fritz. "What Is Ancient Mediterranean Religion?" In *Religions of the Ancient World*, ed. S. I. Johnston (Cambridge, Mass., 2004): 3–16.

Horden, Peregrine, and Nicholas Purcell. *The Corrupting Sea: A Study of Mediterranean History* (Oxford and Malden, Mass., 2000).

Johnston, Sarah Iles. *Religions of the Ancient World* (Cambridge, Mass., 2004).

Lipinski, Edward. *Semitic Languages: Outline of a Comparative Grammar.* Orientalia Lovaniensia Analecta, 80, 2nd ed. (Leuven, 2001).

Martin, Luther. "'Disenchanting' the Comparative Study of Religion." *Method & Theory in the Study of Religion* 16 (2004): 36–44.

McClymond, Kathryn. *Beyond Sacred Violence: A Comparative Study of Sacrifice* (Baltimore, 2008).

McCutcheon, Russell T., ed. *The Insider/Outsider Problem in the Study of Religion: A Reader. Controversies in the Study of Religion* (London, 1999).

Mitchell, Stephen. "The Cult of Theos Hypsistos between Pagans, Jews and Christians." In *Pagan Monotheism in Late Antiquity*, ed. P. Athanassiadi and M. Frede (Oxford, 1999): 81–148.

"Further Thoughts on the Cult of *Theos Hypsistos*." In *One God: Pagan Monotheism in the Roman Empire*, ed. S. Mitchell and P. Van Nuffelen (Cambridge, 2010): 167–208.

Nagle, D. Brendan, and Stanley M. Burstein, ed. *The Ancient World: Readings in Social and Cultural History*, 7th ed. (New York, 2010).

Nongbri, Brent. "Dislodging 'Embedded' Religion." *Numen* 55 (2008): 440–60.

North, J. A. "Pagans, Polytheists and the Pendulum." In *The Spread of Christianity in the First Four Centuries*, ed. W. V. Harris (Leiden, 2005): 125–43.

O'Donnell, J. J. *Review* of M. R. Salzman, *The Making of a Roman Aristocracy: Social and Religious Change in the Western Roman Empire* (Cambridge, Mass., 2002). *BMCR* 2002.06.04, http://ccat.sas.upenn.edu/bmcr/2002–06–04.html.

Oppenheim, A. Leo. *Ancient Mesopotamia: Portrait of a Dead Civilization.* Revised and ed. Erica Reiner (Chicago, 1977).

Paden, William E. "Comparison in the Study of Religion." In *New Approaches to the Study of Religion*, ed. P. Antes, A. W. Geertz, and R. R. Warn (Berlin, 2004): 77–92.

Price, S. R. F. *Rituals and Power. The Roman Imperial Cult in Asia Minor* (Cambridge, 1984).

Rives, James B. *Religion in the Roman Empire* (Malden, Mass., 2007).

"Graeco-Roman Religion in the Roman Empire: Old Assumptions and New Approaches." *CBR* 8.2 (2010): 240–99.

Roller, Lynn E. *In Search of God the Mother: The Cult of Anatolian Cybele* (Berkeley, 1999).

Rüpke, Jörg. "Antike Grossstadtreligion." In *Zwischen Krise und Alltag*, ed. Christophe Batsch, Ulrike Egelhaaf-Gaiser, and Ruth Stepper (Stuttgart, 1999): 13–30.

The Religion of the Romans (Cambridge, 2007).

Smith, Jonathan Z. *Drudgery Divine: On the Comparison of Early Christianities and the Religions of Late Antiquity* (Chicago, 1990).

"Religion, Religions, Religious." In *Critical Terms for Religious Studies*, ed. Mark C. Taylor (Chicago, 1998): 269–84.

Sourvinou-Inwood, C. "What Is Polis Religion?" In *The Greek City from Homer to Alexander*, ed. O. Murray and S. R. F. Price (Oxford, 1990): 295–322.

Stewart, Charles, and Rosalind Shaw. "Introduction: Problematizing Syncretism." In *Syncretism/Anti-Syncretism: The Politics of Religious Synthesis*, ed. Charles Stewart and Rosalind Shaw (London, 1994): 1–26.

Trombley, Frank R. *Hellenic Religion and Christianization*. Religions in the Graeco-Roman World 115 (Leiden, 1993).

Woolf, G. D. "*Polis*-Religion and Its Alternatives in the Roman Provinces." In *Roman Religion*, ed. Clifford Ando (Edinburgh, 2003): 39–57.

"A Sea of Faith." *MHR* 18 (2004), 126–43.

INTRODUCTION TO VOLUME I

MARVIN A. SWEENEY

The conquest of the ancient Near East by Alexander the Great of Macedonia in 333–323 BCE constitutes a major turning point in the religious history of the ancient Near Eastern and Mediterranean worlds.[1] Alexander's conquest marked the first time that a European culture was able to gain political ascendency over the Near East. It presented the opportunity for Alexander and his successors to change profoundly the religious landscape of the ancient world through the promotion of Greek or Hellenistic culture and religion as the ideal form of human life. The introduction of Hellenization to the ancient Near Eastern world laid the groundwork for major change in the religions of the ancient world insofar as the melding of Hellenistic and Near Eastern cultures and religions ultimately produced forms of Judaism, Christianity, and Islam that now constitute the major religious traditions of the western world.

Interpreters of religion have had a mixed reaction to the religious impact of Alexander's conquest of the ancient Near East. On the one hand, many scholars hail the Hellenistic period as a time of great progress in which the light of Hellenistic culture, particularly its values, awakened the ancient Near Eastern world, enabling it to pursue new forms of human religious, cultural, and political expression and achievement.[2] Indeed, Greek thought is widely recognized as the one of the primary foundations for the western intellectual tradition. On the other hand, many other scholars view the promotion of Hellenization as an effort to subvert the nations and cultures that now came under Greek rule and to mold them into a relatively

---

[1] For studies of Alexander, see Green, *Alexander of Macedon;* see also Bosworth, "Alexander the Great, Part 1," "Alexander the Great, Part 2," and *Conquest and Empire.*
[2] See Starr, *A History of the Ancient World,* 407, 413–34.

24   *Marvin A. Sweeney*

cohesive culture that would serve its new Hellenistic masters.[3] Indeed, the Romans, who were always well known for their willingness to learn the lessons of their predecessors, likewise employed Hellenization as an important tool and weapon to serve their own efforts to unite and dominate the ancient Mediterranean and Near Eastern worlds.

The *Cambridge History of Religions of the Ancient World* is an effort to introduce readers to the religious world of the ancient Mediterranean, including southern and western Europe, western Asia, and northern Africa, both before and after the reign of Alexander the Great. Volume I presents the reader with introductions to the religions of the various nations and cultures that constituted the ancient Mediterranean world before the time of Alexander. The ancient Near East was well known for its own conquerors, including the Egyptians, the Sumerians, the Hittites, the Assyrians, the Babylonians, and the Persians, that influenced the religious development of nations under their control, but it was also well known for its religious diversity, insofar as the various cultures and nations of the ancient Near Eastern world also had distinctive forms of religious expression. Volume I thereby presents the seedbeds of the religious development of the western world by enabling the reader to understand both the common features and the distinctiveness of the pre-Alexandrian Mediterranean world.

Volume I approaches its task with a firm grounding in the field of comparative religions. The comparative study of religion has undergone tremendous change from its inception in the eighteenth and nineteenth centuries and through the course of the twentieth and early-twenty-first centuries.[4] Comparative religion necessarily gravitates between concern with those features of religious life and expression that are common or typical among the world's religions and those features that are unique to any given religious tradition. Early study in the field tended to emphasize elements that are common among the religions of the world, largely in an effort to establish a basis for common understanding of humanity's various efforts to give expression to beliefs about the divine or the supernatural.[5] Although such efforts were intended to promote dialogue and peaceful cooperation among the world's religions, interpreters learned to recognize that such universal foci frequently functioned as the means by which

---

[3] See, e.g., Green, *Alexander to Actium*, 312–35, and Isaac, *The Invention of Racism in Classical Antiquity*; cf. Said, *Orientalism*, although it should be noted that Said does not adequately account for the imperial interests of the East, specifically, Islam, in relation to the West (see, e.g., Karsh, *Islamic Imperialism*).

[4] For a convenient overview, see Paden, *Religious Worlds*.

[5] E.g., Eliade, *Patterns in Comparative Religion*.

Introduction to Volume I 25

powerful nations, religions, or cultures would challenge the validity of smaller or weaker nations, religions, or cultures and thereby to undermine and subjugate their smaller and more vulnerable counterparts.[6] History is replete with examples of major religions, such as Christianity, Islam, and Buddhism, that employed comparative criteria to define the validity of other religions in an effort to eradicate them altogether or to bring them under control as the major religions secured their dominant positions in their respective cultures. As a result, interpreters of comparative religion have begun to pay increasing attention to the unique features of a given religious tradition in an effort to understand the distinctive features as well as the conceptual and social integrity of a given religion in order to understand religion's role in influencing and bringing to expression the cultures or societies in which it is rooted.[7]

This issue is of particular importance for the study of religion in the ancient Mediterranean world because this region is the birthplace of the major religions of the modern western world: Judaism, Christianity, and Islam. It is clear that religion plays a major role in defining the distinctive nature of each of the cultures that make up the ancient Near Eastern and Mediterranean worlds, but it is also clear that religion plays a major role in the efforts of many of the nations in this region to spread their influence and gain dominance over their neighbors. Ancient Egypt, Sumer, Babylon, Assyria, Persia, Greece, Rome, and other empires viewed their major deities as ideal expressions or personifications of the values and character of their nations. Relations between nations, whether in the form of treaties that defined the terms of the relationship or in the form of tribute paid by one nation to another, were generally viewed as relations between the gods of the nations in question. Likewise, the relationships between the gods and goddesses within the religious systems of a particular culture often expressed the relationships between its social and political components, such as the cities that made up a larger nation, the bureaucracies that ruled and administered them, the religious functionaries that were established to oversee the life of the people, and even the roles assigned to family groups as well as the men, women, and children within a given culture.[8]

---

[6] See the discussion of the field in Masuzawa, *The Invention of World Religions*.
[7] See Paden, *Religious Worlds*, who stresses the need to construct social and historical context in the interpretation of the unique aspect of any religious system; see also Paden, *Interpreting the Sacred*, which emphasizes the role played by the socio-historical context and perspective of the interpreter in the study of religion.
[8] See, e.g., Handy, *Among the Host of Heaven*.

Numerous issues emerge in the contemporary comparative study of religion in this region. One is the role of deities as the fundamental focus of religion and the means by which each culture employs deities as personifications of the various aspects of its respective worldview. A second is an enhanced understanding of the role that mythology plays in articulating the social and political realities of the cultures in which a given religion functions. A third is the recognition that the social dimensions of religion demand consideration as much if not more so than the focus on religious beliefs insofar as each religion constitutes a paradigm for understanding the social construction of the culture or nation in question. A fourth is the recognition of the political dimensions and functions of religion, both on the part of the religions under study and on the part of the religious contexts in which the work of comparative religion is carried out. A fifth is the recognition of the role that gender plays in religious expression and life, insofar as religion typically defines the roles of men and women in society. And a sixth is the role that texts, whether oral or written, play in the articulation of each tradition. Each of these topics underlies the discussions of the religious traditions treated in this volume.

Volume I treats a very complex religious world in the Mediterranean and the ancient Near East before Alexander's conquest. Although many common elements bind the various religious traditions of the ancient Mediterranean and Near Eastern worlds, each is distinctive in its own right, often based upon the distinctive characteristics and socio-political realities of the nation or culture that produced it. The following chapters, each written by a recognized expert in the field, provide readers with the insights and tools to begin study of these traditions for themselves.

BIBLIOGRAPHY

Bosworth, A. B. "Alexander the Great, Part 1: The Events of His Reign." In *Cambridge Ancient History* VI: *The Fourth Century B.C.*, ed. D. M. Lewis et al. (Cambridge, 1994): 791–845.
"Alexander the Great, Part 2: Greece and the Conquered Territories," in *Cambridge Ancient History VI: The Fourth Century B.C.*, ed. D. M. Lewis et al. (Cambridge, 1994): 846–75.
Conquest and Empire: The Reign of Alexander the Great (Cambridge, 1988).
Eliade, Mircea. *Patterns in Comparative Religion* (New York, 1974).
Green, Peter. *Alexander of Macedon, 356–323 B.C.: A Historical Biography* (Berkeley, 1991).
Alexander to Actium: The Historical Evolution of the Hellenistic Age (Berkeley, 1990).
Handy, Lowell K. *Among the Host of Heaven: The Syro-Palestinian Pantheon as Bureaucracy* (Winona Lake, Ind., 1994).

Introduction to Volume I 27

Isaac, Benjamin. *The Invention of Racism in Classical Antiquity* (Princeton, 2004).

Karsh, Efraim. *Islamic Imperialism: A History* (New Haven, 2006).

Masuzawa, Tomoko. *The Invention of World Religions: Or How European Universalism Was Preserved in the Language of Pluralism* (Chicago, 2005).

Said, Edward. *Orientalism: Western Conceptions of the Orient* (London, 1978).

Paden, William E. *Religious Worlds: The Comparative Study of Religion* (Boston 1988). *Interpreting the Sacred* (Boston, 1992).

Starr, Chester. *A History of the Ancient World* (Oxford, 1965).

PART I

MESOPOTAMIA AND THE NEAR EAST

I

SUMERIAN RELIGION

GRAHAM CUNNINGHAM

Sumer, in the south of what is now Iraq, is celebrated as the region in which writing was invented and the world's earliest urban civilization developed.[1] Temples, as the institutions within which writing is first attested and as the symbolic centers of cities, played a major role in these developments. In addition, a rich and varied body of religious literature was written in Sumerian, bringing order to the world, explaining events within it, and mediating between the human and divine domains. Temples had interrelated functions as the earthly residences of deities and as administrative centers responsible for receiving and redistributing various types of commodities, and much of the religious literature is inseparably related to concepts of kingship. Sumerian religion thus constitutes a complex nexus of what are, from our perspective, theological, socio-economic, and political concerns.

Briefly it can be described as a polytheistic religion, with a strong belief in the efficacy and necessity of ritual, which expressed human dependence on the divine while at the same time enabling a reciprocal relationship between the two. The principal members of the pantheon were anthropomorphic and had joint roles, on a local level being identified with particular cities and on a regional level contributing to the cultural continuity that united Sumer. The pantheon was fluid and, paralleling the human form of deities, was organized on the same principles as human institutions. It was this fluidity that enabled the pantheon to develop, possibly having its origins in speculation about the physical universe, and subsequently expanding to include deities of pastoral and arable farming, and then of skills such as metal working and writing, as well as of objects symbolizing political

---

[1] For the Sumerian sites, see Map 1 in Chapter 2.

status, divine patronage thus stimulating and reinforcing socio-economic and political change.

Writing was invented in Sumer some 5,000 years ago, and Sumerian is attested as a high-status written language throughout much of the ancient Middle East for a period of approximately 2,500 years. The analysis that follows has a more narrow focus, concentrating on Sumer in the third millennium, the place and period during which the language was most extensively spoken and written, and more specifically on the time during this millennium when city-states were the predominant political structure.

Much of our reconstruction of Sumerian religion relies on the textual part of the archaeological record. The analysis therefore begins by contextualizing the written evidence, then locates Sumer in space and time, and concludes by examining in more detail, and in broadly chronological order, the essential parts of that record. First, however, some minor points should be made about how references are given for Sumerian literature, and how Sumerian and Semitic terms are transliterated. The literature is cited according to its modern titles in two online resources, the Diachronic Corpus of Sumerian Literature (*DCSL*) and the Electronic Text Corpus of Sumerian Literature (*ETCSL*),[2] and in the case of the *ETCSL* according to the number a composition has within that corpus. The transliteration conventions are much simpler than those adopted in specialist publications, which use a wide range of diacritics to indicate variations in pronunciation and specify the signs with which words were written.

Transliterated names of deities are hyphenated when they consist of more than one word and are given a literal translation when first mentioned. To map the translations onto the transliterations, the Sumerian genitive case-marker requires a brief description. It is functionally equivalent to the preposition *of*, but like the possessive *'s* in that it occurs at the end of a phrase and is phonologically bound to the word that it follows. The forms of the genitive are complex, and the solution typically taken in transliterating names is not to indicate this case-marker after a word ending in a vowel, as in En-ki, "Lord of (the) earth," and to suffix an *a* after a word ending in a consonant, as in Nin-hursaga, "Lady of (the) foothills." As these examples indicate, Sumerian has no article, nor does it distinguish between singular and plural in inanimate reference. More importantly, the examples also show that many divine names begin with a title.

---

[2] See *Suggestions for Further Reading* at the end of this volume for these resources.

The exact nuances of these titles are difficult to recover, and the status that *nin* confers was also given to some gods.

FROM LITERACY TO LANGUAGE-DEATH

From the invention of writing onward, most of the textual evidence from the ancient Middle East is concerned with administration, including records of the food and drink given to the incarnations of deities in their temples, both on a daily basis and at religious festivals. This administrative focus is particularly pronounced for much of the first half of the third millennium. However, from roughly 2700 onward (all dates are BCE, and are highly approximate), a wider range of textual types is available, including inscriptions incised on durable material such as stone and deposited in temples by rulers.

With their references to rulers, the inscriptions place us more securely in what can be termed history. However, in some cases even establishing the broad outlines of this historical narrative remains difficult. The incompleteness of the textual record is one of the factors contributing to this uncertainty. It is not simply that the accidents of recovery render the record incomplete, but more that most documents were not written with preservation in mind. Although the inscriptions were clearly intended for survival, most writing was instead on clay tablets, which were recycled once they had served their function, although some were discarded to form part of a subsequent building's foundation. It is these discards that are available to us, as well as instances in which the recycling process was interrupted by a building being destroyed or abandoned.

The clay tablets can be divided broadly into two types, administrative and a much smaller group of what can provisionally be termed school texts, many of which are religious in nature, some being lists of deities, structured in terms of their importance and the relationships between them, whereas others are literary compositions, such as hymns in praise of deities. In addition to content and function, fundamental differences are seen between the two types of text: administrative records, unlike school texts, are not attested in multiple exemplars, nor was their content ever transmitted over time.

Our most extensive record of the religious literature comes from eighteenth-century schools and results from such processes of transmission, testifying to the tradition's cultural and ideological significance but often making it difficult to identify when its constituent parts were first composed or how accurately they have been preserved. Similar tablets of an earlier date are less securely provenanced but may also have come from an educational context, again suggesting an association between textualization and incorporation within the curriculum. Further difficulties remain in identifying the contexts in which these compositions were originally performed, whereas other compositions are likely to have been performed but never textualized, thus lying beyond our recovery.

Bearing these qualifications in mind, what the religious literature depicts is a pantheon headed by three gods, each identified with a different part of the cosmos: An, whose name means "The heavens," associated with that part of the universe; En-ki ("Lord of the earth"), associated with what was envisaged as a sacred subterranean ocean, *ki* thus referring not to the surface of the earth but to its substance; and En-lil ("Lord wind"), associated with the space between the two. This vertical axis is reinforced by hymns to temples that describe them as reaching up to the heavens and down to the underground ocean, figurative praise that was physically realized in the monumental scale of the temples.

The two most important female deities are Inana, the goddess of the Venus "star" in its morning and evening aspects, whose name may be a reduction of Nin-ana ("Lady of heaven"), and the various, to some degree syncretized, local forms of a mother-goddess, including Nin-mah ("Majestic lady"), who are associated with birth, child-rearing, and the creation of mankind. According to creation-narratives such as *En-ki and Nin-mah* (*ETCSL* 1.1.2), mankind has been created by the deities to save the latter from having to support themselves, work on the fields thus being a divinely ordained economic necessity, paralleling the ritual presentation of food and drink to deities in their temples.

The aspects of the cosmos with which the deities are associated embrace two categories we regard as distinct: nature, that is, the physical universe, and the human world of social interaction and labor. As is made clear in the distribution of divine offices in *En-ki and the world order* (*ETCSL* 1.1.3), this distinction is alien to Sumerian, both being regarded as dependent upon the divine. This dependence is also expressed in the concept of the *me*, a noun formed from the verb *me* "to be" and thus having a literal meaning as "being," or less literally as "essence," corresponding to one of the other senses of nature in English, that is, as innate quality or character. The *me* were regarded as having a kind of prototype form in the divine domain that could be realized in the human domain, and they included the offices and skills, both social and professional, regarded as essential to civilization. No complete account of the *me* is known, but many, with a particular focus on the cult of Inana, are listed in *Inana and En-ki* (*ETCSL* 1.3.1), a narrative possibly associated with a ceremony held in honor of that goddess.[3]

In addition to being patrons of aspects of the universe, the principal deities were associated with particular cities, An, for example, with Uruk, En-ki with Eridu, and En-lil with Nippur. In terms of political structure, for the middle part of the third millennium these cities can be regarded as the capitals of city-states, that is, small, relatively independent states consisting of an urban center, satellite settlements, and an agricultural hinterland, with varying degrees of cooperation and conflict, and sometimes control, characterizing the relationships between the different states.[4] In some cases, a single state included more than one urban settlement, each having its own satellites and its own patron deity. This description is also likely to apply to the earlier part of the third millennium, although the textual evidence from that period is more limited, as is our understanding of that record. At the end of the preceding millennium the city of Uruk was of particular importance, and its influence and size may have had political consequences. Much of the later third and early second millennia present a more clear-cut political contrast and can be characterized as a period of regional states, under which the city-states lost their political independence and became provinces.

At some stage during this period of primarily regional states, Sumerian ceased to be spoken, although exactly when remains uncertain. The last administrative documents in the language date to as late as the eighteenth century, but these may be following the convention with which writing began rather than reflecting a spoken reality. They are outnumbered by documents in a Semitic language known as Akkadian, first attested during the second half of the third millennium. Akkadian is reasonably well understood because of its similarities to Semitic languages that are still spoken. Sumerian, however, has so far not been convincingly demonstrated to relate to any other group of languages. In consequence, it is much less well understood than Akkadian, and to a large degree our understanding of the language relies on what was taught in ancient schools, lists of Sumerian words, for example, being accompanied by their Akkadian equivalents as well as by guides to their pronunciation.

---

[3] Cohen, *Calendars*, 215–17.
[4] Westenholz, "City-State," 23–42.

CITIES IN THE PLAIN

The first places mentioned in the written record from the ancient Middle East are cities. Expressions for areas are attested only from the second half of the third millennium onward, vary in application, and differ depending on language. We tend to refer instead to Mesopotamia, a loanword from ancient Greek whose literal meaning is "between rivers," the rivers being the Euphrates and Tigris, which rise in the mountains of Turkey and flow down through Iraq to the Persian Gulf. This broad area is divided in two, at a line running slightly to the north of what is now Baghdad, with lower Mesopotamia again being subdivided, at a line running to the north of the ancient city of Nippur.

In Akkadian Sumer corresponds approximately to the south of lower Mesopotamia and Akkad to the north. However, in what we, following Akkadian, call Sumerian, the term for the language is instead *eme-gir*, whereas Sumer is *ki-en-gir* and Akkad *ki-uri*. A literal translation of *eme-gir* is as "native-tongue," noting that in Sumerian a modifier typically follows what it modifies, so the Sumerian sequence is the reverse of the English. In the area names *ki* has the sense of "region," but the other elements are more opaque. One possibility is that *ki-en-gi* is a reduction of a hypothetical *ki-eme-gir*, in which case it can be analyzed as "native-tongue-region," while *uri* is not attested elsewhere in Sumerian, suggesting that it originated in another language. Although analysis of the Sumerian area-terms is uncertain, the Akkadian terminology, deriving words for languages from words for areas, indicates that Akkadian was spoken mainly in the north of lower Mesopotamia and Sumerian mainly in the south, although both areas are likely to have been more multilingual than the written record indicates.

Defining lower Mesopotamia in geographical terms is more straightforward. It consists of the alluvial plain created by the waters of the Euphrates and the Tigris, bounded by mountains in the northeast, desert in the southwest, and marshes leading to the sea in the southeast, with the shoreline of the Persian Gulf lying higher then than it does now. The two rivers enter this area from the northwest, providing transport links to upper Mesopotamia, and within lower Mesopotamia between the cities strung out along the banks of the rivers, the more slowly flowing Euphrates being the most important of the two in relation to the development of Sumer. The geographical distinction within the alluvial plain is between the river-plain in the north and the delta-plain in the south, the flat slope of the land reducing further in the latter, encouraging the Euphrates to split into multiple shifting channels.

Rainfall on the plain is insufficient to support farming. Profiting from the fertility of the alluvial soil consequently required the use of irrigation, while sub-desert outside watered areas provided pasturage for grazing animals. Exactly how this agricultural economy developed into one that supported an urbanized society is much disputed. It is, however, clear that the temples played a significant role in this development. From late prehistory onward they dominated the urban landscape, as they did the flat alluvial plain, and later periods show that this visual dominance had a socio-economic correlate, the temple functioning as a major redistributive center, receiving and reallocating agricultural produce, enabling some members of society to concentrate on maximizing food production while others specialized in artisan-production or administration.

FROM PREHISTORY TO HISTORY

It is to the fifth millennium that the first agricultural settlements in lower Mesopotamia are dated, the evidence coming from the south rather than north of the plain, although agriculture is attested much earlier in upper Mesopotamia. The first temples in lower Mesopotamia also date to this millennium, including one in the far south at Eridu, which the later literary tradition celebrates as the original city (*The Sumerian king list, ETCSL* 2.1.1). In the historical periods Eridu is the earthly residence of the god En-ki, who is associated with the *ab-zu*, the first element in which means ocean, with the second being unclear. This ocean was thought to lie below the surface of the earth and to be the source of the fresh water in springs, wells, and rivers, a concept of central importance given the region's relative lack of rain. However, the origins of the temple may relate less to the god and more to the fresh-water ocean, the marshy environment of lagoons in which it was built being regarded as a manifestation of this essential aspect of the cosmos.

Archaeological evidence from the temple's fifth-millennium levels matches the characteristics of temples in later periods, indicating a combined socio-economic and cultic role. In particular, stamp seals imply that some temple personnel held positions of authority, possibly controlling the movement of commodities in sealed containers, and the large quantities of fish bones suggest divine offerings, and more generally an architectural framing of ritual within a built environment. The temple was repeatedly rebuilt in the same place, respecting the sacredness of the site while at the same time raising the temple ever higher on platforms formed from previous incarnations, each successive stage increasing in grandeur and elaboration over its predecessor. As a result, by the end of the third millennium, when Eridu's economic, but not its religious, significance had diminished, the modest fifth-millennium beginnings had been transformed into a monumental complex consisting of suites of rooms around a central open space with an offerings table, supplemented by a ziggurat, one of the few instances of an Akkadian loanword in English, a multi-staged tower rising in levels of decreasing size, each level having its own terrace.

The fourth millennium, and slightly beyond, is referred to as the Uruk period (4000–2900), named after an immense city in the south of the plain whose influence spread throughout much of Mesopotamia. This was a period of major demographic change, the countryside becoming relatively depopulated while settlements diminished in number but increased in size from the small villages and few towns of the fifth millennium to sites of urban proportions. The largest by far was Uruk itself, the largest city in the world at this time, although other cities increased in importance toward the end of the period.

Densely populated urban centers surrounded by an agricultural hinterland continued to be the pattern for the rest of the third millennium and beyond. One term used for much of the third millennium is Early Dynastic, subdivided into Early Dynastic I (2900–2750), II (2750–2600), IIIa (2600–2450), and IIIb (2450–2350). As the term suggests, this is the first time we have evidence for sequences of hereditary rulers governing city-states. However, the extent to which such dynasties ruled throughout lower Mesopotamia during the Early Dynastic period is uncertain, nor is the existence of hereditary rule in earlier periods necessarily excluded.

This hereditary principle continued to apply to the rulers of the following imperial states, first during an empire whose capital was Agade in the north of the alluvial plain (2350–2150), the city-name being related to the area-term Akkad, and then during an empire whose capital was Ur in the far south of the plain near Eridu (2100–2000). The founder of the first of these regional states was Sargon, an anglicization of the Akkadian Sharru-kin ("The king is legitimate"), and the brief intervening period of renewed city-state independence is referred to as the post-Sargonic period (2150–2100).

The beginning of the second millennium saw further political changes as other Semitic rulers from the north, but this time Amorites, vied for control over Sumer. Two smaller regional states in the south of the plain, centered on Isin and then Larsa, were followed by a third empire, founded in the eighteenth century and centered on Babylon. Babylon's rise shifted political power irreversibly to the north and set in motion the ascent of its patron deity, Marduk, to a position as head of the pantheon. Analysis of this name continues to defy modern scholars; ancient scholars, however, interpreted it as a reduction of a Sumerian phrase, Amar-Utu ("Calf of Utu"), Utu being the sun-god, whose all-seeing daily journey across the sky led to his characterization as a god of justice and truth.

Setting these political changes within a theological framework was one of the concerns of Sumerian literature composed during the Ur and Isin periods, providing the first textual evidence of an interest in assessing, and to some degree appropriating, the recent past. The same narrative that specifies Eridu as the earliest city, *The Sumerian king list*, describes kingship as an institution that descends from heaven and is passed from city to city. This composition is first attested during the period of Ur's domination and appears to promote an imperial ideology, restricting kingship to one city at a time in Mesopotamia, whereas the evidence from the Early Dynastic period suggests that this type of overlordship was rare. According to *The king list*, Ur had already been the dominant city twice before the end of the third millennium, an account that continues to inform modern conventions, the late third millennium often being referred to as the Ur III period.

Although *The king list* illustrates the principle of social institutions as divine gifts, and more broadly the principle of divine intervention within the human domain, it provides no motivation for this intervention. Other compositions, however, elaborate on the ways in which divine decisions necessarily precede political changes. For example, *The cursing of Agade* (*ETCSL* 2.1.5), again first attested in the period dominated by Ur, interprets Agade's fall in traditional terms, that is, as divine punishment of a ruler's transgressions. The various compositions concerned with the fall of Ur develop a different interpretation, presumably because the subsequent Isin rulers, who sought to portray themselves as heirs to the Ur dynasty, wished to have an unsullied inheritance.

These compositions depict divine favor instead as being necessarily impermanent in relation to kingship, its loss therefore being inevitable. Although this was a new theory of political change, it was set within a traditional framework, the compositions lamenting the fall of the Ur empire focusing on the principal religious centers of Sumer: Nippur (*ETCSL* 2.2.4), Uruk (*ETCSL* 2.2.5), and Eridu (*ETCSL* 2.2.6), as well as Ur itself (*ETCSL* 2.2.2 and 2.2.3). The patron god of Ur is a further instance of a major celestial body, the moon, envisaged as a manifestation of a deity. Reflecting the moon's importance for calculating the passage of time, this god had various names, in particular Nanna as the maximal phase of the lunar cycle and Suen as its minimal phase, the moon's crescent-horns also associating the god with cattle and their fertility. In later periods the full moon was referred to as Nannar, presumably reflecting the influence of the Akkadian verb *namaru* "to be bright."

THE FIRST WRITING

Initially, however, writing had a very different function than recording theological accounts of the loss of kingship. It is in Uruk, toward the end of the fourth millennium, that writing is first attested, where it originates not as a way of representing a language but as a form of bureaucratic record-keeping.[5] By the end of the Early Dynastic I period, or possibly later given the provisional nature of our dating of these early tablets, there is evidence of a more widespread distribution of writing, and of its use to represent Sumerian, although still in a very limited way.

In some cases the function of the buildings in which these administrative records were kept remains unclear. However, where the buildings can be identified they are temples. The earliest records are discards found among fill used to raise the platform of a temple-complex dedicated to the goddess Inana. Most of the records from the end of the Uruk period come from the same temple, with a few of the same date being found in a temple of the moon-god in Urum, a city in the north of the alluvial plain. Most of the records dating approximately to the Early Dynastic I period are also associated with a temple of the moon-god, but instead in Ur.

While these administrative records remain difficult to understand, they suggest that the temple played a significant economic role, performing a central function within a redistributive system based on a principle of hierarchical reciprocity, receiving agricultural produce or labor in exchange for providing other supplies or services. The signs in these documents record book-keeping entries, and, like stamp and cylinder seals, they may have originated as a language-independent administrative device. Most are depictions of all or part of what they refer to, or of objects associated with that reference, the sign for the sky-god, for example, being a star. Over time the immediacy of this association was reduced as many signs acquired multiple meanings, and all were reoriented and written using a combination of wedge-like marks, the term we use for this script, cuneiform, coming from the Latin for wedge, *cuneus*. In addition, a small set of signs was also used to represent sound-sequences,

---

[5] Cooper, "Beginnings," 71–99.

Sumerian Religion

41

enabling a wider range of words to be written, and the particular form of a word to be specified more fully.

Some of these administrative documents have been identified more specifically as the first records of food offerings for a deity.[6] Such offerings, dedicated to deities in temples but allotted to their attendants, are central to Sumerian religion, the presence of an honored and therefore benevolent deity being regarded as essential to a city's viability. The hierarchical reciprocity implied in this relationship, that in return for the offerings the deity will bestow blessings, can be interpreted as a sacred counterpart to the temple's redistributive role, providing the foundation on which its more wide-ranging economic activities were based.

Visual evidence of such offerings also comes from Uruk, most strikingly in relief carvings on an alabaster vase dating to the end of the Uruk period (see Fig. 1). The lowest bands on this vase depict water, plants, and domesticated animals. The middle band shows a procession of ritually naked men advancing in unison holding vessels filled with the fruits of the land. The top, and deepest, band portrays a clothed man (partly damaged) whose naked attendant presents offerings to a female figure, Inana, standing in front of her temple. What is thus depicted is a hierarchical and complementary social structure embedded within a natural order headed by a deity, and an agricultural economy dedicated to the service of that deity's urban institution, the temple.

LEXICAL LISTS

The next attested use of writing, for recording lexical lists, differs in crucial ways from the administrative records. These are lists of semantically related words, compiled by scholars for use in the education of trainee scribes, and presumably therefore originating in an educational context, as opposed to the administrative contexts in which trained scribes practiced their trade. The somewhat dry term we use to refer to these compilations obscures the sophisticated ways in which they construct knowledge, and in some cases reconstruct it as their content was transmitted across time.

One of these lexical lists, *The cities list*,[7] first attested in Uruk at the end of the Uruk period, is particularly relevant to the relationship between a city and its patron deity. The principles on which this list is structured remain uncertain. However, the first six names are of important cities in

---

[6] Szarzynska, "Offerings," 115–40.
[7] Matthews, *Cities*, 39–40.

Fig. 1. Uruk (Warka) vase. Water, corn growing from water, sheep, men bearing gifts, and the goddess Inana (Inanna). Five rows of limestone bas-reliefs on a cult vase from Uruk, Mesopotamia (Iraq). Location: National Museum, Baghdad, Iraq. Photo by Erich Lessing. © Art Resource, NY

the south of the alluvial plain: Ur, Nippur, Larsa, Uruk, Kesh, and Zabala. Except for Kesh, probably located farther north than the other cities, each of these names is written in ways that emphasize the city's close identification with its temple and divine patron.

Nippur is written with the same signs as its patron deity En-lil, the two often being distinguished by what is referred to as a determinative, a sign written, but not pronounced, to specify the semantic class of the noun that it accompanies. The writing of the names of the four cities farther south than Nippur follows a different principle.

For Larsa and Zabala the sign for a shrine is combined with the sign used for the cities' respective deities, the sun-god Utu and the Venus-goddess Inana, thus being visually "Utu-shrine" and "Inana-shrine." The sign for a shrine appears to depict the front of a temple raised on a platform, and the sign for Utu is of the sun over the mountains; the sign symbolizing Inana is less straightforward, possibly depicting a temple-doorpost made from bundles of reed tied together. The writings of the city Ur and its patron god Nanna offer a variation on this principle. The city's name is again written by combining the sign for a shrine with the sign symbolizing the deity, also perhaps a depiction of a column-like object made from reeds. However, the writing of the god's name is supplemented by the sign *na*, specifying its pronunciation; over time the initial horizontal wedge in this sign was omitted, the sign thus being reduced to the one we refer to as KI. Uruk itself is written only with a modified version of the sign for a shrine, suggesting that it was regarded simply as the site of *the* shrine, therefore requiring no further specification.

The writing of these city-names indicates the principle of one major deity presiding over one city, although Uruk was the earthly residence of both An and Inana, two originally distinct settlements, Kulaba and Uruk, presumably having merged as one. Typically, a deity presides over only one city. Inana is again an exception, with major sanctuaries in both Uruk and Zabala as well as elsewhere. Local forms of mother-goddesses are also patrons of various cities, including Nin-hursaga ("Lady of the foothills") at Kesh. In addition, the moon-god and the sun-god are guardians of two cities, but here the distribution is geographical, Nanna being patron of Ur in the south of the alluvial plain and Urum in the north, while Utu is patron of Larsa in the south and Sippar in the north.

Their association with a particular deity expresses the individuation of cities. However, their incorporation within such lists suggests that they formed an inclusive community. The deities themselves were also organized into lexical lists, indicating how religion contributed toward this sense of a shared identity. Two fragments of what may be deity lists have been identified at Uruk, from the end of the Uruk period, and at Ur, possibly from the Early Dynastic I period.[8] However, the earliest complete examples date to the Early Dynastic IIIa period,[9] when most of the textual evidence comes from two cities, Shuruppak, upriver from Uruk, and Abu Salabikh (ancient name uncertain), upriver from Nippur.

The Early Dynastic IIIa deity lists, cataloging more than 500 gods and goddesses, are compiled partly on the basis of theological speculation, the first entries following a hierarchical order, and partly on lexical principles, many later entries being grouped together in terms of how they are written. In contrast to administrative documents specifying divine offerings, which provide a vivid record of the deities honored in a particular place at a particular time, the deity lists are more atemporal and regional. The Shuruppak list begins An, En-lil, Inana, En-ki, Nanna, and Utu. As this list indicates, An was considered to be the head of the pantheon; he is, however, a somewhat remote figure, and the other deities appear more frequently, and more actively, in the textual record. The pantheon was fluid rather than fixed, the first six entries at Abu Salabikh being instead An, En-lil, Nin-lil, En-ki, Nanna, and Inana. This sequence places less emphasis on Uruk deities, listing Inana in a lower position, and more on En-lil's city of Nippur, giving third position to his wife Nin-lil ("Lady wind").

Nin-lil's incorporation high in the list from Abu Salabikh further indicates the anthropomorphic nature of Sumerian religion: Deities, in addition to their temple-incarnations requiring food like humans, were related on the model of family relationships, that is, in terms of marriage and parentage, albeit with some degree of flexibility. Consequently, according to one tradition, En-lil and En-ki were sons of An, while Nanna was a son of En-lil, and Utu a son of Nanna. Inana was sometimes a daughter of An, but sometimes of Nanna, then being Utu's sister. Family relationships were constructed on a local as well as a regional basis, En-lil's son in Nippur being the warrior-god Nin-urta, tentatively "Lord of the [arable surface of the] earth," the temple-complex containing subsidiary shrines or separate buildings dedicated to the other members of the divine family.

Confirmation of the complexity of a city's divine household comes from later records of offerings. These show that it was not only the presiding deity who received daily offerings, as well as being clothed and housed in great splendor, but also what were regarded as other members of his

---

[8] Englund, "Texts," 88.
[9] Selz, "Enlil," 212–25.

household, his family, advisors, servants, and sacred possessions, in particular weapons and musical instruments, each of which had its own name. In an extension of this principle, and reflecting the sanctity of the temple, offerings were also given to different parts of the building, such as its gateways and door-bolts.

INSCRIPTIONS

Inscriptions, that is, writing on durable material such as stone artifacts and baked clay, are attested from approximately the Early Dynastic I period onward. Typically these artifacts were deposited in temples, the material marking them as a permanent record thus being reinforced by divine recognition and protection. The earliest inscriptions record the sale by families of that most immovable of assets, land,[10] suggesting a greater emphasis on personalized material wealth. More specifically, this evidence of family-owned property qualifies any suggestion that the temple was the sole landowner, although it should be noted that these sale-records are little attested in the far south of the alluvial plain. Personalization of status also characterizes later inscriptions, attested from the Early Dynastic II period onward, which were used instead to commemorate the deeds of rulers.[11]

These royal inscriptions develop a theology accounting for a ruler's authority, depicting him as the divinely chosen steward of a deity's earthly estates. Typically it is the presiding deity of a city who is said to have selected a ruler, his political and military success being attributed to this divine approval. However, the principal deities often also contribute, Nin-hursaga, for example, being described as nourishing a ruler, En-ki as providing wisdom, and Inana as loving him. Toward the end of the Early Dynastic period, as city-states vied for control over other city-states, En-lil's favor was regarded as the most important. During the subsequent periods of regional states his city of Nippur played a central role in this ideology of kingship, religious authority thus being vested in a single deity at the same time as political authority took the form of a single state. Some city-rulers were further validated as being of divine parentage. In an extension of this principle, some rulers of regional states were not simply associated with the divine but were elevated to that status.

[10] Gelb et al., *Tenure*.
[11] Cooper, "Inscriptions," 227–39.

Administrative records from the Early Dynastic III period provide further qualification to the role of temples as landowners, as well as further evidence of the status of these city-rulers. Most of the records dating to this period come from two cities, Shuruppak again (IIIa, like the deity list) and Girsu (IIIb), located in the east of Sumer and the source of most of the royal inscriptions. The texts from Girsu provide our most complete record of a temple's economic role in the Early Dynastic period, indicating its involvement in irrigation, fishing, arable farming (cultivating cereals, vegetables, and fruit-trees), pastoralism (managing herds of cows and flocks of sheep and goats), artisan-production (of textiles, leather and wooden items, and metal and stone objects), and long-distance trade. However, as is the case at Shuruppak, these records also indicate that the city-ruler had overall responsibility for the temple's estates, in addition to having extensive estates of his own.

Such monarchical rulers constitute a political authority superior to the temple, albeit one with many religious responsibilities, although extrapolating from these limited data is difficult and it is possible that in other places and in earlier periods the head of the temple was the head of the city-state, or that authority had a more distributed form such as an assembly. Some support for the distinctive nature of these rulers, or more exactly their palaces, comes from the language itself. In Sumerian the word *e,* "house," covering a much wider semantic field that includes "household" and "estate," was used to refer to both a human and a divine residence, the latter conventionally being translated as temple. This suggests a communal ethos, with differences of scale rather than of principle. In contrast, a different term was used for a palace, *e-gal,* literally "great house," a compound noun on the basis that it was borrowed into Akkadian as a single word.

The administrative records from Girsu also provide the first extensive references to religious festivals,[12] although given their nature they simply list offerings and provide no description of the rituals that accompanied their presentation. At this time Girsu, whose patron deity, the warrior-god Nin-Girsu ("Lord of Girsu"), is ranked seventh in the deity list from Abu Salabikh, was the capital of a city-state that incorporated various other urban centers on the same branch of the Euphrates, among them Lagash, after which the state was named. The festivals served to unite the state, the ruler's wife leading processions between the various cities and dedicating offerings to the deities in each, including sheep and lambs for the senior deities and goats for those more junior.

---

[12] Cohen, *Calendars,* 37–64.

Sumerian Religion

The inscriptions themselves also provide examples of royal participation in ritual, most commemorating a ruler's rebuilding of a temple or dedication of an object to a deity in a temple. Indicating the instrumental and reciprocal nature of Sumerian religion, many inscriptions specify the divine blessing that was sought in return, namely, that the ruler should have a long life. Temple-building is also the concern of the longest inscription known in Sumerian, which again comes from Girsu, but dates to the post-Sargonic period of renewed city-state independence, under a ruler whose name was Gu-dea, "(The one to whom the) voice has been poured," or less literally "The chosen one." This inscription, *The building of Nin-Girsu's temple* (*ETCSL* 2.1.7), is a masterly recasting in narrative form of the rituals for constructing and inaugurating a temple, and as such can also be classified as literature.

As in the religious festivals, the inscription serves to unite the state of Lagash, recounting how Gu-dea travels between its principal settlements to gain support from their deities for rebuilding the temple, setting the construction-work within a theological framework of divine approval. Like other rulers, he is depicted as a shepherd, thus superior to his people but responsible for their welfare, who has special access to the deities through divination, dreams in particular being vehicles for divine messages. However, although other royal inscriptions offer a somewhat formulaic vision of a prosperous society, this narrative develops a subtle congruence between social structure and physical structure, correlating an idealized social order to the immaculate organization of the temple, the designs for which are said to come from the deities themselves, from Nisaba, the goddess of writing, and Nin-dub, "Lord tablet."

RELIGIOUS LITERATURE

The first evidence of strategies for seeking divine approval other than dedicatory offerings is an isolated inscription containing praise of Nin-Girsu,[13] possibly dating to the Early Dynastic II period. Most of the third-millennium sources for religious literature date instead to the following IIIa period, again coming from Shuruppak and Abu Salabikh. Many of these compositions are written according to a set of conventions that remain opaque to us, and very few are attested later in a more fully written form. The focus in what follows is consequently on those that are most comprehensible, including hymnic, narrative, and didactic compositions, supplemented by

---

[13] Cooper, "Inscriptions," 228.

48 *Graham Cunningham*

references to religious literature preserved on eighteenth-century sources. These compositions depict deities more vividly than the gnomic administrative records, although the vividness often relates as much to the greater glory of rulers as it does to deities.

An early instance of devotional literature is provided by a hymn to Nin-hursaga's temple in Kesh (*The Kesh temple hymn, DCSL*), also attested in a later version (*ETCSL* 4.80.2). Like much other praise of temples, this hymn emphasizes their role in mediating between the human world and the divine domains above and below, describing the temple as embracing heaven and being rooted in the *ab-zu*. Later, however, the focus of praise is deities and regional rulers, the eighteenth-century curriculum being dominated by royal praise poetry and hymns to deities that often request divine blessings for a ruler (*ETCSL* 2.3.1–2.99.e, 4.01.1–4.33.3). This devotional literature stresses the fearsome awesomeness of temples and deities, reflecting the intense nature of many encounters with the divine. However, the rhetoric of terrifying praise is particularly associated with warrior-deities, suggesting that it was also put to political and military ends, as rulers sought to assert authority within their own territories and sometimes beyond them.

Another category of religious composition, referred to as incantations, is also attested from the Early Dynastic IIIa period onward.[14] These differ from other religious compositions in various ways, including, in ancient terms, having only a marginal association with the eighteenth-century curriculum, and, in modern terms, being sufficiently formulaic that they are rarely classified as literature. The incantations have a more explicit instrumental function than the hymns, being used, for example, to provide release from various types of suffering, such as illness, as well as in contexts that focus less on the individual, such as vivifying statues with the presence of a deity. They employ a wider range of verbal strategies than the hymns to achieve these ends. One of these extends the same symbolic significance to sacred purifiers as temples by praising them in similar terms as reaching up to heaven and down to the *ab-zu*. However, another takes a narrative approach to eliding the distance between the human and divine worlds, describing how a junior deity notices a problem in the human domain and then seeks advice from a more remote senior deity, who provides the necessary solution.

In the later periods the senior deity in these narratives is En-ki, the provider of the fresh water of the *ab-zu* essential for agriculture as well for

---

[14] Geller, "Incantations," 269–83.

the purification that is one of the incantations' primary concerns. As such En-ki is rarely associated with the divine awe elaborated in devotional literature, and in other narratives his role is also favorable to mankind. For example, in *En-ki and the world order* (*ETCSL* 1.1.3) he organizes every aspect of the civilized world, and in *Inana and En-ki* (*ETCSL* 1.3.1) he is the holder of the *me* that are essential to human life.

The incantations develop a complex theology to account for the suffering they seek to relieve, to a degree extending on a continuum from random attacks by the A-sag ("Arm-beating") demon to punishment inflicted by En-lil, whose agent is the Namtar ("Fate") demon. Narrative refractions of these two extremes are also attested in the later literary tradition. In *Nin-urta's exploits* (*ETCSL* 1.6.2) the warrior-god defeats the A-sag, while En-lil's relationship with humanity is often depicted as problematic, reflecting his characterization as a storm-god whose tempests manifest divine anger. This is particularly the case in *The flood story* (*ETCSL* 1.7.4), in which he sends a destructive flood, for reasons missing from the fragmentary source. The savior of mankind, who warns of the flood to come, is also missing, although a brief account in another composition credits En-ki (*The death of Gilgamesh*, *ETCSL* 1.8.1.3), thus paralleling his supportive role in incantations and elsewhere.

The importance of the two deities is reflected in their status as creator-gods, each using different technical skills to create mankind. En-ki, in company with the mother-goddess Nin-mah, molds mankind from clay like a potter (*En-ki and Nin-mah*, *ETCSL* 1.1.2), while En-lil, in a pun-filled composition celebrating the hoe, applies that tool's associations with agriculture and building-construction to the fashioning of mankind (*The song of the hoe*, *ETCSL* 5.5.4). Reproduction accounts instead for the creation of minor deities, narratives again being attested in which the two gods play a major role in this sexual process, En-ki with the mother-goddess Nin-hursaga (*ETCSL* 1.1.1) and En-lil with his wife-to-be Nin-lil (*ETCSL* 1.2.1).

The survivor of the flood, sheltering in an ark-like boat, was Zi-ud-sura ("Life of distant days"), a ruler of Shuruppak, appropriately named given that his reward for survival was eternal life. Zi-ud-sura also appears in a didactic composition, but as a prince receiving advice from his father on the correct forms of behavior (*The instructions of Shuruppak*, *ETCSL* 5.6.1). Descriptions of rulers often set their moral and intellectual qualities within a broader framework of praise. In *The instructions*, however, the focus is solely on the ruler as sage, Shuruppak, named after his city, transmitting wisdom rather than might on a hereditary principle.

The instructions is another of the few instances of literature attested in both eighteenth-century and Early Dynastic IIIa versions (*DCSL*). Other compositions are conceptually rather than textually similar across time. For example, in an early cycle of brief hymns, referred to as *zame* hymns (*DCSL*), *zame* being Sumerian for praise, En-lil assigns a series of deities to their cult-centers in the south and north of the alluvial plain. This expression of religious unity is matched in a later collection of hymns to temples (*The temple hymns*, *ETCSL* 4.80.1). However, in the later instance religious unity explicitly mirrors political unity, compilation of the collection being credited to En-hedu-ana ("The lord [is] the abundance of heaven"), a daughter of Sargon, the founder of the empire centered on Agade in the north of the plain.

En-hedu-ana, the first author to receive such a credit, although with what accuracy remains difficult to establish, is also attested in two hymns in which she addresses Inana (*ETCSL* 4.07.2, 4.07.3), the most complex deity in the pantheon. These hymns configure the goddess as a warrior-deity, their imagery exulting in her ferocity and lust for battle. As such Inana is the deity most associated with the terrifying awe elaborated in the devotional literature. Other compositions focus instead on the insatiable nature of the goddess's ambitions, as she contends in one for the underworld (*Inana's descent to the netherworld*, *ETCSL* 1.4.1), and in another for heaven (*Inana and An*, *ETCSL* 1.3.5).

En-hedu-ana was also the high priestess of the moon-god Nanna in his city of Ur in the south of the plain. The gendered complementarity in this ritual relationship can be interpreted as a metaphorical representation of the relationship between the human and the divine, enabling elision of the distance between the two through symbolic union. Visually the relationship is attested much earlier, but with the gender-roles reversed, on the alabaster vase from Uruk at the end of the fourth millennium, which depicts a male figure presenting offerings to Inana.

Textually this relationship is alluded to in royal inscriptions that describe Inana as loving a ruler, and celebrated in several narratives referring to legendary rulers of Uruk (*ETCSL* 1.8.2.1–1.8.2.5). An Early Dynastic IIIa narrative, *Lugal-banda and Nin-sumuna* (*DCSL*), also features one of these rulers, Lugal-banda ("Junior king"), but gives the female role instead to Nin-sumuna ("Lady of the wild cows"). However, the most vivid elaborations of the metaphor are associated with later Ur and Isin rulers. These rulers are often represented as Inana's lover in sexually explicit compositions that equate making love with plant cultivation and animal fertility (such as *ETCSL* 2.4.4.2, 2.5.3.1), thus configuring Inana as a goddess of physical love as well as of battle. While more elaborate than the references in royal inscriptions, these compositions have the same underlying aim: the depiction of a ruler whose selection by a deity ensures the fruitfulness of the land.

A further group of compositions, debates, is much less associated with the elevation of deities and of rulers. In one Inana is wooed by two suitors, the shepherd-god and the farmer-god, whose different merits are debated, the former's butter and milk versus the latter's crops and contribution to irrigation (*Dumu-zid and En-ki-imdu, ETCSL* 4.08.33). Although her choice is the shepherd, the arguments in favor of both dramatize the complementary nature of pastoralism and farming, the agricultural symbiosis at the heart of the economy, and the rejected farmer allows the sheep to graze on the stubble of his fields.

Other debates feature instead personified pairs essential to prosperity: winter and summer, bird and fish, grain and sheep, tree and reed, date-palm and tamarisk, hoe and plough, and copper and silver (*ETCSL* 5.3.1–5.3.7). Although one participant is judged the winner by a deity or ruler, the often-heated arguments enable the importance of both to be fully appreciated. As is generally the case, identifying the context in which these compositions were performed is difficult. However, some evidence associates *The debate between hoe and plough* with a ritual held to celebrate the beginning of the agricultural year, when the two implements were prepared for their coming work on the fields.[15] In their focus on economic prosperity and complementary coexistence these debates can also be compared to the late-fourth-millennium vase from Uruk, and they may constitute a more fundamental aspect of Sumerian religion than the glorification of deities that characterizes much of the religious literature.

CONCLUSION

The preceding account of religion in Sumer during the third millennium is necessarily constrained by the nature of the evidence. However, what emerges clearly is the religion's association with the social, political, and technological developments that took place during this period, maintaining continuity while at the same time promoting and endorsing change. The role of the temple, whether acting independently or under the aegis of a ruler, was of particular importance, being a center for religion as well as for agriculture, writing, craft technology, and economic redistribution. Its

---

[15] Cohen, *Calendars*, 90.

redistributive mechanism followed an institutionalized principle of hierarchical reciprocity in which a privileged central authority received others' products and services, some of which it then redistributed. Hierarchical reciprocity also characterized ritual in Sumer, an instrumental relationship being articulated in which blessings of various kinds were sought in exchange for divinely directed speech and deeds.

This vision of a structured, complementary human society dependent on and congruent to a similarly organized divine one pervades Sumerian religion. Thus the deities were envisaged as having human form and needs, being fed and clothed in their temples, while the relationships between them were expressed in social form, in terms of status, employment, parentage, and marriage. Religion also paralleled technology, the pantheon expanding to include deities associated with, for example, writing and other craft skills. Similarly religion paralleled political organization, divine patronage of a particular city correlating to the importance of city-states while the development of larger regional states saw religious authority being vested more in one god, En-lil, and thus in one city, Nippur.

This horizontal axis expressing solidarity was complemented by a vertical axis that elided the distance between the human domain and the divine domains above and below it. Again this conceptualization was particularly realized in relation to temples, which are typically praised as mediating between the two domains by reaching from the earth up to the heavens of An and down to the sacred underground ocean of En-ki. This tripartite cosmology in turn reflects the dual nature of the principal Sumerian deities, that in addition to being patrons of a particular city whose inhabitants tilled their fields, each was identified with a different aspect of the cosmos.

BIBLIOGRAPHY

Aruz, Joan, ed. *Art of the First Cities: The Third Millennium B.C. from the Mediterranean to the Indus* (New York, 2003).

Black, Jeremy, Graham Cunningham, Eleanor Robson, and Gábor Zólyomi. *The Literature of Ancient Sumer* (Oxford, 2006).

Black, Jeremy, and Anthony Green. *Gods, Demons and Symbols of Ancient Mesopotamia: An Illustrated Dictionary* (London, 1998).

Cohen, Mark E. *The Cultic Calendars of the Ancient Near East* (Bethesda, Md., 1993).

Cooper, Jerrold S. "Inscriptions et textes historiques." *DBSup* 13 (1999): 226–48.

"Babylonian Beginnings: The Origin of the Cuneiform Writing System in Comparative Perspective." In *The First Writing: Script Invention as History and Process*, ed. Stephen D. Houston (Cambridge, 2004): 71–99.

Cunningham, Graham. "A Catalogue of Sumerian Literature (Based on Miguel Civil's Catalogue of Sumerian Literature)." In *Analysing Literary Sumerian: Corpus-Based Approaches*, ed. Jarle Ebeling and Graham Cunningham (London, 2007): 351–411.

Englund, Robert K. "Texts from the Late Uruk Period." In *Mesopotamien: Späturuk Zeit und frühdynastiche Zeit*, ed. Joseph Bauer, Robert K. Englund, and Manfred Krebernik (Freiburg, 1998): 15–233.

Gelb, Ignace J., Piotr Steinkeller, and Robert M. Whiting Jr. *Earliest Land Tenure Systems in the Near East: Ancient Kudurrus* (Chicago, 1991).

Geller, M. J. "Incantations et magie." *DBSup* 13 (1999): 269–83.

Matthews, Roger. *Cities, Seals and Writing: Archaic Seal Impressions from Jemdet Nasr and Ur* (Berlin, 1993).

Postgate, J. N. *Early Mesopotamia. Society and Economy at the Dawn of History* (London, 1994).

Sasson, Jack M. *Civilizations of the Ancient Near East* (Peabody, Mass., 2000).

Selz, Gebhard J. "Enlil und Nippur nach präsargonischen Quellen." In *Nippur at the Centennial. Papers Read at the 35e Rencontre Assyriologique Internationale, Philadelphia, 1988*, ed. Maria deJong Ellis (Philadelphia, 1992): 189–225.

Szarzy ń ska, Krystyna. "Offerings for the Goddess Inana in Archaic Uruk." In *Sumerica. Prace sumeroznawcze*, Krystyna Szarzyńska (Warsaw, 1997): 115–40.

Westenholz, Aage. "The Sumerian City-State." In *A Comparative Study of Six City-State Cultures. An Investigation Conducted by the Copenhagen Polis Centre*, ed. Mogens Herman Hansen (Copenhagen, 2002): 23–42.

2

ASSYRIAN AND BABYLONIAN RELIGIONS

TAMMI J. SCHNEIDER

Modern scholarly understanding of what constituted ancient Assyrian and Babylonian religion is complicated because Assyria and Babylonia were part of the Mesopotamian "stream of tradition"[1] beginning as early as the third millennium BCE and continuing through to the first.[2] Second, owing in part to A. Leo Oppenheim's contention that the history of "Mesopotamian religion" should not be written,[3] religion as a topic has not been thoroughly pursued in the field of Mesopotamian studies. Oppenheim was concerned about the nature of the evidence and "the problem of comprehension across the barriers of conceptual conditioning."[4] Nonetheless, even Oppenheim proceeded, to some degree, to write a history of Mesopotamian religion.

The world of ancient Assyria and Babylonia (see Map 1) was filled with numerous deities whose importance they could not ignore. The responsibilities and power of these gods shifted over time and varied depending on place, affected too by the changing political situation. At the same time, many fundamental components of ancient Mesopotamian religious life continued unchanged for centuries. The basic premise throughout all periods of Mesopotamian history is that humans were created and placed

---

[1] Oppenheim, *Ancient Mesopotamia*, 13. Oppenheim defines this stream as "the corpus of literary texts maintained, controlled, and carefully kept alive by a tradition served by successive generations of learned and well-trained scribes."

[2] "Ever since Jacobsen's penetrating study of the Sumerian king list, it has been clear that unity and linearity were something the Mesopotamians foisted onto their past, rather than qualities which grew from it"; Lieberman, "Nippur: City of Decisions," 128.

[3] Oppenheim, *Ancient Mesopotamia*, 171. Oppenheim suggests the reasons for not writing a Mesopotamian religion are "the nature of the available evidence and the problem of comprehension across the barriers of conceptual conditioning" (172); both issues continue to exist. Despite his cry not to write such a treatise, to some extent in the pages included under this heading he proceeds to do so. The power of Oppenheim's statement on the field is revealed in a recent study of Mesopotamian religion where Oppenheim's claim is invoked in a chapter entitled "The Sources: What We Can Expect from Them"; see Bottero, *Religion in Ancient Mesopotamia*, 26.

[4] Oppenheim, *Ancient Mesopotamia*, 171–2.

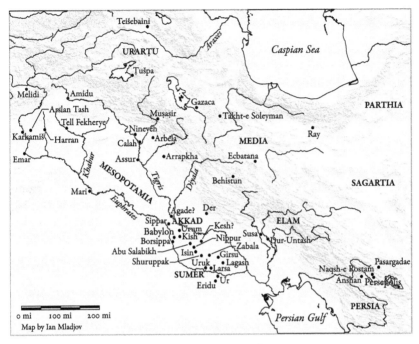

Map 1. Mesopotamia and Persia.

on earth so the gods did not have to work. Each deity controlled different elements of the world order, no one god had full control, and which deity was in charge fluctuated over time and place, affected by political and social changes.

This chapter will begin with a brief introduction to the borders and history of Assyria and Babylonia because political changes in these areas over time affected the religions practiced there, keeping in mind that both are part of a larger Mesopotamian stream of tradition.[5] Our evidence for these religions is fragmented, so scholars must incorporate whatever literary and physical remains survive in an effort to better understand what the Mesopotamians did and what they may have thought about the world around them. In describing these religions, this chapter will identify their key components, focusing on Assyrian and Babylonian mythology, gods, temples, religious personnel, and ritual. My aim is to ascertain the nature of Assyrian and Babylonian religions, their commonalities as well as their differences.

---

[5] W. G. Lambert, "The Historical Development of the Mesopotamian Pantheon," 191, argues that for ancient Mesopotamia, "the historical method is almost the only way open to study religion."

ASSYRIAN AND BABYLONIAN PEOPLES AND HISTORICAL DEVELOPMENTS

The terms "Assyrian" and "Babylonian" refer to inhabitants of Mesopotamia, most of which is modern Iraq, from the second millennium through the middle of the first millennium BCE. The Babylonians occupied the southern part of the flood plain and the Assyrians the north, although these geographical designations do not reveal the complex differences between the two concerning language, historical connection to the Sumerians, political configurations, and religion.

The Babylonians occupied the region extending approximately from modern-day Baghdad to the shore of the Persian Gulf.[6] The name is derived from the city named "Babili" in cuneiform, which becomes Babylon in the Greek.[7] This area coincides mostly with the area occupied by the Sumerians in the third millennium.[8] The last Sumerian political establishment, the Third Dynasty of Ur, fell because of economic and political instability.[9] Part of this demise is attributed to a new group of people in the area: the Amorites.

The first two centuries of the second millennium, the Isin/Larsa period, saw numerous transitional groups try to gain control of Mesopotamia, with limited success.[10] The cultural and religious traditions of the previous millennium were preserved and modified[11] despite the entrance of people grouped under the title "Amorites."[12] Only under Hammurabi did Babylon gain control of all Mesopotamia.[13] Hammurabi's successes were military and political, but they forever changed the role and status of Babylon and its god, Marduk, to some extent identifying and creating the group labeled Babylonians. Hammurabi's heirs did not rule with the authority of Hammurabi, and in 1595 BCE Babylon was sacked in a raid by the Hittites. The Hittites did not stay to control Babylon, but they took with them the statue of Marduk, the city god.[14]

---

[6] Klengel-Brandt, "Babylonians," 256.
[7] Ibid., 256.
[8] See Chapter 1.
[9] Many histories of the ancient Near East will provide discussions of this topic, but the *Lamentation over the Destruction of Sumer and Ur* is the Mesopotamian literary and/or "religious" view of their disaster; see Michalowski, *The Lamentation over the Destruction of Sumer and Ur*.
[10] Van Koppen, "Old Babylonian Period Inscriptions, 88–95.
[11] Sjoberg, "The Old Babylonian Eduba," 159–80; Buccellati, "Through a Tablet Darkly," 58–71.
[12] Heimpel, *Letters to the King of Mari*, 13–25; Schwartz, "Pastoral Nomadism," 249–58.
[13] Horsnell, *The Year-Name System and the Date-Lists* and *The Year-Names Reconstructed*.
[14] "Agum-kakrime and the Return of Marduk," in Foster, *Before the Muses*, 1:273–7.

Even before the Hittites arrived, in the reign of Hammurabi's son and successor, Samsu-ilum, two new groups entered the area of Babylonia. In the south a new dynasty ruled by Iluma-ilum started the Sealand Dynasty, and in his ninth year he referenced another new group: the Kassites.[15] The origin of the Kassites is unclear, as is the reason for their appearance in Babylonia, but they controlled the area for the next four hundred years.[16] Little is known about the Kassite language, and the rulers soon adopted the Babylonian language and customs. Although they are always treated somehow as non-Babylonian, and most scholars argue there is little influence of their national characteristics reflected in the material remains,[17] "the Kassites reigned some four centuries, far longer than any native or for that matter any other dynasty."[18] Babylonian literature flourished during this period.[19] Some argue the return of Marduk under the Kassites is the event that precipitated writing the *enuma elish*, the epic of creation that plays an important role in understanding the Mesopotamian concept of the world.[20]

There is a dramatic westward shift of the Euphrates toward the end of the Kassite period.[21] This led to a population decline in Babylonian cities. In addition, the Assyrians began to threaten Babylonia. Significant in this regard is the conquest of Babylonia by the Assyrian king Tukulti-Ninurta I in 1235 BCE.[22] The conquest of Babylon was not prolonged, but its effects were. It marks the beginning of both the Assyro-Babylonian conflict and the significant Babylonian cultural influence on Assyria. The Kassites were destroyed shortly thereafter in an Elamite raid. Babylon was again sacked, and many of its artifacts taken to Susa.[23]

In the three hundred years following the fall of the Kassites, Babylonia was controlled by a series of local dynasties. Nebuchadnezzar I (1125–1104 BCE) began a new phase of Babylonian history when he attacked the Elamites, recovered the statue of Marduk taken earlier in the sack of Babylon, and referred to Marduk as "king of the gods."[24] The Arameans entered the area

---

[15] Horsnell, *The Year-Names Reconstructed,* 192.
[16] Brinkman, *A Catalogue of Cuneiform Sources.*
[17] Lloyd, *The Archaeology of Mesopotamia,* 172.
[18] Oates, *Babylon,* 86.
[19] Foster, "The Mature Period," 203–9.
[20] See the discussion of that text below.
[21] Brinkman, *Prelude to Empire,* 3–10; Adams, *The Heartland of Cities,* 18, 152, 155–8.
[22] Grayson, *Assyrian Rulers,* 231–79. For the Tukulti-Ninurta Epic, see Foster, *Muses,* 1:209–29.
[23] Dieulafoy, "A History of Excavation at Susa, 20–4. See also Arevalier, "The French Scientific Delegation in Persia," 16–19.
[24] "The Seed of Kingship," line 25, in Foster, *Muses,* 1:292.

around this time and disrupted internal stability, reflected in the paucity of excavated documents. The rise of the Assyrians toward the end of the tenth century, accompanied by the appearance of the Chaldeans[25] in the south, led a Babylonian chronicle to claim "there was no king in the land."[26] Despite non-native Babylonians dominating the area and political instability around 1200 BCE, much Babylonian literature, including texts that are treated as "religious," was standardized.[27]

Conflict between Assyria and Babylonia continued throughout the period of Assyrian hegemony of the ancient Near East from the end of the tenth century until the fall of Assyria in the late seventh century. In this period, depending on the strength or weakness of the Assyrians, other groups, such as the Chaldeans, rose to fill the political vacuum. When Assyria was weaker, such as the period following the reign of Adad-nirari III, the Chaldeans filled the political vacuum. When Assyria was stronger, its kings tried various tactics to gain dominance, ranging from the destruction of Babylon (Sennacherib destroyed Babylon, taking Marduk with him to Assyria)[28] to appeasement (Esarhaddon),[29] with little success, although local Babylonian rulers maintained limited control, often with the help of Assyria. The accession of the Babylonian king Nabonassar in 746 BCE is of key importance for modern scholars because, beginning with his reign, ancient scholars began to keep precise records of historical events, as exemplified in the new-Babylonian chronicle series.[30] Following the destruction of the Assyrian Empire at the end of the seventh century, Nabopolassar (625–605) took the throne of Babylon and established a new dynasty. His son, Nebuchadnezzar, took on the Assyrian goal of controlling Egypt, and it is under his rule that the kingdom of Judah revolted, leading to the destruction of Jerusalem and the exile of its people (2 Kings 24–25). Nebuchadnezzar was also responsible for major building projects in Babylon, making it a major economic and administrative center once more.[31]

Nebuchadnezzar's reign was followed by three kings with no major military or building successes. Nabonidus, who had no hereditary claim to

[25] Delineating the differences between the Chaldeans and the Aramaeans is not easy to do, although the ancient sources do so. See Arnold, "Nebuchadnezzar," 330–55.
[26] Grayson, *Assyrian and Babylonian Chronicles* and *Mesopotamian Chronicles*, 286–7.
[27] Foster, *Muses*, 1:207.
[28] Luckenbill, *The Annals of Sennacherib*, 78.
[29] For an analysis of the different means of his policy see Porter, *Images, Power, Politics*.
[30] Grayson, *Assyrian and Babylonian Chronicles*, 10–24 and 69–111.
[31] Herodotus, *History* 1.186; Berossus 27 in Josephus, *Ant.* 10.11.1.226; Koldewey, *Excavations at Babylon*, 734–9.

the throne, came to power already aged. He is known for his devotion to Sin, the moon god of Haran, likely through the influence of his mother, Adad-guppi, whose tomb inscription has been preserved.[32] What impact this had on his decision to depart Babylon for ten years while he stayed in the Arabian oasis town of Teima and left Babylon unable to carry out the New Year's festival is debated.[33] Shortly after his return, the city of Babylon fell to Cyrus of Persia, marking the end of Babylonian rule and of Babylonian religion in this essay.[34]

Assyrian history follows a different trajectory although it intersects with Babylonian history and culture at various points. The early history of the city of Assur is unknown because of a lack of inscriptional evidence, although all texts indicate the area of Assyria was controlled by the Sumerian and Akkadian south.[35] According to the Assyrian king list, the earliest extant exemplar of which dates to the first millennium BCE,[36] there were seventeen kings who lived in tents, ten ancestor kings, six early kings, and six early Old Assyrian kings with genealogies.[37] Research on this list reveals that, like the Sumerian king list,[38] it serves propagandistic purposes, probably to legitimate the reign of Shamshi-Adad, and shares Amorite attributes with ancestors of the Hammurabi dynasty. As a result, the data provide more information about how the Assyrians later situated themselves than about actual historical leaders.[39] Despite its problems, numerous rulers from this list appear on inscriptions from Assur and are referred to in the texts from the Assyrian trading colony at Karum Kanesh or Kultepe.[40] The documents from Kultepe provide more information about this period in Assyria than any remains from Assur itself.[41] Both sets of documents reveal a city ruled by a person identified as the *issiak assur* or ENSI *Assur*, not the Akkadian term for "king," in concert with city elders.[42]

---

[32] Longman, "The Adad-guppi Autobiography," 477–8.

[33] Beaulieu, *The Reign of Nabonidus*, 178–85.

[34] Herodotus, 1.178, 190–291; Xenophon, *Cyropaedia* 7.5.26–30; Daniel 5:30; Glassner, *Mesopotamian Chronicles*, 237; Cogan, "Cyrus Cylinder," 314–16.

[35] For an example, see Steinkeller, "Administrative and Economic Organization of the Ur III State," 19–42.

[36] Poebel, "The Assyrian King List," 263–7.

[37] Larsen, *The Old Assyrian City-State,"* 36.

[38] Jacobsen, *The Sumerian King List.*

[39] Larsen, *Old Assyrian,* 36.

[40] Ibid., 37–43. For inscriptions of the pre–Shamshi-Adad kings, see Grayson, *Assyrian Rulers,* 7–46.

[41] Despite difficulties in the publication of these materials a new series, Old Assyrian Archives, is making more of these data available. See, for example, Larsen, *The Assur-nada Archive.*

[42] Ibid., 109–59.

During the second millennium, Assyria competed with and was influenced by the Hurrians.[43] Assyria's leaders did not claim the title of "king" until Assur-uballit (1365–1330).[44] His change in title places Assyria on the same international level as the rulers of the major powers of his day: the Egyptians, the Babylonians, and the Hittites. He began ousting the Hurrians,[45] was the first to claim the title of "king," and placed Assyria on the international stage during a period dominated by the Hittites, Egyptians, and Babylonians. He was followed by a series of strong kings under whose leadership Assyria maintained its role as an important power in the ancient Near East.

Many of the ancient Near Eastern powers of the mid-second millennium fell apart toward the end of the century, and new peoples, such as the Arameans, entered the area, modifying what and who constituted Assyria and its religion.[46] Only with the reign of Adad-nirari II (921–891) do we see Assyria recovering as the major political power in the region. His efforts enabled his grandson, Ashurnasirpal II, to turn Assyria into a world power. He expanded the borders of Assyria and began to change the concept of what Assyria was.[47] He moved the capital of Assyria from the traditional home of the national deity Assur in the city of Assur to Calah (modern Nimrud). Shalmaneser III (858–824 BCE) extended the boundaries of Assyria, but his reign ended in turmoil with some of the major cities of Assyria, including Assur, revolting.[48] One of his sons, Shamshi-Adad V, managed to maintain control of Assyria, but the extent and power of the state diminished until the reign of Tiglath-pileser III (745–727 BCE). One of Tiglath-pileser III's many internal changes was to shift the army from an Assyrian-only army to a standing army that incorporated peoples conquered by Assyria and thereby modified the definition of what and who an Assyrian was.

At its height in the eighth–seventh centuries BCE, Assyria controlled most of the ancient Near East. One of the challenges to Assyria's kings was how to control Babylonia. Different methods were tried, alternating brute force[49] with imperial benefactions that included rebuilding the city

---

[43] Wilhelm, *The Hurrians*.
[44] Grayson, *Old Assyrian Rulers*, inscription A.0.73.6, 115. Note reference to him as king of Assyria in letters to the Amarna king of Egypt, Akhenaten. Moran, *The Amarna Letters*.
[45] Harrak, *Assyria and Hanigalbat*.
[46] *The Crisis Years: The 12th Century*, ed. Ward and Joukowsky. For the Arameans, see Sader, "The 12th Century B.C. in Syria," 157–63, and the response by McClellan, "12th Century B.C. Syria," 164–73, and Lipinski, *The Aramaeans*.
[47] Grayson, *Assyrian Rulers*.
[48] Grayson, *Assyrian Rulers II*, 180–8.
[49] Luckenbill, *Annals*, 78.

Assyrian and Babylonian Religions 61

of Babylon using traditional Babylonian rather than Assyrian iconography.[50] Assyria's last major ruler, Assurbanipal, built a significant library and museum in which he gathered all the literature he could find.[51] Modern archaeologists uncovered this library in the mid-nineteenth century, and it is the basis for much of the extant Mesopotamian literature that we have today.[52] Assur-uballit II is Assyria's last ruler (614–609 BCE), and with him the Assyrians disappear as a group from the political stage.

MYTHOLOGY

The Assyrians and Babylonians do not have a word for religion, and so modern scholars must use a wide range of texts to try to understand their views of what we label religion.[53] In the mythology of the Assyrians and Babylonians we see these peoples' (whom I will henceforth refer to as Mesopotamians) answers to questions we would consider religious, namely, the reason for human existence and untimely death, and the nature of the afterlife.

Enuma Elish

One of the most important sources for the mythology that may have infused their religious ideas is the *enuma elish* ("When on High" in Akkadian, also referred to as the Epic of Creation).[54] This long text addresses the origin of the earth, the gods, and the role of humans in the world. One key theme is the notion that the world is full of multiple deities, and man is created simply to serve them. This religious worldview is reinforced by the evidence that the *enuma elish* served ritual purposes. Not only does another text cite it as such, but we also have numerous copies of this text,[55] discovered in diverse locations but displaying far fewer variants than other texts.[56] However, the Assyrian and Babylonian versions differ concerning the most important deity in the text, and this thus provides a paradigm for understanding issues involved with mythological texts. Clearly, these differences

[50] For an analysis of the different means of his policy, see Porter, *Images, Power, Politics*.
[51] Oppenheim, *Ancient Mesopotamia*, 15–18.
[52] Ibid.
[53] The definition of myth is complex. Here mythology will be vaguely defined as a narrative that describes human understanding of the divine realm as explanation for how and why the universe functions as it does, including the divine relationship to humans and their place in the cosmos.
[54] The text has been known since Smith's *A Chaldaean Account of Genesis* and published many times, as recently as the edition by Talon, *Enuma Eliš*.
[55] Cohen, *The Cultic Calendars*, 444.
[56] See Talon, *Enuma Eliš*, xiii–xviii, for the different available manuscripts.

suggest that despite Assyria and Babylonia considering themselves as part of the Mesopotamian stream of tradition, there is dissent about the specifics of the role and importance of the various deities and, probably, about the role of each in the world as a result.

Dating *enuma elish* is difficult. Many scholars have assumed that it was more ancient than its extant copies, which date to the first millennium. The lack of textual variation in the tablets suggests that the text had become canonized for ritual use, perhaps as early as the second millennium.[57] The earliest possible date for the text is the first Amorite ruler of Babylon where Marduk is the patron deity, dating then to the reign of Sumu-la-el (1936–1901).[58] The Kassite ruler Agum-kakrime returned the cult statue of Marduk to Babylon following the sack of Babylon by the Hittites; the cult statue's return to Babylon may have inspired the text.[59] The cult statue of Marduk again was returned from captivity during the reign of Nebuchadnezzar I (1125–1104). A lexical text known as *An-Anum* lists the major gods of the Babylonian pantheon together with their secondary names by assimilation and some of their epithets, and a long section with the names of Marduk includes a subsection that corresponds closely to the names of Marduk appearing on Tablet VII of the epic.[60] A tablet with a list of gods found at the Hittite capital in Anatolia, dating to the second millennium, shows *An-Anum* must have included the *enuma elish* list of Marduk's names, and thus some form of the myth was in play in the second millennium.[61]

The ritual role of *enuma elish* is clear because, as noted, a tablet with ritual instruction for the performance of the New Year festival in Babylon states the text is to be recited (possibly enacted) on the fourth day.[62] The ritual text contains a gap, so it is possible that more than one recital was envisaged. The New Year's festival was one of the major religious events of the Mesopotamian calendar.[63] It originally commemorated the god leaving his temporary residence and entering his permanent residence in his chosen city for the first time[64] and became the ceremony when the king had his mandate to rule renewed by the gods.[65] *Enuma elish* celebrated the

---

[57] Dalley, *Myths from Mesopotamia*, 229.
[58] Ibid.
[59] Ibid.
[60] Ibid., 230.
[61] Ibid.
[62] Cohen, *The Cultic Calendars*, 444.
[63] See below.
[64] Cohen, *The Cultic Calendars*, 405.
[65] Dalley, *Myths*, 232.

Assyrian and Babylonian Religions 63

exaltation of the Babylonian god Marduk (and in Assyria Assur; see below) and ascribed to Marduk the reorganization of the universe with Babylon in the center, making the text a product of Babylonian nationalism.[66] The top officials of the land were called upon to renew their oaths of loyalty to the king and royal family, meaning the ritual reading or enactment was known to a wide swath of the population.[67]

The content of the myth establishes the reason for its importance. The text begins, "when skies above were not yet named nor earth below pronounced by name" (Tablet 1:1).[68] Apsu's (male/father)[69] and Tiamat's (female/mother) waters mix together, gods are born in them, and generations of deities follow. In this process, some of the younger gods are already superior to their fathers (1:11–20). The younger gods become too loud and anger Apsu, who calls out to his vizier to discuss the issue with Tiamat (1:24–5). Apsu wants to abolish their ways, disperse them, and get some sleep, but Tiamat will not hear of it and insists they be patient (1:25–47). The vizier sides with Apsu, the younger gods hear of this, Ea lays out a plan, drenches Apsu with sleep, and slays him (1:46–78). Inside Apsu, the god Marduk is created from Ea and Damkina and eventually annoys Tiamat (79–110). The gods turn on Tiamat, who promotes another god, Qingu. Tiamat confers upon him leadership of the army and command of the assembly, sets him upon the throne, and gives him the tablet of destinies (1:111–159). Fearing Tiamat, the gods turn to An and Ea again, who in this case are too afraid to do anything (2:5). Ea advises Marduk to take the initiative, and Marduk agrees to do so, only after laying out the terms by which he will do it. Ea attacks Tiamat, slays her, and uses her split body to create the heavens (2:127–4:148). Marduk decides to create man from Qingu, who they claim started the war with Tiamat (6:25) so that "the work of the gods shall be imposed (on him) and so that they shall be at leisure" (6:5–8).[70]

Enuma elish contains material concerning how the world was created. The first gods were created from some preexisting material. The younger deities overthrow older gods, a motif found in many other polytheistic mythological texts.[71] Marduk is almost unknown before the first half of

---

[66] Foster, *Muses,* 351.

[67] Cohen, *The Cultic Calendars,* 400–53.

[68] Translation of the text here will be from Dalley, "Epic of Creation," 233–81.

[69] The term *apsu* in Akkadian means, "deep water, sea, cosmic subterranean water, a personified mythological figure, or a water basin in the temple." *Chicago Assyrian Dictionary A II,* 194. The Mesopotamians believed springs, wells, streams, rivers, and lakes took water from and were replenished by a freshwater ocean that lay underneath the earth in the *abzu (apsu)* or *engur.* Black and Green, "Abzu (apsu)," in *Gods, Demons,* 27. See also Horowitz, *Mesopotamian Cosmic Geography.*

[70] The reason for creating man here differs from that of Atrahasis; see below.

[71] For example, from the classical world, see Hesiod's *Theogony,* http://classics.mit.edu/hes.th.html.

64 *Tammi J. Schneider*

the second millennium, and in Assyrian versions of *enuma elish*, the god Marduk is replaced by the god Assur. The role of humans in the universe is clear: They were created from the god Qingu, who began the war between the younger gods and their mother in order that the gods no longer must work. In Assyrian and Babylonian religion, humans were created simply to serve deities.

Atrahasis

The idea that humans were created so the gods did not have to work is reinforced, although not the primary focus, in the myth of Atrahasis,[72] which begins with the line, "When the gods instead of man did the work …"[73] Unlike *enuma elish*, clay tablets with the Old Babylonian version of this myth date to around 1700 BCE, although passages of the text appear as late as Assurbanipal's library.[74] In this text, Atrahasis, a citizen of Shuruppak, saves the world from a flood. Humans are created to do the work for the gods, but in this case they are created from a slain god mixed with clay, and they will hear the drumbeat forever after.[75] After six hundred years the humans become too numerous and, like the gods in *enuma elish*, too loud (2:1:1). First the gods send sickness and drought, but that does not work so they come up with a new plan: a flood (2:6:1).[76] Enki warns Atrahasis of the impending flood and tells him to build a boat and save living things, not possessions (3:1–end of column). The torrent, storm, and flood last seven days and seven nights. A 58-line gap follows the reference to the flood, but when the tablets resume, some human "is putting down and providing food" (3-5-1:1). The gods "gather like flies" over the offering and partake (5:1:5). Now the gods face a dilemma because they had all agreed to destroy humans but are pleased humans are cooking for them again. They decide there will only be one-third of the previous number of people, and to do so they create a category of women who will not successfully give birth, and there will be a demon among the people who will snatch babies from their mother's lap, and thus the gods will control childbirth (5:7:1–7).

---

[72] The name means "exceedingly wise."

[73] The translation for this is also from Dalley, *Myths,* 9.

[74] For a treatment of the manuscripts, see Lambert and Millard, *Atra-Hasis,* 31–9.

[75] For more on the meaning of the noise, "the drumbeat," see Kilmer, "The Mesopotamian Concept of Overpopulation and Its Solution, 160–77, and Moran, "Atrahasis," 51–61.

[76] The concept of a worldwide flood, like that in the biblical book of Genesis, appears in Mesopotamian mythological texts and other texts such as the Epic of Gilgamesh and the Sumerian king list. The flood, in Mesopotamian tradition, is not so much a religious concept as a historical event.

Assyrian and Babylonian Religions   65

This myth agrees with *enuma elish* in that humans are created to provide for the gods, but here the mother is Mami, although Ea is still involved in their creation. This confirms some of the fundamental concepts about the role of humans on earth, although the process by which it comes about is different than in *enuma elish*. The Atrahasis myth addresses the concept of why some women do not bear children and some children die in childbirth or at a young age.

The concept of the netherworld and what happens to humans when they die is addressed in other mythological texts, although no uniform view is easily discerned.[77] The text that focuses most on these topics is Ishtar's descent to the netherworld.[78] Two manuscripts of this text were uncovered from Assurbanipal's library, and an earlier variant version was recovered from Assur.[79] Ishtar, the goddess often described as a goddess of love and war but possibly better described as the goddess of adrenaline,[80] decides to go to the netherworld, the land of her sister, Ereshkigal (1:1).[81] The text does not give a reason for her journey. The netherworld is described as a "dark house," on the road that is "one-way only," where "those who enter are deprived of light," "dirt is their food, clay their bread," they "live in darkness" and are "clothed like birds, with feathers" (1:5–10). The door to the place is bolted, and dust has settled upon the bolt (11).

Ishtar demands that the gatekeeper let her in; if he does not, she will smash the door, shatter the bolt, and "raise up the dead and they shall eat the living so that the dead shall outnumber the living" (1:19). The gatekeeper warns Ishtar's sister, Ereshkigal, who wonders what her sister wants (25–31). Ereshkigal's self-described job is to eat clay for bread, drink muddy water for beer, and weep for young men forced to abandon sweethearts, girls wrenched from their lovers' laps, and the infant child expelled before its time (32–36), a likely reference to miscarriages (see below).

Ereshkigal instructs the gatekeeper to open his gate to her but to treat her according to the ancient rites (37–38). The ancient rites involve taking Ishtar through seven different doors, each time stripping her of an article of jewelry, including the great crown on her head, the rings in her

---

[77] This text is more clearly linked to a Sumerian prototype than many other texts, and the Sumerian text is fuller and explains the association to Dumuzi/Tammuz in a way the Akkadian version does not.

[78] Translation again will be from Dalley.

[79] Foster, *Muses*, 403.

[80] See below for a discussion of some of the different deities.

[81] In another text, "How Nergal Became the King of the Netherworld," Ereshkigal takes a lover who also becomes king of the netherworld. Foster, *From Distant Days*, 85–96.

ears, the beads around her neck, the toggle pins at her breast, the girdle of birth-stones around her waist, the bangles on her wrists and ankles, and the proud garment on her body (40–62).

The problem with Ishtar's presence in the netherworld is that while she is gone, "no bull mounted a cow [no donkey impregnated a jenny], no young man impregnated a girl." (86–89). Ishtar's absence, or presence, naked, in the netherworld, keeps the other world from creating new life. This causes dejection among the great gods until Ea creates a good-looking playboy to cheer up Ereshkigal (91–99). When he asks for water she becomes angry, but somehow Ishtar is sprinkled with the waters of life and leaves through each door, receiving all the jewels originally taken from her (1:100–130). The Akkadian version ends with a reference to "the day when Dumuzi comes back up" (136). In the Sumerian version, food and water are smuggled into Inana, she is told she must be replaced in the netherworld by someone, and when she finds her husband, Dumuzi/Tammuz, having a party she decides to send him to take her place. For reasons that appear in a break, Dumuzi's sister appears to go to the netherworld for part of the year for him. None of this is provided in the Akkadian version.

This text describes the netherworld as a place where people go after life. Though not thoroughly described, it is a concept not challenged by other texts. Once one enters the netherworld, one cannot, with the exception of Ishtar and her replacement, return. It is dark, and the food and beer are not good. The people in the netherworld range from babies who die too young to lovers separated. Ereshkigal, who controls that realm, claims, as her job, the task of weeping over them all. Thus the reality of death is existence in some other, unpleasant, state from which there is no return. Ereshkigal highlights the dark side of the issue and simultaneously expresses a sign of tenderness and caring for her charges through her weeping. The darkness of the netherworld emphasizes the good things to be found before death: good food, beer, love, and light.

THE GODS

The deities in the Mesopotamian pantheon are depicted with strong, lively personalities and are quick to take action, sometimes to the detriment of humans. The Mesopotamian pantheon is a complex one, revealing change and continuity in the identities, functions, and rituals for the deities. References to the various deities appear in mythological texts noted earlier, but also in legal, literary, historical, and ritual remains.

Assyrian and Babylonian Religions 67

Depictions of the gods and their symbols appear on seals, sealings (the impression made on clay by a cylinder seal), wall carvings, and statuary, although no ancient Mesopotamian cult statue has yet been discovered in an archaeological excavation. The data concerning the gods span close to two thousand years. Not surprisingly, then, notions of these deities and their representations show certain inconsistencies that challenge modern, not Mesopotamian, ideas.

The Mesopotamians, from the time of the Sumerians through the first millennium, kept lists, including lists of gods.[82] The Assyrian kings of the end of the second and beginning of the first millennium wrote "annals,"[83] and starting with Tiglath-pileser I (1115–1077 BCE) the annals begin with a list of deities.[84] Not all the gods appear at the beginning of these texts, and different versions of annals within one Assyrian king's reign list different deities in, significantly, the same order as those represented in the earliest god lists.[85] Thus, although the list of deities may change, their ordering defies modification.

In Assyria and Babylonia there was a wide range of deities.[86] The most widely recorded were the gods of the central pantheon, to whom all humans owed some kind of allegiance. Each city was responsible for a deity or, depending on the city, a few deities. There were also personal deities that served to help a particular family connect with the larger pantheon and work on their behalf.[87]

Many of the deities were connected to elements of nature that translated into areas of human civilization. For example, Shamash, the sun-god, was also the god of justice, since the sun eventually sees everything.[88] Ea (Sumerian Enki) was the god of the subterranean freshwater ocean, the clever god, and by extension, the friend of humans.[89] Adad (Sumerian Ishkur), because he was so similar in many areas adjacent to Assyria and Babylonia, such as those occupied by the Hurrians and Hittites, was the god of the wind or storm, but also a foundation for centralized political power.[90] When the gods are depicted, their attributes flow from their

---

[82] Oppenheim, *Ancient Mesopotamia*, 244–8. See too Chapter 1.

[83] Grayson, "Assyria and Babylonia," 140–94.

[84] Rawlinson, *Historical Inscriptions* and Grayson, *Assyrian Royal Inscriptions Part 2*.

[85] Schneider, *Royal Annals of Shalmaneser III*, 44–52.

[86] The total number of Mesopotamian deities has been variously figured as 2,400, according to Tallqvist, *Akkadische Gotterepitheta*, to as high as 3,300 names, according to Deimel, *Pantheon babylonicum*.

[87] See below.

[88] Black and Green, *Gods, Demons and Symbols*, 182–4.

[89] Ibid., 75.

[90] Green, *The Storm-God in the Ancient Near East*, 281; Frymer-Kensky, *In the Wake of the Goddesses*.

shoulders; hence rays emanate from Shamash,[91] water from Ea,[92] and Adad's symbol was lightning or sometimes flowing streams.[93] There were deities for other "arts of civilization" with a separate deity for such diverse elements of the universe as beer and beer-making,[94] healing,[95] and writing.[96]

I will focus here on the principal gods in all of the ancient lists of gods, Ishtar, and the two titular deities of Babylonia and Assyria respectively. These five deities are indicative of the issues surrounding the pantheon; their personas represent the ebb and flow of the history and religious status of the region.

The God An

The first name on the list from Fara (ancient Shuruppak) and Abu Salabikh is An. The word "An" is the Sumerian word for "heaven" and the name of the god labeled the "sky-god."[97] The texts from the Sumerian period delineate three main functions for An: universal god of creation, inhabitant of heaven, and bestower of the royal insignia (founder of earthly royal power), but much of that changed by the time Babylon and Assur were prominent.[98] He is considered the prime deity involved in creation and leader of the gods, but he lost his place of primacy to Marduk, according to *enuma elish*. An should be an important deity well involved in the human world, and yet, "An's nature is ill-defined and, as he is seldom (if ever) represented in art, his specific iconography and attributes are obscure."[99] Thus, An heads the pantheon, although his actual role is almost nonexistent in the religious life of Mesopotamia.

The God Enlil

Enlil is the second major deity on the list and is considered the king of the gods. His role stems from being the offspring of An (*enuma elish*), although he is also described as a descendant of Enki and Ninki.[100] His

---

[91] Black and Green, *Gods, Demons and Symbols,* 183–4.
[92] Ibid., 75.
[93] Ibid., 111.
[94] Beer following Mesopotamian recipes was made by Anchor Steam Brewing Company. For more information see www.anchorbrewing.com/beers/ninkasi.htm.
[95] Black and Green, "Gula," in *Gods, Demons and Symbols,* 101.
[96] Black and Green, "Nabu," in ibid., 133–4.
[97] *Chicago Assyrian Dictionary A part II,* 146.
[98] Wohlstein, *The Sky-God An-Anu.*
[99] Black and Green, "An (Anu)," in *Gods, Demons and Symbols,* 30.
[100] Black and Green, "Enlil," in ibid., 76.

supreme position as ruler of the universe and controller of the affairs of men and gods was guaranteed through his possession of the tablet of destinies (the *mes*) and his crown and throne.[101]

Enlil's primary city was the ancient Sumerian city of Nippur, and this origin may account for the trajectory of Enlil's role in different periods of Mesopotamian history.[102] Nippur became the religious capital of the alluvial plain by 2700, and as long as Enlil reigned as king of the gods, his city served as the religious capital, receiving the veneration of the inhabitants.[103] By the middle of the twenty-fourth century BCE, a king's control of Nippur, and therefore claim to Enlil's call to kingship, provided a divine basis for his kingship.[104] This continued even in the transition from the period of Sumerian hegemony to the first reign of an Amorite ruler, apparent when Ishbi-Irra proclaimed himself king in Isin saying, "Enlil ... has given the kingship to Ishbi-Irra, who is not of the seed of Sumer."[105]

Enlil and Nippur's status declined considerably when Hammurabi and his successors dominated the region.[106] There is a revival of Nippur's fortune during the Kassite period until shortly after 1230 BCE when the king of Elam attacked the city and scattered the people.[107] Approximately 100 years after the onset of Nippur's decline, Enlil handed his kingship over the gods to Marduk of Babylon.[108] Slightly before Enlil's strength waned in Babylon, in Assyria there are traces of attempts to identify Assur with Enlil.[109] In this case, the deity Assur assimilated major deities from the Sumerian and Babylonian pantheon, whereas Marduk replaced them in Babylon.

The Goddess Ishtar

Inana is considered to be represented in the Akkadian world as Ishtar, although there are shifts in the personality of this goddess as a result of this transition. Arriving at an understanding of Ishtar is difficult for it must take into account a diversity of complicated ancient texts along with notions

---

[101] Black and Green, "Tablets of Destinies," in ibid., 173. The tablet of destinies invested its holder with the power to determine the destinies of the world.
[102] For a thorough analysis of Nippur, see Cole, *Nippur in Late Assyrian Times*.
[103] Ibid., 5–6.
[104] Ibid., 7.
[105] Ibid., 9.
[106] There is a change in the course of the river, and it is not clear if this happened because of natural causes or human manipulation. Ibid., 10–11.
[107] Ibid., 12. Grayson, *Chronicles*, 176, tablet iv: 15.
[108] Cole, *Nippur*, 12.
[109] Black and Green, "Assur," in *Gods, Demons and Symbols*, 38.

of the role of women in society, both ancient and modern. Cuneiform literature variously describes her as the daughter of An, the moon-god Sin (Sumerian Nanna), Enlil, or even Enki.[110] Her siblings include her brother the sun-god Shamash (Sumerian Utu) and her sister, queen of the netherworld, Ereshkigal.[111] In general, although there was a diminished role for goddesses from the Sumerian period throughout the Old Babylonian period, and later there were fewer stories about female deities, Ishtar grew in importance.[112] Ishtar's personality has three main components: the goddess of love and sexual behavior, a warlike goddess who is fond of battle, and the planet Venus, the morning and evening star.[113]

Much of the confusion surrounding Ishtar's role in society concerns the different types of texts in which she appears. When she goes down to the netherworld in the "Descent of Ishtar to the Netherworld" (see above), sexuality on earth ceases. She was married, but in the *Epic of Gilgamesh*, Gilgamesh himself refers to her past lovers as a reason not to marry her.[114] She has no children, so her importance for repopulation is not in the act of reproduction but for creating the desire in people and animals to cohabit. She is well known for her interest in and others' interest in taking her into battle.[115] In the Sacred Marriage, an event for which there is only literary evidence dating to the period of the Sumerians, a human priestess representing Inana marries the king.[116] It is not clear if this was an actual event or a ritual, one but if Inana = Ishtar, this links Ishtar closely with the king's legitimacy to rule.[117]

This marriage may be better understood in terms of sexuality and sexual excitement rather than implying anything about love and marriage. These poles are distinct, for example, in stories of rape, an act that is better understood in terms of aggression and dominance than love.[118] In Ishtar's case, the connection between aggression, dominance, and sexual arousal may hold the key to understanding her. Ishtar's interest is in sexuality, not marriage, for either herself or others. She arouses and excites people. This leads to her association with the theater of war, evidenced by some of

---

[110] Black and Green, ibid., 108.
[111] Ibid., 108–9.
[112] Frymer-Kensky, *Goddesses*, 71–7.
[113] Black and Green, *Gods, Demons and Symbols*, 109.
[114] Epic of Gilgamesh, tablet VI, obv. col. i–iii. Gilgamesh lists lovers she has had, and they all met unfortunate fates.
[115] See her "self-praise" in Foster, *Muses*, 1:74.
[116] Black and Green, *Gods, Demons and Symbols*, 158.
[117] Frymer-Kensky, *Goddesses*, 58. For a thorough and detailed analysis of the Sumerian Sacred Marriage in all of its manifestations, see Lavinkivi, *The Sumerian Sacred Marriage*.
[118] Yee, *Poor Banished Children of Eve*.

Assyrian and Babylonian Religions

her attributes: she is described as fierce in terror, exalted (in) the awesome strength of a young bull, a bringer of terror, and able to turn a man into a woman and a woman into a man.[119]

The God Marduk

Marduk was the prime deity for the Babylonians, and the differences between his historical trajectory and that of his rival Assur highlight how they both are part of the stream of tradition. Marduk and Assur are, like other Mesopotamian gods, linked specifically to a city, but because of the power those cities later gain, the role of these deities develops in different trajectories. Moreover, both deities gain power from other deities and from each other.

Marduk was the patron deity of Babylon and is known as early as the Early Dynastic period.[120] Marduk's real power came through the political and subsequent cultural rise of the city of Babylon following the reign of Hammurabi. *Enuma elish* addresses this event on the cosmic level, but the politics behind the shift to Marduk's rise are noted in the Code of Hammurabi, where An and Enlil name the city but give supreme power to Marduk.[121] Because of this close tie between the political and cultural sway of Babylon and Marduk, Marduk's absence, usually because of war and the destruction of Babylon, demanded explanation in both the political and religious realms. Numerous literary texts depict the disaster that ensues whenever Marduk left the city,[122] usually treated as him abandoning the city.[123] Babylon held such sway in Mesopotamia that its embodiment in a deity, Marduk, took on more powers than any other deity – and so the city of Babylon received more status.

The God Assur

Assur was the deity of the Assyrians and probably originated as the local deity of the city Assur. Beginning around 1300 BCE attempts

---

[119] These are all from "Ishtar, Queen of Heaven," which Lambert has shown is a conflation and reworking of various texts about Ishtar. The last attribute refers to sexual deviation, one of her domains. Translation in Foster, *Muses*, 2:501–7.

[120] Black and Green, "Marduk," in *Gods, Demons and Symbols*, 128.

[121] Laws of Hammurabi, Prologue, line 7.

[122] There are numerous texts poetically recounting events concerning Marduk's departure and return, such as "Agum-kakrime and the Return of Marduk," Foster, *Muses*, 1:274–7; "The War with Elam," in *Muses*, 294–5; "The Return of Marduk from Elam," in *Muses*, 299–300; "Nebuchadnezzar and Marduk," in *Muses*, 301; "Nebuchadnezzar to the Babylonians," in *Muses*, 302; and "Marduk Prophecy," in *Muses*, 304–7.

[123] Van de Mieroop, *The Ancient Mesopotamian City*, 48.

72   *Tammi J. Schneider*

began to identify him with Sumerian Enlil, chief of the gods.[124] When Tukulti-Ninurta I defeated the Babylonian Kassite king Kashtiliash IV, he brought back the statue of Marduk. Although the Assyrians assumed responsibility to maintain the cult of the captured Marduk, the background for the event was altered, and Assur replaced Marduk as the chief deity honored during the festival, including the trial of Marduk to avenge the historical wrongs.[125] As Assyria grew in military and political power, so too did its deity. When the Assyrian kings moved their capital to Calah (Nimrud) and Nineveh, the deity Assur maintained his status as deity of the expanded state.[126] The conflict between Babylonia and Assyria, and Babylon's cultural dominance, is reflected in the depiction of each region's titular deity.

This brief overview of some of the major deities of the Assyrian and Babylonian pantheon highlights the connection between the role of a deity and its titular city. Did the kings, priests, or scribes intentionally develop texts to emphasize their deity so the people would follow, or did they believe their deity achieved prominence allowing for the creation of new and the modification of old stories of the deities? Did the "common" people follow these varying traditions, or are the textual references to the gods and their change of rank solely for the elite? The difficulty of dating some of the texts or determining their earliest date of composition means these questions will differ for each deity and text uncovered.

Personal Gods

The bulk of the literary remains from Mesopotamia reflect the attitude or world of the upper echelon of society, consisting mostly of royalty, scribes, and priesthood. For the rest of society there were personal gods. These deities were, like the person they represented, not components of the powerful segment of Mesopotamia, earthly or divine. The function of the personal gods was to see their client's situation received attention by taking their case to the greater gods.[127] This development was a result of the second millennium, when the gods became increasingly identified

---

[124] Black and Green, *Gods, Demons and Symbols,* 38.
[125] Cohen, *The Cultic Calendars,* 422.
[126] For a detailed discussion of how the Assyrian kings incorporated religion with their political powers, see Holloway, *Assur is King!*
[127] Lambert, *Babylonian Wisdom Literature,* 7.

Assyrian and Babylonian Religions

with political ambitions,[128] especially as evidenced with the rise of Marduk and later Assur.

Omens, wisdom literature, and personal prayers provide the evidence for personal gods: "One who has no god, as he walks along the street, Headache [a disease demon] envelopes him like a garment."[129] Luck and good fortune are described as "to acquire a god."[130] In the omen literature, a favorable portent may indicate "that house will acquire a god, that house will endure,"[131] and the reverse, or a bad portent, indicates "that house will grow poor, will not acquire a god."[132] The personal drama placed on the personal god is evident in such texts as *A Man and His God,* where a man complains directly to his personal god when he appears to have no luck.[133] Some texts provide instructions of how to address the personal gods:

Every day worship your god. Sacrifice and benediction are the proper accompaniment of incense. Present your free-will offering to your god, for this is proper toward the gods. Prayer, supplication and prostration offer him daily and you will get your reward. Then you will have full communion with your god.[134]

The "Babylonian Theodicy," an acrostic poem in the form of a dialogue between a sufferer and a friend, sums up the Mesopotamian understanding of the universe in which they lived based on the nature of the relationship between humans and the various divinities.[135] The sufferer exposes the evils of current social injustice, while the friend tries to reconcile these facts with established views of justice and the divine ordering of the universe.[136] Both sufferer and friend begin with the premise that the gods are responsible for maintaining justice among men, yet end by admitting these very gods make men prone to injustice.[137]

THE TEMPLES

The Assyrian and Babylonian temples were the homes of the gods. Because people were on earth to serve the gods, their temples were the ultimate

---

[128] Nemet-Nejat, *Daily Life in Ancient Mesopotamia,* 180.
[129] Lambert, *Wisdom Literature,* 7.
[130] Jacobsen, *Treasures,* 155.
[131] Ibid.
[132] Ibid.
[133] Foster, *Muses,* 2:640–3, and Lambert, "DINGIR SA.DIB2.BA Incantations," 267–322.
[134] Lambert, *Wisdom Literature,* 105, lines 135–40.
[135] Ibid., 65.
[136] Ibid.
[137] Ibid.

74 *Tammi J. Schneider*

manifestations of human service. They were not places for the general populace to confront the gods. Rather, the temples were intended to be the public face of the gods' presence in the city. Viewed as the residences of the gods, temples were critical to the ancient Assyrians' and Babylonians' sense of their role in their cities and of the city's conceptualization of its own identity.

Each Mesopotamian city was the home of a deity, and each of the prominent deities was the patron of a city.[138] Indeed, all of the known temples from Mesopotamia were located in cities.[139] Unlike other ancient Near Eastern religions with urban settings, in Assyria and Babylonia no references are found to cult activity outside the cities, no sanctuaries or cult objects outside cities, nor sacred trees, rocks, rivers, lakes, or seas with cultic power.[140] Even deities whose origins relate to natural phenomena such as the sun and planet Venus had cults located in temples inside cities.[141] The power of the Mesopotamian city is connected to its specific deities, whose divine powers are linked to the political status of their city, a concept revealed in the *enuma elish*, which represents the political and cosmic rise of Babylon.

Mesopotamian religious architecture reflects continuity and change in Mesopotamian religious practices. Despite numerous excavated examples of temples and ziggurats uncovered from ancient Assyria and Babylonia, no standing buildings remain from before the Parthian period (247 BCE–224 CE), and no ziggurat remains to its full original height. The Temple at Eridu, whose first levels date to the Ubaid period, continued to be rebuilt until the first millennium BCE despite the abandonment of the city, and the Kassites rebuilt the Lower Temple at Nippur following exactly the plan of the Isin-Larsa temple, which dates to three hundred years earlier.[142] The Assyrian and Babylonian kings refer to rebuilding dilapidated temples in their annals and year dates and followed the practice of depositing in the foundations or walls of buildings descriptions of their activities, including the information found in the foundation of the building and rebuilding of their predecessors.[143] Because the Mesopotamian kings viewed themselves

---

[138] Van De Mieroop, *City*, 46.

[139] Ibid., 215.

[140] The only rivers deified were used in the river ordeal, a method used to determine the innocence of a person in certain legal situations; the river remained nameless in the texts and was associated in the people's minds with the waters of the underworld. Ibid. and Black and Green, *Gods, Demons and Symbols*, 155–6.

[141] Van De Mieroop, *City*, 216.

[142] Roaf, "Palaces and Temples in Ancient Mesopotamia," 427–9.

[143] Ellis, *Foundation Deposits in Ancient Mesopotamia*.

as the gods' representatives on earth, keeping their homes in order was a primary concern.[144]

All important temples were located within the walled inner city, with the temple of the most ancient patron deity situated in or near the center of town and occupying the highest elevation, although there may have been shrines located in the suburbs.[145] Through numerous rebuilding of the temples, the ground of the oldest tended to be the highest. This may lay behind the concept of the ziggurat, an architectural form developed in the late third millennium. Ziggurats were situated near the temple and connected by courtyards. Although they were built of solid brick and did not house the statue of the deity,[146] their sheer height dominated not only the temple precinct but the city in general.[147]

The temple was literally the "house" of the god that housed the cult image, and where the god lived with his family and servants; it was believed that the god ate, drank, slept, and was entertained in the temple. To thoroughly serve the gods, the temple was equipped like a household containing essential provisions for the gods' meals (kitchens and vessels for making, storing, and serving), sleeping rooms with beds, side rooms for his family, a courtyard with a basin and water for cleansing visitors, and stables for the gods' chariot and draft animals.[148]

Much work has been done in recent years to understand how the ancient Mesopotamians understood the relationship between the anthropomorphized cult statue and the deity the image represented.[149] Ancient texts record that special rituals were carried out to animate the statue of the deity. These indicate the deity had to accept the image for them to take it as their own.[150] Once this was done, the statue served as the god in the context of the temple's rituals. The statue was what the temple housed, and all the temple rituals were anthropomorphized to serve the god/cult statue. The connection between the deity and the deity's cult statue explains why, when temples were destroyed and the image was carried off, usually in times of war, the people viewed it as the deity abandoning them and the city.[151]

---

[144] Cole and Machinist, *Letters from Priests*. The letters edited in this volume reveal the interest the kings Esarhaddon and Ashurbanipal took in the construction and renovation of temple edifices in the major cities of the Assyrian empire, in both the heartland and provinces, even down to minor details of temple and cult.

[145] Van de Mieroop, *City*, 77.

[146] Lloyd, *Archaeology*, 39, 229–30.

[147] Ibid., 180–2.

[148] Wiggermann, "Theologies, Priests."

[149] Winter, "Opening the Eyes," 129–62.

[150] Walker and Dick, *Mis Pi*, 7.

[151] Oppenheim, *Ancient Mesopotamia*, 184.

RELIGIOUS PERSONNEL

There is no native word for "priest." Everyone who served or serviced the gods in the temple setting was considered part of the religious personnel. These included chief attendants, lamentation priests who chanted in the temples, and musicians to sing songs properly, as well as individuals to sweep the floors.[152] Many temple offices were inherited by the eldest son upon division of the estate.[153]

The office of the diviner was important because it was his duty to learn what the gods wanted. The ancient Assyrians and Babylonians believed the gods disclosed their intentions through signs in natural phenomena and world events. However, these needed to be interpreted by those who had devoted prolonged observation and study to these signs, or omens as they were believed to be. The study of omens became a science in Mesopotamia, attested as such by omen treatises.[154] Omens can be divided into two categories, solicited or unsolicited.[155] Diviners were specialists who solicited omens from the gods and then interpreted the signs they received.[156] They could communicate with the divine through extispicy, hepatoscopy, leconomancy, and libanomancy.

There were other avenues for those intent on trying to understand the future and manipulating it. The goal of the magician and sorcerer was to influence man's success on earth. Numerous incantations were used by a range of personnel.[157] *Shurpu* was a collection of spells and rituals for all types of misbehavior: cultic negligence, domestic trouble, uncharitable conduct, cruelty to animals, and unintentional contact with ritually unclean people or places.[158] Astronomy in Mesopotamia associated a sign in the sky with a terrestrial event, usually concerning the king or the country.[159]

Most religious personnel were connected to the state cult and part of a hierarchical organization, although other categories of individuals expressed devotion or connection to gods by what modern people might

---

[152] See list in Postgate, *Early Mesopotamia*, 127.
[153] Nemet-Nejat, *Daily Life in Ancient Mesopotamia*, 192.
[154] For a wonderful introduction to the whole field of extispicy in Babylonia, see Koch-Westenholz, *Babylonian Liver Omens*.
[155] Oppenheim, *Ancient Mesopotamia*, 206–27.
[156] Note their importance to the ruling kings; Star, *Queries to the Sun God*.
[157] Foster, *Muses*, 1:113–45 and 2:840–98.
[158] Nemet-Nejat, *Daily Life*, 197.
[159] Rochberg, "Astronomy and Calendars," 1925–40.

categorize as personal piety. *Nadītu* women apparently chose their form of service, although the regulations concerning these women changed with time and place. In general, *nadītu* were women dedicated to a god, usually unmarried and not allowed to have children.[160] Other examples of *nadītu* women, such as in Babylon, could marry but could not bear children.[161]

Prophetic texts have recently appeared providing new information about an area of Assyrian and Babylonian religion previously unknown and causing Biblicists to rethink the originality of prophecy in Israelite religion.[162] These prophetic texts reveal there was "inspired" prophecy in the ancient Near East, particularly at Mari and Assyria. In the Assyrian context, the prophecies are closely linked to the cult of Ishtar and to Assyrian royal ideology, mythology, and iconography.[163]

RITUAL

Assyrian and Babylonian ritual is where all the categories covered thus far come together: myth, gods, temples, and religious personnel. The Mesopotamian cultic calendar exemplifies the issues addressed repeatedly throughout this survey: continuity and change throughout time and space. Although there was a Mesopotamian calendar with standardized month names, "the almost total lack of writing of the standard Mesopotamian month names impeded determining precisely when this calendar was first introduced into Mesopotamia."[164] The standardization of months was not accompanied by a standardization of religious festivals. Similar types of festivals were observed, although precisely which deity was celebrated, in which month, and in what manner was not standardized.

The *akītu* or New Year's festival was one of the more important and oldest festivals recorded in Mesopotamia, dating as far back as the middle of the third millennium.[165] In Babylon the *akītu* festival was celebrated

---

[160] *Chicago Assyrian Dictionary N Part 1*, 63; Stone, "The Social Role of the Naditu Woman," 50–70.

[161] Code of Hammurabi, paragraph 178–80.

[162] Now that all the Mesopotamian prophetic texts have been published there is a great interest in it in the Society of Biblical Literature. For example, see *Prophecy in Its Ancient Near Eastern Context*.

[163] Parpola, *Assyrian Prophecies*, xv.

[164] Cohen, *The Cultic Calendars*, 299–301. Tiglath-pileser I (1114–1076) adopted the standard Mesopotamian calendar. Tiglath-pileser uses double-dating in one historical inscription, and those who follow him use only the standard Mesopotamian calendar.

[165] Cohen, *The Cultic Calendars*, 401.

78   *Tammi J. Schneider*

in the first and seventh months with detailed descriptions of what events should take place during the eleven days.[166] Prayers were offered,[167] meals were eaten, processions took place, accoutrements of kingship were placed before Marduk, the high priest struck the king's cheek (to instill penitence) and was dragged by his ear before Marduk, the king was struck again to elicit tears so that Marduk accepted him, a white ox and bundled reeds were burned in the courtyard, and gifts were given. On the fourth day, after the second meal, the high priest recited from beginning to end *enuma elish.*[168]

The New Year's festival visually and publicly connected the mythology with the physical image of the god and the king in a powerful social and religious event. In the evening, the king participated in a ceremony where a white bull was sacrificed. The rest of the text is lost, but at some point in the parade the king took the hand of Marduk. The importance of this ceremony is highlighted by the years in which it could not take place. When Nabonidus was in Teima, the king was not there to partake in the festival, no one took Marduk's hand, and the cosmic and earthly world were not united.

Although the New Year's festival was likely the central one of the year, especially as celebrated in Babylon, many *akītu* festivals were carried out more than once a year; moreover, in what city and in which month these were celebrated depended on time and place.[169] Because it was believed that each city originated on behalf of and was devoted to different deities, and the power and place of the deity in the area was connected to the status of the city and its political prominence in any particular period, this is to be expected.

CONCLUSIONS

Assyrian and Babylonian religions are tied to Mesopotamian religion of the third millennium through the pantheon of gods, mythology, temple architecture, and ritual, yet differ from earlier religions and from one another for several reasons; new groups of peoples entering the region, different cities gaining either political or cultural dominance, or both, and the power and charisma of different rulers are key factors. Each deity and component

[166] Ibid., 437.
[167] Ibid., 438–40.
[168] Ibid., 444.
[169] Ibid., 389–481.

of religious cult followed its own trajectory and yet was still part of the stream of Mesopotamian tradition.

BIBLIOGRAPHY

Adams, Robert M. *The Heartland of Cities: Surveys of Ancient Settlement and Land on the Central Floodplain of the Euphrates* (Chicago, 1981).

Arevalier, Nicole. "The French Scientific Delegation in Persia." In *The Royal City of Susa: Ancient Near Eastern Treasures in the Louvre*, ed. Prudence O. Harper, Joan Aruz, and Francoise Tallon (New York, 1992): 16–19.

Arnold, Bill T. "What Has Nebuchadnezzar to Do with David: On the Neo-Babylonian Period and Early Israel." In *Mesopotamia and the Bible: Comparative Explorations*, ed. Mark W. Chavalas and K. Lawson Younger Jr. (Grand Rapids, Mich., 2002): 330–55.

Beaulieu, Paul-Alain. *The Reign of Nabonidus, King of Babylon, 556–539 B.C.* Yale Near Eastern Research 10 (New Haven, 1989).

Black, Jeremy, and Anthony Green. *Gods, Demons and Symbols of Ancient Mesopotamia: An Illustrated Dictionary* (Austin, 1992).

Bottero, Jean. *Religion in Ancient Mesopotamia*, trans. T. L. Fagan (Chicago, 2001).

Brinkman, J. A. *A Catalogue of Cuneiform Sources Pertaining to Specific Monarchs of the Kassite Dynasty.* Vol. 1. *Materials and Studies for Kassite History* (Chicago, 1976).

Prelude to Empire: Babylonian Society and Politics, 747–626 B.C. Occasional Publications of the Babylonian Fund 7 (Philadelphia, 1984).

Buccellati, G. "Through a Tablet Darkly: A Reconstruction of Old Akkadian Monuments Described in Old Babylonian Copies." In *The Tablet and the Scroll: Near Eastern Studies in Honor of William W. Hallo*, ed. Mark E. Cohen, Daniel C. Snell, and David B. Weisberg (Bethesda, Md., 1993): 58–71.

Cogan, Mordechai. "Cyrus Cylinder." In *Context of Scripture: Canonical Compositions from the Biblical World*, ed. William W. Hallo (Leiden, 2000).

Cohen, Mark E. *The Cultic Calendars of the Ancient Near East* (Bethesda, Md., 1993).

Cole, Steven W. *Nippur in Late Assyrian Times c. 755–612.* State Archives of Assyria Studies IV (Helsinki, 1996).

Cole, Steven W., and Peter Machinist. *Letters from Priests to the Kings Esarhaddon and Assurbanipal.* State Archives of Assyria XIII (Helsinki, 1998).

Dalley, Stephanie. *Myths from Mesopotamia: Creation, The Flood, Gilgamesh, and Others: A New Translation* (Oxford, 1989).

Deimel, A. *Pantheon babylonicum* (Rome, 1914).

Dieulafoy, Jane. "A History of Excavation at Susa: Personalities and Archaeological Methodologies." In *The Royal City of Susa: Ancient Near Eastern Treasures in the Louvre*, ed. Prudence O. Harper, Joan Aruz, and Françoise Tallon (New York, 1992): 20–4.

Ellis, Richard S. *Foundation Deposits in Ancient Mesopotamia.* Yale Near Eastern Research 2 (New Haven, 1968).

Foster, Benjamin R. *Before the Muses: An Anthology of Akkadian Literature.* Vols. 1 and 2 (Bethesda, Md., 1993).

From Distant Days: Myths, Tales, and Poetry of Ancient Mesopotamia, Trans. with Introduction and Notes (Bethesda, Md., 1995).

80 *Tammi J. Schneider*

Frymer-Kensky, Tikva. *In the Wake of the Goddesses: Women, Culture, and the Biblical Transformation of Pagan Myth* (New York, 1992).

George, Andrew. "Babylon Revisited: Archaeology and Philology in Harness." *Antiquity* 67 (1993): 734–9.

Glassner, Jean-Jacques. *Mesopotamian Chronicles*. Writings from the Ancient World 19 (Atlanta, 2004).

Grayson, A. K. *Assyrian and Babylonian Chronicles. TCS 5, Chronicle 24* (Locust Valley, N.Y., 1975).

Assyrian Royal Inscriptions Part 2: From Tiglath-pileser I to Ashur-nasir-apli II. (Wiesbaden, 1976).

"Assyria and Babylonia." *Orientalia* (1980): 140–94.

Assyrian Rulers of the Third and Second Millennia BC (to 1115 BC). The Royal Inscriptions of Mesopotamia, Assyrian Periods 1 (Toronto, 1987): 231–79.

Assyrian Rulers of the Early First Millennium BC (1114–859 BC). The Royal Inscriptions of Mesopotamia, Assyrian Periods 2 (Toronto, 1991).

Assyrian Rulers of the Early First Millennium BC II (858–745 BC). Inscription A.o.103.1. The Royal Inscriptions of Mesopotamia, Assyrian Periods 3 (Toronto, 1996).

Green, Alberto R. W. *The Storm-God in the Ancient Near East.* Biblical and Judaic Studies 8 (Winona Lake, Ind., 2003).

Harrak, Amir. *Assyria and Hanigalbat: A Historical Reconstruction of Bilateral Religions from the Middle of the Fourteenth to the End of the Twelfth Centuries B.C.* Texte und Studien zur Orientalistik Band 4 (Hildesheim, 1987).

Heimpel, Wolfgang. *Letters to the King of Mari: A New Translation, with Historical Introduction, Notes, and Commentary.* Mesopotamian Civilizations Vol. 12 (Winona Lake, Ind., 2003).

Holloway, Steven W. *Assur is King! Assur is King! Religion in the Exercise of Power in the Neo-Assyrian Empire.* Culture and History of the Ancient Near East 10 (Leiden, 2001).

Horowitz, W. *Mesopotamian Cosmic Geography.* Mesopotamian Civilizations 8 (Winona Lake, Ind., 1998).

Horsnell, Malcolm J. A. *Chronological Matters: The Year-Name System and the Date-Lists.* Vol. 1, *The Year-Names of the First Dynasty of Babylon* (Hamilton, Canada, 1999).

The Year-Names Reconstructed and Critically Annotated in Light of Their Exemplars. Vol. 2, *The Year-Names of the First Dynasty of Babylon* (Hamilton, Canada, 1999).

Jacobsen, Thorkild. *The Sumerian King List.* Assyriological Studies 11 (Chicago, 1939).

The Treasures of Darkness: A History of Mesopotamian Religion (New Haven, 1976).

Kilmer, Anne Draffkorn. "The Mesopotamian Concept of Overpopulation and Its Solution as Reflected in the Mythology." *Orientalia* 31 (1972): 160–77.

Klengel-Brandt, Evelyn. "Babylonians." *Oxford Encyclopedia of Archaeology in the Ancient Near East,* ed. Eric M. Meyers, trans. Susan I. Schiedel (New York, 1997): 256.

Koch-Westenholz, Ulla. *Babylonian Liver Omens: The Chapters Manzazu, Padanu, and Pan takalti of the Babylonian Extispicy series mainly from Assurbanipal's Library.* CNI Publications 25 (Copenhagen, 2000).

Koldewey, R. *Excavations at Babylon.* English trans. (London, 1914).

Kramer, S. N. "Inanna's Descent to the Nether World: Continued and Revised." *Journal of Cuneiform Studies* 5 (1951): 1–17.

"The Third Tablet of the Ur Version of 'Inanna's Descent to the Nether World'." *Proceedings of the American Philosophical Society* 124 (1980): 299–310.

Lambert, W. G. "DINGIR SA.DIB2.BA Incantations." *Journal of Near Eastern Studies* 33 (1974): 267–322.

"The Historical Development of the Mesopotamian Pantheon: A Study of Sophisticated Polytheism." In *Unity and Diversity: Essays in the History, Literature and Religion of the Ancient Near East*, ed. Hans Goedicke and J. J. M. Roberts (Baltimore, 1975).

Babylonian Wisdom Literature (Oxford, 1960; repr. Winona Lake, Ind., 1996).

Lambert, W. G. and A. R. Millard. *Atra-Hasis: The Babylonian Story of the Flood* (London, 1969).

Larsen, Mogens Trolle. *The Old Assyrian City-State and Its Colonies*. Mesopotamia 4 (Copenhagen, 1976).

The Assur-nada Archive. Old Assyrian Archives. Vol. 1 (Leiden, 2002).

Lavinkivi, Prijo. *The Sumerian Sacred Marriage: In the Light of Comparative Evidence* (Helsinki, 2004).

Lieberman, Stephen J. "Nippur: City of Decisions." *Nippur at the Centennial: Papers Read at the 35th Recontre Assyriologique Internationale, Philadelphia 1988*. Occasional Publications of the Samuel Noah Kramer Fund, ed. Maria de Jong Ellis (Philadelphia, 1992): 127–36.

Lipinski, Edward. *The Aramaeans: Their Ancient History, Culture, Religion* (OLA 100) (Leuven, 2000).

Litke, R. L. *A Reconstruction of the Assyro-Babylonian God-Lists AN:*A-NU-UM and AN:ANU SHA AMELI*. Texts from the Babylonian Collection 3 (Bethesda, Md., 1998).

Lloyd, Seton. *The Archaeology of Mesopotamia: From the Old Stone Age to the Persian Conquest*. Rev. ed. (London, 1984).

Longman, Tremper, III. "The Adad-guppi Autobiography." In *Context of Scripture: Canonical Compositions from the Biblical World*, ed. William W. Hallo (Leiden, 1997).

Luckenbill, Daniel David. *The Annals of Sennacherib* (Chicago, 1924).

McClellan, Thomas L. "12th Century B.C. Syria: Comments on H. Sader's Paper." *The Crisis Years: The 12th Century: From beyond the Danube to the Tigris*, ed. William A. Ward and Martha Sharp Joukowsky (Dubuque, Iowa, 1989): 164–73.

Michalowski, Piotr. *The Lamentation over the Destruction of Sumer and Ur* (Winona Lake, Ind., 1989).

Moran, William L. "Atrahasis: The Babylonian Story of the Flood." *Biblica* 52 (1971): 51–61.

The Amarna Letters. EA 15, line 3, and 16:3 (Baltimore, 1992).

Nemet-Nejat, Karen Rhea. *Daily Life in Ancient Mesopotamia* (Westport, Conn., 1998).

Nissinen, Martti, ed. *Prophecy in its Ancient Near Eastern Context: Mesopotamian, Biblical and Arabian Perspectives*. Symposium (Atlanta, 2000).

Oates, Joan. *Babylon*. Rev. ed. (London, 1979).

Oppenheim, A. Leo. *Ancient Mesopotamia: Portrait of a Dead Civilization*. Rev. ed. completed by Erica Reiner (Chicago, 1977).

Parpola, Simo. *Assyrian Prophecies* (Helsinki, 1997).

Poebel, A. "The Assyrian King List from Khorsabad." *Journal of Near Eastern Studies* 1 (1942): 263–7.

Porter, Barbara Nevling. *Images, Power, Politics: Figurative Aspects of Esarhaddon's Babylonian Policy* (Philadelphia, 1993).

Postgate, J. N. *Early Mesopotamia: Society and Economy at the Dawn of History* (London, 1992).

Rawlinson, H. E. *A Selection from the Historical Inscriptions of Chaldaea, Assyria, and Babylonia*, vol. 1 (London, 1861).

Roaf, Michael. "Palaces and Temples in Ancient Mesopotamia." In *Civilizations of the Ancient Near East*, ed. Jack M. Sasson (New York, 1995): 427–9.

Rochberg, Francesca. "Astronomy and Calendars in Ancient Mesopotamia." In *Civilizations of the Ancient Near East*, ed. Jack M. Sasson (New York, 1995): 1925–40.

Sader, Helene. "The 12th Century B.C. in Syria: The Problem of the Rise of the Aramaeans." In *The Crisis Years: The 12th Century: From beyond the Danube to the Tigris*, ed. William A. Ward and Martha Sharp Joukowsky (Dubuque, Iowa, 1989): 157–63.

Schneider, Tammi J. *A New Analysis of the Royal Annals of Shalmaneser III* (Ann Arbor, 1991).

Schwartz, Glenn M. "Pastoral Nomadism in Ancient Western Asia." In *Civilizations of the Ancient Near East*, ed. Jack M. Sasson (New York, 1995): 249–58.

Sigrist, M. *Les sattukku dans l'Esumesa Durant la periode d'Isin et Larsa* (Mailbu, 1984).

Sjoberg, A.W. "The Old Babylonian Eduba." *Sumerological Studies in Honor of Thorkild Jacobsen on His Seventieth Birthday, June 7, 1974* (Assyriological Studies 20), ed. Stephen J. Lieberman (Chicago, 1975): 159–80.

Smith, G. *A Chaldaean Account of Genesis* (London, 1878).

Star, Ivan. *Queries to the Sun God: Divination and Politics in Sargonid Assyria*. State Archives of Assyria IV (Helsinki, 1990).

Steinkeller, Piotr. "Administrative and Economic Organization of the Ur III State." In *The Organization of Power: Aspects of Bureaucracy in the Ancient Near East*. Studies in Ancient Oriental Civilization 46, ed. McGuire Gibson and Robert D. Biggs (Chicago, 1987): 19–42.

Stone, Elizabeth. "The Social Role of the Naditu Woman in Old Babylonian Nippur." *Journal of the Economic and Social History of the Orient* 25 (1982): 50–70.

Tadmor, Hayim. *The Inscriptions of Tiglath-pileser III, King of Assyria: Critical Edition, with Introductions, Translations, and Commentary* (Jerusalem, 1994).

Talon, Philippe. *The Standard Babylonian Creation Myth: Enuma Eliš*. State Archives of Assyria Cuneiform Texts, vol. IV (Helsinki, 2005).

Tallqvist, Knut. *Akkadische Gotterepitheta* (Helsinki 1938).

Thureau-Dangin, F. "L'inscription des lions de Til-Barsib." *RA* XXVII (1930): 1–21.

van de Mieroop, Marc. *The Ancient Mesopotamian City* (Oxford, 1997).

van Koppen, Frans. "Old Babylonian Period Inscriptions: Isin-Larsa Period." In *Historical Sources in Translation: The Ancient Near East*, ed. Mark W. Chavalas (Malden, Mass., 2006): 88–95.

Villard, Pierre. "Shamshi-Adad and Sons: The Rise and Fall of an Upper Mesopotamian Empire." In *Civilizations of the Ancient Near East*, ed. Jack M. Sasson (New York, 1995): 873–83.

Walker, Christopher, and Michael Dick. *The Induction of the Cult Image in Ancient Mesopotamia: The Mesopotamian Mis Pi Ritual* (Helsinki, 2001).

Ward, William A., and Martha Sharp Joukowsky, eds. *The Crisis Years: The 12th Century: From Beyond the Danube to the Tigris* (Dubuque, Iowa, 1989).

Assyrian and Babylonian Religions

Wiggermann, F. A. M. "Theologies, Priests, and Worship in Ancient Mesopotamia." In *Civilizations of the Ancient Near East,* ed. Jack M. Sasson (New York, 1995): 1861.

Wilhelm, Gernot. *The Hurrians* (Warminster, U.K., 1989).

Winter, Irene. "Opening the Eyes and Opening the Mouth: The Utility of Comparing Images in Worship in India and Ancient Near East." In *Ethnography and Personhood: Notes from the Field,* ed. M. W. Meister (Jaipur, 2000): 129–62.

Wohlstein, Herman. *The Sky-God An-Anu: Head of the Mesopotamian Pantheon in Sumerian-Akkadian Literature,* trans. Salvator Attanasio (Jericho, N.Y., 1976).

Yee, Gale A. *Poor Banished Children of Eve: Woman as Evil in the Hebrew Bible* (Minneapolis, 2003).

3

HITTITE RELIGION

GARY BECKMAN

The term "religion" is employed here in reference to the complex of conceptions concerning the character of parahuman elements in the cosmos and the relationship of men and women to these beings and forces, as well as to the practices by which humans interact with them. Because the Hittites of second-millennium-BCE Anatolia, like all the peoples of the ancient Near East, perceived deities, demons, and the spirits of the dead to be involved in the most mundane aspects of existence, religion was for them an integral part of daily life.

As something so imbricated in the quotidian and self-evident to societal contemporaries, religion was seldom the subject of self-conscious reflection or examination in Hatti (as the Hittites referred to their nation and its territory; see Map 2). Accordingly, the Hittites bequeathed to posterity no theological treatises or surveys of their beliefs, and it is therefore necessary for the modern student to reconstruct their religious life from scattered evidence of the most diverse nature.

MATERIALS

First of all, cuneiform tablets from the Hittite metropolis Boğazköy/ Hattuša[1] (located about a three hour's drive from Turkey's present capital, Ankara) and to a lesser extent from provincial centers such as Maşat Höyük/Tapikka and Kuşaklı/Šarišša elsewhere in central Anatolia include hymns and prayers,[2] detailed programs for ceremonies of the state cult,

---

[1] For a convenient introduction to the current state of the excavations, see Seeher, *Hattusha Guide*.
[2] Singer, *Hittite Prayers*; Lebrun, *Hymnes et prières*; Güterbock, "Some Aspects of Hittite Prayers," 125–39.

Hittite Religion

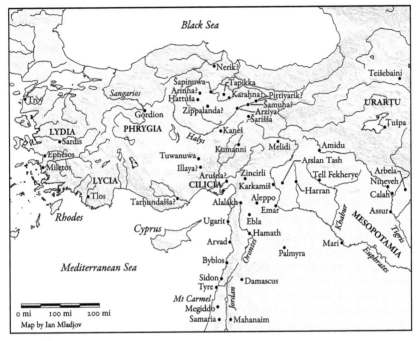

Map 2. Anatolia and Syria.

magical rituals, mythological narratives,[3] records of divinatory procedures, and inventories of the contents of shrines.

The excavated remains of more than thirty temples (each called literally *šiunaš per*, "house of the god[s]") in the capital[4] and several more in lesser cities, some with extensive office precincts and food-storage facilities, demonstrate the important role of religious institutions in Hittite society and administration as well as in the spiritual life of Hatti.[5] The temples were the proprietors of large estates, whose produce, along with additional taxation in kind extracted from other landholders, sustained a substantial redistributive component of the Hittite economy.[6]

Artistic evidence for Hittite religion[7] is provided by images of gods and goddesses in metal, ivory, and other valuable materials;[8] by cylinder and

---

[3] Hoffner, *Hittite Myths*; Beckman, "Mythologie," 564–72.
[4] See Neve, *Hattuša*.
[5] Neve, "Der Große Tempel," 73–79; Güterbock, "The Hittite Temple," 125–32.
[6] Klengel, "Zur ökonomischen Funktion," 181–200.
[7] See in general Bittel, *Die Hethiter*; van Loon, *Anatolia*; Beckman, "Visual Representation," 610–12.
[8] Güterbock, "Hethitische Götterbilder," 203–17.

86 *Gary Beckman*

stamp seals and their impressions on clay tablets, vessels, and *bullae*;[9] by sculpture in low relief on rock faces and free-standing stones;[10] and by ceramics featuring scenes of worship in relief.[11]

PROBLEMS OF RESEARCH

Several difficulties bedevil the student of Hittite religion: First, it must be recognized that almost all of the available written sources pertain to the state cult or to the spiritual needs of the royal family. We have very little information concerning the religious beliefs and activities of the ordinary Hittite man or woman in the street. Second, Hittite religion was an amalgam of elements drawn from various cultural strata: that of the indigenous Hattic people[12] as well as the cultures of the several groups speaking an Anatolian Indo-European language[13] (Hittite, Palaic, or Luwian).[14] To this mix were added influences from Mesopotamia (Babylonia and Assyria) and from the Semitic[15] and Hurrian[16] populations of northern Syria. But it is hazardous to assume, as some commentators have done,[17] that particular spiritual features of these donor cultures documented only elsewhere were equally valid at Hattuša. Finally, the continuous development of central Anatolian civilization throughout the Bronze Ages makes it impossible to present in a short essay a picture accurate in all details across the 500-year history of Hatti. Here I will utilize primarily material from the final century and a half of Hittite history, circa 1350–1180 BCE.

DEITIES

In their cuneiform texts, Hittite scribes placed the divine determinative (DINGIR) not only before the names of proper gods and goddesses, but also before those of demons,[18] topographical features such as springs or mountains,[19] and even parts of temples (for example, the hearth or the

[9] Beran, *Die hethitische Glyptik*; Herbordt, *Die Prinzen- und Beamtensiegel.*
[10] Kohlmeyer, "Felsbilder der hethitischen Großreichszeit," 7–154; Ehringhaus, *Götter, Herrscher, Inschriften.*
[11] Boehmer, *Die Reliefkeramik.*
[12] Klinger, *Untersuchungen.*
[13] On the question of Indo-European relics in Hittite mythology, see Watkins, *How to Kill a Dragon.*
[14] Hutter, "Aspects of Luwian Religion," 211–80.
[15] Hoffner, "Syrian Cultural Influence," 89–106.
[16] Hoffner, "Hurrian Civilization," 167–200; Trémouille, "La religion des Hourrites," 277–91.
[17] As does Haas, *Geschichte der hethitischen Religion.*
[18] Carruba, *Das Beschwörungsritual.*
[19] Lombardi, "Il culto delle montagne," 83–8.

Hittite Religion   87

pillars).[20] That is, this diacritic could be employed to mark any parahuman and immortal force with the power and inclination to intervene in the affairs of humankind.

For the most part, Hittite deities were conceived as human in form, as evidenced by the gods and goddesses sculpted in the relief processions at the shrine of Yazılıkaya[21] (just outside the walls of the capital), but some might also on occasion be depicted theriomorphically. An anthropomorphic divinity is sometimes accompanied by his or her animal manifestation serving as a means of transportation or merely as a mascot. Thus the storm-god might ride in a chariot drawn by bulls, or the goddess of love and war Šaušga stand awkwardly upon the back of her lion-griffon.

For purposes of receiving worship, a god's ultimately ineffable essence could be located in an anthropomorphic or theriomorphic image, in a worked stele or a stone left in its natural state (both called *huwaši*),[22] or in a manufactured symbol such as a disk of gold, and so on. An idea of the sumptuous character of a full-sized cult-image, none of which have yet been physically recovered,[23] may be gleaned from the following introduction to a ritual for establishing the worship of a goddess in a new location:

Thus says the priest of the Deity of the Night: When a person for whom (the matter) of the temple of the Deity of the Night, that is, (the matter) of the Deity of the Night (herself), has become (incumbent) – When it comes about that (s)he[24] builds another temple of the Deity of the Night from (the base of) this temple of the Deity of the Night, and then establishes the deity independently, while (s)he is completing the construction fully, the smiths fashion the deity in gold. They also set about decking her out with the accoutrements appropriate to her. Stuck on her back like beads are sun-disks of silver, gold, lapis-lazuli, carnelian, "Babylon stone," chalcedony (?), quartz, and alabaster, as well as life-symbol(s) and morning stars (?) of silver and gold. They set about fashioning them in that manner. (*KUB* 29.4 i 1–12)

Perhaps more typical was the smaller image included among the inventory of a shrine in an outlying village:[25]

The town Lapana, (chief deity the goddess) Iyaya: The divine image is a female statuette of wood, seated and veiled, one cubit (in height). Her head is plated with gold, but the body and throne are plated with tin. Two wooden mountain

---

[20] Popko, *Kultobjekte in der hethitischen Religion*.
[21] Bittel, *Das hethitische Felsheiligtum*; Alexander, *Sculpture and Sculptors*.
[22] Hutter, "Kultstelen und Baityloi," 87–108.
[23] Given the inherent value of the materials from which such statues were constructed, it is extremely unlikely that any will in fact have survived the ravages of conquest and time.
[24] The Hittite language does not differentiate between masculine and feminine gender.
[25] For a collection of such texts, see Hazenbos, *The Organization of the Anatolian Local Cults*.

sheep, plated with tin, sit beneath the deity to the right and left. One eagle plated with tin, two copper staves and two bronze goblets are on hand as the deity's cultic implements. She has a new temple. Her priest, a male, is a holdover. (*KUB* 38.1 iv 1–7)

The small metal figurines of deities, recognizable as such by their horned headgear, found throughout central Anatolia are probably examples of such local divinities.

In any event, the Hittites were well aware that the divine image, whatever its form, did not constitute or contain the god or goddess. As in Babylonia and Assyria, special ritual was necessary to render a man-made or -selected object a suitable focus for the divine presence. This presence had its true home in that aspect of the cosmos in which it was immanent. (See further below.)

THE PANTHEON

As polytheists,[26] the Hittites could comfortably honor an unlimited number of deities. Indeed, in the course of their imperial expansion, they availed themselves of this flexibility by accepting into their pantheon the gods and goddesses of many conquered areas. This process commenced as early as the Old Kingdom (sixteenth century BCE) with the welcoming of the Storm-god of the Syrian city of Aleppo into Hatti[27] and gained momentum in the fifteenth century with the incorporation of numerous Hurrian deities encountered in southern Anatolia and northern Syria (most importantly the storm-god Teššub and his spouse Hebat, the latter originally the eponymous deity of Aleppo). The community of deities worshiped among the Hittites ultimately grew so large that it came to be referred to as the "Thousand Gods of Hatti."[28]

Most prominent among this myriad of gods[29] were those immanent in the natural phenomena upon which human survival most closely depended: storm-gods, who delivered the rains crucial to the dry-farming economy of central Anatolia and in addition ensured the flow of rivers and springs; sun-deities, whose light was recognized as the basis of all life; and goddesses of the fertile earth. Other deities presided over warfare, sexuality, and reproduction, the world of the dead, particular towns or locations, and so forth. Individual human beings, as well as many

[26] For more detail, see Beckman, "Pantheon," 308–16.
[27] Klengel, "Der Wettergott von Halab," 87–93.
[28] Karasu, "Why Did the Hittites Have a Thousand Deities?" 221–35.
[29] For a full listing, see van Gessel, *Onomasticon*.

Hittite Religion

significant places, objects, and social phenomena, were each watched over by a patron deity (dLAMMA).[30] Thus we meet with the Protective Deity of the King, the Protective Deity of (the town of) Karahna, the Protective Deity of the Army, the Protective Deity of the Quiver, the Protective Deity of the (Palace) Bedroom, the Protective Deity of the Countryside, and many more.

Divinities of similar type often shared a common generic designation; accordingly we find "the Storm-god (dIŠKUR / dU) of (the town of) Pittiyarik" and "the Storm-god of (the town of) Šapinuwa," or "the War-god (dZABABA) of (the town of) Arziya" and "the War-god of (the town of) Illaya." The extent to which such gods were considered "avatars" of a single deity is uncertain: In some cultic texts we find offerings or invocations of, for example, "all the storm-gods of Hatti," whereas in others worship is directed to each individual member of the class.

The explicit identification of Anatolian with Hurrian deities is attested only in the Empire period (mid-fourteenth to early twelfth centuries).[31] The most striking example is provided by an excerpt from a prayer of Queen Puduhepa (mid-thirteenth century): "Sun-goddess of (the town of) Arinna, my lady, you are the queen of all lands! In the land of Hatti you have assumed the name Sun-goddess of Arinna, but in respect to the land that you have made (the land) of cedars (that is, Syria), you have assumed the name Hebat" (*KUB* 21.27 i 3–6). It is significant in this regard that the carved labels accompanying the figures of the gods in the temple of Yazılıkaya present their names in the Hurrian language, not Hittite, thus confirming that this assimilation of pantheons was carried out at the highest level of the state cult.

In certain key respects, the divine world mirrored human societal structure. The pantheon was hierarchical and was ruled by a king, the Storm-god of Hatti (or of the Heavens) – later Teššub – alongside his queen, the Sun-goddess of Arinna – later Hebat. Along with their son (the Storm-god of [the town of] Zippalanda – later Šarrumma) and grandchildren (Mezzula and Zintuhi), these monarchs constituted a family, as did other groups of deities at home in various Hittite towns, for instance, the deities Zašhapuna, Zaliyanu, and Tazzuwašši in Tanipiya.

When warranted by common concerns, such as the witnessing of treaties or the rendering of judgment, all the gods of Hatti met in an assembly whose structure and deliberations undoubtedly mirrored those of the

[30] McMahon, *The Hittite State Cult.*
[31] Wilhelm, "'Gleichsetzungstheologie,'" 53–70.

90 *Gary Beckman*

gathering of Hittite human dignitaries with which it shared the designation *tuliya*.[32] For example, when the Hittite king Tudhaliya IV (late thirteenth century) concluded an agreement with his vassal Kurunta of (the town of) Tarhuntašša, he invoked all the gods as follows: "And in regard to the fact that I have made this treaty for you, the Thousand Gods are now summoned to assembly in this matter. They shall observe and listen and be witnesses!" (An inclusive list of deities follows.)[33] Any violation of the provisions of a treaty thus concluded in the presence of the pantheon would be severely punished by the gods themselves, on occasion even with the death of the culprit.

THE UNIVERSE

We know little concerning how the Hittites conceived the origins or the destiny of their cosmos. However, a ritual passage does relate that in primeval times the celestial and chthonic deities took possession of their respective realms, and that human beings were created by mother-goddesses, presumably from the clay of a riverbank.[34] If we may for once allow ourselves to extrapolate from Mesopotamian evidence, we may speculate that men and women were brought into existence precisely to perform the labor that sustained the leisurely lives of the gods.[35] Such an etiology would certainly be in harmony with the role actually played by humans in the world as illustrated immediately below.

The universe of the Hittites was an integrated system, with no clear-cut boundaries among its levels. Under the right circumstances, gods might mingle with humans, as reported in certain mythological stories.[36] And the euphemism employed for the death of a king or a member of the royal family, "to become a god" (*šiunaš kiš*), shows that a man of sufficient social prominence might attain the status of a minor deity.

As in Mesopotamia, the role of humans was clearly to serve the gods, providing for their sustenance, pleasure, and entertainment.[37] That the gods were actually dependent upon this attention is evident from a passage in a prayer of Muršili II (late fourteenth century), who reminds them of the consequences of a severe outbreak of plague:

[32] Beckman, "The Hittite Assembly," 435–42.
[33] Otten, *Bronzetafel*, iii 78–iv 15.
[34] Otten and Siegelová, "Die hethitischen *Gulš*-Gottheiten," 32–8.
[35] See the discussion of Assyrian and Babylonian religion by Schneider in Chapter 2.
[36] Beckman, "The Anatolian Myth of Illuyanka," 11–25.
[37] Again, see the discussion of Assyrian and Babylonian religion by Schneider.

Hittite Religion

All of the land of Hatti is dying, so that no one prepares the sacrificial loaf and libation for you. The plowmen who used to work the fields of the gods have died, so that no one works or reaps the fields of the gods any longer. The miller-women who used to prepare the sacrificial loaves of the gods have died, so that they no longer make the sacrificial loaves. As for the corral and sheepfold from which one used to cull the offerings of sheep and cattle – the cowherds and shepherds have died, and the corral and sheepfold are empty. So it has come about that the sacrificial loaves, libations, and animal sacrifices are cut off. Yet you come to us, O gods, and hold us responsible in this matter! (*KUB* 24.3 ii 4D–17D)

In return for the necessary maintenance, the satisfied deities would cause crops to thrive, domestic animals to multiply, human society to prosper, and Hittite armies to prevail in battle. This conception is reflected in a prayer in which a god is enjoined:

Give life, health, strength, long years, and joy in the future to the king, queen, princes, and to (all) the land of Hatti! And give to them future thriving of grain, vines, fruit, cattle, sheep, goats, pigs, mules (*sic!*), asses – together with wild animals – and of human beings! (*KUB* 24.2 rev. 12D–16D)

Conversely, a neglected or offended god or goddess could wreak havoc on an individual, a household, or all of Hatti. Attested manifestations of divine displeasure include epidemic, military defeat, and the illness of the king. When confronted with misfortune, it was necessary that the individual sufferer – or the royal establishment on behalf of the community as a whole – determine which deity was angry, the cause(s) of his or her rage, and the appropriate ameliorative measures.

The power of deities to determine human affairs was known as *parā hand(and)atar*, literally "prior arrangement," but often best rendered as "providence." For example, in his "Apology,"[38] Hattušili III attributes the successful course of his career to the intervention of his patron goddess, Šaušga of (the town of) Šamuha. When he had risen in revolt against his nephew, King Urhi-Teššub, "Šaušga, my lady, supported me, and things turned out as she had promised me. Šaušga, my lady, on that very occasion revealed her divine providence (*parā handandatar*) in great measure (by bringing about the defeat of my rival)" (*CTH* 81 iv 16–19).

THE KING

The human monarch[39] stood at the intersection of the divine sphere with that of humans, constituting the linchpin of the entire structure. He had

---

[38] Otten, *Die Apologie Hattusilis III.*
[39] Beckman, "Royal Ideology," 529–43.

92 *Gary Beckman*

been allotted his paramount position in society by the leading deities them-selves: "The gods, the Sun-goddess and the Storm-god, have entrusted to me, the king, my land and my household, so that I, the king, should pro-tect my land and my household on my own behalf" (*KUB* 29.1 i 17–19). In this role he was responsible for ensuring that the people of Hatti properly performed their obligations to their divine masters. In principle, the king directed all communal religious activities, serving as the high priest of all the gods, most importantly that of the Sun-goddess of Arinna, from earli-est days the protector and proprietor of the Hittite state.

Although it was necessary for the king to delegate most of his religious duties, twice yearly, in spring and autumn, he made a progress through the towns of the Hittite heartland, officiating in the sanctuaries of the local divinities. These onerous journeys allowed the monarch to "keep his hand in" the cult of each and every deity worshiped in Hatti. Furthermore, in times of crisis such as the plague addressed above by Muršili II, the ruler appeared in person before the gods to present Hatti's *arkuwar*, "plaidoyer." The parade example of such a brief delivered to a divine authority is that very prayer of Muršili.

COMMUNICATION

As mentioned earlier, it was of the greatest importance that the monarch and the gods maintain a regular exchange of information so that difficulties in the functioning of the cosmos might be rectified to their mutual bene-fit. The king reported directly to his divine lords through his prayers, but traffic in the other direction was necessarily more complex. Accordingly, Muršili II demanded of the gods concerning the cause of an epidemic: "Either let me see it in a dream, or let it be established through an oracle, or let a prophet (*šiunaš antuhšaš*, lit. 'man of god') speak of it. Or all the priests shall perform an incubation rite (lit. 'sleep purely') concerning that which I have instructed them" (*KUB* 14.10 iv 9–13 and dupls.). We may observe that the communication media employed by the gods were of two types: those of which the divinities availed themselves on their own initia-tive (omens), and those whose use was solicited by humans (oracles).

A god might contact a person directly by appearing in a dream,[40] cause a third party to utter a prophecy, or send a portent in the form of unusual human or animal behavior.[41] The sign might also be an astronomical

---

[40] Mouton, "L'importance des rêves," 9–16.
[41] Hoffner, "Akkadian *šumma immeru* Texts," 116–19.

Hittite Religion

occurrence (a solar or lunar eclipse, shooting star, and so forth), a meteorological phenomenon (for example, a lightning strike), or any abnormal terrestrial event.

Alternatively, through various procedures, a specialist serving in the Hittite religious bureaucracy could pose a question to a deity and receive a reply.[42] Divinatory techniques utilized included the examination of the entrails of a sacrificed animal (extispicy),[43] the observation of the flight and other behavior of birds (augury),[44] incubation,[45] and the still mysterious "lot" (KIN) oracle.[46] These various methods were often employed in series as checks upon the results obtained by one another. An excerpt from a lengthy series of such questions is the following:

> In regard to the fact that you, O deity of Arušna, were ascertained to be angry with His Majesty (the King), is this because the Queen cursed (the palace woman) Ammattalla before the deity of Arušna? Because Ammattalla began to concern herself with the deity, yet did not go back and forth (in service to the deity)? Because the son of Ammattalla has dressed himself in garments entrusted to his mother and was summoned to the palace? If you, O god, are angry about this, let the extispicy be unfavorable.... (Here the technical details of the observation are reported.) (Result:) Unfavorable.[47] If you, O god, are angry *only* about this, let the duck oracle be favorable.... (Result:) Unfavorable. (*KUB* 22.70 i 7–11)

THE STATE CULT

The programs of the state cult, probably the most numerous type of text among the surviving Hittite records, prescribe the course of worship in great detail. These religious ceremonies were conducted at regular intervals – daily, monthly, yearly, or at some point in the agricultural cycle (harvest, trimming of the vines, opening of the grain-storage vessels, and so forth) – and are designated by the Sumerogram EZEN, "festival."[48] During these observances, gods and goddesses were lavished with attentions that were likely similar to those customarily enjoyed by the king and his courtiers. The divinities were praised through the recitation of

---

[42] Kammenhuber, *Orakelpraxis, Träume und Vorzeichenschau.*

[43] Schuol, "Die Terminologie des hethitischen SU-Orakels," 73–124.

[44] Archi, "L'ornitomanzia ittita," 119–80.

[45] Mouton, "Use of Private Incubations," 293–300.

[46] Orlamünde, "Überlegungen zum hethitischen KIN-Orakel," 295–311; Beal, "Hittite Oracles," 57–81.

[47] Since the diviner had stipulated that an "unfavorable" response would constitute a "yes" to his query, his supposition as to the cause of the deity's displeasure is thus confirmed. But is there anything else on the god's mind?

[48] Güterbock, "Some Aspects of Hittite Festivals," 175–80.

hymns and provided with much food and drink.[49] They were entertained by singers and dancers[50] and amused by jesters,[51] and they observed the best efforts of athletes in various competitions,[52] including foot races, the shot put, and even mock battles. Strict standards of purity were enforced for officiants,[53] and foreigners were customarily barred from the temple precincts. Celebrations might also include a communal meal[54] for a wider circle of human participants, undoubtedly made up of individuals from the higher ranks of society.

We may gain an idea of the character of regular divine service from the following passage:

The king and queen, while seated, toast the War-god. The *halliyari*-men (play) the large stringed instruments and sing. The clapper-priest claps. The cupbearer brings one snack loaf from outside and gives (it) to the king. The king breaks (it) and takes a bite. The palace functionaries take the napkins from the king and queen. The crouching (cupbearer) enters. The king and queen, while standing, toast the (divinized) Day. The jester speaks; the clapper claps; the *kita*-man cries *"aha!"* (*KUB* 25.6 iv 5–24)

Note that in the rite described in this passage, which is quite typical for the festivals, the duties of the royal couple are rather simple. The more technical aspects of worship were the preserve of religious professionals.

MAGICAL RITUALS

The Hittite scribes employed the Sumerogram SISKUR/SÍSKUR, "ritual," as a label for *rites de passage*, including those concerned with birth,[55] puberty,[56] and death,[57] as well as for ceremonies that were performed only as the need arose – for exigencies such as illness, impotence, miscarriage, or familial strife. These lamentable conditions were held to result from the influence of sorcery or black magic (*alwanzatar*) and/or from infection with *papratar*, "impurity." The immediate goal of treatment was to remove

---

[49] Beckman, "Opfer nach schriftlichen Quellen," 106–11; idem, "Sacrifice, Offerings, and Votives," 336–9.
[50] de Martino, "Music, Dance, and Processions," 2661–9.
[51] de Martino, "Il LÚ.ALAN.ZÚ," 131–48.
[52] Carter, "Athletic Contests," 185–7.
[53] Moyer, "The Concept of Ritual Purity"; de Martino, "Purità dei sacerdoti," 348–62.
[54] Archi, "Das Kultmahl bei den Hethitern," 197–213; Collins, "Ritual Meals," 77–92.
[55] Beckman, *Hittite Birth Rituals*.
[56] Güterbock, "An Initiation Rite," 99–103.
[57] Otten, *Hethitische Totenrituale*; Kassian et al., *Hittite Funerary Ritual*.

Hittite Religion   95

these malign influences, a task to be accomplished largely through the use of analogic magic, which almost always featured a spoken incantation.[58]

Typical in structure, if unusually colorful in its imagery, is this magical speech from a ritual addressed to deities of the underworld: "As a ram mounts a ewe and she becomes pregnant, so let this city and house become a ram, and let it mount the Dark Earth in the steppe! And let the Dark Earth become pregnant with the blood, impurity (*papratar*), and sin!" (*KUB* 41.8 iv 29–32).

It is interesting to observe that women were particularly prominent among magicians,[59] despite their subordinate role among the college of cultic experts in the temples. This is probably because of the special occult knowledge that, as in many other cultures, from classical Greece to early modern France, females were thought to acquire in the process of giving and assisting at birth. Note that one of the most common titles borne by these female practitioners was "the one of birth" (*hašauwaš*), often represented by the Sumerogram ᴹᵁᴺᵁˢŠU.GI, "old woman."

Many of the descriptions of magical rituals found at Hattuša had been collected from practitioners resident in various towns throughout the Hittite realm, seemingly in order to make knowledge of their recommended procedures available to magical specialists attending the royal family, should one of its members suffer from any of the relevant problems. This body of folk remedies gathered from all over Hatti affords a rare window onto the beliefs and practices of the common people of Anatolia.

THE INDIVIDUAL

The birth of each person was overseen by a group of mother-goddesses (DINGIR.MAHᴹᴱˢ/ᴴᴵ·ᴬ) and fate deities (*Gulšeš*), one of whom seemingly accompanied the individual throughout life as a kind of "guardian angel." The relationship of this protector to a man or woman's Protective Deity (ᵈLAMMA) is obscure.

The existence of a son of Hatti did not end with death. Rather, he or she passed to an underworld, about which we are regrettably very poorly informed. We do learn, however, that in this Anatolian Sheol even close relatives failed to recognize one another, and that their daily fare was mud and dirty water.[60] Despite their pitiful lot, the spirits of the dead (*akkant-*,

---

[58] Beckman, "'The Tongue Is a Bridge,'" 519–34.
[59] Beckman, "From Cradle to Grave," 25–39.
[60] Hoffner, "A Scene in the Realm of the Dead," 191–9.

GIDIM; sometimes personalized as the deity Zawalli)[61] could nonetheless intervene for good – but more frequently for ill – in the business of their living descendants.

However, as indicated by the euphemism "to become a god," the king and his closest relatives were thought to enjoy a more pleasant afterlife. A passage from a royal funerary ritual in fact indicates that the deceased monarch became the owner of a herd of livestock grazing in a kind of Elysian Fields, perhaps a fond reminiscence of a simpler lifestyle practiced by his forebears prior to the entrance of the Indo-European groups into the orbit of the civilizations of the ancient Near East. Furthermore, it appears that a change in the ideology of kingship occurred during the final decades of the existence of the Hittite state, and that the ruler came to enjoy a certain divine status even during his lifetime.[62]

CONCLUSION

This survey has revealed that Hittite religious ideology was primarily concerned with the lives of people. Able with their limited technology to intervene only marginally in the basic processes on which their lives depended, the Hittites attributed to their gods power over – and responsibility for – their own survival as individuals and as a group. Positive or negative events were due not to impersonal forces and conditions following their natural development, but were rather the direct expression of divine displeasure with an individual man or woman, or with the king as the embodiment of Hatti.[63] It *was* all about them, and in practice the gods received attention only because of their putative potential influence upon the human level of the cosmos.

With its emphasis on hierarchy, according to which every personage in the universe ideally remained in his or her proper place and fulfilled an allotted role,[64] Hittite religion was also a force for the maintenance of stability within society. In all documented societies of ancient western Asia and northeast Africa the king stood atop both the social and cultic pyramids. The primary distinction between the role of the monarch in Egypt, on the one hand, and in Mesopotamia (Assyria and Babylonia) and Hatti, on the other, is that in the former culture the ruler was himself one

[61] Archi, "Il dio Zawalli," 81–94.
[62] van den Hout, "Tuthaliya IV," 545–73.
[63] Compare Hoffner, "Theodicy in Hittite Texts," 90–107.
[64] Note the "moral of the stories" comprising the cult myths of the *purulli*-festival; see Beckman, "The Anatolian Myth," 11–25.

of the gods, whereas in the latter civilizations he was (merely) first among humans. In either instance resisting his will was ideologically illegitimate. The king had been selected by the gods to be their vicar among humans. Any challenge to the king's paramountcy from below was illegitimate from the outset.[65]

BIBLIOGRAPHY

Alexander, Robert. *The Sculpture and Sculptors of Yazılıkaya* (Newark, Del., 1986).

Archi, Alfonso. "L'ornitomanzia ittita." *Studi micenei ed egeo-anatolici* 16 (1975): 119–80.

"Il dio Zawalli: sul culto dei morti presso gli Ittiti." *Altorientalische Forschungen* 6 (1979): 81–94.

"Das Kultmahl bei den Hethitern." *VIII. Türk TarihKongresi* (Ankara, 1979): 197–213.

Beal, Richard. "Hittite Oracles." In *Magic and Divination in the Ancient World*, ed. L. Ciraolo and J. Seidel (Leiden, 2002): 57–81.

Beckman, Gary. "The Anatolian Myth of Illuyanka." *Journal of the Ancient Near Eastern Society* 14 (1982): 11–25.

"The Hittite Assembly." *Journal of the American Oriental Society* 102 (1982): 435–42.

Hittite Birth Rituals (Wiesbaden, 1983).

"Inheritance and Royal Succession among the Hittites." In *Kaniššuwar: A Tribute to Hans G. Güterbock on His Seventy-Fifth Birthday, May 27, 1983*, ed. H. A. Hoffner, Jr., and G. Beckman (Chicago, 1983): 13–31.

"The Religion of the Hittites." *Biblical Archaeologist* 52(2/3) (1989): 98–108.

"From Cradle to Grave: Women's Role in Hittite Medicine and Magic." *Journal of Ancient Civilizations* 8 (1993): 25–39.

"Royal Ideology and State Administration in Hittite Anatolia." In *Civilizations of the Ancient Near East*, ed. J. Sasson (New York, 1995): 529–43.

"Mythologie (hethitisch)." *Reallexikon der Assyriologie* 8 (1997): 564–72.

"Ištar of Nineveh Reconsidered." *Journal of Cuneiform Studies* 50 (1998): 1–10.

"The Tongue is a Bridge: Communication between Humans and Gods in Hittite Anatolia." *Archiv Orientalní* 67 (1999): 519–34.

"Opfer nach schriftlichen Quellen – Anatolien." *Reallexikon der Assyriologie* 10 (2003): 106–11.

"Visual Representation of Hittite Religion." In *Religions of the Ancient World: A Guide*, ed. S. I. Johnston (Cambridge, Mass., 2004): 610–12.

"Sacred Times and Spaces: Anatolia." In *Religions of the Ancient World: A Guide*, ed. S. I. Johnston (Cambridge, Mass., 2004): 259–64.

"Sacrifice, Offerings, and Votives: Anatolia." In *Religions of the Ancient World: A Guide*, ed. S. I. Johnston (Cambridge, Mass., 2004): 336–9.

"Pantheon. II. Bei den Hethitern." *Reallexikon der Assyriologie* 10 (2004): 308–16.

"How Religion Was Done." In *A Companion to the Ancient Near East*, ed. D. C. Snell (London, 2005): 343–53.

---

[65] It is surely significant that all of the many usurpers of the throne who arose over the course of Hittite history emerged from within the ranks of the royal family itself. See Beckman, "Inheritance and Royal Succession," 13–31.

98 *Gary Beckman*

"Temple Building among the Hittites." In *From the Foundations to the Crenelations: Essays on Temple Building in the Ancient Near East and Hebrew Bible*, ed. M. J. Boda and J. Novotny (Münster, 2010): 71–89.

Beran, Thomas. *Die hethitische Glyptik der Großreichszeit* (Berlin, 1967).

Bittel, Kurt. *Die Hethiter* (Munich, 1976).

Das hethitische Felsheiligtum Yazýilikaya, Boğazköy-Ḫattuša (Berlin, 1975).

Boehmer, R. *Die Reliefkeramik von Boğazköy* (Berlin, 1983).

Carruba, Onofrio. *Das Beschwörungsritual für die Göttin Wišurianza* (Wiesbaden, 1966).

Carter, Charles. "Athletic Contests in Hittite Religious Festivals." *Journal of Near Eastern Studies* 47 (1988): 185–7.

Collins, Billie Jean. "Ritual Meals in the Hittite Cult." In *Ancient Magic and Ritual Power*, ed. M. Meyer and P. Mirecki (Leiden, 1995): 77–92.

"Hittite Religion and the West." In *Pax Hethitica: Studies on the Hittites and Their Neighbours in Honour of Itamar Singer*, ed. Y. Cohen, A. Gilan, and J. Miller (Wiesbaden: 2010): 54–66.

de Martino, Stefano. "Il LÚ.ALAN.ZÚ come 'mimo' e come 'attore' nei testi ittiti." *Studi micenei ed egeo-anatolici* 24 (1984): 131–48.

"Music, Dance, and Processions in Hittite Anatolia." In *Civilizations of the Ancient Near East*, ed. J. Sasson (New York, 1995): 2661–9.

"Purità dei sacerdoti e dei luoghi di culto nell'Anatolia ittita." *Orientalia* 73 (2004): 348–62.

Dussaud, Réné. *Les religions des hittites et des hourrites, des phéniciens et des syriens* (Paris, 1945).

Ehringhaus, Horst. *Götter, Herrscher, Inschriften: Die Felsreliefs der hethitischen Grossreichszeit in der Türkei* (Mainz, 2005).

Furlani, G. *La religione degli hittiti* (Bologna, 1936).

Güterbock, Hans G. "Hittite Religion." In *Ancient Religions*, ed. V. Ferm (New York, 1950): 83–109.

"The Composition of Hittite Prayers to the Sun." *Journal of the American Oriental Society* 78 (1958): 237–45.

"An Initiation Rite for a Hittite Prince." In *American Oriental Society Middle West Semi-Centennial Volume*, ed. D. Sinor (Bloomington, Ind., 1969): 99–103.

"Some Aspects of Hittite Festivals." In *Actes de la XVIIe Rencontre Assyriologique Internationale (1969)*, ed. A. Finet (Brussels, 1970): 175–80.

"The Hittite Temple according to Written Sources." In *Le temple et le cult*, ed. E. Van Donzel (Istanbul, 1975): 125–32.

"Some Aspects of Hittite Prayers." *Acta Universitatis Upsalensis* 38 (1978): 125–39.

"Hethitische Götterbilder und Kultobjekte." In *Beiträge zur Altertumskunde Kleinasiens: Festschrift für Kurt Bittel*, ed. R. Boehmer and H. Hauptmann (Mainz, 1983): 203–17.

Haas, Volkert. *Geschichte der hethitischen Religion* (Leiden, 1994).

Materia Magica et Medica Hethitica (Berlin, 2003).

Hethitische Orakel, Vorzeichen und Abwehrstrategien (Berlin, 2008).

Haas, Volkert, and Heidemarie Koch. *Religionen des Alten Orients: Hethiter und Iran* (Göttingen, 2011).

Hazenbos, Joost. *The Organization of the Anatolian Local Cults during the Thirteenth Century B.C. An Appraisal of the Hittite Cult Inventories* (Leiden, 2003).

Herbordt, Suzanne. *Die Prinzen- und Beamtensiegel der hethitischen Großreichszeit auf Tonbullen aus dem Nişantepe-Archiv in Hattusa* (Mainz, 2005).

Hoffner, Harry A. *Hittite Myths*. 2nd ed. (Atlanta, 1998).

"Hittite Religion." In *The Encyclopedia of Religion*, ed. M. Eliade, vol. 6 (New York, 1987): 408–14.

"A Scene in the Realm of the Dead." In *A Scientific Humanist: Studies in Memory of Abraham Sachs*, ed. E. Leichty, M. de J. Ellis, and P. Gerardi (Philadelphia, 1988): 191–99.

"The Religion of the Hittites." In *Religions of Antiquity*, ed. R. M. Seltzer (New York, 1989): 69–79.

"Syrian Cultural Influence in Hatti." In *New Horizons in the Study of Ancient Syria*, ed. M. W. Chavalas (Malibu, Calif., 1992): 89–106.

"Akkadian šumma immeru Texts and their Hurro-Hittite Counterparts." In *The Tablet and the Scroll: Near Eastern Studies in Honor of William W. Hallo*, ed. M. E. Cohen, D. C. Snell, and D. B. Weisberg (Bethesda, Md., 1993): 116–19.

"Hurrian Civilization from a Hittite Perspective." In *Urkesh and the Hurrians: Studies in Honor of Lloyd Cotsen*, ed. G. Buccellati and M. Kelly-Buccellati (Malibu, Calif., 1998): 167–200.

"Theodicy in Hittite Texts." In *Theodicy in the World of the Bible*, ed. A. Laato and J. C. de Moor (Leiden, 2003): 90–107.

"The Royal Cult in Hatti." In *Text, Artifact, and Image: Revealing Ancient Israelite Religion*, ed. G. Beckman and T. J. Lewis (Providence, 2006): 132–51.

Hutter, Manfred. "Kultstelen und Baityloi: Die Ausstrahlung eines syrischen religiösen Phänomens nach Kleinasien und Israel." In *Religionsgeschichtliche Beziehungen zwischen Kleinasien, Nordsyrien und dem Alten Testament*, ed. B. Janowski, K. Koch, and G. Wilhelm (Freiburg, 1993): 87–108.

"Aspects of Luwian Religion." In *The Luwians*, ed. H. C. Melchert (Leiden, 2003): 211–80.

Kammenhuber, Annelies. *Orakelpraxis, Träume und Vorzeichenschau bei den Hethitern* (Heidelberg, 1976).

Karasu, Cem. "Why Did the Hittites Have a Thousand Deities?" In *Hittite Studies in Honor of Harry A. Hoffner, Jr. on the Occasion of His 65th Birthday*, ed. G. Beckman, R. Beal, and G. McMahon (Winona Lake, Ind., 2003): 221–35.

Kassian, A. S., A. Korolev, and A. Sidel'tsev. *Hittite Funerary Ritual. šalliš waštaiš* (Münster, 2002).

Klengel, Horst. "Der Wettergott von Halab." *Journal of Cuneiform Studies* 19 (1965): 87–93.

"Zur ökonomischen Funktion der hethitischen Tempel." *Studi micenei ed egeo-anatolici* 16 (1975): 181–200.

Klinger, Jörg. *Untersuchungen zur Rekonstruktion der hattischen Kultschicht* (Wiesbaden, 1996).

Kohlmeyer, Kay. "Felsbilder der hethitischen Großreichszeit." *Acta praehistoricae et archaeologicae* 15 (1983): 7–154.

Lebrun, Réné. *Hymnes et prières hittites* (Louvain-la-Neuve, 1980).

Lombardi, Alessandra. "Il culto delle montagne all'epoca di Tudhaliya IV: continuità e innovazione." In *Landscapes: Territories, Frontiers and Horizons in the Ancient Near East*, ed. L. Milano, S. de Martino, F. M. Fales, and G. B. Lanfranchi, vol. 3 (Padua, 2000): 83–8.

100 *Gary Beckman*

Marazzi, Massimiliano. "Ma gli Hittiti scrivevano veramente su 'legno.'" In *Miscellanea di studi linguitici in onore di Walter Belardi*, ed. P. Cipriano, P. Di Giovine, and M. Mancini (Rome, 1994): 131–60.

McMahon, Gregory. *The Hittite State Cult of the Tutelary Deities* (Chicago, 1991).

Mouton, Alice. "Use of Private Incubations Compared to 'Official' Ones in Hittite Texts." In *Offizielle Religion, locale Kulte und individuelle Religiosität*, ed. M. Hutter and S. Hutter-Braunsar (Münster, 2004): 293–300.

"L'importance des rêves dans l'existence de Hattušili III." In *The Life and Times of Hattušili III and Tuthaliya IV. Proceedings of a Symposium Held in Honour of J. de Roos, 12–13 December 2003, Leiden*, ed. Theo van den Hout (Leiden, 2006): 9–16.

Moyer, James. "The Concept of Ritual Purity among the Hittites." Diss. Brandeis University, 1969.

Neve, Peter. "Der Große Tempel in Boğazköy-Hattuša." In *Le temple et le cult*, ed. E. Van Donzel (Istanbul, 1975): 73–9.

Hattuša: Stadt der Götter und Tempel (Mainz, 1993).

Orlamünde, Julia. "Überlegungen zum hethitischen KIN-Orakel." In *Kulturgeschichten: Altorientalische Studien für Volkert Haas zum 65. Geburtstag*, ed. T. Richter, D. Prechel, and J. Klinger (Saarbrücken, 2001): 295–311.

Otten, Heinrich. *Die Bronzetafel aus Boğazköy. Ein Staatsvertrag Tutñalijas IV* (Wiesbaden, 1988).

Hethitische Totenrituale (Berlin, 1958).

"Die Religionen des alten Kleinasien." In *Religionsgeschichte des Alten Orients*, ed. B. Spuler (Leiden, 1964): 92–121.

Die Apologie Hattusilis III: Das Bild der Überlieferung (Wiesbaden, 1981).

Otten, Heinrich, and Jana Siegelová. "Die hethitischen Gulš-Gottheiten und die Erschaffung der Menschen." *Archiv für Orientforschung* 23 (1970): 32–8.

Popko, Maciej. *Kultobjekte in der hethitischen Religion (nach keilschriftlichen Quellen)* (Warsaw, 1978).

Religions of Asia Minor (Warsaw, 1995).

Schuol, Monika. "Die Terminologie des hethitischen SU-Orakels. Eine Untersuchung auf der Grundlage des mittelhethitischen Textes KBo XVI 97 unter vergleichender Berücksichtigung akkadischer Orakeltexte und Lebermodelle, I." *Altorientalische Forschungen* 21 (1994): 73–124.

Seeher, Jürgen. *Hattusha Guide: A Day in the Hittite Capital* (Istanbul, 2002).

Singer, Itamar. *Hittite Prayers* (Atlanta, 2002).

Strauss, R. *Reinigungsrituale aus Kizzuwatna* (Berlin, 2006).

Sürenhagen, Dietrich. "Zwei Gebete Hattusilis und der Puduhepa: Textliche und literaturhistorische Untersuchungen." *Altorientalische Forschungen* 8 (1981): 83–168.

Taggar-Cohen, A. *Hittite Priesthood* (Heidelberg, 2006).

Taracha, P. *Religions of Second Millennium Anatolia* (Wiesbaden, 2009).

Trémouille, Marie-Claude. "La religion des Hourrites: état actuel de nos conaissances." *Studies in the Civilization and Culture of Nuzi and the Hurrians* 10 (1999): 277–91.

van den Hout, Theo P. J. "Tuthaliya IV. und die Ikonographie hethitischer Großkönige des 13. Jhs." *Bibliotheca Orientalis* 52 (1995): 545–73.

van Gessel, Ben H. L. *Onomasticon of the Hittite Pantheon* (Leiden, 1998).

van Loon, Maurits. *Anatolia in the Second Millennium B.C.* (Leiden, 1985).

Watkins, Calvert. *How to Kill a Dragon: Aspects of Indo-European Poetics* (New York, 1995).
Wilhelm, Gernot. "'Gleichsetzungstheologie,' 'Synkretismus,' und 'Gottspaltungen' im Polytheismus Anatoliens." In *Polytheismus und Monotheismus in den Religionen des Vorderen Orients*, ed. M. Krebernik and J. van Oorschot (Münster, 2002): 53–70.

4

ZOROASTRIANISM

PRODS OKTOR SKJÆRVØ

INTRODUCTION

Zoroastrianism (also called Mazdaism) was the religion of peoples speaking Iranian languages who, coming from Central Asia circa 1000 BCE, settled on the Iranian Plateau.[1] Iranian languages are related to the Indo-Aryan languages (Sanskrit, etc.), and the common proto-Indo-Iranian language may have been spoken by peoples inhabiting the area south and southeast of the Aral Sea, who split into Iranians and Indo-Aryans around 2000 BCE. Archaeology has revealed dense settlements in this area of Central Asia, but attempts to correlate them, especially the so-called Bactrian-Margiana Archeological Complex circa 2200–1700 BCE, with the people among whom Zoroastrianism originated remain inconclusive because of the lack of written testimonies.

The Zoroastrian sacred texts collected in the *Avesta* were composed orally between circa 1500 and 500 BCE, but they contain no historical information about the Iranian people who created them. The geographical horizon of the composers of the *Avesta* spans the area from the modern Central Asian republics, through what is modern Afghanistan, to the Helmand River basin, reflecting their southward migration. Since the Iranians did not use writing, the archaeological records from the areas they may have occupied can be only tentatively correlated with them. Thus, the historical-cultural settings of the various stages of the religion of the Iranians before the Achaemenids (550–331 BCE) cannot be determined.

Among the Iranian tribes who migrated onto the Iranian Plateau around the turn of the millennium were the Medes, whose religious practices as described by the early Greek historians were Zoroastrian or variants thereof,

---

[1] For the sites relevant to Zoroastrianism, see Map 1 in Chapter 2.

and the Persians, who formed the Achaemenid dynasty and practiced Zoroastrianism as known from the *Avesta*. The term Parswa, "Persian," is found in Assyrian documents from the ninth century on and indicates that the Persians had migrated southward along the Zagros Mountains before they became settled in what was to become their homeland by the seventh–sixth centuries BCE. According to Herodotus's *Histories*, Persian hegemony began when the Persian Cyrus the Great overthrew the last Median king (550 BCE). When Cyrus's son Cambyses died in an accident on his way from Egypt to Persia, Darius made himself king, claiming descent from Achaemenes, a common ancestor with Cyrus. He and his son Xerxes created the Achaemenid empire (550–331 BCE), which reached from Ethiopia and Libya to the Indus valley, but fell to Alexander in 331/330 BCE. When Alexander died in 323, it was divided among his successors, Iran falling to Seleucus, who founded the Seleucid dynasty, which was followed by the indigenous Parthian Arsacid (247 BCE?–224 CE) and Persian Sasanian dynasties (224–636 CE).

THE *AVESTA*

Like the Old Indic *Rigveda*, but different from much of the Judeo-Christian and Mesopotamian religious traditions, the *Avesta* is a repository of oral texts, transmitted orally in fixed linguistic form until it was written down circa 600 CE.[2] Judging from the language, the older part (*Old Avesta*) was composed between 1500 and 1000 BCE and the later parts (*Young Avesta*) between 1000 and 500 BCE.

The *Old Avesta* contains the five *Gāthās*, "songs," and the *Yasna Haptanghāiti*, "the *yasna* (or sacrifice in seven sections) (*hāitis*)." The principal Young Avestan texts are the *Yasna* (*Yasna* 1–72), the text accompanying the *yasna* ritual (still performed daily), of which the *Old Avesta* is the central part (*Y.* 28–41, 43–51, 53); the *yasht*s, hymns to individual deities; the *Khorda Avesta*, "little *Avesta*," a miscellany of short hymns and other ritual texts; and the *Videvdad* (also *Vendidad*), Avestan *Vi-daēwa-dāta*, literally, "the established rules (*dāta*) (serving to keep) the evil gods (*daēwa*) away (*vi-*)," a collection of texts concerned with purification rituals, including some mythological material. The *Hērbedestān* and *Nīrangestān* are manuals dealing with issues connected with priestly schooling and the performance of rituals.

---

[2] References to the *Avesta* follow K. F. Geldner's edition: *Avesta. The Sacred Book of the Parsis* I–III (Stuttgart, 1896).

The *Gāthās* are composed in a highly elliptic and allusive style, which, together with our incomplete knowledge of the language, makes interpretation difficult. The *Young Avesta* includes no didactic texts explaining the religion in a systematic fashion, and, although the language of the Young Avestan texts is better understood, these too merely allude to myths that are difficult to reconstruct. The Achaemenid inscriptions add little to a detailed understanding of the religious system. Only in the Middle Persian (Pahlavi) texts from Sasanian times, the Zoroastrian oral traditions written down in the ninth century and later, do we find complete narratives that illuminate the older texts.

The *"Author" of the* Old Avesta

Because the *Avesta* consists of ancient oral compositions, its authors are not known. This is also the case of the *Gāthās*, although, in the West, Zarathustra has been assumed to be their author. The anonymous reciter, himself presumably a poet and the performer of the ritual (sacrificer), introduces himself in *Yasna* 28, where he announces his intent to emulate Zarathustra and other famous poets and sacrificers of the past; in *Yasna* 29, the mythical installation of Zarathustra as Ahura Mazdā's human counterpart, who will perform again his cosmic sacrifice in this world, is described; and in *Yasna* 43, the poet identifies himself with Zarathustra and from then on assumes his role.

The *Religion of the* Old Avesta

The *Old Avesta* is a ritual text, which must have accompanied a cosmic renewal ritual (morning or New Year), although the details of the ancient ritual are unknown. The principal verb is *yaza-*, "to sacrifice (to), offer up in sacrifice" (noun *yasna*), and the direct objects either the deities for whom the sacrifice is performed or the consecrated objects offered to them. The *Gāthās* are addressed to Ahura Mazdā, the deity whom the text praises together with his creation and whose opponents he blames or scorns, while the poet of the *Yasna Haptanghāiti* presents himself and his audience as "praisers, not blamers." In the *Young Avesta*, Zarathustra, who first recited the *Gāthās*, is described as the first to praise Order and blame the *daēwa*s (*Yasht* 13.89).

The *Gāthās* are associated with "four holy prayers": The *Ahuna Vairiya* or *Yathā ahū vairiyō*, "as (the new existence) is a worthy (reward [for our sacrifice]) by (the example of) the (first) existence" (first strophe of the first

Gāthā), announces the purpose of the ritual, namely, the renewal of the world under Ahura Mazdā's command; the *Ashem Vohū*, "Order is the best good (reward)" (based on the first strophe of the second *Gāthā*), promises rewards to those who contribute to upholding the cosmic order by their ritual order; the *Yenghyē Hātām*, "He to whom among those that are" (based on the last strophe of the fourth *Gāthā*), promises the sacrificer's praise for all deities in return for his reward; and the *Airyaman Ishiya*, "Let speedy Airyaman (come here)" (last strophe of the last *Gāthā*), sums up the desired results of the ritual. These four texts are recited repeatedly, with varying frequency, throughout all Zoroastrian rituals.

The Old Avestan Ritual

The Old Avestan ritual was performed to regenerate the existence (*ahu*) according to the models (*ratu*) contained in Ahura Mazdā's first ordered existence and to put him back in command (*khshathra*) of the universe as protector of the poor (*Ahuna Vairiya, Y.* 53.9). The forces of Order (*asha*; light, health, life) must overcome those of the Lie, the principle of chaos (darkness, sickness, death), for the ordered cosmos to be reborn in the form of the sunlit new day. This was achieved by strengthening the forces of Order through sacrificial offerings, including hymns of praise, which confer fame and authority, while weakening those of chaos through depriving them of sacrifices and praise and ridiculing and scorning them (*Y.* 53).

The relationship between the poet-sacrificer, performer of the sacrifice, and Ahura Mazdā, its recipient, was that of guest-friends, based on mutual obligations and the giving of gifts (*Y.* 43.14, etc.). The obligations were determined by rules that regulate behavior and relationships, among them the mutual agreements between gods and men (*urwata*s). When the rules were observed, man was rewarded with "brilliant gifts" (*Y.* 33.7): The sun would rise once more, and the human settlements would have peace and prosperity through abundant pasture (*Y.* 29.10, etc.). When the rules were broken, darkness and evil would reign (*Y.* 31). Among the sacrificers' gifts were the sacrificial offerings and their words and actions, but also their bones and life-breath and their "pre-souls" (*frawashi*s; *Y.* 37.3, see below), needed to give solidity and life to the new existence for it to be reborn as a living being (*Y.* 33.14, 43.16). Most of their gifts were themselves gifts from Ahura Mazdā (*Y.* 31.11, etc.).

The sacrificial gifts were sent up to heaven in a race between rival sacrificers, some of them evil (the *kawi*s and *karpan*s). The sacrificer described in the *Gāthā*s took on the role of Zarathustra and was confident that he would be the winner (e.g., *Y.* 46). On the way, the competitors passed the "Ford of the Accountant" (*cinwatō pertu*), the function of which is not specified in the *Gāthās*, but, according to the Pahlavi texts, was where the soul's good and bad thoughts, words, and deeds were weighed on a scale, the balance determining whether they would go to heaven or hell. Those who passed the ford were admitted to a heavenly "audition" (*ya'ah*), during which their performances were judged by the heavenly "arbiters" (*ardra*), comprising the famous poet-sacrificers and heroes of the past, who dwelt in Ahura Mazdā's house (*Y.* 46.14, 50.4). Once the winner was chosen, they proceeded to an exchange of gifts (*maga*, whence *magu*, the priest performing this ritual?), Ahura Mazdā came forward with the prize (*Y.* 51.15), and the winner's hymns were added to those accumulated in Ahura Mazdā's abode (*Y.* 45.8). The successful sacrificer became Ahura Mazdā's guest (*Y.* 31.22), whereas the losers became guests in the house of the Lie (*Y.* 46.11). In return for the gifts presented to him, Ahura Mazdā was asked for a counter-gift of the same (or greater) exchange value (*vasna*), namely, the return of dawn, when the guiding thoughts (*khratu*) of the successful sacrificers (*saoshyant*), as the oxen who pull the new day across the sky, moved forth to uphold the existence of Order (*Y.* 46.3).

The existences, or "worlds" (*ahu*), that are reborn, live, sicken, and die daily (and annually) were two: "the existence that has bones," the world of living beings, and "the existence which is that of thought," the world of (= reached by) thought (*Y.* 28.2). They were regenerated by the combined efforts of Ahura Mazdā and his daughter and spouse, (Life-giving) Humility, the Earth (see below), who contributed to the "thickening" of Order (*Y.* 44.6). With the new day, she would be under Ahura Mazdā's command and protection, "where she sees the sun" and can produce her "works" (*Y.* 43.16).

The principal terms characterizing the good existence are derived from a verb (*spā-/sao-*), which implies "swelling," that is, with vital juices. The good deities in the world of thought, first of all Ahura Mazdā, were all *spenta*, "endowed with swelling (power)," that is, "life-giving, (re)vitalizing," and able to maintain the universe in its pristine state. The daily regeneration of the ordered world is described as a physical birth (*Y.* 43.5, 48.6), implying conception, growth, and birth, while the relapse into chaos is described as an illness (*Y.* 30.6). The regenerated existences are based on the model of the first existence and its elements, which serve as "models" (*ratu*) for every new one (*Ahuna Vairiya, Y.* 31.2), models announced by Life-giving Humility (*Y.* 43.6; similarly in *Rigveda* 2.38.4), which suggests that Order is the web of ordered relations in the universe.

Humans contributed to the maintenance of the ordered universe by their rituals and their behavior; if a ritual was successful, the performer became a *saoshyant*, a "revitalizer." By their efforts, the sacrificers and Ahura Mazdā remade the ordered existence, making it *frasha*, that is, filled with vital juices permitting growth and procreation (*Y.* 30.9, etc.). The last strophe of the last *Gāthā* (*Y.* 53.9) states that Ahura Mazdā has replaced the evil rulers, and the *Airyaman Ishiya* (*Y.* 54.1), the strophe that concludes the *Gāthā* collection, is an invitation to Airyaman, god of peace and healing, to come and heal the ailing existence and support the poet's community. For his contributions, the sacrificer expected a handsome fee (*mizhda*) paid in cows, horses, or camels (*Y.* 44.18, 46.19).

The Old Avestan Divine Beings

Benign beings in the world of thought were those "deserving of sacrifices" (*yazata*), a term found once in the *Old Avesta* referring to Ahura Mazdā (*Yasna Haptanghāiti, Y.* 41.3). Ahura Mazdā's name probably means the All-knowing (*mazdā*) Lord/Ruler (*ahura*), which was still understood in its literal meaning in the *Old Avesta*. Young Avestan Ahura Mazdā and Old Persian Ahuramazdā, however, are simply names.[3]

Divine beings other than Ahura Mazdā include other *ahura*s (*Y.* 30.9, 31.4), perhaps a reference to the male deities featured in the *Young Avesta*, and male and female beings referred to as Life-giving Immortals (*amesha spenta*). These last may be the same as those referred to by this term in the *Young Avesta*, namely, a series of what we would term "abstract" concepts, although they also had "concrete" references: *vohu/vahishta manah*, "good/best thought," was also the sun-lit sky, and *asha (vahishta)*, "(best) Order," was also the sunlit heavenly spaces with the sun (*Y.* 32.2), and both were Ahura Mazdā's children (*Y.* 44.3, 45.4); the *khshathra*, "(royal) command," was generated for Ahura Mazdā in the sacrifice (connected with metal in the *Young Avesta*); *(spentā) ārmaiti*, "(life-giving) Humility,"[4] was Ahura Mazdā's daughter (*Y.* 45.4) and the Earth (already in Indo-Iranian), who patiently supports all that happens on her and by her "works" produces everything needed for life (*Y.* 43.16); and the couple *haurwatāt*, "wholeness," and *amertatāt*, "non-dyingness" (not dying before one's time), were closely connected with water and plants. Their connection with the sacrifice

---

[3] It is therefore misleading to render the name consistently as "Wise Lord" or similar, irrespective of the date of the texts, especially the Old Persian inscriptions and the later texts.

[4] Translation chosen to express her patience with her burden and her status as daughter and wife; similarly, *humility* is from Latin *humus*, "earth."

is obvious, and they probably came into existence as the constituents and results of Ahura Mazdā's primordial sacrifice.

Other divine beings are the Fashioner of the Cow, *sraosha*, "(mutual) readiness to listen" of gods and men, *ashi*, "reward?", Airyaman (Indic Aryaman), the heavenly fire, Ahura Mazdā's son (identical with the ritual fire, *Y.* 36.6), and the heavenly waters, which, together with other nouns of feminine gender, were Ahura Mazdā's "women" (*gnāh, Y.* 38.1). The "women" were also "well deserved" (*vairiya*), which suggests Ahura Mazdā won them as rewards for his successful fight against the powers of evil.

The Old Avestan Ordered Cosmos

The ordered cosmos, "the first existence" (*Y.* 33.1), came about when Ahura Mazdā, like how a poet *thinks* his poem, *thought* (forth) Order and healed the existence (*Y.* 31.19) and when he first "*thought* the free spaces suffused by lights" and "by his guiding thought (*khratu*) spread out the fabric of Order by which he upheld Good Thought (the covering of the sun-lit sky)" (*Y.* 31.7). The sunlit heavenly spaces are the form (*kerp*) of Ahura Mazdā (*Y.* 36.6).

Ahura Mazdā's Order governed the cosmic processes and the ritual and social behavior of men. Everyone and everything that conformed to this principle was said to be a "sustainer of Order" (*asha-wan*, Old Persian *artā-wan*); what opposed it was "filled with/possessed by the Lie" (*drug-want*). The principal agents of chaos were the Lie (*drug*, female), the cosmic deception; Wrath (male), the embodiment of the dark night sky; and the evil gods (*daēwas*). For the (woven) covering (*vyā*) of Good Thought to spread out, (the dark covering of) Wrath needed to be tied down (*Y.* 48.7).

Creatures in the world of living beings were "fashioned" (*tash-*), like the work of a master carpenter (*Y.* 37.2, 38.3), including man, the cow, the waters, and the plants (*Y.* 29.6, 31.11, 44.6, 51.7). Similarly, the poets "fashioned" their thoughts into poems (*manthra*), the first of the poems being "fashioned" by Ahura Mazdā himself, who prepared the ingredients of the ritual (*Y.* 29.7). All that was fashioned was then set in place (*dā-*) by Ahura Mazdā (*Y.* 37.1–2, 44.3–5).

In this ordered cosmos, everyone and everything must choose whether to belong to one or the other side; on one side were those who sustain order, on the other those possessed by the Lie. The primordial choices were made by two *manyu*s, "(cosmic) spirit" and "(poetic) inspiration." In *Yasna* 30, they are described as twin "sleeps," which presumably refers to them as "sleeping" fetuses not yet born. The text seems to imply that, when the two spirits "came together (in strife)," "life" and "non-living" were conceived, and the nature of the new existence was determined as good or bad (*Y.* 30.4). Of the two spirits, the Life-giving one chose to produce order, whereas the one possessed by the Lie chose to produce the "worst things" (*Y.* 30.5). The evil gods, confused by the Lie, made the wrong choices, choosing the "worst thought," and allied themselves with Wrath (*Y.* 30.6). Humans, too, both in the general context of coming of age and in the ritual context, must repeat the primordial choices, and, for their choices, those possessed by the Lie would obtain the "worst existence," to which their "vision-soul" (*daēnā*) would lead them (*Y.* 31.20), whereas the sustainers of order would have "best thought" (*Y.* 30.4).

The Old Avestan Notion of Man

The basic constituents of man were thought (*manah*), breath-soul (*urwan*), vision-soul (*dayanā*, later *daēnā*), guiding thought or "wisdom" (*khratu*), and the "pre-(existing) soul" (*frawashi, Y.* 37.3) and utterances, announcements (*sangha*), statements of choice, and actions (*Y.* 31.11, 45.2). The body contained life-breath (*ushtāna*) and bones (*ast*). Its form (*kerp*) was provided by the bodily tissues (*uta-yuiti*) and breathing (*anman*) by Humility (*Y.* 30.7). The breath-soul was both the breath of the poet, which carried his songs up to heaven (*Y.* 28.4), and the soul that left the body at death and traveled into the beyond to be judged and go on to heaven or hell. The vision-soul was what enabled man to "see" (*day-*) in the other world and hence guided the breath-soul in the other world while successfully fighting off the forces of darkness (*Y.* 39.1–2). In the *Young Avesta*, its appearance is determined by the balance of people's thoughts, words, and actions.

In the exclusively oral Iranian society, thought and speech played crucial roles in the way the poets conceived of the world and their part in it. Thought was essential, because it contained all the memories and knowledge of the professional poet and sacrificer (*zaotar*). Modern Zoroastrians often define their religion as being based on "good thought, good speech, and good action," a formula found for the first time in the *Yasna Haptanghāiti* and frequent in the *Young Avesta*. In the *Gāthās*, the individual terms are omnipresent and basically imply thinking "straight," or true, thoughts and speaking true words about reality as the ordered cosmos established by Ahura Mazdā and performing the actions required to maintain this ordered cosmos. "Sin" is thinking and saying things that disagree with this reality and so are untrue.

Good speech and actions, dependent upon good thought, also refer to ritual activities that can be heard and seen and imply correct performance, crucial for success. The poet-sacrificer's function is to "weave" (*ufya-*) his thought, along with Ahura Mazdā and the other deities, into an orderly poem (*vahma*) to serve as a blueprint for the new existence (*Y.* 28.3).

The Old Avestan Eschatology

Although the references to the (breath-) soul and *daēnā* (vision soul) at a place called the Ford of the Accountant (*Y.* 46.10, 51.13), to the last turn of the existence (*Y.* 43.5, 51.6), and to the fate of the sustainers of order and those possessed by the Lie are primarily referring to a mythical-ritual context, the general nature of the ritual suggests that they also refer to the expectations about what happens to individuals after death, as in the *Young Avesta.* "The last turn" refers to the last turn in the ritual race up to heaven, but perhaps also to the last turn of the heavenly bodies, which measure out time until everything has run its course (*Yt.* 13.58). The Old Avestan *saoshyant*s, "revitalizers," too, refer to the performers of the current rituals, although it is possible they also allude to the final *saoshyant* (see below).

The Poet-Sacrificer and Zarathustra in the Old Avesta

The poet-sacrificer, as the human counterpart of Ahura Mazdā, re-performed on earth the primordial sacrifice by which chaos was overcome and cosmos established. To be successful, he needed the flawless knowledge received from Ahura Mazdā about creation and how man can assist in destroying evil, along with knowledge about rituals and social relationships (e.g., *Y.* 30–33, 44–45). This made him "the knowing one of Ahura Mazdā" (*Y.* 28.4), like a god, a "life-giving man" (*nar spenta, Y.* 34.2, etc.).

The prototype of the human sacrificer was Zarathustra, whose installation is described in *Yasna 29*. Here the cow's breath-soul and that of the poet ascend to the assembly of gods to complain about the world, which has reverted to chaos, in which the cow has no protector, and the Fashioner of the Cow asks Order what model (*ratu*) had been foreseen for the cow (*Y.* 29.1–2). Ahura Mazdā says that although there was none in the first existence (*Y.* 29.6), he has already fashioned the components of the sacrifice, and now someone is needed to take them down to mortals. Someone announces that one has already been found, namely, Zarathustra (*Y.* 29.7–8).

Zoroastrianism   111

In the rest of the *Gāthās*, the sacrificer identifies himself as Zarathustra and imitates his sacrifice (e.g., *Y.* 43.7–8). In the last *Gāthā* (*Y.* 53), it is revealed that Zarathustra's sacrifice, as reputed, was the best. Then, presumably, Zarathustra and his daughter perform a *xwaētuwadatha*, "next-of-kin marriage," matching the union between Ahura Mazdā and Humility (the Iranian form of *hierogamia*),[5] after which Airyaman arrives to heal the world and re-establish peace for the communities of the sustainers of Order (*Y.* 53.8, *Y.* 54.1)

The Religion of the Young Avesta

The *Young Avesta* contains more details about cosmogony and eschatology (*Yt.* 13 and 19), the fate of the soul after death (*Hādōkht nask, Aogemadaēca, Videvdad* 19), and how to deal with the influence of evil (*Videvdad*). These elements of Young Avestan religion are important, as they supplement and amplify the religion described in the *Old Avesta*.

Young Avestan Cosmogony

Ahura Mazdā, the "establisher" (*dātar, dadwāh*), assisted by "the pre-existing souls (*frawashi*s) of the sustainers of Order," fashioned and set everything in place (*dā-*). Predating the creation were the "lights without beginning (*an-agra*)" and the matching "darknesses without beginning" (*Hādōkht nask* 2.33), "the temporal existence (*sti*) of the sustainer of order," and the "firmament" (*thvāsha*). "Time" (*zurwan*) before and after the creation was "unlimited" (*a-karana*), while the duration of the world, which Ahura Mazdā "cut out," was "time long set in place by itself (*dargō-khwa-dāta*). The duration is not specified in the *Avesta*, but an Avestan fragment in the Pahlavi, or Middle Persian, commentary on *Videvdad* 2.20 asks "for how long was the temporal existence (*sti*) in the world of thought established?" which shows that the duration probably was set. In the Pahlavi texts we have four periods of three thousand years: the period of the world of thought, the period from the conception of the world of the living (in the world of thought) to its birth when the Evil One attacks, the period of the world of the living down to the time of Zarathustra and his encounters with Ahura Mazdā, and the three millennia of Zarathustra's three eschatological sons (see below).

---

[5] See Skjærvø, "Marriage: Next-of-Kin Marriage in Zoroastrianism," in *Encyclopædia Iranica* (at http://www.iranica.com).

The elements of the world, in which we live and in which good and evil vie for supremacy (later called the Mixture), were set in place by the Life-giving and Evil Spirits (*Yt.* 13.76). In the *Videvdad*, the Evil Spirit's counter-creations to Ahura Mazdā's good creations are described.

The Young Avestan Pantheon

In addition to the divine beings described above, Ahura Mazdā is surrounded by male and female beings, the generic term for whom is *yazata* "deserving of sacrifices" (only masculine). Several of their names are also found in Vedic religion, but functional similarities are limited, probably because of the long period of independent developments on either side since the two groups parted. Thus, neither pantheon can be considered more original than the other, and both contain archaisms and innovations. Some of the divine beings are explicitly identified with stars (e.g., Tishtriya, the Dog Star).

In the hymns (*yashts*) to these deities, sacrifices are promised to give them the strength to fulfill their cosmic functions and, in return, make them share their wealth with the Aryan (=Iranian) communities. Ahura Mazdā established precedents for Zarathustra and his successors in the world of the living by sacrificing to various deities, including such important ones as the Heavenly River to make Zarathustra support his *daēnā*, to Tishtriya and Mithra to invigorate them and make them benevolent toward men, and to Vāyu to gain the ability to overcome the Evil Spirit and his creations. Ahura Mazdā also sacrificed livestock to the Life-giving Poetic Thought (*manthra spenta*) and to Airyaman in order to allow these to heal him and the world sickened by the Evil Spirit (*Videvdad* 22).

The Heavenly River (*Yt.* 5) is referred to in the *Avesta* as Ardwī Sūrā Anāhitā, "the unattached lofty (water), full of life-giving strength."[6] She came down from the stars at Ahura Mazdā's request and is described as a richly dressed woman. She purifies the semen of males and the wombs of females for conception, and nubile young women pray to her for good husbands. Her sacrifice, from which persons with bodily defects are excluded, should be performed "from sun-rise till sunset," but the libations poured for her at night are rejected and go to the evil gods (*daēwa*s).

---

[6] Her name may refer to the fact that objects in the heavens do not need support to stay aloft. Other translations include "the moist, unblemished one."

Mithra (*Yt.* 10; Indic Mitra), established by Ahura Mazdā to be as worthy of worship as himself, is the personified contract and the guardian of agreements concluded in homes and families, tribes and countries. He is the friend of the truthful and the enemy of the untruthful who break the contract, even when concluded with someone possessed by the Lie (*Yt.* 10.2). He punishes infringements, and even the *daēwa*s and the Evil Spirit fear him. He precedes the sun at dawn, removing all obstacles from its path. When the sun rises, Mithra drives forth over Mount Harā, surveying the Aryan lands and the seven "continents" in a chariot drawn by four white horses and accompanied by other deities.

The god Vāyu (*Yt.* 15; = Indic), originally the wind that blows through the intermediate space between heaven and earth, is described as the space surrounding the spherical earth inside the spherical sky and has an upper, good side and a lower, bad side. The souls of the dead must pass through Vāyu on their way to Heaven or Hell, and he is therefore associated with inflexible destiny.

Communication between humans and gods was crucial for the success of the ritual, and a special deity provided a means of communication between them (*Y.* 28.5). This was Sraosha (*Y.* 56–57), whose name probably meant literally "readiness to listen," that is, the worshipper to the god and the god to the worshipper. As such, this deity was the first to sacrifice to Ahura Mazdā and the Life-giving Immortals by spreading the ritual grass (*barsman*) in correct fashion and causing the *Gāthā*s to be heard. Sleepless, he fights *daēwa*s and other evil beings, especially at night. Wrath, who, at sunset, smites Ahura Mazdā's creation with his "bloody club" and bathes it in blood, is himself struck down and bled at sunrise by Sraosha with his "fearless club." The rooster is his bird, who crows at dawn telling people to "get up, praise Order, and scorn the evil gods" (*V.* 18.16).

Haoma (Indic Soma) was the divine *haoma* plant, which was crushed and its juice made into a drink consumed in the *yasna* ritual (as was the *soma* in the Indic rituals). Haoma bestowed longevity, bodily strength, and victory, effects also produced by the *soma*. The hymn to Haoma (*Y.* 9–11) opens with a description of Zarathustra preparing a sacrifice, building a fire, and reciting the *Gāthā*s. Haoma approaches Zarathustra and exhorts him to press him, drink him, and praise him to make him (Haoma) stronger, so as to provide a precedent for future successful sacrificers (*saoshyant*s). Zarathustra asks him about past precedents and what they gained from the pressing, and Haoma names four, whose rewards were famous sons, the last of them Zarathustra's father. Haoma is also called a sacrificer, installed by Ahura Mazdā (*Yt.* 10.88–89) and so, as his son (*Y.* 11.4), is himself sacrificed to his father.

Airyaman (Indic Aryaman) is a healer and the protector of harmonious relationships, including marriage. He is invoked at the end of the *Gāthās* and the *Videvdad*, presumably as the healer of the ailing world and as the protector of the marriage of Heaven and Earth.

Other deities of note included in the *Young Avesta* are Ashi (*Yt.* 17), goddess of the rewards (?) and protector of marriage; Tishtriya (*Yt.* 8), the Dog Star, who periodically battles Apaosha, the demon of drought; the warrior-god Verthraghna, the "obstruction-smashing force"; Nairyasangha, the divine messenger; and Apām Napāt (= Indic), "Scion of the Waters," perhaps a manifestation of the heavenly fire born from the heavenly waters, who also fashioned and set men in their places (*Yt.* 19.52). These deities coexisted alongside the six "Life-giving Immortals." Headed by their father Ahura Mazdā, these became the Seven Life-giving Immortals (*Yt.* 13.83 = 19.16).

The Young Avestan Evil Beings

The agents of the dark existence are still the Evil Spirit, the Lie, Wrath, and the old, evil, gods (*daēwa*s). Among the *daēwa*s are Indara, Saurwa, and Nānghaithya, originally identical with Old Indic Indra, Sharva (Rudra), and the Nāsatyā twins. Nothing further is said about these three in the *Avesta*, but in the Pahlavi texts they are the opponents of Best Order, Well-deserved Command, and Life-giving Humility. The demon Nasu, "carrion," is the main cause of pollution, and countless other evil beings cause all kinds of illnesses and natural calamities. Numerous harmful beings (*khrafstra*s) belong to the evil existence, among them insects, snakes, and wolves.

The Young Avestan Notion of Man

The *Young Avesta* contains no explicit statement about the origin of mankind, but it is clear that the prototypes of living beings were Gaya Martān and the Cow (later Bull) "established alone" (*gau aēwō-dātā*). In the later tradition, when killed by the Evil Spirit, these two released their semen into the earth, from which men and animals were born. The exact meaning of Gaya Martān is not known, but *gaya* is "life" and *martān* apparently "that which contains something dead." Thus, Gaya Martān may originally be a concept based on the natural birth of the living child and the dead

Zoroastrianism

after-birth, and the two may have been thought of as a pair of twins (as these two are called, e.g., in Persian), perhaps the human counterpart to the Gathic twins.

Man is made up of the "(breath-)soul" (*urwan*), the "vision-soul" (*daēnā*), which sees and is seen in the beyond, the "pre-soul" (*frawashi*), bones (*ast*), which give the body solidity, and the life-breath (*ushtāna*), which gives it life. At death, man's consciousness (*baodah*) is wrenched from his bones by the "Bone-untier" (Astō-widātu), and the soul (*urwan*) leaves the body and wanders into the beyond. Here it is met by its *daēnā*, which guides it to the Ford of the Accountant and whose appearance matches the balance of the person's thoughts, words, and deeds. The soul of the sustainer of Order, whose balance is positive, passes the ford (bridge) and continues on to Ahura Mazdā's dwelling, his House of Songs (*garō.nmāna*), where it is treated as a welcome guest and dwells happily (*shyāta*). The soul of the one possessed by the Lie, whose balance is negative, falls into Hell.

The frawashis *in the Young Avesta*

All good things born have a *frawashi*, "pre(-existing)-soul," which was fashioned by Ahura Mazdā and used by him in their formation, but returns to him at death. The first was that of Ahura Mazdā, who therefore appears to have generated himself. The multitude of *frawashi*s preexistent in the world of thought assisted (*upastām bara-*) Ahura Mazdā when the world of the living was made by helping him "stretch and hold out" (*wi-dāraya-*) both the macrocosmic components of the creation – the sky, the Heavenly River, and the earth – and the microcosmic ones, the sons in the wombs, gathering their body parts in the "coverings" (*vyā*) (*Yt.* 13.2–11). The verb "I weave" (*ufya-*), applied exclusively to the *frawashi*s (*Y.* 17.18, *Yt.* 13.21), suggests their function was to help weave the cosmic "tissues,"[7] and the action expressed by *wi-dāraya-* may have been that of stretching out and attaching these tissues. They then conducted the heavenly (amniotic) waters through them for the rebirth of the ordered cosmos.

Together with Good Thought and the Fire, the *frawashi*s thwarted the schemes of the Evil Spirit (*Yt.* 13.2–13), allowing waters to flow, plants to grow, and winds to blow, sons to be born, and all things to move along their proper paths (*Yt.* 13.14–16). They were thus also closely connected with

---

[7] As the Rigvedic dawn and night weave the day and night skies (*RV.* 2.3.6), the basic concept is Indo-Iranian.

the rain and irrigation, channeling the water to their respective families (*Yt.* 13.68).

Mythical History and the Zarathustra Myth in the Young Avesta

Several of the hymns to individual gods (*yashts*) contain lists of heroes who sacrificed to obtain specific rewards, most of them granted. In the later tradition, these mytho-epic characters, whose stories are merely alluded to in the hymns, became dynasties of early rulers of Iran, who, still later, made it into Islamic and European world histories. There are three distinct groups: The first contains the narratives of Yima and the dragon-slayers; the second the story of the *kawi*s; and the third characters and events connected with Zarathustra. In the later Sasanian and Persian tradition, the three groups are identified with three historical periods, of which the third leads into the Achaemenids and provides the setting for "the historical Zarathustra."

Yima (Indic Yama) was the ruler of the golden age, when living beings were immortal. This resulted in overpopulation, and Yima three times expanded the earth to double its size. Ahura Mazdā then warned Yima that the earth would be decimated by floods caused by harsh winters and told him to build a bunker (*vara*) in which he should admit physically perfect specimen couples of all living beings (including fires) to perpetuate the race (*V.* 2). In the sequel to this story, alluded to in the *Old Avesta* (*Y.* 32.8), Yima was caused to roam the earth for having uttered a falsehood (probably out of hubris, *Yt.* 19.33–34).

There are two dragon-slayers in the *Young Avesta*. The older, Thraētaona, smote the Giant Dragon (Azhi Dahāka), fashioned forth inexpertly by the Evil Spirit to depopulate the earth, and released Yima's two sisters, whom the dragon had abducted (*Yt.* 5.30–34). The younger is the young and curly-haired Kersāspa, slayer of the three-headed dragon, who cooked his noon meal on its back, mistaking it for a hill (*Y.* 9.11). In the later tradition, Azhi Dahāka is not killed, but chained to a mountain, from which it escapes at the end of time and is killed by Kersāspa.

The second period is that of the *kawi*s, probably "poet-sacrificers" (Old Indic *kavi* "poet, seer"), and their war against Frangrasyan and the Turanians, archenemies of the Aryans. This war, in some respects, corresponds to the great war in the Indic *Mahābhārata*. At the end of the war, Haoma seizes Frangrasyan and leads him bound to Kawi Haosrawah, ruler of the Iranians, to be slain by him (*Yt.* 9.18). In the later tradition, the stories of the *kawi*s are quite elaborate, but the Avestan allusions are too brief to decide how much of the later epic material goes back to Avestan times.

The third period is that of a second war, fought over the *daēnā* by Kawi Wishtāspa and other Aryan heroes against Arjad-aspa and his Khiyonians. The narrative features Zarathustra, who asks the deities if he may persuade Kawi Wishtāspa to accompany and support his vision soul (*daēnā*). In the later tradition, this became a story of a historical battle over "religion," but its origin is no doubt the ritual chariot race, as also suggested by the hymn to the Heavenly River, in which the sacrificer asks the goddess that his horses may win the race like those of Kawi Wishtāspa (*Yt.* 5.132). Several of the names in this story are also found in the *Gāthās*, but without details. For instance, Wishtāspa and Frasha-ushtra are said to follow the straight paths of the gift along which the *daēnā* of the successful sacrificer proceeds (*Y.* 53.2).

The Zarathustra myth must be pieced together with the help of later texts. In the Pahlavi texts, Zarathustra's preexisting soul (*frawashi*) enters a *haoma* plant, which is gathered by Zarathustra's father, mixed with milk and drunk by him and his wife, after which she conceives and bears Zarathustra. The connection between Zarathustra, his *frawashi*, and the *haoma* is also found in the *Young Avesta*, which suggests that the later myth is related to that of the first *haoma* pressers. Ahura Mazdā's purpose for Zarathustra was "to help His vision soul (*daēnā*) along in thoughts, words, and actions" (*Yt.* 5.18). Zarathustra is said to have been the first to "think good thoughts," etc. (*Yt.* 13.88). He was also the prototype of three social classes: first sacrificer, first charioteer, and first husbandman (*Yt.* 13.88–89). In other texts and in Pahlavi, the artisans (*hu-uti* "weaver") are added. To what extent this division, which goes back to Indo-European times, corresponded to contemporary Iranian society is not known.

With the birth of Zarathustra, hope that evil will be overcome in the world of the living is rekindled (*Yt.* 13.93–94). He is the first in the Aryan Territory (*airyana vaējah*) to recite the *Ahuna Vairiya*, which made the evil gods (*daēwas*) hide in the ground; before this time, these evil gods went about in the shape of men, abducting women (*Y.* 9.14–15, *Yt.* 19.80–81). As the "first guide of the lands," Zarathustra then declared that sacrifices were not to be made to the *daēwas* (*Yt.* 13.90).

Zarathustra's encounters with the Evil Spirit are described in epic style. In the hymn to Ashi, Zarathustra wields the *Ahuna Vairiya* like an enormous stone with which to smash the Evil Spirit, and he uses the *Ashem Vohū* as a hot iron with which to burn him, finally forcing him to flee from the earth (*Yt.* 17.19–20). In *Videvdad* chapter 19, the Evil Spirit tries to tempt him with great fortunes if only he will "back-praise" the *daēnā* of those who sacrifice to Ahura Mazdā. Zarathustra refuses and performs a

118 *Prods Oktor Skjærvø*

purification ritual, by which the Evil Spirit and the *daēwas* are chased back to hell and darkness.

Eschatology in the Young Avesta

The return to the origins begins when Zarathustra chases the *daēwas* and the Evil Spirit from the world of the living. Later, three sons will be born from his seed, preserved in the Kansaoya Sea (*Yt.* 13.62), each of whom will bring the cycle of existences closer to the end. The last is the final *saoshyant*, Astwad-arta "he who shall make order have bones (permanently)" (*Yt.* 13.142, *Yt.* 19.92). When he comes with his companions, the dead will rise; he will see "with the eyes of the guiding thought (*khratu*)" and "with the eyes of the milk-libation (*īzhā*)"; and he will make the world of the living permanently full of the juices of life, bringing about *frashō-kerti*, the "Renovation." Good Thought will overcome Evil Thought, Wholeness and Undyingness will overcome Hunger and Thirst, and the Evil Spirit will flee, forever deprived of power (*Yt.* 19.11–12, 89–96, *V.* 19.5).

In the later eschatological myth, Zarathustra's son Isad-wāstar will call an assembly, in which the good will be separated from the bad; the Fire and Airyaman will melt the metal in the mountains into a river, through which all must pass to be cleansed of their sins; and, finally, Ahura Mazdā goes down into the world of the living and, together with Sraosha as his assistant, performs the very last sacrifice, by which evil will be banned from the creation forever.

The Rituals in the Young Avesta

The morning ritual, the *yasna*, originally began before sunrise to coincide with the recital of *Yasna* 62, the hymn to the Fire. Patterned on the myth of the primordial creation of the world, the *yasna* aims at placing Ahura Mazdā back in command (*Y.* 8.5–6). It begins by reordering all the elements in the worlds of thought and of living beings by announcing and consecrating their models (*ratu*). Omitting and angering one of them would spell failure, and the sacrificer repeatedly asks for forgiveness for this eventuality (*Y.* 1.21–22). The story of Zarathustra's birth from the *haoma* ritual follows, and the *yasna* ritual culminates in the preparation and offering of the *haoma* drink (*Y.* 27), at which point Zarathustra is presumably "reborn" in the persona of the sacrificer and proceeds to recite his *Gāthās* (*Y.* 28–53). The *Yasna* continues with the hymn to Sraosha, who battles and overcomes the powers of darkness (*Y.* 56–57), hymns to the Fire

Zoroastrianism 119

(*Y.* 62.1–10) and the heavenly waters (*Y.* 65), and praise of the creations, to produce the rebirth of the sun and the new day. The ritual was performed in the presence of a fire and an area covered with sacrificial grass or twigs (*barsman*, later *barsom*).

The *videvdad sade*, a purification ritual, begins at midnight. It is accompanied by a modified *Yasna*, in which the chapters of the *Videvdad* enfold the *Old Avesta*. According to the *Videvdad*, its purpose is to heal Ahura Mazdā and his creation from the 99,999 illnesses made by the Evil Spirit (*V.* 22.2).

Rituals to individual deities described in the *Avesta* include that to Mithra: Libations to him should be consumed after two days of washing the entire body and undergoing rigorous austerities including twenty whiplashes daily (*Yt.* 10.121–122). Some of these deities were the object of animal sacrifices, although these are mentioned only occasionally. Haoma complains about the sacrificers who do not give him his allotted portion of the victim, a cheek with the tongue and the left eye (*Y.* 11.4–6), and, according to the *yashts*, mythical sacrificers killed hundreds of stallions, thousands of bulls, and ten thousand sheep to strengthen the deities.

Numerous rituals had to do with human life, among them the coming-of-age ceremony, in which the fifteen-year-old for the first time tied on the girdle (*aiviyāŋhana*; *Yt.* 8.14), woven in a particularly complex manner, and donned a white shirt (*vastra*, "garment") made out of one large piece of woven fabric. Before this age, the person's good and bad deeds would accrue to the parent's "account," but from then on they are the young person's responsibility. The shirt symbolizes Good Thought and its weaving the "weaving" of the sunlit sky, which is the visible aspect of Good Thought. It covers the upper part of the body, which is governed by good impulses and is separated by the girdle from the lower part, which is governed by evil impulses. The girdle itself represents the Mazdayasnian *daēnā*.

Pollution and Purification in the Young Avesta

The *Videvdad* provides a glimpse into the concerns of the Young Avestan society, listing in detail things that are counter to Ahura Mazdā's creation, their degree of sinfulness, and how one can cleanse what is polluted and atone for crimes. The most serious contaminants were "dead matter" (*nasu*), dead bodies and what has been secreted from bodies and is no longer alive, including blood, hair, and nails, all of which need to be disposed of appropriately (*V.* 17). Exposure to blood from birth, spontaneous abortion, and menstruation through external contact or intercourse posed

a particular risk to male believers, and menstruating women were seques-
tered until the bleeding stopped, after which they had to undergo severe
cleansing rituals, washing with animal urine and water. Human urine
was not used, except that of men and women in "next-of-kin marriages"
(*xwaētuwadatha*). Accidental pollution in nature (contact with unnotice-
able feces from evil animals, etc.) constituted no crime, because, if it did,
it would have made the whole world "guilty" (*V.* 5.3–4).

Crimes included harm to living beings (especially dogs and the otter)
and activities considered to strengthen the powers of evil, among them
prostitution, which creates the risk of mixing the semen of the good and
the evil (*V.* 18.62), and abortion (*V.* 15.12–14). Among inexpiable crimes
were interring dead bodies, a crime against the Earth (*V.* 3.38–39), and
intercourse between men, which is counter to the nature and purpose of
Ahura Mazdā's creation and turns men into *daēwa*s (*V.* 8.26–32).

The most common penalty was whipping, but some crimes were atoned
for by killing harmful animals and/or giving firewood to the fire (*V.* 14.1–6,
for killing an otter). Both of these were supremely good actions, which
contributed to the defeat of the forces of evil and the final victory of the
forces of goodness.

ACHAEMENID RELIGION

The royal inscriptions, the Elamite tablets (reigns of Darius and Xerxes,
ca.522–465 BCE) recording goods expended for religious services, and the
theophoric proper names preserved in Babylonian, in the Aramaic letters
from Elephantine (mostly fifth century BCE), and in Greek documents show
that the main elements of Achaemenid religion were those of the *Avesta*.
The Achaemenid kings sacrificed (*yada-* = Avestan *yaza-*) to Ahuramazdā
(as he is now called), fought against the Lie (*drauga*, masculine) and its
machinations, and repudiated the evil gods (*daivas*) and decreed that they
not receive sacrifices. They followed the straight path, exercised impartial
justice, and believed the good would be "happy" (*shyāta*) in life and "one
with order" (*artā-van*) after death. The later kings, Artaxerxes II and his
son Artaxerxes III, also name Mithra and Anāhitā as their protectors.

The basic religious terminology is that of the *Avesta*: Ahuramazdā is
"the greatest of the gods" (cf. *Yt.* 17.16), although Old Persian has *baga*,
"god" (originally "the one who distributes things"), differing from Avestan
yazata. Ahuramazdā was the one who set in place (*dā-*) the earth and
heaven, who made "happiness" (*shyāti*) for men, made the king king, and

supported (*upastām bara-*) him in all his undertakings. The king, chosen by Ahuramazdā and his representative, maintained His order on earth, and those ruled by him must conform to the king's law (*dāta*).

Certain key terms were interpreted to reflect current realities: The *daivas* were the gods of the non-Iranians, the Elamites and the Babylonians; the Lie was the force that made men oppose the king and his law; and the old Old Avestan term *frasha*, which denoted the state of the reborn cosmos, was used by the Achaemenid kings of their building activities, implying that the building of palaces reflected the rebuilding of the cosmos. The royal gardens (Greek *paradeison*) represented paradise on earth.

The Elamite texts mention offerings made to Ahuramazdā, Ashi, Nairyasangha, Spentā Ārmaiti, the "preexisting souls" (*frawashis*) of the sustainers of Order, as well as to "all the gods." In addition, there is mention of a goddess "who grants rewards" (Mizhdushī); divinities of rivers, mountains, places, and cities; the Elamite deity named Humban; "the Great God"; the Babylonian weather god, Adad; and KI, the Earth. Numerous personal names in the Elamite and Aramaic texts from Persepolis and in the Aramaic letters contain names of Zoroastrian deities and other Zoroastrian terms; these include Baga-pāna, "whose protection is from the gods"; Baga-zushta, "favored by god/the gods"; Mithra-pāta, "protected by Mithra"; Mithra-dāta, "(child) given by Mithra"; Hauma-dāta, "(child) given by Hauma"; Spanta-dāta and Ārmati-dāta, "(child) given by Life-giving Ārmaiti"; Mazda-yazna, "who sacrifices to (Ahura) Mazdā"; and Mithra-yazna, "who sacrifices to Mithra."

The principal ritual was the (Elamite) *lan*, celebrated in honor of various deities, but, presumably, mainly Ahuramazdā, whose name is rarely mentioned, however. Other rituals were the *dauça*, "libation service" (Av. *zaothra*), or *dauçiya*, and *baga-dauçiya*, "libation ritual for the god(s)." The main priest was the (Elamite) *shaten*, while the others, the *magush*, were chiefly involved with the *lan* ritual. We also hear of the *yashtā* "sacrificer" (Av. *yashtā*), and the *ātru-wakhsha* (Av. *āter-wakhsh*), the priest in charge of the fire. Among offerings were grain (barley) for cakes (Av. *draonah*) and wine for libations.

The Achaemenid kings had themselves buried in rock-cut tombs at Naqsh-e Rostam, except for Cyrus the Great, who was buried in a stone monument at Pasargadae. Presumably, this represents a compromise with the practice of exposure: In the rock and stones the possibility of contaminating the earth is minimized. The kings also left reliefs in the rock and on buildings representing their roles as protectors against evil and as worshippers of Ahuramazdā. In reliefs accompanying their tombs at Naqsh-e Rostam, we see the king with the sacred bow in his hand approaching a fire altar, above which there hovers a winged disk representing the sun and the cosmic order, and a deity, who is most likely to be Ahuramazdā, the kings' protector. This is matched by Xerxes' statement that he "sacrificed to Ahuramazdā, according to Order, in the height." The New Year's ceremony is depicted along the great staircase at Persepolis, where representatives from all the provinces of the empire are shown bearing gifts to the king.

Archaeological remains provide some additional information about the rituals practiced by the Achaemenids. At Persepolis, for example, mortars and pestles were found that were used in the ritual for pounding the *haoma*, and, at Naqsh-e Rostam, two structures thought to be outdoor fire altars remain.

The Greek writers provide additional information. Herodotus (*Histories*, ca.425 BCE) mentions that sacrifices were made on high mountains to heaven, which they called Zeus (1.131), bodies of dead males were buried after being torn by dogs or birds of prey, and priests would kill animals, especially ants, snakes, and other flying or creeping things (1.140). Ctesias of Cnidus, a hostage and physician at the court of Artaxerxes II (404–359 BCE), in his *History of the Persians*, mentions the story of Queen Semiramis of Babylon and Bactria, which, from around 100 CE on, also involved Zarathustra as a Bactrian king. Xenophon (ca.430–354 BCE), who wrote about the upbringing of Cyrus, mentions animal sacrifices to Zeus, the sun god, and the Earth (8.3.24).

These three do not mention Zarathustra, but Xanthus of Lydia, who lived slightly before Herodotus, allegedly reported that the Persians claimed it was Zoroaster who had made the rule against burning dead bodies or otherwise defiling the fire, that the *magoi* cohabited with their close female relatives, that Zoroaster lived six thousand years before Xerxes' Greek expedition, and that "Zoroaster the Persian" ruled five thousand years before the capture of Troy. In the chronology of the Sasanian sources, Alexander arrived 258 years after Zarathustra's revelation.

Still missing in the archaeological and literary records, which focus on royalty and aristocracy, is information about popular religion. If the religion of Persia was that of the *Avesta*, it is likely that they observed the same kind of private rituals as modern Zoroastrians. Hopefully new excavations, especially in the workers' quarters around the major sites, may provide this information in the future.

THE STUDY OF ZARATHUSTRA AND ZOROASTRIANISM
IN THE WEST

By the first century BCE, Zoroaster was associated with the "Chaldean" astrologers, to which we may owe the deformation of his name (Greek *astēr*, "star"). On the basis of the Classical sources, throughout the Middle Ages, Zoroaster was viewed as the prince of the magi; and, by the seventeenth century, he was commonly presented as a philosopher and law-giver, as well as a religious reformer and the founder of the Persian religion. All the available information was incorporated by Thomas Hyde in his book (in Latin) on the religion of the Persians and Medes (Oxford, 1700), in which Hyde subscribed to the view that Zarathustra was a prophet, reformer, theologian, and philosopher.

In 1755–58, a young Orientalist, Abraham Hyacinthe Anquetil-Duperron, traveled to Surat, India, where he studied the religion and (imperfectly) the languages of the local Zoroastrians (Parsis). His translations, published in 1771, disappointed those who expected the sublime revelations of the great law-giver of the Orient, and they concluded that either the texts were not by Zarathustra or Zarathustra was not who he was thought to be. Anquetil's translations were inexact by modern standards, but the judgment of his contemporaries was based mainly on the litanies of the *Yasna* and repetitive purification rules of the *Videvdad*. In 1843 the Reverend John Wilson published a lengthy study of Zoroastrianism in which he demonstrated the inferiority of Zoroastrianism to Christianity.

In the nineteenth century, it was proved that Avestan was related to Old Indic and that the *Avesta* was a genuine text. The first complete editions of the *Avesta* and its Pahlavi translation and the first grammars appeared between 1852 (N. L. Westergaard, F. Spiegel) and 1867 (F. Justi, Spiegel). The German scholar Martin Haug was the first to suggest that only the *Gāthās* were by Zarathustra, which led him to distinguish between a monotheistic speculative philosophy of the prophet and a later dualist teaching reflected in other texts, which relieved the prophet of ritualistic narrow-mindedness (1862). Spiegel, however, doubted the historicity of Zarathustra, arguing that it was impossible to determine whether the *Gāthās* were by one or more authors and that the mythical Zarathustra figure in the *Gāthās* was the same as in the *Young Avesta*.[8]

---

[8] F. Spiegel, 1867, 340–1.

In the second half of the nineteenth century, scholars argued for the historicity of Zarathustra by what they perceived as the realistic Zarathustra image seen in the *Gāthās*, which, to them, proved he was a real person. The obviously mythical Zarathustra figure and polytheism in the *Young Avesta*, it was assumed, reflected *post*-Zarathustrian developments or a return to *pre*-Zarathustrian beliefs kept intact outside of the church of the prophet. This argument became standard in descriptions of Zoroastrianism throughout the twentieth century and was adduced by A. V. W. Jackson, who, in his *Zoroaster the Prophet of Ancient Iran* (1899), based his reconstruction of the life of Zarathustra and his interpretation of the *Gāthās* on the traditional sources.[9]

About the end of the nineteenth century, western scholars began using the term *gāthā* for each of the sections (*hāiti*s, altogether seventeen) into which the *Gāthās* are subdivided, a practice that provided the basis for attempts to arrange the "*Gāthās*" in chronological order and to correlate them with events in what was thought to be the prophet's real life, but was reconstructed from the later hagiography.

The focus at the end of the nineteenth century on Zarathustra's original teachings and the construction of an "orthodox" Zoroastrianism led to the labeling of elements that were not felt to be worthy of Zarathustra as "pagan" and "pre-Zoroastrian" or as "unorthodox" or "heretical." Among the most studied of such heresies is "Zurvanism," according to which Ahura Mazdā and the Evil Spirit were twin brothers engendered by Zurwān, (male) god of time. The labeling of this belief as part of a heretical movement is found in the Christian and Muslim writers on heresies, but scholars cannot verify whether this was an organized religion or not or if it existed as such before the end of the Achaemenids.

C. Bartholomae's Avestan dictionary (1904) and translation of the *Gāthās* (1905) became the basis for work on Zoroastrianism for most of the twentieth century. His ideas about Zarathustra, based on his "realistic image," cemented the image of the historical prophet Zarathustra and his "sermons," the *Gāthās*. Bartholomae's grammatical and lexical analysis, however, was still based on an imperfect understanding of the language and was subordinated to his views of Zarathustra and his teachings.

As similarities between the *Avesta* and the Old Indic texts were increasingly studied, it became clear that they shared many religious terms and

---

[9] He was criticized for not distinguishing clearly between what *can* be historical and what *must* be historical. It has been pointed out that his book appeared at the acme of the *Leben-Jesu-Forschung*, and his reconstruction was based on Jewish, Christian, and Islamic models (Stausberg, *Die Religion Zarathustras*, vol. 1, 47).

literary formulas. To reconcile this with the notion of Zarathustra, the reformer who rejected the pagan religion, it was suggested that he used ancient formulas, but imbued them with *higher, ethical,* meaning, a notion developed especially by H. Lommel. The apparent Christian-type ethics of the *Gāthās,* however, as well as their historical interpretation, resulted from the translations of key terms: *asha,* "righteousness"; *asha-wan,* "righteous"; *spenta,* "holy"; *spenta manyu,* "holy spirit"; *yazata,* "angel"; *amesha spenta,* "archangel"; *saoshyant,* "savior"; *frawashi,* "guardian spirit" or "guardian angel"; *manah,* "intent" (for "thought"); *sraosha,* "obedience"; the two *rānas,* "religious factions" (for "thighs, legs," part of the chariot race imagery); *ahu,* "lord"; *ratu,* "master"; etc. The translations of *kawi* as "prince, ruler" and *daēnā* as "religion" supported the interpretation of Kawi Wishtāspa as the enlightened ruler who fought for Zarathustra's new religion and the other *kawis* as kings of eastern Iran, for whom there is no other evidence, however. The common translation of the verb *yaza-* as "worship" made everything in the world the object of "worship" and exposed the Zoroastrians to the eighteenth- and nineteenth-century criticism of being the ultimate polytheists.

Beginning in the 1950s, the focus returned to the texts and their language. H. Humbach explored the ritual terminology of the *Gāthās* and the role of the guest-friendship and gift-exchange. He emphasized the need to take grammatical forms at face value and to adhere to the meanings won from philological analysis, rather than from the presumed contents. For instance, K. Hoffmann had shown that the verbal form "injunctive" expresses timelessness rather than future, which eliminated numerous apparent references to eschatology. To Humbach, the *Gāthās* were not sermons, but hymns in praise of God and his work, and their literary heritage was Indo-Iranian. At the same time, M. Molé maintained the *Gāthās* were ritual texts with a religious function that needed to be analyzed. He suggested that, already in the *Gāthās,* the historical Zarathustra had been transformed into a mythical-ritual prototype, whose sacrifice was aimed at the renovation of the cosmos and with whom every sacrificer identified himself. Molé emphasized the improbability of the traditional construct of Zarathustra philosopher and reformer preaching a largely mental worship in the first, let alone the second, millennium BCE. After his premature death, Molé's opinions were widely disregarded and refuted by reference to the traditional arguments and the common opinion.[10]

---

[10] E.g., Boyce, *Zoroastrianism,* 1:182 n. 4.

The first modern English translation of the *Gāthās* was that of Stanley Insler and therefore gained wide distribution. Insler, too, took for granted the existence of Zarathustra, author of the *Gāthās*, and his higher, ethical teachings, as well as the traditions about his princely patron Wishtāspa. Quite differently, Jean Kellens and Eric Pirart based their interpretation of the poems on the assumption that most of the text referred to the rituals.

Mary Boyce was the most prolific writer on Zoroastrianism from the 1970s to her death in 2006. She was the first in recent times to date Zarathustra to the second millennium BCE, and she was the only western Zoroastrian scholar to have studied Iranian Zoroastrians up close for any length of time. Her descriptions were flawed, however, by her failure to distinguish clearly between what she learned from modern Zoroastrians and her own ideas about ancient Zoroastrianism. Criticism has been leveled at her tendency to assign to Zarathustra and his religious reform elements from the later tradition, thereby creating the continuity and conservatism she claimed were the religion's characteristic features. She used existing translations of the *Gāthās* eclectically, favoring those of Bartholomae and Lommel, and basically accepted the traditional Zarathustra *vita*.

ZARATHUSTRA'S TEACHING AND REFORM

Twentieth-century scholars agreed that the *Gāthās* are extremely obscure, yet argued that they are didactic texts, whose message can be well understood. We know nothing about earlier Iranian religion, yet the *Gāthās* were assumed to express a religious reform, the nature of which was disputed. To Bartholomae it had been monotheism; to W. B. Henning (Boyce's teacher), dualism; to Humbach, Zarathustra's vision of the imminent beginning of the end of the world; to Boyce, reinterpreting beliefs at a nobler and subtler level and the system of the seven Life-giving Immortals as divine aspects of Ahura Mazdā, representing exalted ethical concepts; and to J. Kellens and E. Pirart, a modified ritual.

On the implicit assumption that the *Gāthās* contain all of Zarathustra's teaching, it was argued that the absence from the *Old Avesta* of Mithra and *haoma* and apparent disparaging references to the *haoma* and the bloody sacrifice expressed the prophet's disapproval. The condemnation of the *haoma* sacrifice was deduced from *Yasna* 32.14 and 48.10, which both contain serious grammatical and lexical problems, but clearly refer to the misuse of the *haoma*. The abolition of the bloody sacrifice was deduced from *Yasna* 29 (see above); from *Yasna* 32.14, which refers to the practices of evil people; and from *Yasna* 32.8, a passage featuring Yima that

Bartholomae, following the Pahlavi tradition, thought referred to Yima's sinful behavior in teaching people to eat meat, but this text is now considered incomprehensible. The demotion of the Indo-Iranian *daiwa*s, which is particularly hard to explain historically, was simply ascribed to Zarathustra's reform.[11]

Faced with such fundamental disagreements, historians of religions have tended to shy away from Zoroastrianism or simply refer to one or another existing description. What is needed at this juncture is the application to this religion of the same methodologies as are applied to other ancient religions. On the one hand, it needs to be studied as an archaic religion descended from Indo-Iranian and Indo-European traditions. On the other hand, it needs to be defined what the beliefs were at various times. For instance, the *Gāthā*s obviously did not "mean" the same in Achaemenid times as they did when they were composed.

BIBLIOGRAPHY

Boyce, M. *Zoroastrianism* I–II, in *Handbuch der Orientalistik*, I, viii: *Religion* 1, 2, 2A (Leiden, 1975–82).

Forrest, S. K. M. *Witches, Whores, and Sorcerers: The Concept of Evil in Early Iran* (Austin, 2011).

Humbach, H. *Die Gathas des Zarathustra*, 2 vols. (Heidelberg, 1959).

Insler, S. *The Gāthās of Zarathustra* (Tehran, 1975).

Kellens, J. *Essays on Zarathustra and Zoroastrianism*, trans. and ed. P. O. Skjærvø (Costa Mesa, Calif., 2000).

Kellens, J., and E. Pirart. *Les textes vieil-avestiques*, 3 vols. (Wiesbaden, 1988, 1990, 1991).

Lamberg-Karlovsky, C. C. "Archaeology and Language. The Case of the Bronze-Age Indo-Iranians." In *The Indo-Aryan Controversy. Evidence and Inference in Indian History*, ed. E. F. Bryant and L. L. Patton (London, 2005): 142–77.

Malandra, W. W. *An Introduction to Ancient Iranian Religion. Readings from the Avesta and the Achaemenid Inscriptions* (Minneapolis, 1983).

Molé, M. *Culte, mythe et cosmologie dans l'Iran ancien. Le problème zoroastrien et la tradition mazdéenne* (Paris, 1963; posthumously).

Rose, J. *Zoroastrianism: An Introduction* (London, 2011).

Skjærvø, P. O. "Smashing Urine: on Yasna 48.10." In *Zoroastrian Rituals in Context*, ed. M. Stausberg (Leiden, 2004): 253–81.

"The Achaemenids and the *Avesta*." In *Birth of the Persian Empire*, ed. V. S. Curtis and S. Stewart (London, 2005): 52–84.

"Poetic and Cosmic Weaving in Ancient Iran. Reflections on Avestan *vahma* and Yasna 34.2." In *Haptačahaptāitiš. Festschrift for Fridrik Thordarson*, ed. D. Haug and E. Welo (Oslo, 2005): 267–79.

---

[11] E.g., ibid., 1:251. Old Indic *deva* (related to Latin *deus*) is a term applied to several benevolent deities.

128   *Prods Oktor Skjærvø*

"Gifts and Counter-Gifts in the Ancient Zoroastrian Ritual." In *Classical Arabic Humanities in Their Own Terms: Festschrift for Wolfhart Heinrichs on His 65th Birthday from His Students and Colleagues*, ed. M. Cooperson and B. Gruendler (Leiden, 2007): 87–114.

"Zarathustra: A Revolutionary Monotheist?" In *Reconsidering the Concept of Revolutionary Monotheism*, ed. B. Pongratz-Leisten (Winona Lake, Ind., 2011): 325–58.

"Zoroastrian Dualism." In *Light against Darkness: Dualism in Ancient Mediterranean Religion and the Contemporary World*, ed. E. M. Meyers et al. (Göttingen, 2011): 55–91.

The Spirit of Zoroastrianism (New Haven, 2011).

Spiegel, F. *Grammatik der altbaktrischen Sprache, nebst einem Anhange über den Gâthâdialekt* (Leipzig, 1867).

Stausberg, M. *Faszination Zarathushtra. Zoroaster und die Europäische Religionsgeschichte der Frühen Neuzeit* (Berlin, 1998).

Die Religion Zarathustras. Geschichte – Gegenwart – Rituale, 3 vols. (Stuttgart, 2002–4).

Zarathustra and Zoroastrianism: A Short Introduction, trans. M. Preisler-Weller with a postscript by A. Hultgård (London, 2008).

5

SYRO-CANAANITE RELIGIONS

DAVID P. WRIGHT

Religion is a constructed reality.[1] As C. Geertz has observed, it is "a system of symbols which acts to establish powerful, pervasive, and long-lasting moods and motivations in men by formulating conceptions of a general order of existence and clothing these conceptions with such an aura of factuality that the moods and motivations seem uniquely realistic."[2] One of the ways that religion's symbolic system is constituted is through the operation of conceptual analogy or metaphor (for our purposes the terms are interchangeable).[3] This is where what is unknown, mysterious, hoped for, or threatening is described in terms of the known. The use of analogy for the production of knowledge is basic to human conceptualization generally and part of the language instinct. Even modern science employs analogy to explain new discoveries on the basis of the known. In religion, where conceptual creativity is presumably more prevalent, metaphorical conceptualization is fundamental. It not only concretizes elements of religious belief and practice, but also provides the psychological motivation, energy, and rationale for continued belief. Therefore religious beliefs and customs informed by analogy are not merely matters of tradition, but have a life and logic for their current practitioners. It is through the theoretical framework of the analogical construction of religious ideas that we will here explore the history of the religious traditions of ancient Syria and Canaan of approximately the first three millennia BCE. This will help in the observation of a creative continuity and development over time.

---

[1] For the sites relevant to Syro-Canaanite religions, see Map 2 in Chapter 3 and Map 3 in this chapter.
[2] Geertz, *Interpretation of Cultures,* 90 (his enumeration is omitted). For a critique of Geertz's dichotomy implied here, see Bell, *Ritual Theory,* 25–9.
[3] See Wright, "Analogy," and Brettler, "Metaphorical Mapping," for theoretical considerations.

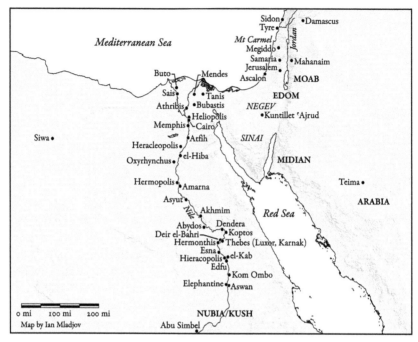

Map 3. Egypt and Canaan.

HISTORICAL OVERVIEW

Evidence does not allow the writing of a detailed and continuous history of the religions of ancient Syria and Canaan across the first three millennia BCE. The textual record, the best evidence for reconstructing the history of religion, is extremely meager and spotty. Relevant material finds, while evocative, are even less consistently evidenced and hard to interpret. The uneven historical record leads most scholars to base their studies and descriptions on the texts from Ugarit (see below), the most extensively attested corpus. The body of this chapter will follow this custom and will bring in textual and material perspectives from the other traditions when applicable. An outline of the documentary evidence here will provide a chronological backdrop for the discussion that follows.

The earliest relevant texts come from excavations conducted at Tell Mardikh, Syria (ancient Ebla), between the westernmost corner of the Euphrates and the Mediterranean. These include nearly two thousand rather complete tablets (plus many more fragments), dating to the twenty-fourth century BCE. The majority are administrative texts and do not record data pertaining to religion in a primary way. Lists of offerings, however, do provide some help in reconstructing the pantheon, which included primary Syro-Canaanite gods, including Hadda (=Baal), El, and Dagan. Some incantation texts have been found, but these are of Mesopotamian origin.

After the time of Ebla, from the end of the third millennium and the beginning of the second millennium, Amorite personal names hint at the basic inventory of Syro-Canaanite gods. The Amorite homeland was located on the eastern borders of the Syro-Canaanite world along the middle Euphrates and lower Khabur rivers and surrounding steppe areas. Amorite names include gods such as Hadda, Dagan, and El.

Principal textual data begin around 1500 BCE, including individual texts, such as the inscription of Idrimi of Alalakh (on the north bend of the Orontes River, from just after 1500), which contain incidental reference to religious customs. A more substantial body of texts comes from Emar, located at the large bend of the Euphrates in Syria. These date to the fourteenth and thirteenth centuries and include numerous important festival texts written in Akkadian but reflecting Syro-Canaanite customs to some extent.

Most important and substantial are the tablets discovered at and near Ras Shamra (ancient Ugarit) in Syria, just off the Mediterranean coast. These texts, dating to around 1275 BCE, include documents written in various international languages, such as Akkadian, Hurrian, and Hittite. The most significant for the reconstruction of Syrian-Canaanite religion are those written in Ugaritic, the regional dialect. These documents number more than thirteen hundred, and the longer texts pertain to religious issues. They include myths, legends, incantations, prayers, hymns, votive texts, god lists, festival catalogs, sacrificial lists, ritual prescriptions or descriptions, liturgies, and omen texts.

Several distinct branches of Syro-Canaanite religion are documented in the first millennium. One is the Israelite/Judean religious tradition as attested primarily in the Hebrew Bible. Because this is the focus of another chapter, it will be noted only incidentally and comparatively here. Two other branches are the Aramean and Phoenician traditions. The former, more amorphous and of broader geographical scope than the latter, is attested in various Aramaic texts. These are generally dedicatory and building inscriptions, although some amulet texts exist. They encode religious ideas in an incidental but sometimes notable manner. Some of the Aramaic texts important in the review below include the Zakir Inscription (*KAI* 202; ca.775 BCE), the Sefire Inscriptions (*KAI* 222–224; before 740), the Panammu I Inscription (*KAI* 214; mid-eighth century), and the

Akkadian-Aramaic bilingual inscription on a statue from Tell Fekherye (ninth century, on the upper west branch of the Khabur River). Phoenician texts from the area of what is now Lebanon, along with later Punic texts (i.e., texts in the Phoenician dialect of the western Mediterranean starting in the fifth century BCE), are rather plentiful but of limited use because of genre. Many of these are dedicatory or building inscriptions. Some Punic lists of offering materials (tariffs) exist, which cast light on the scope of sacrificial practice. Some of the Phoenician and Punic texts of importance in this chapter include the inscriptions of Yahimilk (*KAI* 4; middle of tenth century BCE), Azatiwada (*KAI* 26; ca.720), Yehawmilk (*KAI* 10; ca. fifth–fourth centuries), and the Marseilles and Carthage Tariffs (*KAI* 69 and 74; ca.200 BCE). Some late sources throw light on both Syrian and Phoenician religion but must be critically used. These include the *History of the Phoenicians* by Philo of Byblos (ca.100 CE; preserved mainly by Eusebius) and *The Syrian Goddess* purportedly by Lucian of Samosata (second century CE). The Hebrew Bible also contains information on Aramean and Phoenician religions.

Other texts attest first-millennium traditions in a limited way. The Mesha Inscription (ca.850 BCE) may be noted. This is the major source of information about the religion of the Moabites, one of the Canaanite ethnic subgroups and neighbor of ancient Israel. This includes information about the Moabite chief god Kemosh (attested much earlier as Kamish at Ebla). Another key text is the fragmentary inscription dealing with the prophet Balaam from Deir 'Allah (ca.700 BCE, on the east side of the middle course of the Jordan River), written in a unique Northwest Semitic dialect with similarities to Aramaic.

NATURAL PHENOMENA

Analogy is visible in the association of deities with natural phenomena. This involves the perception that just as notable effects in the observable world are produced by sentient agencies – primarily by humans (such as making tools, providing shelter, controlling fire, dominating animals) – so inexplicable events and phenomena of nature (such as the regular rising and setting of the sun, the cycle of the seasons, calamitous droughts or floods, death and birth) must be produced by sentient agencies that are not entirely different from humans, only more powerful. The analogical association of deities with natural phenomena in Syro-Canaanite religion lies in prehistory, inasmuch as such deities appear fully established already at Ebla (for example, Hadda, the storm-god; Suinu, the moon-god; ^{d}UTU, the sun-god; Kabkab, an astral deity) and are part of ancient Semitic religion more broadly.

The storm-god was primary in Syro-Canaanite religious tradition. His name is Hadda/Hadad, "The Thunderer," and is often called simply Baal, "Lord." His preeminence had to do in part with the dependence of Syria and Canaan on rain for fertility. The Baal Cycle from Ugarit tells of this god's rise to power over other gods. It includes an account of his death and consequent restoration as an effectual power. A sign of his revitalization is the appearance of rain and fecundity, such as described in the predictive dream that the high god El had of Baal's resuscitation. In this "the sky rained oil and the wadis flowed with honey" (*CAT* 1.6 iii 14–21). The Aqhat story tells about a famine caused after the murder of the boy Aqhat. His father, Daniel, exclaims:

May the clouds bring precipitation on the summer-fruit, let dew distill on the grapes! Baal could be missing for seven years, eight, the cloud-rider – without dew, without rain, without the surge of the deep waters, without the sweetness of Baal's voice! (*CAT* 1.19 i 40–46)

The sea and death were associated with supernatural powers. The Baal Cycle describes battles that Baal fought with each of these gods. El originally ordained the royal status of Yam ("Sea"). Baal protests this and eventually overcomes Yam to rule in his place (*CAT* 1.1–1.2). The battle with the sea is known in the Hebrew Bible in poetic passages and in some passages reapplied to the crossing of the Red Sea (Exod 15:8–10; Isa 27:1; Hab 3:8; Ps 74:12–17, 77:16–20, 114:2–6). The battle with Mot ("Death") in the Ugaritic Baal Cycle provides a structural parallel with the Yam battle (*CAT* 1.5–1.6). After a palace is built for Baal, Mot complains about not being invited to the dedication feast. For reasons not entirely clear, Baal submits to Mot's power and enters into Mot's gullet and the underworld. After being rescued by Anat, Baal's vicious ally, and by the sun-goddess Shapsh, Baal wins a battle with Mot by decision from Shapash. An echo of the battle with Mot is found in the Bible in the statement that Yahweh "victoriously swallows Death" (Isa 25:8) – an inversion of what Mot did to Baal. Some have argued that Baal's rise to power in the Baal Cycle is evidence of the late addition of the storm-god to the pantheon. This is unlikely given that the storm-god is evidenced a millennium earlier at Ebla. The Baal Cycle may seek to single Baal out for praise or celebrate the building and dedication of his temple. Phenomenologically it seeks to describe the empirical importance of fructifying rain over threatening phenomena.

Well-being was not exclusively Baal's province. The high god El provided blessing in general. In the Ugaritic texts El is called the "creator of creatures" (*bny bnwt*; cf. *CAT* 1.4 ii 11, iii 32). El's creative power, coupled with his interest in providing healing, is found in the Kirta story, where he creates the female healing being Shataqat to heal Kirta, who is deathly ill (*CAT* 1.16 v 24–vi 9). Shataqat's activity involves a small-scale battle with Mot, a structural echo of the Baal Cycle in which female deities help rescue an ailing male. El's role as lord of creation is found in his title **qny 'rṣ* "creator/possessor of the earth" (for example, *KAI* 26 A iii 18; cf. Gen 14:19). This title is found permutated to Elkurnisa in a myth about the god preserved among the Hittite texts (*COS* 1.55) and that is contemporary with the Ugaritic texts. In this text El seeks to punish Baal for consorting with his wife Ashertu (=Ugaritic Athirat and biblical Asherah). The goddess Anat-Astarte warns Baal, but he is injured and requires healing. The tension between El and Baal in this text is comparable to the tension between the gods found in the Ugaritic Baal Cycle, although in the latter the tension never develops into outright theomachy, and El eventually supports the advancement of Baal.

Although El, Baal, and other gods provide blessing (for example, Phoenician Eshmun in *KAI* 66), various other deities were connected with the suffering of evil. The god Resheph was a god of plague and illness. Anat, a west Semitic goddess known from at least the beginning of the second millennium through the first, was a goddess of violence. Some of the high gods could show a demonic side. Athirat, for example, makes Kirta ill, apparently for not bringing to her his promised vow offering (*CAT* 1.15 iii 25–30).

Astronomical phenomena, such as the sun, were associated with deities. In Ugaritic literature the sun-god (Shapsh) is female, although elsewhere it is generally male. At Ebla, the sun-god was prominent in having one of the gates of the city named after him (ᵈUTU). In the Ugaritic texts and especially the Baal Myths the sun-goddess was a benevolent figure. She also had some association with the underworld, through which she made her nightly journey. The moon (Yarih at Ugarit) and stars or visible planets (such as Kabkab at Ebla) were also considered deities. A Canaanite astral myth was taken up in Isaiah 14 to figuratively describe the rise and fall of the king of Babylon. He is compared to the "shining one, son of the dawn," who was brought down to the underworld after seeking supremacy over the "stars of El."

The association of deities with natural phenomena was not a simple personification of those phenomena. Although in some cases, the gods are

Syro-Canaanite Religions 135

described as if they were the phenomena, such as astronomical bodies, the gods more often stand behind the phenomena, such as storms, the sea, death, disease, and well-being. As we will see, when the gods are described bodily it is often in human form. This is explainable in terms of the analogical production of the conceptions: The natural phenomena are *effects* that the gods direct. A final consideration should be observed. Although the association of deities with natural phenomena is characteristic of the pantheon, other factors created the religious traditions whose complexity goes beyond being mere nature religions.

ANTHROPOMORPHISM

Syro-Canaanite gods were generally conceived of in the physical, emotional, and social image of human beings. This becomes significant in the larger context of analogical construction of the religious ideas and customs. Believing that natural phenomena result from the *willful* agency of unseen beings is one aspect of the anthropopathic imagining of deity.

The human form of the deities is found in both visual representations and textual descriptions. Perhaps the most famous representation is the stela from Ugarit, dating to around 1500 BCE, that portrays the storm-god Baal as a man who stands with a weapon in his raised right hand and a stylized shaft of lightning in his left.[4] He has long hair and beard, and wears a kilt, belt and dagger, and pointed or conical hat, with two horns protruding to mark his divinity. Numerous other representations from the second and first millennia portray deities with weapons or in a threatening pose.[5] Forms of female deities often emphasize sexual organs, perhaps to indicate their ability to provide for reproductive success and fertility.[6] A fourteenth-century ivory carving from Minet el-Beida near Ugarit shows a very attractively carved topless goddess, with necklace and flowing full skirt. She holds stalks of grain and is surrounded by two goats standing on their hind legs.[7] The goddess identified as Qadesh-Astarte-Anat is found in multiple representations from Egypt or in local art following Egyptian models and in human shape.[8]

The human form of the gods allowed humans to interact with them in artistic representations.[9] For example, the Phoenician king Yehawmilk

---

[4] *ANEP* 490; cf. 489. For representations of Baal, see Cornelius, *Iconography*.
[5] Cornelius, *Iconography* (cf. *ANEP* 468, 476, 481, 486, 491, 494, 496, 499, 500, 501, 827).
[6] Cornelius, *Many Faces* (cf. *ANEP* 465, 467, 469, 829).
[7] Ibid., no. 2.7 (*ANEP* 464).
[8] Cornelius, *Many Faces* (cf. *ANEP* 471, 472, 473, 474, 830).
[9] E.g., ibid., 5.14, 5.15 (*ANEP* 472, 485, 487).

stands before and makes an offering to the Lady of Byblos.[10] In an engraving from Ras Shamra from the thirteenth century a person stands before a figure, perhaps El, seated on a throne with footstool. He wears a conical crown with horns protruding from both sides. One hand is raised in what seems to be a welcoming salute while the other holds an object, perhaps a cup.[11] This motif may be coordinated with the description of blessing in the Kirta and Aqhat texts (*CAT* 1.15 ii 16–20; 1.17 i 34–43).

Human emotions and behaviors along with human form are attributed to the gods in the Ugaritic myths. Baal wields weapons in his hands as he angrily and forcefully battles Yam (*CAT* 1.2 iv). The goddess Anat shows rage when she threatens El in the Baal Cycle and in the Aqhat story (*CAT* 1.3 v 19–25; 1.18 i 6–14). In the former, when she makes a request of El that he create a palace for Baal, she preempts his refusal by saying: "[In the building of] your mansion, O El, … do not rejoice.… [I] will smite your head, I will make your white hair flow [with blood], your white beard with gore" (*CAT* 1.3 v 19–25). El himself acts as a human when he learns that Mot had vanquished Baal. He "descended from his throne, he sat on the footstool.… He sat on the ground. He poured straw of mourning on his head.… He covered himself with a waistcloth. He scraped his skin with a stone.… He cut his cheek and chin" (*CAT* 1.5 vi 12–19). El shows another side of his human disposition when he celebrates a feast and urges the other gods who were invited: "Eat, gods, and drink, drink wine to the full, new wine to inebriation!" El himself goes home drunk, at which point the text says that "he had fallen in his excrement and urine; El was like a dead person; El was like those that descend to the underworld" (*CAT* 1.114).

The human appetite for sex is also attributed to the gods. In one miscellaneous mythic text, El has sex with two goddesses: "The 'hand' of El became long like the sea, the 'hand' of El like the flood. He took the two hot ones (the goddesses).… He took (them) and put (them) in his house. El lowered his staff" (*CAT* 1.23: 34–37). In the Baal Cycle, El welcomes Athirat with food and an offer of sex: "Does the 'hand' of king El excite you? Does the love of the Bull (i.e., El) stimulate you?" (*CAT* 1.4 iv 38–39). When Baal is told to descend to the netherworld, "he makes love to a heifer in the steppe.… He lies with her seventy-seven times, mounts (her) eighty-eight

---

[10] *ANEP* 477 (for the accompanying text, see *KAI* 10).

[11] Caquot and Sznycer, *Ugaritic Religion*, plate 7 (*ANEP* 493); compare the figurine in a similar gesture in plates 8 (*ANEP* 826), 22, and 23.

times" (*CAT* 1.5 vi 18–22). A similar story appears to be told in a separate mythic text (*CAT* 1.10; here the cow is not to be identified as the goddess Anat). Although figurines of female deities with exaggerated sexual organs may indicate use as fertility symbols, the sexual activity of deities in narrative is not necessarily a sign that they are specifically fertility gods.

As in iconography, so in story the human form of the gods allows humans to interact with them. El can approach and bless Kirta and Daniel, as noted above. In the Aqhat story, the goddess Anat attends a feast celebrating Aqhat's maturity. She enters into dialogue with him and asks him to give her the bow and arrows that he had been given on the occasion. She offers him riches, which he refuses. He tells her to have Kothar-wa-Hasis, the craftsman-god, make a weapon for her. She then offers Aqhat eternal life, which he rejects because he realizes that death is inescapable. He then adds that, as a woman, she does not need a weapon (*CAT* 1.17 vi). Angered, Anat eventually kills Aqhat, although she transforms herself into a vulture to furtively carry out the act (*CAT* 1.18 iv).

Because humans were believed to be higher than the animals (cf. Ps 8:4–9), the gods were constructed primarily as humans. But aspects of the animal world could be brought in to aggrandize the description of a god's power or to populate the divine world, as seen in a few cases above. A notable case is the description of Yam as "Litan, the elusive serpent … the twisting serpent, the savage with seven heads" (*CAT* 1.5 i 1–3). The multi-headed sea monster Litan appears as Yahweh's enemy Leviathan in the Bible (Isa 27:1; Ps 74:14; Job 41:1). In these descriptions, Sea is not a normal sea creature, but has an exaggerated form. This accords with the embellishment of the gods in other respects. For example, Mot is gigantic; his opened mouth extends from the ground to the stars (*CAT* 1.5 ii 2–4). Divine animals also exist as subordinate beings in the divine world, to be used by the gods for work or transportation (or sex).[12] A few engravings or figurines portray deities riding animals (lions). The bulls or calves in the Hebrew Bible that are considered as idolatrous are probably to be connected associatively with Yahweh in a similar way (Exod 32; 1 Kings 12:25–33). Gods could also be stylized as natural phenomena, such as the sun-disk (with wings, hence partial animal form) that hovers over Yehawmilk even as he reverences the human form Lady of Byblos. Such stylizations are symbolic representations of the gods that could still be conceived of in human form.

---

[12] See Cornelius, *Many Faces*, 4.1–26 (*ANEP* 470–474, 479, 486; 500, 501, 835).

SOCIAL ORGANIZATION OF THE GODS

The human social categories applied to the divine world included familial relationships. The gods bore children. El was the father, of particular deities (*CAT* 1.14 ii 24–25) and a father in general (*CAT* 1.1 iii 24; 1.2 I 10). Athirat had children (*CAT* 1.6 i 40). Anat is described as the sister of Baal (*CAT* 1.6 ii 13). The genealogy of the gods was not fully or systematically worked out, at least according to what the texts choose to tell us, although the *History* of Philo of Byblos comes closest to providing a theogony. Family relations are seen in the theology of the Phoenician cities; each had at the head of the pantheon a male-female pair: at Byblos, Baal-Shamem (=earlier Baal/ Hadda) and Baalat (the "Lady" of Byblos, perhaps identifiable with Anat; *KAI* 4, 5, 6, 7, 10); at Sidon, Eshmun and Astarte (biblical Ashtoreth; *KAI* 13, 14); and at Tyre, Melqart (the Tyrian form of Baal) and Astarte.[13] Family conceptualization allowed power relationships between various cities and kingdoms to be articulated symbolically on the religious level. It also allowed for systematic correlations to be established among religious cults that mainly developed locally with their own particular characteristics.

The notion of the divine council, a basic theological motif within Syro-Canaanite religion, also grew out of an analogy from human social organization, particularly the dynamics of the royal court and to some extent the judicial court. This developed out of an urban context and imposed on a presumed pre-urban or non-urban religion primarily connected with natural phenomena. The operation of the divine council is found in the Kirta story. El assembles the gods to determine how to cure Kirta. He asks, seven times, "Who among the gods can cast out sickness, dispel disease?" No one responds, in contrast to the similar scenes of Yahweh's council in Isa 6:8–10 or 1 Kings 22:19–23. El himself, therefore, has to take on the requested task. Phoenician tradition also continued the notion of a divine council as "the assembly of the holy gods of Byblos" (*KAI* 4:1–4; cf. 26 A iii 19).

In addition to the specific notion of a divine council, the larger hierarchical and even bureaucratic relationship of the gods reflected human administrative institutions.[14] A concrete manifestation of this analogical construction is the description of various high-level gods as kings. The power of the analogical construction in religion is such that the analogical may be perceived as primary with the original phenomenon or description in the human world viewed as derivative from the divine model. Hence, royal power, for example, is seen as coming from the gods. The Lady of

---

[13] See Esarhaddon's treaty with Tyre, *ANET*, 533–4.
[14] Handy, *Host*.

Syro-Canaanite Religions 139

Byblos made Yehawmilk king (*KAI* 10:2), and Baal-Shamayn appointed Zakir of Hamath (*KAI* 202:3–4). The familial and royal models were combined in the view that the king was a *son* of the gods, as found of Kirta or biblical kings (*CAT* 1.16 i 20–23; 2 Sam 7:14).

THE CULT

The cult – the temple and ritual practices associated with it – was primarily fashioned after the protocol followed in engaging a king or other leaders in order to maintain their favor. This conceptualization is inextricably tied to the anthropomorphic conceptualization of the deity as discussed above. Sacrifice, the central activity of the cult, was conceived of as a meal given to the deity. In the Aqhat story, the pious patriarch Daniel provides several such meals for the gods. The text specifically says he *feeds* them and *gives them drink* (1.17 i 2–15; ii 26–42; v 3–33). The gods thus feasted include Baal, El, the Kotharat (birth-goddesses; cf. *CAT* 1.24), and Kothar-wa-Hasis. The narrative context allows these sacrifices to be described clearly as meals, similar to the hospitality meals of Genesis 18 or Judges 13, at which supernatural beings are hosted. The Baal Cycle, in which the characters are solely deities, features feasts that are similar in nature to the repasts that humans might offer to the gods. Baal holds an elaborate feast when his palace is completed. Numerous deities are present and enjoy slaughtered oxen and flock animals and an abundance of wine (*CAT* 1.4 vi 40–59; cf. 1.3 i 2–17). This is apparently what sacrifice looks like from the perspective of the gods in their temples.

The analogy involved in sacrifice is made clear in a text from the Hittites, neighbors and even overlords of Ugarit, who shared a similar view of sacrifice. Their "Instructions to Temple Officials" (*KUB* 13 i 21–26; cf. *ANET* 207b) asks, "Are the minds of man and the gods somehow different?" It answers "No! ... When a servant stands up before his master he is washed and wears clean (clothing). He gives him (the master) (something) to eat and to drink." Thus the master "is relieved in his mind." This same perspective is found in the book of Malachi (1:8): "When you offer a blind animal for sacrifice, is there nothing wrong? Present it to your governor – will he accept you or show you favor?" In both of these texts, making an offering to the gods is like presenting a feast to a human leader.

The Bible elsewhere reflects the notion that sacrifice is the deity's food, although it resists taking this idea literally (cf. Psalm 50).[15] It is likely that Israel's neighbors would have also seen sacrifice as figurative, despite the

---

[15] Wright, *Ritual*, 32–6.

polemic in the apocryphal Bel and the Dragon (Greek Daniel Chapter 14). Analogical conceptualization allows but does not require literal understanding of the metaphors employed. The analogical notion of sacrifice is attested more broadly in the Syro-Canaanite world. The Panammu I Inscription (*KAI* 214) expresses the hope: "May [the gho]st of Panammu [eat] with you (Hadad), and may the [gh]ost of Panammu dri[nk] with you." In the Ebla texts, animals as well as bread, beer, wine, and oil were offered to the gods. A menu of this sort continues into the first millennium. The Punic tariffs from Marseilles (*KAI* 69) and Carthage (*KAI* 74), reflecting traditions of the Phoenician homeland, list animals and other food items that are to be presented to the gods. The Syro-Canaanite menu may be augmented with incense, which gratifies the gods' sense of smell (*CAT* 1.19 iv 24–25).

Different modalities lie behind sacrifices. They may be brought in positive spirit to praise the gods, thank them, and seek future blessing. Daniel's sacrifices, mentioned above, have these goals. In other cases offerings may be brought to appease an offended deity. A ritual text from Ugarit (*CAT* 1.40) describes the offering of a ram and donkey (or bull?) in the case of sin. The animal is borne aloft to the gods by means of the sacrificial process. This achieves a purpose described by the noun *npy*, sometimes translated "atonement" or "well-being." In cases of sacrifice for positive and negative circumstances the same basic psychology applies: The stylized meals curry the favor of the gods. This effect assumes that the gods have emotions and rational powers similar to those possessed by humans.

Other gifts were given to the gods. The texts from Ebla list objects of precious materials given as offerings. Phoenician and Aramaic texts refer to statues of the giver (*KAI* 5, 6, 43; 201; Tell Fekherye Inscription), ornaments (*KAI* 25), weapons (*KAI* 38), altars (*KAI* 43), thrones (*KAI* 17), and various building structures (*KAI* 7; *KAI* 17). Stone anchors, perhaps votive offerings, were found at the Baal temple of Ugarit. The Kirta story tells of that patriarch's promise to give to Athirat gold and silver several times the weight of his bride-to-be (*CAT* 1.14 iv 34–43). Although all gifts to the gods operate in a similar symbolic fashion, food offerings stand apart as distinct by reason of the operative metaphor. Food is a daily requirement of humans; the other gifts are not. As such, the offering of food gifts developed a regularity and a context not associated with non-food gifts.

A unique gift to the deity was the sacrifice of a child, found in Phoenician religion, particularly in the Punic tradition at Carthage. Early documentation for the practice is found in two stelae from Malta from the sixth century (*KAI* 61 A, B). These were erected to Baal-Hammon, who was native to Phoenicia but who became the chief god at Carthage and the god associated there with child sacrifice. Child sacrifice, as a deviant or foreign practice, is also documented in the Hebrew Bible (cf. Lev 20:5; Isa 30:33; Jer 19:5). A chief example is the offering made by the Moabite king (2 Kings 3:26–27). Child sacrifice should be considered an intensified form of animal sacrifice and gift-giving to the gods rather than the original form of sacrifice, which was later replaced by animal sacrifice.

Sacrifices as food gifts to the deities were primarily offered at temple structures, considered the permanent or temporary dwelling places of the deities. Syrian-Canaanite temples generally consisted of a large hall with one or two ante-chambers. Ugarit had at least two main temples, perhaps for the veneration of Baal (the image of Baal holding the thunderbolt, described above, was found there) and Dagan, built on the acropolis of the city. These temples perhaps had a tower-like appearance, visible from a distance. The royal complex contained a palatial temple, and numerous minor shrines dotted the city. In the latter incense stands, vessels for libations, and small images were found.

The Baal Cycle shows a concern about providing the deities with temples. Although in these myths the gods could be described quite visually as taking up residence and feasting, in real life the gods were unseen. To complete the cultic analogy, the gods' presence was therefore made concrete in their images or cult symbols. These images or symbols were probably not conceived of as the gods themselves, but a representation of their being and power. The presence of the deity in the temple may seem to be contradicted by the description of the gods as being or living in the sky, on Mount Sapanu/Saphon (the Mount Olympus of the Syro-Canaanite world), or remote locales in the world. Such tension was tolerated, perhaps because of the discrete contexts and functions of the descriptions and the cogency of the individual analogical constructs.

Festivals were held in connection with temples and based on the lunar calendar, adjusted to fit the seasons of the year. The subdivisions of the approximately 28-day-long lunar month into halves and quarters is perhaps what led to the importance of the seven-day unit in ritual throughout the Syro-Canaanite and Semitic worlds and eventually the notion of the week. This division of the month is particularly visible in the Ugaritic texts that describe the course of festivals over various months (e.g., *CAT* 1.41/87; 1.106; 1.112; 1.119; 1.126).[16] Emar also had celebrations in certain

---

[16] Olmo-Lete, *Canaanite Religion*, 24–7.

months.[17] The seven-day *zukru* rite took place on the year's first new moon for Emar's chief deity Dagan, whose main center of worship was originally in the area of the middle Euphrates. Other festivals include a nine-day rite for the installation of a NIN.DINGIR, a priestess of the storm-god and an eight-day rite for the installation of the *maš 'artu* (another type of priestess) of Aštart of Battle. Ebla had special feasts for different gods distributed over the months of the year. In the Phoenician and Punic texts, new and full moons are important ritual occasions (cf. *KAI* 37; 43).

A ritual feast known as the *marzeah* is widely attested geographically and chronologically. It is known from the third to the first millennium and is apparently mentioned in Ebla tablets and clearly featured in Phoenician texts (*KAI* 6916, 60:1), an Elephantine ostracon, Nabatean inscriptions, Palmyrene inscriptions, as well as the Bible.[18] A month at Emar takes its name from the institution. An Akkadian economic text documenting the acquisition of a vineyard for a *marzeah* shows that wine was a key element in the group's activities (RS 18.01 = PRU 4, 230, pl. 77). The nature of these feasts is not well known. It is unclear if they are connected with veneration for the dead. The various *marzeah* "clubs" had buildings and/or rooms dedicated to them, and they were supported by the city and state officials. Thus gatherings may have been frequent, if not regular. A prescription to cure a hangover (*CAT* 1.114) shows that the deities were imagined to enjoy this very human social institution, even to inebriation.

Various functionaries performed the rites of the temples. Kings served as priests in various locales (*KAI* 13; 14). Their participation is particularly visible in the practical ritual texts from Ugarit, that is, texts that prescribe or describe actual ritual practice, as opposed to narratives where ritual is ideally depicted. Kings were also responsible for building or rebuilding temples (*KAI* 14). A professional class officiated under the direction of the kings in the day-to-day operation of the temples. Ugarit had a class of *khnm*, "priests," with a *rb khnm*, "chief priest," although this class of officiant does not appear in the prescriptive or descriptive ritual texts. Other personnel included, for example, *'rbm*, "those who enter (the temple)," and *tnnm*, "guards" (?) (*CAT* 1.23:7). Most of the Emar texts were found in a temple supervised by a diviner ($^{l\acute{u}}$*HAL*), who was apparently an overseer of cultic activities in the larger region. All of the temple functionaries operated on the analogy of servants attending to the needs of the king and his palace.

---

[17] Fleming, *Time*.
[18] Wright, *Ritual*, 62–5.

The notions of holiness and purity were companion concepts and operated primarily in connection with temple phenomenology. Holiness was the quality that prevailed by virtue of the presence of the deity in the temple. Purity was necessary to sustain holiness. Purity was mainly a matter of housekeeping and personal decorum in the divine master's court. This notion is manifested in the Hittite temple official instructions, noted above. In Ugaritic narrative, Kirta needs to purify in order to make an offering (*CAT* 1.14 iii 52–54). In practical ritual texts from Ugarit the king alternates between states of purity (ritual preparedness) and profaneness (off-duty, normal status). While pure he can makes sacrifices.[19] Ritual washing in and of itself entails analogy. It is based on washing from physical, mundane dirt. Stylized for ritual contexts, it becomes effective against unseen supernatural filth.

PRAYER, PROPHECY, AND DIVINATION

Various means of communication bridged the unseen and visible worlds. Humans spoke to the gods through prayer, and the gods communicated to humans by means of visions, dreams, prophecy, and omens. The liturgy for the month of *Iba'lt* at Ugarit in addition to offerings prescribes the following prayer: "O, Baal, drive away the strong one from our gates.... O Baal, we shall consecrate a bull (to you), we shall fulfill a vow.... We shall ascend to Baal's sanctuary, we shall walk the paths of Baal's temple" (*CAT* 1.119). Hymns of praise may also be recited. One from Ugarit extols Baal who "sits like a mountain foundation, Hadad ... like the flood. In the midst of his mount, Saphon, in the mount of conquest.... His head is awe-inspiring, dew drips down between his eyes" (*CAT* 1.101 rev. 1–6). The text may represent Anat as singing this song, to the accompaniment of a lyre. In another prayer, Baal with the title "Healer, Eternal King" is called upon for help (*CAT* 1.108). The prayer urges him to drink wine and speaks of his being honored with music. Music thus complements the larger cultic analogy of feasting by providing entertainment for the god. The prayer ends with the words: "Let your might, grace, power, guidance, and glory be in the midst of Ugarit, for days, months, and favorable years of El." Some hymn-related texts include the recitation of mythological episodes (*CAT* 1.23; 1.24). Apart from Ugarit, some Phoenician or Aramaic votive inscriptions embed requests for long life for their sponsors (*KAI* 26 iii 2–6; Tell Fekherye Inscription).

---

[19] *CAT* 1.42//1.87; 1.46:9–10; 1.105:10; 1.106:23–27, 32; 1.108:9–11, 15–17; 1.109:2; 1.119:1–8.

144   *David P. Wright*

The gods may answer prayer through prophets. The Zakir Inscription describes how the king received Baal-shamayn's help against attacking enemies:

I lifted my hands to Baal-sha[may]n; Baal-shamay[n] answered me; Baal-shamayn [spoke] to me by means of seers and prophets; Baal-shamayn [said to me]: "Don't fear, for I have made you [king, and I will stan]d with you, and I will deliver you." (*KAI* 202:11–14)

In the Egyptian Report of Wen-Amon, which tells of the author's journey to Phoenicia, we read about a youth who was seized with ecstasy and made a divine pronouncement (cf. COS 1.41, p. 90). The Deir 'Allah text tells of a vision of Balaam son of Beor, who was "seer of the gods" (cf. Numbers 22–24). The gods visit Balaam at night in council, whose chief is El. The gods tell Balaam, and he tells the people, that the gods will punish the land with darkness for the socially inverted behavior of people and animals. The ninth-century-BCE Amman Citadel Inscription announces its contents as the "[words of Mi]lcom," the chief Ammonite god, implying prophetic revelation (*COS* 2.24, p. 139). Similarly the Mesha Inscription has Kemosh speaking to the Moabite king Mesha (*KAI* 181:14).

In addition to prophecy, the supernatural world communicated to humans through omens, visible in animal entrails and behavior, birth abnormalities, and astrological phenomena. The Idrimi stela refers to omens by birds and entrails (*ANET* 557). The Ugaritic corpus contains a few short texts of dream omens (*CAT* 1.86), lunar omens (*CAT* 1.63), an astronomical report (*CAT* 1.78), omens of abnormal births of animals and humans (*CAT* 1.103; 1.140), and clay models of livers and lungs on which omens were written (*CAT* 1.127; 1.141–144, 1.155). These were influenced by the Mesopotamian tradition of divination, but have been taken over and integrated into the native religious practice. Divination was attractive because of its seeming empiricism supported by the assumption of supernatural control of natural phenomena.

HEALING AND CURSE

Various rituals sought to alleviate evils such as sickness, natural catastrophe, witchcraft, and sorcery. At Ebla numerous incantations sought to "bind" demonic evil and to oppose serpents and scorpions. A ritual from Ugarit provides a remedy for sorcery (*CAT* 1.169). This text uses explicit analogical formulation (lines 1–4): "You (the evil) shall depart at the voice of the *t'y*-priest, like smoke through a hatch-hole, like a snake from a wall, like mountain goats to the summit, like lions to the lair." The similes here may be viewed analytically as compressed analogy. In this case, the analogy operates on a case-specific level to characterize an otherwise indescribable desired result, which can consequently be manipulated conceptually. In the Aqhat text, Daniel recites prayers in which he embraces and kisses plants calling upon them to grow, to remedy the drought in his land (*CAT* 1.19 ii 21–25). The embrace gesture is analogical, transferring notions of human attachment to the plant. Two Ugaritic texts deal with healing from snakebite (*CAT* 1.100, 1.107). In the first, a dozen gods are called upon for a cure, with Horon finally being able to perform the task. This is similar to the scene in the Kirta text where El successively calls upon gods to heal the sick father.

Two amulets from Arslan Tash seek to avert evil. Their authenticity has been questioned, but there is reason to believe that they are legitimate. One has an illustration showing a demonic animal eating a child, representing the evil that is to be averted. The reverse of the amulet has a deity carrying an axe, apparently symbolizing power over the evil. A Ugaritic text for healing a child appears to require giving myrrh to Horon and Baal and perhaps also placing a figurine in a temple (*CAT* 1.124). Analogical play may exist here: Something evil (*mr,* "sickness, bitterness") is to be replaced by something positive (*mr,* "myrrh").

Curses, which seek to bring evil upon another, are found in treaty texts. The Sefire inscriptions (*KAI* 222–224), partly dependent upon Mesopotamian treaty forms, list hyperbolic descriptive curses to befall one who breaks the treaty stipulations. Part of the texts includes analogical curses, some of which were likely performed by the participants as illustrations. One clause says, "Just as this wax is burned with fire, so shall M[ati'el] be burned [with fi]re" (202 A:37–38). When Daniel buries his son, he curses vultures who might disturb the grave: "May Baal break the wings of the vultures, may Baal break their pinions, if they fly over my son's grave, and disturb him in his sleep" (*CAT* 1.19 iii 42–45). This is similar to curses against disturbing graves, found in Phoenician inscriptions (*KAI* 14; KAI 225), or altering the Tell Fekherye Inscription.

THE AFTERLIFE

Another factor in constructing a view of the supernatural world was the hope for some sort of continued existence beyond death. This led to the belief in the human ghost. For the common person, this afterlife apparently was of little consequence and substance. The Hebrew Bible, which reflects aspects of the larger Syro-Canaanite view of the afterlife, describes the world of the dead as dark and underground. Its inhabitants, called "the dead" and "the shades" (*rěpā'îm*; v. 11), do not praise deity, and deity pays no heed to them (Psalm 89). Thus when Aqhat exclaims to Anat that the fate of humans is not to live forever, he does not mean that human identity ceases altogether but only that one does not obtain a life like the gods'.

The ghosts of kings, however, were viewed differently. At Ugarit, they were thought to live on as the *rapa'ūma*, a term cognate with Hebrew *rěpā'îm*. The notion of royal divinity is found in the Kirta story when his family bewails his impending death: "Kirta is a son of El, the offspring of the Gracious One (epithet of El).... Do gods die?" (*CAT* 1.16 i 20–23). In some practical ritual texts, the dead kings were called upon together with the chief gods, and offerings were made to them to secure their blessing (cf. *CAT* 1.39; 1.48; 1.105; 1.106). An apparent funeral liturgy speaks of the descent of the recently deceased king Niqmaddu to the netherworld (*CAT* 1.161). The *rapa'ūma* are invoked, offerings are made, and well-being is proclaimed for the new king and the kingdom. Another ritual text (*CAT* 1.108) appears to celebrate the deification of the dead king. It begins "Lo! the *rap'u*, the eternal king, has been established," referring to the dead king.

The Panammu I text (*KAI* 214) says that a person who sacrifices at the statue of Hadad is to "remember the ghost of Panammu with (the storm-god) [Ha]dad" and that the ghost of Panammu is to share food with Hadad. The feasting of a dead individual and the enduring life of his soul in a monument is a theme of the recently discovered Kuttamuwa inscription from Zincirli.[20] Phoenician inscriptions set out curses against one who would disturb the sarcophagi of dead kings or alter their inscriptions (cf. *KAI* 1, 10, 13, 14, 30). This may imply their special status in the hereafter. Offerings may have been given to the dead at Emar, as indicated by some legal documents and a liturgy for the month of Abu, but these kings are not necessarily considered deified. Veneration of the dead has a long prehistory in Syro-Canaan, indicated by the plastered and decorated skulls found at Jericho from around 7000–5500 BCE.[21]

---

[20] Pardee, "Inscription," 51–71.
[21] See *ANEP* 801; Wright, *Ritual*, 147–53.

MYTH AND RITUAL

A continuing debate in the study of Syro-Canaanite religion is the connection of the Ugaritic myths and legends with ritual practice. Mythic episodes are clearly used in practical rituals, such as instructions for reciting a myth about the "Gracious Gods" (*CAT* 1.23), snakebite cures (1.100 and 1.107), the cure for a hangover with a *marzeah* feast myth (1.114), and perhaps a cure for a child (1.124). In these cases the mythic episodes appear to illustrate what is hoped for on the practical level. This raises the question whether the longer myths and legends, particularly the Baal Cycle and Kirta and Aqhat stories, have a ritual context. Some influential earlier scholarship argued that one or more of these texts were part of the annual liturgy because they appear to reflect the annual seasonal cycle. This, however, is doubtful, even for the Baal Cycle, which most overtly exhibits a concern with natural phenomena, because of ultimate imprecision in correlations. Other interpretations for the Baal Cycle, which may be situated in a ritual context, include seeing it as a cosmogonic myth (explaining fertility and the hierarchy of the gods), a myth that analogically defines a new political order in the human world (e.g., it was written in support of a new dynasty at Ugarit), or a myth that describes the limited exaltation of Baal precisely because this deity symbolizes and mediates the blessings of the natural order important to society.[22]

An interpretation of the Baal Cycle, Kirta, and Aqhat texts may consider their common themes, and not just the unique features of each. These common themes suggest that the stories were, as a group, of interest to the ruling class. The three stories center on an individual, god or human, who is a king, potentially a king, or at least king-like. This individual lacks something crucial to his kingship or line (a temple, a wife and children, a male heir). The chief god El is instrumental, in different ways, in rectifying this deficiency and moving the fate of the lead character along. The stories' plots for the most part devolve around challenges to royal or family succession, where rebellion or impiety leads to the death or sickness of the king/father or his heir, and where alternative successors are considered and rejected. El's plan or will is challenged by female deities (Anat or Athirat). At the same time, subordinate female characters (divine or human) help restore the balance of power. These stories also manifest a thick weave of ritual scenes and motifs, which are often used to help characterize the piety or impiety of particular characters.[23] The main characters in particular seek

---

[22] Smith, *Ugaritic Baal Cycle I*, 58–114.
[23] Wright, *Ritual*, esp. 223–9.

148   *David P. Wright*

to maintain proper ritual practice (despite some failures or interruptions), which is crucial to the maintenance of order among the gods or between the gods and humans. These commonalities provide hints that the stories may have been used in connection with the installation of a king or more generally in royal celebrations. It may be wondered if Baal's victory feast described in the Baal Cycle itself (*CAT* 1.3 i 2–27) points to the type of ritual setting where these stories were used, where meat and wine are enjoyed and Baal is celebrated in song.

CONCLUSION

The power of the Syro-Canaanite religious traditions lay in the interconnection of analogical constructs operative in different phenomenological facets, which fit together like puzzle pieces to form a larger coherent picture. The form and mind of the gods were suited to the method of their worship and how humans communicated with them. Upon death humans might even join the realm of gods in some degree or manner, and elite humans might even be worshipped as gods. The primary power in such a construct was its ability to make the gods real despite their invisibility and to enable them to provide benefit to humans. As Syro-Canaanite religious tradition developed further in the hands of Jewish and Christian tradents, with the dawn of Hellenistic rationalism to the Age of Enlightenment and beyond, the analogical content of the tradition was constrained. The original personality of the divine, when preserved, ended up in the truncated and philosophically purified figure of a prime mover or designing intelligence. Deity's body, including his politically incorrect gender, was shed and only a mind remained, a mind that remains nonetheless remarkably human.

BIBLIOGRAPHY

A. Primary Texts in Translation (Some with Commentary)

Attridge, H. W., and R. A. Oden. *The Syrian Goddess (De Dea Syria)* (Missoula, Mont., 1976).
Philo of Byblos: The Phoenician History (Washington, D.C., 1981).
Dearman, A., ed. *Studies in the Mesha Inscription and Moab* (Atlanta, 1989).
Donner, H., and W. Röllig. *Kanaänaische und aramäische Inschriften* (Wiesbaden, 1971–1976).
Greenfield, J. C., and A. Shaffer. "Notes on the Akkadian-Aramaic Bilingual Statue from Tell Fekherye." *Iraq* 45 (1983): 109–16.

Hallo, W. W., and K. L. Younger, eds. *The Context of Scripture* (Leiden, 2003).

Levine, B. "The Balaam Inscriptions from Deir 'Alla." *Numbers 21–36* (New York, 2000): 241–75.

Pardee, D. *Ritual and Cult at Ugarit* (Atlanta, 2002).

"A New Aramaic Inscription from Zincirli." *Bulletin of the American Schools of Oriental Research* 356 (2009): 51–71.

Parker, S. B., ed. *Ugaritic Narrative Poetry* (Atlanta, 1997).

Pritchard, J. B., ed. *Ancient Near Eastern Texts Relating to the Old Testament* (Princeton, 1969).

Smith, M. S. *The Ugaritic Baal Cycle*, vol. 1 (Leiden, 1994).

The Rituals and Myths of the Feast of the Goodly Gods of KTU/CAT 1.23 (Atlanta, 2006).

Wyatt, N. *Religious Texts from Ugarit* (Sheffield, U.K., 1998).

B. Material Finds

Caquot, A., and M. Sznycer. *Ugaritic Religion* (Leiden, 1980).

Cornelius, I. *The Iconography of the Canaanite Gods Reshef and Baal: The Late Bronze and Iron Age I Periods (c. 1500–1000 BC)* (Fribourg, 1994).

The Many Faces of the Goddess: The Iconography of the Syro-Palestinian Goddesses Anat, Astarte, Qedeshet, and Asherah c. 1500–1000 BCE (Fribourg, 2004).

Pritchard, J. B. *The Ancient Near East in Pictures* (Princeton, 1969).

Yon, M. *The City of Ugarit at Tell Ras Shamra* (Winona Lake, Ind., 2006).

C. Other Bibliography

Bell, Catherine. *Ritual Theory, Ritual Practice* (New York, 1992).

Brettler, M. Z. "The Metaphorical Mapping of God in the Hebrew Bible." In *Metaphor, Canon and Community*, ed. R. Bisschops and J. Francis (Bern, 1999): 219–32.

Chavalas, M. W., ed. *Emar: The History, Religion, and Culture of a Syrian Town in the Late Bronze Age* (Bethesda, Md., 1996).

Clifford, Richard. "Phoenician Religion." *BASOR* 279 (1990): 55–64.

Conklin, Blane W. "Arslan Tash I and Other Vestiges of a Particular Syrian Incantatory Thread." *Biblica* 84 (2003): 89–101.

Fleming, D. E. *Time at Emar: The Cultic Calendar and the Rituals from the Diviner's House* (Winona Lake, Ind., 2000).

Geertz, C. *The Interpretation of Cultures* (New York, 1973).

Greenfield, J. C. "Aspects of Aramean Religion." In *Ancient Israelite Religion*, ed. P. D. Miller (Philadelphia, 1987): 67–78.

Handy, L. K. *Among the Host of Heaven* (Winona Lake, Ind., 1994).

Mullen, T. *The Divine Council in Canaanite and Early Hebrew Literature* (Chico, Calif., 1980).

Olmo Lete, G. del. *Canaanite Religion According to the Liturgical Texts of Ugarit* (Bethesda, Md., 1999).

Stieglitz, R. R. "Ebla and the Gods of Canaan." In *Eblaitica: Essays on the Ebla Archives and the Eblaite Language*, vol. 2, ed. C. H. Gordon (Winona Lake, Ind., 1990): 79–89.

Walls, N. H. *The Goddess Anat in Ugaritic Myth* (Atlanta, 1992).

Watson, W. G. E., and N. Wyatt. *Handbook of Ugaritic Studies* (Leiden, 1999).

Wright, D. P. "Analogy in Biblical and Hittite Ritual." In *Internationales Symposion: Religionsgeschichtliche Beziehungen zwischen Kleinasien, Nord-syrien und dem Alten Testament im 2. und 1. vorchristlichen Jahrtausend*, ed. K. Koch, B. Janowski, and G. Wilhelm (Freiburg, 1993): 473–506.

Ritual in Narrative: The Dynamics of Feasting, Mourning, and Retaliation Rites in the Ugaritic Tale of 'Aqhat (Winona Lake, Ind., 2001).

6

ISRAELITE AND JUDEAN RELIGIONS

MARVIN A. SWEENEY

The religions of ancient Israel and Judah constitute the primary religious foundation for the development of the western monotheistic traditions, including Judaism, Christianity, and Islam. Ancient Israelite and Judean religions emerge in the land of Canaan during the late-second millennium BCE. They are known primarily through the writings of the Hebrew Bible, which form the Tanakh, the foundational sacred scriptures of Judaism, and the Old Testament, the first portion of the sacred scriptures of Christianity.[1] Archaeological remains and texts from ancient Israel and Judah and the surrounding cultures also supply considerable information.[2]

Israelite and Judean religious traditions focus on the worship of the deity, YHWH, and function especially as national or state religious traditions from the formation of the Israelite monarchy during the twelfth–tenth centuries BCE through the subsequent history of the separate kingdoms of Israel and Judah (see Map 4). Although Israel and Judah share the same basic religious tradition based in the worship of YHWH, each appears to have distinctive conceptualizations of YHWH and the means by which YHWH should be represented and worshiped. Unfortunately, literary evidence concerning religion in northern Israel is limited, because most of the Hebrew Bible was written and transmitted by Judean writers and reflects distinctive Judean viewpoints. But the destruction of the northern kingdom of Israel by the Assyrian Empire in 722/1 BCE, the destruction of the southern kingdom of Judah by the

---

[1] For a critical edition of the Hebrew text of the Bible, see Elliger and Rudolph, eds., *Biblia Hebraica Stuttgartensia*. For standard English translations and study notes, see Berlin and Brettler, *The Jewish Study Bible*, and Meeks et al., *The HarperCollins Study Bible*. For a critical, historical introduction to the Hebrew Bible, see Collins, *An Introduction to the Hebrew Bible*.

[2] For archaeological surveys of the land of Israel during the Bronze, Iron, and Persian periods, see Mazar, *Archaeology of the Land of the Bible*; Stern, *Archaeology* II.

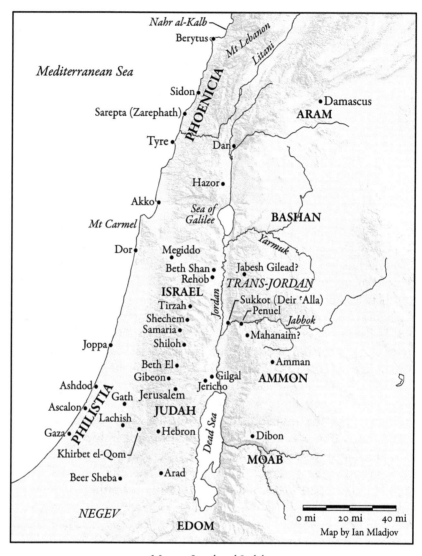

Map 4. Israel and Judah.

Babylonian Empire in 587/6 BCE, and the reconstitution of Judah as a Persian province in the late-sixth through the late-fourth centuries BCE prompted the development of Judaism as a monotheistic religion practiced by Jews in the land of Israel itself and throughout the Persian and Greco-Roman world.

Israelite and Judean Religions   153

THE ORIGINS OF YHWH: CREATOR AND GUARANTOR
OF FERTILITY AND ORDER

YHWH is the ineffable name of the deity worshiped in ancient Israel and Judah. The correct pronunciation of the divine name is uncertain since the holy character of the name proscribed its pronunciation in liturgical and common practice. The only exception to this proscription was the annual observance of Yom Kippur, "the Day of Atonement," when the high priest would enter the Holy of Holies of the Jerusalem Temple to invoke YHWH's name as part of the annual liturgy to atone for the sins of the nation. The modern scholarly reconstruction, Y-hw-h (spelled with a and e), is based on Greek transcriptions by early Church Fathers: Ιαουε[3] and Ιαβε or Ιαβαι.[4] To avoid pronunciation of the holy name, Jewish tradition calls for the use of terms such as *'ădōnāy*, "my Lord," *haššēm*, "the Name," in Hebrew, or *šĕmā'*, "the Name," in Aramaic, as substitutes. The widely known term Jehovah is not the divine name. It is based on a combination of the four Hebrew consonants for the divine name combined with the vowel pointing for the term *'ădōnāy*, "my Lord." Abbreviated forms of the divine name appear as *Yhw*, "Yahu," in northern Israel and southern Judah, *Yw*, "Yau," in texts associated with northern Israel, and *Yh*, "Yah," in texts associated with southern Judah. Abbreviated forms of the divine name frequently appear as an element of theophoric Hebrew personal names, for example, *ḥḥizqîyāhû*, *ḥḥizqîyâ*, and *yĕḥḥizqîyāhû*, all forms of the name Hezekiah, which mean "YHWH has strengthened" in the first two examples or "may YHWH strengthen" in the third.

The name YHWH appears to be based on a finite third masculine singular Hebrew verbal form with a preformative *yôd* followed by the verb root *hwy/hwh*, "to be." The stem of the verb is uncertain; it could be the basic *Qal* form, which would mean "he is," or the causative *Hiphil* form, which would mean, "he causes to be/brings into being." This interpretation is based in part on the interpretation of the divine name in Exod 3:14, *'ehyeh 'ăšer 'ehyeh*, "I am who/what I am," when YHWH answers Moses' question concerning the divine name in the burning bush episode. Because this expression is an interpretation of the name rather than a scientific etymological analysis, many scholars look to Arabic roots to explain the meaning of the name, which first appears in regions associated with ancient Edom and Midian to the south of the land of Israel. The Arabic

---

[3] Clement of Alexandria, *Stromata* 5.6.34.5.
[4] Epiphanius of Salamis, *Adv. haer.* 1.3.40.5; Theodoret of Cyrus, *Quaest. In Ex. XV*; *Haer. Fab.* 5.3.

verb root *hwy* can mean "to desire, be passionate," "to fall," or "to blow." The last two meanings have been especially attractive because they suggest YHWH's character as a nature deity of the desert, that is, "he causes (rain) to fall" or "he causes (wind) to blow." Nevertheless, the original etymology of the name remains uncertain.

Although YHWH is best known as the deity of ancient Israel and Judah, YHWH's origins lie in the regions of ancient Edom and Midian to the south and the east of the land of Israel. The earliest attestation of the name appears as the toponym "Yahu in the land of the Shosu-bedouins" in Egyptian texts from the reigns of Pharaohs Amenophis III (early-fourteenth century BCE) and Ramesses II (thirteenth century BCE). The earliest known occurrence of the divine name YHWH in a West-Semitic text appears in the ninth-century-BCE Moabite Stone, a stela written by King Mesha of Moab to celebrate his victory over Israel in the Trans-Jordan.[5] The association of YHWH with these regions accords well with biblical narratives that point to YHWH's association with Israel in the Exodus from Egypt and the wilderness traditions of the Pentateuch (see esp. Exodus, Numbers, and Deuteronomy) in which Israel journeys through the wilderness along the southern borders of Canaan and enters the land of Israel from across the Jordan River to the east. It also accords well with the identification of YHWH with the Kenites, that is, the descendants of Cain who are associated with the early worship of YHWH (see Genesis 4, esp. v. 26), most notably Jethro the Kenite priest of Midian and father-in-law of Moses (Exodus 3, 18 and Judg 1:16)[6] and the Rechabites, a Kenite Bedouin group known for its devotion to YHWH (2 Kings 9–10 and Jeremiah 35). The YHWistic prophet Elijah is likewise associated with the Trans-Jordan and the wilderness (1 Kings 17 and 19), and his successor Elisha prompts the revolt of Jehu against the northern Israelite Omride dynasty with the support of the Rechabite Jehonadab (2 Kings 9–10).

Various hymnic texts from the Bible associate YHWH with Edom and the Trans-Jordan, viz., "YHWH came from Sinai and shone upon them from Seir; He appeared from Mount Paran and approached from Ribbeboth-kodesh" (Deut 33:2); "O YHWH, when you came forth from Seir" (Judg 5:4); "God comes from Teman and the Holy One from Mount Paran" (Hab 3:3); and "I have seen the tents of Cushan under guilt; the curtains of the land of Midian tremble" (Hab 3:7). Although YHWH's association with the sun is evident in each of these texts (see also Psalms

---

[5] For discussion of the Mesha inscription, see Dearman, ed., *Studies in the Mesha Inscription*.
[6] N.b., Jethro is also known as Hobab in Num 10:29 and Judg 4:11 or Reuel in Exod 2:18.

68 and 104), lightning flashes and rain also symbolize YHWH's ability to sustain and protect Israel in the Song of Moses (Deuteronomy 33), the Song of Deborah (Judges 5), and the Psalm of Habakkuk (Habakkuk 3). Israel's ability to enter the land of Canaan from across the Jordan River likewise points to associations with the Trans-Jordan and to YHWH's control of nature, insofar as the Jordan River parts to allow Israel's crossing (Joshua 5). The parting of the Jordan is correlated with the parting of the Red Sea at the Exodus from Egypt in Exodus 14–15 to bracket the wilderness traditions of the Pentateuch. Jacob's relationship with his brother Esau, the eponymous ancestor of Edom, likewise points to YHWH's origins in Edom and Midian (see Genesis 25–35). Such traditions correlate with extra-biblical textual evidence, such as the fourteenth-century-BCE Amarna letters, written by the rulers of various Canaanite city-states to their Egyptian overlords, which report that semi-nomadic tribal groups, labeled in Akkadian as *habiru*, "barbarians," were moving into the land of Canaan and acting in concert with the city of Shechem, and thereby presented a threat to other cities such as Megiddo and Jerusalem.[7]

YHWH may originate in Edom and Midian as a Kenite or Bedouin nature deity, but YHWH's role as deity of Israel and Judah indicates a movement from the wilderness regions of the Trans-Jordan and southern Negev into the land of Canaan itself as Israel emerges in the land from the twelfth century BCE on. The traditions of Israel's origins relate how Jacob, the eponymous ancestor of Israel, is able to supplant Esau as the heir of Isaac by convincing Esau to give up his right as the first-born (Gen 25:27–34) and by convincing Isaac to grant him the blessing of the father in place of Esau (Genesis 27). Although Jacob is presented as the grandson of Abraham, he is especially associated with northern Israelite and Trans-Jordanian locations, such as Beth El, Shechem, Mahanaim, and Penuel, whereas Abraham is especially associated with southern Judean sites, such as Hebron and Jerusalem. Biblical tradition points to YHWH's role in the north as well as in the south and to YHWH's supplanting or absorbing the Canaanite and Aramean deities, such as the Canaanite creator deity, El, the Canaanite fertility deity, Baal, or the Aramean storm deity, Hadad.[8] Genesis 14 states that Abram venerated El Elyon (God Most High) at Salem or Jerusalem, and Exodus states that YHWH was previously known to Abraham, Isaac, and Jacob as El Shaddai. Both names are renditions of the Canaanite divine name El. The Elijah and Elisha traditions

---

[7] For an English translation of the Amarna letters, see Pritchard, *Ancient Near Eastern Texts*, 483–90.
[8] For the contention that El is the original God of Israel, see Smith, *The Origins*, esp. 135–48.

156   *Marvin A. Sweeney*

point to the overthrow of the northern Israelite Omride dynasty, which was allied with the Phoenicians and thereby associated with the fertility deity Baal. Elijah's own association with nature, his feeding of the widow and her son in the Phoenician city of Zarephath, and his contest with the prophets of Baal and Asherah to see which deity would bring rain to the land, all point to an effort to demonstrate that YHWH and not Baal (or El) is the true creator and fertility deity (1 Kings 17–18). Likewise, Elisha's role in instigating the revolt of Jehu against the house of Omri ensures the installation of an Israelite dynasty aligned with YHWH over against Baal (2 Kings 9–10).

YHWH's role as creator and fertility deity is expressed throughout the Hebrew Bible. Gen 1:1–2:3, a later text written by the Jerusalem priesthood, relates YHWH's creation of the world in seven days, beginning with the creation of light on the first and culminating with the Sabbath day of rest in all creation on the seventh as the fundamental account of the ordering of the world. Deuteronomy relates YHWH's power to bring rain and fertility as well as YHWH's ability to protect the people from foreign enemies as a fundamental incentive to ensure observance of the civil and religious instruction in YHWH's will that forms the basis for the relationship between YHWH and Israel (see esp. Deuteronomy 28–30; cf. Leviticus 26). YHWH's role as creator is evident in the prophets as well, who frequently point to chaos in the natural world to symbolize YHWH's dissatisfaction with the people's actions (e.g., Isaiah 24, Hosea 4, or Haggai) or to stability and fertility in the world to symbolize YHWH's satisfaction or promises of restoration (e.g., Isaiah 11, Ezekiel 47–48, or Amos 9). Much like the Mesopotamian and Canaanite traditions, which posit that Marduk or Baal create order in the world by defeating chaos deities, Psalms 74 and Job 38 portray YHWH's taming of various chaos monsters to ensure the stability and moral order of creation. YHWH's role as creator also appears in the wisdom tradition, which maintains that YHWH created the world with wisdom and that human beings must observe and study that world in order to understand how to live in it (Proverbs 8 and 30).

YHWH AS DEITY AND PROTECTOR OF THE ISRAELITE
AND JUDEAN MONARCHIES

YHWH's role as creator and guarantor of fertility and order in the natural world coincides with YHWH's role as deity and protector of the Israelite and Judean monarchies. Although biblical narrative emphasizes the unity of the twelve tribes of Israel as descendants of the patriarchs Abraham,

Isaac, and Jacob, separate kingdoms of Israel in the north and Judah in the south existed for most of Israel's history in the land. Both the Israelite and Judean monarchies play important roles in defining the understanding of YHWH expressed in the Bible. Northern Israel was the larger and more powerful kingdom, but its early destruction by the Assyrian Empire in 722/1 BCE left Judah as the surviving monarchy until its own destruction by the Babylonians in 587/6 BCE. Judah's survival into the sixth century and beyond ensured that the Bible would reflect a predominantly Judean viewpoint.

Despite the Bible's projection of a united twelve tribes of Israel, the key ancestral figures are closely associated with either southern Judah or northern Israel. Abraham is especially associated with Judean areas, particularly Hebron, the original capital of Judah during King David's early reign. Jacob and Joseph are especially associated with northern Israel. Jacob is renamed Israel in Genesis 32 and 35 and founds the northern Israelite sanctuary at Beth El in Genesis 28. Joseph is the son of Jacob and the father of Manasseh and Ephraim, the two key tribes that later form the core of the northern kingdom of Israel. Moses is especially associated with northern Israelite tradition, particularly because his son Gershom founds a line of priests at the northern Israelite sanctuary at Dan (Judg 18:30, but note that the Hebrew text is altered by the addition of a superscript letter *nun* to the name Moshe [Moses] to describe him as the son of Menasheh [Manasseh] rather than as the son of Moses). Joshua is especially associated with Gilgal and Shechem, key sites in the northern kingdom of Israel (Joshua 4–5 and 24). Although the book of Judges presents Israel as a unity of twelve tribes throughout the pre-monarchic period, it is noteworthy that with the exception of the first judge (n.b., the Hebrew term *šōpēṭ*, "judge," also means "ruler" in biblical Hebrew), Othniel of Judah, all of the judges are localized rulers of various tribal groups in northern Israel. Indeed, the Judges narrative relates the efforts of the tribe Ephraim to impose its rule over the other northern tribes during the pre-monarchic period. Several temples are identified in biblical narrative prior to the monarchic period. In addition to the temples at Beth El and Dan, which later became the temples of the northern kingdom of Israel, Judges 21 and 1 Samuel 1–4 identify the Temple at Shiloh as the central Israelite sanctuary where the Ark of the Covenant was kept prior to its capture by the Philistines. Temple sites are found at Gilgal, Arad, Beer Sheba, and elsewhere.[9]

---

[9] For discussion of the archaeological sites, see the respective entries in Stern, *New Encyclopedia*.

Saul of the small tribe of Benjamin is presented as the first king of a unified Israel in 1 Samuel. Nevertheless, his kingdom appears to be a weak federation of the northern tribes of Israel and the southern tribe of Judah that was held together by a common interest in resisting the Philistines, who were based along the Mediterranean coast and attempted to extend their rule over the Israelite and Judean hill country. Following Saul's defeat and death in battle against the Philistines in 1 Samuel 31, 2 Samuel relates how Saul's protégé and rival, David of the tribe of Judah, was able to unite Judah and Israel, defeat the Philistines, and extend his rule over other neighboring nations, such as Edom, Moab, Ammon, and Aram. The Davidic dynasty would rule for some four hundred years, first over a united kingdom of Israel and Judah and later over Judah alone, from circa 1000 BCE until 587/6 BCE. As founders of the Davidic dynasty, David and his son Solomon play key roles in establishing the foundations of ancient Judean religion.

David's choice of the city of Jerusalem, a Jebusite or Canaanite city located along the borders of Judah and Israel in the tribal territory of Benjamin, was an important factor in uniting his kingdom and establishing its religious institutions. Because Jerusalem was Jebusite and seized without bloodshed by David's own mercenaries, neither Judah nor Israel could claim the city as its own, which helped to alleviate tensions between the two major components of David's kingdom. Because kings in the ancient world ruled on behalf of their respective patron deities, Jerusalem had to become the religious capital of Israel as well as its political capital. 2 Samuel 6 therefore relates how David brought the Ark of the Covenant, a wooden chest overlaid with gold that symbolized YHWH's presence among the people from the Mosaic period, into Jerusalem where it would be housed in a tent shrine until a permanent temple could be constructed. 2 Samuel 7 then relates YHWH's covenant with David in which YHWH promises that David's sons will rule over Israel "forever," although individual monarchs may suffer punishment when they do wrong. King David thereby establishes the cultic center for the veneration of YHWH as the national deity of Israel/Judah, and YHWH in turn guarantees the rule of the house of David and the security of the city of Jerusalem and the nation Israel/Judah. Such a relationship is typical of the monarchies of the ancient Near East.

THE JERUSALEM TEMPLE

The Jerusalem Temple, built by King Solomon, is the central religious institution of ancient Israel/Judah (1 Kings 5–8; 2 Chronicles 2–7). The

Israelite and Judean Religions 159

Temple is located at the threshing floor of Araunah (2 Samuel 24), a small hill located at the highest point on the northern edge of ancient Jerusalem. Such a location enables the Temple to overlook the city and thereby highlights YHWH's role as sovereign national deity, and it facilitates the processing of grain brought to the Temple as offerings since high locations are ideal for catching the wind that separates grain from chaff during the threshing process. Although the narratives reflect the embellishment of later writers who would have idealized the portrayal of the Temple and its dedication, the basic structure and features of the Temple reflect the structure and imagery of temples in the ancient Syro-Palestinian world.[10] Solomon's Temple, built with the assistance of Hiram (Ahiram), King of Tyre, is a typical three-room temple structure that reflects the patterns of Syro-Palestinian royal palaces. Such a correlation between temples and royal palaces in the ancient world emphasizes the role of deities as national gods, viz., since the monarch rules on behalf of the national deity, the deity is the ultimate sovereign of the nation, and the temple therefore serves as the deity's royal palace. Insofar as national deities are generally conceived as creator gods, ancient temples also symbolize the center of creation. Solomon's Temple is no exception, insofar as it reflects YHWH's role as sovereign ruler of Israel/Judah and of all creation.[11]

Solomon's Temple measured sixty cubits long, twenty cubits wide, and thirty cubits high. Because the ancient royal cubit is approximately 20.9 inches, this results in dimensions of approximately one hundred five feet long, thirty-five feet wide, and fifty-two feet high. The building was constructed of undressed stone to symbolize the pristine purity of YHWH's creation. The interior of the Temple was overlaid with cedar, cypress, and olivewood inlaid with gold images of cherubs, palm trees, plants, and the like, to symbolize creation in the Garden of Eden. The Temple faced to the east, which enables the rising sun to illuminate the interior of the Temple during the morning liturgy and thereby symbolizes creation each morning insofar as light was the first creation in Genesis 1. The *'ûlām*, "portico," which served as the entry way to the structure, measured ten cubits long and twenty cubits wide. Its entrance was flanked by bronze pillars, named Jachin and Boaz, to symbolize the pillars or foundations of the earth and thus the role of the Temple as the center of creation. The *hêkal*, "palace" or "great hall" of the Temple, measured forty cubits long and twenty cubits wide. In addition to the table for the bread of the presence, it contained the

[10] Meyers, "Temple, Jerusalem," 6:350–69.
[11] See Levenson, "The Temple and the World," 275–98.

ten bronze incense burners and the ten bronze candelabra that together fill the *hêkal* with smoke and flashing lights in keeping with the theophanic imagery of cloud, smoke, fire, and lightning associated with YHWH's presence (see Exodus 19 and 40). The *dĕbîr* or "inner sanctum" (also called the "holy of holies"), which housed the Ark of the Covenant to represent the throne of YHWH, measured twenty cubits wide and twenty cubits long. Built with two cherubim or composite animal figures (in addition to the two cherubim built onto the Ark), it was enclosed with olivewood doors, incised with gold images of cherubim, palms, and so on, to symbolize the sacred character of the *dĕbîr* as the throne room of YHWH and entrance to the Garden of Eden. Cherubim or composite animal figures are frequently built beside royal thrones and city gates in the ancient Near East to symbolize divine power and protection, and images of gods and goddesses are frequently depicted as mounted or enthroned upon animal figures that symbolize divine qualities (cf. Psalms 18 and 68 and Ezekiel 1). Because the term *dĕbîr* is related to the Hebrew term for speech, the *dĕbîr* functions as the place where YHWH's presence and will are manifested, particularly to the high priest who enters the *dĕbîr* to experience the presence of YHWH on Yom Kippur (Leviticus 16). The Temple structure was enclosed on three sides (north, west, and south) by a three-story structure containing storerooms.

The courtyard of the Temple contained several major installations that served the liturgical purposes of the Temple and symbolized YHWH's relationship with the nation and creation. The Temple altar, constructed of uncut stones (Exod 20:19–23) to symbolize the purity of creation, was located before the entrance to the Temple structure. It was employed for the presentation and burning of sacrifices offered to YHWH as part of the tribute due to YHWH as sovereign of creation and the nation. Ezekiel 43:14 designates the altar as *ḥḥêq hā'āreṣ*, "the bosom of the earth," to symbolize its role at the center of creation. The "molten sea," a cast bronze tank of water set atop twelve cast-metal bulls, was also located in the Temple courtyard. The twelve bulls, with three facing in each of the four directions of the compass, symbolize fertility and divine strength. The water tank enabled the priests to immerse themselves in water in preparation for their service at the altar, and it symbolizes YHWH's creation of the world out of the sea as well as Israel's crossing of the Red Sea at the exodus from Egypt. The Temple courtyard serves as the place of assembly for the people during the sacrifices and singing of the Temple liturgy, and it is the location where festival meals were prepared and eaten following the offering of festival sacrifices.

Although Solomon's Temple was destroyed by the Babylonians in 587/6 BCE, the Second Temple was built at the outset of Persian rule during the years 520–515 BCE under the supervision of Joshua ben Jehozadak, the high priest, and Zerubbabel ben Shealtiel, the Persian-appointed governor of Judah and the grandson of the last reigning monarch of the house of David (Ezra 3–6). Very few details concerning the structure of this Temple are preserved in biblical literature, although it follows the general three-room pattern of Solomon's Temple. Because the Ark of the Covenant was lost, likely taken away as booty by the Babylonians, the *děbîr* remained empty throughout the Second Temple period.

THE PRIESTS OF ANCIENT ISRAEL AND JUDAH

The priests of ancient Israel and Judah were fundamentally responsible for overseeing the sanctity of the people and the temples. They served as intermediaries between YHWH and the people, conducted the temple liturgies and sacrifices, and instructed the people in YHWH's Torah (Hebrew, *tôrâ*), "instruction," concerning what was holy or pure and profane or unclean (Lev 10:10–11). The Hebrew Bible emphasizes that the tribe of Levi serves as the priests of Israel and Judah and therefore will have no tribal inheritance of land like the other tribes (Numbers 3–8 and 17–18; cf. Exodus 32). They are supported instead by the offerings of the people.

The priestly role of the Levites was likely a later development insofar as Israelite tradition notes that the first-born sons of the people served as priests until the tribe of Levi was designated for the priestly role (see Num 3:40–51).[12] Aaron, the brother of Moses and son of Amran and his wife Jochebed of the tribe of Levi (Num 26:59), was designated by YHWH as the first chief priest of Israel. His sons Nadab and Abihu died when they made inappropriate incense offerings to YHWH, leaving his sons Eleazer and Ithamar and their descendants to continue the priestly line (Leviticus 10). This tradition conveys the seriousness with which YHWH's and the priesthood's holiness are considered, and many interpreters believe it may represent conflict or displacement in the priestly lines of Israel and Judah. Eleazer emerges as the ancestor of the Zadokite line of priests that served in the Jerusalem Temple. He is given charge of the Levitical family of the Kohathites, who carry the Ark of the Covenant and serve as the primary

---

[12] N.b., to the mother; see Exod 22:28 and 34:19–20; Samuel, the first-born son of Hannah, the wife of Elkanah of the tribe of Ephraim, was placed in the sanctuary at Shiloh to be trained as a priest in 1 Samuel 1.

162 *Marvin A. Sweeney*

priests who officiate in YHWH's central sanctuary (Numbers 4). Ithamar becomes the ancestor of the subsidiary priestly line of Abiathar, who was expelled from the Jerusalem Temple by Solomon (1 Kings 2). He is given charge of the Levitical families of the Gershonites and Merarites, who were assigned secondary tasks and ultimately developed into a secondary priestly line known as the Levites, who likely served in sanctuaries outside of Jerusalem and later performed secondary duties in the Jerusalem Temple, such as preparing sacrificial animals for the altar, cooking food, and gate supervision. Priests serve in the sanctuary from the age of thirty (but Num 8:23–26 specifies twenty-five) through the age of fifty (Numbers 4). They are ordained for service during a seven-day ceremony in which they are isolated, cleansed with water, dressed in pure priestly garments, and consecrated by sacrifice (Exodus 28–29, Leviticus 8, and Numbers 8).

WORSHIP OF YHWH AT ISRAELITE AND JUDEAN TEMPLES AND THE FESTIVAL CALENDAR

Worship of YHWH at Israelite and Judean temples was centered on the offering of incense and animal sacrifices at specified times to honor YHWH and to provide support to the sanctuary; the singing of psalms that would praise YHWH, recount YHWH's deeds and expectations, and enable the people to petition YHWH; the recital of prayers that would enable the priests and the people to address YHWH; and festival dancing, meals, and the like that would facilitate the celebration of appointed times and festivals that marked the sacred calendar. The Bible contains some descriptions of worship, such as Abram's offering of his tithe to El Elyon at Salem or Jerusalem (Genesis 14); the appearance of God to Jacob at Beth El (Genesis 28, 35); Hannah's prayer during worship at the Shiloh sanctuary (1 Samuel 1); the dancing and hymns that marked the parting of the Red Sea (Exodus 14–15); Joshua's celebration of Passover at Gilgal (Joshua 5); the celebration of Sukkot at Shiloh (Judges 21); David's bringing of the Ark of the Covenant into Jerusalem (2 Samuel 6 and 1 Chronicles 16); Solomon's dedication of the Jerusalem Temple (1 Kings 8 and 2 Chronicles 5–7); Jeroboam's offering of incense at the northern Israelite sanctuary at Beth El (1 Kings 13); Elijah's sacrifice to YHWH at Mount Carmel (1 Kings 18); the celebration of Passover during the reign of kings Hezekiah and Josiah (2 Chronicles 30 and 35); the dedication of the altar and later the Second Temple by the priest Joshua ben Jehozadak (Ezra 3 and 6); and Ezra's reading of the Torah to the people at Sukkot (Nehemiah 8–10). The variety of liturgical practices found in these narratives indicates the differing liturgical practices that might be found at individual sanctuaries as well as the historical development of Israelite and Judean liturgies.

The Israelite and Judean festival calendar includes a number of observances that emphasize YHWH's roles as sovereign of both the nation and creation (see Exodus 23 and 34, Leviticus 23, Numbers 28–29, and Deuteronomy 16). Although the 354-day lunar calendar was adapted from the Babylonians at some point during the Second Temple period, a 364-day solar calendar was apparently employed throughout the monarchic period. The three major festivals of the liturgical year emphasize YHWH's role as creator by sanctifying the key times of the agricultural season together with key elements of Israel's and Judah's sacred history. The people are expected to appear at the Temple for each of these festivals to bring offerings or tithes of one-tenth of their flocks and harvests to honor YHWH and to support the Temple and the state. The first festival, *pesaḥḥ*, "Passover," celebrated for a total of eight days beginning on the fourteenth day of the first month in the spring, marks the beginning of the grain harvest as well as the Exodus from Egyptian slavery. The festival combines the one-day observance of Passover, which marks the beginning of the birth season for livestock, and the seven-day observance of Matzot, "Unleavened Bread," which marks the beginning of the grain harvest. The second major festival, *šābû'ôt*, "Weeks (Pentecost)," is celebrated fifty days after Passover to mark the conclusion of the grain harvest in the late spring. Shavuot later came to commemorate the revelation of the Torah at Mount Sinai as well. The third major festival, *sukkôt*, "Booths" or "Tabernacles," is celebrated for a total of eight days beginning on the fifteenth day of the seventh month in the fall to mark the conclusion of the fruit harvest and the beginning of the rainy season in the land of Israel. The name Sukkot is drawn from the temporary shelters or booths in which the people lived while out in the fields and orchards bringing in the harvest. This image also associates the festival with the forty years of wilderness wandering as the people traveled through the Sinai wilderness from Egypt to the Promised Land. Other observances are also included in the liturgical calendar. Daily worship includes morning, afternoon, and evening sacrifices that commemorate YHWH's act of creation each day. Weekly celebration of the *šabbāt*, "Sabbath," marks the seventh day of the week, Saturday, as the day that YHWH rested following the six days of creation. The New Moon marks the beginning of the month in keeping with the thirty-day lunar cycle. The New Year, *rō'š haššanâ*, marks the beginning of the liturgical year on the first day of the seventh month with celebration of the day on which YHWH created the world.

The Day of Atonement, *yôm kippûr*, is an annual fast day observed on the tenth day of the seventh month to atone for the sins of the nation.

The Israelite and Judean sacrificial system calls for only a limited number of animals considered fit for sacrifice to YHWH and for human consumption (Leviticus 16 and Deuteronomy 14), apparently as a reminder of the limitations imposed by YHWH on the human capacity for violence and bloodshed (Genesis 9). The hind portions of the animal are to be offered only to YHWH (Genesis 32), perhaps because they are associated with life or reproduction, and the rib cage and shoulder portions of the animal may be eaten by humans after all blood has been drained from the animal and returned to the ground. The *'ôlâ*, "whole burnt offering," is the most common type of animal sacrifice offered every day and on all festival occasions (Leviticus 1). It is accompanied by a *minhhâ*, "gift" or "grain offering" of unleavened bread (Leviticus 2) and by libation offerings. The *zebahh šĕlāmîm*, "Sacrifice of Well-being," is an animal sacrifice that is offered on occasions of special gratitude or celebration (Leviticus 3). The *hhathhtā't*, "Sin Offering," is offered as a means of purification when one has become impure through the commission of a cultic or moral wrong, and the *'āšām*, "Guilt Offering," is offered as a means of reparation in such circumstances (Leviticus 4–5).

The hymns sung as part of the Temple liturgy appear primarily in the book of Psalms, although selected examples appear in narrative or prophetic literature (e.g., Exodus 15, Judges 5, Isaiah 12, and Habakkuk 3). They include a variety of different types. The songs of praise recount YHWH's qualities and actions on behalf of the nation (Psalms 8, 105, and 106). Songs of lament or complaint petition YHWH to act in times of crisis on behalf of both individuals and the nation (Psalms 6 and 7). Songs of thanksgiving are sung at times of individual or national deliverance from some danger or calamity (Psalms 30, 34, and 118). Royal psalms recall YHWH's sovereignty and relationship with the royal house of David (Psalms 2, 89, 96–99, and 110). Songs of Zion celebrate YHWH's relationship with Zion or Jerusalem (Psalms 46, 48, and 76) and the Songs of Ascent (to Zion) were likely sung at major festivals at the Jerusalem Temple (Psalms 120–134).

YHWH'S EXPECTATIONS OF TEACHING (*TÔRÂ*)

Israelite and Judean religion viewed YHWH as the source for holiness and moral order in the world. The temples and priesthood therefore played important roles in promulgating YHWH's expectations or teaching (*tôrâ*) among the people in the form of collections of law that would govern Israelite worship and sanctity and provide the basis for a viable and stable social and economic life for the nation. In keeping with typical patterns throughout the ancient Near East, the Jerusalem Temple (and presumably other Israelite and Judean temples) serves as the center of creation. The construction of the wilderness tabernacle, a precursor to Solomon's Temple in biblical narrative, appears as the culmination of creation in the pentateuchal narrative concerning the origins of Israel and creation in general. Following the ancestral or patriarchal period in Genesis, the pentateuchal narrative in Exodus, Leviticus, Numbers, and Deuteronomy relates the Exodus from Egyptian bondage, the revelation of divine Torah at Mount Sinai including instructions for the construction of the Ark of the Covenant, and the final journey to the Promised Land. Indeed, the narratives concerning the revelation of divine Torah at Mount Sinai portray the mountain as a holy temple-like site, insofar as YHWH is revealed there and the people must purify themselves and avoid contact with the mountain. Moses, the Levitical priest, then mediates the revelation of Torah to the people. In later times, the Temple would continue to serve as the source for divine instruction, including the development, regulation, interpretation, and implementation of the Israelite and Judean legal system. Although judges were selected from the common people and the priests, the priesthood served as the final court of appeal in the Israelite and Judean judicial system (Deuteronomy 16–17; cf. Exodus 18). Kings sometimes exercised judicial authority (see 2 Samuel 12 and 1 Kings 3), but the narratives view such power critically, and pentateuchal tradition calls for the Levitical priests to oversee royal authority (Deut 17:14–20).

The pentateuchal narratives concerning the revelation of divine Torah include two basic accounts, viz., the initial revelation at Mount Sinai and later in the wilderness in Exodus 19–40, Leviticus, and Numbers, and Moses' repetition of YHWH's Torah in the land of Moab east of the Jordan River in Deuteronomy immediately prior to Israel's taking possession of the Promised Land. Although both narratives are presented synchronically as coherent accounts of the origins of Israel's and Judah's legal systems, interpreters recognize that the various law codes embedded in the narrative presuppose a number of distinct historical and cultural settings.

Following the portrayal of YHWH's presence at Mount Sinai in Exodus 19, the first collections of Israelite law appear in the Ten Commandments and the so-called Covenant Code of Exodus 20–24. The Ten Commandments are not law per se, but a form of legal instruction that articulates the basic principles of piety and justice that underlie Israel's and Judah's world views as, for example, recognition of YHWH alone as God; observance of YHWH's religious requirements, such as the sanctity of YHWH's name and the Sabbath; and observance of YHWH's social requirements concerning respect for parents and forbidding murder, theft, adultery, and so on. The Covenant Code may constitute Israel's earliest law code from the tenth-eighth centuries BCE. Many of its provisions find parallels in the major Mesopotamian law codes, such as the Code of Hammurabi (eighteenth century BCE), which points to the antiquity of the Covenant Code and to the possibility of Mesopotamian legal influence in Israel and Judah. The Covenant Code includes a wide array of civil law concerning debt-slavery, manslaughter, assault, property matters, personal liability, financial regulations, cursing God and king, treatment of the poor, and observance of religious festivals including the obligation to bring offerings to the Temple. Exodus 25–30 contains instructions for constructing the Tabernacle, the Ark of the Covenant, and various items associated with the Temple and priesthood.

Following a narrative concerning cultic apostasy with the Golden Calf, a revised law code in Exodus 34, perhaps from a later period in Israel or Judah, addresses problems of religious observance. Exodus 35–40 relates the construction of the Tabernacle and the Ark, which then serve as YHWH's de facto Temple until the construction of the Jerusalem Temple by Solomon. Leviticus 1–16 includes regulations concerning Temple sacrifices and cultic matters, generally dated to priestly circles from the exilic or early Second Temple period. The Holiness Code of Leviticus 17–26 likewise considers cultic matters, such as the treatment of blood, marriage relations, social behavior, conduct of the priesthood, the festival calendar, property matters, and obligations to the Temple. Some interpreters date this material to the reign of the eighth-century Judean monarch Hezekiah (715–687/6 BCE) although many consider it to be exilic or post-exilic. Numbers contains a mixture of narrative concerning the wilderness wanderings and regulations concerning the role and authority of the Levitical priesthood, the organization of the community, cultic matters, and civil matters such as the inheritance of property by women. Interpreters are divided concerning the setting of this material. Although much is priestly, it appears to presuppose periods earlier than the exile.

Deuteronomy presents Moses' repetition of YHWH's Torah in the form of a Levitical sermon prior to Israel's movement into the land of Canaan. This account also begins with a version of the Ten Commandments in Deuteronomy 5 that reiterates the basic principles of Israel's world view. Close analysis of the laws of Deuteronomy indicates that they are frequently revisions of earlier laws that give greater rights to various disadvantaged groups, particularly the Levites, resident aliens, women, and the poor of the land in general. Deuteronomy emphasizes that worship of YHWH should be concentrated in only one central sanctuary in the land (Deuteronomy 12 and other passages). Although some interpreters argue that Deuteronomy's origins lie in northern Israel, the northern kingdom maintained sanctuaries in Dan and Beth El. The requirement for a central sanctuary fits with Judean practice, insofar as Judean kings such as Hezekiah (715–687/6 BCE) and Josiah (640–609 BCE) attempted to centralize Judean worship in Jerusalem. Most interpreters maintain that Deuteronomy represents a law code employed in King Josiah's program of religious reform and national restoration following the collapse of Assyrian power over Judah and western Asia in the mid-seventh century BCE. Although Deuteronomy gives greater rights to the people of the land, the very group that put Josiah into power following the assassination of his father King Amon (642–640 BCE), it is ascribed originally – like the other law codes – to YHWH and Moses.

The pentateuchal law codes played important roles in governing both religious and civil life in ancient Israel and Judah during the monarchic period. Following the Babylonian exile, when Judah was reconstituted as a province of the Persian Empire, the Pentateuch provided the means for Jews to govern themselves according to their own laws in keeping with Persian imperial practice (see Nehemiah 8–10). Later periods saw the Pentateuch or Torah emerge as the basis for Jewish life outside of the land as well during the Greco-Roman period and beyond.

ALTERNATIVES TO THE JERUSAELEM TEMPLE: OTHER FORMS OF RELIGIOUS PRACTICE AND VIEWPOINTS

The Jerusalem Temple played a constitutive role in defining ancient Judean religious tradition, but the Hebrew Bible and archaeological evidence point to other forms of religious practice and viewpoint as well. Some may be characteristic of the northern kingdom of Israel, which is frequently presented in polemical terms in the largely Judean Hebrew Bible. Others may be characteristic of popular religion practiced among the people outside of the Jerusalem Temple or syncretistic practices that combine elements of Judean and Israelite religious practice with those of the surrounding cultures.

Although Judean reform movements frequently emphasize the Jerusalem Temple as the central and exclusive sanctuary for the worship of YHWH,

Israelite and Judean religions generally presuppose multiple sanctuaries. Early practice would call for sacrifice to be made to YHWH or other gods by family representatives at high places throughout the land (see, e.g., Elijah's sacrifice at Mount Carmel). Worship of family gods was known at the popular level,[13] and burials indicate offerings on behalf of the dead. Established sanctuaries appear in the north at Gilgal, Shiloh, Beth El, Dan, Shechem, Megiddo, and elsewhere, and southern sanctuaries appear at Jerusalem, Gibeon, Beer Sheba, Arad, and other locations. Archaeological excavation indicates that many of these sites were founded in the Bronze Age long before the emergence of Israel beginning in the twelfth century BCE and may therefore have served as Canaanite sanctuary sites that later were identified with YHWH.

The northern kingdom of Israel maintained two national temple sites at Beth El and Dan, probably because the greater size of the kingdom required two sites to ensure that the people could reach a sanctuary in order to make their offerings at the festivals. Because the Hebrew Bible is largely a Judean work, it tends to portray northern worship sites and practices polemically as apostate or as deviations from YHWH's will. Although northern Israelite practice displays some Canaanite features, the same may be said for Judah. It is doubtful that northern Israel deliberately set out to engage in sinful religious practice, and it is therefore necessary to set aside some of the religious polemics when reading narratives about the northern kingdom. Jeroboam's establishment of the sanctuaries at Beth El and Dan, for example, include the installation of golden calf images, which 1 Kings 12 depicts as idolatrous. The golden calves, however, were not gods per se. Such images are typical mounts for deities in the ancient Near Eastern world, and it is likely that they functioned as mounts for YHWH much as the Ark of the Covenant functioned as YHWH's throne in the Jerusalem Temple. The charge that Jeroboam appointed non-Levitical priests is likely true, although it would presuppose the practice noted above of designating first-born sons as priests prior to the designation of the tribe of Levi as priests. The celebration of the festival of Sukkot on the fifteenth day of the eighth month, rather than on the fifteenth day of the seventh month, likely presupposes a somewhat different festival calendar in the north. The circumstances under which Passover may be celebrated on the fourteenth day of the second month, rather than the fourteenth day of the first month, may also presuppose a different northern calendar (Numbers 9).

---

[13] See the reference to the household idols (*tĕrāpîm*) of Laban in Genesis 31 and 35.

The installation of uninscribed cultic pillars or *maṣṣḥēbôt* likely represents a male fertility symbol associated with the Canaanite god Baal, but they come to represent YHWH in Israelite sanctuaries, such as Beth El (Genesis 28), or the excavated Judean sanctuary at Arad. Likewise, the planting of a cultic tree (*'ăšērâ*) by Ahab (1 Kings 16), Manasseh (2 Kings 21), and others originally represents the Canaanite fertility goddess Asherah, but such imagery is incorporated into the Jerusalem Temple insofar as the seven-branched candelabra or *mĕnōrôt* represents the tree associated with Eve in the Garden of Eden (Genesis 3). The charges that various kings sacrificed children or caused their sons to pass through the fire may represent Canaanite or Moabite forms of child sacrifice (see, e.g., Mesha's sacrifice of his son in 2 Kings 3). By contrast, Israelite and Judean practice maintains that the first-born belong to YHWH (Exod 34:19–20), but rejects human sacrifice and instead calls for the first-born sons to be redeemed to serve as priests (see Genesis 21 and 1 Samuel 1), a role later taken in Judah by the tribe of Levi (Numbers 3–4 and 8).

It is also possible that women played liturgical roles in the north. Exodus 15 portrays Miriam, a prophet and Levitical sister of Moses and Aaron, leading the women of Israel in worship, dance, and liturgical song at the parting of the Red Sea. Judges 4–5 depicts Deborah, a prophet and judge, singing a liturgical psalm together with the warrior Barak upon their victory over Sisera. The mourning of Jephthah's daughter prior to her sacrifice in Judges 11 may reflect mourning rituals conducted in Canaanite, Mesopotamian, Israelite, and Judean traditions during the late-summer dry season prior to the onset of the rainy season in the fall (see also Ezekiel 8, which notes the women mourning for Tammuz, the Mesopotamian fertility god who must be brought back from the underworld by Ishtar to inaugurate the rainy season). 1 Samuel 1–2 portrays Hannah praying at the Shiloh temple during the festival celebrated there, and it notes how Hophni and Phineas, sons of the high priest Eli, lay with the women who were congregating at the Tent of Meeting or sanctuary. Inscriptional evidence also points to potential cultic roles for women. The Khirbet el-Kom tomb inscriptions, a site located in Judah west of Hebron dated from the eighth through the sixth centuries BCE, refer to both YHWH and the goddess Asherata or Asherah.[14] The Kuntillet 'Ajrud inscriptions, discovered at the site of a ninth-eighth-century-BCE northern Israelite trading station located in the eastern Sinai, refer to "YHWH of Samaria," "YHWH of Teman," and YHWH's "Asherah." Drawings associated with the inscriptions also depict

---

[14] See Zevit, *The Religions*, 359–70.

a woman playing an instrument while two male figures dance.[15] The proliferation of mother or mother-goddess figurines in Israel and Judah may represent vestiges of popular religion, Canaanite practice, or even earlier Israelite and Judean religious practice.[16] Consulting the spirits of the dead may reflect Canaanite or popular practice, but it was forbidden in Israel (see Exod 22:17 and 1 Samuel 28). The *marzēahḥ*, a funerary observance that calls for copious drinking (Isaiah 28), was a Canaanite practice known from Ugarit that found its way into Israel and Judah.[17]

Finally, prophets play an important role in both northern Israel and southern Judah as figures who communicate oracles from YHWH to the people. Prophets are known throughout the ancient Near Eastern world as oracle diviners, poets and singers, and cultic functionaries who advise monarchs, priests, and other figures concerning the will of the gods. An example of an oracle diviner in the Bible is the Mesopotamian *baru*-priest Balaam, a figure known from an eighth-century-BCE Trans-Jordanian wall inscription from Deir 'Allah,[18] who unsuccessfully attempts to curse the Israelites prior to their entry into the promised land (Numbers 22–24). Moses also functions in this role, insofar as he communicated directly with YHWH throughout the pentateuchal narratives and veiled his face as a result of that experience (see esp. Exodus 33–34). Prophets could also serve as the singers of psalms in the Temple liturgy (see 2 Chron 29:25 and 35:15; cf. 2 Kings 3, which portrays Elijah delivering an oracle to music). Although priests could serve as prophets (e.g., Jeremiah, Ezekiel, or Zechariah), non-priestly figures could also serve (e.g., Amos, Isaiah, or Micah). Women could serve as prophets in northern Israel (e.g., Deborah, Judges 4–5) and in southern Judah (e.g., Huldah, 2 Kings 22).

The prophets are key figures in interpreting events in relation to their understandings of YHWH's will. Insofar as they argue that catastrophe takes place as a result of human – and not divine – failings, the prophets engage in theodicy or the defense of divine power and righteousness.[19] Amos, a Judean agriculturalist who brought Judean tribute to the northern Israelite sanctuary at Beth El, argued that northern Israel was unjust in its treatment of its vassal Judah and that YHWH would destroy the Beth El temple and restore Davidic rule over the north. Isaiah advised

---

[15] See ibid., 370–406.
[16] See ibid., 267–74.
[17] See Lewis, *Cults of the Dead*, 80–94.
[18] For discussion of the Deir 'Allah inscription, see Dijkstra, "Is Balaam," 43–64.
[19] Such assertions may also be challenged. See, e.g., Job, which raises questions about YHWH, and Esther, in which YHWH does not appear at a time of threat.

King Ahaz against turning to the Assyrians when Judah was attacked by the allied forces of Aram and Israel based on the Davidic-Zion tradition that YHWH would defend Jerusalem and the Davidic king. Jeremiah, a Levitical priest charged with teaching divine Torah, argued that Judah must ally with Babylon rather than with Egypt, Israel's oppressor in the Torah, or suffer destruction as a punishment from YHWH. Ezekiel, a Zadokite priest exiled to Babylonia, saw visions of YHWH based on the imagery of the Ark of the Covenant from the Jerusalem Temple, as part of his efforts to argue that destruction of the Temple entailed YHWH's attempt to purify the defiled Temple and all creation. An anonymous prophet from the exile known only as Second Isaiah argued that the fall of the Babylonian Empire to Persia was an act of YHWH and that the Persian king Cyrus was YHWH's anointed who would see to the restoration of the exiles to Jerusalem. Zechariah, a Temple priest returned to Jerusalem from Babylonian exile, portrayed the rebuilding of the Temple as a signal of YHWH's recognition as sovereign by the nations of the world.

CONCLUSION

In sum, the religions of ancient Israel and Judah provided the basis for national and social self-identity and religious practice from the time of the formation of an independent monarchy during the early tenth century BCE until the respective destructions of the northern kingdom of Israel by the Assyrian Empire in 722/1 BCE and the southern kingdom of Judah by the Babylonian Empire in 587/6 BCE. Both appear to have grown out of pre-Israelite Canaanite religious practice, and both were heavily influenced by other religious traditions, such as those of Egypt, Aram, Phoenicia, and Mesopotamia. Nevertheless, both Israelite and Judean religions represent distinctive approaches to the worship of the deity, YHWH, as creator of heaven and earth and the patron deity of the kingdoms of Israel and Judah. Throughout the period of the Israelite and Judean monarchies, temples at Shiloh and later at Beth El and Dan in northern Israel and Jerusalem in southern Judah constituted the focal points for religious ideology, liturgy, and observance in each kingdom. With the return of exiled Judeans to Jerusalem in 539 BCE and the reconstruction of the Jerusalem Temple in the early years of the Achaemenid Persian Empire (520–515 BCE), Judean religion began to develop into the religious tradition of Judaism that would be practiced not only in the land of Israel but throughout the ancient Mediterranean world and beyond.

172 *Marvin A. Sweeney*

BIBLIOGRAPHY

Ackerman, Susan. *Under Every Green Tree: Popular Religion in Ancient Judah.* Harvard Semitic Monographs 46 (Atlanta, 1992).

Albertz, Rainer. *A History of Israelite Religion in the Old Testament Period.* 2 vols., trans. John Bowden (Louisville, 1994).

Anderson, Gary A. *Sacrifices and Offerings in Ancient Israel: Studies in their Social and Political Importance.* Harvard Semitic Monographs 41 (Atlanta, 1987).

Berlin, Adele, and Marc Brettler. *The Jewish Study Bible* (Oxford, 2003).

Bloch-Smith, Elizabeth. *Judahite Burial Practices and Beliefs about the Dead.* Journal for the Study of the Old Testament Supplements 123 (Sheffield, U.K., 1992).

Boecker, Hans Jochen. *Law and the Administration of Justice in the Old Testament and Ancient East,* trans. Jeremy Moiser (Minneapolis, 1980).

Busink, T. *Der Tempel von Jerusalem. Von Salomo bis Herodes.* 2 vols. (Leiden, 1970–1980).

Collins, John J. *An Introduction to the Hebrew Bible* (Minneapolis, 2004).

Cryer, Frederick H. *Divination in Ancient Israel And Its Near Eastern Environment: A Socio-Historical Investigation.* Journal for the Study of the Old Testament Supplements 142 (Sheffield, U.K., 1993).

Dearman, Andrew, ed. *Studies in the Mesha Inscription and Moab.* Society of Biblical Literature Archeology and Biblical Studies 2 (Atlanta, 1989).

Dijkstra, Meindert. "Is Balaam Also among the Prophets?" *Journal of Biblical Literature* 114 (1995): 43–64.

Elliger, Karl, and Wilhelm Rudolph, eds. *Biblia Hebraica Stuttgartensia,* 3rd ed. (Stuttgart, 1987).

Gerstenberger, Erhard S. *Psalms, Part 1, with an Introduction to Cultic Poetry.* The Forms of the Old Testament Literature 14 (Grand Rapids, 1988).

Klawans, Jonathan. *Impurity and Sin in Ancient Judaism* (Oxford, 2000).

Knohl, Israel. *The Sanctuary of Silence: The Priestly Torah and the Holiness School* (Minneapolis, 1995).

Levenson, Jon D. "The Temple and the World." *Journal of Religion* 64 (1984): 275–98.

Sinai and Zion: An Entry into the Jewish Bible (Minneapolis, 1985).

Lewis, Theodore J. *Cults of the Dead in Ancient Israel and Ugarit.* Harvard Semitic Monographs 39 (Atlanta, 1989).

Mazar, Amihai. *Archaeology of the Land of the Bible 10,000–586 B.C.E.* (New York, 1990).

Meeks, Wayne A., et al., eds. *The HarperCollins Study Bible* (San Francisco, 2006).

Meyers, Carol. "Temple, Jerusalem," in *The Anchor Bible Dictionary,* ed. D. N. Freedman et al. (Garden City, N.Y., 1992), 6:350–69.

Milgrom, Jacob. *Cult and Conscience* (Leiden, 1976).

Pritchard, James B. *Ancient Near Eastern Texts Relating to the Old Testament* (Princeton, 1969).

Rehm, Merlin D. "Levites and Priests." *ABD* 4: 297–310.

Rooke, Deborah W. *Zadok's Heirs: The Role and Development of the High Priesthood in Ancient Israel.* Oxford Theological Monographs (Oxford, 2000).

Smith, Mark S. *The Origins of Biblical Monotheism: Israel's Polytheistic Background and the Ugaritic Texts* (Oxford, 2001).

Stern, Ephraim, ed. *The New Encyclopedia of Archaeological Excavations in the Holy Land.* 4 vols. (Jerusalem, 1993).

Archaeology of the Land of the Bible. Volume II: *The Assyrian, Babylonian, and Persian Periods (732–332 B.C.E.)* (New York, 2001).

Sweeney, Marvin A. *The Prophetic Literature.* Interpreting Biblical Texts (Nashville, 2005).

Van der Toorn, Karel. "Y-hw-h," *DDD²*, 910–19.

Family Religion in Babylonia, Syria, and Israel. Studies in the History and Cultures of the Ancient Near East 7 (Leiden, 1996).

Weinfeld, Moshe. *Deuteronomy and the Deuteronomic School* (Oxford, 1972).

Zevit, Ziony. *The Religions of Ancient Israel: A Synthesis of Parallactic Approaches* (London, 2001).

PART II

EGYPT AND NORTH AFRICA

7

EGYPTIAN RELIGION

DENISE M. DOXEY

Along with its great antiquity,[1] ancient Egyptian religion presents unique obstacles to interpretation.[2] The absence of a coherent written doctrine has required scholars to rely on a variety of disparate sources, including funerary spells, literary works, instructional treatises, biographical inscriptions, artistic representations, and archaeological evidence to attempt to understand the ancient Egyptians' relationship to the divine. Fortunately, Egypt's climate and the Egyptians' own practices have left an unusually rich corpus of textual and archaeological evidence.

The study of Egyptian religion is also complicated by the seemingly alien nature of Egyptian deities and beliefs when viewed from the perspective of cultures accustomed to an anthropomorphic deity or deities. From Greco-Roman times, representations of gods and goddesses with combined human and animal characteristics aroused confusion and suspicion. The esoteric nature of surviving funerary texts, with their enigmatic denizens of the afterlife, only increased the sense of alienation. In addition, the Egyptians' understanding of their pantheon was subject to review and alteration over its three-thousand-year history. Towns and districts each worshipped their own deities and even held different beliefs regarding creation and the nature of the cosmos. In Lower Egypt the principal creator-god was Atum, the patron god of Heliopolis. At Memphis, the Memphite god Ptah was seen as a manifestation of Atum. Meanwhile in southernmost Egypt, Khnum, a god associated with the source of the Nile, was the primary creator. The Egyptians apparently saw no contradiction in the presence of multiple gods of creation. Deities therefore shared overlapping functions and characteristics, and two or more could share attributes.

---

[1] For the sites relevant to Egyptian religion, see Map 3 in Chapter 5.
[2] Quirke, *Religion*, 7–19.

For example, Amen-Ra, the supreme state god of Egypt during the New Kingdom, arose from the combination of the traditional solar god Ra with the local god of Thebes, Amen, after Thebes became Egypt's capital.

The study of Egyptian religion has also suffered from attempts to view ancient beliefs and practices through the lens of contemporary religious teaching. One of the foremost questions having engaged scholars is the extent to which Egyptian religion was monotheistic. Many early interpretations were guided by the preconception that monotheistic religions were more "advanced" than animist or polytheistic religions and that Egyptian religion should somehow "progress" from polytheism to monotheism. The history of scholarly thought about Egyptian religion is well covered by Hornung in his *Conceptions of God in Ancient Egypt*.[3] Many nineteenth-century Egyptologists, either consciously or not, sought to establish an underlying monotheism behind the apparent multiplicity of Egyptian deities. It was once believed that monotheism preceded polytheism in the development of Egyptian religion. Near the end of the century Maspero first argued the opposite – monotheism had developed out of polytheism. The discovery of the first Predynastic and Early Dynastic cultures supported his theory by demonstrating that the earliest Egyptians worshipped multiple deities. Later, the early twentieth century saw the search for monotheism give way to a widespread belief that the Egyptians were henotheistic, worshipping different deities, but only one at any given time. Yet by mid-century, scholars, following Drioton, adopted what Hornung terms "neomonotheism," a belief that the Egyptians worshipped numerous manifestations of a single, hidden deity. Hornung's study led him to support the notion of a multiplicity of deities. Still more recently Assmann has argued in *Solar Religion in the New Kingdom* for belief in a transcendent solar deity, at least during the eighteenth dynasty. New evidence and new approaches will undoubtedly continue to bring new and revised interpretations.

THE EGYPTIAN CONCEPT OF GOD AND GODS

Although the Egyptians did not have a word for "religion," they had a word for "god," translated today as *netjer* and rendered *noute* in Coptic, *theos* in Greek, and *Eloha* in Aramaic.[4] The hieroglyph for *netjer*, an outstretched banner attached to a pole wrapped in bandages, appears among

[3] Hornung, *Conceptions*, 15–32.
[4] Dunand and Zivie-Coche, *Gods and Men*, 7–13; Hornung, *Conceptions*, 33–65.

the earliest preserved hieroglyphs, around 3100 BCE, indicating that its symbolism dates to prehistory. The interpretation of this emblem is unclear, but flagpoles were standard features of temple façades, and evidence for them occurs even in the remains of predynastic temples (3650–3300 BCE). Other hieroglyphs for "god" include a falcon perched on a standard and a seated, cloaked human. The fact that the word "gods" frequently occurs in the plural demonstrates that it cannot refer to a single "God," although certain types of texts, particularly autobiographies and instructions, use *netjer* to designate an unspecified deity. It was this usage that led scholars to see it as a word for an overarching, monotheistic, god.

Although Egyptian deities were believed to be incorporeal, they required a physical form to interact with humans. A statue, for example, could serve as the temporary "body" of a deity, enabling it to receive offerings of food and incense. This transformation required the performance of rituals to animate the statue. The best known is the Opening of the Mouth ceremony, believed to enable a cult statue to eat and breathe. The situation is thus directly opposite to that of Judaism and Islam, which expressly forbid the creation of idols.

In giving a physical structure to natural forces, Egyptian gods took both anthropomorphic and zoomorphic forms, as well as combinations of the two. Animals later identified with gods and goddesses appeared in Predynastic amulets and other representations, but it is uncertain whether they were already at that point believed to be divine. Certain anthropomorphic figures of the same period, including females with upraised arms and males with distinct, pointed beards have been interpreted as deities, but the identification is not universally accepted. By the Early Dynastic Period, both zoomorphic and anthropomorphic deities are clearly identifiable.

A deity could have a single or multiple manifestations, both human and animal, based on its function. Despite the interpretations of early writers such as Herodotus, the Egyptians did not worship animals per se. Animal cults are documented during the later parts of Egyptian history, but in these cases only a single animal, not an entire species, was believed to serve as the god's representative. The best known of these cults is the Apis bull of Memphis. Some deities, such as Amun, Ptah, and Osiris, appeared solely in human form. Several funerary gods, notably Anubis but also Khentiamentiu, Wepwawet, and Duamutef, took the form of a jackal, a creature regularly seen in cemeteries. The multifaceted Thoth could appear as a baboon, an ibis, or an ibis-headed human. Amen-Ra, the preeminent deity of the New Kingdom and later, was represented as a human, as a falcon or falcon-headed man, and as a ram or ram-headed man. Several

Fig. 2. Representation of Ra from the temple of Ramesses III, Medinet Habu, dynasty 20. Photo by Denise M. Doxey.

gods associated with virility appeared as bulls, and maternal goddesses as cows or cow-headed women. A ram could symbolize one of several gods, including Ra, Khnum, or Harsaphes. In these cases, barring an identifying inscription, the gods' headdresses are the best means of distinguishing them, because they often incorporate identifying symbols of a particular deity. For example, a falcon wearing the double crown of Upper and Lower Egypt can be understood as Horus, the patron of kingship, and a falcon wearing a solar disk represents the sun-god Ra (Fig. 2).

COSMOGONY AND COSMOLOGY

Evidence for ancient Egyptian cosmology and cosmogony derives from an array of texts and scenes from tombs, royal mortuary complexes, and

Egyptian Religion

temples. The texts are complex and at times contradictory, and ancient glosses indicate that even the Egyptians themselves had difficulty understanding them.[5] Information can nevertheless be gleaned from a careful study of inscriptions from the late fifth dynasty Pyramid Texts of Unas (ca.2353–2323 BCE), through the Middle Kingdom (ca.2140–1640 BCE) Coffin Texts and the New Kingdom (ca.1550–1070 BCE) Books of the Afterlife and Book of the Dead.[6]

The Egyptians had no single version of cosmogony, the creation of the universe, but rather several accounts that varied over time and location. One of the most important is known today as the Heliopolitan Cosmogony because it derives from Heliopolis, the center of solar cult near the ancient capital, Memphis.[7] Features of this version first appeared in the Pyramid Texts, but they surely existed in oral form earlier and continued with some variations throughout Egyptian history. In this cosmogony, the creator-god Atum is said to have ejaculated to beget the air and moisture, personified, respectively, by the god Shu and goddess Tefnut. They in turn gave birth to the earth, Geb, and the sky, Nut, who then became the parents of the next generation of gods, Osiris, Isis, Nephthys, and Seth, whose story is discussed below. This group of nine primeval deities is known today as the Heliopolitan Ennead.

The influence of Egypt's location and environment on its concept of the universe, or cosmology, can hardly be overstated.[8] The Nile, running through virtually rainless northern Africa, created a fertile strip of land through an otherwise inhospitable climate. Annual floods provided layers of fertile silt on which the Egyptians depended for their agriculture. The valley was thus perceived as the hospitable "black land" while the deserts to either side were the "red land," inhabited by chaotic and threatening elements such as wild animals, foreign enemies, and a relentlessly unfriendly climate. The regularity of the floods and resulting harvests infused Egyptian belief with a strong sense of repetition and rebirth. The daily cycle of the rising and setting sun and nightly movements of stars and other heavenly bodies reinforced this view. Hence, to the Egyptians, the functioning of the world and the entire cosmos depended upon a constant cycle of birth, death, and rebirth. To maintain this cycle, it was necessary to remain vigilant against forces continuously threatening to disrupt it.

---

[5] Shafer, ed., *Religion*, 89–90; Simpson, ed., *Religion and Philosophy*, 29–54.
[6] Allen, *Genesis*, 1–7; idem, *Pyramid Texts*; Hornung, *Afterlife*.
[7] Shafer, ed., *Religion*, 91–4.
[8] Ibid., 117–22.

Fig. 3. Osiris and king Amenhotep II from the tomb of Amenhotep II, Thebes, dynasty 18. Photo by Denise M. Doxey.

The story of Osiris and Seth, a cornerstone of Egyptian belief, is best understood in this context.[9] According to the myth, Osiris, the prototypical king of Egypt, presided over the fertile valley in the company of his sister and wife, Isis, the embodiment of marital fidelity and motherhood. His brother, the storm-god Seth, occupied the inhospitable desert beyond. Envious of Osiris, Seth murdered and dismembered him, scattering his body parts throughout Egypt. Isis, a powerful magician, retrieved and reassembled the remains, reviving Osiris successfully enough to conceive by him his son, Horus, who would go on to defeat Seth and avenge his father. Horus thereby became the personification of divine kingship, while Osiris became the ruler of the underworld, or *Duat* (Fig. 3).

Among the best illustrations of the Egyptians' perceived cosmos are New Kingdom scenes such as those on the ceilings of the cenotaph of Seti I (ca.1290–1279 BCE) at Abydos and the tomb of Ramesses VI (ca.1143–1136

[9] Ibid., 92–3.

BCE) in the Valley of the Kings at Thebes.[10] These and similar scenes on funerary papyri depict the sky as the goddess Nut, whose star-covered body stretches over the earth, supported by the atmosphere in the form of the god Shu. Geb, usually shown in human form, personifies the earth. Nut gives birth to the sun at dawn and devours it again at dusk. The *Duat*, the world of the gods and the deceased, is sometimes said to lie within the body of Nut, although other sources place it below the earth.[11] Surrounding both worlds was a limitless expanse of impenetrably dark water known as *Nun*. The daily cycle of the sun took place at the point of intersection between the known world and what lay beyond.

SOLAR RELIGION

The sun-god Ra and his travels through the heavens played a highly signifi-cant role in Egyptian religion, and many other deities were at times under-stood as manifestations of the sun-god. From the dawn of their history, the Egyptians had a deep appreciation of the sun's importance, and just as early they identified it with a falcon, initially the sky-god Horus, who later was associated with the rising and setting sun in the form of Ra-Horakhty (meaning "Horus of the horizon"). From the time of the Pyramid Texts, Ra was treated as a manifestation of the creator-god, Atum. As such, he was believed to have created himself spontaneously.

During the New Kingdom, both texts and tomb scenes emphasize the all-encompassing significance of the sun-god in his many forms. The royal tombs of the Valley of the Kings featured a scene and accompanying text known as the "Litany of Ra," which appeared later in non-royal funerary papyri as well.[12] Here the sun-god was named and portrayed in seventy-five different forms, including those of other major deities. Contemporary non-royal monuments also demonstrate the increased prominence of solar religion. For example, the stele of the twin brothers Suti and Hor, from the reign of Amenhotep III (ca.1390–1352 BCE) and now in the British Museum (BM 826), bore a pair of hymns and prayers to the sun-god,[13] referring to him as "the creator, uncreated, the sole one, the unique one," and assert that when the sun sets the earth's creatures "sleep as in a state of death." The primacy of the sun-god soon thereafter reached an unprece-dented level during the reign of Akhenaten (ca.1352–1336 BCE).

[10] Allen, *Genesis*, 1–7; Hornung, *Afterlife*, 115, fig. 64.
[11] Allen, *Genesis*, 6–7.
[12] Hornung, *Afterlife*, 141–7.
[13] Lichtheim, *Literature*, 2:86–9.

In both art and hieroglyphic texts, the solar god took a number of forms in addition to that of the falcon. To symbolize the self-creative process, the Egyptians drew an analogy to the scarab, or dung beetle, which laid eggs in a ball of dung and rolled it across the sand, after which the new generation of scarabs hatched and emerged from the ball as if self-engendered (Fig. 4). The moving ball was likened to the solar disk and the newly hatched beetles to the emergence of the sun at dawn. Hence, from the late Old Kingdom onward the scarab, known to the Egyptians as Khepri, "one who comes into being," became one of the most ubiquitous symbols of rebirth in Egyptian religion. Another solar symbol derived from the natural world was that of the first mound of earth to emerge from the primeval waters at creation, on which the sun-god appeared in the form of a heron, the *benu*, which later inspired the Greek concept of the phoenix. A third solar emblem is the blue lotus blossom, which closed at night to reopen again at dawn. From the New Kingdom onward the infant sun-god, as well as the king as the sun-god, could be represented emerging from an open lotus at the start of the solar cycle.

The journey of the sun-god through the heavens by day and the afterlife by night became the principal subject of royal tomb decoration in the New Kingdom, appearing in burial chambers, shrines, and mummy wrappings.[14] Like the Litany of Ra, the journey later became a feature of non-royal funerary papyri as well. Beginning in the early part of the eighteenth dynasty, when only the nocturnal journey was represented, the portrayal of the sun's travels appeared in several different versions, known collectively today as the Books of the Afterlife or Books of the Underworld. Certain fundamental aspects of the journey occur in all versions. Ra travels in a boat accompanied by other deities imbued with powers to guide and protect him. In the course of his journey, he faces numerous challenges, most notably the serpent Apophis, who attempts to ground the vessel as if on a sandbank. Thus, the sun-god, and by association the king, was required to defeat dangerous forces to ensure the continuation of life. At the depths of the underworld and in the middle of the night, the most important part of the nocturnal cycle occurred when the *ba*, or mobile spirit, of the sun-god became one with Osiris, the deceased king and ruler of the afterlife, in order to be reborn.

---

[14] Hornung, *Afterlife*, 27–112.

Fig. 4. The sun-god in the form of the beetle, Khepri, from the White Chapel of Senwosret I, Thebes, dynasty 12. Photo by Denise M. Doxey.

186   *Denise M. Doxey*

THE IDEOLOGY OF KINGSHIP

The ideology of kingship and social order was inextricably linked to cosmology and solar religion.[15] On the one hand, the king was believed to be the living embodiment of Horus, the son of Osiris, and therefore the direct descendant of the Heliopolitan Ennead and the creator-god.[16] In this capacity he was responsible for protecting Egypt against the forces of chaos represented by Seth. Thus, the Horus falcon was linked to royal iconography throughout Egyptian history. At the time of Egypt's earliest kings, about 3100 BCE, the king's name was written in a stylized palace façade, known as a *serekh*, atop which sat a falcon. By the Old Kingdom, the first of the king's five formal titles was "the Horus." The king was also associated from the earliest times with Ra and was known from the late Old Kingdom onward as the "son of Ra," a phrase of such significance that it immediately preceded the king's personal name in the royal titulary.[17] Inscriptions on monuments of the New Kingdom (ca.1550–1070 BCE) and later liken the king so closely to the sun-god that the two can be seen as separate manifestations of the same entity, with the king taking corporeal form on earth for a limited time before returning to the heavens.

The divine ancestry of the king was documented in art and writing throughout Egyptian history. In the New Kingdom, the female pharaoh Hatshepsut (ca.1473–1458 BCE) justified her right to the throne with a cycle of images in her mortuary temple at Deir el-Bahri, in which the god Amen-Ra takes the form of Hatshepsut's father, the king, engendering Hatshepsut as his divine heiress, whose birth he then oversees. The sequence suggested that the king was not a mere mortal, but rather the offspring of the sun-god. A literary work of the early Middle Kingdom (ca.2061–1780 BCE) preserved in the "Westcar Papyrus" made this point even more strongly.[18] In this text, a prophet foretells the end of the fourth dynasty with a tale of the divine conception and birth of the first kings of the fifth. The sun-god in this case was said to select a non-royal woman, the wife of a solar priest, to be the mother of the next dynasty. The story is set at precisely the time that the title "son of Ra" became a standard part of the kings' titles, perhaps reflecting a historical reality in the growing importance of the solar cult.

---

[15] Frankfort, *Kingship*; Quirke, *Cult of Re*, 7–8; Shafer, ed., *Religion*, 91.
[16] Assman, *Search*, 119–23; Quirke, *Cult of Re*, 7–8; Shafer, ed., *Religion*, 93.
[17] Assman, *Search*, 118–19; Quirke, *Religion*, 21.
[18] Berlin Papyrus, 3033.

The semi-divine position of the king formed the basis of Egypt's social hierarchy. In Egyptian thought, the king functioned as the direct and only intermediary between humankind and the gods. In this capacity, he sustained and appeased the gods with offerings, in exchange for which they made it possible for him to maintain world order.[19] In temple decoration, the king appeared as the quintessential high priest. He was the ultimate judge, responsible for maintaining order, or *maat*, throughout the realm. Activities such as dedicating temples, waging wars, and organizing trading missions all were perceived as acts of devotion to the gods. Foreigners were included among the potentially chaotic forces that needed to be subdued to maintain order and divine good will. A series of songs in honor of king Senwosret III (ca.1878–1841 BCE), preserved on papyri from the town of Illahun, exemplify these principles.[20] The first hymn recalls Senwosret's military prowess, crediting him with "overwhelming the foreign lands with your crown." The next is more all-encompassing, describing Senwosret's deeds in satisfying the gods, the Egyptian people, deceased ancestors, the young, the elderly, and the land of Egypt itself. Another hymn likens him to Ra, calling him a dam against floods, a bastion against enemies, shade in summer, warmth in winter, and protection against storms. Some of the phrasing evokes later Jewish and Christian tradition, such as the reference to the king as the shepherd of his people, a metaphor also found in other Egyptian hymns in praise of the king.

For the rest of the Egyptian population, access to the divine world and to eternal salvation came only through service to the king or his representatives. Where the king could be said to appease the gods directly, his immediate subordinates claimed to have pleased the king, while receiving the love and beneficence of the gods only indirectly through royal favor.[21] In turn, local governors and other senior officials depicted themselves in their tombs as intermediaries between the king and the lower ranks of society, dispensing justice and collecting offerings for the royal coffers, while caring for their constituents and ensuring their survival in times of trouble.

SANCTUARIES AND FESTIVALS

The earliest identifiable remains of an Egyptian temple were discovered at Hieraconpolis, ancient Nekhen and modern Kom el-Ahmar, in southern

[19] Quirke, *Cult of Re*, 17–22.
[20] Simpson, ed., *Literature*, 301–6.
[21] Doxey, *Epithets*, 80–151.

Egypt, already an important center of worship some four centuries before Egypt's first king.[22] The complex consisted of a large parabolic-shaped court surrounded by a wattle-and-daub wall with the main temple on the south side and the entrance, along with a series of subsidiary buildings, on the north. At the center of the apse was a large pole, possibly bearing a cult statue of the local falcon-god. The temple was faced with a series of massive posts, which the excavators identified as likely precursors of the flagpoles that later stood before the pylons of Egyptian temples.

Most surviving Egyptian temples date to the later years of ancient Egyptian history, the New Kingdom through the Greco-Roman period (ca.1550 BCE–364 CE). Although it is somewhat hazardous to extrapolate backward to earlier periods, the archaeological evidence suggests a degree of continuity. The ancient Egyptian term for a temple, *hut-netjer*, translates literally as "god's house," and the name conveys accurately how the temples functioned. They were not places of public worship, and the majority of the population was restricted from entering most areas of the temple. Rather, they functioned as estates for deities or deceased kings, in which their cult statues were clothed, fed, and cared for by an entourage of priests. The most common priestly title, *hem-netjer*, translates literally as "god's servant." In addition to the temple, cult property included wharfs, agricultural land, industrial workshops, bakeries, slaughterhouses, storehouses, offices, treasuries, libraries, and other facilities that made the temples a vital component of the Egyptian economy. Massive walls protected these complexes, creating what were essentially fortified palaces for their divine inhabitants.

The preserved temples adhere to a relatively standard plan. Moving from the exterior of the temple through to the sanctuary, a visitor would proceed through a series of courtyards and rooms that rose gradually in elevation, had increasingly low ceilings, and received a decreasing amount of light as they became smaller and more contained. The innermost and least accessible part of the temple was the sanctuary. There, the god's cult statue was housed within a sealed shrine, accessible only to select priests. For the general public, access to the sacred statues took the form of frequent festivals and processions, during which the cult images were carried outside in boats, symbolically "sailing" as Ra did through the heavens (Fig. 5). Processional ways lined with sphinxes and shrines for the divine barque connected the temples to the world of the living.

[22] Wilkinson, *Temples*, 17–18; Friedman, "Ceremonial Centre," 16–35.

Fig. 5. Procession of the solar barque, from the temple of Ramesses III, Medinet Habu, dynasty 20. Photo by Denise M. Doxey.

The temples' decoration was intimately connected to the function of its various parts. The entrance was through a pylon shaped like the hieroglyph for the horizon, or *akhet*, over which the sun-god entered the world of the living on its daily course. In front of the pylon was a pair of massive flagpoles. The decoration of the pylon often incorporated the motif of the king holding Egypt's traditional enemies by the hair, his raised arm holding a mace and poised to strike them (Fig. 6). It has been suggested that this violent image was intended magically to ward off potential threats to the temple.[23] From at least the New Kingdom obelisks and colossal royal statues stood before the pylons, commemorating important events in the kings' reigns. Immediately within the pylon was a colonnaded courtyard, probably the only area of the temple accessible to the general public. The decoration of the court often incorporated the hieroglyph for "common person," a lapwing bird with human arms raised in supplication.[24] Statues of kings and non-royal officials crowded the outer courtyards and were believed to function as intermediaries between the living and divine

[23] Derchain, "Réflexions," 18.
[24] Wilkinson, *Temples*, 62–3.

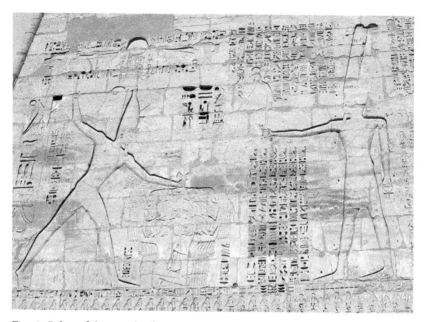

Fig. 6. Pylon of the temple of Ramesses III, Medinet Habu, dynasty 20, showing the king smiting foreign enemies. Photo by Denise M. Doxey.

realms. In exchange for prayers and offerings to the statues, worshippers could hope for intervention with the temples' resident god or goddess. Beyond the courtyard was a roofed hypostyle hall featuring closely spaced columns around a central processional way. The floral motifs of the capitals and bases of the columns evoked the fertile vegetation of the primordial marshes of creation.

A series of doorways varying in number depending on the size of the temple led through the central axis of the temple to the sanctuary that housed the cult image. The door lintels were decorated with the motif of a winged solar disk, and ceilings often bore patterns of stars to evoke the heavens. The walls of these rooms, as well as the preceding courtyards, showed the king making offerings to the resident deity in his role as high priest. Such scenes have enabled scholars to re-create the daily cult ritual that formed the basis of temple activity. The most complete pictorial account of temple ritual survives in the temple of Seti I (ca.1294–1279 BCE) at Abydos.[25] In the morning and again in the evening, a priest would enter the sanctuary, open the shrine, purify the air with incense, recite prayers

---

[25] David, *Ritual*, 289; Sauneron, *Priests*, 75–109; Shafer, ed., *Temples*, 18–27.

Egyptian Religion 191

and present offerings. He would then remove the cult statue from the shrine and wash, anoint, and dress it. When the statue was suitably attired, he offered a specifically prepared meal of food and beer. Once the god was perceived as satisfied, the meal was removed and distributed among the temple personnel. The statue was resealed in its shrine and the footsteps of the priests swept away. The elite priests who performed these ceremonies were considered highly privileged, boasting in their autobiographies to have seen the face of the god.[26]

Before the New Kingdom, Egypt lacked a dedicated, full-time priesthood, with otherwise secular officials serving as priests on a rotating basis. Only from the eighteenth dynasty was there a priestly class made up of men whose roles were in part hereditary. At all periods, priests were required during their active service to observe strict standards of purity, including bathing twice daily, shaving off their hair, being anointed with sacred oils, abstaining from sex, eating prescribed food, and washing their mouths with natron.[27] Although important changes occurred over time, several priestly roles and titles can be identified.[28] In general the term *hem-netjer*, or "god's servant," designated an upper category of priests allowed to enter the sanctuary and perform the daily ritual. A lower rank known as *wab* priests, or "pure priests," carried out lesser temple duties and did not enter the sanctuary itself. Specialists also existed. The *kheri-hebet*, or lector priests, for example, were literate and trained in sacred texts, making them among the most elite of practitioners. Once the priesthood became a full-time position, high priests were at least nominally appointed by the king and often wielded considerable political and economic power. The temple personnel also included women who served as priestesses, musicians, and singers.[29] For most of Egyptian history, they played primarily a supportive role.

An exception is the title of "god's wife," first held by Ahmose Nefertari, the wife of king Ahmose, the founder of the eighteenth dynasty (1550–1525 BCE), which, based on scenes depicting temple ritual, appears to refer to actual priestly duties. "God's Wives of Amun" came to have significant religious and political importance during the twentieth dynasty (1186–1070 BCE), when centralized royal authority weakened and eventually collapsed, leaving southern Egypt under the control of the High Priests of Amun at Thebes.[30] The title was bestowed on the king's daughter, who

---

[26] Doxey, *Epithets*, 104–9.
[27] Sauneron, *Priests*, 35–43.
[28] Ibid., 51–74; Shafer, *Temples*, 9–17; Wilkinson, *Temples*, 90–4.
[29] Robins, *Women*, 142–9.
[30] Ibid., 149–56.

resided at Thebes and passed the office through "adoption" to the daughter of his successor in order to legitimize his claim to the throne. Both the conquering Kushite rulers of the twenty-fifth dynasty (760–664 BCE) and the native Egyptian kings of the twenty-sixth dynasty (664–525 BCE) who replaced them justified their rule by having their daughters "adopted" by the presiding God's Wife. Although male officials actually administered the Theban government, preserved records indicate that the estates and endowments of the God's Wives rivaled those of the kings.

Numerous festivals punctuated the Egyptian calendar, including several extended holidays of national importance. Two of the best-documented festivals took place at Thebes and involved the procession of Amen-Ra's cult statue from the great temple at Karnak.[31] The "Beautiful Festival of the Valley" took place at the beginning of the summer harvest season, from at least the early Middle Kingdom (ca.2040 BCE). Statues of Amen, his consort Mut, and their son Khonsu were carried from their temples in the sprawling complex on the east bank of the Nile, ferried across to the west bank, the site of the Theban cemeteries, and taken to visit royal mortuary temples and other sacred sites. During the festival, families visited their dead relatives and held meals in the courtyards of their tombs. During the Opet festival, which can be securely documented only from the eighteenth dynasty on, Amen-Ra's cult image again traveled from the Karnak temple, this time to the temple of the royal life force, or *ka*, at Luxor, located on the east bank south of Karnak.[32] Taking place over the course of several weeks during the inundation season, the Opet was the most important Theban holiday, aimed at re-invigorating both Amen-Ra and the king. Festival processions in which sacred statues traveled from one temple to another are also attested at other sites, including the sanctuaries of Horus at Edfu and Hathor at Dendera.

Among Egypt's most important cult centers was Abydos, the burial place of Egypt's earliest kings and the location of important early dynastic temples. By the time of the Old Kingdom it was the site of a temple to the canine funerary god Khentiamentiu, "Foremost of the Westerners," who was later assimilated with Egypt's principal funerary god, Osiris. The early Middle Kingdom (ca.2060–1926 BCE) witnessed a major renovation of the sanctuary, after which it took on nationwide importance. The tomb of the first dynasty king Djer was identified as the burial place of Osiris and became the focal point of festivals that continued for the rest of ancient

[31] Wilkinson, *Temples*, 95–8.
[32] Shafer, *Temples*, 157–79.

Egyptian history. The festival of Osiris, culminating in a procession from the temple of Osiris Khentiamentiu to the "tomb of Osiris," drew pilgrims from throughout Egypt. The vast cemeteries west of the city became popular burial places not only for the local population but also for officials and dignitaries from other cities. Wealthy visitors who came to Abydos on business or as pilgrims commissioned small shrines and stelae along the processional way. Kings built temples along a stretch of desert between the city and its vast cemetery fields. At least two of them, Senwosret III of the late twelfth dynasty (ca.1878–1841 BCE) and Ahmose, founder of the eighteenth dynasty (ca.1550–1525 BCE), built mortuary complexes in southern Abydos. The temples of nineteenth-dynasty kings Seti I (ca.1294–1279 BCE) and Ramesses II (ca.1279–1213 BCE), along with Seti's Osireion, or ceremonial tomb of Osiris, are among the best-preserved monuments at the site.

A stela dedicated at Abydos by the late Middle Kingdom official Ikhernofret contains one of the few preserved contemporary accounts of an ancient Egyptian festival.[33] Sent by Senwosret III to refurbish Osiris's cult statue, Ikhernofret participated in the ceremony, leading the procession. According to his description, the day's activities included, in addition to visiting the site believed to be Osiris's burial place, a mock battle between Osiris and Seth. Centuries later, a similar reenactment, featuring Horus and Seth, appeared in the Ptolemaic temple of Horus at Edfu.

THE AMARNA PERIOD

Solar religion increased in significance throughout the eighteenth dynasty, but during the reign of Amenhotep IV/Akhenaten (ca.1352–1336 BCE) both it and the cult of divine kingship were advanced to unprecedented levels. Acceding to the throne as Amenhotep IV, the king initially emphasized traditional manifestations of the sun. Shortly thereafter, however, he changed his name to Akhenaten ("One who is effective for the Aten"), rejecting anthropomorphic and zoomorphic representations of deities and allowing only images of the solar disk, or Aten. His sole concession to anthropomorphism was in relief representation, where the Aten's rays ended in hands, enabling it to bestow benefits on the king and his queen, Nefertiti. Like the king and unlike Egypt's traditional gods, the Aten had multiple names written in cartouches, signifying his close association with kingship. The fact that the Aten was a visible, functioning part of the world of the living, rather than an abstract, invisible deity, makes Akhenaten's version

---

[33] Lichtheim, *Literature*, 1:123–5.

194   *Denise M. Doxey*

of monotheism significantly different from that of modern religions such as Judaism, Christianity, and Islam.[34]

Akenaten's zealotry for his new religion led him to build a new capital on a previously unoccupied site in Middle Egypt, which he named Akhetaten, "Horizon of the Aten." Its modern name, Amarna, has become the moniker of Akhenaten's era and its revolutionary beliefs. The boundary stelae surrounding the site assert that it was chosen specifically because no other cult could lay claim to it. Elsewhere, the traditional gods, in particular the state god Amen of Thebes, were abandoned and their images and monuments destroyed. Egypt's great sanctuaries fell into disrepair, and their associated festivals were abruptly halted.

Evidence for Akhenaten's beliefs derives mainly from the tombs of his officials in the cliffs near Akhetaten. Here traditional tomb decoration was replaced by scenes of the royal family traveling around the capital, worshipping in the city's temples, celebrating feasts, and bestowing honors on their supporters, all under the protective watch of the Aten. It is as though the king himself replaced the sun-god as the center of funerary iconography. Several tombs also included versions of the superbly poetic "Great Hymns to the Aten," among the most important works of Egyptian literature and our best source for understanding Akhenaten's new religion.[35] Certain aspects of the hymns, like earlier hymns to the king, bear comparison to the Judeo-Christian Psalms. The poems focus on joy at the Aten's creation of the world and its human and animal inhabitants. At sunrise the creatures awaken and give praise, while the sun's resurrection parallels the animals' procreation of young. The hymns also describe the Aten's salient characteristics, calling him the sole deity and creator, without whom the world could not exist. He was a universal god, caring for foreigners as well as Egyptians and providing solace and happiness to all. He was a father figure, but Akhenaten was his only son. The rest of humanity continued to rely on the king for access to the divine world.

Akhenaten's religion did not long survive the king. Even during his reign, there is evidence that common people continued to worship the traditional gods, in particular household deities, to the extent possible. Figurines, amulets, and votive offerings to the apotropaic god Bes and the fertility goddess Taweret, as well as Thoth and even Amen, have been found in the workmen's village at Amarna. The failure of Atenism may have more to do with what was missing from its beliefs and practices than what was

[34] Dunand and Zivie-Coche, *Gods and Men*, 35.
[35] Freed et al., *Pharaohs of the Sun*, 99–105.

Egyptian Religion

expressed. Although the king had always held a central place in Egyptians' interaction with their gods, the significance of Akhenaten's own personality to the religion made it almost impossible for a successor to fill his role. Amarna religion also failed to address the everyday dangers against which traditional religion offered protection in the form of spells and amulets. Finally, and most significantly, Atenism completely failed to address the afterlife. Life after death was said to be eternal, but neither the decoration of tombs nor the accompanying hymns offered an adequate explanation of the form it would take, focusing instead on earthly existence.

PERSONAL RELIGION AND DOMESTIC CULTS

As with all pre-industrial societies, life in pharaonic Egypt was precarious and often short. To combat life's many dangers the Egyptians relied on what was known to them as *heka*, and would today be considered magic. *Heka* had no inherent negative connotations and could be used for both good and evil, depending upon the user. From the dawn of Egyptian history, amulets and other implements were called upon to facilitate prowess in hunting, to ward off enemies, and to promote strength, fertility, and even love. Eventually, they would assist in guiding the deceased to the afterlife.

The ancient Egyptians perceived each person as composed of a number of parts, including the body itself, the heart, the name, the shadow, the *ka*, and the *ba*.[36] The heart was the center of intellect and personality. The name was an essential component of survival both in life and after death, and its destruction meant the destruction of the individual. The *ka*, present in texts from the Old Kingdom onward, was a potent life force present at birth and after death, which needed continual sustenance in the form of food and offerings. In art, the *ka* was shown as a sort of twin (Fig. 7). The *ba*, also attested from the Old Kingdom on, embodied the ability to move around and manifest oneself in the world. By the New Kingdom, it was portrayed as a human-headed bird that moved back and forth between the tomb and the world of the living. The *bas* of the deceased were believed to be capable of affecting the living. It was therefore necessary to appease them on an ongoing basis. A significant part of Egyptian funerary cult involved nurturing the *ba* and *ka*.

Pregnancy, childbirth, and infancy were especially dangerous, and the Egyptians elicited the aid of various deities during these times. Foremost

---

[36] Quirke, *Religion*, 105–12.

Fig. 7. Senwosret I and his *ka*, from the White Chapel of Senwosret I, Thebes, dynasty 12. Photo by Denise M. Doxey.

among them were the goddess Taweret and the god Bes. Both of these composite creatures – Taweret had the body of a pregnant hippopotamus and the tail of a crocodile, and Bes was a dwarf with a lion's mane and serpentine tongue – were fearsome in appearance but benevolent in averting dangers to mothers and babies. In the Middle Kingdom, they appeared among other apotropaic creatures on ivory wands used to draw protective boundaries around the beds of expectant mothers. Later their images adorned beds and headrests. Other deities associated with childbirth included the god Khnum, who formed individuals on his potter's wheel,

Egyptian Religion 197

the frog-goddess of fertility Heqet, the personified birth brick Meskhenet, and the serpent-goddess Renenutet. Many of these gods and goddesses would also be called upon again to assist with rebirth in the afterlife.

The treatment of injuries and illnesses involved what would today be considered a combination of medicine and magic.[37] Medico-magical papyri describe three categories of care. The term *shesau* included diagnosis and prognosis. Prescriptions and recipes for medications were known as *pekheret*. Finally and of equal importance were the *ruu*, spells and incantations that accompanied the *pekheret*. Magical and medical practitioners were one and the same, being equipped with wands, amulets, and spells as well as medicinal plants and surgical tools. During the Late Period (760–332 BCE) the infant god Horus, with or without his mother Isis, was particularly associated with healing.

FUNERARY BELIEFS AND PRACTICES

Due to the nature of Egyptian burial practices and the relatively good state of cemetery preservation, funerary religion is among the best-studied aspects of Egyptian religion. The earliest known burials already demonstrated a belief in an afterlife. Predynastic (3950–2960 BCE) bodies were placed in pit graves, in a fetal position and wrapped in animal skins or matting, where the dry sand naturally mummified them. The accompanying grave goods were small and portable, including pottery, figurines, jewelry, amulets, and cosmetic equipment. Without texts, their underlying significance remains uncertain, but some of Egypt's later beliefs appear already to have been forming. Figurines, notably ivory tags in the form of bearded men and bird-faced pottery figurines with upraised arms, have been interpreted as gods and goddesses.[38] Amulets of cattle, falcons, and other animals may already have been linked to specific deities. Scenes reminiscent of later tomb decoration, such as ships and hippopotamus hunts, decorated pottery made specifically for burials, and early boat models hinted at the later significance of ships as transportation to the afterlife. The earliest decorated tomb, of the Naqada II period (ca.3650–3300 BCE), was discovered at Hieraconpolis.[39] Tomb 100 was a rectangular mud-brick structure, one wall of which bore a scene of boats sailing through a desert landscape, surrounded by humans and animals engaged in activities suggesting both

---

[37] Ibid., 111–12.
[38] Wilkinson, *Gods and Goddesses*, 15.
[39] Quibell and Green, *Hieracopolis*, pls. 75–9; Hoffman, *Egypt*, 132–3.

ritual and warfare. One group included the earliest known depiction of the king smiting foreigners, later one of Egypt's most ubiquitous portrayals of royal authority. Another figure, the "Master of Animals," may reflect contact with western Asia.

Early Dynastic kings built the first monumental royal tombs (ca.2960–2649 BCE), multi-chambered subterranean structures of mud brick topped by increasingly large superstructures.[40] Enormous mud-brick enclosures, evidently destroyed shortly after the burial, stood closer to the cultivated land and must have served the royal cults.[41] Grave goods became far more numerous and varied, and courtiers, servants, and animals were interred by the hundreds around the tombs and mortuary structures, a practice that did not outlast the second dynasty. A fleet of full-sized boats buried alongside the mortuary enclosure of the second dynasty king Khasekhemwy (ca.2676–2649 BCE) but now believed to belong with an earlier, dynasty 1 enclosure were evidently intended to ferry the king to the afterlife.

Although the architecture of tombs changed over time, the fundamental elements would remain in place for much of Egypt's history: a subterranean or otherwise hidden burial place and a memorial temple. Still, the transition from the Early Dynastic Period to the Old Kingdom brought changes in funerary practices reflecting what must have been substantial underlying developments in religious beliefs. With the advent of wooden coffins, the need to preserve the body led to the practice of mummification. Beginning with the third dynasty tomb of Djoser at Saqqara (ca.2630–2611 BCE), stone pyramids became the norm for royal tombs (Fig. 8). Typical mortuary complexes consisted of a temple at the base of the pyramid and another close to the edge of the cultivated and inhabited land, connected by a causeway. Although the temples were decorated and housed statuary to support the memorial cults, the hidden burial chambers remained unadorned until the reign of the fifth dynasty king Unas (ca.2353–2323 BCE), when the world's oldest preserved religious texts, the Pyramid Texts, were introduced. The texts contained a combination of spells against earthly dangers such as snakebites, and guides for navigating the route to the afterlife. The deceased king was for the first time identified with Osiris, while also being said to become one with Ra in the heavens.

The tombs of officials and royal family members typically clustered around the royal pyramids, although by the late Old Kingdom provincial governors were usually buried in their home cemeteries. Non-royal, elite

---

[40] Wilkinson, *Early Dynastic Egypt*, 230–42.
[41] O'Connor, "Boat Graves," 5–17.

Fig. 8. Step pyramid complex of Djoser at Saqqara, dynasty 3. Photo by Denise M. Doxey.

tombs took two basic forms. Cemeteries in the low desert had subterranean burial shafts, with bench-shaped mud-brick or stone superstructures known today as *mastabas* (Fig. 9). Although their decoration was initially limited to a single stele, the chapels became increasingly complex and elaborately decorated. Where the valley was narrower, the chapels were cut into cliffs, with chapels above ground and descending burial shafts below. Until the late New Kingdom, most of their decoration – scenes of agriculture, crafts, and hunting – was devoted to furnishing provisions for the *ka* and the burial. The accompanying texts consisted of offering formulas and biographical texts justifying the maintenance of the cult. The focal point of worship was the "false door," through which the *ka* was believed to pass to and from the afterlife. In front of this nonfunctional representation of a doorway, survivors left not only offerings but also messages for the dead requesting assistance with problems or intercession with the gods in the afterlife. Statues served as temporary repositories for the *ka* and intermediaries between earth and the afterlife.

The tombs' essential features continued into the Middle Kingdom, but burial furnishings reveal significant changes in funerary beliefs. Most notable

Fig. 9. Mastaba complex of the Senedjemib family, Giza, dynasty 5. Photo by Denise M. Doxey.

was a marked increase in the importance of Osiris, who replaced Anubis as Egypt's principal funerary deity, a development also reflected in the rise of Abydos as a cult center. For the first time, non-royal people were designated "the Osiris," demonstrating their potential to become one with the god after death. The interiors of certain elite, but non-royal coffins now bore inscriptions, known today as Coffin Texts, derived from the Pyramid Texts and providing the spells necessary for reaching the afterlife. Accompanying them on some coffins was the Book of Two Ways, a schematic map illuminating the routes to the *Duat*. Other burial goods paralleled features of the offering chapel, including wooden models depicting houses, boats, animal husbandry, and other activities related to equipping the tomb. Magical implements such as figurines of hippopotami and ivory wands illustrated with apotropaic creatures suggest a new interest in warding off dangerous beings or harnessing their powers for self-protection. In the late Middle Kingdom came the first of the funerary "servants" known as *ushabtis*, figurines intended to labor on behalf of the deceased in the afterlife.

Although non-royal tombs remained largely unchanged into the early New Kingdom, royal tombs were now constructed in the Valley of the Kings west of Thebes, with mortuary temples located alongside the cultivated land. Royal tomb decoration featured new funerary texts and scenes, in which Osiris featured most prominently, but Ra continued to play a prominent role as well. The Litany of Ra appeared for the first time, and early-eighteenth-dynasty burial chambers featured scenes from the *Amduat*, literally "what is in the afterlife," which traced the nightly journey of the sun-god, during which he ultimately united with Osiris prior to being reborn in the morning. The *Amduat* derived from the Middle Kingdom Book of Two Ways. Probably because the *Amduat* was copied from an original text on papyrus, the figures and their accompanying texts are executed schematically in black and red outline, as if an enormous scroll were spread around the walls of the burial chamber. The Coffin Texts at this time developed into the Book of Going Forth by Day in the Afterlife, better known today as the Book of the Dead, which culminated in the scene of judgment, in which the deceased were required to defend their actions in life while their hearts were weighed against a feather symbolizing *maat*. Now written on papyrus or burial shrouds, the texts gradually became available to an increasingly wide segment of the population.

The Amarna interlude brought about a transformation in Egyptian funerary religion. Following the return to the traditional religion, non-royal tomb decoration focused on the funeral and afterlife and for the first time showed the deceased interacting directly with gods. Royal tombs introduced variants on the *Amduat*, including the Book of Gates and Books of Heaven and Earth, which included not only the solar journey but also scenes of retribution against the damned. The images no longer copied papyrus, but were now vividly colored. The solar aspects of funerary religion manifested themselves on the ceilings of burial chambers with elaborate renderings of the sky.

The later years of ancient Egyptian history witnessed an increased blurring of the distinction between royal and non-royal funerary practices. Elaborately decorated anthropoid coffins bore imagery associated with divine judgment, the protective goddesses Isis and Nephthys, the myth of Osiris, winged scarabs, and scenes of resurrection. Books of the afterlife remained popular on both papyrus and burial wrappings. Traditional Egyptian burial practices continued alongside their Greco-Roman counterparts, and mummification survived even into the early days of Christianity.[42]

---

[42] Dunand and Lichtenberg, *Mummies*, 123–8.

MORALITY IN ANCIENT EGYPT

Like most cultures, the Egyptians believed that entrance to an eternal afterlife required moral behavior while alive. Evidence for Egyptian moral values derives from biographical texts, instructional literature, and, to a lesser degree, the "negative confessions" included in funerary texts. The behavior of literary characters offers further insight. Instructions for living, which have been closely linked to texts such as the biblical Proverbs, began to be written down in the Old Kingdom and continued throughout Egyptian history. Phrased as rules from fathers to sons or teachers to students, "wisdom literature" encouraged readers to behave in the interest of public good, to respect parents and the elderly, honor the king, care for the poor, and display modesty, humility, and generosity.[43] Autobiographies in tombs and on votive stelae claim that officials appeased the gods, pleased the king, and saw to the welfare of their families and communities.[44] They applauded careful speech, obedience, knowledge of one's responsibilities and, increasingly, personal piety. The judgment scenes in the Book of the Dead included a series of "negative confessions," in which the deceased argued that they have done nothing contrary to *maat*, including both committing what would today be considered sinful acts and engaging in unnatural actions such as eating excrement and walking upside down.

SUMMARY

Egyptian religion reflected a close connection to the natural world, knowledge of the needs of the community, and an adherence to one's place in a hierarchy including the gods, the king, the family, peers, and dependents. The landscape of Egypt was a critical influence, centering on the Nile with its regular, replenishing floods, the daily rising and setting of the sun, moon, and stars, and the potentially threatening desert beyond. Maintenance of a balanced world order required constant vigilance, especially on the part of the king. For most of its history, Egypt's great gods remained distant from most of the population, but both household deities and the spirits of the deceased were invoked for assistance and protection. Festivals brought the human and divine worlds together at regular intervals. Surviving the transition to the afterlife involved the preservation of the body and the sustenance of the many aspects of the

---

[43] Lichtheim, *Moral Values*, 77–89.
[44] Lichtheim, *Autobiographies*, 129–35; Doxey, *Epithets*, 224–9.

spirit, as well as moral behavior toward the living and piety toward the gods. The tomb served as an interface between the worlds of the living and dead, who ideally would continue to interact to their mutual benefit in perpetuity.

BIBLIOGRAPHY

Allen, James. *Genesis in Egypt: The Philosophy of Ancient Egyptian Creation Accounts* (New Haven, 1988).
The Ancient Egyptian Pyramid Texts (Atlanta, 2005).
Assmann, Jan. *Der König als Sonnenpriester* (Glückstadt, 1970).
Solar Religion in the New Kingdom: Re, Amun, and the Crisis of Polytheism (London, 1995).
The Search for God in Ancient Egypt, trans. David Lorton (Ithaca, 2001).
David, A. R. *Religious Ritual at Abydos (c. 1300 BC)* (Warminester, U.K., 1973).
Derchin, Philippe. "Réflexions sur la decoration des pylones." *Bulletin de la Société Française d'Égyptologie* 46 (1966): 17–24.
Doxey, Denise. *Egyptian Non-Royal Epithets in the Middle Kingdom: A Social and Historical Analysis* (Leiden, 1998).
Dunand, Françoise, and Roger Lichtenberg. *Mummies and Death in Ancient Egypt*, trans. David Lorton (Ithaca, 2006).
Dunand, Françoise, and Christiane Zivie-Coche. *Gods and Men in Ancient Egypt, 3000 BCE to 395 CE* (Ithaca, 2004).
Frankfort, Henri. *Kingship and the Gods* (Chicago, 1948).
Freed, Rita, Yvonne Markowitz, and Sue D'Auria, eds. *Pharaohs of the Sun: Akhenaten, Nefertiti, Tutankhamen* (Boston, 1999).
Friedman, Renée. "The Ceremonial Centre at Hieracopolis Locality HK29A." In *Conceptions of God in Ancient Egypt: The One and the Many*, ed. Erik Horning, trans. John Baines (Ithaca, 1982).
Hoffman, Michael A. *Egypt before the Pharaohs* (New York, 1990).
Hornung, Erik. *Conceptions of God in Ancient Egypt. The One and the Many* (Ithaca, 1982).
The Ancient Egyptian Books of the Afterlife (Ithaca, 1999).
Lichtheim, Miriam. *Ancient Egyptian Literature*, vols. 1–3 (Los Angeles, 1975–1980).
Ancient Egyptian Autobiographies chiefly of the Middle Kingdom (Göttingen, 1988).
Moral Values in Ancient Egypt (Göttingen, 1997).
O'Connor, David. "Boat Graves and Pyramid Origins." *Expedition* 33 (1991): 5–17.
Quibel, J. E., and F. W. Green. *Hieraconpolis II* (London, 1902).
Quirke, Stephen. *Ancient Egyptian Religion* (London, 1992).
The Cult of Re: Sun-Worship in Ancient Egypt (New York, 2001).
Robins, Gay. *Women in Ancient Egypt* (Cambridge, 1993).
Sauneron, Serge. *The Priests of Ancient Egypt*, trans. David Lorton (Ithaca, 2000).
Shafer, Byron, ed. *Religion in Ancient Egypt: Gods, Myths and Personal Practice* (Ithaca, 1991).
Temples of Ancient Egypt (Ithaca, 1997).
Simpson, William K., ed. *Religion and Philosophy in Ancient Egypt* (New Haven, 1989).

The Literature of Ancient Egypt (New Haven, 2003).

Spencer, A. J., ed. *Aspects of Early Egypt* (London, 1996).

Wilkinson, Richard H. *The Complete Temples of Ancient Egypt* (New York, 2000).
The Complete Gods and Goddesses of Ancient Egypt (London, 2003).

Wilkinson, Toby A. H. *Early Dynastic Egypt* (London, 1999).

Winlock, Herbert E. *The Temple at Deir el-Bahri* (London, 1894–1908).

8

PHOENICIAN-PUNIC RELIGION

PHILIP C. SCHMITZ

The term "religion" is oversupplied with meaning.[1] There is no corresponding universal cultural taxon. The inefficiency of cultural recurrence is problematic for *meme* theories of cultural and religious evolution,[2] despite the notion's attractive fit with evolutionary biology.[3] Reducing religion to intergroup competition – "a space in which competing sets of social interests meet"[4] – postpones the question of definition indefinitely. A useful taxonomy of religion may be possible, and seems necessary, but is beyond the scope of the present undertaking. Rather than delineate a subspecies "Punic religion," the following discussion will depend on traditional categories of religious behaviors: sacrifice, offerings, prayer, purity regulations, cultic sites, cultic personnel, festivals, and funerary practices.[5]

The word "Phoenician" derives from *phoinikes*, which Homer (*Il.* 23.744; *Od.* 13.272; 14.288; 15.415, 419, 473) and later Greek writers used to designate foreign traders from the Levant. The Greek word entered Latin as *Poeni*, "Punic" being derived from the Latin adjective *Punicus.* Thus both the Greek and Latin terms label the same group. English uses "Phoenician" to refer to the East and "Punic" for the West, particularly in reference to language. The Phoenician language developed new features in the West, warranting the distinct label Punic. With respect to the practice of religion there are fewer contrasts between East and West, weakening the rationale for distinct labels. Religious practice within the Phoenician and Punic city-states remained largely a matter of local custom.[6]

---

[1] For the Punic sites, see Map 3 in Chapter 5, Map 4 in Chapter 6, Map 5 in the current chapter, and Map 6 in Chapter 9.
[2] Sperber, "Objection," 163–73; Atran, *In Gods We Trust*, 17.
[3] Dennet, *Breaking the Spell*, 379–86.
[4] McCutcheon, *Religion and the Domestication*, 4.
[5] Capps, *Religious Studies*, 1–52; Masuzawa, *Invention*, 12–13.
[6] Bonnet and Xella, "La religion," 316–17.

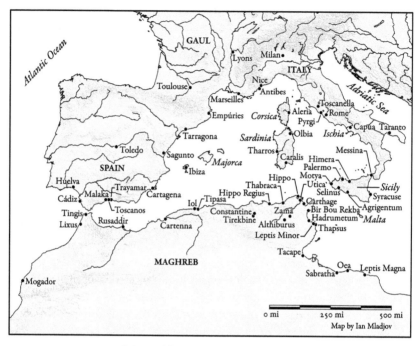

Map 5. The western Mediterranean.

HISTORY OF THE PHOENICIANS

Phoenician-Punic presence in the western Mediterranean lasted from the ninth century BCE until the fifth or sixth century CE. From the perspective of world history, the Phoenicians built a trade diaspora,[7] perhaps initiated in response to external stimuli,[8] but rapidly taking new form through state-directed market development.[9] Whatever its initial conditions,[10] the Phoenician expansion created settlements in the western Mediterranean along the North African coast, on the islands of Ischia (Pithecoussai), Sicily, and Sardinia, and along the Mediterranean and Atlantic coasts of the Iberian peninsula.[11] Phoenician and Punic settlements on the Atlantic coast of Africa ranged from Tingis (Tangier) in the north to Mogador (founded from Gadir, modern Cadiz) in the south. Over such a broad geographic expanse, the homogenous elements of Phoenician and later Punic

[7] Cohen, *Global Diasporas*, 83.
[8] Frankenstein, "The Phoenicians in the Far West"; idem, *Arqueología del colonialismo*, 15–64.
[9] Aubet, *Phoenicians and the West*, 142–3.
[10] Boardman, "Early Euboean Settlements," 195–200.
[11] Lipiński, *Itineraria Phoenicia*, 337–434.

settlements maintained a significant degree of linguistic, cultural, and religious similarity. From the selection of settlement sites to the construction of walls, in pottery manufacture and metallurgy, in the script styles of their documents, and in the burial of their dead, Phoenician-Punic civilization replicated and adapted models and life patterns that originated in the Canaanite coastal region of western Asia.

The period from the beginning of Phoenician colonization to the end of the Pyrrhic war (275 BCE) was the age of the ascent of Carthage. Carthage flourished in a time of significant change. World population tripled from 1000 to 200 BCE, and the geographic extent of political empires grew by a factor of fifteen; the number of cities with populations greater than thirty thousand more than doubled. The density of world trade expanded, not least because of Phoenician efforts. Paradigmatically, while growing complexity benefited Carthaginian elites, maladaptive forces eventually checked growth, leading to stasis and decline.[12]

With an estimated area of 25 to 60 ha,[13] and six known cemeteries, in which (a mere) three thousand burials have been excavated,[14] Carthage was a large city. A conservative estimate of the Carthaginian population in 146 BCE, the time of its Roman destruction, would be 200,000.[15] Carthage probably accounted for 30 to 40 percent of the western Phoenician population, distributed in about fifty major Phoenician and Punic settlements in the western Mediterranean islands, Iberia, and North Africa. Individual settlements varied considerably. Toscanos, a Phoenician settlement on the Andalusian coast of Spain, had a walled area no greater than 15 ha, with a population estimated at fifteen hundred.[16] Nearby Malaka (modern Málaga), a Punic foundation of the early sixth century BCE, rapidly became a major port and population center despite its nearly identical size.[17] On the African coast, Tipasa, about 60 km west of Algiers, with an area less than 10 ha, possessed two large cemeteries and a child cemetery.[18] Iberian trade centers on the Atlantic, such as Gadir, Doña Blanca, and Huelva, and Mediterranean settlements on the Andalusian coast, such as Trayamar, held affluent nuclei of Phoenician merchants.[19] Phoenician

---

[12] Sanderson, *Social Transformations*, 117–33.
[13] Niemeyer, "Early Phoenician City-States," 104.
[14] Benichou-Safar, *Les tombes puniques*, 13–60.
[15] Fantar, *Carthage*, 1:176–7.
[16] Niemeyer, "Phoenicians in the Mediterranean," 484.
[17] Aubet, "From Trading Post to Town," 58.
[18] Lancel, *Carthage*, 95–9.
[19] Aubet, *Phoenicians and the West*, 336.

208 *Philip C. Schmitz*

settlement began at Lixus on the Atlantic coast of Africa early in the eighth century BCE.[20]

Moscati[21] located the transition from a Phoenician or colonial horizon to a Punic or Carthaginian horizon in the decade between 545 and 535 BCE. Carthaginian ascendancy fostered growing imperialism enforced by a powerful navy and a mercenary army.[22] The defeat of Punic forces at Himera in Sicily in 480 BCE checked the advance for a generation while Carthage occupied itself with plans and preparation for a second massive assault.[23] The Sicilian campaign of 409 BCE destroyed Selinunte and Himera, and in 406 BCE the Carthaginian forces successfully sacked Agrigentum after a siege.[24] Soon, however, plague felled the mercenaries and storms wrecked the fleet. The young general Himilco took his own life.[25] By 301, Agathocles was able to invade Africa and wreak havoc in Carthaginian territory. The following quarter century brought Carthage into alliance with Rome in Sicily, then to fatal war with Rome. In other North African sites, Punic culture would survive, and the Punic language would continue in use, until the end of the Byzantine period.

SOURCES

There are literary and epigraphic sources about Punic religion. The literary sources are mostly ancient writings, very few of them from Phoenician authors, transmitted through a scribal process for centuries. Biblical texts, for example, provide a foil against which Canaanite religious practices stand out – although sometimes in a distorted form. Greek and Latin translations of the Bible provide occasional evidence for germane interpretive practices.

Writings by classical and Hellenistic Greek authors and both pagan and Christian Latin authors are also highly significant. With respect to the Phoenicians, Movers's *Die Phönizier* (1841–56) is still consulted for its full treatment of Greek and Latin sources. Bunnens's *L'expansion phénicienne* (1979) is comprehensive, and Gsell's *Histoire ancienne de l'Afrique du Nord* (1920–24) was long a standard reference. *Fonti classiche* (edited by Mazza, Ribichini, and Xella) anthologizes nearly every relevant passage in Greek literature.

[20] Aranegui, ed., *Lixus*, 94.
[21] Moscati, "Dall'età fenicia," 213.
[22] Fariselli, *I mercenari di Cartagine*, 1–400.
[23] Diodorus Siculus, 13.79–91; Bondì, "Carthage, Italy," 39–48.
[24] Diodorus Siculus, 13.79–90; Krahmalkov, "Carthaginian Report," 171–7.
[25] Diodorus Siculus, 19.3.1–2.

In Tunisia, excavations at Carthage since 1973 have reached the earliest occupation levels in the late ninth or early eighth century BCE.[26] Delattre's campaigns in the ancient Carthaginian cemeteries of Douïmès, St Louis (Byrsa), Junon, and Bordj Djedid whetted the public appetite for antiquities and inscriptions,[27] but his destructive methods foreclosed future excavations.

After finds of stelae there in 1817, the later identification of the so-called *tophet* of Carthage attracted attention chiefly because of the site's macabre association with infant sacrifice, but also because of the votive stelae and cippi unearthed there.[28] Icard directed the first excavation of the tophet in 1922,[29] and Poinssot and Lantier[30] continued the work. In 1925 Kelsey directed a season of fieldwork supported by the University of Michigan, but his death the following year led to the suspension of excavation until 1934. Lapeyre conducted two seasons in the Carthaginian tophet with significant results.[31] Pierre Cintas directed further digging from 1945 to 1950. A later American excavation refined the pottery chronology of the tophet and established a continuous stratigraphy.[32] The Carthage tophet has yielded the preponderance of Punic inscriptions (just under six thousand, or 97 percent of the extant epigraphic corpus of Phoenician and Punic). Most of the inscribed cippi and votive stelae now find shelter in the Bardo Museum in Tunis or in the Carthage Museum.

Archival documents that survive only as cited in literary texts are a significant category of sources for all aspects of Phoenician and Punic history. Several Greek histories of the Phoenicians once existed. Josephus cited a work by the enigmatic Mochus (*FGrH*, 87 F67; 784 F6), a Phoenician history by Philostratus (Josephus *A.J.* 10.228; *C. Ap.* 1.143–4; *FGrH*, 789 F1a–b), and the Tyrian king list compiled by the Hellenistic historian Menander of Ephesus (*C. Ap.* 1.116–19, 121–5, 156–8; Josephus *A.J.* 8.144–9, 324; 9.284–7). Herennius Philo of Byblos (fl. 100 CE) translated into Greek a much older Phoenician history by Sanchuniathon. Eusebius cited portions of this history in his *Praeparatio evangelica.*[33]

During the Second Punic War, Hannibal concluded a treaty with Philip V of Macedonia (Polybius 7.9). The unusual features of the Greek text of

---

[26] Lancel, *Carthage*, 38–46; Aubet, *Phoenicians and the West*, 218–28; Docter et al., "Carthage Bir Massouda," 37–89; Niemeyer et al., eds., *Karthago*.

[27] Frend, *Archaeology of Early Christianity*, 69–72, 123–4, 183–4.

[28] Gsell, *Histoire ancienne*, 2:80–1; 4:416–17.

[29] Dussaud, "Trente-huit ex voto," 243–60.

[30] Poinssot and Lantier, "Un sanctuaire de Tanit," 32–68.

[31] Lapeyre, "Fouilles récentes à Carthage" [1935]; idem, "Les fouilles du Musée Lavigerie" [1939].

[32] Stager, "The Rite of Child Sacrifice," 1–11.

[33] See Attridge and Oden, *Philo of Byblos*, 19–21; Baumgarten, *Phoenician History*, 8–30.

210 *Philip C. Schmitz*

the treaty – especially Semitisms – indicate a Punic original. The treaty includes lists of divine witnesses:

In the presence of Zeus, Hera, and Apollo; in the presence of the Genius (Gk. *daimonos*) of Carthage, of Herakles and Iolaus; in the presence of Ares, Triton, and Poseidon; in the presence of the gods who battle for us and of the Sun, Moon, and Earth; in the presence of Rivers, Lakes, and Waters; in the presence of all the gods who possess Carthage; in the presence of all the gods who possess Macedonia and the rest of Greece; in the presence of all the gods of the army who preside over this oath. (Polyb. 7.9.2–3)

The text may witness a sort of Punic pantheon, and several scholars have attempted to establish equivalencies between Greek and Punic deities. But even Barré's equation of the Greek divine name *Diòs* with Baal Ḥamon remains inconclusive.[34] The treaty does show that in diplomacy Carthage recognized foreign pantheons (note the acknowledgment of "all the gods who occupy Macedonia and the rest of Greece," Polyb. 7.9.3).

The Roman historian Livy also recorded examples of Hannibal's religious behavior and, implicitly, Carthaginian religious attitudes. After the Punic victory at Cannae, a Punic emissary to Carthage declared it proper to express and feel gratitude to the immortal gods (Liv. 23.11.7); Hannibal left Capua with a portion of his troops to visit Lake Avernus, "with the pretext of sacrificing" (24.12.4); a clearing sky after foul weather that had prevented Hannibal from attacking Rome became "for the Carthaginians ... a solemn warning" (26.11.4); summering near the temple of Juno Lacinia to avoid a plague, Hannibal erected a Punic-Greek bilingual inscription (28.46.15–16).[35] These details tell us little about the content, structure, or organization of Punic religion at the time.

Archaeologically recovered Punic texts have been carefully studied but not exhausted as historical sources. The following section presents several examples of close readings that cast light on important cults and rituals in Punic religion and the problems they present for understanding Punic religious history.

THE CULTS OF ADONIS AND ASTARTE

Two epigraphic sources provide ambiguous evidence that the Adonis myth was influential and enduring in Phoenician-Punic religious practice. From late-sixth-century-BCE Etruria, the Phoenician-inscribed gold lamina

[34] Barré, *God-list*, 57; Bonnet, *Melqart*, 179–82.
[35] See also Ribichini and Xella, *La religione fenicia*, 40–2.

Phoenician-Punic Religion 211

discovered at Pyrgi concerns a sacrifice by the Etruscan ruler Thefarie Vel(i)unas in celebration of the Adonis festival: *byrḥ zbḥ / šmš bmt n'*, "in the month *zbḥ šmš*, at the death of (the) Handsome (one)" (*KAI* 277.4–5).[36] The Phoenician word *n'*, "Handsome (one)," signifies Adonis, a youth so handsome, says Greek myth, that Aphrodite (=Astarte) could not bear to be parted from him.[37] Phoenician *n'* is equivalent to Middle Hebrew *nā'eh*, "handsome."

The month *krr* mentioned in line 4 began with the first new moon after the summer solstice,[38] corresponding to July. The traditional date of the Adonis festival was at the predawn or heliacal rising of the star Sirius, 19 or 20 July, the beginning of the Egyptian Sothic year. The day of the ceremony is *'ym qbr 'lm*, "the god's burial day" (*KAI* 277.9).[39]

Scholars have identified the deity (Punic [Pun.] *'lm*) in the Pyrgi inscription (*KAI* 277.9) as either Adonis or Melqart, with the weight of opinion favoring Melqart.[40] It is nearly impossible to establish a clear conceptual distinction between the two deities. Lines 4–5 of the inscription as interpreted here confirm that the Pyrgi ceremony celebrated the burial of the deity known to the Greeks as Adonis.

The dedicator of the Pyrgi inscriptions, the Etruscan ruler Thefarie Vel(i)unas, also constructed a *tw*, a ritual enclosure generally translated "cella." As a further contribution to the festival, Thefarie Vel(i)unas copied or replaced a deity image: *wšnt l m'š 'lm / bbty*, "And I copied / transferred a statue of the deity in(to) her temple for her" (lines 9b–11).[41]

The reference to a sculpture of the deity brings to mind Etruscan artistic representations of Adonis, whose tragic beauty and untimely death became a significant theme in Etruscan art. Images of the lovers – Aphrodite and Adonis – decorated Etruscan mirrors. A late-fifth-century bronze mirror, for example, portrays the nude and winged youth labeled in Etruscan *Atunis* (Adonis) with the seated goddess labeled *Turan* (Aphrodite-Astarte).[42] Sculptures of the dead or dying Atunis were made in wax or terracotta to be carried in processions, at the conclusion of

---

[36] See Schmitz, "Adonis in the Phoenician Text from Pyrgi?" 9, 13.

[37] Ribichini, *Adonis*, 80–6.

[38] Koffmahn, "Sind die altisraelitischen Monatsbezeichnungen," 217; Stieglitz, "Phoenician-Punic Calendar," 695.

[39] Krahmalkov, *Phoenician-Punic Dictionary*, 424.

[40] Lipiński, "La fête d'ensevelissement," 34–46, 47–8; Ribichini, *Adonis*, 163; Bonnet, *Melqart*, 287–8; Amadasi Guzzo, *Iscrizioni fenicie*, 96; Ribichini and Xella, *La religione fenicia*, 133–5; Mettinger, *Riddle of Resurrection*, 117–37.

[41] Translation by Schmitz.

[42] Servais-Soyez, "Adonis," 224, no. 16.

which the images would be thrown into a body of water.[43] The deity image copied or transferred by Thefarie Vel(i)unas (*KAI* 277.9–11) might have been an image of *Atunis* (Adonis) and might have been later disposed of in a similar manner. Ceremonial sculptures certainly inspired the famous Hellenistic terracotta figure of the dying Atunis supine on a catafalque, found in 1834 during excavations at Toscanella, one of the masterpieces of Etruscan plastic arts.[44]

A Late Punic inscription from Althiburus (modern Henchir Medeine) in Tunisia may involve the same festival attested in the Pyrgi text. The Althiburus inscription refers to a celebration to dedicate a new addition to a temple or sanctuary (Pun. *mqdš*) in the city.[45] The text provides a rare glimpse of the social and religious networks in a provincial center. Located 175 km southeast of Carthage, Althiburus constituted, by the mid-second century BCE, the eastern boundary of the Punic *'rṣt tšk't* (*KAI* 141.1), Greek *chōra Tuscan* (*Punica* 59), Latin *pagus Thusca*, the southeastern administrative district of Carthage.[46] Althiburus absorbed considerable Carthaginian influence despite its distant location and had a tophet.[47]

The inscription, apparently from the second century CE, is complete in nine lines of Neo-Punic script (*KAI* 159).[48] The inscription commemorates a vow to the god Baal Ḥamon made in honor of eleven men, each of whose names precedes their father's name in the text (*KAI* 159.2–4). Eight of the honorees have Libyco-Berber names, two have Latin names, and one has a Punic name. The text mentions as their friends or allies (Pun. *ḥbr*) a Roman cavalry unit or *turma* (Pun. *mzrḥ* [*KAI* 159.4]). The group responsible for the inscription, denominated *'bd mlqrt*, "servants of Melqart," sponsored the restoration of a meeting place (Pun. *kns*, line 1), and constructed a cella or chamber (Pun. *tw* [*KAI* 159.5]) adjoined to a local temple or sanctuary (Pun. *mqdš* [*KAI* 159.5, 8]). In the month *krr* (*KAI* 159.5; see above), that is, July, a nocturnal sacrifice (Pun. *zbḥ* [*KAI* 159.5]) took place. The last two lines of the inscription (*KAI* 159.8–9) are only partly legible, but appear to refer to types of sacrifices. There is mention of "holocausts" (Pun. *'lt* [*KAI* 159.8])[49] and "offerings" (Pun. *mnḥt* [*KAI* 159.8])[50] as well as a vow (Pun. *ndr* [*KAI* 159.9]).

---

[43] Vellay, *Le culte et les fêtes*, 141.
[44] Gregorian Etruscan Museum, Vatican, cat. 14147.
[45] Schmitz, "Large Neo-Punic Inscription."
[46] Manfredi, *La politica amministrativa*, 443–7.
[47] Lipiński, ed., *Dictionnaire*, 23; Ben Younès, "Tunisie," 817–20.
[48] Jongeling and Kerr, *Late Punic Epigraphy*, 39–40; Lidzbarski, *Handbuch*, 437, hand copy, Taf. XVII; Bron, "Notes sur les inscriptions néo-puniques de Henchir Medeina," 147, photograph.
[49] Février, "Le vocabulaire sacrificiel," 50.
[50] Février, "Molchomor," 17; Krahmalkov, *Phoenician-Punic Dictionary*, 295.

The officiating priest, *wrswn*, son of *'rš* (*KAI* 159.7), is designated the *khn* (cf. Hebrew *kôhēn*, "priest") of the god Baal Ḥamon. Priests (Pun. *khnm*) are associated with sacrifice (Pun. *zbḥ*) in the Marseilles tariff (*KAI* 69.3–15), a Carthaginian inscription from the third century BCE (see Figs. 10 and 11).

Mention of a sacrifice and the construction of a cella (*tw*) during the month *krr* in both the Pyrgi text and the Althiburus inscription invites the supposition that the "servants of Melqart" in Althiburus were celebrating an Adonis festival. The construction of sacred buildings, which at Pyrgi in the sixth century BCE is part of the portfolio of the head of state, had become a matter of public service by a private sodality in Roman Althiburus. Sacrifice takes place in connection with the celebration at Pyrgi and at Althiburus. The priest is unmentioned in the Pyrgi inscription but is associated with Baal Ḥamon/Saturn in the North African town. At Pyrgi the dedication is to Astarte, and sacrifice and construction occur at her sanctuary. At Althiburus, the dedication is to Baal Ḥamon, but the temples (*mqdšm, KAI* 159.5, 8) of the city probably served a number of deities. This late text provides one source possibly connecting the god Melqart with the Adonis myth, a link that scholars have suggested or assumed in the past.

The goddess Astarte is more abundantly attested and has received considerable attention from specialists. According to Sanchuniaton, as represented by Philo of Byblos, "The Phoenicians say that Astarte is Aphrodite."[51] Astarte and her Greek interpretation Aphrodite are sometimes difficult to distinguish.[52] Paphian Aphrodite, for example, the quintessential manifestation of the goddess on Cyprus, had an equivalent, "Astarte of Paphos," attested in a Phoenician inscription of the third century BCE from Paphos.[53] Lucian (*De syria dea* 6) claimed to have seen the great temple of Aphrodite at Byblos where secret rites for Adonis were enacted.[54] Although we cannot be certain that the goddess of Byblos was identical to Astarte,[55] Lucian's comment implies the identification.[56]

At Delos, Lindos, and other sanctuaries of the Greek goddess Aphrodite, Phoenician or "orientalizing" influence is sometimes evident. The Egyptian goddess Isis and the Greek goddess Demeter cohere with Astarte in inscriptions, and the cults of Aphrodite Pontia and Aphrodite Ourania bear impressions of the oriental cult of Astarte. The myth of Cythera has

---

[51] Attridge and Oden, *Philo of Byblos*, 55.
[52] Delcor, "Astarte," 1077; Bonnet and Pirenne-Delforge, "Deux déesses."
[53] Masson and Sznycer, *Recherches*, 81–2; Bonnet, *Astarté*, 76.
[54] Bonnet, *Astarté*, 28.
[55] Ibid., 19–30.
[56] Oden, *Studies*, 78.

Fig. 10. Punic priest officiating at altar. Photo by Philip C. Schmitz.

Fig. 11. Plaque inscribed with eleven lines in Punic (*CIS* 5510). Photo by Philip C. Schmitz.

many elements undoubtedly arising from contacts with Phoenician and other ancient Near Eastern deity cults. The reciprocal syncretisms between Astarte and Aphrodite profoundly influenced Mediterranean religions.[57]

Many associations link Astarte to Adonis, especially at Pyrgi. The Pyrgi inscription provides important evidence that the Adonis festival took place at a temple of Astarte. At Pyrgi the myth of Adonis appears still to have been vital, whereas in the context of Roman North Africa the myth had probably become latent. No document links Astarte to Baal Ḥamon in the Adonis celebration at Pyrgi in the sixth or fifth century BCE, and although Baal Ḥamon appears to be somehow associated with Melqart at late-Roman Althiburus, Astarte is absent from the textual source. The implicit association among these three deities may have a basis in history or may be a mirage induced by the insufficiency of sources.

SACRIFICIAL PRACTICES

Temple sacrifice is an area in which inscriptional evidence is crucial. Carthaginian temples regulated the procedures of and payments for

---

[57] Bonnet, *Astarté*, 87–96.

216 *Philip C. Schmitz*

sacrifices by *khn*-priests according to public standards. We have as an example a sacrificial tariff inscribed on a plaque that once hung in the temple of Baal Saphon in Carthage (*CIS* I 165; *KAI* 69). Found in 1844 or 1845 near the old harbor of Marseilles, France, the inscription dates paleographically to the third century BCE. (The inscription probably arrived at Marseilles from Carthage as part of a ship's ballast.) The Marseilles tariff (*KAI* 69) concerns (by line): (1–2) administrative authorities, namely, the "thirty men in charge of payments," probably municipal officials; (3–12) payments to officiating priests and the distribution of portions of sacrificial victims according to type of victim, type of sacrifice, and type of recipient; (13) summary of procedures for sacrifices of the type *ṣw't* (meaning uncertain), in which a portion of the victim is retained by the sacrificer; (14) procedures for inanimate sacrificial materials; (15) exemption for additional simultaneous sacrifices; (16–17) liability for group sacrifices; (18–19) payments for sacrifices not stipulated in the inscription (the reader is referred to another document); and (20–21) fines for receipt by priests of illicit payments and failure of sacrificers to pay (see also Fig. 10 and Table 1).

A fragment found at Carthage in 1858 holds seven partial lines of a similar tariff (*CIS* I 167; *KAI* 74). Chabot later collated *CIS* I 167, 168, and 170 with three pieces found by Lapeyre at Carthage (*CIS* I 3915–3917), establishing a more or less common text, labeled by Février 167C (for "complete"). The reconstructed tariff witnesses to a text that follows the same topical order as the Marseilles tariff (except for the placement of the exemption for additional simultaneous sacrifices [*KAI* 74.6]; see Fig. 11 and Table 2), but involves a different number of sacrifices. The Marseilles tariff and 167C constitute our chief source of information about Phoenician-Punic temple sacrifice.

The tone of the documents is strikingly bureaucratic. At least in the portion of the text that survives, there is no hint of enforcement by a deity. The tariff anticipates malfeasance and assesses fines, but no malediction threatens divine retribution. Nor are blessings apportioned for compliance. From our limited viewpoint, Phoenician-Punic sacrificial legislation appears not to have acknowledged a divine law or a single human lawgiver. Religious practices were customary, regulated at the level of the city-state. This is comparable to the situation in Greek religion (see Chapter 11 by Kearns).

The similarity of the temple tariffs to non-cultic documents becomes clearer by comparison with a fourth-century-BCE Punic inscription

Table 1. *Analysis of Marseilles Tariff*

Lines	Topic	Sacrifice	Victim	Payment	Recipient
1–2	Administrative authorities				30 men in charge of payments
3–4	Blood sacrifices Large quadripeds	kll, ṣwʿt, šlm kll	ʾlp (bull)	10 pieces silver each	khnm
5–6	Large quadripeds	kll	ʿgl (calf); ʾyl	5 pieces silver each; 150 shekels meat	khnm
		ṣwʿt	(hind)	5 pieces silver each, additional portions of victim	khnm; meat to sacrificer
		šlm kll		5 pieces silver each	khnm
7–8	Medium quadripeds	kll	ybl (ram); ʿz	1 shekel, 2 zr each	khnm
		ṣwʿt	(she-goat)	1 shekel, 2 zr each; additional portions of victim	khnm; meat to sacrificer
		šlm kll		1 shekel, 2 zr each	khnm
9–10	Small quadripeds	kll	ʾmr (lamb); gdʾ	¾ shekel, 2 zr each	khnm
		ṣwʿt	(kid); šḥrb ʾyl	¾ shekel, 2 zr each; additional portions of victim	khnm; meat to sacrificer
		šlm kll	(young ram)	¾ shekel, 2 zr each	khnm
11–12	Birds	kll, ṣwʿt, subtypes šṣp, ḥzt	ʾgnn, ṣṣ	¾ shekel, 2 zr each	khnm; meat to sacrificer
13	Summary	ṣwʿt [text broken]		Additional portions of victim	khnm
14	Inanimate sacrifices	bll, ḥḥlb, zbḥ, mnḥ[t]		Additional portions of material	khnm
15	Exemption	Additional simultaneous sacrifice	mqnʾ, ṣpr	None	khnm
16–17	Distributed liability	By family or sodality		Payment according to text of [this inscription?]	Referred to a separate document
18–19	Additional payments	Not written in this inscription		Payment according to text of [?]	
20	Fines	Accepting illicit payments		Not according to text of this inscription	Against priests
21	Fines	Failure to pay			Against sacrificers

Table 2. *Analysis of CIS I 167C (KAI 74) + (KAI 75)*

Lines	Topic	Sacrifice	Victim	Payment	Recipient
KAI 75.1	Administrative authorities				30 men in charge of payments
2	Blood sacrifices Large quadripeds	*kllm, ṣwʻt*	[ʾlp] (bull)	Skin to priests	*khnm* *tbrt to* sacrificer
3	Large quadripeds	*kllm, ṣwʻt*	[ʾgl (calf); ʾyl (hind)]	Skin to priests	*khnm* *tbrt to* sacrificer
4	Medium quadripeds	*kllm, ṣwʻt*	ybl (ram); ʻz (she-goat)	Skin to priests	*khnm* ʻšl[bm] to sacrifice
5	Small quadripeds	*kllm, ṣwʻt*	ʾmr (lamb); gdʾ (kid); ṣrb ʾyl (young ram)	Skin to priests	*Khnm*
6	Exemption	Additional simultaneous sacrifice	mqnʾ, ṣpr	None	*Khnm*
7	Birds (bipeds)		ʾgnn, ṣṣ	2 *zr* each	[*khnm*]
8	Summary	ṣwʻt [text broken]		Additional portions of victim	*Khnm*
9	First fruits	[*qdmt*] qdš, ṣhd (game), šmn (oil)			
10 = *KAI* 75.1	Inanimate sacrifices	bll, ḥḥlb, zbḥ mnḥt		Additional portions of material	*khnm*
11 = *KAI* 75.2	Additional payments	Not written in this inscription		Payment according to text of [?]	
3	Fines	Accepting illicit payments		Not according to text of this inscription	Against priests
4	Fines	Failure to pay Selling			Against sacrificers
5					
6	[Fines?]	Defacing inscription			
7	Colophon	[Artisan]	pds bn ʾšmnḥl[sḥ]		

unearthed at Carthage in 1966.[58] The inscription acknowledges administrative, financial, and material support for construction work near one of the city gates and is one of the few Carthaginian Punic inscriptions not dedicated to a deity. It stipulates a fine of one thousand (pieces) of silver for some offense – probably defacement of the inscription itself – mentioned in a now-broken portion of the stone plaque. The fine is levied by *hmhšbm 'š ln*, "our comptrollers" (*KAI*, 5th ed., 303.7). In both cases – sacrifice and public works – the governance structures of municipal administration provide the regulatory mechanisms.

At the linguistic level, the Phoenician-Punic vocabulary of sacrifice draws on an archaic common Semitic lexical stock: words for sacrificial actions, such as *zbḥ* (< *δbiḥ-*), "slaughter, sacrifice" (n.), *šlm* (< *šalim-*), "intact" (adj.), and names of domestic animals and products from them, such as *'gl* (< *'igl-*), "calf" (n.), and *ḥlb* (< *ḥalab-*), "fat" (n.).[59]

As a cultural practice, the *zbḥ* is an institution and a ritual that represents political affiliation and social order. When the eighth-century-BCE Anatolian ruler Azatiwada had established a city, subdued its opponents, fortified its dependencies, and strengthened its military forces, then regular sacrifice (*zbḥ*) began to be offered to Baal *krntryš*, a Syro-Anatolian deity: *wylk zbḥ l kl hmskt*, "and all the river-lands (?) brought sacrifice to him" (*KAI* 26 Aii19–iii1). The text is bilingual (hieroglyphic Luwian and Phoenician), the practice multicultural, the god regional, the Phoenician word *zbḥ* ubiquitous. We can envision historical levels or "shells" of relatedness between sacrificial language and sacrificial practice. Reading in a biblical text, for example, that Phoenician priests performed *zĕbaḥîm*, "sacrifices," in a temple of Baal in Samaria (2 Kgs 10:24) occasions no surprise. Seeing *'ôlôt*, "holocausts," as the next word in the sentence (2 Kgs 10:25) piques curiosity – why is this sacrificial category absent from the Punic tariffs? In the Late Punic text from Althiburus, particular mention is made of the exemplary worshipper, *'š h'l' [k]' 'lt 'w m[n]ḥt bmqdš*, "The man that brings up there his holocausts or offerings in the temple" (*KAI* 159.8). If the practice was typical, why single it out in this way? If it was unusual, why was it so?

The sacrificial practice represented in the tariffs has clear similarities with the system of sacrifices found in the Hebrew Scriptures. For example, the Phoenician and Punic sacrificial term written *mnḥt*, "offerings,"

---

[58] Mahjoubi and Fantar, "Une nouvelle inscription carthaginoise," 201, 209.
[59] Fronzaroli, "Studi sul lessico commune semitico IV," 264; idem, "Studi sul lessico commune semitico VI," 314.

has a Hebrew cognate, *minḥōt*. In the Pentateuch, Hebrew *minḥōt* (always written without vowel letters)[60] is found in non-Priestly legislation.[61] The pairing and order of "holocausts" (Pun. *'lt*) and "offerings" (Pun. *mnḥt*) in the Althiburus inscription (*KAI* 159.8) is replicated in biblical Hebrew (e.g., Lev 23:37; Josh 22:23; Jer 14:12; Ezek 45:25).

Besides the linguistic similarity of the names of Phoenician sacrifices to those in the pentateuchal legislation,[62] there are structural similarities. In the Marseilles tariff, cases not explicitly covered by the inscription are referred to a separate document (*KAI* 69.17). Similarly, in Lev 5:10, the procedure for offering the second of two birds in a sin offering is referred outside the immediate context (i.e., to be done "lawfully" [Hebrew *kammišpāṭ*).[63] The procedure is legislated in Lev 1:14–17. Both the biblical legislation and the Punic tariff illustrate the thoroughly textual character of ancient Near Eastern law and cultic regulations.

THE PUNIC PANTHEON AND THE SIGNIFICANCE
OF THE RITES OF THE TOPHET

With a basic grasp of the significance of sacrifice in Punic religion, we can turn now to the major deities of the Punic culture area before considering the rites of the tophet. One of the earliest inscriptions from Carthage is the inscribed gold pendant discovered in a tomb of the Douïmès necropolis (*KAI* 73).[64] Peckham dated the inscription no earlier than the mid-eighth century,[65] partly because the shape of the letter *kap* was unattested before the late seventh century.[66] Recent epigraphic finds create a window between 800 BCE and about 720 BCE in which the *kap* of the Carthage pendant fits.[67] The text is a dedication to Astarte and Pygmalion[68] by *yd'mlk*, a son of *pdy* (*KAI* 73.3–4). The paleographic date of the pendant inscription leaves no further grounds to reject an interpretation of this text as referring to the historical king of Tyre known from Menander's list of Tyrian rulers.[69]

---

[60] See Anderson and Forbes, *Spelling*, 11–14.
[61] Anderson, "Sacrifices," 873.
[62] Février, "Le vocabulaire sacrificiel," 49–63; idem, "Remarques," 35–43; idem, "L'évolution des rites sacrificiels," 22–7; Levine, *In the Presence*, 118–22; Amadasi Guzzo, "Sacrifici e banchetti," 115.
[63] See Baker, "Leviticus 1–7," 194.
[64] Peckham, *Development*, 119–24.
[65] Ibid., 124.
[66] Ibid., 152.
[67] Schmitz, "Deity and Royalty."
[68] Bonnet, *Astarté*, 101.
[69] On Pygmalion, see Aubet, *Phoenicians and the West*, 51, 215; on the pendant inscription, see Krahmalkov, "Foundation of Carthage,"186–8.

As Krahmalkov argues, the name of the donor's father, *pdy*, could be the name known as Bitias, commander of the Tyrian fleet according to Virgil (*Aen.* 1.738). In this context the final clause, *'š ḥlṣ pgmlyn*, "who Pygmalion equipped," makes sense, for *ḥlṣ*, "to equip, arm for war," is the sort of action a military commander would have the resources to undertake. The dedication to Astarte is consistent with the legend associating the expedition of Elissa with the priesthood of Astarte.[70] In later periods Astarte is less in evidence as a major deity of Carthage or other Punic sites. Personal names, however, attest to a vigorous domestic cult of the goddess Astarte.

The goddess whose name is written *tnt*, conventionally read as *Tanit* but possibly to be vocalized *tinnit* or *tinneit*, remains mysterious. Studies of this goddess rapidly mire themselves in etymologies of her name and debates about her place of origin. A good deal can be known about her role and function in religious practice quite apart from the genealogical quest. Once again, Punic texts provide the source. This section presents a current consensus, but also moves past it.

The earliest occurrences of the divine name *tnt* appear on funerary stelae of the late seventh or early sixth century from the Tyre necropolis[71] and somewhat later at Carthage.[72] The ivory plaque from Sarepta dedicated to Tinnit-Ashtarte (*tnt 'štrt*) is of about the same date (*KAI*, 5th ed., 285.3–4). Personal names compounded with the theophoric element *tnt* occur in two fifth-century ink-written ostraca from the temple of Eshmun at Sidon (*KAI*, 5th ed., 283.13; 284b, e). Lipínski[73] observes that the names would have been given by parents who lived in the late sixth century. There are several other attestations of *tnt* from Lebanon and the eastern Mediterranean.[74] Regarding the emergence of the ubiquitous "sign of Tanit," Sader[75] elaborates Garbini's view[76] that the sign involves a combination of the Egyptian *ankh* (life) with the isosceles triangle (perhaps representing fertility). In particular, the ankh was adapted to represent the sacred betyl on a stool, a symbol found in Phoenician iconography.[77]

---

[70] Aubet, *Phoenicians and the West*, 216.

[71] Sader, *Iron Age Funerary Stelae*, 26–7, 1.4.d; 38–9, stela 13.1.

[72] Hvidberg-Hansen in Niemeyer, Docter, "Grabung unter dem Decumanus Maximus von Karthago: Vorbericht," 241–3; idem in Niemeyer, Docter, "Grabung unter dem Decumanus Maximus von Karthago: Zweiter Vorbericht," 491–4.

[73] Lipínski, "Tannit et Ba'al Hḥammon," 218.

[74] Ibid., 218–20.

[75] Sader, *Iron Age Funerary Stelae*, 130–1.

[76] Garbini, *I fenici*, 179.

[77] Sader, *Iron Age Funerary Stelae*, 131.

222   *Philip C. Schmitz*

In the western Mediterranean, *tnt* is attested in inscriptions from Sicily,[78] Sardinia,[79] Malta,[80] and Spain.[81] The name *tnt* does not appear in the votive inscriptions from Motya, an island adjoining western Sicily.

In North Africa, Carthage was her main seat. A large room or house excavated in early-fifth-century levels at Carthage has a paved floor inlaid with the "sign of Tanit" and outfitted with a drainage installation, possibly to facilitate libations.[82] The religious significance of this locus remains controversial.[83] Outside Carthage, the name *tnt* appears in Punic votive stelae from Sousse (ancient Hadrumetum, in modern Tunisia), Bir Bou Rekba (Tunisia), and Constantine (in modern Algeria), and in Late-Punic inscriptions from Constantine and Tirekbine (Algeria). The element *tnt* may also appear in two personal names inscribed in Neo-Punic script on ostraca from Mogador.[84]

The goddess is linked to the tophet area in Carthage, where votive stelae and cippi from the fifth century onward place her name in initial position, before the name of the god Baal Hḥamon. The implications of this textual feature for the pantheon and cult are not clear. Almost invariably she is addressed as *rbtn*, "our Lady;" her name is frozen in the phrase *tnt pn b'l*, spelled in Greek *thinith phane bal* (*KAI* 175.2) and *thenneith phenē bal* (*KAI* 176.1–2). A coin minted at Ascalon during Hadrian's reign carries the "sign of Tanit" and the Greek legend *phanēbalos*.[85] The widespread translation of *pn b'l* as "face of Baal" is supported by a Tannaitic text from the Cairo Genizah that records a dysphemic midrash on the injunction in Deut 12:3, *wĕ'ibbadtem 'et-šĕmām*, "and you shall abolish their names": *šm't šmm pny b'l qr' šmm pny klb*,"When you hear their names 'face-of-Baal,' say their names 'face-of-a-dog.'"[86]

In the earliest votive inscriptions from Carthage, from the late seventh or early sixth century, *tnt pn b'l* does not appear. By the fifth century, however, she figures in a variety of texts and contexts. The epigraphic witnesses are eloquent, but ambiguous. Lapeyre excavated more than a thousand inscribed votive objects (published as *CIS* I 3922–5275) in the tophet area of Carthage. Among these is a plaque inscribed with eleven lines in Punic

---

[78] Ribichini, Xella, *La religione fenicia*, 50.

[79] Ibid., 96.

[80] Guzzo Amadasi, *Le iscrizioni fenicie e puniche delle colonie in occidente*, Malta 10, 11.

[81] Ibid., Spa. 10 B3.

[82] Groenewoud, "Use of Water in Phoenician Sanctuaries," 139–59.

[83] Müller, "Religionsgeschichtliche Aspekte," 230–1.

[84] Février, "Inscriptions puniques et néopuniques," pl. VI.52, 53.

[85] Hill, *Catalogue*, pl. XIII, 18.

[86] Flusser, *CRINT* I (1976) 1075 n. 2.

(*KAI*, 5th ed., 302; see Fig. 11). A similar fragment has seven incomplete lines of text inscribed in a very similar script (*CIS* I 5511). These texts, composed in 406–405 BCE, are of considerable historical importance.[87] The first nine lines allow us to glimpse Carthaginian religious beliefs up close.

The text of *KAI* 302 includes powerful maledictions, directed probably against persons who dishonor or damage the votive installation that the plaque once marked. Below are two key sentences from the text (line numbers in parentheses):

(1) ... *k bd h'dmm hmt rbtn* [*tnt pn b'l w'dn b'l hmn yš*(2)*ptbr*]*ht h'dmm hmt wbrht 'zrtnm w'p* ...

"... by those persons, our Lady [Tinnit Phane Baal and Lord Baal Ḥamon will punish the s]ouls of those persons and the souls of their families and ..."

The formula *špt brh* is restored on the basis of its occurrences in *KAI* 79.10–11; *CIS* I 4937.3–5 (subject Tinnit), as well as in 5632.6–7 (subject Baal Ḥamon). A cognate construction in biblical Hebrew, *tišpoṭ bām*, "punish them" (2 Chron 20:12), is part of Jehoshaphat's prayer for protection against military attack. The Punic construction has the same meaning, "punish." Punishment of the soul (Pun. *rh*) takes place after death. We can deduce this because Punic religious belief also anticipated a state of rejoicing after death.

The third-century-BCE Punic epitaph of Milkpilles refers to the blessed state of the deceased: *mṣbt l'zr yšr 'nk 'šsp*[*y bn*] *lskr 'l m'spt 'ṣmy ṭn't k rh dl qdšm rn*, "A stela for a just minister (have) I, *'šspy*, his son, erected as a memorial over his gathered bones, for his soul is rejoicing with (the) holy ones" (*CIS* I 6000bis.3b–4). Tinnit Phane Baal does not appear in this text, which mentions a sacrifice at the temple of Isis (line 8). The son singles out his father's pious devotion toward the holy deities as praiseworthy (line 5).

For the Punic believer, the future life could offer bliss or terror. In the maledictions of *KAI* 302, Tinnit Phane Baal is a terrifying judge. But her power is not limited to the afterlife, as the next passage, *KAI* 302.4–5, demonstrates:

(4) [*wkl'*]*dm 'š 'ybl mšrt wkpt rbtn tnt pn b'l w'*(5)*dn b*[*'l*] *hmn 'yt 'dmm hmt bhym 'l pn šmš dl 'zr*(6)*tm w'* [...] *nm*

"And as for any person who does not serve, our Lady Tinnit Phane Baal and the Lord Baal Ḥamon will bind those persons in life before the sun, with their families and their...."

---

[87] Krahmalkov, "Carthaginian Report," 171–7; Schmitz, "The Name 'Agrigentum,'" 1–13.

The Punic word *mšrt*, translated "serve," refers to religious or cultic service. A religious boundary is set, and transgression anticipated. This binding will not be mystical or secret, but will take place in broad daylight (cf. 2 Sam 12:12).

The so-called tophet is the resting place of infants – in their thousands – and must be sanctified. Any violation of its sanctity, by commission or omission, invites punishment in this life and in the next. *KAI* 302 introduces the deities who protect the sacred space. Its maledictions set the tone of awe infusing all transactions there.

Was the tophet a place of ritual infanticide?[88] Two lines of evidence bear on this question. Recent research on the contents of cinerary urns from the Carthage tophet excavations leads in several directions. Generally, the remains of one individual are represented in an urn.[89] As many as seven different sets of remains may, however, be combined in a single urn. Sexing indicates 41 percent male, 59 percent female, between two and twelve post-natal months of age, with circa 40 percent of the sample definitely perinatal and 20 percent prenatal. The authors consider these distributions consistent with normal infant mortality.[90] The prenatal remains rule out the possibility that all tophet interments represent sacrificed infants.

Another study of remains from 459 urns from the Carthage tophet reports 95 percent of the sample aged between one and twelve months, with 51 percent dying between birth and one month; prenatal remains are not reported.[91] The authors conclude that the age distribution detected in the sample differs from anticipated patterns of infant mortality and "strengthens the claim that infants at Carthage were indeed sacrificed."[92]

The better controlled excavation of the tophet of Tharros in western Sardinia provided an important comparative sample. The analysis of remains from the cinerary urns reveals a pattern of coordination of animal and human remains: Overall, for each set of human remains there is a set of remains of a lamb, one human plus one animal accounting for 52 percent of the sample.[93] The lambs ranged in age from seven to twenty-seven days. Because lambs are born during a period of about fifty days centered on 1 March, the authors concluded that the lambs died on the same day or on a small number of separate days.[94] The same point arises in a recent

---

[88] Ribichini, "La questione del *tofet* punico," 293–304.
[89] Schwartz, *What the Bones*, 51–2.
[90] Schwartz et al., "Human Sacrifice," 138; Schwartz et al., "Skeletal Remains from Punic Carthage."
[91] Avishai, Smith, "Cremated Infant Remains," 39.
[92] Ibid.
[93] Fedele, Foster, "Tharros," 43.
[94] Ibid., 41.

Phoenician-Punic Religion

study of remains from six Carthage urns in the Allard Pierson Museum, Amsterdam.[95] The forensic evidence leaves little doubt that lambs were routinely killed and burned in the tophets of Carthage and Tharros on one or more days between late February and early April.[96] The timing suggests a coordinated ritual.

The admixture of human and animal incinerations is difficult to explain unless it was intentional. But how does this fit with the evidence that 60 percent of the infants were newborn or stillborn? Can it be possible that Punic society engaged in ritually controlled fertility?[97]

To sketch a possible response to this question we return to the Adonis celebration discussed above. Was the Adonis festival part of a larger cycle? A perplexing element of the Adonis cult is the ritualized sexual license associated with it.[98] If a woman engaged in ritualized sex and conceived between the new moons before and after the Sothic new year (20 July), the resulting birth would be likely to occur in the month after the vernal equinox. In other words, these (illegitimate?) infants would be neonatal during the time when lambs lost their lives in the tophets. The *cui bono* test must be applied to this hypothesis, but it gives us a possible framework in which to reconsider this portion of Punic religion with regard to the lived experience of women.

To establish the cycle of Phoenician-Punic festivals, we must know the months of the annual calendar sequentially, but the order of most of the Phoenician months must be determined by comparison with better-known calendars and is thus hypothetical throughout the first millennium BCE. We can be fairly certain that the heliacal rising of the Egyptian constellation *S3ḥ*-Orion, associated with Osiris, would occur during the second half of the month – probably *zbḥ šmš* – that precedes the Phoenician month *krr*, in the second week of the waning phase of the moon. The heliacal rising of the Dog Star Sirius-Sothis, associated with Isis-Hathor-Astarte and the occasion of the Egyptian new year's day, would take place during the second week of the waxing phase of the moon in the month *krr*. Building on this assumption, and comparing the dates of a number of Phoenician votive inscriptions, particularly from Cyprus, we can detect what may be a seasonal pattern in the cults of Melqart and Osiris: Offerings are made to Melqart during the occultation of the constellation *S3ḥ*-Orion (April

---

[95] Docter et al., "Interdisciplinary Research," 424.
[96] Cf. Bernardini, "Leggere il tofet," 21 n. 15.
[97] Stager, "The Rite of Child Sacrifice," 1–11.
[98] Vellay, *Le culte et les fêtes*, 169–73; Ribichini, *Adonis*, 161–4; Lipiński, ed., *Dictionnaire*, 7; Bonnet, *Astarté*, 28.

226 *Philip C. Schmitz*

to June) and during the preceding waning period (January to March); offerings to Osiris are made during the waxing period of the constellation *S3ḫ*-Orion (July–December), although we have evidence only from the first month of that period. We can conjecture that offerings to Osiris would have begun after the heliacal rising of the constellation *S3ḫ*-Orion and continued at least until the heliacal rising of the star Sirius-Sothis (corresponding to the Egyptian new year celebration).

If one accepts the chronological deduction made above from the evidence of lamb remains mixed with human remains from the tophets of Tharros and Carthage, then we might associate the interments in the tophet with the occultation of the constellation *S3ḫ*-Orion and inferentially with the cult of Melqart. This calendrical inference would then associate the *ym qbr 'lm*, "god's burial day" (*KAI* 277.9), with the appearance of constellation *S3ḫ*-Orion and the heliacal rising of Sirius, which perhaps inaugurated the annual veneration of Osiris. Precisely how the cult of Melqart-Adonis fits in this calendrical pattern remains speculative.

About inter-cult conflict and its toleration in Phoenician religion we are poorly informed. Apparently the cult of Melqart was a matter of controversy in Punic Carthage, because the Punic inscription *KAI* 302.6–7 stipulates its toleration: *qr' lmlqrt ysp 'lty lšlm wlyrḥy / bmqm* [z], "As for one who worships Melqart(-Adonis?) they shall continue to greet him and make him welcome in this city."[99] What scenarios of competition would have made this injunction necessary? Was the god under symbolic rehabilitation as part of "a major reorganization of the entire Carthaginian colonial network" during the fifth century?[100] Did Melqart-Heracles offer a model of successful endogamy, addressing colonial anxieties?[101] Should we see the divine pair implied by Melqart's presence?[102] Or was the tide of imperialism at Carthage buffeting older loyalties to the *metropolis*? At this stage of our knowledge of Punic religion, silence is the appropriate answer.

MORTUARY RITES

The discovery of cremation burials and funerary stelae from the ninth to the sixth century BCE in the al-Bass necropolis of Tyre[103] has allowed scholars to place older discoveries of tomb assemblages at Phoenician-Punic

[99] Krahmalkov, *Phoenician-Punic Dictionary*, 462, s.v. Š-L-M I.
[100] Van Dommelen, "Ambiguous Matters," 130.
[101] Bonnet, "Melqart in Occidente," 21.
[102] "Non c'è Melqart senza Astarte"; Bonnet, "Melqart in Occidente," 21.
[103] Aubet, *Phoenician Cemetery of Tyre al-Bass*, 465.

Phoenician-Punic Religion   227

sites in the West, particularly at Cádiz[104] and Carthage,[105] in a firmer context of interpretation. Simultaneously, the discovery of new Phoenician and Aramaic texts, and the reinterpretation of the Pyrgi text and some Punic texts from Carthage (illustrative examples of which appear above), have permitted a clearer view of Phoenician-Punic beliefs about the spirit and its possible experiences in the afterlife.

One of the distinctive features of Phoenician-Punic mortuary rites now identifiable at all known Phoenician and Punic burial sites is a ritual involving the breaking of ceramic ware, particularly plates, cups, and jugs.[106] The cremation burials in the Tyre al-Bass cemetery reveal a consistent pattern: After the two urns containing the cremated remains of a single individual were placed in an excavated space and a few simple offerings stacked atop them, the urns and their associated grave goods were covered with reeds, branches and leaves from white poplar, fig, and olive trees, and vine stems, and set alight. As the fire burned down, plates, cups, and jugs that probably had been used in a funerary meal were deliberately broken and thrown into the fire (indicated by surface scorching).

This practice has similarities with the much older Egyptian funerary ritual *sḏ ḏšrwt*, "smashing the redware," and could possibly derive from Egyptian influence. A related but distinct practice of Egyptian funerary rituals involves "killing" pots by perforating or smashing them.[107] Breaking containers at the conclusion of a ritual would prevent their subsequent profane use. Ritual breaking *as a constituent of a ritual*, on the other hand, might eliminate unwholesome powers believed to have accumulated in ritual objects during the course of their ritual use. The former case implies a purificatory purpose for the breaking, the latter an apotropaic purpose. If, as seems likely, the fire into which shattered pottery was thrown during burials at the Tyre al-Bass cemetery had a purificatory purpose, then the ritual itself probably implied purification, although protection is not ruled out. The ceramic evidence for this pottery-smashing ritual implies that Phoenicians throughout their western Mediterranean settlements practiced similar funerary rites and mortuary cult banquets. The ritual is associated with both inhumation and cremation burials.

The funerary stelae discovered in excavations at the Tyre al-Bass cemetery cannot be confidently associated with individual interments. The

---

[104] Niveau de Villedary y Mariñas, "Banquetes rituales en la necropolis púnica de Gadir," 35–64.
[105] Benichou-Safar, *Les tombes puniques*, 278–82.
[106] Aubet, "Phoenician Cemetery of Tyre," 40.
[107] Budka, *Bestattungsbrauchtum und Friedhofsstruktur im Asasif*, 405–10.

228   *Philip C. Schmitz*

paleography of the inscribed stelae indicates a range of time from the ninth to the fifth century BCE. The inscriptions on stelae from the Tyre al-Bass cemetery are brief, the longest being five words.[108] The texts are entirely labels: the name of the deceased, in a few cases with the father's name added (and in one case [no. 31] the grandfather's also). Thus the Phoenician stelae discovered in the Tyre al-Bass cemetery originally preserved the essential details necessary for mortuary commemoration: the name of the deceased and the location of the interment.

CONCLUSION

Punic religion enjoyed about five centuries of practice as a relatively coherent tradition. Although never entirely free from external influence, the Canaanite elements inherited from the Late Bronze Age and Early Iron Age remained recognizable until the Roman period. Egyptian religious imagery and magical practice infused Punic piety throughout its history. One thinks, for example, of Herodotus's *logos* (3.37.2) concerning the image of Hephaistos (Ptah) in his temple at Memphis and its similarity to the *pataikoi* (Ptah-images) of the Phoenicians. The Egyptian goddess Isis had a temple in Hellenistic Carthage as well (*CIS* I 6000bis.8). Evidence of Persian religious influence is slight. Phoenicia was in long and sustained contact with the Greek world[109] and exerted considerable influence on Greek religion.[110] As the earlier discussion of the Adonis cult indicates, Phoenician-Punic religion was receptive to Greek religious influence also. For example, Carthage adopted the Hellenistic cult of Demeter and Persephone.[111] The relatively weak textual base on which the present reconstruction rests characterizes the difficulties awaiting future attempts to understand the religion of Phoenician settlers in the western Mediterranean world.

BIBLIOGRAPHY

Amadasi Guzzo, M. G. "Sacrifici e banchetti: Bibbia ebraica e iscrizioni puniche." In *Sacrificio e società nel mondo antico*, ed. C. Grottanelli and N. F. Parise (Rome, 1988): 97–122.

Iscrizioni fenicie e puniche in Italia. Itinerari 6 (Rome, 1990).

"Le plurilinguisme dans l'onomastique personnelle à l'époque néopunique." *Antiquités africaines* 38–39 (2002–2003): 281–8.

---

[108] Sader, *Iron Age Funerary Stelae*, 56–7, no. 31.
[109] Wenning, "Griechischer Einfluss auf Palästina," 29.
[110] López-Ruiz, *When the Gods Were Born*, 23–47.
[111] Xella, "Sull'introduzione del culto di Demetra e Kore a Cartagine," 215–16.

Anderson, F., and A. D. Forbes. *Spelling in the Hebrew Bible* (Rome, 1986).

Anderson, G. "Sacrifices and Sacrificial Offerings." *ABD* 5 (1992): 870–86.

Aranegui Gascó, C., ed. *Lixus: colonia fenicia y ciudad púnico-mauritana* (Valencia, 2001).

Atran, S. *In Gods We Trust: The Evolutionary Landscape of Religion* (Oxford, 2002).

Attridge, H. W., and R. A. Oden, Jr. *Philo of Byblos: The Phoenician History* (Washington, D.C., 1981).

Aubet, M. E. "From Trading Post to Town in the Phoenician-Punic World." In *Social Complexity and the Development of Towns in Iberia: From the Copper Age to the Second Century AD*, ed. B. Cunliffe and S. Keay (Oxford, 1995): 47–65.

———. *Phoenicians and the West*, 2nd ed. (Cambridge, 2001).

———. "Burial, Symbols, and Mortuary Practices in a Phoenician Tomb." In *Across Frontiers: Etruscans, Greeks, Phoenicians, and Cypriots. Studies in Honor of David Ridgway and Francesca Romana Serra Redgway*, ed. E. Herring et al. Accordia Specialist Studies on the Mediterranean 6 (London, 2006): 37–47.

Avishai, G., and P. Smith. "The Cremated Infant Remains from Carthage: Skeletal and Dental Evidence for and against Human Sacrifice." *American Journal of Physical Anthropology* suppl. 34 (2002): 39.

Bacigalupo Pareo, E. "I supremi magistrati a Cartagine." In *Contributi di storia antica in onore di Albino Garzetti* (Genoa, 1976): 61–87.

Baker, D. W. "Leviticus 1–7 and the Punic Tariffs: A Form Critical Comparison." *ZAW* 99 (1987): 188–97.

Barré, M. L. *The God-list in the Treaty between Hannibal and Philip V of Macedonia* (Baltimore, 1983).

Baumgarten, A. I. *The Phoenician History of Philo of Byblos: A Commentary*. EPRO 429 (Leiden, 1981).

Ben Abdallah, Z. *Catalogue des inscriptions latines païennes du Musée du Bardo* (Rome, 1986).

Ben Younès, H. "Tunisie." In *La civilisation phénicienne et punique: manuel de recherche*, ed. V. Krings (Leiden, 1995): 796–827.

Benichou-Safar, H. *Les tombes puniques de Carthage* (Paris, 1982).

———. "Les fouilles du tophet de Salammbô à Carthage (première partie)." *Antiquités africaines* 31 (1995): 81–200.

Bernardini, P. "Leggere il tofet: sacrifice e sepulture. Una riflessione sulle fasi iniziali del tofet." In *Fra Cartagine e Roma*, ed. P. Donati Giacomini (Faenza, 2002): 15–28.

Boardman, J. "Early Euboean Settlements in the Carthage Area." *Oxford Journal of Archaeology* 25 (2006): 195–200.

Bondì, S. F. "Carthage, Italy, and the 'Vth Century Problem'." In *Phoenicians and Carthaginians in the Western Mediterranean*, ed. G. Pisano (Rome, 1999): 39–48.

Bonnet, C. *Melqart* (Leuven, 1988).

———. *Astarté* (Rome, 1996).

———. "Melqart in Occidente: Percorsi di appropriazione di acculturazione." In *Il Mediterraneo di Herakles*, ed. P. Bernardini and R. Zucca (Rome, 2005): 17–28.

Bonnet, C., E. Lipiński, and P. Marchetti, eds. *Religio Phoenicia*. Studia Phoenicia 4 (Namur, 1986).

Bonnet, C., and V. Pirenne-Delforge. "Deux déesses en interaction: Astarté et Aphrodite dans le monde égéen." In *Les syncrétismes religieux dans le monde méditerranéen antique*, ed. C. Bonnet and A. Motte (Rome, 1999): 249–73.

Bonnet, C., and P. Xella. "La religion." In *La civilisation phénicienne et punique: manuel de recherche*, ed. V. Krings (Leiden, 1995): 316–33.

Bron, F. 2009. "Notes sur les inscriptions néo-puniques de Henchir Medeina (Althiburos)." *Journal of Semitic Studies* 54: 141–7.

Bunnens, G. *L'expansion phénicienne en Méditerranée* (Brussels, 1979).

Camps, G. "Liste onomastique libyque. Nouvelle édition." *Antiquités africaines* 38–39 (2002–2003): 211–58.

Capps, W. H. *Religious Studies: The Making of a Discipline* (Minneapolis, 1995).

Chabot, J. B. "Sur deux inscriptions puniques et une inscription Latine d'Algerie." *CRAI* (1916): 242–50.

Cintas, P. *Manuel d'archéologie punique* (Paris, 1970).

Manuel d'archéologie punique II, ed. S. Lancel (Paris, 1976).

Cohen, R. *Global Diasporas: An Introduction* (Seattle, 1997).

Delcor, M. "Astarte." *LIMC* 3.1 (addendum) (1986): 1077–85.

Dennett, D. C. *Breaking the Spell: Religion as a Natural Phenomenon* (New York, 2006).

Docter, R. F., et al. "Interdisciplinary Research on Urns from the Carthaginian Tophet and Their Contents." *Palaeohistoria* 43–44 (2001–2002): 417–33.

"Carthage Bir Massouda: Second Preliminary Report on the Bilateral Excavations of Ghent University and the Institut National du Patrimoine (2003–2004)." *Babesch. Bulletin Antieke Beschaving* 81 (2006): 37–89.

Donner, H., and W. Röllig. *Kanaanäische und aramaische Inschriften* (Wiesbaden, 1966–1969).

Dussaud, R. "Trente-huit ex voto provenant du sanctuaire des ports à Carthage." *Bulletin archéologique du Comité des Travaux historiques et scientifiques* (1922): 243–60.

Facchetti, G. M. *Carthage: Approche d'un civilisation* (Tunis, 1993).

L'enigma svelato della lingua etrusca, 2nd ed. (Rome, 2001). Glossary online: http://it.wikipedia.org/wiki/Lingua_etrusca_(vocabolario).

"Le tophet du Salammbô." In *L'Afrique du Nord antique et médiévale: mémorie, identité et imaginaire*, ed. C. Briand-Ponsart and S. Crogiez (Rouen, 2002): 13–24.

Fantar, M. H. *Carthage: Approche d'un civilisation* (Tunis, 1993).

Fariselli, A. C. *I mercenari di Cartagine* (La Spezia, 2002).

Fedele, F., and G. V. Foster. "Tharros: ovicaprini sacrificali e rituale del tofet." *RSF* 16 (1988): 29–46.

Février, J. G. "Molchomor." *RHR* 143 (1953): 8–18.

"Le vocabulaire sacrificiel punique." *JA* 243 (1955): 49–63.

"Remarques sur le grand tarif dit de Marseille," *Cahiers de Byrsa* 8 (1958–1959): 35–43.

"L'évolution des rites sacrificiels à Carthage." *Bulletin archéologique du Comité des Travaux historiques et scientifiques* (1959–60): 22–7.

"Inscriptions puniques et néopuniques." In *Inscriptions antiques du Maroc*, ed. R. Rebuffat (Paris, 1966): 82–131.

Frankenstein, S. "The Phoenicians in the Far West: A Function of Neo-Assyrian Imperialism." In *Power and Propaganda: A Symposium on Ancient Empires*, ed. M. T. Larsen (Copenhagen, 1979): 263–96.

Arqueología del colonialismo. El impacto fenicio y griego en el sur de la Península Ibérica y el suroeste de Alemania (Barcelona, 1997).

Frend, W. H. C. *The Archaeology of Early Christianity* (Minneapolis, 1996).

Friedrich, J., and W. Röllig. *Phönizisch- punische Grammatik*, 3rd ed., rev. M. G. Amadasi Guzzo and W. R. Mayer (Rome, 1999).

Fronzaroli, P. "Studi sul lessico commune semitico IV. La religione." *Rendiconti degli Atti dell'Accademia Nazionale dei Lincei, Classe di scienze morali, storiche e filologiche* 8th ser. 22 (1965): 246–69.

"Studi sul lessico commune semitico VI. La natura domestica." *Rendiconti degli Atti dell'Accademia Nazionale dei Lincei, Classe di scienze morali, storiche e filologiche* 8th ser. 24 (1969): 285–320.

Garbini, G. *I fenici, storia e religione* (Naples, 1980).

González de Canales, F., L. Serrano, and J. P. Garrido. "Nuevas inscripciones fenicias en Tarteso: su contexto histórico." In *Actas del IV Congreso Internacional de Estudios Fenicios y Punicos Cádiz, 2 al 6 Octubre de 1995*, ed. M. E. Aubet and M. Barthélemy (Cádiz, 2000): 1:227–38.

Gsell, S. *Histoire ancienne de l'Afrique du Nord*, 8 vols., 2nd ed. (Paris, 1920–1924).

Guzzo Amadasi, M. G. *Le iscrizioni fenicie e puniche delle colonie in occidente* (Rome, 1967).

Hill, G. F. *Catalogue of the Greek Coins of Palestine* (London, 1914).

Hvidberg-Hansen, F. O. *La déesse TNT: une étude sur la religion canaanéo-punique*, trans. R. Arndt (Copenhagen, 1979).

Jacoby, F. *Die Fragmente der griechischen Historiker*, 3 vols. in 10 pts., 2nd ed. (Leiden, 1957–1964).

Jongeling, K., and R. M. Kerr. *Late Punic Epigraphy* (Tübingen, 2005).

Katzenstein, H. J. "Tyre in the Early Persian Period (539–486 B.C.E.)." *BA* 42 (1979): 23–34.

Kelsey, F. W. *Excavations at Carthage 1925: A Preliminary Report* (New York, 1926).

Koffmahn, E. "Sind die altisraelitischen Monatsbezeichnungen mit den kanaanäisch-phönikischen identisch?" *BZ* 10 (1966): 197–219.

Krahmalkov, C. R. "A Carthaginian Report of the Battle of Agrigentum 406 B.C. (CIS I 5510.9-11)." *RSF* 2 (1974): 171–7.

"The Foundation of Carthage, 814 BC: The Douïmès Pendant Inscription." *JSS* 26 (1981): 177–91.

Phoenician-Punic Dictionary (Leuven, 2000).

A Phoenician-Punic Grammar (Leiden, 2001).

Krings, V., ed. *La civilisation phénicienne et punique: manuel de recherche* (Leiden, 1995).

Lancel, S. *Carthage: A History*, trans. A. Nevill (Oxford, 1992).

Lapeyre, G. G. "Fouilles récéntes à Carthage." *CRAI* (1935): 81001E7.

"Les fouilles du Musée Lavigerie à Carthage de 1935 à 1939. I. Temple de Tanit." *CRAI* (1939): 294001E300.

Leglay, M. *Saturne africain* (Paris, 1961–1966).

Levine, B. A. *In the Presence of the Lord: A Study of Cult and Some Cultic Terms in Ancient Israel* (Leiden, 1974).

Lidzbarski, M. *Handbuch der nordsemitischen Epigraphik* (Weimar, 1898).

Lipiński, E. "La fête d'ensevelissement et de la résurrection de Melqart." In *Actes de la XVIIe Rencontre Assyriologique Internationale*, ed. A. Finet (Ham-sur-Heure, 1970): 30–58.

"Tannit et Ba'al Hḥammon." *Hamburger Beiträge zur Archäologie* 15–17 (1988–1990): 209–49.

ed. *Dictionnaire de la civilisation phénicienne et punique* ([Brussels], 1992).

Itineraria phoenicia (Leuven, 2004).

Mahjoubi, A., and M. Fantar. "Une nouvelle inscription carthaginoise." *Rendiconti degli Atti dell'Accademia Nazionale dei Lincei, Classe di scienze morali, storiche e filologiche* 8th ser. 21 (1966): 201–11.

Manfredi, L. I. *La politica amministrativa di Cartagine in Africa Roma* (Rome, 2003).

Markoe, G. E. *Phoenicians* (Berkeley, 2000).

Masson, O., and M. Sznycer. *Recherches sur les Phéniciens à Chypre* (Paris, 1972).

Masuzawa, T. *The Invention of World Religions* (Chicago, 2005).

Mazza, F., S. Ribichini, and P. Xella, eds. *Fonti classiche per la civiltà fenicia e punica* (Rome, 1988).

McCutcheon, R. T. *Religion and the Domestication of Dissent* (London, 2005).

Mettinger, T. N. D. *The Riddle of Resurrection* (Stockholm, 2001).

Montfaucon, B. de. *Palaeographia graeca* (Paris, 1708).

Moscati, S. "Dall'età fenicia all'età cartaginese." *Rendiconti degli Atti dell'Accademia Nazionale dei Lincei, Classe di scienze morali, storiche e filologiche*, 9th ser. 4 (1995): 203–15.

Movers, F. C. *Die Phönizier* (Berlin, 1841–1856).

Müller, H. P. "Religionsgeschichtliche Aspekte." In *Karthago: die Ergebnisse der Hamburger Grabung unter dem Decumanus Maximus* (Mainz am Rhein, 2007): 228–32.

Niemeyer, H. G. "Die Phönizier und die Mittelmeerwelt im Zeitalter Homers." *Jahrbuch Des Römisch-Germanischen Zentralmuseums Mainz* 31 (1984): 1–94.

"The Phoenicians in the Mediterranean: A Non-Greek Model for Expansion and Settlement in Antiquity." In *Greek Colonists and Native Populations*, ed. J.-P. Descoeudres (Oxford, 1990): 469–89.

"The Early Phoenician City-States on the Mediterranean: Archaeological Elements for their Description." In *A Comparative Study of Thirty City-State Cultures*, ed. M. H. Hansen (Copenhagen, 2000): 89–115.

Niemeyer, H. G., et al., eds. *Karthago: Die Ergebnisse der Hamburger Grabung unter dem Decumanus Maximus* (Mainz, 2007).

Niveau de Villedary y Mariñas, A. M. "Banquetes rituales en la necropolis púnica de Gadir." *Gerión* 24:1 (2006): 35–64.

O'Connor, M. *Hebrew Verse Structure* (Winona Lake, Ind., 1980).

Oden, R. A. *Studies in Lucian's* De Syria dea (Missoula, Mont., 1977).

Peckham, J. B. *The Development of the Late Phoenician Scripts* (Cambridge, Mass., 1968).

Poinssot, L., and R. Lantier. "Un sanctuaire de Tanit à Carthage." *RHR* 87 (1923): 32–68.

Pritchard, J. B. "The Tanit Inscription from Sarepta." In *Phönizer im Westen*, ed. H. G. Niemeyer (Mainz, 1982): 83–92.

Renfrew, C., and P. Bahn. *Archaeology: Theories, Methods, and Practice*, 4th ed. (London, 2004).

Ribichini, S. *Adonis* (Rome, 1981).

Il tofet e il sacrificio dei fanciulli (Sassari, 1987).

"La questione del *tofet* punico." In *Rites et espaces en pays celte et mediterraneen: etude comparee a partir du Sanctuaire d'Acy-Romance (Ardennes, France)*, ed. S. Verger (Rome, 2000): 293–304.

Ribichini, S., and P. Xella. *La religione fenicia e punica in Italia* (Rome, 1994).

Sader, H. *Iron Age Funerary Stelae from Lebanon* (Barcelona, 2005).

Sanderson, S. K. *Social Transformations: A General Theory of Historical Development* (Lanham, Md., 1999).

Schmitz, P. C. "Tophet." *ABD* 6 (1993): 600–1.

"The Name 'Agrigentum' in a Punic Inscription (CIS I 5510.10)." *JNES* 53 (1994): 1–13.

"The Phoenician Text from the Etruscan Sanctuary at Pyrgi." *JAOS* 115 (1995): 559–75.

"A Research Manual on Phoenician and Punic Civilization." *JAOS* 121 (2001): 623–36.

"Adonis in the Phoenician Text from Pyrgi? A New Reading of KAI 277.5." *Etruscan News* 8 (2007): 9, 12.

"The Large Neo-Punic Inscription (*KAI* 159) from Henchir Medeine (Althiburus) Translated and Interpreted." *Studi Epigrafici e Linguistici* 27 (2010): 39–57.

Schwartz, J. H. *What the Bones Tell Us* (New York, 1993).

Schwartz, J. H., et al. "Human Sacrifice at Punic Carthage?" *American Journal of Physical Anthropology* suppl. 34 (2002): 137–8.

"Skeletal Remains from Punic Carthage Do Not Support the Systematic Sacrifice of Infants." *PLoS ONE* 5 (2010) 5(2): e9177. doi:10.1371/journal.pone.0009177.

Servais-Soyez, B. "Adonis." *LIMC* I (1981): 222–9.

Sperber, D. "An Objection to the Memetic Approach to Culture." In *The Electric Meme: A New Theory of How We Think and Communicate*, ed. R. Aunger (New York, 2002): 163–73.

Stager, L. E. "The Rite of Child Sacrifice at Carthage." In *New Light on Ancient Carthage*, ed. J. Pedley (Ann Arbor, 1980): 1001–11

Stiebing, W. H. *Uncovering the Past: A History of Archaeology* (Oxford, 1993).

Stieglitz, R. R. "The Phoenician-Punic Calendar." *ACFP* 4 (2000): 691–5.

Sznycer, M. "L'emploi des termes 'phénicien', 'punique', 'néopunique'. Problèmes et méthodologie." In *Atti del secondo Congresso Internazionale di Linguistica camito-semitica, Firenze, 16–19 aprile 1974*, ed. P. Fronzaroli (Florence, 1978): 261–8.

Tekoğlu, R., and A. Lemaire. "La bilingue royale louvito-phénicienne de Çineköy." *CRAI* (2000): 961–1007.

Van Dommelen, P. "Ambiguous Matters: Colonialism and Local Identities in Punic Sardinia." In *The Archaeology of Colonialism*, ed. C. L. Lyons and J. K. Papdopoulos (Los Angeles, 2002): 121–47.

Vellay, C. *Le culte et les fêtes d'Adônis-Thammouz dans l'orient antique* (Paris, 1904).

Xella, P. *Baal Hamon: Recherches sur l'identité et l'histoire d'un dieu phénico-punique* (Rome, 1991).

PART III

GREECE AND THE EASTERN MEDITERRANEAN

9

MINOAN RELIGION

NANNO MARINATOS

HISTORY OF SCHOLARSHIP

The bases of Minoan religion were set by the excavator of Knossos, Sir Arthur Evans (1851–1941). Evans realized at once that he was unearthing a magnificent civilization that, although under the strong influence of Egypt, had never become enslaved to it and had thus managed to maintain its own cultural identity (see Map 6). It was a highly literate culture with two different hieroglyphic and two Linear scripts (Hieroglyphic A and B, Linear A and B). The fact that all but Linear B remain undeciphered is an accident of history due to the dearth of preserved materials. There may be little doubt, however, that Minoan culture had myths and ritual texts of which we are unfortunately ignorant due to the perishable nature of the material on which they were written. Such texts would have helped better to elucidate Minoan religion.

As a consequence of this lack of evidence, Evans had to create his own narrative about Minoan mythology based partly on intuition, partly on observance, partly on projection of Greek myth backward, and partly on his solid knowledge of Egypt and the Near East. His basic assumptions as regards Minoan religion were three: (1) Early Crete had aniconic cults. (2) The aniconic objects as well as trees were possessed by the spirits of the divinity. For this idea he was indebted to Edward B. Tylor's theory of animism.[1] (3) The principal goddess of the Minoans was a Great Mother, as he called her. He detected her on the images on seals and wall paintings. Next to her often stood a youthful god, which he sometimes called the goddess's consort, but most times he identified him as her son. A most important observation of Evans is that Minoan religion may be elucidated through

---

[1] Tylor, *The Origins of Culture*.

Map 6. The Aegean.

comparisons with Egypt and the Near East. The Minoan Goddess was similar to Hathor. She was the dominant deity in the pantheon, and thus Minoan religion was virtually monotheistic. Moreover it was a palatial religion; the Great Goddess was also the protectress of the king.

Martin Persson Nilsson subsequently synthesized the study of Minoan and Mycenaean religion in a book that he wrote while Evans was still alive.[2] Nilsson, however, was not as systematic as it might at first seem, and the picture of Minoan religion that he adumbrates is not a coherent one; rather, it is a collection of archaeological data, which he assembled with great meticulousness. His main interest in this religion was the detection of the origins of Greek myth in Minoan times. He lacked Evans's intuitions concerning the meaning of Minoan images and, most importantly, the latter's intensive engagement with the Minoan world. On several occasions Nilsson was critical of Evans, such as Evans's interpretation of Minoan monotheism centering on the Great Goddess. Nilsson in some ways

---

[2] 1st edition, 1927; 2nd revised edition, 1950.

Minoan Religion 239

undermined the coherence of Evans's narrative without really replacing it. The accomplishment of Nilsson must, however, not be underestimated.

Evans's view of Minoan religion is still with us today, although its basis has often been distorted. Popular scholarship and the feminist movement adopted the idea of the Mother Nature Goddess as a primeval deity going back to the Neolithic and Paleolithic eras.[3] In the imagination of moderns, Crete became a utopian paradise, a cradle for peaceful men who seldom fought wars, who worshipped trees and assigned their male gods to a lower order. But such a Mother Nature Goddess is nowhere testified in the second millennium BCE.

This misunderstanding and popularization of Evans's ideas led some scholars to skepticism about our ability to read any narratives into Minoan religion. The deconstruction movement of Jacques Derrida reached the Minoan field as well. Method was emphasized over interpretation, and accuracy of description was favored over meaning. A substantial contribution has been made by Colin Renfrew in his *Archaeology of Cult*.[4] He introduced criteria about how to distinguish the object of worship from the means of worship, how to detect the focal point, how to distinguish the cult room from the storage area. Following this line of reasoning, Christiane Sourvinou-Inwood's analysis of the images on gold rings provides an exemplary model for reading images without presumptions.[5]

A BRIEF HISTORY OF MINOAN CULTURE AND ITS RELIGION

Crete was an independent island culture, which turned into a palatial society in the beginning of the second millennium BCE. From that time on, the kings of the island became partners with other kings across the Aegean. Letters found in the archives of king Zimri-Lim at Mari in the eighteenth century speak about objects of the Keftiu (this is what Cretans were called by their neighbors). Ugaritic texts mention the island of Kaphtor. The Keftiu are depicted in Egyptian tombs during the eighteenth dynasty.[6]

The historical periods of Crete were divided into three main phases by Evans: Early Minoan, Middle Minoan, and Late Minoan. These phases are based on correlations with the Egyptian Old, Middle, and New Kingdom. New methods of dating, based on natural science, are currently also used

---

[3] Gimbutas, *The Language of the Goddess*.
[4] Renfrew, *The Archaeology of Cult: The Sanctuary at Phylakopi*.
[5] Sourvinou-Inwood, "On the Lost 'Boat' Ring from Mochlos," 60–9; Sourvinou-Inwood, "Space in Late Minoan Religious Scenes in Glyptik."
[6] Evans, *Palace of Minos* II (1928), 658ff.

by archaeologists, but they have proved to be anything but reliable. A more historically oriented division of Minoan chronology was proposed by the Greek scholar Nikolaos Platon, who suggested First Palace (ca.1990–1650) and Second Palace Period (ca.1650–1375 BCE) instead of Middle and Late Minoan. In about 1375 BCE, the palace of Knossos was destroyed by earthquakes. From then onward Crete seems to have played a secondary role in the Aegean, being supplanted by the kingdom of Mycenae on the mainland of Greece. Why the palace of Knossos fell is a highly debated question;[7] at any rate, its fall did not signify change in the religious tradition. Post-palatial Crete has the same religious symbols as the preceding era, but it is clear that the fall of kingship necessitated a major social reform as regards the priesthood. Although the king was high priest during the palatial period,[8] after the fall of Knossos this could no longer be the case. Also, the palaces could no longer function as cult centers. Yet, the deities and their symbols were preserved.

SOURCES AND METHOD

One of the early scripts used in Crete, Linear A, remains undeciphered, and consequently no myths are preserved of the second millennium. We must therefore rely on archaeology and especially images to reconstruct religion. Imagery has the advantage that it has vocabulary and syntax, as language does. Yet, pictures too have limitations: How do we read them without knowledge of the visual conventions of a culture and, most importantly, the mental apparatus of this culture? And how can we appreciate meaning if we do not know who commissioned the representation? These are real difficulties, but they need not be exaggerated. Evans's decision was to study Minoan religion as part of an interconnected East Mediterranean world with emphasis on parallels from Egypt and Anatolia. These were fruitful paths.

The method adopted here pursues the same approach and will consider Minoan religion in a Near Eastern perspective, contextualizing it in its Eastern Mediterranean second millennium setting, and connecting it with other theocratic religions of the Ancient Near East and Egypt. Given these links, we should expect a king who was also high priest and a close connection between sanctuary and palace. This is the case in all Near Eastern

---

[7] See, for example, Hood, *The Arts in Prehistoric Greece*.
[8] For analogies with the Hittite kingdom see Beckman's discussion of Hittite religion in Chapter 3.

Minoan Religion   241

kingdoms. Parallels from the Hittite and Egyptian empires strengthen this hypothesis greatly.[9]

There remains, still, the question of whether or not it is legitimate to assume continuity of tradition between Minoan Crete and Classical/ Hellenistic/Roman Greece. Is it possible that Minoan cults, gods, and their myths survived? The answer to this complex question is that *yes*, there is a possibility of continuity, but it must be *proven* rather than *assumed*. There are circumstances that make survival of myths and cults possible within the *same* region. One such factor is the continuity of language and written tradition. In the case of Crete, however, it must be noted that Minoan is not Greek, and, if one is to posit continuity between the two cultures, regions, and eras, one must also posit that myths were translated into Mycenaean, and that they were somehow inherited by later Greeks after a thousand years. Further it must be assumed that the preservation was deliberate, as happened with Jewish literature. These are possibilities, but, to this author, they seem rather implausible ones. The once widely held view that Greek myths reflect Minoan precursors cannot be taken for granted; such a view must be demonstrated rather than stated as axiomatic truth.[10]

On the positive side, Minoan and Greek myths were both part of a larger religious pool, a *koine*, that lasted over three millennia in the Eastern Mediterranean. For this reason, common elements between Greek and Minoan probably do exist, but contemporary Near Eastern cultures may furnish closer models than Greek myth.

THE KING

No account of Minoan religion is possible without taking into account the role of the king because he was the high priest of the gods and the main legitimate intermediary between the human community and the divine world. Evans's vision of a Priest King, whom he detected in the famous relief painting from Knossos, is doubted by several scholars today, but it is certainly entirely consistent with the traditions of the Ancient Near East.[11] The king presided in all major state festivals.[12] It would be unthinkable for

[9] See ibid.
[10] See also Rutherford's discussion of Mycenaean religion in Chapter 10.
[11] Van de Mieroop, *A History of the Ancient Near East*; Marinatos, *Minoan Kingship and the Solar Goddess*.
[12] Frankfort, *Kingship and the Gods*.

242 *Nanno Marinatos*

Near Eastern specialists to write an account of rituals without references to the king.[13]

In the heart of the palace of Knossos and west of the central court, Evans found the oldest stone throne of the Aegean world. From the beginning he identified it as the seat of King Minos in an attempt to associate a figure and a name with the throne. But if this is accepted, we must wonder how this modest area could be the audience hall of a king. The problem may be solved if the throne room is interpreted as a sanctuary (a house of god; see below) situated within the palace.[14] The throne of the deity is also the throne of the king; the king thus becomes a partner with the god or goddess and sits on the throne. The benches accompanying the throne were designed for a restricted elite who could witness the king's intimacy with his patron deity. The German scholar Helga Reusch made another suggestion: The throne was designed for a female divinity. Hittite texts provide us with a scenario that supports this hypothesis of the partnership between king and goddess. During the festival of the storm-god, the Hittite king and the queen entered the sanctuary and sat on the throne of the deity. There they performed various rituals of libation and handled the sacred objects of the god. The ritual was witnessed by the master of ceremonies and other officials, but most people stayed outside. They knew what happened but did not witness it directly.[15] Another parallel comes from Egypt. The pharaoh sat on the throne of Isis, who was his mother and protector. Note also that the name "Hathor," the mythical mother of the pharaoh, means in Egyptian "house of Horus," that is, his palace.[16] The function of the Knossos throne room may thus be deduced from unexpected sources: texts of the Hittite and Egyptian kingdoms.

The role of the king at Knossos required both administration and religious performance, especially participation in public sacrifices. King and queen had to demonstrate that they were closer to the gods than ordinary people, and this could be achieved only by processions in which the royal couple, dressed in magnificent paraphernalia and carrying the emblems of the gods, displayed their special status. This may be the reason why, in the iconography of Minoan Crete, it is difficult to distinguish king from god: The two look exactly the same, and the ambiguity was no doubt intentional. In one case a king is accompanied by a griffin (see Fig. 12). We also understand why the palaces of Crete had large courts. The latter were

---

[13] See Beckman in Chapter 3, who says that the king served as a high priest in every major festival. For Egyptian religion, see Doxey's contribution to this volume, Chapter 7.

[14] On the designation house of god in Hittite documents, see Chapter 3.

[15] See ibid. for this rite.

[16] See Chapter 7 for these deities.

Fig. 12. King accompanied by griffin. Source: *CMS* I, 223.

designed to accommodate large crowds to witness the performances of the royal couple in their priestly capacities. Lavish banquets must have taken place following sacrifices. The queen mother and the royal children as well as other relatives of the king undoubtedly took part. This scenario matches what we know about Hittite festivals rather well.[17]

HOUSE OF GOD

Minoan Crete presents us with a seeming paradox. Temples, which typify most palatial societies in Egypt and the Near East, seem to be missing. House-shrines are detectable, and so are nature sanctuaries in caves or on

---

[17] See Chapter 3.

mountains tops. What are missing are independent monumental buildings with a cela and a base for a cult image. This paradox may be easily solved when we realize that the term "temple" is a conceptual term and not an architectural category, and that our notion of temple is colored by notions of Greco-Roman temples. Even in the Near East temples do not conform to a strict typology: Hittite temples are huge buildings with many rooms and storage areas.[18] Canaanite shrines, on the other hand, are far more modest, and there is great variation between them. Egyptian temples contain inner shrines with cult images but also a host of ceremonial halls and storage areas.[19] A notorious case is the interpretation of the biblical *bamah* (Ezek 20:29). Is it an altar, a "high place," or any open air shrine?[20]

A first step toward clarity is that we replace "temple" with the term "house of god" (Hebrew, *bêt elohim*). Such a term defines the edifice as a dwelling place of the deity without specifying its size or design, whether it has a roof or it is just an enclosure. A second step is to define how the "house of god" was conceptualized by the Minoans themselves, and this may be accomplished only by the investigation of imagery.

Such a house of god is represented on a gold ring recently found in a tomb at Poros, near Herakleion (see Fig. 13). This building is located on a mountain top and is surmounted by a horn-like object. Evans originally interpreted such M-objects as horns of bulls but, as many scholars increasingly have come to realize, the object is a symbol of a a cosmic mountain (*axis mundi*) with twin peaks. Below it is an incurved design. In front of the building is a woman who makes a gesture of greeting or adoration; this shows that the edifice is a house of god. The woman may be the queen, who at the same time is high-priestess.

These two examples suffice to demonstrate the existence of a codified visual vocabulary for the representation of the house of god. The house of god has the same form as the palace of the king. This means that no distinction was made between divine palace, royal palace, and temples: The deities were imagined as living in the palace along with the king and queen.

A second type of house of god is an open air sanctuary with a tree as its focus of worship (see Fig. 14). Such types are attested in other cultures of the East Mediterranean and fit the description of holy places in biblical texts: "You shall not plant for yourself any tree, *as a wooden image*, near the altar which you build for yourself to the Lord your God" (Deut 16:21).

---

[18] See ibid.

[19] Wilkinson, *The Complete Temples of Ancient Egypt*.

[20] Biran, *Temples and High Places in Biblical Times*.

Fig. 13. Divine palace. Ring from Poros, Crete. Source: *Archäologischer Anzeiger* 2005, Fig. 1.

Fig. 14. Man shaking tree and woman dancing; scene of ecstatic divination. Ring from Vapheio, Peloponnese. Source: CMS I, 126.

246 *Nanno Marinatos*

Thus, the house of god is a *conceptual category that includes* palace as well as open air shrine.

HOUSE CULT

Domestic cults in Minoan households were detected already by Evans, but it was Nilsson who systematically investigated the subject, devoting one chapter to "House Sanctuaries" in his *Minoan Mycenaean Religion.* In 1985 Geraldine Gesell made a thorough and updated study in which she introduced the important distinction between town, house, and palace cult.[21] In the house shrines we may envisage a smaller clientele with the master of the house officiating and members of his household, servants and dependents, taking part. The size of the house and its storage capacity approximately indicate the scale of the sacrificial banquets. It must be stressed that a religious feast is primarily a banquet, of which only a part is dedicated to the gods; the rest is consumed by the community. For this reason, we must always expect storage jars, cups, and pots to accompany religious paraphernalia, such as portable altars or incense burners.

At Akrotiri at Thera (Santorini), each house had its own cult rooms, most of them decorated with murals.[22] From Cretan sites we have no painted house shrines because murals are seldom preserved. But they have distinctive architectural features, such as benches on which idols or aniconic emblems of the deity stood. In front of these benches offering tables and jars with liquids were placed. The type of shrine with benches and cult images is evident also on the Mycenaean mainland, as well as in Syria and Palestine.[23] The shrines with benches and idols may thus be viewed as part of a Near Eastern and Aegean religious *koine.*

RITUALS

In most ancient religions the act of worship involves sacrifice of animals or bloodless offerings to the gods. Scenes of animal sacrifice are attested on seals. On the painted sarcophagus from Hagia Triada, a woman prays in front of a sacrificed bull or cow. She is most likely the queen acting in her role as high priestess.

Processions and festivals are depicted on the murals of the palace of Knossos. The splendid life-size mural from the West Entrance stands

---

[21] Gesell, *Town, Palace, and House Cult in Minoan Crete.*
[22] Marinatos, *Art and Religion in Thera.*
[23] Keel and Uehlinger, *Gods, Goddesses, and Images of God in Ancient Israel.*

out as one of the best examples of one such procession. It consists of tribute bearers who bring vessels and other luxury objects to the palace. The focal point is unfortunately not preserved, but we may assume that the objects were delivered to the king and queen and/or their patron goddess.

Recently scholars have laid emphasis on rites of passage. For example, it has been noted that many of the participants on the murals from the Minoan-influenced island of Thera (Santorini) are youths. The ages of the participants may be inferred from their shaved heads, a feature that characterizes only children and adolescents in Minoan and Egyptian art. The youths are shown in various activities: The girls gather crocus flowers whereas the boys wrestle, fish, or hunt. One scene is fraught with drama. It concerns a girl seated on a rock who has suffered a wound to her foot. A fallen crocus next to her suggests that the wounding occurred while she was collecting flowers. This may be a reference to a myth that we have no way of reconstructing. The flowing of blood, however, cannot be fortuitous and most likely marks her symbolic status as a woman; it may thus well be a myth alluding to the entry of the girl into womanhood (see Fig. 15).[24]

A group of gold rings from Crete and the mainland show another peculiar rite that, however, is not a puberty rite because adults are involved. A man or a woman shake a tree or lean passively over a rounded rock. As Evans was the first to realize, these rites are of an ecstatic nature. But what was the purpose of the ecstasy? A reasonable explanation is this: When a tree is shaken, the rustling of its leaves makes sounds, which may be interpreted as the "word of the tree." Exactly such a phrase occurs in Ugaritic texts: *a word of tree and whisper of stone*.[25] On certain seals and ring impressions, a female ecstatic rests on a rock and seems to see a vision consisting of a pair of enormous butterflies (see Fig. 16). This activity is best interpreted as an ecstatic rite of prophecy similar to those practiced in the Near East.

The Minoans certainly practiced aniconic worship, as may be inferred from the presence of votives among stalagmites in the Cretan caves, Psychro, Amnissos, Skoteino, and others. The former included altars as well. The cult of the Cretan caves must have been related to deities of the Underworld, and a plausible case was made by Evans that the goddess of the Underworld and the goddess of earth and sky was the same. Her symbol was the double axe.

---

[24] Marinatos, *Art and Religion in Thera*, 43–72.
[25] *KTU* 1.3. iii 21 ff; N. Wyatt, *Religious Texts from Ugarit*, 78.

Fig. 15. Wounded girl. Mural from Thera (Santorini). Source: Marinatos *Art and Religion in Thera*, 74.

Finally, a few words must be said about the most spectacular public festival of Minoan Crete, acrobatics and bull games. The palace of Knossos seems to have been behind the organization because it used the theme as a subject on its murals. Also, Knossos had a large west court to host such festivals. In this way it provided entertainment to the people, enhanced its glory, and showed its reverence for the Great Goddess, to whom the games were dedicated. Evans comprehended all this but committed one

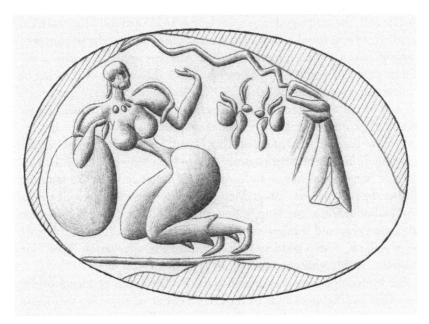

Fig. 16. Woman leaning over a stone; scene of ecstatic divination. Ring impression from Hagia Triada, Crete. Source: CMS II, 6, 4.

mistake. He thought that women performed the bull-leaping sport along with men. He was wrong about that because all the participants (white or red in color) have male anatomy: They wear male costumes with phallus sheaths and have no breasts.

THE GREAT GODDESS AND THE DOUBLE AXE

Evans was quite right that the dominant goddess of the Minoan pantheon was a female one, and that her symbol was the double axe. Representations of this goddess abound in murals, rings, and seals even on objects found on the mainland of Greece. A few statuettes representing her as a snake handler were found in the palace of Knossos itself. After the fall of the palace of Knossos in 1400, many more were found in chapels of private houses and towns which means that this type of worship survived the demise of the palaces and was spread from the center to the periphery.

Evans also perceived, correctly in the view of this author, that the Minoan Great Goddess was the mother of the major male god. There are parallels in Near Eastern mythologies for such a pair. The mother of the chief warrior god (the storm-god, for example) has an exalted role. The mythical paradigm reflects social reality, namely, that the goddess is the patroness of both the queen or queen mother and her son. For mythical examples see Ninsun, the cow-goddess in Gilgamesh. She is the mother of the king of Uruk and intervenes on his behalf with the sun-god.[26] The dowager queen is a very important figure in royal households of the Near East and Egypt because she controls lineage. Of some interest in this context is the important role of Bathsheba, mistress of King David, for the selection of her son Solomon as king.[27] In Mesopotamia this goddess may be identified with Ishtar or Ningirsu, or Mami. In Egypt she is Hathor and Isis.[28] Among the Hittites she is Hepat, the sun-goddess of Arinna, whereas her son Sharuma is an embodiment of the king.[29] Note that the Hittite queen receives the title *tawananna* and is priestess of the sun-goddess of Arinna.[30] In Ugarit she is Athirat. These goddesses often receive the appellation "great" or "mistress." In Mycenaean Linear B, she is named *po-tni-ja*.[31]

The Minoan goddess was similar to these other queen goddesses of the Near East and Egypt, a type of Egyptian Hathor or Isis. Like them, she was most likely a solar deity. On a ring found at Thebes she is shown with the sun above her (see Fig. 17). On a gold ring from Tiryns (see Fig. 18), the goddess is seated on a throne receiving libations from demons with a leonine form, reminiscent of the Egyptian goddess Taweret. Here again we see the enthroned goddess associated with luminaries of heaven, the sun and moon.

The Great Goddess is thus a celestial and chthonic goddess at the same time, a deity who controls the *entire universe*. She is also the patroness and mother of the young god and the king alike.

Regarding the name of the Solar Goddess, we must note that Linear A has not been deciphered. Nevertheless, we can perhaps associate her name with an inscription that occurs many times on stone libation vessels and other votives. The inscriptions read *A-sa-sa-ra*. The phonetics of the syllables cannot be equated with any name in Greek mythology. However, the name may be the equivalent of Ugaritic *Athirat* or biblical *A-she-rah*. The Asherah is both a goddess and a palm tree in Israelite cult, and this constitutes a further connection between the Minoan goddess, who is

---

[26] *Gilgamesh* iii, ii; Dalley, *Myths from Mesopotamia*, 65.

[27] 1 Kings 17–22.

[28] Troy, *Patterns of Queenship in Ancient Egyptian Myth and History*.

[29] See Chapter 3.

[30] Bin-Nun, *The Tawannana in the Hittite Kingdom*.

[31] See Chapter 10 for further discussion of the deities in the Linear B tablets.

Fig. 17. Goddess and young god or king greeting each other under a solar sign. Ring from Thebes. Source: CMS V, 199.

Fig. 18. Seated goddess receiving offerings from lion-creatures under sun and moon. Gold ring from Tiryns. Source: CMS I, 179.

252   *Nanno Marinatos*

closely associated with the palm tree, and her counterparts in Syria and early Israelite cult.[32]

THE GREAT STORM-GOD

Evans perhaps underestimated the importance of the male god, whom he thought of as being inferior to the Great Goddess but he discussed him nevertheless. He called him sometimes a boy-god and other times a youthful divinity, martially arrayed. This god supposedly died and was reborn; he was a type of Tammuz or Greek Adonis who was mourned by the mother goddess.[33]

The Swedish scholar Nilsson followed the basic outline drawn by Evans, and so did his compatriot Axel W. Persson: They both viewed the male deity as a hunting-god, "a relic of a nature demon," a god of yearly death who would be mourned by his consort. The myth of the tomb of Zeus, as presented in Hellenistic poetry, was invoked as evidence of the survival of this dying god into Greek myth. The mythical *persona* of the dying god thus became fixed in Minoan studies, and it has rarely been systematically challenged. But there is no visual evidence that points to such a dying god. The youthful male divinity is always depicted as a lord and master of his domain, as facing the seated solar goddess, as dominating over wild animals or as a warrior smiting enemies.[34] All these characteristics suggest a very powerful warrior deity and not a god of vegetation. He is equivalent to the storm-/warrior-gods of the Near East: Baal, Hadad, Marduk, Seth, and Horus, all of which combat enemies and establish order over chaos. Sometimes they also kill the monsters that threaten the cosmic harmony of the universe. That such a god existed is not only evident in the iconography, but is also historically plausible. If we press the social analogy between gods and royalty, the Minoan god embodies the ideal king.[35]

Deeds and accomplishments of such a god would lend themselves to mythological narratives. The following example, a ring impression from Knossos, may be such a mythological narrative. We see here a youthful male combating a monster, the head of which emerges from the waters (see Fig. 19). The youthful man stands in a boat, and although his weapons

[32] Discussion of the connections and further references in Marinatos, *Art and Religion in Thera*, 63–4, 95–6.
[33] Evans, *The Palace of Minos*, 3:464–5; cf. Frazer, *The Golden Bough*, 327–9. For criticism see Wyatt, "Religion at Ugarit"; idem, "There's Such Divinity." For a recent revival of the year god see Otto, "Der Altkretische Jahresgott und seine Feste," 27–48.
[34] For all these images see Marinatos, *Art and Religion in Thera*, 167–85.
[35] Marinatos, *Minoan Kingship*.

Fig. 19. God (?) in a boat attacking Leviathan-type sea monster. Ring impression from Knossos. Source: CMS II. 8. 234 (slightly restored).

are not preserved, it is clear from the position of his hands that he held two weapons, a spear and perhaps also a sword. The male is most likely the god combating a sea-dragon such as the Ugaritic Litanu, the biblical Leviathan, or the Egyptian Apophis, all of which monsters threaten the universe and are defeated by the storm-gods Baal, Jahweh, and Seth. If this pattern is applied to the ring impression from Knossos, we may indeed get a glimpse of a genuine Minoan mythological narrative akin to that of the Near East.

Was there polytheism in Crete? Certainly this was the case. Yet, only the Solar Goddess and the storm-god have recognizable iconographical features because they were the chief deities with a clear mythological profile.

CONCLUSION

This account of Minoan religion has been dominated by two assumptions. The first is that kingship is essential for the appreciation of the social as well as the mythical aspect of Minoan religion. The second is that Near Eastern texts and representations offer an invaluable guide for the "reading" of Minoan images and religion. This comparative approach to Minoan religion was fruitfully applied by Sir Arthur Evans first, and it remains still the best approach, although now the social and economic realities of cult can also be taken into consideration.

However, a problem still remains. What were the connections between Minoan and Mycenaean religions? That there was a connection cannot be doubted. The images yielded by the finds of Mycenaean Greece are similar to those of Crete; we see in both cases a female deity and a warrior-god. On the other hand, the decipherment of Linear B as Greek has introduced a different paradigm (or "assumption" as I called it above) in the study of Mycenaean religion. Instead of reading it through its extant iconography, specialists interpret it through the prism of Linear B and, because the latter is Greek, through Greek myth. The results are puzzling since the Greek gods attested in the tablets – Zeus, Hera, Poseidon, Athena, Dionysus – cannot be detected as distinct personalities in the images of deities found on the Mycenaean mainland. On the other hand, the enthroned Great Goddess is attested in paintings and rings in all the major Mycenaean sites. Perhaps, then, the Minoan model of mother and son fits the Mycenaean evidence best. More finds may shed further light on Mycenaean religious identity in the near future.[36]

BIBLIOGRAPHY

Bib-Nun, Shoshana. *The Tawannana in the Hittite Kingdom.* Texte der Hethiter S. (Heidelberg, 1975).

CMS = Corpus der minoischen und mykenischen Siegel, ed. F. Matz, H. Biesantz, and I. Pini. Akademie der Literatur and Wissenschaften, Mainz (Berlin, 1964–).

Dalley, S. *Myths from Mesopotamia: Creation, the Flood, Gilgamesh, and Others.* (Oxford, 1998).

Dimopoulou, N., and G. Rethemiotakis. "The 'Sacred Conversation' Ring from Poros." In *Minoisch-mykenische Glyptik: Stil, Ikonographie, Funktion: Ergebnisse eines Internationalen Siegelsymposiums, Marburg, September 1999*, CMS Beiheft 6, ed. W. Müller (Berlin, 1999): 39–56.

Evans, A. J. *The Palace of Minos.* 4 vols. (London, 1921–1935).

Frazer, James G. *The Golden Bough: A Study of Magic and Religion.* Abridged ed. (London, 1922).

Gimbutas, M. *The Language of the Goddess* (San Francisco, 1995).

Hood, S. *The Minoans: Crete in the Bronze Age* (London, 1971).

---

[36] For the problems of Linear B and the new models to approach Mycenaean evidence see Chapter 10.

Koehl, Robert. "The Chieftain Cup and a Minoan Rite of Passage." *Journal of Hellenic Studies* 106 (1986): 99–110.

Marinatos, N. *Art and Religion in Thera: Reconstructing a Bronze Age Society* (Athens, 1984).

Minoan Religion: Ritual, Image, and Symbol (Columbia, S.C., 1993).

Minoan Kingship and the Solar Goddess (Urbana, 2009).

Marinatos, S. "Μινωική και Ομηρική Σκύλλα." *Archaologikon Deltion* X (1926): 51–62.

"Le Temple géometrique de Dréros." *Bulletin de Correspondence Hellenique* 60 (1936): 214–256.

Matz, F. *Göttererscheinung und Kultbild im minoischen Kreta. Abhandlungen der Geistesund Sozialwissenschaftlichen Klasse,* Akademie der Wissenschaften und der Literatur in Mainz vol. 7 (Wiesbaden, 1958).

Nilsson, M. P. *The Minoan-Mycenaean Religion and Its Survival in Greek Religion.* 2nd ed. (Lund, 1950).

Otto, B. "Der Altkretische Jahresgott und seine Feste." In *Kreta und Zypern: Religion und Schrift. Von der Frühgeschichte bis zum Ende der Archaischen Zeit. 26.–28.2.1999, Ohlstadt/Oberbayern – Deutschland,* ed. A. Kyriatsoulis. Verlag für Kultur und Wissenschaft (Ohlstadt, 2001).

Persson, A. W. *The Religion of Greece in Prehistoric Times* (Berkeley, 1942).

Platon, N. "Inscribed Libation Vessel from a Minoan House at Prassa, Herakleion." In *Minoica, Festschrift Grumach,* ed. H. Reusch (Berlin, 1958): 305–18.

Renfrew, C. *The Archaeology of Cult: The Sanctuary at Phylakopi,* BSA Suppl. 18 (London, 1985).

Rethemiotakis, G., and Dimopoulou, N. "The Sacred Mansion Ring from Poros, Herakleion." *Athenische Mitteilungen* 118 (2003): 1–22.

Reusch, H. "Zum Wandschmuck des Thronsaales in Knossos." In *Minoica, Festschrift Grumach,* ed. Reusch (Berlin, 1958): 334–58.

Rutkowski, B. *The Cult Places of the Aegean* (New Haven, 1986).

Sourvinou-Inwood, C. "On the Authenticity of the Ashmolean Ring 1919.56." *Kadmos* 10 (1971): 60–9.

"On the Lost 'Boat' Ring from Mochlos." *Kadmos* 12 (1973): 149–58.

"Space in Late Minoan Religious Scenes in Glyptik: Some Remarks." In *Fragen und Probleme der Bronzezeitlichen Ägäischen Glyptik: Beiträge zum 3. Internationalen Marburger Siegel-Symposium 5–7 September 1985.* CMS Beiheft 3, ed. Walter Müller (Berlin, 1989): 241–57.

Troy, Lana. *Patterns of Queenship in Ancient Egyptian Myth and History.* (Stockholm, 1986).

Watson, W. G., and N. Wyatt, ed. *Handbook of Ugaritic Studies.* Handbook of Oriental Studies, Part 1: The Near and Middle East 39 (Leiden, 1999).

Wilkinson, R. H. *Reading Egyptian Art: A Hieroglyphic Guide to Ancient Egyptian Painting and Sculpture* (London, 1992).

Wyatt, N. *Religious Texts from Ugarit: The Words of Ilimilku and His Colleagues.* The Biblical Seminar 33, 2nd ed. (Sheffield, 2002).

Wyatt, Nicolas. "There's Such Divinity Doth Hedge a King." In *Selected Essays of Nicolas Wyatt on Royal Ideology in Ugaritic and Old Testament Literature.* Society for Old Testament Study Monographs (Ashgate, 2005).

10

MYCENAEAN RELIGION

IAN RUTHERFORD

Mycenaean religion means the religion of mainland Greece in the Late Helladic (LH) period, when we know from the evidence of Linear B that the language of administration was Greek.[1] The principal centers in this period are Mycenae and Pylos in the Peloponnese, Thebes in Boeotia, and Knossos in Crete, which Greeks must have taken over sometime around 1400 BCE. Our picture of Greek civilization in this period is still incomplete; above all, we do not know whether there was a single center of power, or if so, where it was (Mycenae and Thebes are the likely contenders). Hittite records from the fourteenth and thirteenth centuries refer to Ahhiyawa, which is now generally identified with Mycenaean Greece.[2]

Research on Mycenaean religion can be divided into two phases, before and after the decipherment of Linear B in 1952. The most comprehensive survey of the archaeological and iconographical sources was by Martin Nilsson,[3] who argued for a unified Mycenaean/Minoan religion, which was a distant ancestor of the Greek religion of the alphabetic period. The decipherment of Linear B as Greek enabled scholars to explore in a more focused way the relationship of Mycenaean religion to the religion of the Minoans (whose language was not Greek; see discussion of Mycenaean religion and Minoan religion) and to Greek religion of the alphabetic period (see discussion of Mycenae and Greek religion of the alphabetic period). Archaeological excavations in the last fifty years have also been important, for example, at the Cult-Center at Mycenae (see discussion of cult places) and at Phylakopi on the Aegean island of Melos, and new archaeological discoveries continue to be made, as at Kalapodi in Phokis, where a major

---

[1] For the Mycenaean sites, see Map 6 in Chapter 9.
[2] See Hawkins, "Tarkasnawa," 1–31.
[3] Nilsson, *The Minoan-Mycenaean Religion.*

256

temple of the classical period seems to have been built on the foundations of a Mycenaean structure.[4] Problems of interpretation remain, however, as can be seen from the recent controversy surrounding newly published Mycenaean tablets from Thebes; the editors claimed these showed evidence for religious festivals, but those claims were later disputed.[5]

Two recent trends in the research can be mentioned. First, ritual practice in the Mycenaean palace is now understood better due to recent work on feasting, drawing on both texts and material culture (including zooarchaeology) to build up a comprehensive picture.[6] Second, since the decipherment of Linear B, scholars have been interested in understanding the place of religion within the general economic structures of Mycenaean society, and in particular whether Mycenaean Greece had centralized temple-states of the sort known from the Ancient Near East. Lisa Bendall's recent study of the subject[7] suggests that this was not the case, and that the religious and political spheres were distinct.

TEXTUAL EVIDENCE

Linear B tablets are attested from Pylos, Thebes, Knossos, Mycenae, and, to a lesser extent, Tiryns and Khania. Those from the mainland are dated to the end of LHIIIB (around 1200 BCE), whereas those from Knossos have generally been placed around 1400 BCE, although they too may be from the thirteenth century.[8] Linear B is still imperfectly understood: the syllabary is ambiguous because it does not usually write the final consonant of syllables, or introductory "s" before consonants, and not all the values of the signs are certain (uncertain signs are transcribed * + a number). The most reliable guide to the vocabulary is Aura Jorro, *DMic*, and the most convenient commentary on religious texts is still Gerard-Rousseau.[9]

Typically, a name or word attested in Linear B can be represented either (a) as an alphabetic transcription of the syllables, for example, *pa-ki-ja-ne* (the name of the main sanctuary at Pylos),[10] or (b) as many scholars believe it would have been written in an alphabetic script: *Sphagianes*. In addition, (c) when a word or name indisputably continues in alphabetic Greek, it is common to use this form (hereafter cited as AG).

---

[4] See Jacob-Felsch, "Die Spätmykenische," 102–5.
[5] See Palaima, Review of Aravantinos (2001).
[6] See Wright, *Mycenaean Feast*.
[7] Bendall, *Economics of Religion*, esp. 290–2.
[8] Ibid., 10–14.
[9] Gerard-Rousseau, *Les mentions*.
[10] NB: the letter "j" is conventionally written for the "y," i.e., a glide between vowels.

All surviving texts are administrative records, dealing with personnel, livestock, metals, vessels, cloth, or weapons. Each published tablet has an inventory number of the form Fr 1219, where the first letter encodes the class of tablet (e.g., F is conventionally used for offerings tablets with the ideogram for oil). Inventory numbers are usually preceded by a two-letter prefix indicating the provenance (PY for Pylos, KN for Knossos, etc.). The most important class of tablets for the study of Mycenaean religion are records of offerings or contributions, which survive from Pylos (Fr: olive oil), from Knossos (Fp, Fh: oil; Gg: honey), and now from Thebes in the form of seals (the Wu series). Records of personnel are also important (e.g., some of the PY A class) and inventories of utensils (PY Ta, Tn). These documents are usually extremely simple, for example, KN Gg 702: *pa-si-te-o-i/me-ri* AMPHORA 1 /*da-pu$_2$-ri-ti-jo/po-ti-ni-ja meri* AMPHORA I (One jar of honey to all the gods / One jar of honey to the Mistress of the Labyrinth). At the other extreme, the most illuminating of all tablets for the study of Mycenaean religion is PY Tn 316, which records gift-giving of vessels to deities during a specific month of the sacred calendar. Another text from Knossos (KN V 280) could be part of a sacred calendar, specifying that certain activities are inappropriate on certain days, but the interpretation is uncertain (see discussion of ritual and sacrifice). Thus, the most the texts tell us is the names of deities, other official offerings made, and the occasions of the offerings, but nothing about how the deities were perceived, or about popular, sub-official religion.

How problematic interpretation is can be illustrated with a few examples. First, the Fp offering tablets from Knossos preserve a name *qe-ra-si-ja*, which has been interpreted in three ways: (a) as a theonym, "the goddess of Thera"; (b) as a theonym, "the goddess of the beasts" (AG *ther*; cf. Homer, *Il.* 21.470: *potnia theron*); or (c) as title of a religious official connected with omens (cf. AG *teras*, Tiresias). A second example comes from Pylos. In the Fr tablets, the word *di-pi-si-jo-i* has been interpreted as "the thirsty ones," either a theonym or a euphemism for the dead (cf. below), but it could also mean "at the *dipsia*-festival."[11] The Fr series also has the word *wa-na-so-i*, which has been often interpreted as "*wanassoiïn*," that is, "to the two ladies," but other interpretations are possible as well.

Among the numerous obscurities in the Pylos material, PY Tn 316, we may single out the deity *pe-re-*82*, who has been interpreted as *Peleiwa* (Dove) but in several other ways as well. Similarly, the new tablets from Thebes contain many disputed words. For example, the sequence *ma-ka*

---

[11] Cf. Trümpy, "Nochmals," 191–234.

Mycenaean Religion 259

(Fq series) suggested to the original editors the expression Ma Ga, used by the fifth-century-BCE Greek poet Aeschylus apparently in the sense of "Mother Earth" (*Suppliants* 890), but other interpretations of *ma-ka* may be preferable, for example, the unpretentious noun *maga* (AG *mage*), "kneading."[12]

ARCHAEOLOGY AND MATERIAL CULTURE

Archaeologists recognize three types of Mycenaean sites as showing signs of religious activity: the *megaron* (ceremonial hall) of the royal palace, where the *wanax* (king) no doubt presided over state rituals; specialized cult centers attached to palaces, the best preserved of which is the one at Mycenae; and shrines not apparently attached to palaces, of which a few are known. Religious activity probably also took place in open-air sites that lacked architectural structures (see discussion of cult places).[13]

Rings and gems found in Mycenaean sites seem to depict aspects of cult activity and religious experience. Because these are Minoan in design and may be primarily artistic objects, they do not necessarily reflect the religious beliefs of their owners. Careful work is necessary to distinguish Mycenaean features. One example of a ring with a religious symbol that is likely Mycenaean is the ring from the Acropolis Treasure at Mycenae depicting a figure-of-eight shield, directly comparable to the "Palladion" from Tsountas' House (*CMS* I, n.17; see discussion of the pantheon).[14]

Clay figurines are one of the characteristic features of Mycenaean religion. Most of them are small female figurines, called *phi*, *psi*, or *tau* depending on the posture.[15] A few larger statues have been found, at Asine, Mycenae (from the "House of the Idols"), and Phylakopi, and some of these could be cult icons. The larger figurines also tend to be female, although male ones were found at Phylakopi. There are indications that figurines were used in ritual: One thinks of the term *te-o-po-ri-a* (=*theophoria*, "carrying the god"), and such usage seems to be illustrated in some frescoes: K-P71 from Mycenae and K-P106–7 from Tiryns.[16] An ivory trio of a boy and two adult female figures survives from Mycenae[17] and has been linked to later Greek ideas about the Eleusinian triad.[18] Mycenaean frescoes are strikingly

---

[12] Aravantinos et al., *Thèbes*, 190; for criticism, Palaima, review in *Minos* (2001).
[13] Wright, *Spatial Configuration*.
[14] See Niemeier, "Cult Scenes," 165–70.
[15] French, "The Development," 101–87.
[16] With Boulotis, "Zur Deutung," 59–67.
[17] Wace, *The Ivory Trio*; Poursat, *Catalogue*, 20–1.
[18] Vermeule, *Greece in the Bronze Age*, 292.

260   Ian Rutherford

Minoan in style and technique, and, as in the case of seals, it is hard to know whether they reflect indigenous religious practice. One way out of this difficulty is to concentrate on features that are different from Minoan art. Kontorli-Papadopoulou[19] concludes that the following features are distinctive of the mainland: the warrior-goddess, symbolized by figure-of-eight shields and a helmeted figure carrying a griffin; female processions, which probably represent votaries; material offerings; and lions accompanied by griffins. For frescoes, see the next section.

THE PANTHEON

The polytheistic nature of Mycenaean religion is established by Linear B texts, principally from Knossos and Pylos, which contain many words that can safely be identified as theonyms due to parallels with AG. The word for god is *te-o* (AG *theos*), and we find the phrase *pa-si-te-o-i* ("to all the gods") at Knossos; a common title for goddesses is *po-ti-ni-ja* (AG *potnia*), often in combinations (see below). In some cases a theonym is not attested directly but can be inferred on the basis of an anthroponym: For example, *a-pa-i-ti-jo*/Haphaistios implies the theonym Haphaistos (later Hephaistos); *s-mi-te-u* may imply Smintheus, a name of Apollo.

The only deities attested at both Knossos and Pylos are *po-si-da-o* (AG Poseidon), *di-we* (AG Zeus),[20] and possibly *di-u-ja* (i.e., *Diwia*). *di-wo-nu-so* (Dionysus) is attested in Pylos and Khania.[21] Otherwise we find different gods in Crete and the mainland: in Knossos *A-re* (=AG Ares), *da-pu₂-ri-to-jo po-ti-ni-ja* ("lady of the Labyrinth"), *pa-ja-wo-ne* (AG Paian, Paiaon), *a-ta-na-po-ti-ni-ja*, *e-re-u-ti-ja* (= AG Eleithia, Eleithuia), *e-ri-nu* (AG Erinus, "Fury"), *qe-ra-si-a* (see discussion above), *a-ne-mo* ("winds"),[22] *e-nu-wa-ri-jo* (AG Enualios), perhaps *e-ne-si-da-o-ne* (=AG Ennosidas), *da-nwa* (AG Danae?), *me-na* (the moon?), *pi-pi-tu-na* (wholly obscure); *pe-ro₂-* at KN E842.3 may be Apellon, an early form of Apollon; in Pylos, various forms of Potnia, as well as *e-ra* (Hera, also attested in Thebes), *po-si-da-e-ja* (*Posidaheia*), *a-ti-mi-ti* (AG Artemis), *ma-te-re te-i-ja* (*Mater Thehia*: Divine Mother), *i-pe-me-de-ja* (cf. AG Iphimedeia), *e-ma-a₂* (AG Hermes), *di-ri-mi-o* (a son of Zeus); *qo-wi-ja* (*Gwowia*, a cow-goddess

---

[19] Kontorli-Papadopoulou, *Aegean Frescoes*, 161–2.
[20] *Di-we*, i.e., *diwei* is the dative; the nominative in MycG is not attested, but it could have been *diweus*.
[21] For the Khania tablet see Hallager et al., "New Linear B Tablets," 61–87; for Dionysus, Antonelli, "Dionisio," 169–76; Palaima, "Die Linear B Texte," 205–24.
[22] On the cult of the wind, cf. Hampe, *Kult der Winde*, esp. 24.

Mycenaean Religion 261

[cf. AG *bous*]?); *ko-ma-we-te-ja* ("she of the hairy one"?);[23] *ma-na-sa, ti-ri-se-ro-e* ("Thrice-hero"; see discussion below), *do-po-ta* ("lord of the house"). The difference between Pylos and Knossos is likely to be partly a matter of chance, since the number of texts surviving is comparatively small, but some of it may be due to local variation: At Pylos, Poseidon is important (as Homer still remembers: see *Od*.4.43, for example), whereas some of the deities attested at Knossos may be indigenous to Crete.

A striking feature of the Mycenaean pantheon are theonyms formed with the title *po-ti-ni-ja*, usually preceded by another word in the genitive case. The simplex *po-ti-ni-ja* is also attested.[24] The compound forms are indicated by find site.

A) From Knossos:

da-pu₂-ri-to-jo po-ti-ni-ja (KN Gg 702), lady of the "Labyrinth," presumably a sacred structure of some sort.

A-ta-na po-ti-ni-ja (KN V 52), possibly Athanas potnia, "mistress of Athens" (?),[25] suggests the Homeric Greek *potni' Athenaia* (*Od*.6.305), "lady Athene."

B) From Pylos:

i-qe-ja po-ti-ni-ja: the first element means "horsey" (AG *hippeia*), possibly to be associated with a Mycenaean statue of a goddess on a horse.[26]

u-po-jo po-ti-ni-ja: the first element is obscure; Sucharski and Witczak[27] suggest it means "baetyl" or "sacrificial post," comparing Sanskrit *yupah*.

po-ti-ni-ja A-si-wi-ja: "mistress of Asia" (?) (*potnia Aswias*) (see discussion below).

C) From Mycenae:

Si-to-po-ti-ni-ja (MY Oi 701): possibly "lady of the grain," which suggests the later Greek goddess Demeter.[28]

Excavations at Mycenae have revealed fragments of frescoes with representations of female figures who could be goddesses. The Room of the Frescoes has a goddess with sheaves of grain (K-P74a), and in

---

[23] Cf. del Freo, "Osservazioni," 145–68; *DMic* suggests that this could be the name of a ritual.

[24] Finkelberg, "Ino-Leukothea between East and West" has claimed to identify the theonym *potnia* in a Semitic inscription in the Levant.

[25] Cf. Gulizio et al., "Religion," 452–61.

[26] Levi, "La dea," 109–25; see EIEC, 279–80.

[27] Sucharski and Witczak, "U-po-jo," 5–12.

[28] The recent attempt to interpret *Ma-ka* and *Ko-wa* in the Thebes tablets as *Ma Ga* ("mother earth," i.e., Demeter) and Korwa is too speculative; see Palaima's review of Aravantinos in *Minos* 35–6 (2000–2001), 481–2.

the panel above the lower part of two goddesses, with between them a down-pointed sword and figures floating (K-P74b). In the Tsountas' House Shrine was found the so-called Palladion, a stucco panel showing a figure-of-eight shield, perhaps representing a goddess, with two votaries on either side (K-P78).[29] Similar shield-frescoes have been found in the Megaron in the Cult Center (K-P80), at Tiryns (K-P 88), and at Thebes (K-P108). And compare K-P73, a helmeted female figure apparently carrying a griffin, found outside Tsountas' House. It is natural to try to link these with known theonyms: K-P74a suggests Sitopotnia; the shield-goddess could be a war-goddess;[30] in K-P74b the goddess with the sword could be either a war-goddess, that is, Athanaspotnia,[31] or a goddess of death both because the small figures floating between could be chthonic, and because of the sword, which it is thought to have a parallel in the funerary symbolism of Hittite Yazılıkaya, where he represents the deity Ugur or Nergal.[32]

Some of the texts give clues about the organization of deities in cult. In PY Tn 316, rites at four shrines are described, each in honor of several deities:

A) At *pa-ki-ja-ne*, for Potnia, Manasa, Posidaeia, Triseros, Dopotas.
B) At the sanctuary of Poseidon, for Gwowia, Komawenteia.
C) At the sanctuary of *Pere*82*, Iphimedeia and Diwia, for *Pere*82*, Iphimedeia, Diwia, and Hermes.
D) At the sanctuary of Zeus, for Zeus, Hera, and Drimios, son of Zeus.

The last of these resembles a classical triad with mother, father, and son.[33] In Khania, Zeus and his son Dionysus were worshipped together. One might have expected that Diwia would be worshipped with Zeus and Posidaeia with Poseidon, but these pairings are not attested.

It is sometimes claimed that the Mycenaean pantheon included zoomorphic deities, but the evidence is at best inconclusive: The tablets have the "horsey" mistress from Pylos, who need not have been represented as a horse; a horse-god has also been alleged (PY Ea 59); from Pylos also comes the goddesses *qo-wi-ja* ("Bovine") and *pe-re-*82*, which might mean

---

[29] The term "Palladion" is a misnomer: see Marinatos, "The Palladion," 107–14.
[30] See Rehak, "The Mycenaean 'Warrior Goddess,'" 232–6.
[31] Rehak, "New Observations," 535–45; idem, "The Mycenaean 'Warrior Goddess,'" 227–39.
[32] Marinatos, "The Fresco," 245–8; Morgan, "The Cult Centre," 159–71; Haas, *Geschichte*, 366–7; Gallou, *The Mycenaean Cult of the Dead*, 37.
[33] This point first made in Gallavotti, "La triada lesbia," 225–36; cf. Tarditi, "Dionisio Kemelios," 107–12.

Mycenaean Religion 263

"dove" (cf. the famous fresco of the singer). Other animal-deities have been alleged in the new Thebes tablets.[34]

Considering that Greek is an Indo-European language, surprisingly little of the religion is demonstrably Indo-European in origins, with the exception of the name Diweus/Zeus and the title *potnia* (cf. Sanskrit *patni*: mistress). Nor is there any trace of the Dumezilian "trifunctionality" often associated with Indo-European culture.[35] It is unfortunate that our only certain source for Mycenaean religion from outside Greece is a Hittite oracular text from the thirteenth century BCE, which attests cult honors paid to a "deity of Ahhiyawa" and a "deity of Lazpa" (Lesbos), apparently in the Hittite court, which had imported these deities for some reason. We do not know the MycG name for either deity.[36]

CULT PLACES

Linear B tablets have several terms for sanctuaries of the gods. General words used are *i-je-ro* = sanctuary (AG *hieron*); *na-wi-jo*, an adjective occurring only on one tablet (PY Jn 829), which may imply the word *naos*: temple; *wo-ko* = alphabetic Greek *oikos*, dwelling place; and *do* = house. Specific places include in Pylos *pa-ki-ja-ne*; *sa-ra-pe-da* in PY Un 718; and several other places mentioned in Tn 316, including *po-si-da-i-jo* (sanctuary of Poseidon), *pe-re-*82-jo* (sanctuary of Pere-*82), and *di-u-jo* (sanctuary of Zeus); and a series of places in the area of Knossos including the *da-da-re-jo*/*daidaleon* and perhaps the *da-pu$_2$-ri-to*/*labyrinthos*, terms that foreshadow Greek traditions about Crete in the alphabetic period.[37]

To turn to the archaeology, the most significant types of structure are the following:

A) The *megaron* (ceremonial hall) of the palace, which seems likely to have been the locus for rituals performed by, on behalf of, and in the presence of the *wanax* (king); a focal point in the *megaron* was the hearth, which may have had religious significance.[38]

B) Independent cult centers within the citadel.[39] The best preserved is the one on the SW side of the Citadel at Mycenae, excavated from 1959

---

[34] See Rousioti, "Did the Mycenaeans Believe?" 305–14.
[35] See Palaima, "The Nature of the Mycenaean *Wanax*," 121–3.
[36] *KUB*5.6; Sommer, *Die Ahhijava Urkunden*, n.10; on the deity of Lazpa, see Singer, "Purple-Dyers in Lazpa," 32.
[37] On the *da-pu$_2$-ri-to* see Hiller, "Amnisos," 63–72. For cult places near Knossos, see DMG 304–5.
[38] Wright, *Spatial Configuration*, 55–7.
[39] See Albers, *Spätmykenische Stadtheiligtümer*; Wright, *Spatial Configuration*, 61–4.

to 1969, apparently connected to the palace via a processional way.[40] It comprised the following rooms:

- The "Temple Complex" (Rooms XI, 18, and 19), also known as "House of Idols," which yielded a number of clay figurines that could be gods or worshippers, as well as an anthropomorphic vase and terracotta snake figures.
- The "House of the Frescoes" (Room 31), laid out with a bench along one side, and a "low rectangular stone base or table" in the middle. K-P74a and 74b were found there. In front of the House of Idols and the House of Frescoes was a circular altar with a fresco fragment representing dancing asses (K-P76).
- The "Tsountas House Shrine," source for the Palladion-panel (K-P79 above). The floor of one room has a horse-shoe shaped hearth, which may have been used for libations, with a stone block that could have been used for sacrifice.
- The so-called Megaron, to the East of the House of Idols and to the North of Tsountas' House, which has yielded important fragments of frescoes, e.g., the Mykenaia (K-P70), and the shield (K-P 80) from LHIIIB and the lady with lily (K-P72 from LHIIIC).

  Other citadel cult centers are found at Phylakopi on the island of Melos, where there were two buildings with religious function ("West Shrine" and "East Shrine"), and a possible baetyl,[41] and at Asine, where Room XXXII, of house G, is the source of a clay figurine, the "Lord of Asine."

C) Open-air sanctuaries. Unlike in Minoan Crete, caves are not major centers of religious activity,[42] and evidence for ritual activity on peaks is also rare, although there are exceptions, including Mount Oros on the island of Aegina (the later seat of Zeus Hellanios), and the site at Mount Kynortion near Epidauros (later Apollo Maleatas).[43]

Several sites known to have been cultic centers in the alphabetic period were built on Mycenaean sites, such as Eleusis.[44] Some of these sites seem to have had a religious function already in the Mycenaean period, such as Kalapodi, Mount Kynortion, and the sanctuary at Ayia Irini on the island of Ceos.

---

[40] See Moore and Taylour, *Temple Complex*, whose system of enumeration I follow.
[41] Renfrew, *The Archaeology of Cult*, esp. 361–91.
[42] However, see Hägg, "Mykenische Kultstätten," 49–52.
[43] See Wright, *Spatial Configuration*, 68–70.
[44] See Darcque, "Les vestiges," 593–605.

Mycenaean Religion

RITUAL AND SACRIFICE

The Linear B evidence demonstrates the practice of sending offerings to sanctuaries, sometimes specifying that they are "*qe-te-jo*" ("payment" or even "fine").[45] Offerings sent are primarily oil, honey, grain, and wool, less often animals and even human beings. The practice of sending offerings can be compared with frescoes from Thebes and from Pylos that illustrate processions and sometimes allow us to identify the thing being offered to the deity, for example, a pyxis, flowers, and a jar on the procession of women from the Kadmeia in Thebes (K-P106).

Animal sacrifice is a significant ritual in all ancient Mediterranean and Near Eastern cultures. Frescoes illustrate sacrifice occasionally (e.g., K-P96 from Pylos), and archaeology confirms that animal sacrifice took place. It used to be believed on archaeological grounds that sacrifice in Mycenaean Greece did not involve burning of parts of the animal reserved for the god, but that view has now been challenged.[46] The tablets mention contributions of animals, but make no reference to sacrifice itself (although the word *sa-pa-ka-te-ri-ja* in KN C 941.B has been interpreted as *sphakteria*, animals to be sacrificed). The usual AG word for sacrifice, "*thu-*," is used only for incense in Linear B. The verbal form "*i-je-to*" (*hiyetoi*) in PY Tn 316 may be related to *i-je-ro* (AG *hieros*, "sacred"), and *i-je-re-u* (= *hiereus*) "priest," and mean "sacred action takes place, there is a sacrifice." Archaeology also suggests that libation was an important part of ritual,[47] and the oil and honey offerings that the tablets mention may well have been used for this purpose.

Several names of rituals and/or festivals are known from the texts, including the following: *te-o-po-r-i-a* from Knossos, "carrying the god" (AG *theophoria*, a ritual where the statue of a deity is carried around, a practice that seems to be confirmed from rituals; *po-re-no-zo-te-ri-ja* from Pylos, festival of girdling of *porenas* (see below), to be compared with a reference in a Thebes tablet to offerings of wool for *porenas* (TH Of 26.3); similarly *po-re-no-tu-te-ri-a*: festival of the sacrifice of victims (?); *me-tu-wo ne-wo* from Pylos: festival of new wine (or is it the name of a month?); *to-no-e-ke-ter-i-jo* from Pylos: often interpreted as "*thorno-helkterion*," that is, "drawing the throne," but there are a number of other possibilities as well (see

---

[45] See Hutton, "The Meaning," 105–32.

[46] The earlier view appears in Bergquist, "The Archaeology," 21–34; idem, "Bronze Age," 11–43; for the new view see Isaakidou et al., "Burnt Animal Sacrifice," 76; Hamilakis and Konsolaki, "Pigs for the Gods," 135–51.

[47] Hägg, "The Role of Libations," 177–84; Konsolaki-Yannopoulou, "New Evidence," 213–20.

DMic); *re-ke-e-to-ro-te-ri-jo* from Pylos: interpreted as *lekhe-stro-terion*, that is, "spreading the couches." There is no alphabetic Greek equivalent, although one can consider the Latin *lectisternium,* the term indicating the ritual for "spreading the couches" for the gods.[48]

At least some of these rituals or festivals are likely to have coincided with major feasts, and the Linear B texts seem to provide evidence for the provisioning of festivals or feasts. This practice was first inferred on the basis of clay nodules from Thebes bearing the imprint of seals (the Wu-series), which revealed the sending of payments from numerous places in the region.[49] Similar patterns have been detected in tablets from Pylos[50] and in other archaeological remains from Pylos.[51]

That the Mycenaeans practiced human sacrifice has been argued for on the basis of (a) archaeological evidence, which is at best uncertain,[52] and (b) textual evidence, specifically PY Tn 316, where the offerings to various gods include the ideogram for man and woman; it has even been suggested that the term *poren,* pl. *porenes,* in this tablet and elsewhere might refer to sacrificial victims.[53] On balance, the case is not strong.

Offering tablets from Pylos and Knossos suggest that offerings were organized on a monthly basis. For Knossos it is possible to reconstruct a system of offerings over several months to different sanctuaries (*DMG,* 304–5). One tablet from Knossos (KN V280) has been interpreted as a sort of religious calendar, where unknown activities are designated "*o-te-mi,*" which could be AG "*ou themis,*" "not religiously correct."[54]

Offerings were sometimes sent a considerable distance and may have been an expression of long-distance relations between states. A collection of seals published in 1990 seemed to indicate that contributions were sent to Thebes from various towns including Karystos and Amarynthos on the island of Euboea, suggesting that the palace at Thebes controlled a large region and used the institution of religious festivals to impose its authority. Knossos sent offerings to Amnisos,[55] possibly Kydonia/ Khania in western Crete, and Nauplion on the mainland. Konsolaki suggests that the presence of a Mycenaean cult in Methana overlooking

---

[48] Milani, "Osservazioni," 231–42.
[49] Pitiros et al., "Les inscriptions," 103–84; Killen, "Thebes Sealings," 67–84.
[50] Killen, "Thebes Sealings"; Bendall, "A Time for Offerings," 1–9.
[51] Stocker and Davis, "Animal Sacrifice," 59–76.
[52] See Gallou, *The Mycenaean Cult of the Dead,* 110–12.
[53] See Buck, "Mycenaean Human Sacrifice"; on Th316, Palaima, "PO-RE-NA"; idem, "KnO2-Tn316."
[54] So *DMG* but *DMic* disagrees.
[55] Taillardat, "Une panégyre," 365–73.

the Saronic Gulf points forward to the later "Calaurian Amphictiony" in the region.[56] Godart and Sacconi argued that the new Thebes tablets showed evidence of offerings being sent as far as the Ptoion and Mount Kithairon (TH Av 106 [+] 91), but this claim has not found general acceptance,[57] nor has the hypothesis that one of the Thebes seals refers to Aphaia in Aegina.[58]

RELIGIOUS PERSONNEL

The word for priest is "hiereus," as in AG; priestess is "hiereia," best attested in Pylos-texts. A priestess of the winds is attested for Knossos (KN Fp 1, 13). One tablet (PY Ep74) seems to record, inter alia, a conflicting claim about a god's ownership of land between the priestess Eritha and the people (*da-mo*): "Eritha the priestess holds and claims that the god holds an *e-to-ni-jo*; but the local community says that he holds an interest consisting in *ko-to-na ke-ke-me-na*."[59]

Many other religious officials have been identified in the tablets, but often we do not know whether we are dealing with religious officials or some other sort of official. Examples are the following:

ka-ra-wi-po-ro = *klawiphoros*: "key-bearer" (cf. AG *kleidoukhos*).

ka-ru-ke, to be analyzed as *karux*, "herald" (AG *kerux*); the herald had a religious role in Greek religion during the alphabetic period.

i-je-ro-wo-ko = *iyeroworgos* (AG *hierourgos*): doer of ritual.

ki-ri-te-wi-ja = *krithewia*: perhaps "barley-scatterer," a class of female ritual specialist.

pu-ko-wo = *purkowos*: "fire-priest," to be identified with the AG *purkoos*.

wo-ro-ki-jo-ne-jo in PY Un718.11 has been related to AG *(w)orgeones* ("ritual initiators"), but there are other possibilities also (*DMic*.2.446).

ke-re-ta in PY Cn 1287.6 could be an early form of AG *khrestes* "prophet" (cf. *DMic*.1.348).

di-pte-ra-po-ro: possibly someone who wears the skin of an animal. In contemporary Hittite texts, there were cultic officials called "wolf-men" and "bear-men";[60] were the *di-pte-ra-po-ro* analogous?

---

[56] Konsolaki, "A Mycenaean Sanctuary," 25–36.
[57] Godart and Sacconi, "Les dieux thébains," 99–113.
[58] Hiller, "TH Wu 94."
[59] See Hooker, "Cult Personnel," 174.
[60] Cf. Pecchali-Daddi, *Mestieri*, 233–4, 473–5.

The tablets attest hierodules, that is, slaves (*do-e-ra* female, *do-e-ro* male, corresponding to AG *doule, doulos*) of the god. At least some of these may have been honorific positions, not implying low social status, because they own land. In addition, some individuals (smiths, women, a perfumer) are specified as *po-ti-ni-ja-we-jo* = *potniaweios*, "belonging to potnia" or "potnian," a usage that suggests that religious institutions played a significant social and economic role within the state (see the next section).

RELIGION AND THE STATE

A rough idea of the Mycenaean state has emerged over the last fifty years. The basic structure of society is likely to have been quasi-feudal, with the *wanax* or king in charge of the palace, and various levels of landowners and officials under him. The palace kept records of people and livestock in the territory it controled and oversaw the gathering and distribution of materials through a system of bureaucratic mechanisms.

A significant, but not preponderant, part of the palace economy was devoted to making contributions to cult.[61] One tablet from Pylos (PY Un718) seems to register contributions by different members of society to a cult of Poseidon: by an individual named *e-ke-ra₂-wo* (Egkhes-lawon?), generally thought to be the *wanax*, by the *damos* (people, AG *demos*), by the *lawagetas*, another official, and by the obscure *wo-ro-ki-jo-ne-jo ka-ma*. The *wanax* gives by far the most, followed by the *damos*. For the contribution of the *damos* here, compare PY Tn 316 VI, where the *wa-tu* (*wastu*, town) may be involved.

Comparison with other Bronze Age cultures suggests that the *wanax* is likely to have had religious authority as well as political authority.[62] This may be indicated by the apparent ritual function of the *megaron* in the palace. One Pylos-text (PY Un2) seems to refer to rituals on the occasion of his initiation.[63]

Within this system, it is possible that some religious institutions may have enjoyed a level of economic autonomy. Attention has focused particularly on persons as "potnian"; in particular the "potnian" smiths, whose existence suggests that temples served as manufacturing centers.[64] However, the surviving textual evidence is heavily weighted in the direction of elite- or palace-sponsored cult. This does not preclude the likelihood that religion worked at a popular level as well, possibly focusing on

---

[61] See Bendall, *Economics of Religion*, esp. 290–2.
[62] Palaima, "Nature," 119–42; Kilian, "*Wanax* Ideology," 291–302.
[63] Palaima, "Nature," 131; Bendall, *Economics of Religion*, 27.
[64] See most recently Lupack, *Role of the Religious Sector*, esp. 114–18.

Mycenaean Religion

different shrines, and some archaeological evidence has been claimed for this area of religious life as well.[65]

CULT OF THE DEAD?

In view of the extensive evidence for Mycenaean mortuary practice,[66] it might be expected that it would be possible to make inferences about those parts of religion that have to do with death, specifically about people's beliefs about the afterlife and the realm of the dead, and about the cult of the dead, if there was any. Both issues are very hard to address.

As for the ideology of death, several of the painted *larnakes* from Tanagra in Boeotia depict winged female creatures, which could be either the soul of the deceased or a deity;[67] one of the frescoes from the cult center at Mycenae (K-P74a) depicts floating figures, and the goddess with the sword has been interpreted as a symbol of death (see discussion above). The Pylos tablet Tn 316 mentions offerings to a figure called *ti-ri-se-ro-e*, which has generally been interpreted as "*tris-heros*," "thrice hero," perhaps meaning an ancestor (cf. AG *tritopatores*), and another called *do-po-ta*, which might mean "lord of the house," another type of ancestor. On the *di-pi-si-jo-i* ("the thirsty ones?"; see discussion above).

As for the cult of the dead, a key focus for discussion here has been the fact that at Mycenae the LHI burials in "Grave Circle A" were later enclosed within the city wall and separated off in a monumental *temenos* or sacred precinct, where they may have become a focus for some form of cult. Some scholars have suggested that the nearby cult center may have been used for activities connected with the veneration of the dead.[68]

MYCENEAN RELIGION AND MINOAN RELIGION

The relation between the two religions is likely to be complex. The standard view is that Greek religion was influenced by the religion of Minoan Crete in the sixteenth century BCE but that subsequently Minoan influence waned.[69] It follows that "Mycenaean religion" as we find it in the

---

[65] See Hägg, "Official and Popular Cults," 35–9; Killen, "Religion at Pylos," 435–43.

[66] Cavanagh and Mee, *A Private Place*, 103–20.

[67] Vermeule, "Painted Mycenaean Larnakes," 123–48; Gallou, *The Mycenaean Cult of the Dead*, 35–6.

[68] Van Leuven, "The Religion of the Shaft Grave Folk;" Gallou, *The Mycenaean Cult of the Dead*, 16–30.

[69] Renfrew, "Questions," 31–2; Hägg, Mycenaean Religion," 213. For Minoan religion, see Chapter 9 by Marinatos.

LH period is a blend of Minoan and mainland elements. Which elements of the resulting amalgam are originally Minoan and which not Minoan is a very difficult issue: The only controls are the few demonstrably Indo-European elements that cannot be Minoan (see above), and elements of material culture that seem non-Minoan, such as figurines, and certain elements of frescoes (see discussion of archaeology and material culture above).

The case of Mycenaean administration in Crete is likely to have been a special case. Thus, the name *Di-wi Di-ka-ta-i-o* (AG Zeus Diktaios), attested in Knossos tablets, may be either an *interpretatio Graeca* (Greek interpretation) of a Cretan deity worshipped on Mount Dikte (whose name may already be represented in Linear A tablets), or a syncretic deity, combining Greek and Minoan elements.[70] Other theonyms in the Knossos tablets could also be originally Minoan gods, or Minoan gods translated into Greek religious idiom. So, for one, *Pajawon* is attested only in KN V 52, whom later Greek tradition remembered as specially associated with Crete.[71]

RELATIONS WITH CULTURES OF THE NEAR EAST AND ANATOLIA

The main period of oriental influence on Greece is the eighth century BCE,[72] but there must have been influence in the Late Bronze Age as well. We know that there were diplomatic contacts between Greece/Ahhiyawa and other Late Bronze Age states (cf. the deity of Ahhiyawa at the Hittite court; see discussion of the pantheon). In addition, although Mycenaean Greece was not a "temple economy,"[73] its palace-centered organization still had similarities to the social-political structures of the Late Bronze Age Near East.[74] Some correspondences in the organization of religion are to be expected on that basis. The institution of hierodules might, for example, be considered a Near Eastern feature,[75] as might the focus on the ruler; so, for example, with the "initiation of the *wanax*" ritual (Un 2), we might compare a Hittite text that describes a ritual for the initiation of a prince.[76] The administrative technique of listing offerings by month found in Mycenaean documents has parallels in the Near East, for example, at

---

[70] For syncretism in this context, see Lévêque, "Le syncrétisme," 19–73; Hägg, "Religious Syncretism," 163–8.
[71] Huxley, "Cretan Paiawones," 119–24.
[72] Burkert, *The Orientalizing Revolution*, 6.
[73] Hiller, "Tempelwirtschaft," 94–104; Bendall, *Economics of Religion*, 4–9.
[74] de Fidio, "Mycènes," 173–96.
[75] Already in Palmer, *New Religious Texts*, 26–7.
[76] See Güterbock, "An Initiation Rite," 111–14.

Alalakh.[77] Similarities between Hittite and Mycenaean administrative texts have been investigated by Uchitel, and this reinforces the ties between these two cultures.[78]

Parallels with Late Bronze Age Anatolia are particularly likely, because the Mycenaean Greeks are known to have been active on the West Coast of Asia Minor. The key pieces of evidence are the theonym *po-ti-ni-ja A-si-wi-ja* (PY Fr 1206), if it is rightly analyzed as "mistress of Asia";[79] the probable attestation of the theonym Apollo in a treaty between the Hittites and the Luvian king Alaksandus of Wilusa, a city that was likely in contact with the Mycenaeans;[80] and the parallel between the down-pointed sword in the Room of the Frescoes at Mycenae and the iconography of Yazılıkaya, Chamber B.

MYCENAE AND GREEK RELIGION OF THE ALPHABETIC PERIOD (FIRST MILLENNIUM BCE)

We use Greek religion of the alphabetic period as a tool to help us reconstruct Mycenaean religion. The problem then arises of how the Mycenaean religious system, so reconstructed, looks in comparison to Greek religion of the alphabetic period, and how the former might have evolved into the latter. The limitations of Mycenaean Greek sources are a problem here, for we face not just the paucity of documentary material, but the lack of narrative texts as well.

Some continuities are attested. We find many theonyms: Zeus, Poseidon, Dionysus, Paion, Hermes, Ares, Enualios, possibly Apollo, Hera, Artemis, Eileithuia, and Athene in the form "mistress of Athana," as well as the title *potnia*. In this regard, we can note here that some Mycenaean Greek theonyms appear as divine epithets in alphabetic Greek, such as Paion of Apollo and Enualios of Ares. We also find a limited number of other religious terms that continue in use: *theos* (god), *naos* (temple), *hieros* (sacred, etc.). On the other hand, some ritual terms have no parallel, such as *po-re-na*. All things considered, the Mycenaean Greek pantheon looks very different from AG. Many Mycenaean Greek deities have no later attestation, and several important deities of AG period are absent, for example, Aphrodite and Demeter (although cf. on *Si-to-po-ti-ni-ja* above). Moreover, the

---

[77] *DMG* 305, with Wiseman, *The Alalakh Tablets,* 93; cf. Pardee, *Ritual and Cult,* 26–40, for monthly offerings at Ugarit.
[78] Uchitel, "Assignment of Personnel," 51–9.
[79] See Morris, "Potniya Aswiya," 423–34.
[80] *CTH* 76; translated in Beckman, *Hittite Diplomatic Texts,* 82–8.

272   Ian Rutherford

presence in some cases of pairs of male and female theonyms from the same root (*Diwia* versus *Diweus* and *Poseidaja* versus *Poseidaon*) suggests that the structure of the pantheon was radically different from the later one (although a theonym Diwia is attested from Hellenistic Pamphylia).[81]

CONCLUSION

In the ancient world religion cannot be distinguished from the political structures of the societies in which it is found. A necessary condition for continuity of religious practice is that there is continuity in respect of political organization. But most scholars would see the political structures of archaic Greece as both discontinuous with and radically different from those of the Late Bronze Age. It follows that the religious system of the Mycenaean palaces and that of the classical Greek city-states is not likely to have been very close.

BIBLIOGRAPHY

Textual Sources

General introduction to the language and script: *DMG* (M. Ventris and J. Chadwick, *Documents in Mycenaean Greek*[2] [1973]) and J. T. Hooker, *Linear B: An Introduction* (Bristol, 1980), both of which contain selections of religious inscriptions.

Knossos

Killen, J.-T., and J.-P. Olivier. *The Knossos Tablets* 5. Minos Suppl. 1 (Salamanca, 1989).

Pylos

Bennett, E. L. *The Pylos Tablets Transcribed*. 2 vols. (Rome, 1976).

Thebes

Aravantinos, V. L., L. Godart, and A. Sacconi. *Thèbes. Fouilles de la Cadmée I. Les tablettes en linéaire B de la Odos Pelopidou. Édition et commentaire* (Rome, 2001).
Spyropoulos, T. G., and John Chadwick. *The Thebes Tablets* II. Minos Suppl. 4 (Salamanca, 1975).

Mycenae

Melena, J. L. and J. P. Olivier. *Titherny. The Tablets and Nodules in Linear B from Tiryns, Thebes and Mycenae. A Revised Transliteration* (Salamanca, 1991).

---

[81] See Brixhe, *Dialecte Grec*, 139.

Mycenaean Religion 273

Khania

Hallager, E., and M. Vlasaki. "New Linear B Tablets from Khania." In *La Crète mycénienne*. BCH Supplément 30, ed. J. Driessen and A. Farnoux (Paris 1997): 169–74.

Material Culture

Archaeology

Iakovidis, S. *Late Helladic Citadels on Mainland Greece* (Leiden, 1983).
Moore, A. D., and W. D. Taylour. *Well-Built Mycenae*, Fascicle 10: *The Temple Complex* (Oxford, 1999).
Whittaker, H. *Mycenaean Cult Buildings: A Study of Their Architecture and Function in the Context of the Aegean and the Eastern Mediterranean*. Monographs from the Norwegian Institute at Athens 1 (Bergen, 1997).

Frescoes

Kontorli-Papadopoulou, L. *Aegean Frescoes of Religious Character*. SIMA 117 (Göteborg, 1996).

Seals

Available in *CMS* (=*Corpus der minoischen and mykenischen Siegel*, ed. F. Matz, H. Biesantz, and I. Pini. Akademie der Literatur and Wissenschaften, Mainz [Berlin, 1964–]), in particular:
Sakellariou, A. *Athen Nationalmuseum*. *CMS* 1 Suppl. (Berlin, 1982).
Die Minoischen und Mykenischen Siegel des Nationalmuseums in Athen. *CMS* 1 (Berlin, 1964).
For minor Greek collections, see the various volumes of *CMS* V.

Mycenaean Ivories

Poursat J.-C. *Catalogue des ivoires mycéniens du Musée national d'Athènes*. Bibliothèque des Écoles françaises d'Athènes et de Rome 230 (Athens, 1977).

Secondary Materials

Albers, G. *Spätmykenische Stadtheiligtümer: Systematische Analyse und vergleichende Auswertung der archäologischen Befunde*. BAR International Series 596 (Oxford, 1994).
"Rethinking Mycenaean Sanctuaries." In *POTNIA. Deities and Religion in the Aegean Bronze Age*, Aegaeum 22, ed. R. Laffineur and R. Hägg (Liège, 2001): 131–41.
Antonelli, C. "I santuari micenei ed il mondo dell'economia." In *Politeia, Society, and State in the Aegean Bronze Age*, vol. 2, ed. Robert Laffineur and W.-D. Niemeier (Liège, 1995): 415–21.
"Dioniso: Una divinità micenea." In *Atti e memorie del secondo Congresso internazionale di micenologia*, Incunabula Graeca 98, ed. E. De Miro, L. Godart, and A. Sacconi (Rome, 1996): I:169–76.

274   *Ian Rutherford*

Aravantinos, V. L., L. Godart, and A. Sacconi. *Thèbes. Fouilles de la Cadmée I. Les tablettes en linéaire B de la Odos Pelopidou. Édition et commentaire* (Rome, 2001).

Baumbach, L. "The Mycenaean Contribution to the Study of Greek Religion in the Bronze Age." *Studi miceneni ed egeo-anatolici* 20 (1979): 143–60.

Beckman, Gary. *Hittite Diplomatic Texts* (Atlanta, 1996).

Bendall, L. M. "A Time for Offerings: Dedications of Perfumed Oil at Pylian Festivals." In *A-NA-QO-TA. Studies Presented to J. T. Killen*, ed. J. Bennet and J. Driessen (= *Minos* 33–4) (Salamanca, 1998–9): 1–9.

"The Economics of Potnia in the Linear B Documents: Palatial Support for Mycenaean Religion." In *POTNIA. Deities and Religion in the Aegean Bronze Age. Aegaeum* 22, ed. R. Laffineur and R. Hägg (Liège, 2001): 445–52.

Economics of Religion in the Mycenaean World: Resources Dedicated to Religion in the Mycenaean Palace Economy. School of Archeology Monograph 67 (Oxford, 2007).

Bergquist, B. "The Archaeology of Sacrifice: Minoan-Mycenaean vs. Greek." In *Early Greek Cult Practice*, ed. R. Hägg, N. Marinatos, and G. Nordquist (Göteborg, 1988): 21–34.

"Bronze Age Sacrificial *Koine* in the Eastern Mediterranean? A Study of Animal Sacrifice in the Ancient Near East." In *Ritual and Sacrifice in the Ancient Near East*, ed. J. Quaegebeuer. Orientalia Lovaniensia Analecta 55 (Louvain, 1993): 11–43.

Boulotis. "Zur Deutung des Freskofragmentes Nr. 103 aus der Tirynther Frauenprozession." *Arch Korr Bl* 9 (1979): 59–67.

Brixhe, C. *Le dialecte Grec de Pamphylie. Documents et grammaire* (Paris, 1976).

Buck, R. J. "Mycenaean Human Sacrifice." *Minos* 24 (1989): 131–7.

Burkert, W. *Greek Religion. Archaic and Classical* (Oxford, 1985).

The Orientalizing Revolution (Cambridge, Mass., 1992).

Cavanagh, W., and C. Mee. *A Private Place. Death in Prehistoric Greece* (Jonsered, 1988).

Chadwick, J. "What Do We Know about Mycenaean Religion?" In *Linear B: A 1984 Survey*, ed. A. Morpurgo Davies and Y. Duhoux (Louvain-la-Neuve, 1985): 191–202.

Darcque, P. "Les vestiges mycéniens découverts sous le Télésterion d'Eleusis." *Bulletin de correspondance hellénique* 105 (1981): 593–605.

de Fidio, Pia. "Mycènes et Proch-Orient ou le théorème des modèles." In *Mykenaika*, ed. J.-P. Olivier (Paris, 1992): 173–96.

del Freo, M. "Osservazioni su miceneo ko-ma-we-te-ja." *Minos* 31–32 (1996–97): 145–58.

Felsch, R. C. S. "Zur Stratigraphie des Heiligtums." In *Ergebnisse der Ausgrabungen im Heiligtum der Artemis und des Apollo von Hyampolis in der antiken Phokis* II, ed. R. C. S. Felsch (Mainz, 2007): 1–27.

Finkelberg, M. "Ino-Leukothea between East and West." *Journal of Ancient Near Eastern Religions* 6 (2006): 105–21.

French, E. "The Development of Mycenaean Terracotta Figurines." *Annual of the British School at Athens* 66 (1977): 101–87.

Gallavotti, C. "La triada lesbia in un testo miceneo." *Rivista di Filologia Classica* 34 (1956): 225–36.

Gallou, C. *The Mycenaean Cult of the Dead*. BAR International S1372 (Oxford, 2005).

Gérard-Rousseau, M. *Les mentions religieuses dans les tablettes mycéniennes* (Rome, 1968).

Gilmour, G. "Aegean Sanctuaries and the Levant in the Late Bronze Age." *Annual of the British School at Athens* 88 (1993): 125–34.

Godart, L. "Il Labirinto e la Potnia nei testi micenei." *Rendiconti dell'Accademia di Archeologia, Lettere e Belle Arti* 50 (1975): 141–52.

Godart, L., and Sacconi, A. "Les dieux thébains dans les archives mycéniennes." *Comptes rendus de l'Académie des inscriptions et belles letters* (1996): 99–113.
Gulizio, G., K. Pluta, and T. G. Palaima. "Religion in the Room of the Chariot Tablets." In *POTNIA. Deities and Religion in the Aegean Bronze Age. Aegaeum* 22, ed. R. Laffineur and R. Hägg (Liège, 2001): 452–61.
Güterbock, H. C. "An Initiation Rite for a Hittite Prince." In *Perspectives on Hittite Civilization: Selected Writings of Hans Gustav Güterbock*, ed. H. A. Hoffner (Chicago, 1997): 111–14.
Haas, V. *Geschichte der hethitische Religion* (Leiden, 1994).
Hägg, R. "Mykenische Kultstätten im archäologischen Material." *Opuscula Atheniensia* 8 (1968): 39–60.
"Official and Popular Cults in Mycenaean Greece." In *Sanctuaries and Cults in the Aegean Bronze Age*, ed. R. Hägg and N. Marinatos (Stockholm, 1981): 35–9.
"Mycenaean Religion: The Helladic and the Minoan Components." In *Linear B: A 1984 Survey*, ed. A. Morpurgo Davies and Y. Duhoux (Louvain-la-Neuve, 1985): 203–25.
"The Role of Libations in Mycenaean Ceremony and Cult." In *Celebrations of Death and Divinity in the Bronze Age Argolid*, ed. R. Hägg and G. C. Nordquist (Stockholm 1990): 177–84.
"State and Religion in Mycenaean Greece." In *Politeia, Society, and State in the Aegean Bronze Age*, Vol. 2, ed. Robert Laffineur and W.-D. Niemeier (Liège, 1995): 387–91.
"The Religion of the Mycenaeans Twenty-four Years after the Mycenological Congress in Rome." In *Atti e memorie* II (1996): 599–612.
"Religious Syncretism at Knossos and in Post-Palatial Crete?" In *Crète mycénienne* (Paris, 1997): 163–8.
"Ritual in Mycenaean Greece." In *Ansichten griechischer Rituale: Geburtstags-Symposium für Walter Burkert* (Stuttgart, 1998): 99–113.
Hallager, E., M. Vlaski, and B. P. Hallager. "New Linear B Tablets from Khania." *Kadmos* 31 (1992): 61–87.
Hamilakis, Y., and Konsolaki, E. "Pigs for the Gods: Burnt Animal Sacrifices as Embodied Rituals at a Mycenaean Sanctuary." *Oxford Journal of Archaeology* 23 (2004): 135–51.
Hampe, R. *Kult der Winde in Athen und Kreta* (Heidelberg, 1967).
Hawkins, J. D. "Tarkasnawa King of Mira: 'Tarkondemos,' Bogazköy Sealings and Karabel." *Anatolian Studies* 48 (1998): 1–31.
Henshaw, R. A. *Female and Male: The Cultic Personnel: The Bible and the Rest of the Ancient Near East* (Philadelphia, 1994).
Hiller, S. "Mykenische Heiligtümer: Das Zeugnis der Linear-B Texte." In *Sanctuaries and Cults in the Aegean Bronze Age*, ed. R. Hägg and N. Marinatos (Stockholm, 1981): 95–125.
"Amnisos und das Labyrinth." *Ziva Antika* 31 (1981): 63–72.
"Tempelwirtschaft im mykenischen Griechenland." *Archiv für Orientforschung* Beiheft 19 (1982): 94–104.
"TH Wu 94, a2-pa-a2-de: Aphaia, Theben und Aigina." *Ziva Antika* 50 (2000): 117–24.
Hooker, J. *Linear B. An Introduction* (Bristol, 1980).
"Cult Personnel in the Linear B. Texts from Pylos." In *Pagan Priests*, ed. M. Beard and J. North (London, 1990): 159–74.
Hutton, W. F. "The Meaning of *qe-te-o* in Linear B." *Minos* 25–6 (1990–1): 105–32.
Huxley, G. "Cretan Paiawones." *Greek Roman and Byzantine Studies* 16 (1975): 119–24.

276   *Ian Rutherford*

Iakovidis, S. *Late Helladic Citadels on Mainland Greece* (Leiden, 1983).

Immerwahr, S. A. "Death and the Tanagra Larnakes." In *The Ages of Homer: A Tribute to Emily Vermeule*, ed. J. B. Carter and S. P. Morris (Austin, 1995): 109–21.

Isaakidou, V., P. Halstead, J. Davis, and S. Stocker. "Burnt Animal Sacrifice at the Mycenaean 'Palace of Nestor,' Pylos." *Antiquity* 76 (2002): 86–92.

Jacob-Felsch, M. "Die spätmykenische bis frühprotogeometrische Keramik," in *Kalapodi: Ergebnisse der Ausgrabungen im Heiligtum der Artemis und des Apollon von Hyampolis in der antiken Phokis*, ed. R. C. S. Felsch (Mainz, 1996): 1–213.

Kilian, K. "Zeugnisse mykenischer Kultausübung in Tiryns." In *Sanctuaries and Cults in the Aegean Bronze Age*, ed. R. Hägg and N. Marinatos (Stockholm, 1981): 49–58.

"The Emergence of *Wanax* Ideology in the Mycenaean Palaces." *Oxford Journal of Archaeology* 7 (1988): 291–302.

Killen, J. T. "The Knossos Ld(1) tablets." In *Colloquium Mycenaeaum. Acte du sixième colloque international sur les texts mycéniens et égéens tenu à Chaumont sur Neuchâtel du 7 au 13 septembre 1975*, ed. E. Risch and H. Mühlstein (1979): 151–81.

"Thebes Sealings, Knossos Tablets, and Mycenaean State Banquets." *BICS* 39 (1994): 67–84.

"Religion at Pylos: The Evidence of the Fn Tablets." In *POTNIA. Deities and Religion in the Aegean Bronze Age. Aegaeum* 22, ed. R. Laffineur and R. Hägg (Liège, 2001): 435–43.

Koehl, R. B. "The Functions of Aegean Bronze Age Rhyta." In *Sanctuaries and Cults in the Aegean Bronze Age*, ed. R. Hägg and N. Marinatos (Stockholm, 1981): 179–87.

Konsolaki-Yannopoulou, E. "New Evidence for the Practice of Libations in the Aegean Bronze Age." In *POTNIA. Deities and Religion in the Aegean Bronze Age. Aegaeum* 22, ed. R. Laffineur and R. Hägg (Liège, 2001): 213–20.

Kontorli-Papadopoulou, L. *Aegean Frescoes of Religious Character. SIMA* 117 (Göteborg, 1996).

Lévêque, P. "Le syncrétisme créto-mycénien." In *Les syncrétismes dans les religions de l'antiquité*, ed. F. Dunand and P. Lévêque (Leiden, 1975): 19–73.

Levi, Doro. "La dea micenea a cavallo." *Studies Presented to David Moore Robinson* (St. Louis, 1951): 1:109–25.

Lupack, S. M. "Palaces, Sanctuaries, and Workshops: The Role of the Religious Sector in Mycenaean Economics." In *Rethinking Mycenaean Palaces: New Interpretations of an Old Idea*, ed. M. L. Galaty and W. A. Parkinson (Los Angeles, 1999): 25–34.

The Role of the Religious Sector in the Economy of Late Bronze Age Mycenaean Greece (Oxford, 2008).

Marinatos, Nannos. "The Fresco from Room 31 at Mycenae: Problems of Method and Interpretation." In *Problems in Greek Prehistory. Papers Presented at the Centenary Conference of the British School of Archaeology at Athens, Manchester, April 1986* (Bristol, 1988): 245–8.

"The Palladion across a Culture Barrier? Mycenaean and Greek." In *Ithaka, Festschrift J. Schäfer*, ed. S. Böhm and K.-V. von Eickstedt (Würzburg, 2001): 107–14.

Milani, C. "Osservazioni sul latino lectisternium." *Rendiconti dell'Instituto Lombardo* 110 (1976): 231–42.

Moore, A. "The Large Monochrome Terracotta Figures from Mycenae: The Problem of Interpretation." In *Problems in Greek Prehistory. Papers Presented at the Centenary*

Conference of the British School of Archaeology at Athens, Manchester, April 1986 (Bristol 1988): 219–28.

Moore, A. D., and W. D. Taylour. *Well-Built Mycenae* Fascicle 10: *The Temple Complex* (Oxford, 1999).

Morgan, Lydia. "The Cult Centre at Mycenae and the Duality of Life and Death." In *Aegean Wall Painting. A Tribute to Mark Cameron*, ed. L. Morgan (London, 2005): 159–71.

Morris, S. P. "Potnia Aswiya: Anatolian Contributions to Greek Religion." In *POTNIA. Deities and Religion in the Aegean Bronze Age. Aegaeum* 22, ed. R. Laffineur and R. Hägg (Liège, 2001): 423–34.

Mylonas, G. E. *The Cult Center of Mycenae* (Athens, 1972).

Mycenaean Religion, Temples, Altars and Temene (Athens, 1977).

"The Cult Centre of Mycenae." *Proceedings of the British Academy* 67 (1982): 307–20.

Negbi, Ora. "Levantine Elements in the Sacred Architecture of the Aegean at the Close of the Bronze Age." *Annual of the British School at Athens* 83 (1988): 339–57.

Niemeier, W.-D. "Zur Ikonographie von Gottheiten und Adoranten in den Kultszenen auf minoischen und mykenischen Siegeln." In *Fragen und Probleme der bronzezeitlichen ägäischen Glyptik, CMS* Beiheft 3, ed. W. Müller (Berlin, 1989): 163–84.

"Cult-Scenes on Gold-Rings from the Argolis." *Celebrations of Death and Divinity in the Bronze Age Argolid*, ed. R. Hägg and G. C. Nordquist (Stockholm, 1990): 165–70.

Nilsson, M. P. *The Minoan-Mycenaean Religion and Its Survival in Greek Religion* (Lund, 1927).

The Minoan-Mycenaean Religion and Its Survival in Greek Religion. 2nd ed. (Lund, 1950).

Olivier, J.-P. "'Les collecteurs': Leur distribution spatiale et temporelle." In *Economy and Politics in the Mycenaean Palace States*, ed. S. Voutsaki and J. Killen. Cambridge Philological Society Suppl. 27 (Cambridge, 2001): 139–57.

Palaima, T. G. "The Nature of the Mycenaean *Wanax*: Non-Indo-European Origins and Priestly Functions." In *The Role of the Ruler in the Prehistoric Aegean. Aegeum* 11, ed. P. Rehak (Liège, 1995): 119–42.

"PO-RE-NA: A Mycenaean Reflex in Homer? An I-E Figure in Mycenaean?" *Minos* 31–2 (1996–1997): 303–12.

"Die Linear-B Texte und der Ursprung der hellenischen Religion: DI-WO-NU-SO." In *The History of the Hellenic Language and Writing: From the Second to the First Millennium B.C., Break or Continuity?* (Weilheim, 1998): 205–24.

"KnO2-Tn316." *FSM* 2 (1999): 437–61.

Review of Aravantinos (2001), *Minos* 35–6 (2000–1): 475–85.

"Sacrificial Feasting in the Linear B Documents." In *The Mycenaean Feast*, ed. J. C. Wright (Princeton, 2004): 97–126.

Palmer, L. "New Religious Texts from Pylos." *TPS* (1958): 1–35.

Mycenaean Greek Texts (London, 1963).

Pardee, Dennis. *Ritual and Cult at Ugarit* (Leiden, 2002).

Pecchioli Daddi, F. *Mestieri, professioni e dignit` nell'Anatolia ittita* (Rome, 1982).

Pitiros, C., J.-P. Olivier, and J.-L. Melena. "Les inscriptions en linéaire B des nodules e Thèbes (1982): La fouille, les documents, les possibilités d'interprétation." *Bulletin de correspondance hellénique* 104 (1990): 103–84.

278   Ian Rutherford

Poursat, J.-C. *Catalogue des ivoires mycéniens du Musée national d'Athènes*. Bibliothèque des Écoles françaises d'Athènes et de Rome 230 (Athens, 1977).

Rehak, P. "New Observations on the Mycenaean 'Warrior Goddess.'" *Archäeologische Anzeiger* 1984: 535–45.

"The Mycenaean 'Warrior Goddess' Revisited." In *POLEMOS. Le contexte guerrier en Égée à l'Âge du Bronze*. Aegaeum 19, ed. R. Laffineur (Liège, 1999): 227–39.

Renfrew, C. "Questions of Minoan and Mycenaean Cult." In *Sanctuaries and Cults in the Aegean Bronze Age*, ed. R. Hägg and N. Marinatos (Stockholm, 1981): 27–33.

Renfrew, C., et al. *The Archaeology of Cult: The Sanctuary at Phylakopi* (London, 1985).

Rousioti, D. "Did the Mycenaeans Believe in Theriomorphic Divinities?" In *POTNIA. Deities and Religion in the Aegean Bronze Age. Aegaeum* 22, ed. R. Laffineur and R. Hägg (Liège, 2001): 305–14.

Ruijgh, C. J. "Wánax et ses dérivés dans les textes mycéniens." *FSM* 2 (1999): 521–35.

Rutkowski, B. *Cult Places in the Aegean World* (Warsaw, 1972).

Singer, I. "Purple-Dyers in Lazpa." In *Anatolian Interfaces: Hittites, Greeks, and Their Neighbours. Proceedings of an International Conference on Cross-Cultural Interaction, September 17–19, 2004*, ed. B.-J. Collins, M. Bachvarova, and I. Rutherford (Oxford, 2008).

Sommer, F. *Die Ahhijava Urkunden* (Munich, 1932).

Stavrianopoulou, E. "Die Verflechtung des Politischen mit dem Religiösen im mykenischen Pylos." In *Politeia, Society, and State in the Aegean Bronze Age*, vol. 2, ed. R. Laffineur and W.-D. Niemeier (Liège, 1995): 423–33.

Stella, L. A. "Considerazioni sul politeismo miceneo." *Atti e memorie* 2 (1996): 901–9.

Stocker, Sharon R., and Jack L. Davis. "Animal Sacrifice, Archives, and Feasting at the Palace of Nestor." In *The Mycenaean Feast [= Hesperia* 73:2 (2004). The American School of Classical Studies at Athens], ed. J. C. Wright (Princeton, 2004): 59–76.

Sucharski, R., and K. Witczak. "U-po-jo po-ti-ni-ja and the cult of Baetyls." *Ziva Antika* 46 (1996): 5–12.

Taillardat, J. "Une panégyre en Crète Mycénienne?" *Revue des Études Grecques* 97(1984): 365–73.

Tarditi, G. "Dioniso Kemelios (Alceo, fr.129, 8L.-P.)." *Quaderni Urbinati di Cultura Classica* 4 (1967): 107–12.

Taylour, W. D. "New Light on Mycenaean Religion." *Antiquity* 44 (1970): 270–80.

Trümpy, C. "Nochmals zu den mykenischen Fr-Tuäfelchen. Die Zeitangaben innerhalb der pylischen Ölrationserie." *Studi micenei ed egeo-anatolici* 27 (1989): 191–234.

Uchitel, A., "Assignment of Personnel to Cultic Households of Mycenaean Greece and the Hittite Empire (PY Tn316 and KBo XVI.65)," *Kadmos* 4 (2005): 51–9.

Van Leuven, J. C. "The Mainland Tradition of Sanctuaries in Prehistoric Greece." *World Archaeology* 10 (1978): 139–48.

"Problems and Methods of Prehellenic Naology." In *Sanctuaries and Cults in the Aegean Bronze Age*, ed. R. Hägg and N. Marinatos (Stockholm 1981): 11–25.

"The Religion of the Shaft Grave Folk." In *Transition. Le monde égéen du bronze moyen au bronze recent. Aegeum* 3, ed. R. Laffineur (Liège, 1989): 191–201.

"Tombs and Religion at Mycenaean Prosymna." *Journal of Prehistoric Religion* 8 (1994): 42–61.

Vermeule, E. *Greece in the Bronze Age* (Chicago, 1964).

"Painted Mycenaean Larnakes." *Journal of Hellenic Studies* 85 (1965): 123–48.

Götterkult. Archaeologica Homerica III.V (Göttingen, 1974).

Wace, H. *The Ivory Trio: "The Ladies and Boy from Mycenae"* (Athens, 1939).

Whittaker, H. *Mycenaean Cult Buildings: A Study of Their Architecture and Function in the Context of the Aegean and the Eastern Mediterranean.* Monographs from the Norwegian Institute at Athens 1 (Bergen, 1997).

"Reflections on the Socio-Political Function of Mycenaean Religion." In *POTNIA. Deities and Religion in the Aegean Bronze Age. Aegaeum* 22, ed. R. Laffineur and R. Hägg (Liège, 2001): 355–60.

"Religion and Power. The Nature of Minoan Influence on Early Mycenaean Religion." *Opuscula Atheniensia* 27 (2002): 151–7.

Wiseman, D. J. *The Alalakh Tablets* (Ankara, 1953).

Wright, J. C. "The Spatial Configuration of Belief: The Archaeology of Mycenaean Religion." In *Placing the Gods. Sanctuaries and Sacred Space in Ancient Greece*, ed. S. Alcock and R. Osborne (Oxford, 1989): 37–78.

ed., *The Mycenaean Feast* [= *Hesperia* 73.2 (2004)]. The American School of Classical Studies in Athens (Princeton, 2004).

II

ARCHAIC AND CLASSICAL GREEK RELIGION

EMILY KEARNS

What do we mean by "Greek religion"?[1] First and foremost, the limits of time need some definition. It is traditional in accounts of the ancient Greek world to begin as a sort of preface with a brief treatment of the Bronze Age Aegean ("Minoan-Mycenaean religion"), to proceed to a somewhat agnostic version of the relationship between Homer and the "Dark Ages," and to take "archaic and classical" and "Hellenistic" as significant dividers in what follows. This may not be the only set of categories we can apply to a diachronic treatment of the subject, but it has two advantages: At least at the upper end, it fits the nature of the evidence as it shifts in the different periods, and it corresponds roughly to far-reaching changes in social and political organization, with which religious expression is intimately connected. Thus it is possible to view the religion of the archaic and classical period as mediated to us to a great extent through contemporary literature and epigraphy, unlike that of earlier periods, and, as we shall see, we can also characterize it as "polis-religion," corresponding as it does (and not merely chronologically) to the heyday of the polis between the eighth or seventh century and the world of Alexander and his successors. Other ways of dividing up the extent of pre-Christian Greek religion may reveal other characteristics, and it is undeniable that much in Hellenistic religion is continuous or even identical with earlier periods, but it is certainly convenient and frequently helpful to take the archaic and classical period as a unit.

There is no sudden break between "Minoan-Mycenaean" and "Greek" religion, although tracking the continuities through the so-called Dark Ages is an extraordinarily difficult task. And certain things present contrasts: The political structure of the societies is obviously different (no

---

[1] For the sites relevant to Greek religion, see Map 6 in Chapter 9.

Archaic and Classical Greek Religion 281

palaces in later Greece), and so is the predominant form of sanctuary (the monumental temple that dominates the physical appearance of most larger Greek sanctuaries develops from the eighth century onward and owes something to Egyptian models). Continuity is seen most obviously in the names of the deities worshipped. Alongside some unfamiliar cult recipients, Linear B texts have shown versions of Zeus, Hera, Athena, almost certainly Dionysos, and many others. In fact, most of the divine names that have emerged from the Mycenaean palace sites are remarkably similar to those of the main deities known to all later Greeks through the epic and early hexameter – Homer and Hesiod, whom Herodotus (2.53.2) perceived to be crucial in crystallizing the forms of the gods of the Greeks. Whatever the ultimate origins of the names – and the majority defy a certain explanation in Greek or proto-Indo-European – they were at least well established by the end of the first millennium BCE.

THE GODS: LOCAL AND PANHELLENIC, OLD AND NEW

Whether the later gods themselves, as well as their names, were "the same" as the Mycenaean deities is perhaps a philosophical rather than a historical question, but it may serve to introduce some more tangible issues surrounding the identity of the gods. The panhellenic pantheon[2] familiar from the poets is only one of many. Every city, every locality, had its own group of deities familiar not from texts such as those of Homer and Hesiod, but from ritual. Of course, each local pantheon had a degree of overlap with the panhellenic, literary equivalent, and it is reasonable to suppose that both the local cult group and the shared literary depictions of the gods will have been influential in forming conceptions of divinity. But discrepancies there were, apparent at various levels.

Simplest of all, the names most conspicuous in the texts were not always those actually accorded worship in any given locality. Hephaistos, for instance, is an important character in the *Iliad*, but outside it he was worshipped in few places other than Lemnos and Athens. The Peloponnesians, northern Greeks, and most islanders, who knew about Hephaistos from Homer and were familiar with his name as equivalent in poetic language to fire, had no direct religious experience onto which to map this literary version of divinity. Again, Hesiod's *Theogony*, which as the name implies deals with the gods through the medium of their births and origins, tells largely of very early times and includes many divine figures who, it claims,

---

[2] On "pantheons" see the discussion of trends in interpretation.

flourished before the reign of Zeus and the Olympians. The coup masterminded by Zeus might explain why no one worshipped Ouranos and Kronos and Koios and Phoibe (or not much), but we are still left with the curious phenomenon of a whole set of "deities" essentially without cult. The tradition of a war between two groups of superhuman beings – Gods and Titans, devas and asuras, and so on – presumably goes back to proto-Indo-European times, and the Greek version was evidently refreshed by later contact with West Asian myths, but the elaborate individuation of the losing side, the creation of a sort of alternative pantheon, is distinctively Greek, although one struggles to see what purpose it serves.[3]

The literary tradition, then, knew more deities than were worshipped in any one place, and some who were hardly worshipped at all. Conversely, the local pantheons included some deities with little or no part in the panhellenic group. Who, for instance, were Kourotrophos "nurturer of children" or Daeira in Attica, Despoina or Areion in Arcadia, the Tritopatores in many parts of the Greek world?[4] Writers sometimes conjecturally identified these locally important figures with names familiar from universal mythology, but there was no consensus on such matters, and their true contexts are those of cult and local tradition rather than the world of epic or theogony. Comparably, Hestia, the hearth – the name is a simple Greek word, unlike the names of most Greek divinities – was often a prominent figure in cult, as she typically received the first offering in a religious ceremony, and yet she has been only half-mythologized in the poetic tradition; she is the virgin daughter of Kronos and Rhea, sister of Zeus, but beyond this she has no mythical personality.[5]

The gods of panhellenic myth are single individuals in just the same way as the humans who worship them and with whom, in myth, they interact. In cult things are much less clear-cut, and each apparently unitary deity may become many. In a common perception, a different deity inhabits each different sanctuary: Thus, for instance, in Athens, Athena Polias ("of the city") on the Acropolis is different from Athena Ergane in the agora or Athena Soteira ("savior") in Peiraieus. This is nicely illustrated

---

[3] See, however, Faraone, "Kronos and the Titans," esp. 398–9, citing *Iliad* 14.273–9 and *Homeric Hymn to Apollo* 331–42, depicting the collectivity of Titans as underworld entities and witnesses and enforcers of oaths, though in both passages it is a goddess, Hera, who thus invokes them.

[4] Kourotrophos: Hadzisteliou Price, *Kourotrophos*. Daeira: Nilsson, *Opuscula selecta*, vol. 2, 545–7; Despoina, Areion: Jost, *Sanctuaires et cultes d'Arcadie*; Tritopatores: Jameson et al., *Lex Sacra*, 107–14.

[5] In company with Hermes, Hestia is the subject of a famous essay by Vernant, *Myth and Thought among the Greeks*.

*in Menander's comedy *Dyskolos*, set near a cave of Pan and the Nymphs: Hearing that the hero's mother has had a dream of Pan, the cook Sikon asks, "This one here, you mean?"[6] Where the epic-mythological view focuses on the gods as characters in a narrative, this conception is worshipper based: It relies on the fact that the deities in different sanctuaries look different, that different cult actions may be appropriate for them, and possibly different benefits may be expected. Nonetheless, there is a sort of intermediate position between the two: In one sense, each "epic" divinity (Zeus, Apollo, Athena, and so on) can be divided into several types, recognizable in different places of worship. Thus cults of Apollo Agyieus ("of the streets"), Zeus Meilichios (understood as "the kindly one"), and Aphrodite Ourania ("heavenly"), to name but a few, are known with essentially the same characteristics in most parts of the Greek world, and they are quite different from other types of Apollo, Zeus, or Aphrodite.

Finally, in some cities or regions the predominant form of a deity might be of a type different from that universally acknowledged. In Crete, for instance, Zeus was sometimes a young god, rather than the mature and majestic "father of gods and men."[7] In Lokroi Epizephyrioi (southern Italy), Persephone is primarily concerned with marriage, rather than appearing as the dread queen of the Underworld, her usual form.[8] Arcadian deities are especially idiosyncratic: There, Artemis is seldom associated with Apollo, whereas Demeter is linked with Poseidon and has as much to do with animals as with crops.[9]

Local religious practice also included quasi-divine figures such as nymphs, heroes, and heroines; a glance at any one of the sacrificial calendars that have in part survived from the fifth and fourth centuries confirms that offerings to these figures were not just an add-on, but a conspicuous part of the religious observance of both the city and its subgroups.[10] Nymphs were known everywhere, but generally each local set had a different name and was considered distinct from others. Some heroes, such as Herakles or Agamemnon, for example, were names familiar to all Greeks through*

---

[6] Menander, *Dyskolos* 412.

[7] See Verbruggen, *Le Zeus crétois*, who, however, counsels caution in differentiating the Cretan Zeus too completely from the "normal" version.

[8] Sourvinou-Inwood, "Persephone and Aphrodite at Locri," 13–37.

[9] On Arcadian deities, see Jost, *Sanctuaires et cultes d'Arcadie*.

[10] On heroes, see most recently Boehringer, *Heroenkulte in Griechenland*, and Ekroth, *Sacrificial Rituals*, each with further bibliography. Nymphs: Larson, *Greek Nymphs*. On sacrifice calendars, see below and inscriptions collected in Sokolowski, *Lois sacrées de l'Asie mineure*, *Lois sacrées: supplément*, and *Lois sacrées des cités grecques* (*LSAM*, *LSS*, *LSCG*, respectively) and Lupu, *Greek Sacred Law* (*NGSL*).

panhellenic mythology, but many were obscure characters of interest only to their local worshippers, and because the worship of heroes took place typically at what was considered to be the hero's tomb, there were obvious limits to the spread of any individual hero's cult.

But none of these differences and divergences was mutually exclusive. No pantheon, no way of looking at the gods or a god, was the only approach that an individual knew, however logically incompatible the different possibilities might be. To put it at its most basic, every Greek was familiar with both the epic-mythological pantheon and with the group of deities and quasi-deities worshipped locally. Concomitantly, Greek religion as a whole displays both centripetal and centrifugal elements. Centripetal, because obviously mobility created mutual influences, not least in the great panhellenic festivals, the games of Olympia, Delphi, Nemea, and the Isthmus, and also because of the canonical status of Homer, Hesiod, and other early hexameter poetry, a phenomenon that comes to be matched in the second half of the fifth century by a canonical visual style of representing the gods. Centrifugal, because of the major local differences mentioned above; because participation in the cults of another city was often limited; and because beside the creations of Pheidias and Praxiteles, there were older and often more venerable cult statues depicting and embodying deities in ways specific to the locality and the particular cult. These two tendencies held each other in check, so that views of the gods and religious practice had always a local and a panhellenic dimension.

The multiplicity of possibilities in conceptualizing and naming divinity indicates a degree of flexibility and open-endedness that is constantly open to change. Although doing things "according to ancestral custom" (*kata ta patria*) carried a powerful charge for the Greeks, and was frequently backed up by the responses of oracles, in practice the list of the gods changed and developed over time. Contact with others – Greeks or non-Greeks – brought about many modifications to the pantheon, either as additions of new deities or as identifications of a deity with a more familiar one. These changes came about in different ways, sometimes gradually and "organically," sometimes as the result of a deliberate decision, and the new deities occupied all points on a spectrum varying from utmost respectability to a very dubious reputation. But however much the gods of foreigners might be mocked in comedy (in which god-mockery is frequent), or indeed in certain kinds of oratory, there was no sense that they were objectively less real than the gods of the Greeks, nor were the categories of Greek and foreign gods watertight.

RELIGION AND THE *POLIS*

Variability is then a prime characteristic of Greek pantheons, but the most important of all variables is locality. Yet so far we have only touched on political structures in this regard. What we have chiefly seen is that locality, in a weak sense, determines the gods one worships, but there is also a strong sense for the statement, in which the local political structure determines and deliberately lays down the basis of religious practice. The role of the *polis* is indeed one of the defining features of Greek religion, and one that has been much emphasized in recent years.[11] "The *polis* anchored, legitimated, and mediated all religious activity" is the epigrammatic formulation of one scholar in the field,[12] and although this may be overstated, it at least draws attention to the intimate relationship between religion and the state – and also expresses what many Greeks, including Plato,[13] felt was the ideal. But how more precisely, and why, was the relationship thus?

In a nutshell, the *polis* fulfilled many of the functions that in other societies were the preserve of religious experts. Structures of overall religious authority were notably lacking in the Greek world. Priests were neither born into a caste nor formed *collegia* with quasi-political power as they did at Rome. A priest or priestess (they appear in similar numbers) had an air of grandeur when engaged in his or her office[14] and was worthy of respect; he or she, if adult, was probably an expert on the particular cult and deity served, but the priestly office by itself conveyed no other religious expertise or authority. Seers (*manteis*) were usually practitioners of a craft, men who had learned a particular skill; they seldom claimed any direct insight into the ways of the gods, and more extravagant claims on their part risked seeming merely eccentric. There were also, at least in fourth-century Athens, officials called *exēgētai*, "explicators," whose job it was to advise on appropriate ritual action across the board. These men must have had considerable knowledge and expertise, but they were not essential to the operation of the religious system, and they were not figures of power.[15]

Authority might be held to derive directly from the gods in the form of responses from the great oracular shrines – Delphi, Dodona, Didyma, or Branchidai near Miletos, and others. Such pronouncements were

---

[11] See Section, *Trends in Interpretation* this chapter.
[12] Sourvinou-Inwood, "What Is Polis Religion?" 15.
[13] For instance, *Laws* 10 909d–910d.
[14] Thus Plato, *Politicus* 290c.
[15] On priests, seers, and exegetes, see Garland, "Religious Authority," 75–123, and "Priests and Power," 73–91, and Parker, *Polytheism and Society*, 89–99, 116–20.

frequently made on religious and ritual matters at the request of official *polis* delegations, and their authority was incontrovertible. But most cities were at some distance from the major, most prestigious oracles, and consultation was not an everyday affair. Practices they recommended might fall into disuse – they did not issue reminders, but only responded when asked a question. Again, there was often doubt about their accuracy. When the Lydian Croesus tested the oracles, according to Herodotus (1.46–9), only Delphi and perhaps the Amphiareion at Oropos got the right answer. Further, the human mediators of the god's word were fallible and perhaps corruptible: Herodotus again records, and seems to endorse, suspicions that the Pythia at Delphi had been manipulated by a particular interest group (5.90).

It was left therefore to the *polis* structure itself to regulate the management of religion within its boundaries – although which is cause and which effect in this equation may be debated. Did the rise of the *polis* effectively quash other potential control, or did the *polis* move into a gap waiting to be filled? What is clear is that during our period religious activity took place not merely *in* the *polis*, but to a great extent within a framework laid down by the *polis*. This is perhaps most obviously and tangibly demonstrated by the system of publicly funded sacrifices that we can observe in Attica. Almost all of the most important and prestigious rituals regularly observed in Athens, and some in other parts of Attica, were under the financial control of the *dēmos* (people), and a good deal of the income necessary to perform the correct sacrifices and other rites was generated not directly from the sanctuaries themselves, but from central *polis* funds, supported by taxation. The finances of the deities involved were in the charge of treasurers, who were appointed annually by lot in accordance with the norms of the democracy, and were responsible to the state. Athens also appointed officials called *hieropoioi* ("sacred/ritual doers"), whose business concerned sacrifices in general; this name and those of *hieromnēmones*[16] and *hierophylakes* ("rememberers" and "guardians" of sacred rites) are found in many other cities, all referring to religious administrators, although the precise duty and the importance of the office varied from place to place. Other Athenian magistrates, including the holders of the three chief offices – the (eponymous) *archon*, the *basileus*, and the *polemarchos* – were responsible for the proper performance of many specific festivals and presided over some sacrifices in the place of a priest – although the significance of this is

---

[16] But *hieromnēmones* may also be attached to particular sanctuaries, and there are other uses of the word that do not concern us here.

somewhat lessened when we recall that a priest was by no means a formal or theological necessity for a sacrifice (see below).[17]

It was very similar with smaller groups within the city, and here again it is Athens and Attica that give us our clearest evidence. Most, although not quite all, of the smaller groups that met for worship were clearly integrated as units into the *polis* structure. The most obvious example is the deme, the basis of Attic local government. Large chunks of the inscribed sacrificial calendars of several demes survive and show that at this level too it was the "people" (what we call "deme" is simply *dēmos*, "people" in Greek) who were responsible for the financing and conduct of sacrifices; the calendars were public documents issued by the deme assemblies. Other divisions of the population such as "tribe" (*phylē*) and "phratry" (*phratria*) were very clearly integrated into the Athenian system of government, and in many ways their cults, although limited in scope, were managed similarly. They too issued public notices in the form of inscriptions recording and regulating their religious activity, on the model of the *polis* itself, and their meetings for sacrifice – and the associated meal – served to integrate the group and highlight its role within the city, as also to confirm the civic identity of those participating. Even the household (*oikos*), another unit of cult, can be viewed as a subset of the *polis*. Before taking office, the archons had to show that they had a "Zeus of the enclosure" (Zeus Herkeios, the Zeus of their household) alongside an Apollo Patroös who guaranteed their phratry membership.[18] In both cases the unit is an exclusive one – you can worship only one Apollo Patroös and one Zeus Herkeios – but each household and each phratry performs similar worship, and this acts as a guarantee of citizen status.

What we see, then, is a system in which religion is "embedded," to use the favored terminology, in the socio-political structure – or perhaps the other way 'round – and also a system in which the ultimate authority on most religious matters was the state itself.[19] A glance at the so-called sacred laws – inscriptions regulating ritual conduct – emanating from all over the Greek world is enough to show that in very many cases the issuing authority is either one of the deliberative bodies of the state – assembly, council, or similar – or officials directly appointed or elected by such bodies or allotted from them.[20] Many fewer can be shown to emanate directly from

---

[17] The system as it worked in the later fourth century is set out in Aristotle, *Constitution of the Athenians* 42–69.
[18] Ibid., 55.
[19] Which is not to say that a good deal of "unofficial" religious activity did not take place.
[20] These inscriptions are collected in Sokolowski, *LSAM, LSS, LSCG,* and Lupu, *NGSL.*

288 *Emily Kearns*

priests, although their expert knowledge of a particular cult makes them quite a likely source for some of those that are unattributed. Priesthoods were sometimes allotted from all eligible citizens, sometimes (at least from the beginning of the fourth century) available for purchase, and sometimes confined to a particular kin group, including many of a city's "well-born" families, but however a priesthood was acquired, a priest's essential job was the same: to perform the appropriate rites in order to maintain a good relationship between the community (including its constituent individuals) and the deity. In this sense, as Plato argues in the *Statesman*,[21] the priest is a public servant.

As for the worshipping community itself, much admirable work has been done that shows the crucial significance (in Greece as elsewhere) of common worship in constituting group identity, whether that group be the city, or one of its subdivisions large or small, or some entity beyond the city, such as an amphictiony (a regional grouping of cities that are felt to have some common traditions), an ethnic group (such as Dorians or Ionians), or even the Greeks in general.[22] Given the pivotal position of the *polis* among these groups, the phenomenon is another major way in which the term "*polis*-religion" can be understood. It is important also to note that the role of cult in constituting the group did not operate entirely on an unconscious level: The idea of "common sacrifices" was always a potent one for the Greeks, evoking ties that must be respected. Nonetheless, the point has sometimes been emphasized to the detriment of equally or more important rationales for worship. The Greeks were aware that common cult fostered a sense of belonging and appreciated the value of festivals as recreation and refreshment, "respites from toil" as Thucydides makes Pericles say;[23] but neither of these human-centered aims was the main reason for worshipping the gods. The gods were worshipped, as Aristotle's pupil Theophrastos put it, "to give them honor, or to render thanks, or to ask for something that we need."[24]

RELATIONS WITH THE GODS

As a preliminary to discussing the nature of that worship, let us now consider the conceptions of the gods and of their relations with human beings that accompany worship. Some theorists have argued that ritual,

---

[21] Plato, *Politicus* 290c.
[22] See Section, *Trends in Interpretation*.
[23] Thucydides 2.38.
[24] Fr 12 Pötscher, from *On Piety*.

including religious ritual, is per se meaningless.[25] It is true that ritual is to an extent self-propelling and self-perpetuating (within the grammar of the specific ritual system, one action suggests another, and the completed ritual demands to be performed again), but even if not all the details are understood, ritual is normally very far from meaningless to those who participate in it. The concept of "orthopraxy" (meaning that doing, rather than believing, the right thing is what counts) explains a great deal about Greek religion,[26] but it should not be taken to mean that beliefs and viewpoints are unimportant, or that they have no connection with the cult that is offered to the gods.

Theophrastos's dictum, quoted above, seems to describe Greek practice well. Setting aside literary testimonia, we can deduce much from excavations of sanctuaries throughout the Greek world, which have produced countless offerings both of individuals and of groups. These are not only the remains of animals offered in sacrifice, usually seen as the central act in Greek religious practice (see below), but also and more conspicuously and often more revealingly, the more durable offerings instantiated or commemorated on stone. Statues, tablets or pictures (*pinakes*), and reliefs were commonly dedicated, as were other objects often itemized in sanctuary inventories even where the originals have not survived, and the Greek "epigraphic habit" often shows us what the dedicator wanted to commemorate about the dedication and the reason for it. The votive offering was extremely common; the dedicator made an offering that was given to the sanctuary and perhaps exhibited there, in thanks for a benefit attributed to the deity in question, very often in fulfillment of a vow. "Do such-and-such, and I will give you this-and-that" was a common prayer, and seldom was any need felt to soften this *do ut des* formula. Indeed, after thanks were given, a common request was to make another dedication possible. The majority of such requests and thanks were made on an individual level.[27]

The first of Theophrastos's motives for worship, "to give honor," needs a bit more explication. Some element of giving honor is always present in worshipping a deity, even when it is not the primary motive; in fact, a very common Greek word expressing what we call cult is simply *timai*, honors. But sometimes to honor the deity can be seen as the main purpose of the cult action; this is the case with the regularly recurring sacrifices and

---

[25] Notably Staal, *Rituals without Meaning*.
[26] On orthopraxy, see, for instance, Bell, *Ritual*, 191–7.
[27] On dedications and votive offerings, see *ThesCRA* I.269–450, van Straten, *Gifts for the Gods*, and Bartoloni et al., *Anathema*. On prayer, see Versnel, *Religious* Mentality, and Pulleyn, *Prayer in Greek Religion*.

festivals offered by the city and its subdivisions, and those that occur in a set pattern in different sanctuaries. Of course, here too there are other reasons for the action: For instance, there is the importance of doing things according to ancestral custom, mentioned above. And the giving of honor itself is not without self-interest. Even where no immediate favor is at issue, there is an idea of reciprocity inherent in worship. There is an expectation that worship properly and generously carried out – according to one's means – will be pleasing to the gods, and therefore that it is likely to dispose them more certainly in one's favor. There is a ready model for this in the human world, where – as the Greeks were quick to see – the exchange of gifts and good offices is intrinsic to relationships of fondness (*philia*). It is too simplistic to reduce this complex system to "currying favor with the gods"; rather the operation of reciprocity or *charis* is like a thread running through relations between gods and humans, sometimes remarked on, sometimes less emphasized, but in no way incompatible with an affective relationship. That the gods are concerned for human beings (and therefore that there is a relationship to cultivate) is one of the three tenets mentioned in Plato's *Laws* as essential for the citizens of the fictional Magnesia to accept; Yunis has shown that it was also a baseline for normal Greek belief.[28] Certain mythological and literary contexts, notably tragedy, show a developed awareness that the ways of the gods actually appear a great deal more complicated than a simple understanding of *charis* would suggest. But in Greece as elsewhere, it would have taken a great deal more than this negative evidence to destroy such an appealing assumption.

There is only very limited and partial evidence for a more intense, more god-centered sense of a relationship comparable to what many modern traditions call devotion (or similar names). We find no explicit statements that a normal cult action is carried out without the wish for any benefits, but for sheer love of the deity. The nearest approach is in the words of two characters from tragedy – Hippolytos and Ion, in Euripides' plays of those names. Both are young, both cultivate purity of life and have a special devotion to one deity, and both, crucially, wish to spend their lives performing actions that are felt to be particularly pleasing to that deity. Neither is an ordinary character, even within the larger-than-life framework of tragedy, and their sentiments are clearly not usual, either. Yet they must have had some distant analogue in contemporary experience, or their feelings would have made no sense to the audience. Although it was always proper

---

[28] Plato, *Laws* 10 885b; Yunis, *A New Creed*, 38–44. Plato's third tenet shows that he is very far from accepting some of the ways in which the *charis* relationship was supposed to operate.

Archaic and Classical Greek Religion 291

to worship all the gods (here is where Hippolytos goes wrong), a special enthusiasm for one deity seems not to have been anomalous. We find evidence for such enthusiasm in contemporary inscriptions, for instance, in the testimony of Archedamos of Thera, a resident of Attica whose pride and joy was the cave of the nymphs at Vari, and who describes himself as *nympholēptos* – "possessed by the nymphs."[29] Although worshippers of this stamp will naturally tend to attribute any good fortune to their divine favorite, their relationship will also tend to diminish the more formulaic *do ut des* elements of the *charis* complex and emphasize the more affective side. It is nonetheless significant that relations of this sort are scarcely discussed by Greek writers tackling the subject of religion.

TA NOMIZOMENA – "THINGS CUSTOMARILY DONE"

We must now discuss the means by which the Greeks were able to express the various sentiments they felt toward the Gods and the ways in which their religious system worked in practice. It is probably fair to say that the central action in Greek worship was animal sacrifice, although it was not necessarily the action most frequently performed.[30] It was central in that it was the normative action of a group gathered together for worship, it was a part of almost every religious celebration beyond the smallest in scale, and it was assumed, with a few exceptions, to be what every deity wanted. Modern writers have made much to hang on the ritualized killing of animals,[31] and indeed the fact that slaughter is involved is by no means played down in the sacrificial process; but still more apparent perhaps is the sense that the deity is being pleased by the worshippers' action. A sacrifice was usually (not always) a happy and positive occasion, as well as one that increased the solidarity of the group. There were different roles to play in the action: Women, for instance, were required to ululate at the moment of the kill, while only a man would normally wield the knife (he was often a specialist, a butcher-cook or *mageiros*).[32] If the sacrifice was of a reasonable size, the practical need to get the animal to the altar would result in a procession, with participants leading the animal and carrying the sacrificial accoutrements and other offerings such as incense and sweetmeats

---

[29] IG I³ 980; discussed (together with 974–9, 981–2) notably by Connor, "Seized by the Nymphs," 155–89, and Purvis, *Singular Dedications.*

[30] The centrality of animal sacrifice is however challenged from various perspectives in the collection of Faraone and Naiden, *Greek and Roman Animal Sacrifice.*

[31] See Section, *Trends in Interpretation.*

[32] Berthiaume, *Les rôles du mageiros;* also Osborne, "Women and Sacrifice," 293–405.

Fig. 20. *ThesCRA* I, plate 5 no (Athens, National Museum, 16464). Wooden votive tablet (*pinax*) dedicated to the Nymphs by Euthydika and Eucholis. A sacrificial procession leads a sheep to the altar. From Pitsa, near ancient Sikyon, ca.540–530 BCE.

(see Fig. 20). Hymns were sung during the procession and on arrival at the altar – again, something in which the deity might take pleasure. One person normally presided over the sacrifice by making the appropriate prayers over the victim. Often, of course, this was the priest or priestess, whose central role was precisely this, but it was by no means necessary to have a priest in order to perform a sacrifice. Indeed, the Homeric poems, although they are well aware of priests and priestesses, seldom show them performing sacrifice but instead have sacrificial scenes where the senior male present presides over the ceremony. In later times, this continued as the pattern in household cult and on occasions such as the sacrifices before a meeting of the Athenian assembly.[33] But priestless sacrifices were also conducted in regular sanctuaries when the priest was absent, for it was only the very largest sanctuaries that were constantly attended – being a priest was seldom a full-time job. A fourth-century inscription from a sanctuary in Chios instructs visitors to call three times for the priest, and then if he does not appear to perform the sacrifice themselves.[34] Again, at the Amphiareion at Oropos on the Attic-Boeotian border – a healing sanctuary, where many individuals would have a motive for their own particular worship – the regulations state that the priest will perform the sacrifice when he is present, and at the main festival he will pray over the publicly

---

[33] Household cult: e.g., Isaeus 8.16. Sacrifice before the assembly: Parker, *Polytheism and Society*, 404; Meritt and Traill, *The Athenian Agora* (= *Agora* XV), 4–5.
[34] *LSS*, 129.

offered victims, while each individual prays over the victim he himself has provided.[35]

Sacrifice was a messy business. The altar was splashed or at least dribbled with the animal's blood, although paradoxically in most contexts blood was considered impure, and the animal was then butchered.[36] The god's portions – somewhat less appetizing than those destined for human consumption, a fact that clearly bothered the Greeks – were burned on the altar, while the rest was cooked and served to the participants, the priest or priestess usually being allocated an honorific portion. It is easy to imagine the scene as something like that at a Greek village *paniyiri* today. However, every community knew sacrifices that diverged from this norm. Most of them were marked out as different because the victim was burned entire, or the meat was given to only a small group, or no wine was used – all variations likely to lessen the merriment of the occasion. We even hear of a sacrifice that was supposed to be performed in a gloomy and apprehensive mood, contrasting with the good cheer normally prevalent.[37] In fact, it seems that there was a whole grammar of sacrifice, only part of which we can recover, by which, consciously or unconsciously, different approaches to the divine could be expressed.

What of the physical setting? A prerequisite for sacrifice is an altar or similar construction at which the animal is killed and on which, usually, the god's portion is burned. Typically this was a square or rectangular block of stone of medium size, but some altars in larger sanctuaries were huge, stepped constructions designed for the simultaneous sacrifice of many animals, whereas others, often associated with heroes and Underworld powers, were simple hearths on the ground. Most altars were in the open air; they may be thought of as the primary element in a sanctuary. The area around an altar was naturally felt to belong to the god and acquired sacred status. In practical terms, this meant that certain purity regulations, varying to some extent from place to place, had to be observed within the boundaries, and that anything produced within the area was the property of the god. The third element, at least chronologically, was the temple, whose name in Greek, *naos*, suggests its function as the deity's dwelling place. It was in essence a grand shelter for the cult statue and was usually positioned so that the deity in the form of the statue could view the altar through the open doors. Of course, temples often became elaborate and beautiful

---

[35] *LSCG*, 69.

[36] On the practicalities of sacrifice, Van Straten, *Hiera Kala* is an excellent general conspectus, with an emphasis on visual evidence.

[37] The Diasia at Athens, for which see Lalonde, *Horos Dios*, 58–61, 107–10.

294 *Emily Kearns*

constructions, ornamented with friezes and pedimental sculptures. They further became places where objects dedicated to the deity could be affixed and displayed and also often stored when no longer on display, but this is secondary to the feeling that the deity somehow lives in the temple. The statue was often the focus for prayer and attention, particularly of a more individual sort, and offerings of a more durable kind were usually made to the deity in statue form, as, for instance, a peplos (woman's dress) was offered to Athena both in Athens, at the Panathenaia festival, and at Troy in the *Iliad* (6.302–3). The philosopher Heraclitus speaks scornfully of those who pray to statues, as though they were to address houses.[38] Cult statues were variable in form, from the admired creations of great sculptors such as Pheidias (whose Zeus at Olympia was particularly famous), often on a huge scale and made of precious materials, to simple, barely iconic wooden constructions that were thought to be of great antiquity (sometimes attributed to the mythical sculptor Daidalos) and were usually regarded as particularly venerable.

Many sanctuaries show features other than the basic altar and sacred area (*temenos*, though this word can also apply to sanctuary-owned estates) and the usual temple (see Fig. 21).[39] A spring or fountain was common, since water was required both for purification and for worship. There were also often dining rooms (*hestiatoria*) in which worshippers could enjoy the sacrificial meal – more necessary during the winter months. The larger sanctuaries sometimes developed special buildings in which to house the more precious and durable dedications. Sanctuaries such as Olympia or Delphi, which people visited from all over Greece, or their regional equivalents, had associated buildings, usually outside the sacred area proper, for the holding of contests – athletic and poetic – which was such a conspicuous feature of large-scale, particularly supra-*polis*, religious festivities, and for the accommodation of worshippers. In addition to this, a large sanctuary might contain many subordinate shrines or at least altars belonging to gods or heroes other than the main deity. Within the sanctuary of Apollo at Delphi, for instance, was the tomb and cult place of the hero Neoptolemos and an altar of Poseidon, and just outside was another sanctuary, that of Athena Pronaia ("in front of the temple").[40]

Sanctuaries often clustered together, particularly in the middle of cities. The Athenian acropolis is an obvious example of what may almost be called

---

[38] Fragment 5, Diels-Kranz.
[39] The most recent treatment of sanctuaries in their religious context is Pedley, *Sanctuaries and the Sacred*.
[40] See ibid., 135–53.

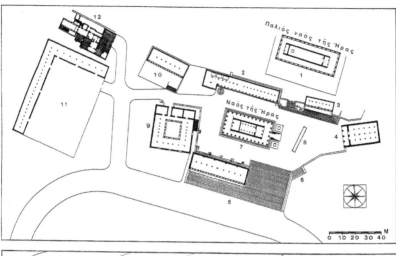

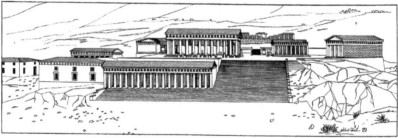

Fig. 21. Line drawing. N. D. Papahatzis, Παυσανίου Ελλάδος Περιήγησις (Athens, 1976), vol. 2, 144, fig. 141. Plan (and reconstruction) of the Argive Heraion, a major extra-urban sanctuary built on a terraced slope. Ancillary buildings were added over a period of several centuries; no. 12 dates from the Roman period. No. 1 is the earliest temple (burned down in 423 BCE), no. 7 the later one, with its altar, no. 8.

a cult complex, containing not only the Erechtheion, the Parthenon, and the temple of Athena Nike, which remain obvious, but other sanctuaries such as those of Hermes and the Charites, Artemis Brauronia, Artemis or Hekate Epipyrgidia, Zeus Polieus, and many others.[41] All were inevitably linked by proximity, some by more. Intricate strands of cult and myth connected Athena, Poseidon, the heroes Erechtheus and Erichthonios, and the heroines Aglauros and Pandrosos, among others, and none of these can properly be considered in isolation from the others. At the other extreme, we find the isolated extra-urban sanctuary, of which the finest surviving

[41] Ibid., 186–204.

example is the sanctuary of Apollo Epikourios at Bassai near – but not that near – Phigaleia in Arcadia. Some deities had a penchant for such rural locations: Artemis, for instance, not infrequently had her sanctuaries in marshy or mountainous areas. Sometimes the extra-urban sanctuary actually honored the chief protecting deity of the city, as with the Heraia of Argos and of Samos. In this case, the sanctuary was usually important in expressing a link between the city and its territory.

With an extra-urban sanctuary, the sacrificial procession was of necessity emphatic, but in other cases too processions at different festivals had different traditions, and these were often marked out as special characteristics of the festival. Indeed, most festivals and celebrations contained some special ingredient that marked them out from others, so much so that ancient scholars wrote books on the subject, giving us a fair amount of information, particularly about the festivals of Attica.[42] Thus we know, for instance, that at the Oschophoria, a ritual connected with Dionysos and Athena Skiras in Phaleron, vine branches with grapes were carried by two young men dressed as women, the sacred herald garlanded his staff rather than his own head, and a strange and apparently contradictory shout of acclamation was made after the pouring of the libations. Athenians explained these peculiar features by referring to myths of Theseus, their national hero, who was supposed to have returned from Crete on that day; modern scholars analyze this and similar observances on a different level, referring in this case to the remnants of a rite of passage for young males. Neither type of explanation tells us exactly what the participants thought they were doing. At the Pyanopsia, perhaps celebrated on the same day, larger numbers took part by boiling up grains and pulses (the name means "bean-boiling"), while children took a decorated branch from house to house, singing a special song and begging. In this case, it may seem easier to gain an idea of the "feel" of the occasion, as the actions seem closer to our category of folk custom than to worship; but we really cannot know how close a connection they were felt to have with Apollo, the deity connected with the festival in our sources.

What is abundantly clear is the immense diversity of practice in the annual round of the city's religious celebrations, and although no individual would have taken part in all the festivals (some were open to only a few participants, and a significant number confined to women),[43] when we add

---

[42] On Attic festivals, see Deubner, *Attische Feste;* Simon, *Festivals of Attica;* and most recently Parker, *Polytheism and Society,* esp. 155–383.

[43] For "women's festivals" see, for instance, Dillon, *Girls and Women in Classical Greek Religion,* and Goff, *Citizen Bacchae.*

Archaic and Classical Greek Religion 297

the observances of local and kin groups, we can see that the sheer quantity of celebrations was also very considerable. But not all religious activity took place on a regularly recurring basis. We have seen that individuals and small groups might offer sacrifice in accordance with specific needs or as a thanksgiving, and there were also cults and sanctuaries of a specialized nature that offered divine help in more particular ways. Perhaps the most characteristic of these was the oracle.[44] Although the art of prophecy (*mantikē technē*)[45] was well established in the hands of professionals and deeply embedded in Greek practice (for instance, it was essential to take note of the sacrificial omens before a battle), the oracular sanctuary is a different phenomenon: There, the answer came not from a learnable technique but from the god himself, through a priest or other consecrated person (often, as at Delphi, a woman). Oracles of a small sort may have been dotted around the Greek world, but they were not everywhere: Clearly there was none of much repute in Attica in the classical period, for instance. Thus the consultation of an oracle was often a major event, involving a fair amount of traveling, and much of the business of the best-reputed oracles was with state inquiries rather than with individuals. Thus it has been possible to speak of Delphi in particular as almost a political player, encouraging the sending out of colonies and later perhaps counseling submission to the Persian invasion. Foul play was sometimes suspected, but the oracle maintained its prestige in a way that would not have been possible if such human contamination had been obvious and consistent.

Even apart from the journey that was usually involved, the process of oracular consultation was often a difficult and awe-inspiring one. At Delphi, the oracle was open for the full form of consultation, with the Pythia giving responses from her tripod in the inmost part of the temple, on one day a month, probably nine months of the year. This must have severely limited the numbers able to benefit from the procedure. Various sacrifices were necessary beforehand, and only those actually making a consultation were allowed into the temple. Consulting the oracle of Trophonios at Lebadeia in Boeotia was well known to be a terrifying experience, involving an underground descent and supposed to leave the enquirer unable to laugh.[46] Fortunately, there were easier alternatives. The oracles of Delphi and Dodona (in northern Greece) both had a much more widely available procedure involving the use of the lot or a similar method.

---

[44] A great deal has been written on oracles: Convenient starting places are Parker, "Greek States," Bowden, *Classical Athens*, and Stoneman, *The Ancient Oracles*.

[45] On which see Flower, *Seer*.

[46] Aristophanes, *Clouds* 506–8; Semos of Delos, *FGrH* 396 F 10.

298 *Emily Kearns*

At Dodona questions were written on thin metal plaques, many of which have survived. The questions pose alternatives and speak eloquently of the concerns of ordinary people: "Is the child mine?" "Shall I get my freedom?"[47] The lot was often held to be a way of determining divine choice, and so even in this less prestigious form of consultation the inquirer was in communication with the god and soliciting a direct response.

Comparable in some ways to oracles were healing shrines, in which the deity was asked to cure the ailments of individuals. Although any deity might receive prayers and sacrifices for this purpose, in some sanctuaries it was customary for the worshipper to "consult" the god by making offerings and then sleeping in a special building in the complex in the hope of meeting the deity in a dream and being healed by him (less often her). The similarity with the oracle is not far to seek, and indeed the sanctuary of Amphiaraos at Oropos began life as a general oracle and later (by the early fourth century) became a healing sanctuary where incubation was practiced. Again, dreams were a common medium in which gods might communicate with humans – dedications were often made in response to a command in a dream, or more rarely a waking vision – but to solicit the dream is something different. This type of sanctuary, and especially the cult of its most famous subject, Asklepios, can be observed spreading geographically and growing in popularity during the last quarter of the fifth and first half of the fourth centuries.[48]

A different form of contact with the divine is to be found in the realm of Mysteries (*mystēria*) and initiations (*teletai*, although the word has a slightly wider application).[49] Here we are dealing with a very diverse body of ritual. Many belong in the category of official, regularly recurring ceremonies, whereas others seem to have been performed in accordance with demand. What they all have in common is that the participants went through an experience in conditions of secrecy; this related to the deities of the ritual and was felt to convey special benefits, often of an eschatological nature. The experience was often intense and might generate a strong affective bond between worshipper and divinity. Nevertheless it is not correct to

---

[47] Preparation of the corpus of these inscriptions, which was to have been published by A.-F. Christidis before his untimely death, is currently in progress. Meanwhile, Lhôte, *Les lamelles oraculaires,* has the fullest collection and analysis, and Eidinow, *Oracles, Curses, and Risk,* an important book in its own right, contains additional examples.

[48] There is no up-to-date comprehensive treatment of healing sanctuaries in general, but Edelstein, *Asclepius,* remains a wonderful compendium on the cult of Asklepios. For Amphiaraos and other Attic figures, see Verbanck-Piérard, "Les héros guérisseurs."

[49] A good general treatment is Burkert, *Ancient Mystery Cults.*

think of Mysteries, still less "mystery religions," as offering the individual an alternative to "state religion." The most reputed and venerable of all Mysteries, those of Eleusis, were firmly integrated into the Athenian system of state finance and control – and national pride – and there is no reason to suppose the same was not true of similar celebrations in other localities.[50] On the other hand, the elements of secrecy and soteriology that we find at Eleusis are also common to much of what Parker has called "unlicensed religion."[51] Plato speaks disapprovingly of itinerant initiators; Demosthenes, attacking his enemy Aeschines, depicts him as assisting his mother in initiations, holding books and instructing the initiate to declare, "I have escaped the bad, I have found the better."[52] However distorted this might be as an account of Aeschines' activities, the law-court jurors were clearly expected to recognize the sort of rite referred to and to despise it, or at least those who were "professionally" involved in it. "Unlicensed" religion may sometimes involve its practitioners in more than just one-off rituals, as we see with (often rather amorphous) groups labeled as "Orphic" or less often "Pythagorean," who had their own sacred discourse and variants on mythology, and who practiced an austere lifestyle aimed at a more than usual purity, sometimes including practices like vegetarianism that ran counter to accepted religious mores. Such groups tended to be treated as marginal at Athens, although they appear to have been more respectable in the cities of southern Italy.

Of course, there were also more conformist ways in which religious activity took place away from the festival calendar and outside the sanctuary. Dreams of the gods appear to have been rather common, suggesting their importance in most people's lives. Prayer and small offerings were frequent, and not only in moments of crisis: "Sacrifice to the immortal gods ... and at other times propitiate them with libations and offerings, both when you go to bed and when the holy light appears, so that they may have a favorable heart and mind towards you," says Hesiod (*Works and Days* 334–40). Libations indeed were a very common offering, being poured regularly at meals and drinking parties as well as at sacrifice (see Fig. 22), and there were countless such occasions where the Greeks regularly acknowledged the presence of the gods, hoping to retain a good relationship with them.

---

[50] We can see this in great detail for Andania in Messenia (*Syll.³* 736 = IG V.1 1390) at a rather later date.
[51] Parker, *Polytheism and Society,* 116 (chapter heading).
[52] Plato, *Republic* 364b–65a; Demosthenes, 18.258–260.

Fig. 22. *ThesCRA* IV, plate 52, no 74e (= ARV² 1635). Basel, Antikenmuseum Kä 423. Attic red-figure oinochoe (wine jug), ca.480 BCE, showing a man pouring a libation onto the flames lit on an altar.

TRENDS IN INTERPRETATION

It is impossible in such a short compass to deal even briefly with every item of importance in Greek religion. In particular, I am aware that I have scarcely touched on the importance of gender roles, and I have not tried to give an account of the role of mythology, or of controversial or apparently negative opinions of the gods. Works cited in the notes, along with the separate bibliography at the end of the volume, may help to fill the gaps. It may also be helpful in conclusion to give a very brief sketch of the trends of the last century in scholarship on Greek religion. Where not noted, references to representative works are to be found in the volume-end bibliography.

The "Cambridge ritualists" (Murray, Cornford, A. B. Cook, and above all, Jane Harrison),[53] flourishing in the 1920s, in some ways set the tone for much of the work of the succeeding eighty years, in which the study of ritual has been dominant. The group's views on the relationship between ritual and myth and their indulgence in reconstructions of a supposed ritual system in prehistoric Greece did not find lasting favor, but an underlying belief in the primacy of ritual has aged better and forms the basis for a great deal of important work by many distinguished scholars, ranging from studies of individual festivals through works on the cults of a particular place or deity to ambitious general theories. Noteworthy among the last, and particularly admired in the 1970s and 1980s, has been the work of Walter Burkert linking Greek ritual practice with evolutionary biology. Building on the work of Karl Meuli, Burkert worked out in *Homo necans* (1972), a hugely influential theory of sacrifice that explains the action in terms of the containment of violence and the unease supposedly felt by primitive hunters at the kill. In later works he has taken sociobiological approaches further, explaining aspects of religious activity with reference to the behavior of primates and other nonhuman species, although his writing spans a much wider range than this, and his *Greek Religion* (1977 and revisions) is still the standard general work.

A quite different approach has been taken by the "Paris school" (notably Vidal-Naquet, Vernant, Detienne, and Loraux), whose innovation was the application of structuralist techniques to Greek religious material, above all to mythology, resulting in some classic studies of the meanings of religion and mythology within society and an emphasis on the inner workings of "the pantheon." Greek myth has also been studied from diverse

---

[53] See Calder, *Cambridge Ritualists.*

comparativist and historical perspectives, for instance, by Geoffrey Kirk and Martin West.

The study of Greek religion in its socio-political context goes back at least to Fustel de Coulanges in the nineteenth century and was the subject of important work by Louis Gernet, who combined it with anthropological theory, from the 1930s onward. But the "*polis*-religion" approach really became popular in the last quarter of the century, and in Anglophone scholarship began to loom large only in the mid-1980s, coinciding with a greater willingness on the part of more traditional Greek historians to take religion seriously.[54] Parallel with this development, and sometimes expressing itself as a reaction to it, has been a smaller stream of work stressing cognitive approaches and investigating the religious mentalities of the Greeks, as they can be recovered both from traditional texts and from archaeological data.[55]

Archaeology and epigraphy, although they cannot in themselves be classified as "approaches" to the study of religion, have in fact contributed immensely to the subject over the course of the late nineteenth and twentieth centuries. The layout of sanctuaries, the analysis of faunal remains (from sacrifice), and the recovery of works of art have all had a part to play, but it is perhaps the yield of new and different types of text that has been most important. It would be hard to exaggerate the importance that the study of inscriptions has for the subject, although we must recognize that (as with literary texts) there are generic constraints that limit the type of information they can give. Beyond monumental inscriptions, other forms of text have emerged: Notably, a number of texts incised on small metal plaques (the so-called Orphic gold leaves or lamellae)[56] and some on bone have added considerably to our knowledge of Orphism and related phenomena, an area illuminated also by one of the few papyri found outside Egypt, the Derveni papyrus.[57]

BIBLIOGRAPHY

Bartoloni G., G. Colonna, and C. Grottanelli, eds. *Anathema: Atti del convegno internazionale, Scienze dell'Antichità* 3–4 (1989/90).

---

[54] Notable exponents of this approach are Sourvinou-Inwood, e.g., "Persephone and Aphrodite" and "What Is *Polis* Religion?" and Parker, e.g., "Greek States and Greek Oracles" and *Polytheism and Society.*

[55] This last trend, prominent in the work of Rudhardt, *Notions fondamentales,* is also seen, for instance, in Gladigow, "Der Sinner der Götter," Kearns, "Order, Interaction, Authority," Lowe, "Thesmophoria and Haloa," and Harrison, *Divinity and History.*

[56] See Pugliese Carratelli, *Le lamine d'oro orfiche;* Graf and Johnston, *Ritual Texts;* Tzifopoulos, *Paradise Earned.*

[57] The long-awaited official publication of this enigmatic text is Kouremenos et al., *Derveni Papyrus.*

Bell, C. *Ritual: Perspectives and Dimensions* (Oxford, 1997).

Berthiaume, G. *Les rôles du mageiros: Étude sur la boucherie, la cuisine et le sacrifice dans la Grèce ancienne*. Mnemosyne suppl. 70 (Leiden, 1982).

Boehringer, D. *Heroenkulte in Griechenland von der geometrischen bis zur klassischen Zeit: Attika, Argolis, Messenien* (Berlin, 2001).

Bowden, H. *Classical Athens and the Delphic Oracle* (Cambridge, 2005).

Burkert, W. *Homo Necans: The Anthropology of Ancient Greek Sacrificial Ritual and Myth* (Berkeley, 1983; German original, 1972).

Greek Religion: Archaic and Classical (Oxford, 1985; German original 1977).

Ancient Mystery Cults (Cambridge, Mass., 1987).

Calder, W. M., III, ed. *The Cambridge Ritualists Reconsidered*. Illinois Classical Studies suppl. 2 (Atlanta, 1991).

Connor, W. R. "Seized by the Nymphs: Nympholepsy and Symbolic Expression in Classical Greece." *Classical Antiquity* 7.2 (1988): 155–89.

Deubner, L. *Attische Feste* (Berlin, 1932)

Dillon, M. *Girls and Women in Classical Greek Religion* (London, 2002).

Edelstein, E. J., and L. Edelstein. *Asclepius: Collection and Interpretation of the Testimonia*. 2 vols. (Baltimore, 1945; repr. in one volume, 1998).

Eidinow, E. *Oracles, Curses, and Risk among the Ancient Greeks* (Oxford, 2007).

Ekroth, G. *The Sacrificial Rituals of Greek Hero-Cults in the Archaic to the Early Hellenistic Periods*. Kernos supplement 12 (Liège, 2002).

Faraone, C. "Kronos and the Titans as Powerful Ancestors: A Case Study of the Greek Gods in Later Magical Spells." In *The Gods of Ancient Greece: Identities and Transformations*, ed. J. N. Bremmer and A. Erskine (Edinburgh, 2010).

Faraone, C., and F. Naiden, eds. *Greek and Roman Animal Sacrifice: Ancient Victims, Modern Observers* (Cambridge, 2012).

Flower, M. A. *The Seer in Ancient Greece* (Berkeley, 2009).

Garland, R. "Religious Authority in Archaic and Classical Athens." *BSA* 79 (1984): 75–123.

"Priests and Power in Classical Athens." In *Pagan Priests: Religion and Power in the Ancient World*, ed. M. Beard and J. North (London, 1990; rev. but abbrev. version of above): 73–91.

Gladigow, B. "Der Sinner der Götter: zum kognitiven Potential der persönlichen Gottesvorstellung. " In *Gottesvorstellung und Gesellschaftentwicklung*, ed. P. Eicher (Munich, 1979): 41–62.

Goff, B. *Citizen Bacchae: Women's Ritual Practice in Ancient Greece* (Berkeley, 2004).

Graf, F., and S. I. Johnston. *Ritual Texts for the Afterlife: Orpheus and the Bacchic Gold Tablets* (London, 2007).

Hadzisteliou Price, T. *Kourotrophos: Cults and Representations of the Greek Nursing Deities* (Leiden, 1978).

Harrison, T. *Divinity and History: The Religion of Herodotus* (Oxford, 2000).

Hitch, S., and I. Rutherford, eds. *Animal Sacrifice in the Ancient Greek World* (Cambridge, forthcoming).

Jameson, M. H., D. R. Jordan, and R. D. Kotansky. *A Lex Sacra from Selinous*. GRBS monographs 11 (Durham, 1993).

Jost, M. *Sanctuaires et cultes d'Arcadie*. Études Peloponnésiennes IX (Paris, 1985).

Kearns, E. "Order, Interaction, Authority: Ways of Looking at Greek Religion." In *The Greek World*, ed. A. Powell (London, 1995).

Kouremenos, T., G. M. Parassoglou, and K. Tsantsanoglou. *The Derveni Papyrus, Edited with a Translation and Commentary* (Florence, 2006).

Lalonde, G. V. *Horos Dios: An Athenian Shrine and Cult of Zeus* (Leiden, 2006).

Larson, J. *Greek Nymphs: Myth, Cult, Lore* (Oxford, 2001).

Ancient Greek Cults: A Guide (New York, 2007).

Lhôte, E. *Les lamelles oraculaires de Dodone* (Geneva, 2006).

Lowe, N. J. "Thesmophoria and Haloa: Myth, Physics and Mysteries." In *The Sacred and the Feminine in Ancient Greece*, ed. S. Blundell and M. Williamson (London, 1998): 149–73.

Lupu, E. *Greek Sacred Law. A Collection of New Documents (NGSL)*. Religions in the Graeco-Roman World 152 (Leiden, 2005).

Meritt, B., and J. S. Traill. *The Athenian Agora: Results of the Excavations Conducted by the American School of Classical Studies in Athens*, volume XV, *Inscriptions: The Athenian Councillors* (Princeton, 1974).

Nilsson, M. P. *Opuscula selecta*, vol. 2 (Lund, 1952).

Ogden, D., ed. *A Companion to Greek Religion* (Malden, Mass., 2007).

Osborne, R. "Women and Sacrifice in Classical Greece." *Classical Quarterly* 43:2 (1993): 392–405.

Parker, R. "Greek States and Greek Oracles." In *Oxford Readings in Greek Religion*, ed. R. G. A. Buxton (Oxford, 2000; original publication, 1985): 76–108.

Polytheism and Society at Athens (Oxford, 2005).

Pedley, J. *Sanctuaries and the Sacred in the Ancient Greek World* (Cambridge, 2005).

Pugliese Carratelli, G. *Le lamine d'oro orfiche* (Milan, 2001).

Pulleyn, S. *Prayer in Greek Religion* (Oxford, 1997).

Purvis, A. *Singular Dedications: Founders and Innovators of Private Cults in Classical Greece* (New York, 2003).

Rudhardt, J. *Notions fondamentales de la pensée religieuse et actes constitutifs du culte dans la Grèce classique*, 2nd ed. (Paris, 1992; 1st ed., 1958).

Simon, E. *Festivals of Attica: An Archaeological Commentary* (Madison, Wis., 1983).

Sokolowski, F. *Lois sacrées de l'Asie mineure* (Paris, 1955 = *LSAM*).

Lois sacrées: supplément (Paris, 1962 = *LSS*).

Lois sacrées des cités grecques (Paris, 1969 = *LSCG*).

Sourvinou-Inwood, C. "Persephone and Aphrodite at Locri: A Model for Personality Definitions in Greek Religion." *JHS* 98 (1978): 101–21.

"What Is *Polis* Religion?" In *Oxford Readings in Greek Religion*, ed. R. Buxton (Oxford, 2000; original publication, 1990): 13–37.

Staal, F. *Rules without Meaning: Ritual, Mantras, and the Human Sciences* (New York, 1989).

Stoneman, R. *The Ancient Oracles: Making the Gods Speak* (New Haven, 2011).

van Straten, F. T. "Gifts for the Gods." In *Faith Hope and Worship: Aspects of Religious Mentality in the Ancient World*, ed. H. S. Versnel (Leiden, 1981): 65–151.

Hiera Kala: Images of Animal Sacrifice in Archaic and Classical Greece (Leiden, 1995).

Suárez de la Torre, E., ed., *Héros et héroïnes dans les mythes et les cultes grecs*. Kernos suppl. 10 (Liège, 2000): 281–332.

Tzifopoulos, Y. *Paradise Earned: The 'Bacchic-Orphic' Lamellae of Crete* (Cambridge, Mass., 2007).

Archaic and Classical Greek Religion

Verbanck-Piérard, A. "Les héros guérisseurs: des dieux comme les autres! À propos des cultes médicaux dans l'Attique classique." In *Héros et héroïnes dans les mythes et les cultes grecs*, ed. V. Pirenne-Delforge and E. Suárez de la Torre. Kernos suppl. 10 (Liège, 2000): 281–332.

Verbruggen, H. *Le Zeus crétois* (Paris, 1981).

Vernant, J.-P. *Myth and Thought among the Greeks* (London, 1983; original version, *Mythe et pensée chez les Grecs. Étude de psychologie historique,* 2 vols. [Paris, 1965; 2nd ed., 1985]).

Versnel, H. S. "Religious Mentality in Ancient Prayer." In *Faith Hope and Worship: Aspects of Religious Mentality in the Ancient World*, ed. H. S. Versnel (Leiden, 1981): 1–64.

Yunis, H. *A New Creed: Fundamental Religious Beliefs in the Athenian Polis and Euripidean Drama.* Hypomnemata Heft 91 (Göttingen, 1988).

PART IV

THE WESTERN MEDITERRANEAN AND EUROPE

12

ETRUSCAN RELIGION

NANCY T. DE GRUMMOND

FRAMEWORK

The evidence for the study of Etruscan religion is fragmentary, much more than it is for Greek or Roman religion. Very little survives of original Etruscan writings on this subject. The most authoritative primary evidence comes from archaeological excavations in Etruscan sacred places, representations in art, and a few surviving texts in the Etruscan language ranging from circa fifty to thirteen hundred words, as well as some eleven thousand short inscriptions. After that come the numerous references in Greek and Latin authors, always to be read with appropriate caution as to time and place, and a few documents purporting to be translated from Etruscan into Latin or Greek. All of these sources must then be interpreted to seek a coherent picture.

Given these severe restrictions, it is still possible to use these sources to argue that the religion of the Etruscans should be studied as a system that had a profound connection with what they regarded as their sacred history. Key pieces of evidence indicate that both spoken and written words were controlling factors in formulating communication with the gods, and the result was that the Etruscans had a collection of books with an authority for them comparable to that of the Bible or the Q'uran, encompassing the origins of their religious practices, the pronouncements of their prophets, and a particular view of history as a record of the destiny of individuals, cities, and the Etruscan people as a whole.

Etruscan ritual thus was informed by a constant preoccupation with fate and destiny, and centered on attempts to learn the will of the gods and somehow to affect their decisions and thus the outcome of human affairs. The well-known Etruscan science of haruspication, involving the scrutiny and interpretation of the entrails of a sacrificial animal, epitomizes Etruscan praxis, but there is evidence of various other techniques of divination, such as reading the flight and activity of birds, interpreting the significance of lightning and thunder, drawing lots in a sacred setting, and recognizing and accounting for abnormalities in nature.[1] These persisting practices have been characterized as "archaic" and "magico-religious,"[2] and emphasis has been given rightly to the superstitious nature of official rituals that evidently had to be performed with scrupulous attention to minutiae. Arnobius, writing around 300 CE, made reference to "Etruria, the begetter and mother of superstition" (*Adversus Nationes* 7.26).[3] Still, Etruscan religion should not be thought of as crudely primitive, given its dependency on sacred writings and the degree of sophisticated study and training that Etruscan priests must have undertaken. It is possible to note certain characteristics of religion in the Archaic period (ca.600–450 BCE) and continuity as well as change at a later date, it would be rash to attempt a developmental history of Etruscan religion on the basis of the little knowledge we have of Etruscan history as a whole. This problem will be reviewed at the end of the chapter. Rather, the method adopted here, as noted above, will focus on Etruscan religion as part of a communicative system between humans and gods.

THE SOURCES

The most consistent and reliable picture of the practice of Etruscan religion may be obtained by studying the evidence from archaeology. Excavations have revealed altars, temples, boundary markers, and sanctuaries, as well as abundant votive deposits documenting rituals that existed from the earliest periods, the Villanovan (ninth–eighth century BCE) and Orientalizing (750–600 BCE), down to the final centuries of Etruscan civilization in the second and first centuries BCE. Funerary remains, the most ubiquitous of Etruscan material culture, provide a record showing the similarities and differences of ancestor cult through the centuries and across the map of Etruria proper (largely modern Latium, Tuscany, and Umbria) and in Etruscan-controlled or -influenced territories of northern Italy and Campania in the south (see Maps 7 and 8).[4]

[1] Maggiani, "La divinazione in Etruria," 52–78.
[2] Torelli, "La religione," 162–3.
[3] See de Grummond, "Selected Latin and Greek Sources," 191 and throughout for texts and translations of literary sources cited in this article.
[4] For Roman religious, see Chapter 13.

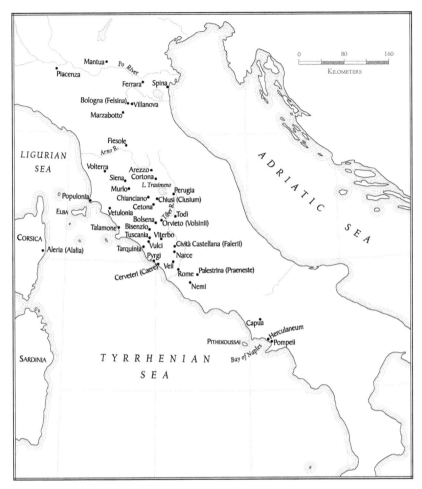

Map 7. Etruscan Italy.

Particular objects from controlled excavations and chance finds illuminate Etruscan religion. Most famous is the bronze model of a sheep's liver that was found at Piacenza (see Fig. 23; third-second century BCE; Rix, *ET* Pa 4.2), evidently a priest's guide to interpreting the actual liver of a sacrificed animal;[5] Etruscan mirrors (see Fig. 24) and gems show a number of images of the priest holding the liver and showing the conditions under which the liver was interpreted. Many thousands of individual votive offerings display a rich spectrum of concerns of devotees, from uteri and

[5] Van der Meer, *Bronze Liver;* Maggiani, "Qualche osservazione," 53–88.

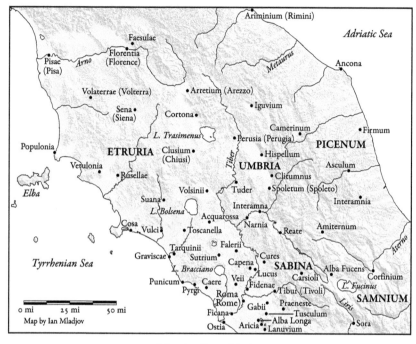

Map 8. Central Italy.

Fig. 23. Bronze model of a sheep's liver found near Piacenza. Third-second century BCE. Piacenza, Museo Civico.

Etruscan Religion 313

Fig. 24. Bronze Etruscan mirror from Tuscania, with scene of Pava Tarchies reading a liver in the presence of Avl Tarchunus; third century BCE. Florence, Museo Archeologico Nazionale. Source: Mario Torelli, "Etruria principes disciplinam doceto," Studia Tarquiniensia (Archeologia Perusina 9), 110, Fig. 1. © Giorgio Bretschneider Editore, Rome.

swaddled babies to weavers' implements, ceramic and metal vessels, luxury goods, and statuettes of the worshippers or the gods.[6] Representations in art convey information, depicting priests in full regalia, altars, processions, games, prophetic scenes, and instruments of cult. Temple decorations of terracotta often feature images of the gods, sometimes as part of a narrative that conveys a message to worshippers.

Much attention has been given to writings in Etruscan[7] and other languages. The best known of all Etruscan inscriptions are found on a group of metal tablets from Pyrgi, the port city of Cerveteri and site of the greatest Etruscan international sanctuary (ca.500 BCE; Rix *ET* Cr 4.3–4.5). Three are in gold, and a fourth fragmentary one is of bronze; one of the gold ones is a paraphrase in Phoenician/Punic, conveying a message similar to that in the other two gold tablets, in Etruscan. All refer to the worship of Uni, equated in the tablets with Astarte.

The highest importance is attached to the amazing Etruscan linen book, found cut into strips wrapped around an Egyptian mummy, now in the National Museum of Zagreb (second century BCE; length, twelve to thirteen hundred words; probably from the area of Perugia-Cortona; Rix *ET* LL). Unfortunately, only parts of it can be translated or interpreted with confidence, but enough can be read to say that it is a liturgical book, containing texts and prescriptions for ritual acts set out in the form of a calendar, with instructions for each particular day.[8] It seems to be the only surviving example from the ancient world of what the Romans called a *liber linteus*, a sacred linen book. This type of book is represented in Etruscan art as early as circa 500 BCE, in the Etruscan Archaic period. Another calendrical text, the Capua Tile, was found inscribed on a terracotta tile discovered at Santa Maria di Capua (ca. three hundred words surviving; now Berlin, Staatliche Museen; ca.500 BCE; Rix *ET* TC).[9] There is little in common between the items in the two calendars, a fact that is not surprising given that in the ancient world local religion quite commonly conditioned the entries on the calendar of a place.

Yet another Etruscan calendar is known, this time in Greek translation, based on a Latin version in turn perhaps translated and edited from the Etruscan in the first century BCE. This is the Brontoscopic (Thunder) Calendar preserved by Nigidius Figulus, an erudite contemporary of

---

[6] Turfa, "Votive Offerings," 90–115.
[7] Bonfante, "Etruscan Inscriptions," 9–26.
[8] Roncalli, *Scrivere etrusco*, 52.
[9] Cristofani, *Tabula Capuana;* Edlund-Berry, "Etruscans at Work and Play," 330–7.

Cicero, transmitted in Greek by Johannes Lydus, a Byzantine cleric and scholar of the sixth century CE.[10] In spite of its late date and remote geographical connection, it remains a most valuable source for revealing the type of predictions that were made on the basis of thunder on a particular day, concerning agriculture, politics, health, and natural phenomena.

Much antiquarian literary evidence for Etruscan religion has been preserved by Roman and occasionally Greek writers of the late Roman Republic and early empire.[11] Livy (5.1.6) declared that the Etruscans were "a people more than any other dedicated to religion, the more as they excelled in the practice of it."[12] The Roman polymath Varro frequently made references to Etruscan practices and teaching, such as how the Etruscans ritually founded a town by plowing around its boundaries (*De lingua latina* 5.143). Aulus Caecina, from an Etruscan family of Volterra and another contemporary of Cicero, wrote a Latin treatise, *De etrusca disciplina*, "On the Etruscan Discipline," that was much studied and quoted. The phrase *etrusca disciplina* is probably the Latin translation of some Etruscan expression that described the compilation of precepts and practices in their religious literature.

SACRED TIME: PROPHECY AND CALENDARS

A remnant of Etruscan prophecy describing the origin of the universe survives in a Roman treatise on measuring land.[13] Vegoia, Vecuvia in Etruscan, declares that after the sea was separated from the sky, the original division of the lands of Etruria was carried out by "Jupiter," that is, the chief deity of the Etruscan pantheon, Tinia. With a fervor worthy of some of the fiercest prophets of the Old Testament, Vegoia warns that violation of the boundaries will lead to dire consequences.

The origin of the *Etrusca disciplina*, taught by the prophet called Tages in Latin, belongs to an early period in Etruscan sacred history, although the evidence concerning this is quite late. According to Johannes Lydus, Cicero, and others, Tages suddenly popped out of the ground as it was being plowed by a farmer at Tarquinia. The prophet – a baby, but with the features of a wise old man – began to sing out the principles of the *disciplina*. According to one version, the noble Tarchon, founder of Tarquinia, took down his words and conveyed all his teachings to the twelve major

---

[10] Turfa, "Etruscan Brontoscopic Calendar," 173–90.
[11] De Grummond, "Introduction: History of the Study," 2–4.
[12] Eadem, "Latin and Greek Sources," 191.
[13] Ibid., 191–2.

peoples of Etruria. Much of the content of the prophecy related to the arts of soothsaying, with special attention to haruspication. A possible representation of this fundamental Etruscan myth appears on an engraved mirror from Tuscania, near Tarquinia (Fig. 24; third century BCE),[14] where a youth (not a baby), holds and interprets a liver, while a bearded man labeled Avl Tarchunus (possibly = Tarchon) listens intently, as if learning from the boy. The name inscribed next to the haruspicator, Pava Tarchies, has been argued to be the equivalent of Latin *puer Tages*, that is, "child Tages."

The Etruscan view of their sacred history included a chronology based on the generic time designator of the *saeculum* ("age," "generation," "lifetime"). They believed that their people had a destiny, and that the end of their name would come after ten *saecula* (Censorinus, *De die natali* 17.5–6). Various authors give bits of information on the doctrine of the *saecula*, revealing how the calculations were made and the number of years in each *saeculum*. At the time of the founding of the Etruscan nation, the first *saeculum* began from the time of the birth of the first child and lasted until the time of his death. An omen would be sent from the gods to announce the end of each age, for example, a trumpet blast from the sky (Plutarch, *Life of Sulla*, 7.3–6). The lengths of the *saecula* are quite peculiar, for they scarcely match with the lifetime of a man. As far as the evidence we have, the first four *saecula* were each of one hundred years; the following ones were of 123, 119, and 119 years, and one late one seems to have been of forty-four years.

Given the importance of the calendar to Etruscan religion, it is no accident that two of the longest Etruscan texts surviving are calendrical. Unfortunately we know very little about the feasts, sacrifices, and celebrations recorded in the calendar of the Etruscan year. As in early Rome, the year started in March, and the Romans and Etruscans evidently counted their months in the same way, starting with the new moon, and using divisions of the month to identify the days. In fact, the Latin calendrical word Ides, a lunar term, is believed to be derived from Etruscan *itus*.

It is certain that at least some of the months were named after important deities: July, called Traneus in its Latin form (*TLE* 854), is surely the month of Turan, the Etruscan goddess of love and sex, and September, Celius (*TLE* 824), was sacred to Cel Ati, mother earth. The Zagreb mummy wrappings give quite particular instructions for sacrifices to certain deities on individual days of the months of June, August, and September, but often

---

[14] Eadem, *Etruscan Myth*, 23–7, Fig. II.2. Pallottino, "Uno specchio," 679–709.

the specific meaning of the terms used for ritual details is not known. The passages for which the translations can be agreed upon are nevertheless not rich in detail: "In the month of Cel, on the twenty-sixth day, the offerings to Nethuns (=Neptune) must be made and immolated."[15]

THE PANTHEON

Several sources, notably Martianus Capella (fifth century CE) and the Piacenza Liver, give evidence that the Etruscans regarded the heavens as divided into sixteen major parts, and that each of these segments provided abodes for the gods.[16] Some gods had more than one habitation; Tinia, the head of the Etruscan pantheon, had multiple houses in the sky on the north and east, as well as on the liver, and in addition had a connection with the Underworld. His consort Uni (called Juno in Latin) also had more than one celestial house, including one on the darker, western side of the sky. In short, there was no Olympus for the Etruscan gods, and although we may make up tidy-looking charts of their Greek and Roman counterparts, it is certain that they had their own powers and places in the Etruscan cosmos.

Of the first importance was the authority the Etruscans attributed to lightning and thunder. Nine gods were recognized as having the power and the right to throw the thunderbolt, including – to use the names provided by Roman writers – Jupiter, Juno, Minerva (=Etr. Menrva), Vulcan (=Sethlans), Mars (=Laran), and Saturn (=Satre).[17] The unusual significance of lightning for the Etruscans is made clear by the passage in Seneca, who noted, "This is the difference between us and the Etruscans, who have consummate skill in interpreting lightning. We think that because clouds collide, lightning is emitted. They believe that clouds collide in order that lightning may be emitted" (*Quaestiones naturales* 2.32.2).[18] The doctrine of lightning was exquisitely detailed, with several different systems of classification on record. It was important for a priest to know which deity

---

[15] Bonfante and Bonfante, *The Etruscan Language*, 183.
[16] Weinstock, "Martianus Capella." The text of Martianus is conventionally referred to as *De nuptiis Mercurii et Philologiae* (relevant passage: I.45–61; for text and translation, see de Grummond, "Selected Latin and Greek Sources," 2006, 199–200). For a concise review of the most important Etruscan gods, see Simon, "Gods in Harmony." For more extensive treatment, see de Grummond, *Etruscan Myth*, especially chapter III.
[17] Pfiffig, *Religio etrusca*, 130. The names of the other three are not certain, but Hercules was described by Seneca as a lightning god, and the Roman deity Summanus who could throw the thunderbolt is probably Etruscan in origin.
[18] Trans. T. H. Corcoran, Seneca, *Quaestiones naturales* (Cambridge, Mass., 1971), 151; de Grummond, "Latin and Greek Sources," 213–14.

318   *Nancy T. de Grummond*

had sent forth the lightning or thunder; in order to interpret the omen, he had to have a knowledge of the sixteen parts of the sky and the sphere of influence that was affected. No doubt the reading of livers had a similar system: The *haruspex* had to know which gods controlled each section or cell of the liver.

Major deities and many minor ones[19] were at work transmitting messages from the macrocosm of the sky as well as from the microcosm of the liver. Martianus Capella provided names of deities practically unknown outside of his survey of the heavens – Neverita, Lynsa Silvestris, Janitores Terrestres – whose function can only sometimes be conjectured, while the liver mentions, in addition to Tinia and Uni and recognizable deities such as Nethuns, Fufluns (=Bacchus), and Selvans (=Silvanus, more or less), problematic names such as Thuflthas, Tec, and Letham. Hercle (Hercules) is also present on the liver, worshipped as a god of cult in Etruria.

Still other deities are known mainly from dedicatory inscriptions. Śuri, the principal deity of the south sanctuary at Pyrgi, has been equated with Soranus, an epiclesis of Apollo worshipped in Latin territory, who seems to have both solar and Underworld connections.[20] The sphere of Śuri's consort, Catha (variously spelled), may be similar, but given the fluidity of the Etruscan pantheon, she (if Catha is indeed female) could have other duties. Lur and Leinth in the Etruscan artisans' sanctuary at Cetamura del Chianti (near Siena) are evidently deities of fate and fortune.[21]

Myths and legends told in Rome mention Etruscan deities, such as Vertumnus, described by Varro as the "chief god of Etruria" (*De lingua latina* 5.46). It is almost certain that this was a variant name for Tinia, occurring in several forms in Rome, and probably also on the Pava Tarchies mirror as Veltune (Fig. 24; a Tinia-like figure on the far right). Vertumnus appears in descriptions by Propertius (4.2) and Ovid (*Metamorphoses*, 14.623–771), which have a ring of truth in that the god is able to change sex and demonstrates a flexibility in identity and spheres of influence.

Representations of themes of myth and legend in Etruscan art, beginning in the seventh century BCE, help to define Etruscan deities, but even so, much remains unclear. As Pallottino put it, "The Etruscan concept of supernatural beings was permeated by a certain vagueness as to numbers, sex, attributes, and appearance."[22] Thus in art some deities may be

---

[19] Simon, "Gods in Harmony," 45–65.
[20] Colonna, "L' Apollo di Pyrgi," 345–75.
[21] De Grummond, "Sanctuary of the Etruscan Artisans," 115–17.
[22] Pallottino, *The Etruscans*, 140.

Etruscan Religion

represented as double and some deities change gender, but the significance of these variations is seldom clear. Menrva and Turms (=Mercury) each appear as twins on mirrors, where the theme of doubling makes reference, perhaps, to two different divisions of the cosmos, inside the mirror and out. The cult of the twin Dioskouroi may have been popular precisely because of the dualism inherent in their nature. An infant named Mariś (*not* identifiable with Mars, but perhaps rather a parallel to Genius) appears as triplets, each time with an additional byname of as yet little understood purpose. Martianus refers to vague, elusive gods in groups, such as the Janitores Terrestris, "Doorkeepers of the Earth," and the Favores Opertanei, "Secret Gods of Favor," while Seneca (*Quaest nat.* 2.41) records the dark, mysterious Dii Involuti ("Shrouded Gods"), who advised Jupiter when to hurl thunderbolts. The Etruscans had four types of Penates, who served the spheres of Jupiter and Neptune (i.e., the heavens and the waters), as well as the Underworld and the domain of men (Arnobius 3.40); these and other group gods recognized by the Romans, such as the Lares and the Manes, may well be Etruscan in origin.[23]

The change of sex is particularly typical of personification deities, who probably were not normally thought of as having a specific gender, nor did the Etruscan language assign a gender to their abstract nouns, as happened in Greek and Latin. Thus Alpan, a deity of good will and gladness, appears as either male or female, and Thalna, a popular spirit who attends scenes of birth, childhood, romance, revelry, and prophecy, may appear as a robust youth or a lovely goddess. Other gods who appear as both male and female are Leinth, Achvizr, and Evan, and in addition the ubiquitous flying spirit Lasa, whose name may mean something like "nymph," except that such a comparison does not fit in the one inscribed instance where Lasa is clearly male.[24]

Foreign gods were adopted in Etruria. Hercle, who has a rich mythological life in early Italy, was chief of these. Apollo was worshipped as Apulu or Aplu, and his sister Artemis is named as Artumes or Aritimi. Fufluns evidently took such a firm hold in Etruria that his cult got out of hand, provoking the famous Roman senatorial decree *de Bacchanalibus* (186 BCE). The presence of the name Astarte (=Uni) in the harbor at Pyrgi provides a rare instance of a Punic cult at an Etruscan site.[25]

---

[23] Ibid., 142–3.
[24] Rallo, *Lasa*, 23–4.
[25] Colonna, "Il santuario di Pyrgi," 209–17. For the Etruscan-Punic relations and the differences in their cult practices, see Turfa, "International Contacts," 77–8. On Punic religion see Schmitz's discussion in Chapter 8.

320   *Nancy T. de Grummond*

THE ROLE OF MYTH

Representations of myths played an important part in ritual and surely also in instruction. There are many representations in art that show activity at an altar, although the import of the scenes is not always clear, especially when the story depicted is a myth imported from Greece.[26] Stories of Troy and Thebes, with heroic characters based on the Greek myths, were common, sometimes mainly for entertainment or sensual pleasure, but at other times because of their echoes of serious concerns in Etruscan religion. Cinerary urns from Volterra and sarcophagi from Tarquinia (third–second centuries BCE), from a time and place in which the conflict was between Etruscan identity and Roman power, portray various themes of bloodshed at an altar or tomb, seemingly making reference to human sacrifice, although by this period, the actual practice would have been rare. Strangely popular in the fourth century was the theme of Achilles sacrificing Trojan prisoners at the tomb of Patroclus, a motif that received very little attention in Greece. Perhaps the best explanation for the choice of this theme and various battle scenes is the desire to refer symbolically to the shedding of blood, a substance needed by the ancestral dead in the tomb in order to revivify. As Arnobius notes (*Adv. nat.* 2.62), "They promise this in the *Acherontic Books* in Etruria, that when the blood of certain animals is given to certain numinous spirits the souls become divine and they are led away from the laws of mortality."[27]

Other ritual motifs crop up in representations of Etruscanized Greek myths. Themes with lightning are frequent, with the thunderbolts often represented with particular care or emphasis. The hammer and nail, both instruments associated with ceremonial actions, are depicted in several contexts. A surprising representation of the fate-goddess Atropos, called Athrpa in Etruscan, shows her without spinning attribute and working alone without her sisters Clotho and Lechesis, as she hammers a nail into the wall to affix a boar's head (mirror in Berlin). On either side of her are pairs of lovers who experienced a sad destiny because of a boar: Turan and Atunis (=Aphrodite and Adonis) and Atlenta and Meliacr (Atalanta and Meleager). The reference is patent, for the nail played a sacred role in Etruscan religion. It symbolized the inexorable passage of time, as, for

---

[26] Ambrosini, "Le raffigurazioni," 197–233; Steuernagel, *Menschenopfer.*

[27] Arnobius, *Adv. nat.* 2.62: *Quod Etruria libris in Acheronticis pollicentur, certorum animalium sanguine numinibus certis dato divinas animas fieri et ab legibus mortalitatis educi.* See too de Grummond, "Selected Latin and Greek Sources," 217, for my earlier translation, superseded by the present rendering.

Etruscan Religion

321

example, when a nail was hammered each year into the wall of the temple of the goddess Nortia, a custom imitated by the Romans in the Capitoline temple.[28] Nails are sometimes found as offerings in sanctuaries (e.g., Cetamura del Chianti),[29] a usage that may relate to fortune and fate. The hammer may also have a fatal import, appearing as it does as the attribute of the death-demon Charu(n), who escorted the dead into the afterlife.[30]

PRIESTS, PRIESTESSES, AND POLITICS

Representations of Etruscan priests are numerous, providing abundant evidence for the dress of these officiants, as well as clues about their posture, gestures, and attributes.[31] The characteristic tall hat with pointed or slightly flattened top is found widely, for example, on the Pava Tarchies mirror and on a series of bronze statuettes now in Göttingen. Much of the evidence belongs to the fourth or third century BCE, but at least one image comes from the sixth century, and it is generally agreed that the strange archaic hat originated in Villanovan times, perhaps having a connection with the Villanovan helmet topped by a flame-like crest. Often the *apex* (as it was called by the Romans, whose *flamines* and Salian priests wore a similar hat) was affixed to an animal-skin cap, the *galerus* (again, a Latin term), tied beneath the chin in a complex loop. All of these priests are clean shaven and the feet are always bare, but the garment varies. Typical is the fringed mantle, probably originating as an animal skin (perhaps one sacrificed by the priest), fastened by a large archaic fibula as it hangs down in front rather like a coat, but there are other ways of draping the mantle. The Göttingen bronzes include a figure with the mantle hanging in a low loop across the front, resembling the *laena* of the Roman *flamines* and the chasuble of the Catholic priest.

The *haruspex* has a characteristic pose, best demonstrated by Pava Tarchies, who props his left leg up on a mound of earth, and holds out the liver in his left hand so that he may manipulate it with his right. Sometimes the *haruspex* is bearded and wears a mantle draped to expose the shoulder. Other figures who seem to have served a sacred function may have a bare chest, for example, a bronze statuette of an augur (Paris, Louvre; sixth century BCE), which shows the priest with head twisted to look up at the sky,

---

[28] Aigner-Foresti, "Zur Zeremonie der Nagelschlagung," 144–6.
[29] De Grummond, "Sanctuary of the Etruscan Artisans," 41–3.
[30] Mavleev and Krauskopf, "Charu(n)," 235.
[31] Maggiani, "Immagini," 1557–63; Torelli, *Gli etruschi*, 278–80, 455, 591–3; de Grummond, "Prophets and Priests," 35–8; Roncalli, "Haruspex."

perhaps to discern the flight of birds or study some celestial phenomenon. Occasionally the priestly figure carries a staff, most prominent of which is the wand curved in a shape rather like a question mark, known in Latin as the *lituus*. It was adopted in Roman religion as the tool of the augur that marks out the area for observation of omens.

There is limited evidence for the terminology of priests in Etruria. By a fortunate stroke, a bilingual inscription from Pesaro (Rix *ET* Um 1.7; first century BCE), gives the Latin titles of one Larth Cafates as *haruspex fulguriator*, "reader of entrails, reader of lightning," and provides the Etruscan version of these titles: *netśvis trutnvt frontac*. It is agreed that *netśvis* is the equivalent of *haruspex*, but *fulguriator* seems to relate to two Etruscan words, and so there is uncertainty about their precise equivalency. Yet another word for an Etruscan priest, *cepen* (variant spellings occur), seems to be generic. *Cepen* occurs four times with another word, *maru*, which seems to refer to the activities of a magistrate who may also have priestly duties.[32] The latter term also is found with a collective ending, in the word *maruχva* (Rix *ET*, AT 1.96, 1.161), interpreted as referring to an association or *collegium* of priest-magistrates. Very rare is the word *eisnev*, which is nevertheless suggestive in that it is etymologically related to Etruscan words referring to a god (*ais-*) or something divine (*aisna/eisna*).

Images survive showing female religious functionaries performing animal sacrifice,[33] and there are several representations of women in what seems to be ritual dress, all coming from a funerary context as images on sarcophagi from the Tarquinia area.[34] They wear tall hats as well as grand, conspicuous necklaces of possibly ceremonial import and a coiffure with the hair divided into six major locks on each side of the head (cf. the *seni crines* of the Roman Vestal Virgins). Some carry attributes that are suggestive – a patera, a kantharos, a bird – and one seems to offer a drink to a deer. There may be an Etruscan word for priestess, *hatrencu*, but for it, too, the evidence is only funerary, and the term is found only at Vulci.[35] In the Hellenistic Tomb of the Inscriptions were found five instances of the word *hatrencu*, used in juxtaposition with women's names as if in a title. It has been argued that they were members of a *collegium* that had a right to burial in a special place.

It is likely that authority in controlling religious activity and therefore political life among the Etruscans was in the hands of the nobility, as it was

---

[32] De Grummond, "Prophets and Priests," 34 and 42 (note 19).
[33] Donati, "Sacrifici," 155–7 (nos. 160, 162, 176).
[34] De Grummond, "Prophets and Priests," 38–9.
[35] Nielsen, "Sacerdotesse," 45–67.

in Rome. Some inscriptions use the term *zilc* (alternate spellings occur), generally agreed to be a magistracy roughly equivalent to the *praetor* at Rome, in combination with *cepen* or some form of *maru*. The epitaph of Arnth Churcles from Norchia describes his offices with the words *zilc* and *cepen*, as well as *marunuχ* in combination with *spurana*, "pertaining to the city" (Rix *ET* AT 1.171; third century BCE). Specific information comes from the famous inscription on a scroll held by L(a)ris Pulenas of Tarquinia. His grand sarcophagus from the tomb of the prominent Pulenas family (250–200 BCE) shows the deceased holding a document that traces his lineage through four generations; the *curriculum vitae* notes that he wrote a book on haruspication, and that he served the cults of Catha and Pacha.

An important tomb painting from Vulci (François Tomb, ca.350–325 BCE) depicts Vel Saties, principal figure of a distinguished family.[36] He is depicted gazing upward, as an assistant controls a woodpecker on a string, ready for release so that the magistrate may take auspices. Vel Saties wears a laurel wreath and a fine mantle, purple with rich embroidered or painted decoration, featuring three shield-bearing naked dancing males. It is clear that he exercised both military and augural power, appearing here as a victorious general. The image of dancing soldiers is not the only one in Etruria, and it may be that there was an Etruscan priesthood such as the Salians at Rome. An urn from Bisenzio depicts naked shield-bearing soldiers dancing in a circle around a wolf-like monster, clearly a ritual act.[37]

SACRED SPACE: SANCTUARIES, TEMPLES, ALTARS

To a certain extent it is possible to describe the historical development of Etruscan sanctuaries. Stunning discoveries on the Pian di Civita of Tarquinia in the "Sacral-Institutional Complex"[38] have revealed a quite early rectangular cult building (Bldg. Beta; early seventh century BCE) adjoining a natural cavity in the earth. Within Beta was a stone platform – an altar – from which a channel would conduct liquid offerings into the cavity. At the entrance to a rectangular precinct surrounding Beta was a remarkable votive pit with a bronze shield and a bronze *lituus*-shaped trumpet, both folded, and a bronze axe head. The close connection between the offering of the paraphernalia of a magistrate and the sacrifices at the altar is patent.

---

[36] Roncalli, "La decorazione pittorica," 99–100.
[37] Torelli, *Gli etruschi*, 541 (no. 15); Camporeale, "Purification," 59–60.
[38] Bonghi Jovino, "Area Sacra," 21–2.

The overall picture becomes quite breath-taking when we consider that near the altar and the cavity were found a burial of a child, about nine years old, judged to have had epilepsy, and scattered bones of other infant burials. Further, burials of adults, clearly human sacrifices, also occur in the Sacral-Institutional Complex.

Although highly unusual (evidence for Etruscan human sacrifice is otherwise very rare), the Pian di Civita site is in some ways typical of Etruscan sanctuaries, with its altar, rectangular temple-like building and precinct with votive pits. There is also evidence of water being channeled and stored in the precinct, probably also for ritual purposes, as found at many Etruscan sacred sites. Other early temple-like buildings have been excavated at Piazza d'Armi, Veii (late seventh–early sixth century BCE), where the roof was already being decorated with the characteristic Etruscan terracotta antefixes and plaques, and at Rusellae (also late seventh–early sixth century),[39] which featured a rectangular precinct with a circular building inside and abundant weaving implements probably intended as offerings. The simple rectangular type of precinct, with rectangular shrine, is also documented as late as the third century BCE (Grasceta dei Cavallari and Poggio Casetta at Bolsena).[40]

Around 580 BCE there occurs a change in sacred architecture, in which the simple rectangle begins to have a deep front porch with *antae* (projecting walls) and/or columns, as well as a podium to raise the temple up higher, occasioning a need for a frontal staircase. The monumentalizing of the building seems to have a parallel development in the introduction of true cult statues into Etruria.[41] Within a short while, these features were associated with a building type known as the Tuscanic (i.e., Etruscan) plan, described in precise terms, although at a much later date, by the Roman architect Vitruvius (*De architectura* IV.7; second half of the first century BCE).[42] The Vitruvian plan was a nearly square building, divided into a front part (*pars antica*) with a deep front porch and a rear part (*pars postica*) featuring three cellas or a central cella and two wings (*alae*). The front porch typically had two rows of four columns. No Etruscan temple fits perfectly the description given by Vitruvius, but there are many variations on the Tuscanic plan that generally are consistent with the Vitruvian parameters, and it is also possible to find hints of the plan in a few Etruscan houses, as

[39] Colonna, *Santuari*, 53–9; Comella, "Aedes," 140.
[40] Colonna, *Santuari*, 155–6; Comella, "Aedes," 140–1.
[41] Colonna, *Santuari*, 23–4. But cf. the critique of the tenuous evidence for cult statuary by Rask, "New Approaches," 89–112.
[42] Colonna, "Sacred Architecture," 152–5.

Etruscan Religion

well as in several tombs at Cerveteri that seem to imitate the architecture of grand houses. Thus there is good reason to believe that in this period the temple became for the Etruscans a house of the god, as it was for the Greeks, whereas earlier it may have had more of a function for ritual.[43] Still, the deep front porch, taking up the front half of the building, would have served well for ritual activities, especially of divination, perhaps previously practiced outdoors. The word *templum* itself, used in Latin in contexts that show strong Etruscan influence and connotations, originally referred to a designated area of sky or earth within which the priest would look for omens. The functionary normally took his stance facing south, with the east on his left – lucky – side, and thus it is not surprising that many Etruscan ritual sites face the south or southeast.[44]

The temple at the Portonaccio sanctuary at Veii, dated to the end of the sixth or beginning of the fifth century BCE, featured a square plan divided in half, with a triple cella in back, oriented toward the east/southeast. A large cistern-like pool flanked the temple and provided water for rituals, and a rectangular altar was placed well in front of the temple, turned to the east at an angle from the orientation of the building. Associated with this mature Etruscan temple structure are rich polychrome terracotta decorations, including the famed statue of the Apulu of Veii and ante-fixes with the head of Medusa. They typify the decoration of Etruscan sacred architecture, which unlike Greek and Roman temples did not show a development in the usage of stone sculpture. Greek influence is evident, though, in the mythological subjects chosen to decorate the buildings as well as in the idea of having an anthropomorphic image of the chief deity set inside the building. There is relatively little evidence for the appearance of Etruscan cult statues, hypothesized to have appeared around 580 BCE, replacing aniconic images.[45] An intriguing painted terracotta plaque from Cerveteri (ca.540 BCE) shows a statue of a goddess standing upon an altar-like base, and representations on Etruscan mirrors also suggest that the Etruscans may have thought of the gods as present on the flat surface of an altar.

Great temples were built at Cerveteri and its port Pyrgi, as well as at Tarquinia, Vulci, Marzabotto, and Orvieto in the period from the sixth to the fourth century BCE.[46] A newly discovered temple within the city at

---

[43] Cf. the discussion of cult statuary below.
[44] Torelli, "Templum," 340–7; Prayon, "Sur l'orientation," 357–71.
[45] Colonna, *Santuari*, 23–4; Rask, "New Approaches," 89–112.
[46] Colonna, *Santuari*, 60–6, 70–83, 88–92; Colonna, "Sacred Architecture," 152–62; Comella, "Aedes," 139–42.

Marzabotto, dating to the fifth century BCE, shows a unique plan, with a rectangular single cella, and a colonnade going all around the temple. There were four columns in front, five in back, and six along each side. Smaller temples of the latest period (third-first century BCE) occur at Fiesole and Volterra, with a ground plan of a single cella or a single cella with wings on the side. There is some evidence for the continued construction of grand temple structures.[47]

Historically speaking, altars provided the focus for worship considerably before temple architecture appeared.[48] They show remarkable diversity, and it is evident that even relatively rudimentary forms known in Archaic times survived into the late years of Etruscan civilization. Altars of rubble occur at the south sanctuary at Pyrgi (sixth–fourth century BCE) and appear also at Cetamura del Chianti in the late second century BCE.[49] Larger, monumental altars have received more attention. At Pieva a Socana (Arezzo) is the famous rectangular sandstone platform with handsome moldings (4.99 × 3.75 m.; fifth century BCE), its blocks held together by lead clamps.[50] On the heights above the city at Marzabotto, two monumental altar podiums were found in a sequence of religious edifices all in a row, facing south.[51] Numerous examples of stone altars of smaller size are known, varying in shape, and altars are frequently represented in art, on reliefs from Chiusi of the Archaic period, on Etruscan mirrors, and on reliefs of the latest period from Volterra (third–first century BCE).[52] The most common type is roughly like an hour glass, with a broad base and a broad altar table, often enriched with moldings, and concave or narrowed sides, as seen, for example, on a well-preserved sandstone altar from Fiesole.[53]

GIFTS TO THE GODS

Among the animals[54] sacrificed at the altars were those commonly offered in Greek and Roman rites: hoofed creatures, bulls, pigs, sheep, horse, and deer. Dogs seem to have been a frequent offering, and there is also surprising evidence of the sacrifice of foxes (unknown in Greece or Rome) at

---

[47] Sassatelli and Govi, "Cults of Marzabotto"; Colonna, "Sacred Architecture," 163.
[48] Comella, "Altare," 165–71; Colonna, "Sacred Architecture," 132–43.
[49] De Grummond, "Sanctuary of the Etruscan Artisans," 40, 67.
[50] Thuillier, "Autels," 244; Comella, "Altare," 168 (no. 4).
[51] Santuari, 88–92.
[52] Thuillier, "Autels," 247; Ambrosini, "Le raffigurazioni," 199–201, 204–5; Steuernagel, Menschenopfer.
[53] Santuari, 45 (interpreted as a base for a donation) and Comella, "Altare," 168 (no.8).
[54] Donati, "Sacrifici," 139–57.

Pyrgi and Pian di Civita of Tarquinia. Tortoise, hare, fish, chicken, dove, and other birds are all recorded. Bloodless offerings at the altar of grain, fruits, and the like were probably more frequent than appears from the examples actually identified in excavation. At Pian di Civita, spectacular results in analysis of vegetal remains showed that a votive pit of the seventh century BCE contained fig, poppy, mulberry, hazel nuts, peas, lentils, parsley, celery, barley, and several other cereals.[55] At Cetamura, the gods received a pot of cooked chickpeas.[56]

Material offerings to the Etruscan gods show a wide spectrum of dedications made by individuals of varying status. The gold plaques of Pyrgi relate that Thefarie Velianas, king of Caere, made a dedication to Uni of something very imposing, possibly a temple or even a whole sanctuary, in the third year of his reign, because the goddess supported him. The names of other prominent political figures such as Tulumnes and Avile Vipiiennas (Vipenas) occur incised on pottery dedications at Veii.[57] The former, a royal family name, occurs in both Etruscan and Latin, including one dedication to Menerva. The latter is identical with the name of a general active in Vulci, Rome, and elsewhere who achieved legendary status and was even represented in art. At the other end of the social spectrum were the humble artisans and workers of Cetamura and other sites, who appear to have made dedications relating to their production, such as loom weights, spools and spindle whorls (weavers), miniature bricks (kiln workmen), and iron objects such as nails (iron workers). A weight of bronze and lead from Cerveteri (third century BCE), perhaps used by a merchant in commercial transactions, was inscribed to Turms.[58]

Among the most common offerings were clay vases,[59] often in miniature so that it was clear that the vessel was for the usage of the gods only. The forms of the vessels show that most often they were the kind of vessels used for preparation and serving of food as well as actual eating and drinking. Many different fabrics were utilized, from bucchero and impasto in the earlier centuries, to Greek imports in the sixth and fifth centuries, and the ubiquitous Etrusco-Campanian black gloss in the latest period. All through these periods there occurs a great variety of local uncolored wares of coarse or fine paste. It is clear that in some cases the pottery was ritually

---

[55] Bagnasco Gianni, "Il deposito reiterato," 197–219.
[56] De Grummond, "Sanctuary of the Etruscan Artisans," 89–90, 189–90.
[57] Turfa, "Votive Offerings," 98–9, 101, 104.
[58] Edlund-Berry, "Italien. Dedications," 379 (no. 470).
[59] Ibid., 371, 373, 377; Turfa, "Votive Offerings," 103.

328   *Nancy T. de Grummond*

broken and/or burned before being deposited, and only part of it was left for the deity.

Weapons, incense burners, fish hooks, coins, rings, and other metal objects were among the more expensive offerings. There were, of course, metal statues and statuettes, some of them quite ambitious.[60] Hollow cast bronzes such as the *putto Graziani,* dating to the third century BCE, and the life-size "Orator" in Florence, as well as numerous small bronze statuettes, have inscriptions. The bronze *putto* depicts a baby wearing an amuletic *bulla,* playing with a bird and a ball. Dedicated to the little-known god Tec Sans, he is one of a number of examples of babies, children, or heads of babies, actually more often made of terracotta, that have been found in Etruscan votive contexts, and that suggest the parent's wish for fertility or for the birth or health of a child. Of the smaller bronzes, two splendid images of gods – Culsans and Selvans – were found beside one of the gates of the city of Cortona, revealing a liminal ritual seeking the favor of these gods and perhaps purification.[61] Other gods to whom inscribed dedications were made, besides ones already mentioned above, include Tinia, Turan, Vei, Catha, Cel Ati, Artumes, and Hercle.

One of the most remarkable phenomena of Etruscan votive ritual relates to the thousands of "anatomical" terracottas, offered to various deities at sites in Etruria itself, but also in non-Etruscan Latium as well as north of Etruria proper.[62] These belong to the period of the fourth to first centuries BCE and are so common as to lead to the conclusion that a wide range of deities might be operative in the vows made and the results desired. They relate directly to concerns of fertility, birth, and healing, and practically any part of the body might be offered: hands, feet, legs, torsos, heads, hearts, uteri, breasts, penises, and viscera in general. The anatomical votives are almost never inscribed, an exception being the uteri inscribed to Vei, a fertility deity who has been compared to the Greek Demeter.[63]

How were the votives deposited or distributed in the sanctuaries? A revealing case is found in the sanctuary of Fontanile di Legnisina outside a city gate of Vulci,[64] where a temple was flanked by an altar made of the local fine tufa, adjoining a grotto and a spring. Dating from the fourth and third centuries, the votives were distributed somewhat according to type

---

[60] Simon, "Italien. Dedications," 349–59.
[61] Ibid., 355 (no. 224), 356 (no. 236).
[62] Turfa, "Votive Offerings," 96–8, 101–2, 104–5; Turfa, "Italien. Dedications," 359–68.
[63] Found at the Fontanile di Legnisina, for which see the next footnote.
[64] Turfa, "Votive Offerings," 101–2; Colonna, "Sacred Architecture," 143; Ricciardi, "Il santuario etrusco."

Etruscan Religion 329

with terracotta models of uteri at the entrance to the grotto while terra-cotta statuettes of babies were deposited northeast of the grotto and the uteri. Still farther north was found the majority of the ceramic material. Bronze statuettes of offerants were wedged in between the cliff and the back wall of the altar precinct. A similar phenomenon of placing particu-lar types of offerings in a special area may be observed at the sanctuary at Graviscae (the port city of Tarquinia), where in Room G the terracottas were placed parallel to the walls, uteri on the north, and heads, statues, and figurines on the south and west.[65]

CULT OF THE DEAD

There is an enormous variety in burial customs and tomb construction in Etruria and the Etruscan-influenced areas to the north and south, but at the same time it is evident that there was a rather consistent belief in the nature of the afterlife and in the immortality of the deceased.[66] Hence, the Etruscans prepared the dead for burial by laying out the corpse on a couch in a shroud, with the face exposed, as if sleeping. Women served as func-tionaries, in some cases plying alabastra filled with unguents for anointing the deceased.[67] The unguents may have served as purificatory, or possibly to help make the deceased immortal. Etruscan tombs frequently featured deposits of alabastra to accompany the dead so that they could continue to enjoy the usage of the unguents in the afterlife. The deceased made a jour-ney to the beyond, on foot, on horseback, in a wagon, or over water (or in a combination of these means). He or she then passed through a gate into another world where life continued as above ground, particularly the more pleasant aspects of eating, drinking, dancing, sporting, and making love. The survivors accordingly made elaborate preparations for the deceased in the afterlife. The Etruscans attempted to reproduce in the tombs the conditions in which they were comfortable while alive. The necropoleis were sometimes laid out along a grid pattern, for example, at Cerveteri and Orvieto, as if to indicate that the city of the dead should follow the rules of the *Etrusca disciplina* for laying out a city of the living. The houses constructed for the dead varied considerably. At Cerveteri, rooms carved out of the tufa bedrock featured doors, windows, columns, grand chairs, tables, beds, and benches to make the dead feel at home. The Tomb of the

[65] Turfa, "Votive Offerings," 97.
[66] Krauskopf, "The Grave and Beyond," 66–89; Torelli, "La religione," 222, 231–4.
[67] Camporeale, "Purification, Etr," 49.

330   *Nancy T. de Grummond*

Reliefs takes the concept to the ultimate, with its sculptured representations of all manner of equipment and household goods depicted as if hung
on the walls. At Tarquinia and elsewhere the walls of the tombs of the elite
were covered with paintings showing a celebratory banquet with musicians
and dancing, perhaps a commemoration of the actual funeral feast but also
intended to transport the festivities magically to an eternal venue.[68]

Games in honor of the dead were a common and widespread feature of
Etruscan funerary ritual, as in early Greece and Republican Rome.[69] There
were contests of wrestling and races, as known in Greece, but the Etruscan
games were quite particular, including masked performances and a bloodshed ritual that constituted a prototype for gladiatorial combat in a funeral
context.[70] In the Tomb of the Augurs at Tarquinia (sixth century BCE), a
masked man, labeled Phersu, wearing a tall headdress and a bizarre mot-
tled shirt, directs a dog on a leash to bite an adversary with a bag over his
head. The latter, deprived of sight and with legs bleeding, defends himself
by swinging a club toward the dog.

The history of Etruscan burials is throughout concerned with grave furnishings. These might be spectacularly elaborate, as in some of the great
inhumation burials of the Orientalizing period (ca.750–600 BCE; e.g.,
the Regolini-Galassi tomb at Cerveteri) or modest, including only an ash
urn, and one or two grave gifts, as in cremation burials of the Villanovan
period, and freedmen's burials of the latest period. Most burials had an
offering of food and drink, as may be deduced from the numerous vessels
found in tombs, and occasionally from the actual foodstuffs, while the
tombs of nobles often included items demonstrating status. Fine ladies
needed grooming equipment (hence the abundance of surviving Etruscan
mirrors), and gentlemen required allusions to their military prowess, political offices, and priesthoods.

Altars have been found in Etruscan cemeteries, in some cases quite
monumental, as in the staircase and platform attached to the tomb Melone
del Sodo II at Cortona, and in the round stone altar at Grotta Porcina
(sixth century BCE), decorated with pacing animals and surrounded by a
rectangular precinct, on three sides of which step-like benches are cut out
of the bedrock, presumably to seat spectators at the funeral sacrifice or
performance. At the necropolis of Cannicella at Orvieto, a terrace sanctuary featured a cylindrical altar, basins for water, and a remarkable marble

---

[68] Steingraber, *Etruscan Painting*.
[69] Thuillier, *Les jeux athlétiques*.
[70] Jannot, "Phersu," 281–320.

statue of a nude goddess, one-half life size (late sixth century BCE), providing rare evidence for the appearance of cult statues. Altars could be inside the tomb as well, as in a noted example from Cerveteri, where the altar takes the form of a throne.

In the latest period in Etruria, there is a dramatic change in the view of the afterlife, evidenced in the depictions of the journey to the Underworld and the banquet of eternity, perhaps related to important changes in the political and daily life of the Etruscans. Aita and Phersipnei (Hades and Persephone) make their first appearances at the banquet, and the sunny atmosphere of the Elysian-style parties turns gloomy and dark. Frightening demons first occur around 400 BCE, in the Tomb of the Blue Demons at Tarquinia, where they escort the deceased on the journey. Throughout the Hellenistic period, in the paintings of chamber tombs at Tarquinia and the reliefs on ash urns from Volterra, appear the leading demonic figures, the winged goddess Vanth and the hammer-god Charu.[71] Unlike the Greek Charon, the Etruscan demon does not have a boat, but instead normally wields his hammer, which he may swing toward the deceased, as if to finalize death, or possibly to bang on the gates of the Underworld. Charu is often represented with discolored or diseased skin, serpents in his hair, and anger upon his ugly face. His counterpart Vanth, often shown as beautiful, has generally a more kindly aspect, carrying a torch that will light up the dark Underworld for the traveler.

ETRUSCAN RELIGION – HISTORICAL CONSIDERATIONS

It is not possible now and likely never will be to give a coherent historical and developmental account of Etruscan religion. When, for example, did the Etruscans begin to practice haruspication, or divination from birds and other phenomena in the sky? And when were the paradigmatic myths of the prophecies of Tages and Vecuvia first told? We might argue that the usage of augury is closely related to the temple with the deep front porch, which manifests itself in the Archaic period, and is certainly documented by the statue of an augur turning his head sharply to look up at the sky dated circa 500 BCE. The earliest representation of the act of haruspication in art may be dated around 450–400 BCE, and the possible images of the famous Etruscan prophets date between 350 and 300 BCE. In fact, there is a concentration of representations and *realia* (e.g., liver models,

---

[71] De Grummond, *Etruscan Myth*, 213–35.

objects for drawing lots [*sortes*]) related to divination in the late period of the third and second centuries BCE. So it is probably fair to say that some of these quintessential Etruscan religious practices already existed in the Archaic period, but divination and prophecy attracted more attention in later Etruscan times.

The temples themselves certainly show an evolution from early hut-like structures to the grand structures of the sixth–fourth centuries BCE. It has been argued that there is little change in temple development after that period, and that the impetus for monumentality and affluent display decreases.[72] At the same time the cults of healing spread far and wide, as indicated by the proliferation of anatomical votives. The changed view of the Underworld as a frightening place populated by demons is precisely contemporary with this phenomenon and also with the popularity of divination. The alteration of mood and customs has often been associated with the conquest of the Etruscan cities by Rome that took place especially in the fourth and third centuries.[73] Thus concerns about production, reproduction, and health and the perception of the afterlife as grim were an extension of the prevailing view of daily life, in which the individual had to cope with radical changes in society and the economy.

The final phase of Etruscan religion relates to its transference to Rome, as a subject of fascination to priests and antiquarians such as the Romanized Etruscans Caecina and Nigidius Figulus and intellectuals such as Cicero. Etruscan influences had been present since the Archaic period, when Etruscan kings ruled Rome, but in the late Republic Etruscan religion became a subject for scholars, who recorded practices of the past in the light of their own times. The absorption of Etruscan culture by the Romans makes it difficult for scholars today to sort out what was long established and what was truly Etruscan as opposed to adaptations made in a Roman context. At any rate, haruspices were evidently fully integrated into Roman state cultic practice, although carrying out rites that were foreign in origin. They continued to exert influence into Late Antiquity, though periodic imperial edicts against their activity in the fourth century CE show how they, along with other components of public cult, were no longer authorized by the state.

---

[72] Turfa, "Watershed," esp. 62, 64.

[73] For a concise review of the events of the crises and decline in Etruria in later centuries, see Haynes, *Etruscan Civilization*, especially 261–4, 327–30. For the pessimistic atmosphere and change in the concept of the afterlife, see de Grummond, *Etruscan Myth*, 9 and 212–28.

Etruscan Religion

BIBLIOGRAPHY

Primary Sources

Bonfante, Giuliano, and Larissa Bonfante. *The Etruscan Language: An Introduction* (Manchester, 2002).

De Grummond, Nancy T. "Selected Latin and Greek Sources on Etruscan Religion." In *The Religion of the Etruscans*, ed. Nancy T. de Grummond and Erika Simon (Austin, 2006): 191–218.

Martianus Capella. *Martianus Capella and the Seven Liberal Arts*, trans. W. H. Stahl and R. Johnson (New York, 1977).

Pallottino, Massimo, ed. *Testimonia linguae Etruscae* (Florence, 1968) (=*TLE*)

Rix, Helmut. *Etruskische Texte, Editio Minor* (= Rix *ET*), 2 vols. (Tübingen, 1991).

Roncalli, Francesco. *Scrivere etrusco* (Milan, 1985).

Thulin, C. O. *Die etruskische Disciplin*. Repr. of I. *Die Blitzlehre* (1905); II. *Die Haruspicin* (1906); III. *Die Ritualbücher und zur Geschichte und Organisation der Haruspices* (1909) (Darmstadt, 1968).

Van der Meer, L. Bouke. *The Bronze Liver of Piacenza: Analysis of a Polytheistic Structure* (Amsterdam, 1987).

Wallace, Rex. *Zikh Rasna, A Manual of the Etruscan Language and Inscriptions* (Ann Arbor, 2008).

Other Works Cited

Aigner-Foresti, Lucia. "Zur Zeremonie der Nagelschlagung in Rom und in Etrurien." *AJAH* 4 (1979): 144–56.

Ambrosini, Laura. "Le raffigurazioni di operatori del culto sugli specchi etruschi." In *Gli operatori cultuali*, ed. M. Rocchi, P. Xella, and J. A. Zamora (Verona, 2006): 197–233.

Bagnasco Gianni, G. "Le *sortes* etrusche." In *Sorteggio pubblico e cleromanzia dall'antichità all'età moderna*, ed. Federica Cordano and Cristiano Grottanelli (Milan, 2001): 197–219.

"Tarquinia, Il deposito reiterato: una preliminare analisi dei comparanda." In *Offerte dal regno vegetale e dal regno animale nelle manifestazioni del sacro*, ed. Maria Bonghi Jovino and Federica Chiesa. *Tarchna*, suppl. 1 (Rome, 2005): 91–7.

Bonfante, Larissa. "Etruscan Inscriptions and Etruscan Religion." In *The Religion of the Etruscans*, ed. Nancy T. de Grummond and Erika Simon (Austin, 2006): 9–26.

Bonghi Jovino, Maria. "'Area sacra/complesso monumentale' della Civita." In *Tarquinia etrusca, una nuova storia*, ed. Anna Maria Moretti Sgubini (Rome, 2001): 21–9.

Camporeale, Giovannangelo. "Purification, Etr. Mondo etrusco." *ThesCRA* II (2004): 36–62.

Colonna, Giovanni. "Il santuario di Pyrgi alla luce delle recenti scoperte." *Studi Etruschi* 33 (1965): 191–219.

ed. *Santuari d'Etruria* (Milan, 1985).

"L'Apollo di Pyrgi." In *Magna Graecia, etruschi, fenici: Atti del trentatreesimo convegno di studi sulla Magna Graecia, Taranto, 8–13 Ottobre 1993* (Taranto, 1994): 345–75.

"Sacred Architecture and the Religion of the Etruscans." In *The Religion of the Etruscans*, ed. Nancy T. de Grummond and Erika Simon (Austin, 2006): 132–68.

Comella, Annamaria. "Aedes." *ThesCRA* IV (2005): 139–42.

"Altare." *ThesCRA* IV (2005): 165–71.

Cristofani, Mauro. *Tabula Capuana* (Florence, 1975).

De Grummond, Nancy T. *Etruscan Myth, Sacred History and Religion* (Philadelphia, 2006).

"Introduction: The History of the Study of Etruscan Religion." In *The Religion of the Etruscans*, ed. Nancy T. de Grummond and Erika Simon (Austin, 2006): 1–8.

"Prophets and Priests." In *The Religion of the Etruscans*, ed. Nancy T. de Grummond and Erika Simon (Austin, 2006): 27–44.

Donati, Luigi. "Sacrifici, etr., Repertorio dell specie; Criteri dell scelta delle vittime." *ThesCRA* I (2004): 142–60.

Edlund-Berry, I. E. M. "Etruscans at Work and Play: Evidence for an Etruscan Calendar." In *Kotinos, Festschrift für Erika Simon* (Mainz, 1992): 330–7.

"Dedications, Rom. Italien. Other Votive Objects." *ThesCRA* I (2004): 368–79.

Haynes, Sybille. *Etruscan Civilization, A Cultural History* (Los Angeles, 2000).

Jannot, J.-R. "Phersu, Phersuna, Persona." In *Spectacles sportifs et scéniques dans le monde étrusco-italique: actes de la table ronde / organisée par l'Equipe de recherches étrusco-italiques de l'UMR 126 (CNRS, Paris) et l'Ecole française de Rome: Rome, 3–4 mai 1991* (Rome, 1993): 281–320.

Krauskopf, Ingrid. "The Grave and Beyond in Etruscan Religion." In *The Religion of the Etruscans*, ed. Nancy T. de Grummond and Erika Simon (Austin, 2006): 66–89.

Maggiani, Adriano. "Qualche osservazione sul fegato di Piacenza." *Studi Etruschi* 50 (1982): 53–88.

"Immagini di aruspici." In *Secondo Congresso internazionale etrusco, Firenze 26 maggi–2 giugno 1985.* Vol. 3 (Rome, 1989): 1557–63.

"La divinazione in Etruria." *ThesCRA* III (2005): 52–78.

Nielsen, Marjatta. "Sacerdotesse e associazioni cultuali femminili in Etruria: Testimonianze epigrafiche e iconografiche." *Analecta Romana* 19 (1990): 45–67.

Pallottino, Massimo. *The Etruscans*, trans. J. Cremona, ed. David Ridgway (Bloomington, 1975).

"Uno specchio di Tuscania e la leggenda etrusca di Tarchon." In *Saggi di Antichità*. Vol. 2 (Rome, 1979): 679–709.

Pfiffig, A. J. *Religio etrusca* (Graz, 1975).

Prayon, Friedhelm. "Sur l'orientation des édifices cultuels." In *Les plus religieux des homme, État de la receherche sur la religion étrusque*, ed. Françoise Gaultier and Dominique Briquel (Paris, 1997): 357–71.

Rallo, Antonia. *Lasa, Iconografia e esegesi* (Florence, 1974).

Rask, Kathryn. "New Approaches to the Archaeology of Etruscan Cult Images," in *The Archaeology of Sanctuaries and Ritual in Etruria*, ed. N. T. de Grummond and I. Edlund-Berry. *JRA* Supplementary Series 81 (2011): 89–112.

Ricciardi, Laura. "Il santuario etrusco di Fontanile di Legnisina a Vulci. Relazione delle campagne di scavo 1985 e 1986: l'altare monumentale e il deposito votivo." *Notizie degli Scavi* 42–43 (1988–89): 137–209.

Roncalli, Francesco. "La decorazione pittorica." In *La Tomba François di Vulci*, ed. Francesco Buranelli (Rome, 1987): 79–114.

Simon, Erika. "Dedications, Rom. Italien. Offerte in forma di figura umana, Bronzo." *ThesCRA* I (2004): 349–59.

"Gods in Harmony." In *The Religion of the Etruscans*, ed. Nancy T. de Grummond and Erika Simon (Austin, 2006): 45–65.

Steingräber, Stephan. *Etruscan Painting: Catalogue Raisonné of Etruscan Wall Paintings*, ed. David and Francesca Ridgway (New York, 1986).

Steuernagel, Dirk. *Menschenopfer und Mord am Altar. Griechischen Mythen in etruskischen Gräber* (Wiesbaden, 1998).

Thuillier, J. P. *Les jeux athlétiques dans la civilisation étrusque* (Rome, 1985).

"Autels d'Etrurie." In *L'Espace sacrificiel dans les civilisations méditerranéennes de l'antiquité, Actes du Colloque tenu à la Maison de l'Orient, Lyon, 4–7 juin, 1988*. Publications de la Bibliothèque Salomon-Reinach, 5 R, ed. M.-T. Etienne (Paris, 1991): 243–7.

Torelli, Mario. "La religione." In *Rasenna: Storia e civiltà degli etruschi* (Milan, 1969): 159–240.

Gli etruschi (Milan, 2000).

"Templum." *ThesCRA* IV (2005): 340–7.

Turfa, Jean MacIntosh. "International Contacts: Commerce Trade and Foreign Affairs." In *Etruscan Life and Afterlife: A Handbook of Etruscan Studies*, ed. Larissa Bonfante (Detroit, 1986): 66–91.

"Dedications, Rom. Italien. Anatomical Votives." *ThesCRA* I (2004): 359–68.

"Votive Offerings in Etruscan Religion." In *The Religion of the Etruscans*, ed. Nancy T. de Grummond and Erika Simon (Austin, 2006): 90–115.

"Appendix A: The Etruscan Brontoscopic Calendar." In *The Religion of the Etruscans*, ed. Nancy T. de Grummond and Erika Simon (Austin, 2006): 173–90.

"Etruscan Religion at the Watershed: before and after the Fourth Century BCE." In *Religion in Republican Italy*, ed. Celia E. Schultz and Paul B. Harvey, Jr. (Cambridge, 2006): 62–89.

Weinstock, Stefan. "Martianus Capella and the Cosmic System of the Etruscans." *JRS* 36 (1946): 101–29.

13

ROMAN RELIGION THROUGH
THE EARLY REPUBLIC

JÖRG RÜPKE

If Greek culture is late compared to the city-states and empires of the Ancient Near East, Roman culture is late and peripheral to Greek culture. It entered the international stage by the very end of the sixth century BCE, but contemporary literary sources or reliable later accounts are not available before the second half of the third or fourth century BCE. By this time, the Romans and their allies' armies started to build an empire that comprised the whole of the Mediterranean and much of its hinterland, that is, the whole of western Europe including Britain and much of southeastern Europe, including modern Austria, Hungary, Bulgaria, and Romania, and Asia Minor as far as Armenia by the beginning of the second century CE. Rome defended a hostile borderline against the Sassanian Persian empire and influenced political and cultural patterns throughout its realm with lasting effects for two millennia. It is this later history that accounts for an interest in Rome's origins. But such an interest must be disappointed here. Nothing supports the assumption that any of the religious elements from the period before the fourth century BCE should be part of a causal explanation of the later expansion of the city-state into a world empire.

THE SITE OF ROME AND ARCHAIC RELIGION

Most of the discussion of and evidence for archaic Roman religion of necessity focuses on the city of Rome. Situated on or near a crossing of the Tiber, a distance of some twenty-five kilometers from the open sea, the Palatine Hill in Rome attracted settlements already as early as in the Paleolithic Age.[1] Any notion of continuity, however, could not be entertained before the turn of the first millennium BCE. Now, in the incipient

---

[1] Anzidei and Gioia, "Rinvenimenti," 29–32.

Roman Religion through the Early Republic 337

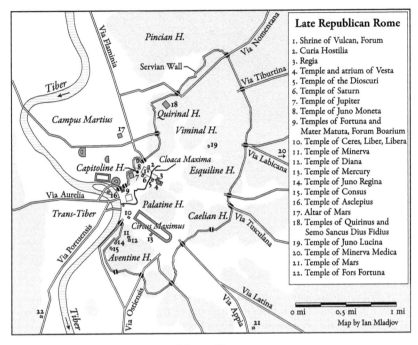

Map 9. Rome.

Iron Age, the ethnogenesis of the Latins, distinguished from the Osco-Umbrians to the west and south and the Villanovan culture to the north, led to a distinguishable culture.[2] Given the small range of comparable evidence, the hut-urns – small round urns with a roof and a little modeled door – were the most important feature. Judging by later inscriptional evidence, the Latin language, a variant of the older Italian branch of the Indo-European dialect as were the Venetian and the Osco-Umbrian (or "Sabellian") dialects, was restricted to the small area between the Tiber in the north and the Liris in the south.[3] If continuous settlement in the area of the later city of Rome started in the tenth century, one has to keep in mind that the Tiber, even if a large river compared to other Italian streams, was but one of the relatively short west-flowing rivers that structured the western slopes of the central Italian Appenine chain (see Map 9; see also Maps 7 and 8 in Chapter 12).

---

[2] Smith, *Early Rome and Latium*, 24–43 for the Latins; for Italy in general, see Moscati, *Così nacque d'Italia*; Pallottino, *Dinamiche*.
[3] To the north, the Faliscan dialect should be added.

Fig. 25. Model of the city of Rome displayed in the Museo della Civiltà Romana (Rome). It recalls the topographic characteristics of the City on the Seven Hills situated at the Tiber. The photo views the model from the north, as an observer from the Quirinal would have seen the city. To the right, overlooking the river, the two summits of the Capitoline Hill can be discerned, the rear one (Capitolium) dominated by the late regal temple of Iuppiter Capitolinus. One can also see how the Palatine (center) overlooks the Forum (left center), whose most imposing buildings are the early republican temple of the Castores (Castor and Pollux) and, to the right of it, the temple of Saturn, situated directly below the slope of the Arx (the nearer summit of the Capitoline). The Campus Martius to the right and the Isola Tiberina are outside the urbanized region. Moving left along from the Tiber bridge (presumably representing a wooden predecessor of the Pons Aemilius), one can pick out the valley of the Circus immediately behind and below the Palatine; beyond it is the Aventine, as yet barely inhabited. Photo by Ulrike Egelhaaf-Gaiser.

Of necessity, and for methodological reasons, this chapter restricts the first part of this introductory account to what can be gathered about early Rome and its religion from the archaeological evidence; this coincides with the major architectural achievements in the city of Rome (see Fig. 25).

According to the archaeological finds from the end of the nineteenth century CE, the topographical center of the city, what would later be the Roman Forum, was still used as a cemetery down through the early eighth century when, however, the settlements on the Palatine and on the Quirinal were joined together. But urbanization proper begins at Rome only at the beginning of the so-called late Orientalizing period

Roman Religion through the Early Republic 339

(ca.650/640 BCE), indicated by three interconnected processes. The Roman Forum was paved in tamped earth, even if some huts had to be removed for this purpose; a stone pavement followed around 625. Second, by the sixth century BCE, the *cloaca maxima*, a monumental tunnel, was created to drain the area. Already before and increasingly after this date, houses of stone and tiled, not thatched, roofs, indicating the later atrium type with a number of rooms around a courtyard, were built on the slopes of the Palatine and on the Velia and occupied for many centuries.[4] The Forum was built up relatively quickly. An assembly area of circular shape, comparable to Greek places for political assemblies, was created, called the *Comitium*.[5] North of this, a building that can be interpreted as the first *curia*, called *"Hostilia"* (Varro, *ling.* 5.155), identified as a roofed meeting structure for the Senate, would have been part of this earliest monumentalization of the political center.

It is from this area, beginning around 580 BCE, that we find several of the earliest and most intriguing "religious" monuments (see Map 9). The first stone-built shrine that was built in the *Comitium* dates to this period. Here an inscribed five-sided block (*cippus*) has been found offering one of the earliest Latin texts, a regulation pertaining to a king (*recei [sacrorum?]*) (*ILLRP* 3). The foundation-deposit beneath this stone includes a fragment of an Attic black-figure vase, dated to circa 575–550 BCE, showing Hephaestus, the Greek smith-god, riding a mule. This might point to the identification of the structure as a shrine for the god Vulcan, a *Volcanal*, an impressive indicator of the material and conceptual presence of Greek culture and religion in the very beginning of Roman religion. Another early building marks the southern boundary of the Forum area; the name later applied to this building, the *Regia*, "Royal Palace," might point to the earliest usage of this cult-center reserved to the *rex sacrorum* and the *pontifex maximus*.[6] Nearby, in the Forum, the (later) "House of the Vestals" (*atrium Vestae*) was among the first stone buildings.

Around the same time, 580 BCE, the earliest full-fledged podium temple was built on the northern edge of the *Forum Boarium* or Cattle Market near the banks of the Tiber and the *pons sublicium* (see Fig. 25, covered by the Capitoline hill). This is identified as the nucleus of the later double sanctuary of Fortuna and Mater Matuta (see Fig. 26). By the mid-sixth century, this temple was decorated with terracottas of the Greek gods

---

[4] Carandini, "Palatium e sacra via," in Carandini, ed., *Palatium e Sacra Via I*, 31–33.
[5] Kolb, *Agora und Theater*; Coarelli, *Il Foro Romano* I, 1–19.
[6] Coarelli, *Il Foro Romano* I, 56–79.

Fig. 26. Terracotta figures of Herakles (Hercules) and Athena from the Temple of Mater Matuta in the Forum Boarium; second half of the sixth century BCE. Location: Capitoline Museum, Rome. Photo by Jörg Rüpke.

Hercules and Minerva.[7] Clearly, Greek influence in terms of the media and narratives present at Rome is visible at a very early date.

The building of religious monuments in the city of Rome reached its first climax with the construction of the temple on the Capitol (see Fig. 25). Completed at the end of the sixth century, it had a base measuring 61 by 55 meters and must have been one of the largest temples of its time in the

---

[7] Short critical account: Smith, *Early Rome and Latium*, 161–3.

entire Mediterranean area. Because of its size, visibility, and the choice of deities, the sanctuary was indicative of the influence of the Greek culture dominating the eastern Mediterranean, present also in Italy in places like Gravisca or Pyrgi. The temple was dedicated to Jupiter Optimus Maximus (Jove the Best and Greatest), Juno, and Minerva, and competed with the largest Greek sanctuaries in places like Athens, Corinth, and Olympia to the deities Athena, Hera, and Zeus, respectively. The investment in the quality of the terracotta statuary (see Varro in Plin. *NH* 35.157) points to the same Greek influence. One other indication of this emulation is the temple of the Dioscuri, dedicated in the Forum at the beginning of the fifth century. Although smaller than the Temple of Jupiter, this temple's foundations still reached a breadth of circa 29 and a depth of circa 39 meters.[8] But a new wave of monumental additions to the city center had to wait for the new political formation in Rome at the end of the fourth century BCE.

The extraordinary size of the city by the end of the sixth century BCE, forming a capital of perhaps thirty thousand inhabitants, presupposes economic success and regional military expansion. The former is attested by the traces of Etruscan and Greek presence in the *Forum Boarium*, mentioned above in connection with the terracotta decorations of the Temple of the Mater Matuta and Fortuna (see Fig. 26). The latter is attested by the text of a treaty, preserved by the Greek historian Polybius, who explains the rise of Rome in his *History* composed in the middle of the second century BCE. The treaty was arranged between Rome, the regional power, and the Carthaginians, at the end of the sixth century. The latter, descendants of the Phoenicians, who had been sailing the Mediterranean Sea since the late second millennium, not only dominated Sicily and the western Mediterranean, but were extensively present along the coasts of central Italy as well. The Punic and Etruscan texts on the gold tablets from Pyrgi reveal that they maintained a cult of Astarte in that town, which is a mere fifty kilometers from Rome.[9]

The broad outlines derived from the archaeological record are at odds with the detailed image depicted by historians of the late second century BCE. Modern interpreters are justifiably skeptical concerning the reliability of supposedly oral or written traditions that could have been attached to and supported by institutional patterns, temples, laws, and genealogical narratives. Only a rough sketch of the relevant political institutional

---

[8] Hesberg, *Römsche Baukunst*, 80–4.
[9] Pyrgi (AA.VV.).

342   *Jörg Rüpke*

developments of the sixth to fourth centuries is possible here. The period of kingship (partly of Etruscan origins) ended by circa 509 BCE, and it was replaced by a system of aristocratic government that allotted to assemblies of Roman citizens the right to choose between different candidates, especially for the highest office of two annual consuls, and to give consent to "laws." Politically, a conflict between a "patrician" nobility (that might have taken shape only in the transition from monarchy) and a new "plebeian" elite led to specific institutions (tribunal of the people, binding resolutions of the plebeian assemblies, etc.) and was much elaborated in later narratives. A codification of laws ("Twelve Tables," the text of which was only stabilized by the commentators of the second century BCE) by the mid-fifth century, experiments in multiple rulership (consular tribunes), and a full plebeian participation in the office of consuls from the mid-fourth century onward, mark a process closed only around the turn of the third century by laws on the opening of priesthoods (*lex Ogulnia*) and the acceptance of the binding force of plebiscites (*lex Hortensia;* dated 287 BCE). Regionally, the capture of the Etruscan town of Veii (a mere fifteen kilometers from Rome) at the beginning of the fourth century and the sack of Rome by the Gauls shortly afterward indicate military vicissitudes. The decisive defeat of the Latin League in the "Latin Wars" of 340–338 BCE marks the beginning of Rome's hegemony over central Italy, a dominance that the Romans extended over the whole of Italy in the century to come.

INTEREST IN EARLY ROMAN RELIGION

Interest in early Rome and its religion was old. Probably, the massive changes of the third, and especially late third century, triggered such an interest, which is visible in texts of Greek observers like Timaeus of Tauromenion already by the start of the century. Romans developed aetiological myths as well as narratives about formative norms and values that took the form of "history." The universalizing – temporally and geographically – grid of Greek and Hellenistic mythology and history was known, but it was embraced as a framework for the Romans to locate themselves in the Mediterranean only from the end of the third century BCE onward.[10] These efforts occurred in the Greek form of "historiography," making use of Latin only from the second century BCE on. The modern, and indeed the Roman imperial, view of early Roman history, is dominated by writers from the end of the Republic (Cicero, Varro) and the Augustan age

---

[10] Rüpke, "Kulturtransfer," 42–64.

(Livy, Vergil, the Greek Dionysius of Halicarnassus), who engaged in establishing a canonical version as well as in criticizing what they considered party narratives of Roman history. These authors acknowledged that the founding fathers, that is, the first kings of Rome (Romulus, Numa), planted the seeds of civil war (the killing of Romulus's brother Remus) at the same time as they laid the groundwork for empire (through ecumenical recruitment and early expansion).

Given the enormous prominence of religion and the degree of its change, interest in religion on the part of the authors named above is understandable. Polybius, the Greek statesman and historian who tried to explain the Roman dominance to his Greek contemporaries, had recently witnessed the enormous expansion of Roman power in the Hellenistic East during the first half of the second century BCE. Beginning with his works, Roman piety (which Polybius considered as superstition) was addressed as a central factor for Rome's military success. Because much of our knowledge about earlier Roman religion rests on these texts – or, to put it in the words of Christopher Smith, "the evidence we have for Roman religion is often ancient interpretation"[11] – it is important to grasp the concept of religion these authors entertained.

Republican and imperial writers, like Romans and Greeks in general, did not have a coherent concept of "religion." The existence of the gods and their character, that is, their stance toward humans, was a matter of philosophy, or "philosophy of religion" as we would say. If the existence of the gods was taken for granted, "piety" (*pietas*) was a natural consequence and resulted in what could be termed *religio:* a sense of obligation, the concept that honors should be paid to an immortal god or gods (Cic. *Nat. deor.* 1.3; 1.117; 3.5). These honors would find the form of temples, rituals (*sacra*), and specialists (*sacerdotes*), obliged to care for these places and rituals. *Cultus* might occasionally be used as an umbrella term for all the above. Hence, epiphanies (critically reviewed) and divination, the foundations of temples, public rituals, and changes in the public priesthoods gained the interest of writers who gave special emphasis to exceptional rites in times of crisis; these gave them the opportunity to comment on participation (and even individual ritual activities), an aspect invisible elsewhere.

Details of cult, theological speculation, routine rituals, or the daily running of sanctuaries do not figure in the literary tradition. Conversely, votive deposits or burial practices, so prominent in the archaeological record, do not enter into the textual one. More is learned about the financing

---

[11] Smith, "Worshipping Mater Matuta," 136.

of cults than about the reflections on divinity, more about institutionalized than embedded or diffused religion. Usually, it is on the building or
restoration of temples that archaeological records and literary references
concur – inviting quick identifications. To give just one example, the location and description of the pair of temples of Mater Matuta and Fortuna
in Livy 33.27.4 (*in foro Boario*) have led to the identification of the archaic
double temple in the area of San Omobono,[12] now considered as one of the
most important archaic sanctuaries.

For the modern interpreter, the evidence suggests a concept of religion
that is not too far removed from the concept underlying this evidence. A
relational definition of "religion," tying its usage to cultural practices and
signs that refer to "gods," itself a class of religious signs (names, images),
seems most fruitful. "Religion" as used here refers to an ensemble of practices, institutions, habits, and beliefs, even if incoherent at times. It is the
place of religious communication within the spectrum of social interactions and institutions that form a society that I will be attempting to bring
into relief for purposes of cross-cultural comparison. Before I start to suggest new perspectives to study archaic Roman religion, I will briefly review
earlier approaches. To orient the reader and researcher it is helpful to take
a look at the most important etic models applied by people to those who
were not members of the culture in question.

INTERPRETIVE MODELS AND APPROACHES

Due to the successful application of comparison in nineteenth-century
linguistics and its reconstruction of a genealogical tree of Indo-European
languages, Roman religion has been seen as a variant of an original
Indo-European religion and compared to other such traditions, from Celtic
myths to Vedic rituals. Drawing on the addressees of a highly prestigious
and probably archaic group of three "major flamens" (*flamines maiores* were
the priests of Jupiter, Mars, and Quirinus), Georg Wissowa, in his still fundamental handbook, had identified a triadic structure of deities that seem
to antedate the Capitoline triad mentioned above.[13] Contested by some
as an irrelevant and late grouping, the French scholar Georges Dumézil
nonetheless saw the earlier triad as modeled on an Indo-European system
of social ordering, including the three functions of priest/king, warrior,
and agriculture, corresponding to the major orders of the Hindu caste

---

[12] See Ziolkowski, *Temples of Mid-Republican Rome*, 105.
[13] Wissowa, *Religion und Kultus*, 23.

Roman Religion through the Early Republic

system. This "trifunctionalism" instigated attempts to detect other common inheritances, such as the connection of Latin *flamen* with Sanskrit *Brahman* or *ritus* with *ṛta*. For Dumézil, it served as a hermeneutical key for many a Roman narrative and his reconstruction of archaic Roman religion.[14] Dumézil's system, not his often astute observations, has been severely (and rightly) criticized.[15]

On balance, one cannot deny the Indo-European roots of certain terms, names, and even constellations of deities. But, for the reconstruction of complex rituals and their conceptualization by the Romans, the comparison with Vedic terms and rituals has not proven heuristically fruitful. The same holds true for other less far-fetched etymological approaches to religious institutions. Typically, phonetics, the sound of words, proved more stable than semantics, meanings, and pragmatics, that is, the institutional contexts of the usage, of words, thus rendering etymological approaches futile.

Primitivism is another approach (rather than model) toward archaic (and, indeed, later) Roman religion. It comes in two forms. One, inspired by evolutionary theories of religion, applies supposedly primitive concepts. Aniconic forms of worship are a favorite one (conforming to ancient notions about the purity of a religion without images). Without doubt, the production of statuary had a history in Italy, detectable in both votive deposits and ancient historical accounts. Without doubt, Greek statuary (that itself could draw on Near Eastern models) was highly attractive and – first in terracotta, then in bronze – sought after or copied from the sixth century onward. Yet, aniconic worship existed side by side with iconic ones in many Mediterranean societies and did not betray a historical stratification. Compared to Greek narratives and genealogies, Roman gods occasionally appear to be lacking in personality, family, and adventures. This is, however, no sufficient reason to postulate pre-personal conceptions of deity, where metaphorical usage could explain certain materials in ritual sequences. A stone need not be a *Iuppiter Lapis* ("Jupiter the Stone").[16] In the 1940s, Hendrik Wagenvoort's "dynamism" – the title of his book published in 1947 that concerned itself with impersonal conceptions of divine power – was one of the last exponents of a whole generation of scholars, whose interpretations linger on in isolated forms and beyond the validity

---

[14] Dumézil, *Jupiter, Mars, Quirinus* 1–2; idem. *Archaic Roman Religion*.
[15] For criticism, see Momigliano, "Premesse," 245–61, and "Georges Dumézil," 135–59; Belier, *Decayed Gods*.
[16] Shown by Rüpke, *Domi militiae*, 112–14.

of, again, many new observations, such as the lack of addressees of gods in fetial rites.[17]

Primitivism occurs in another form, less easily associated with this term. Here Roman society is modeled on contemporary face-to-face societies known in detail by the classics of twentieth-century anthropologists. It is seen as constituted by age groups, all individuals of which are subjected to initiation rituals, as a community whose economic and social activities are dictated by a common and detailed calendar.[18] Again, this is not to deny the notion of "initiation" altogether, but its application is in analogy, only, if applied to (self-appointed or aristocratically defined) representatives of an age group in a city of some twenty or forty thousand inhabitants. An important variant of this approach could be termed a household approach toward state religion. The Roman polity is interpreted as the king's household writ large. As a family's cult is focused on the hearth (among other things), the king's daughters (i.e., the priesthood of the Vestal virgins) care for the city's hearth (i.e., the fire in the "House of Vesta," *aedes Vestae*).[19] Ritual tasks, which might have been the duty of the king (evidence is lacking), were performed by the supreme pontiff (*pontifex maximus*) and the "King of the sacrifices" (*rex sacrorum*). No conclusion has been reached so far, as to whether the *rex sacrorum* was heir to the sacral duties of the king,[20] later to be overshadowed by the *pontifex maximus*, or whether a *rex sacrorum* existed already in regal times to (at least partly) fulfill the religious duties of the king, whose legal competences later fell to the pontiffs (who might have antedated the Republic, too). The Romans' own view (the emic perspective) clearly followed the first route, regarding the "sacrificial king" as a successor to the king proper (Livy 2.2.1; Dion. Hal. 4.74.4).

Emic models for Roman religion abound, fueled by a comparative interest as well. "What are Romans that the others are not?" and "Why are the Romans as Greek as the Greeks?" were the main questions to be answered by late Republican or early imperial writers. The direct or indirect addressees could vary. The questions could even take the form "Why are some Romans superior (or: equal) to others?" For reasons that might relate to Rome's small hinterland and the dramatic process of Romanization in the

---

[17] Wagenvoort, *Roman Dynamism*; many studies by H. J. Rose; even in Robert Muth, "Vom Wesen römischer 'religio,'" *ANRW* II.16,1 (1978), 290–354.

[18] E.g., Ulf, *Das römischer Lupercalienfest*; Torelli, *Lavinio e Roma*.

[19] For criticism see Beard et al., *Religions of Rome*, 52; for an alternative model, see Wildfang, *Vestal Virgins*.

[20] Thus Wissowa, *Religion und Kultus*, 504–5 with the ancient evidence. For criticism and the alternative model, see Beard et al., *Religions of Rome*, 54–8.

Roman Religion through the Early Republic 347

wake of the "Civil War" with its own Italian allies (91–89 BCE),[21] Roman authors of the first century BCE were fond of narrating Rome's early history and its religion as a process of accretion from other middle-Italian cultures, Etruscan, Sabine, Oscan. The rape of the Sabine women, abducted in order to supply the male founders with the possibility of procreation, is the most drastic example of this type of story, as is the association of a central Roman god, Quirinus, with the Sabine municipality of Curiae.[22] The stories of synoicisms and immigrating groups need not be taken at face value. They demonstrate that political and military hegemony could be balanced in the cultural and religious realm and offer models for the integration of an empire. At the same time they point to historical adaptations and common features among the peoples of central Italy, as will be shown below. They need not, however, be read as direct evidence of Roman religiosity.

Not surprisingly, Greek attempts to integrate the ascending city of Rome into their mythological network were not easily readily received either. The ancestry from Troy, advocated already by the Greek historian Timaios of Sicilian Tauromenion at the beginning of the third century BCE, was not enthusiastically embraced before the first century BCE. Then, however, the story of the fugitive Trojan prince Aeneas moved into the heart of Roman self-conceptualization. Given the massive impact of Greek culture in all areas connected with writing, Roman authors tend to minimize this factor and stress the differences despite common ancestry. Rome's massive share in Greek culture and religion (directly received from "Greater Greece," Greek settlements in southern Italy or Sicily, or indirectly via Etruscans or Campanians) is not adequately represented in the literary tradition. Archaeology demonstrates the Greek presence in the temples of the sixth century (as shown above) or, for example, the presence of Dionysian imagery in fourth- and third-century Rome.[23]

Emic (and following etic) perspectives on religious competences are informed by gender and social order. Therefore, the Romans' historical image of female religious competence was distorted. The major roles enjoyed by Roman women, matrons in particular, in the late Republic,[24] were not systematically retrojected into the earlier period. Female religious activities were thought to be concentrated on the Vestals. It was the contrast between patricians and plebeians that dominated the reconstruction

---

[21] Mouritsen, *Italian Unification*.
[22] For the latter, see Smith, *Early Rome and Latium*, 201.
[23] Wiseman, "Liber"; earlier Altheim, *Griechische Götter*.
[24] Schultz, *Women's Religious Activity*; Šterbenc-Erker, *Religiöse Rollen*.

348   *Jörg Rüpke*

of early Roman religion (Livy 6.41). The right to divination in the form
of auspices (observing of birds, lightning, and more) as well as to membership in the priestly colleges and their communicating with the gods
lay exclusively with the patricians. It must be stressed that the Ogulnian
Law of 300 BCE that opened up religious offices to non-patricians did not
diminish the number of patrician priests, but simply added plebeian pontiffs and augurs.[25]

ARCHAIC ROMAN RELIGION IN A REGIONAL PERSPECTIVE

The teleological perspective displayed by Roman (and modern) authors
tends to identify uniqueness in Roman religion as well as in the acquisition of an empire. This is perhaps unavoidable, given the exceptional (if
late) evidence for this city. By the end of the third century, Romanization
(in a vague socio-political as well as cultural sense) appears as an irresist-
ible force. Yet inscriptional evidence tells us not only about the flower-
ing of other Italian languages by the first century BCE, but of complex
and diverging ritual systems. The Roman solar calendar, in use at Rome
since the late fourth century, was neither used by neighboring Latin townships nor by the Etruscan sacrificial calendar of the *liber linteus* ("Agramer
Mumienbinden").[26] By the end of the second century BCE, Latin cities like
Praeneste or Tibur could still engage in architectural rivalry with Roman
temple sites. Some decades later, the allies of the Marsian war imagined
an Italian future without Roman hegemony. The fact that the direction
of cultural transfer is often far from clear could be taken as an indicator
of a region characterized by intense cultural exchange. In the following
paragraphs some ritual and organizational features of early Roman religion
are reviewed within their regional context with the aim of recovering this
interchange between Roman and Italic religions analyzed within a communicative model of religion.

Burial

Burial is an archaeologically well-documented complex ritual and mechanism to preserve material culture for later inquiry. Its religious importance
(in the substantialist sense as defined above) is more difficult to assess.

---

[25] Rüpke, *Fasti sacerdotum*, 1621–3.
[26] Rüpke, *Zeit und Fest*, 45–9; for the dating of the Roman calendar; see Rüpke, *Kalender und
Öffentlichkeit*, 170–2, for diverging Italian calendars.

Although rituals addressed to deities might accompany burials, there is hardly any evidence to support the view that burial was considered part of Roman religious practice; this contrasts to its role in a number of contemporary religions and a topos of religious ethnography, a view in large part due to its religious significance in (early) modern Christianity. Archaeologically speaking, burial is often taken as providing evidence for individual religious affiliation, but this is probably not an important factor in comparison to larger group or local traditions. For instance, at Rome, inhumation and cremation coexisted for centuries, preferences changing again and again without any accompanying evidence indicating religious changes. The concept of the *Di Manes,* the "good gods," that embody the dead, did not appear regularly on tombstones before imperial times. The collective plural seems to accompany tendencies of individualization, the stress on the divine status of the dead seemingly implied in the wording was not as strongly felt as to hinder Christians to employ the formula. Yet, for the badly attested society that forms the object of this chapter, such burial practices provide some sorts of evidence for questions of cultural exchange.

Most significant is the change in burial practice throughout Latium and Etruria during the sixth and fifth centuries BCE as it points to a shift in the social outlook of elites. The Orientalizing period (ca.730–630 BCE) had produced numerous luxury tombs, princely burials with highly valuable and prestigious objects in sites around Rome (Praeneste, Ficana, Castel di Decima), although (so far) not in Rome itself.[27] Social power had offered the possibility of acquiring wealth and long-distance contacts; such contacts and goods served to further prestige. The following period, characterized at Rome by urbanization and monumentalization (processes, however, that happened earlier in some Etruscan places), witnessed a substantial decline in number and quality of grave goods. Probably, funerary expenditure during this period was lavished on "prospective" public display, that is, on aristocratic competition in the form of banquets and entertainments or the building of palace-like houses in stone-masonry, rather than on "retrospective" treasure assigned privately to the dead.[28] In the long run this would help to create urban centers and public space, and to invest in the latter. There is no indication that such a decline was due to changing conceptions of the fate of the dead.

[27] Cornell, *The Beginnings of Rome,* 81–92; in greater detail: Meyer, *Pre-Republican Rome.*
[28] Cornell, *The Beginnings of Rome,* 105–8.

Jörg Rüpke

Sanctuaries

Cult sites have already been mentioned for the city of Rome. A sanctuary need not contain a temple building. Open spaces could focus on an altar that need not be constructed in stone. A number of votive deposits indicate such places. Such a pit – directly used to deposit votive offerings or occasionally filled when a larger number of offerings had to be removed from the premises[29] – allows archaeological identification of a sanctuary. In the city of Rome, such deposits preceded the oldest temple at San Omobono in the Cattle Market.[30] Such deposits were widespread in Italy and beyond, and also frequent in Rome and its surrounding territory. Characteristic of Rome and Latium are human (often female) terracotta statuettes (and sometimes statues approaching life size as in Lavinium from the early fifth century onward), heads and busts from the sixth century onward, and anatomical votives from the fourth century onward. Even if reinforced by anatomical votives associated with the Greek cult of Asklepios, the frequency of such representations of parts of the body remained characteristic down to the first century BCE.[31]

The building of temples from the second half of the sixth century BCE onward was shared by Rome and other Etruscan places. A high podium gave access on one side only, the other sides having neither steps nor wall openings. This foundation was completed by a building dominated by wooden columns and roof constructions decorated with colorful terracotta reliefs. Such a construction clearly marked boundaries of everyday life and marked off sacred space.[32] Yet its usage was not restricted to the housing of a cult statue (besides the statues decorating the tympanon and the roof). A threefold cella at the back of the building offered at least two rooms for different types of activities (and does not indicate the veneration of a triad of deities); the rooms of the high podium could likewise be put to different uses. Storage and shop functions of the basement would be completed by storage functions, political assemblies, and banquets and ritual activities above – as architectural forms and later practice suggest.[33] "Religion," here, offered a defined and public space for different forms of communication.

---

[29] See Glinister, "Reconsidering 'Religious Romanization,'" 11.
[30] Smith, *Early Rome and Latium*, 159–60.
[31] Baggieri, *Speranza*; de Cazanove, "Some Thoughts," 71–6; Simon et al., "Weihgeschenke," 332–40, 359–68; Schultz, *Women's Religious Activity*, 95–120. For cult places, see Edlund, *The Gods and the Place*.
[32] Izzet, "Tuscan Order," 34–53.
[33] Hesberg, *Römische Baukunst*, 84–6.

Roman Religion through the Early Republic 351

Our knowledge about cult-places and temples at Rome is limited; chance finds supplement a literary tradition that might be reliable in the sanctuaries named but is hardly complete. Urban (not necessarily public) sanctuaries of the period down to the Latin Wars ending in 340/338 BCE include Jupiter Optimus Maximus (with Juno and Minerva) and Jupiter Feretrius; Juno Moneta on the Capitol Hill (resp. in the Arx), Vulcan, Vesta, Saturn, and Castor in the Roman Forum; the Lupercal and altars for the Carmentae on the slopes of the Palatine; Fortuna and Mater Matuta in the Forum Boarium (San Omobono), the altar to Hercules nearby; Mercury, Consus (altar), and the "plebeian triad" Ceres, Liber, Libera in or above the circus valley; Diana, Minerva, and Juno Regina on the Aventine; Quirinus, Dius Fidius (Semo Sancus), and unidentified votive deposits at Sta Maria della Vittoria and S Vitale on the Quirinal; Juno Lucina (first a *lucus*) and Minerva Medica on the Esquiline Hill, and again a cult-place characterized by a votive-deposit close to the later Colosseum.[34] Mars had an altar in the Campus Martius and later a temple directly outside the Porta Capena (388 BCE), Fors Fortuna in Trastevere.

When in the century following the Latin Wars nearly fifty new temples were founded,[35] the difference in the religious and social implications of the act of temple-building and the communicative functions of these temples is obvious. Individuals, mostly victorious generals, were able to implement their own choice of cult into public religion. The resulting list comprises a heterogeneous ensemble with regard to gods and venerators addressed. Cult-places dominated by votive-deposits and healing cults (Carmentae, Minerva Medica) mix with cults organized on the principle of exclusion of the other sex (Mater Matuta, Vesta, Hercules) or for special groups (plebeians, Vesta, Fors Fortuna?). Special spatial arrangements, a grotto (?) at the Lupercal, a well (?) for Anna Perenna[36] and the Carmentae, do without temple buildings. Some cults clearly reflect import (the Capitoline triad, Vulcan, Castor, Fortuna, Hercules, Diana, Juno Regina). Such decisions need not be due to immigrant groups, but might reflect decisions of the political elite. "Greek" cults and prominent cults of neighboring towns dominate in this group. Apart from a dominant strand of caring for personal needs, such religious practices reflect an elite's trans-local

---

[34] I follow Ziolkowski, *The Temples of Mid-Republican Rome*, in referring to the temples (and attested cult-places) of the Penates and Vica Pota on the Velia to the third century BCE. Dating the shrine of Minerva Medica before the late fourth century is not certain, nor is it certain for that of the Carmentae.

[35] Ziolkowski, *The Temples*, 187–9.

[36] The early identification (Piranomonte, *Il santuario*) is not tenable.

352   *Jörg Rüpke*

communication: Imported statues of gods or ritual practices into Rome
signaled acknowledgement of equality toward the regions of origin.

Ritual

Communication is not restricted to contacts between humans. Ritual
communication between humans and deities that are not as present, visible, and touchable as human participants in face-to-face communication
needs reinforcements to ensure a successful transmission of messages and
to make a positive outcome of the communicative effort more probable.
Hence the communicative model is fruitful for analyzing forms of representation of the divine.

Archaeological finds and later literary description suggest that rituals at
Rome share the spectrum of ritual forms present in Mediterranean societies: vegetable and animal sacrifice, libations, votives (with the many variations according to material resources), economy, diets, and artisanship. As
mentioned before, representation of the human supplicant was important.
We do not know to what degree mass production was individualized by the
addition of painting. Differentiation was made in terms of sex and (at least
roughly) life-phase (infant, youth, adult). Using a model of communication, one may tend to interpret this primarily in terms of the perpetuation
of communication: The temporary, difficult, and uncertain communication with the divine is made to transgress the limit of the time (defined
by the visiting of a shrine) by permanently representing the human actor
in a place closer or more visible to the deity. The subterranean deposit of
the votives might be made directly into a trench or pit. However, archaeologically identified deposits might be of secondary origin, too – the results
of a periodical removal of votives from visible spaces, thus leading to new
ensembles in the deposit space.[37] The many findings in the Tiber close to
the sanctuary of Asklepios probably originated from such cleanings.

Apart from the representation of a deity's presence and power, the statuary representation of the deity is another (and not mutually exclusive)
strategy to improve ritual communication. Such a strategy – not supplanting, but supplementing the representation of the humans – was present
at Rome at least from the late sixth century BCE onward. Life-sized or
nearly life-sized painted terracotta statues dominated the period analyzed
here (e.g., Dion. Hal. 1.68.2) and were more and more rivaled by metal
and marble statues later on. Occasionally wooden statues are found. Such

---

[37] See Bouma, *Religio votiva*, for examples.

Roman Religion through the Early Republic 353

permanent epiphanies[38] tended to be housed in temple buildings, marking their presence (see above) as well as restricting access. Precise identification by attributes and imagery from narratives on the architecture poses the problem of trans-local identity and encourages narratives of transfer or spontaneous movement. At least potentially, the users and spectators are engaged with such rivalries and trans-local relationships. Of course, the same holds true – in an even more emphatic sense – for the producers, the initiator and the actual builders, in a number of cases probably drawn from other towns. Yet for literary texts as for temples, reconstruction of potential "meanings" cannot be restricted to the moment of creation, but has to cover the long period of usage (and maybe different usages, too).[39] In the case of early Rome, references would have included Greek and Carthaginian/Punic culture as well as Etruscan and Latin culture and localities. In many a Latin town, as mentioned before on the so-called princely tombs, artistic techniques were at least as developed as in Rome. Apart from the terracotta fragments from the San Omobono finds, the terracotta acroterion statue of Apollo from the Portonaccio temple at Veii, figures from the larger temple of Pyrgi (both in the Museum of the Villa Giulia, Rome), or the statue of Juno Sospita from Lanuvium give an impression of what the statues in the Capitoline temple might have looked like.

Without a reliable textual tradition – the nonfictitious sources of the late Republican and Augustan authors that are the basis for our reconstruction hardly antedate the second or third centuries BCE – ritual action is even more difficult to reconstruct than its material ingredients. First-century narratives about the institution of cults by Romulus and Numa are as unreliable as twentieth-century projections of the calendar (*fasti*) into the regal period. In fact, the list of festivals was codified in the late fourth-century-BCE calendar and is known from first-century copies.[40]

Evidence from Etruscan tombs, for instance, the Tomba delle Bighe at Tarquinia or the Tomba della Scimmia at Chiusi, suggests the existence of athletic competitions and processional rites in (at least some) Etruscan towns from the sixth or even seventh centuries BCE onward.[41] Reliefs and vase paintings from the sixth and fifth centuries, for example, an amphora from Ponte di Micali, dated 520–510 BCE,[42] confirm games that include different types of competitions and, by the end of the sixth

---

[38] Gladigow, *Religionswissenschaft*, 62–84.
[39] Cf. Smith, "Worshipping Mater Matuta," 142 and 152.
[40] Rüpke, *Kalender und Öffentlichkeit*, 261–6.
[41] Bernstein, *Ludi publici*, 25–30.
[42] Bruni, "Le processioni," no. 29; photo: *ThesCRA* 2, tab. 93, no. 15.

354 *Jörg Rüpke*

century, processions. Thus, the later Roman narratives about the introduction of circus games by the Tarquins (Livy 1.35.7–9), that is, Etruscan kings of Rome, and scenic games in the middle of the fourth century BCE from Etruria (Livy 7.2.1–12) seem to offer a convincing reconstruction of these rituals.[43] The Greek Dionysius of Halicarnassus's image of the institution of a circus procession at Rome in the beginning of the fifth century agrees (7.72–3). And it is of some interest that the neighboring town of Veii is credited for comparable competitions in the sixth century BCE (Plin. *NH* 8.65; Fest. p. 340–2 L). Yet, there can be no doubt about the "international" character of such games, mirroring the Greek institution and involving members of middle Italian elites. It should be added that gladiatorial games, probably known in Etruria for centuries, were attested for Roman funeral cult practices only in 264 BCE (Val. Max. 2.4.7). If such practices were a necessary ritual element of Etruscan burials of nobles, at Rome they are discussed only for their demonstration of the economic status of the dead (and his heirs). Ritual semantics might shift due to cultural transfer.

Religious Specialists

Roman tradition attributed the institutionalization of several priesthoods to the first kings. There is no reliable evidence for Roman priests before the fifth and especially the fourth centuries BCE.[44] Here Italian evidence is not helpful, either. Evidence for the divinatory specialists called *haruspices* in Latin sources and *netśvis* in Etruscan texts (Rix, *ET* Um 1.7; Cl 1.1036) does not antedate the fifth century, neither does the evidence for the priestly role of *cipen* or *cepen*, assumed by magistrates.[45] Priesthoods from Italian townships, offering striking similarities to Roman institutions, belong to late Republican and imperial times; they might have been the result of early exchange processes, in which Rome could have been giving as well as receiving. The evidence, however, does not offer any clues to the chronology of such exchanges. Since a differentiated Roman priesthood of the late Republic need not be postulated for Archaic Rome, the question of how to imagine priests in the regal period could be broken down to a limited set of problems.

[43] Bernstein, "Complex Rituals," 222–34.
[44] Rüpke, *Fasti sacerdotum*, 24–38.
[45] Estienne, "Personnel de culte," 67.

Specialists for divination ("seers" with a number of different techniques) are attested in numerous Mediterranean societies; Latin literary tradition develops the figure of the charismatic seer, such as the augur Attus Navius,[46] in opposition to such figures as the mythical king Numa. Such specialists were at times attacked (see, for example, the Marcius or Marcii of the third century) or derided (the *harioli*, "charlatans" of the first century BCE), but they probably existed throughout Roman history. The high prestige of the college of the augurs in the early Republic marks an institutionalization of some of them during the regal period and their ascent to positions that made their belonging to the "patricians" by the end of the monarchy probable, as the right to the auspices seems to have been a kernel of patrician self-definition.[47]

The existence of an unknown number of religious specialists (not necessarily all male) caring for individual cults (and probably cult-places) can be reasonably assumed; their name *flamen* points to a much older institutional pattern, as shown above. In contrast to the augurs or pontiffs, *flamines* tended to be appointed at a very young age, if third- and second-century-BCE evidence can be trusted. Groups of aristocratic youths (that is, an elite close to the king) might hold the duty to care for some very important cults. The Vestal Virgins would fit into such a pattern, as would the *Salii* and the badly attested Salian virgins in the cults of Vesta and Mars (Fest. 439.18–22 L). If the invitation to banqueting, as offered by the Salian priests,[48] is given to an organized "public" group, that might well have been related to "the disappearance at the end of the sixth century of terracotta friezes depicting banqueting scenes" that has been suggested to reflect "the disappearance of the private banquet as well, as part of the realignment of social affairs consequent on the fall of the last king."[49] Associations caring for other cults probably sprang up and died; we have no idea of the origins of such religious groups as the *Mercuriales*, the Arval brethren or the *sodales Titii*.[50] It cannot be ruled out that the latter went back to the regal period, as was thought in Augustan times (Tac. *Ann.* 1.54; *Hist.* 2.95). Some of these groups probably came to be regarded as "public priests" (*sacerdotes publici*) by the late Republic. Before the Augustan revival, most of these were socially and politically without importance.

---

[46] Beard et al., *Religions of Rome*, 23–4.
[47] Smith, *Early Rome and Latium*, 263–8; his projection of the later priestly system into the regal period (260–2) is problematic.
[48] Rüpke, "Collegia sacerdotum," 41–67.
[49] Smith, *Early Rome and Latium*, 316, referring to Zaccaria Ruggiu, *More regio vivere*, 361–401.
[50] Varro, *De lingua latina* 5.85. See Rüpke, *Fasti sacerdotum*, for prosopographical details.

356   *Jörg Rüpke*

Salii and *Vestales,* more prominent in our record, were out of the political realm proper by reasons of sex or age.

Much prestige was given to the Roman pontiffs, for whom we have evidence of interaction between different priesthoods. This includes not only appointing or punishing *flamines* or Vestals by the supreme pontiff, but also ritual interactions with the *Salii* (*Fast. Praen.*) and with the *Luperci* (Ov. *Fast.* 2.21–2). There were many occasions where they acted together with *flamines* or Vestals.[51] The pontiffs, represented by the *pontifex maximus,*[52] presided over an ancient assembly of the *curiae* (*comitia calata*) that was charged with the continuation of families and their cults (Cic. *Leg.* 2.48). In his important role as regulator of the calendar, the *rex sacrorum* is paired with a "minor" pontiff on the *Kalends*, the first of each month (Macr. *Sat.* 1.15.9–12) or with the pontiffs on the *Tubilustrium*, a March festival to Mars.[53] The pontiffs as a prominent public priesthood were the result of a conscious effort at religious centralization, based on the presupposition of the existence of the *comitia centuriata* (in order to free the *comitia* [*curiata*] *calata* for their presidency) and of a *rex sacrorum,* which could have been a position already during the late monarchy. Attributing centralization to a major restructuring of society as might be supposed for the termination of the monarchy seems the easiest hypothesis.[54] If there had been people called "pontiffs" before, there is no need to believe that their role had been comparable. It should be stressed that all the other colleges were modeled on the form of the pontifical college; the augural college (with its eldest member serving as *augur maximus* but without specific authority) was far less important compared to the individual augur's power.[55]

Calendar

Calendars provide an apt conclusion to a regional consideration of Roman religion. They can shed light on economic, political, and ritual activities in specific areas. Here the Etruscan *Tabula Capuana* from the beginning of the fifth century BCE, a text of some four thousand letters, offers comparative material.[56] This fragmentary list of rituals, summarily described,

---

[51] Wissowa, *Religion und Kultus,* 516–8.
[52] Ibid., 509, points to the easy substitution of the *pontifex maximus* by his colleagues.
[53] Aul. Gell., *Noct. att.* 15.27.1–3; Rüpke, *Kalender und Öffentlichkeit,* 214–21.
[54] The latter is stressed by Smith, *Early Rome and Latium,* 307. Linke, *Von der Verwandtschaft,* 149–51, too, relates this process to the (early) Republic.
[55] See Linderski, "Augural Law," 2146–2312, for individual and collective duties and powers.
[56] Cristofani, *Tabula Capuana*; Woudhuizen, *Etruscan Liturgical Calendar*; Rüpke, "Review, Cristofani, *Tabula Capuana,*" 272–4.

Roman Religion through the Early Republic

corroborates the Roman antiquarian claim that the structuring of the months by the Ides was Etruscan; it shows a system of week-like periods (although not necessarily of constant length) from full moon to full moon: *iśveita – celuta – tiniana – aperta* (institutionally corresponding to Latin *Idus – Tubilustrium – Kalendae – Nonae*). At Rome, these days concentrate routine cultic activities of the *rex* and *regina sacrorum*, the *Flamen Dialis* (priest of Jupiter), the pontiffs and *Tubicines* (trumpeters), engaging in rituals addressed to Jupiter, Juno, and the moon, and monthly adapting this civic rhythm to the lunar cycles, as is typical for a lunar calendar. It was only with the reforms of Appius Claudius Caecus and Gnaeus Flavius in the final years of the fourth century BCE that calendar months were of fixed length and no longer correspond to the lunar phases, resulting in a pure solar calendar that is the basis of today's Julio-Gregorian calendar.[57]

REPUBLICAN POLITICAL DEVELOPMENTS AND ROMAN RELIGION

The early Republic was characterized by internal social and political conflicts. Later Roman tradition shaped the complexity of the processes into the dichotomy of patricians and plebeians, thus summarizing processes that comprised the institutionalization and codification (the "Twelve Tables," ca.450 BCE), of growing social distinction, and the establishment of the *gentes* as structures to ensure inheritance within long-lived social institutions larger than families, and as structures to distribute political and priestly positions more evenly, thus reducing strife and frustration.[58] By the second half of the fourth century, a unified elite had evolved that did not remove the distinction of patricians and plebeians, but gave equal access to offices. The passing of the *lex Ogulnia* in the year 300 BCE opened even the priestly colleges of the augurs and pontiffs to plebeians. Under the pressure of a citizenship that was necessary for successful warfare and had powers of decisions in popular assemblies, an ethos had been developed that oriented the drive for distinction toward "publicly" useful activities and thus opened the way toward external military success.[59]

Social developments would have affected public ritual, too. Hypothetically, an important change in the Roman *ludi* ("games") could thus be explained. If aristocratic competition was restricted to publicly

---

[57] Rüpke, *Kalender und Öffentlichkeit*; the codification is redated from the period of the decemviri ("ten men"), i.e., mid-fifth century BCE, to the end of the fourth century in Rüpke, *Zeit und Fest*. On Claudius see Humm, *Appius Claudius Caecus*.

[58] Smith, *Early Rome and Latium*; for the sources of the "conflict of orders," see Eder, *Staat und Staatlichkeit*, 92–217.

[59] Hölkeskamp, *Die Entstehung*; Rüpke, *Domi militiae*.

useful fields as warfare, the fight for distinction by athletic victories might have been scorned. First, the organization was monopolized by patrician priests, organizing chariot races in March (*Equirria*), August (*Consualia*), or October (*Equus October,* "October horse"), the outcome of which did not earn prestige to the winners. The "Roman" and the "Plebeian Games" in September and November, respectively, were probably exempted, as were games organized by returning victors. Second, participation shifted from aristocratic youths to professional or local amusement (*ludi Capitolini* in October). Only later did the organization of the games come to be connected with different stages of the magistrates' careers and developed into a field of rivalry and distinction in itself. Games came to be concentrated at Rome, offering financial opportunities for foreign professionals and spectators from the large hinterland of Rome,[60] but restricting the field of elite competition to the splendors of organization.

The situation should not be regarded as stable, but as an ever-shifting equilibrium. If prestigious display and consumption in the form of grave goods had been widely eliminated by the fifth century, gentilician and family power had been publicly stressed by the building of monumental houses from the same time onward. By the end of the fourth century, temple-building by victorious generals turned into a highly competitive field, even if many of them opted for the prestigious consumption in the form of victory games (*ludi votivi*).[61] Such activities – and probably likewise the return of a victor into a city and his attempts at the display of statues of himself[62] – were subjected to public control by ritualization and senatorial decisions. In the face of military expansion and direct contact with the cultural and political sophistication of the Hellenistic world, Romans continued to reshape and expand their religion for centuries to come.[63]

Could findings at Rome be generalized for a comparative study of ancient Mediterranean religions? A few remarks might be in order. First, no religious traditions developed isolated from one another. Long-distance contacts are proven already for the prehistoric periods; Phoenician and Greek and Babylonian and Hittite expansion as well as Egyptian cultural export established routes that provided easy traveling for technical experts, warriors, and elite members interested in luxury goods and alliances. Religion could be part and parcel of such transferences of media,

---

[60] See Cancik, "Auswärtige Teihlnehmer."
[61] Orlin, *Temples, Religion, and Politics*; Ziolkowski, *The Temples.*
[62] This hypothesis is argued in Rüpke, *Zeit und Fest.*
[63] See Rüpke, *Religions of the Romans*, 24–38, 54–61.

political institutions, and concepts. Thus "Greek" images and architecture are among the earliest traces of "Roman" religion and continue to influence local practices down to late Antiquity and Greek-speaking Christianity.

Second, even archaic religion was a complex religion. Religious practices reflected interests and potentials of different social groups, even individuals. For a city of some ten thousand inhabitants, the resulting topography of temples, cults, and practitioners was far from conceptually unified. As a result, any attempts to parallel social and religious elements must be partial and demand careful handling.

Finally, "religion" was no clearly separated and unified realm in archaic and early Republican Rome. To analyze "religion" necessitates a clear explanation of the researcher's interest and his or her definition of religion. In this chapter, communication has been used as a way to contextualize evidence within social and regional human interaction, and to interpret religious practices and artifacts with regard to the presupposed interests of the humans in order to get in touch with and grasp the divine.

BIBLIOGRAPHY

Textual Sources

Bernstein, Frank, *Ludi publici: Untersuchungen zur Entstehung und Entwicklung der öffentlichen Spiele im republikanischen Rom.* Historia Einzelschriften 119 (Stuttgart, 1998).

Cristofani, Mauro, *Tabula Capuana: Un calendario festivo di età arcaica.* Istituto nazionale di studi etruschi e italici: Biblioteca di Studi Etruschi 29 (Florence, 1995).

Rüpke, Jörg. *Kalender und Öffentlichkeit: Die Geschichte der Repräsentation und religiösen Qualifikation von Zeit in Rom.* Religionsgeschichtliche Versuche und Vorarbeiten 40 (Berlin, 1995).

"Kulturtransfer als Rekodierung: Zum literaturgeschichtlichen und sozialen Ort der frühen römischen Epik," in Rüpke (ed.), *Von Menschen und Göttern erzählen: Formkonstanzen und Funktionswandel vormoderner Epik.* Potsdamer altertumswissenschaftliche Beiträge 4 (Stuttgart, 2001): 42–64.

Zeit und Fest: Eine Kulturgeschichte des Kalenders (Munich, 2006).

Fasti sacerdotum: Prosopographie der stadtrömischen Priesterschaften römischer, griechischer, orientalischer und jüdisch-christlicher Kulte bis 499 n. Chr. Potsdamer Altertumswissenschaftliche Beiträge 12/1–3 (Stuttgart, 2005); trans. David Richardson (Oxford, 2008).

Woudhuizen, Fred. *The Etruscan Liturgical Calendar from Capua* (Amsterdam, 1996).

Material Culture

Anzidei, A. P., and P. Gioia. "Rinvenimenti preistorici nell'area del Tempio della Vittoria al Palatino." *Archeologia Laziale* 12 (1995): 29–32.

360 *Jörg Rüpke*

Baggieri, G., ed. *"Speranza e sofferenza" nei votivi anatomici dell' antichità: complesso monumentale del S. Michele di Roma, Sala degli aranci, ott.-nov. 1996* (Rome, 1999).

Bispham, Edward, and Christopher Smith, eds. *Religion in Archaic and Republican Rome and Italy: Evidence and Experience* (Edinburgh, 2000).

Bouma, J. W. *Religio votiva: The Archaeology of Latial Votive Religion. The 5th–3rd cent. BC Votive Deposit South-west of the Main Temple at "Satrium" Borgo Le Ferriere*, 3 vols. (Groningen, 1996).

Coarelli, Filippo. *Il Foro Romano 1: Periodo arcaico* (Rome, 1983).

Il Foro Boario: Dalle origine alla fine della repubblica (Rome, 1988).

Il Campo Marzio: Dalle origini alla fine della repubblica (Rome, 1997).

Edlund, Ingrid. *The Gods and the Place: Location and Function of Sanctuaries in the Countryside of Etruria and Magna Graecia (700–400 B.C.)* Skrifter utgivna av Svenska institutet i Rom, 4°, 43 (Stockholm, 1987).

Fraschetti, Augusto. *The Foundation of Rome*, trans. Marian Hill and Kevin Windle (Edinburgh, 2005).

Hesberg, Henner von. *Römische Baukunst* (Munich, 2005).

Izzet, Vedia. "Tuscan Order: The development of Etruscan sanctuary architecture." In *Religion in Archaic and Republican Rome and Italy: Evidence and Experience*, ed. Edward Bispham and Christopher Smith (Edinburgh, 2000): 34–53.

Kolb, Frank. *Agora und Theater, Volks- und Festversammlung.* Deutsches Archäologisches Institut: Archäologische Forschungen 9 (Berlin, 1981).

Meyer, Jørgen Christian. *Pre-Republican Rome: An Analysis of the Cultural and Chronological Relations 1000–500 B.C.* Analecta Romana Instituti Danici Suppl. 11 (Odense, 1983).

Moscati, Sabatino. *Così nacque l'Italia: Profili di antichi popoli riscoperti* (Turin, 1997).

Orlin, Eric M. *Temples, Religion, and Politics in the Roman Republic.* Mnemosyne Suppl. 164 (Leiden, 1997).

Piranomonte, Marina. *Il santuario della musica e il bosco sacro di Anna Perenna* (Milan, 2002).

Simon, Erika, et al. "Weihgeschenke: Altitalien und Imperium Romanum." In *ThesCRA* 1, ed. A. Comella and J. M. Turfa (Los Angeles, 2004): 327–450.

Zaccaria Ruggiu, A. *More regio vivere: il banchetto aristocratico e la casa romana di età arcaica.* Quaderni di Eutopia 4 (Rome, 1992).

Ziolkowski, Adam. *The Temples of Mid-Republican Rome and Their Historical and Topographical Context.* Saggi di Storia antica 4 (Rome, 1992).

General Bibliography

AA.VV. *Akten des Kolloquiums zum Thema "Die Göttin von Pyrgi:" Archäologische, linguistische und religionsgeschichtliche Aspekte (Tübingen, 16–17 Januar 1979).* Istituto di Studi etruschi ed italici: Biblioteca di Studi etruschi 12, ed. Aldo Neppi Modona and Friedhelm Prayon (Florence, 1981).

Altheim, Franz, *Griechische Götter im alten Rom*, RGVV 22.1 (Giessen, 1930).

Beard, Mary, John North, and Simon Price. *Religions of Rome. 1: A History. 2: A Sourcebook* (Cambridge, 1998).

Roman Religion through the Early Republic

Belier, Wouter W. "Decayed Gods: origin and development of Georges Dumézil's 'Idéologie tripartie.'" Studies in Greek and Roman Religion 7 (Leiden, 1991).

Bernstein, Frank. "Complex Rituals: Games and Processions in Republican Rome." In *A Companion to Roman Religion*, ed. Jörg Rüpke (Oxford, 2007): 222–34.

Bruni, Stefano. "Le processioni in Etruria." In *ThesCRA* I (Los Angeles, 2004): 21–32.

Bruun, Christer, ed. *The Roman Middle Republic: Politics, Religion, and Historiography c. 400–133 B.C.* Acta Instituti Finlandiae 23 (Rome, 2000): 265–99.

Cancik, Hubert. "Auswärtige Teilnehmer an stadtrömischen Festen." In *Festrituale in der römischen Kaiserzeit*, STAC 48, ed. Jörg Rüpke (Tübingen, 2008): 5–18.

Carandini, Andrea. *La nascita di Roma: Dèi, Lari, eroi e uomini all'alba di una civiltà* (Turin, 1997).

    ed. *Palatium e Sacra Via I: prima delle mura, l'età delle mura e l'età case arcaiche.* Bollettino di archeologia (Rome, 2000).

Cornell, Timothy J. *The Beginnings of Rome: Italy and Rome from the Bronze Age to the Punic Wars (c. 1000–264 BC)* (London, 1995).

De Cazenove, Olivier. "Some Thoughts on the 'Religious Romanisation' of Italy before the Social War." In *Religion in Archaic and Republican Rome and Italy: Evidence and Experience*, ed. Edward Bispham and Christopher Smith (Edinburgh, 2000): 71–6.

Dumézil, George. *Jupiter, Mars, Quirinus 1: Essai sur la conception Indo-Européenne de la société et sur les origines de Rome*, 2nd ed. (Paris, 1941).

    Jupiter, Mars, Quirinus 2: Naissance de Rome (Paris, 1944).

    Archaic Roman Religion: With an Appendix on the Religion of the Etruscans, 2 vols., trans. P. Krapp (Chicago, 1970).

Eder, Walter, ed. *Staat und Staatlichkeit in der frühen römischen Republik* (Stuttgart, 1990).

Estienne, Sylvia. "Personnel de culte: monde romain I. Définitions." In *Thesaurus cultus et rituum antiquorum* 5 (Los Angeles, 2005): 67–8.

Gabba, Emilio. *Roma arcaica: Storia e stroiografia.* Storia e letteratura 205 (Rome, 2000).

Gladigow, Burkhard. "Religionswissenschaft als Kulturwissenschaft." In *Religionswissenschaft heute* I, ed. Christoph Auffarth and Jörg Rüpke (Stuttgart, 2005).

Glinister, Fay. "Reconsidering 'Religious Romanization.'" In *Religion in Republican Italy*, Yale Classical Studies 33, ed. Celia E. Schultz and Paul B. Harvey (Cambridge, 2006): 10–33.

Hölkeskamp, Karl Joachim. *Die Entstehung der Nobilität: Studien zur sozialen und politischen Geschichte der Römischen Republik im 4. Jhdt. v. Chr.* (Stuttgart, 1987).

Humm, Michel. *Appius Claudius Caecus: La république accomplice* (Rome, 2005).

Latte, Kurt. *Römische Religionsgeschichte.* Handbuch der Altertumswissenschaft 5:4 (Munich, 1960).

Linderski, Jerzy. "The Augural Law." *ANRW* II.16:3 (1986): 2146–312.

Linke, Bernhard. *Von der Verwandtschaft zum Staat: Die Entstehung Politischer Organisationsformen in der Frührömischen Geschichte* (Stuttgart, 1995).

Momigliano, Arnaldo. *Contributi alla storia degli studi classici e del mondo antico*, 9 vols. (Rome, 1955–92).

    "Premesse per una discussione su Georges Dumézil." *Rivista Storica Italiana* 15 (1983): 245–61.

362   *Jörg Rüpke*

"Georges Dumézil and the Trifunctional Approach to Roman Civilization." *History and Theory* 23:3 (1984): 312–30.

Mouritsen, Hendrik. *Italian Unification: A Study in Ancient and Modern Historiography* (London, 1998).

Paoletti, Orazio, and Giovannangelo Camporeale, eds. *Dinamiche di sviluppo delle città nell'Etruria meridionale: Veii, Caere, Tarquinia, Vulci, Atti del XXIII Convegno di Studi Etruschi ed Italici*, 2 vols. (Pisa, 2005).

Rüpke, Jörg. *Domi militiae: Die religiöse Konstruktion des Krieges in Rom* (Stuttgart, 1990).

Kalender und Öffentlichkeit: Die Geschichte der Repräsentation und religiösen Qualifikation von Zeit in Rom. Religionsgeschichtliche Versuche und Vorarbeiten 40 (Berlin, 1995).

"Review of F. Cristofani, Tabula Capuana …" *Gnomon* 71 (1999): 272–4.

"Kulturtransfer als Rekodierung: Zum literaturgeschichtlichen und sozialen Ort der frühen römischen Epik." In *Von Menschen und Göttern erzählen: Formkonstanzen und Funktionswandel vormoderner Epik.* Potsdamer Altertumswissenschaftliche Beiträge 4, ed. J. Rüpke (Stuttgart, 2001): 42–64.

"Collegia sacerdotum: Religiöse Vereine der Oberschicht." In *Religiöse Vereine in der römischen Antike: Untersuchungen zu Organisation, Ritual und Raumordnung, Texte und Studien zu Antike und Christentum* 13, ed. Ulrike Egelhaaf and Alfred S. Gaiser (Tübingen, 2002): 41–67.

Zeit und Fest: Eine Kulturgeschichte des Kalenders (Munich, 2006).

ed. *A Companion to Roman Religion* (Oxford, 2007).

The Religions of the Romans: An Introduction, ed. and trans. Richard Gordon (Oxford, 2007).

Fasti sacerdotum: Prosopographie der stadtrömischen Priesterschaften römischer, griechischer, orientalischer und jüdisch-christlicher Kulte bis 499 n. Chr. Potsdamer Altertumswissenschaftliche Beiträge 12/1–3 (Stuttgart, 2005); Engl. trans. David Richardson (Oxford, 2008).

Schilling, Robert, and Jörg Rüpke. "Roman Religion: The Early Period." *Encyclopedia of Religion* 12, 2nd ed. (New York, 2005): 7892–911.

Schultz, Celia E. *Women's Religious Activity in the Roman Republic* (Chapel Hill, 2006).

Smith, Christopher John. *Early Rome and Latium: Economy and Society c. 1000 to 500 BC* (Oxford, 1996).

"Worshipping Mater Matuta: ritual and context." In *Religion in Archaic and Republican Rome and Italy: Evidence and Experience*, ed. Edward Bispham and Christopher Smith (Edinburgh, 2000): 136–155.

The Roman Clan: The Gens from Ancient Ideology to Modern Anthropology (Cambridge, 2006).

"The Religion of Archaic Rome." In *A Companion to Roman Religion*, ed. J. Rüpke (Oxford, 2007): 31–42.

Šterbenc Erker, Darja. *Die religiösen Rollen römischer Frauen in "griechischen" Ritualen.* Potsdamer altertumswissenschaftliche Beiträge (Stuttgart, forthcoming).

Ulf, Christoph. *Das römische Lupercalienfest: Ein Modellfall für Methodenprobleme in der Altertumswissenschaft.* Impulse der Forschung 38 (Darmstadt, 1982).

Wagenvoort, Hendrik. *Roman Dynamism: Studies in Ancient Thought, Language, and Custom* (Oxford, 1947).

Wildfang, Robin Lorsch. *Rome's Vestal Virgins: A Study of Rome's Vestal Priestesses in the Late Republic and Early Empire* (London, 2006).

Wiseman, Timothy Peter. "Liber: Myth, Drama, and Ideology in Republican Rome." In *The Roman Middle Republic: Politics, Religion, and Historiography c. 400–133 B.C.*, ed. Christer Bruun. Acta Instituti Finlandiae 23 (Rome, 2000): 265–99.

14

CELTIC RELIGION IN WESTERN
AND CENTRAL EUROPE

DOROTHY WATTS

An account of the religion of the Celts of Western and Central Europe is beset with many difficulties, the most significant being a debate over the existence of "the Celts" as a definable people with a common religious tradition. It is true that modern concepts of the Celts are only perhaps two hundred years old at most; but that a people known as Celts or Keltoi did exist in the ancient world, and that even beyond these tribes were others who had similar language, religion, and art, cannot be disputed.[1] This commonality of culture is the determining factor for scholars in identifying the Celts, whose material remains may be traced from Ireland in the west to Romania and even Turkey in the east, to the north as far as southern Germany, and south to parts of the Iberian Peninsula and to Italy north of the Po River (see Map 10).[2]

Granted this commonality of culture, scholars in search of creating as comprehensive a picture as possible of Celtic religious systems have heavily drawn on archaeological evidence from these regions to supplement the ancient written sources. Apart from the First Botorrita Inscription found in Spain, the Coligny Calendar, and the Chamalières and Larzac Tablets from France (Roman Gaul), some bilingual texts such as the Vercelli Inscription from Italy, and an occasional dedication, there is virtually nothing written by the Celts themselves relating to their religion.[3] Writing had little or no part in their culture, and such

---

[1] This view is taken by many scholars, European and British (see bibliography). Most of the opposing views come from British scholars, especially Collis, *Celts*, and James, *Atlantic Celts*. See also Carr and Stoddart, *Celts*.
[2] Haywood, *Atlas*.
[3] Maier, *Dictionary*, 41–2, 70, 77, 166; Birkhan, *Celts*, 81–2.

Map 10. Celtic Europe.

inscriptions mostly used the Greek or Latin alphabets.[4] Our main written sources, texts by Greek or Roman authors of the fifth century BCE on, were not interested in giving a point of view that might reflect that of those whom they were describing. At best they portray the Celts with a certain sympathy; at worst the emphasis is on their barbarity and their "otherness," and the ancient exaggerations and fabrications are repeated uncritically by successive writers. For example, the first-century-BCE Greek historian Diodorus Siculus (5.32) writes of cannibalism in Ireland, and this is repeated half a century later by Strabo (*Geog.* 4.5.4) who adds incest to the crimes, although he concedes that he does not have "trustworthy witnesses" for his information. The Irish and Welsh myths come closest to the actual Celtic world, although their stage is populated by supernatural heroes, warriors, and devotees of cults from the upper classes. Because these tales were recorded sometimes centuries after composition,

---

[4] Known "Celtic" scripts include the Cisalpine-Gaulish, Leopontine, and Iberian (this last borrowed from Phoenician); as Birkhan points out (*Celts,* 81–2 and fig. 331), none of these was particularly suited to the recording of a Celtic language.

366 *Dorothy Watts*

and by Christian monks often using them to spread their proselytizing message, they present additional problems of interpretation.

ORIGINS OF CELTIC RELIGION

There have been few modern discussions on the origins and interpretation of Celtic religion, doubtless because there has been such little evidence to dispute. A succinct summary by Cunliffe[5] is that, as Celtic society progressed, the emphasis on solar and lunar cycles gave way to matters concerning things on and in the earth. A more detailed view was advanced by one of the earliest twentieth-century writers on the subject, MacCulloch,[6] who saw its development reflecting the evolution of the Celts from primitive hunters to tillers of the soil. Nature spirits evolved into vegetation (trees/groves), earth, and fertility deities. Animals that had been hunted for human survival were given a cult, their hunters in effect "apologizing" for the slaughter. With settlement and the domestication of animals, war became an intrinsic part of Celtic life; war-gods emerged, and deities came to be recognizable by gender: Earth was the fruitful mother, vegetation and corn spirits were female, while the Celtic migration and expansion in Europe contributed to the evolution of war-gods. This definition of deities by gender was fluid, however, and an earth-god might replace the earth mother, or stand as her consort, while female war divinities also emerged with Celtic tribal expansion. Contact with Rome meant the development of a hierarchy, but, according to MacCulloch, Celtic religion never completely lost its primitive associations with the earth spirits.[7]

A similar view of the evolution of Celtic religion as tied to socio-cultural change has been presented by the present writer: Primitive chthonic and weather-gods, as also found in ancient civilizations such as the Egyptians, Mesopotamians, Hittites, and Persians, gave up preeminence to deities of nature, war, fertility, and then healing.[8] A growing sophistication and contact with the cultures of the Mediterranean – notably the Greeks, Etruscans, and Romans – led to anthropomorphism to some extent, which reached its full form only with the Roman conquest of Gaul by Caesar in the first century BCE. Although some aspects remained the same, others changed with the times: Nature spirits still existed in the air, the earth, in watery contexts, and as animals or birds, whereas the intensification of the

---

[5] Cunliffe, *Ancient Celts*, 184; see also Green, *Celts*, 39, for a similar view.
[6] MacCulloch, *Religion*, 3–4.
[7] Ibid.
[8] Watts, *Religion*, 59–60, 116–17.

Celtic Religion in Western and Central Europe 367

healing attributes of deities such as Sulis and Belisama may have reflected the conflating by the Romans of these goddesses with the Roman Minerva (Medica). By themselves the Celts did not take the further step of creating salvation cults; these were to come later from the East, Greece and Rome, the most influential being Christianity. Life was controlled by the gods, and propitiation was necessary to ensure favorable outcomes: Rituals, sacrifice, and offerings provided the means.

Given the differing views of the evolution of Celtic religion, it is not surprising that so too do historians adduce different explanations for the origins of Celtic cultic practices, although these are not known. So, for one, Green[9] has proposed that water cults in Central Europe came to prominence around 1200–1100 BCE with wetter conditions as a result of climate change. On another aspect, Ross[10] has written extensively on a "Cult of the Head." She sees evidence for it from France in the stone pillar decorated with human heads at a shrine at Entremont and another with actual skulls at a sanctuary at Roquepertuse. These finds support the view of several classical writers that the Celts saw the head as the location of the soul.[11] From these texts as well as material evidence of "skull" and "decapitated" burials in Britain and Ireland, other interpretations have been advanced,[12] the most detailed being that the practice of decapitated burial, with the relocation of the skull away from its anatomically correct position, represented a Celtic belief in the transmigration of souls; at death the spirit moves on to another person, so death itself is not the end of life, but merely a stage in it.[13]

HISTORICAL CONTEXT

Identifiable Celtic religious practices, sacred places, and burials began to appear in the Middle to Late Bronze Age. In Central Europe, around 1200 BCE, a refinement of the existing Urnfields culture emerged. This culture was given the name Hallstatt from the location of the original discovery in Austria. It was a hierarchical society of small chiefdoms comprising hill forts, hamlets, and isolated farms. Considerable wealth came from the mining of salt, which was widely traded. Iron objects were increasingly brought in during this time, and with them knowledge of iron working;

[9] Green, *Gods*, 3.
[10] Ross, *Pagan Britain*, 94–171.
[11] Diodorus Siculus 5.29; Livy 10.26, 23.24; Strabo 4.4.5 (quoting Posidonius).
[12] Summarized in Watts, *Religion,* 82–3.
[13] Ibid., 74–89. See Strabo 4.4.4; Caesar *B.G.* 6.14; Pomponius Mela 3.2.19; Lucan 1.455–8.

368   *Dorothy Watts*

by the beginning of the period known as Hallstatt C (around 800/700–600 BCE), a fully developed Iron Age civilization was flourishing. Little is known about the religion of early Hallstatt culture, but the discovery in 1846 of around a thousand graves dating from circa 700 BCE gives some insight into burial practices and beliefs of the later Hallstatt period.

It is fairly certain that Celtic languages dominated Central Europe by this time, but Hallstatt cultural influence was much more widespread, extending to Britain, northern Germany, Spain, and northern Italy.[14] By circa 600 BCE the economic and political focus had shifted westward to the region of the upper Rhine, upper Danube, and eastern France. This change was undoubtedly related to the establishment of a Greek settlement at Massilia (Marseille) and the resultant increase in trade in the Rhône valley. Rich barrow burials attest to a wealthy elite, now with trade links to the Mediterranean cultures and an acquired taste for luxuries like wine.

Ritual sites are rare for this time, the best known being a large open air sanctuary at Libenice in the Czech Republic, where the focus was apparently on a standing stone and posts. Further cult practices from the Hallstatt period are difficult to determine, mainly because the distinction between sacred and secular is not clear cut, but the deposition of an everyday object such as a sickle in what might be seen as a sacred place (for example, a swamp, rocky crag, or cave) points to the belief in a connection between the place and a fruitful harvest.[15] The most extensive find of this type is from the Býčí-Skála cave at Blansko, north of Brno. Items included weapons, bronze and pottery vessels, jewelry, tools and implements, and horse and wagon trappings; there were also the remains of at least forty humans and five wagons. While the human remains allow a funerary interpretation for the cave, the wagons and the discovery of burnt grain and a cup made from a human skull suggest cultic practices.[16] It is thought that the cave had been in continuous use as a cult site since the Neolithic.[17] Sacrificial burnt offerings have also been interpreted for remains at Farchant near Garmisch-Partenkirchen, Osterstein in Bavaria, and Dellingen in the Black Forest.[18] At the same time, metalwork as offerings in watery places became more common. Undoubtedly less durable offerings were also made in such locations.

[14] See Menghin, *Hallstattzeit*; Haywood, *Atlas*, 32–3.
[15] Weiss, "Hallstattzeit," 20.
[16] Pare, *Wagons,* 319–21.
[17] Birkhan, *Celts,* 95.
[18] Weiss, "Hallstattzeit," 21.

Celtic Religion in Western and Central Europe 369

Other cults may be suggested, besides those of fertility and water. It is likely that there was a solar cult at least as early as the Urnfields period, and probably much earlier. Solar symbols such as circles and swastikas are found on Hallstatt artifacts; these and representations of the bull are seen by Potrebica[19] as indicating a connection with Greek civilization, and in particular the worship of Apollo, the Greek sun-god. Potrebica also identifies a "cult of heroes" manifested in pairs of burials of warriors with the same status, in which he sees a further link between the Hallstatt and Greek cultures.

The Hallstatt itself was to be subsumed by a still more developed culture, and a more warlike society, as hill-forts became fewer but larger, and warrior kingdoms replaced petty chiefdoms. The influence of the La Tène culture (ca.475–450 BCE), named after a settlement and ritual site on Lake Neuchâtel in Switzerland, was even more widespread than Hallstatt; its features are better known because the region and its inhabitants now came into direct contact with those of the Mediterranean. Celtic mercenaries fought in Hellenistic and Roman armies (e.g., Xen. *Hell.* 7.1.20; Justin 25.2.9), Roman traders were active in Celtic territory (e.g., Cic. *Font.* 33; Caes. *B. Gall.* 7.55), and by the end of the second century BCE proto-towns or *oppida* appeared in the landscape. Classical writers began to be interested in the peoples to the north of the Po, especially as they came to pose a political threat. There was considerable emphasis on their "barbarian" nature, their conflict with the civilizations of Greece and Rome, including the invasion of Rome by the Gauls in 387/386 BCE (Livy 5.35–49), the attack on Delphi in 279/278 (Justin 24.4–8), and the effects of their migration across Europe. Livy (5.33–35) and Caesar (*B. Gall.*1.2-5), both describe the movement of tribes. Caesar is also one of the main sources for information on Celtic religion and religious practices, information that he supposedly gleaned during his campaigns to Britain (55 and 54 BCE) and his conquest of Gaul (58–51 BCE).[20] The religion of the Celts did not disappear with the coming of the Romans into Celtic regions. Because Roman religion was polytheistic, it was well suited to the absorption of further deities, and, apart from the banning of Druidic practices from the time of Augustus and attacks on the Druids themselves in the reign of Nero, Rome did not interfere.

---

[19] Potrebica, "Greek Elements," 29–35.

[20] The value of Caesar as a source on Celtic religion and indeed on Celtic society is much debated. Some of his material, at least, can be contradicted by archaeology; for other information, he is the main or only source.

CELTIC DEITIES

From the early La Tène period (fifth century BCE), and as a result of contact with the cultures of the Mediterranean, Celtic religion had become more visible as deities were increasingly depicted in three-dimensional anthropomorphic form, although their identification as deities in the earliest finds has relied on archaeological context. The native names of some deities came to be known to the Romans and were recorded on Roman inscriptions. This wealth of information demonstrates the diversity and complexity of Celtic religion. There are over three hundred different names recorded only once in about five hundred inscriptions.[21] Some deities were found in several parts of the Celtic world. For example, a Mother goddess was worshipped from Galatia in Anatolia to the British Isles. Lugh ("shining light") was found from Ireland to Spain and France and may have been a fertility god. Epona, a Gallic goddess, patron of horses and having some connection with death and fertility, was found in inscriptions from France to Hungary; she was probably also worshipped in Britain, and had an equivalent in Wales and Ireland. Taranis, the god of thunder, was found in varying forms from Britain to the Balkans. Cernunnus, a horned hunter deity usually associated with a stag and snake or snakes and depicted on the well-known Gundestrup cauldron found in Denmark, was also known in Britain and France. The Deae Matres or triple Mother goddesses who were connected to fertility and childbirth were found at least in Italy, Germany, France, and Britain (*RIB* 88) and in Slovenia. Deities whose names incorporated the Celtic *nemeto* ("sacred grove") or its derivatives were also widely distributed in Britain and France, with outliers in the Iberian peninsula and in Galatia.[22]

In addition to such widespread deities, there were others that were restricted to their particular geographical locations. Sequana was a goddess at the source of the Seine, Clota the goddess of the Clyde, Sinann linked to the Shannon, and Sulis the divinity of the hot springs at Bath. Danuvius was either the god of the Danube, or the river itself. As these rivers played a vital role in the sustaining of life, it is likely that they were revered from very early times.

Although some were undoubtedly older than others,[23] there does not appear to have been a hierarchy of Celtic gods. Nor did the Romans attempt

---

[21] MacCulloch, *Religion*, 24.

[22] Haywood, *Atlas*, 64–5.

[23] It has been proposed by Ross, *Pagan Britain*, 80, that the popularity of gods such as Cernunnus, Lugh, Taranus, Teutates, and Esus may represent a deliberate policy by the Druids to create "national" gods.

Celtic Religion in Western and Central Europe

to create such a hierarchy, although they did in many instances equate and pair Celtic deities with their own – the *interpretatio romana* described by Caesar (*B. Gall.* 6.17) and Tacitus (*Germ.* 43). One of the most primitive deities, the sky- or thunder-god Taranis, was seen as equivalent to Jupiter, chief of the Roman pantheon. He appears in Romano-Celtic art holding not only a thunderbolt, Roman style, but also a wheel or solar disc; he is recorded by the first-century-CE Roman poet Lucan (*Phars.* 1.444–446) among the deities worshipped in Gaul.

Caesar (*B. Gall.* 6.17) claims that Mercury was the god most revered, and although this is not necessarily borne out by epigraphy and archaeology for the Celtic world as a whole, it may be true for Gaul. Many temples to Mercury have been found in the tribal area of the Allobrogi and also numerous bronze statues. Caesar says Mercury's preeminence was due to his being the god of travelers, trade, and money. On the other hand, it could have been Mercury's much more ancient association with agriculture, and thus with fertility, that made him so popular. In continental inscriptions, the god was paired with at least nine other Celtic deities.[24] In Britain almost all known dedications are to Mercury alone, although one inscription includes the emperor's *numen* and the otherwise unrecorded god Andescociuoucus (*RIB* 193).

Other gods that Caesar says the Gauls worshipped included Mars, Apollo, and Minerva. He also says that the Gauls believed that these gods descended from Dis Pater, god of the Underworld and death, probably associated also with regeneration. It is certain that a Mars-type war-god had an important place in the Celtic pantheon, given the early evidence of weapon deposition in what were presumably sacred places. Mention has already been made of such finds in the Late Hallstatt period, and the practice continued. In Switzerland, the great deposit of weapons and shields at La Tène, by Lake Neuchâtel, signaled a new, more warlike Celtic culture in the fifth century BCE; at Llyn Cerrig Bach, in Wales, there was a similar accumulation of metalwork, including weapons and chariot fittings, dated from about 500 BCE to after 120 CE; in England, two fine La Tène bronze shields were recovered, one from the River Witham dated to the second century BCE, the other from the Thames attributed to the first century CE. It has been observed that, at least in Switzerland in the La Tène period, votive offerings from or relating to females are virtually nonexistent.[25] That seems also to be the case in the many later Romano-Celtic inscriptions that

---

[24] Maier, *Dictionary*, 193.
[25] Müller, Lüscher, *Kelten*, 146.

link Mars with war deities. In Britain, for example, of eighty-eight known dedications to Mars or to Mars paired with one of over a dozen Celtic gods, one only (*RIB* 213) is by a woman.

In contrast Apollo, in the Greco-Roman pantheon, was associated with a sun cult, as well as being a god of flocks, of the arts, and of medicine and healing (the father of Aesculapius and grandfather of Hygieia). The Celts also had gods of health and healing, and it was this attribute of Apollo that apparently led to the pairing with at least ten different Celtic deities. In France evidence for the god is often found at healing springs. In Britain there are inscriptions to Apollo-Maponus, Apollo-Grannus, and Apollo-Cunomaglos. A further Celtic healing-god, Nodens, is attested in Ireland and Britain and another, Lenus, in Britain and France. Curiously, they are both equated with Mars, but it has been shown that, in the Roman period (after 50 BCE), Mars came to lose his martial attributes, and he too became a healer, especially in Gaul: There was a major healing cult of Lenus-Mars at Trier.[26]

Caesar's inclusion of Minerva among the gods most worshipped by the Celts (*B. Gall.* 6.17) is somewhat surprising, as there is little obvious archaeological evidence for her cult. A patron of crafts and industry, Minerva or a Minerva-type deity may have been the focus of devotion by Celtic women occupied in spinning and weaving. As Minerva Medica she was also associated by the Romans with the art of healing, which would explain her being linked with the Celtic goddess at Bath, and also explain the depositions of votive items associated with women in the hot springs.[27] At St Lizier, in Gaul, Minerva was linked to the Celtic Belisama, and the name of this goddess has echoes in various place names in modern France.[28] Belisama may have been the same as the Irish Brigit, herself a goddess of knowledge.[29] A recent inscription from Baldock, in England, has revealed a hitherto unknown deity, Senua, also believed to be equated with Minerva.[30]

Other Celtic deities, known by name but not linked with those of Rome, abound, and the names of still others are unknown. Some were seen as anthropomorphic, others were revered in animal form as the Celts believed that gods could change their shape. Not all creatures may have

[26] Green, *Gods,* 158.
[27] Objects such as hair- and dress-pins, items of jewelry and, significantly, a pair of miniature carved ivory breasts – a reminder that women's complaints such as cancer of the breast and mastitis had a long history.
[28] Maier, *Dictionary,* 35.
[29] MacCulloch, *Religion,* 68.
[30] Kennedy, "Senua."

Celtic Religion in Western and Central Europe

been deities, but rather were attributes of a deity, or tribal totems. There are few, if any, certain examples of animals as gods. In Irish myth, the sacred salmon in the Finn saga may have been a manifestation of Nodens. At Langres in France, a Celtic boar-god, possibly Moccus ("swine"), is thought to be associated with a fertility cult as there was an ancient European rite of mixing the flesh of these animals with grain and then burying it to ensure a successful harvest; and a stylized boar is depicted on the bronze shield found in the River Witham in Essex. The bull was revered in the religions of many ancient civilizations, from the cultures of the Indus Valley, Middle East, Crete, and Mycenaean Greece. It represented strength, virility, and fertility. From France there are two depictions linking a bull with three birds: Tarvos Trigaranus ("bull with three cranes") is found on a relief from Paris[31] and another from Trier. Such triplism is a feature of Celtic religion, for example, triple *Genii loci*, Matres, and human heads, and many bronze figurines of bulls with three horns have come from France. However, the significance of the Gallic bull with three cranes and their association with a known god, Esus, is unknown. It seems to be part of a long tradition. Bulls and marsh birds appeared on zoomorphic wagon fittings, probably attached to cult objects, from as early as the Urnfields period.[32]

Julius Caesar's conquest of Gaul meant the effective end of the Celtic religion as a force in itself in the West. The *interpretatio romana* was a one-sided affair, as Celtic deities were seen as equating to Roman ones, and given Roman names and attributes, with few escaping this Romanizing tendency. Even that most Celtic of gods, the torque-wearing, stag-horned Cernunnus, was transformed into a Roman deity by the first century CE. It is likely that the bronze deity found in Bouray-sur-Juine, a truncated figure with Roman hair style and eye of glass, is a Romano-Celtic representation of the god: The torque, the cross-legged pose, and the cloven hoofs are all that remain of a once fantastic hybrid creature. By the reign of the emperor Tiberius, Cernunnus and two other Celtic deities, Esus and Smer[trius], sit in the company of the classical Castor and Pollux on the Pilier des Nautes (*Nautae Parisiaci*), a monument found under Nôtre Dame in Paris and recently restored.[33] Only in the outposts of Empire, such as in Britain, does it seem that devotion to the native gods survived and held greater importance for the native population. At the classical temple of Minerva-

---

[31] *Le Pilier des Nautes*: see below.
[32] Pare, *Wagons*, 28, 42.
[33] Saragoza, "Pilier," 15–27.

374   Dorothy Watts

Sulis in Bath, for instance, most of the *defixiones* or curse tablets dedicated to the goddess are to Sulis, and others to Sulis-Minerva or Minerva-Sulis. There are none to Minerva alone.[34] The inscriptions date from the late-second to the fourth century CE, an indication that even after centuries of Romanization the Celtic deities in Britain retained some hold over the native population.

DRUIDS

Loss of knowledge of the ancient native cults was the result not only of the dominance by the Romans, but also of their breaking down, if not eliminating, the aristocratic priestly group who held such knowledge, the Druids. According to Pliny (*HN* 16.95) the term "Druid" had connections with the Greek δρῦς ("oak"), while some modern scholars see the word as having a Celtic root *dru* meaning "wise man."[35] Either interpretation would be acceptable, as the oak was regarded by the Celts as the most sacred of all trees, and the Druids were the repositories of all tribal knowledge. They were often close relatives of the tribal chieftains, but, more significantly, it was they who had the knowledge of tribal history, law and lore (including the Celtic calendar), religion and ritual, all of which they had committed to memory. Caesar (*B. Gall.* 6.13–16) tells us much of what we know of them, and this is supplemented by other Greek or Roman authors, especially those quoting the lost account of Posidonius.[36] Virtually nothing can be gleaned from archaeology, and what is known from the classical sources relates to Gaul and Britain only. The Irish legends provide fairly similar information.

Caesar says it was thought that the Druids came to Gaul from Britain, although the Elder Pliny (*HN* 30.4) thinks the reverse was true. Whatever their origins, every year they held an assembly at a sacred site in the tribal territory of the Canutes in Gaul. Here they settled disputes and elected their leader, the archdruid who had himself gone through the long twenty-year process of training from Bard to Seer to Priest. They prophesied, acted as overseers of religious observances and sacrifices, and carried out augury and divination; they were teachers of the aristocratic youths of the tribe, instructing them in astronomy, science (including medicine), and religion.

---

[34] Tomlin, *Tabellae Sulis*.
[35] See Chadwick, *Druids*, 12–13.
[36] See Tierney, "Posidonius," 189–275.

Celtic Religion in Western and Central Europe   375

They were also said to be advisors to the kings and, in Ireland at least, accompanied them on campaign.

Such men[37] had immense power within the tribe and were rightly seen by the Romans as a rallying point for anti-Roman sentiment. Caesar would have been well aware of Druidic power during his long campaign in Gaul. It was probably this political motive, as well as the "horrible and savage cults of the Druids" (Suet. *Claud.* 25), which led the emperor Augustus to prohibit any Roman citizen from taking part in Druidic cults – a move that suggests that some Roman citizens had, indeed, been attracted to them. Augustus's successor, Tiberius, supposedly banned the Druids themselves (Pliny *HN* 30.4), but this ban seems to have been ineffective because they were still there when Claudius became emperor in 41 CE. Claudius legislated to ban Druidic practices. It is quite clear from events that soon followed that banning human blood sacrifices could not be done without bloodshed: In the reign of Nero, the governor of Britain, Suetonius Paulinus, declared war on the Druids and drove many of them onto the island of Anglesey, where they were massacred (Tac. *Ann.* 14.29–30).

Roman law and Roman legions did not, however, cause the disappearance of the Druids in either Britain or Gaul, although the most abhorrent of their practices would eventually have ceased. Pliny, who died in 79 CE, says that in his time Druids were numerous in Britain and that they still practiced human sacrifice (*HN* 30.3). It is very likely that they ultimately became respected members of society, acting as priests for the Romano-Celtic cults and temples that sprang up under Roman rule. They were probably still called Druids. Certainly some of the ancient writers thought so. Sources from the second, third, and fourth centuries CE mention them in Gaul as prophets and magicians, and as associated with temples.[38]

RITUALS

While evidence for Druidic rituals is confined mainly to the literary sources, it is almost certain that, as the guardians and leaders of the Celtic religion, the Druids had a role in those rituals that have been revealed by archaeology: for example, at Ribemont-sur-Ancre where, along with the remains of animals apparently sacrificed, were those of at least a thousand humans aged from fifteen to forty years old. Their bodies had been

---

[37] Druidesses are also mentioned by the ancient sources, but their training and roles are unknown. See Chadwick, *Druids*, 78–83; Ross, *Druids*, 17, believes that they had the same training as men.

[38] Clem. Al. *Strom.* 1.15.17; Hippolytus *Phil.* 1.25; Lampridus *Alex. Sev.* 59.5; Vopiscus *Numer.* 14; Auson. *Prof. Burd.* 4.7–10, 10.20–30.

decapitated or dismembered, and carefully stacked. Lindow Man, the "bog man" found in Cheshire, had been the victim of a "triple death" by being bludgeoned and garrotted, and then having his throat cut. The victim has been thought to be from the upper classes of Celtic society, and his murder may have been ordered by the Druids to appease the gods, or to prevent an imminent catastrophe. Two further "bog men" recently found in Ireland have been thought to be offerings to the gods for fertility or good harvest.[39] Caesar tells us that the Druids presided over human sacrifice (*B. Gall.* 6.16).

The ritual dress and paraphernalia found in various parts also give a little insight into priestly activities. The headdresses and scepters from Hockwold and Wanborough were found at the site of Romano-British temples; and similar objects as well as crowns and rattles have been found elsewhere in Britain.[40] They were probably part of priestly accoutrements during rites held on important festivals in the Celtic and later Roman calendars. Ross describes a Druid in Ireland wearing a bull's hide and the headdress of a white speckled bird with fluttering wings.[41] Some sympathetic magic may have been involved here.

What the actual rituals were, and their relationship to the conceptualizing of deity, is somewhat difficult to determine. The sacrifice of animals and humans was a custom from distant prehistoric times, its purpose seemingly to achieve favorable outcome in respect to weather or harvest or fertility, to prevent a calamity, to ensure survival, to appease the gods for perceived wrongdoing, or to allow the examination of the entrails of the victim in order to prophesize future events. Examples of many of these are known from literary works: Agamemnon's sacrifice of his daughter Iphigenia to obtain propitious winds for his journey to Troy is one of the most dramatic events of the Trojan War. Here the offering of a virgin is to the virgin goddess Artemis (Aesch. *Ag.* 198–217). In Livy (8.6), animal sacrifices during the war with the Latins in the fourth century BCE were to the gods of the Underworld and to Mother Earth – such sacrifices were to ensure military victory. That these gods were also associated with regeneration and fertility attests to the antiquity of live sacrifice – human or animal.

Even from Rome as late as the year 216 BCE, there was a report of the suicide of one Vestal Virgin and the burial alive of another, supposedly for

---

[39] Owen, "Bog Man."
[40] Green, *World of the Druids,* 60–3.
[41] Ross, *Pagan Britain,* 83.

Celtic Religion in Western and Central Europe

unchastity (Plut. *Fab. Max.* 18). This kind of propitiation was most likely directed to Vesta, goddess of the hearth, to whom the lives of Vestals were dedicated. Livy (22.57) tells the same story, and also that two Greeks and two Gauls were buried alive in the Forum Boarium after the defeat of the legions in the battle at Cannae in the same year. At the time, this was the greatest defeat that Rome had ever suffered, and it is probably significant that Gauls and Greeks had fought with Hannibal in the struggle with Rome. In both these cases there is an element of punishment along with appeasement of the gods.[42]

This same concept was found among the Celts. Caesar (*B. Gall.* 6.16), in his discussion on the practice of human sacrifice, relates that the Druids offer one human, usually a criminal, to save another, in order to "propitiate the god's wrath." The punishment motive is again obvious; but Caesar goes on to say that if there are no criminals available, an innocent man will do. The discovery in Linz, Austria, of a large pit with evidence of human sacrifice by immolation has given scholars cause to believe this represents the type of mass human sacrifice described by both Caesar (ibid.) and Strabo (4.4.5),[43] where a huge wicker figure was stuffed with victims and burnt. It was observed that most of the victims appear to have had physical deformities. This would appear to confirm that sacrifice of the weak or wounded was an acceptable practice in times of stress.[44] A similar account of a sacrificial pyre is given by Diodorus Siculus (5.32), who says that the victims were offered to honor the gods. Neither source says which gods are to be honored, but the Berne *scholia* of the fourth and eighth/ninth century on the work of Lucan, a poet of the first century CE, say that these types of sacrifices were to Taranis. Lucan (*Phars.* 1.444–446) does write of human sacrifice to Taranis, and also to Teutates and Esus. Taranis has been mentioned earlier as an ancient thunder- or sky-god; and Teutates was probably equated with Mars and thus a war- or even a fertility-god – there is a Mars-Toutatis in Britain (*RIB* 219); of Esus little is known, except that he is depicted on the Pilier des Nautes and the relief from Trier as a woodman pruning or cutting down a tree, and that the Romans may have seen him as Mercury or Mars. The connection between human sacrifice and these deities is not immediately clear, although fertility may be the common thread; and in both cases Esus is associated with the Tarvos Trigaranus, the "bull with three cranes."

---

[42] Pliny, *HN* 30.3, says that the Roman Senate banned the practice of human sacrifice in 97 BCE and that it ceased in public, and for some time altogether.

[43] Both probably drawing on Posidonius.

[44] Birkhan, *Celts,* 96. See also Diodorus 22.9. The assumption here is that people who were physically less than perfect were also appropriate sacrificial victims.

378   Dorothy Watts

Live offerings were not the only type made to the gods. Much more common were offerings found in the ground, or in shafts or underground caves. These can readily be identified as offerings to fertility deities, especially the Earth Mother, and also the gods of the Underworld, as a pit or shaft was seen as the entrance to the Underworld. Among the most spectacular ritual shafts excavated thus far were those from the Vendée region in France. More than thirty were found in an area of about four square kilometers, dating to the first century BCE. One of these was more than twelve meters deep, and divided by stone layers into four compartments, each with distinctive deposits such as animal bones, charcoal, and pottery. The lowest level contained antlers and, at the very bottom, a statuette of a seated female figure. Another pit held a four-meter-high cypress tree. Three similar shafts were discovered at Holzhausen in Bavaria, one almost forty meters deep, and one holding a wooden pole. Shafts such as these have a history going back to the Bronze Age, one example from Hampshire in Britain containing a post dated to circa 1000 BCE.[45]

The practice continued into the Roman period, at least in the western provinces. At Newstead, in southern Scotland, a series of pits, wells, and shafts from early Roman date and excavated almost a century ago contained material that is believed to have ritual significance.[46] More certainly so was another group of nine pits from Cambridge dating to the late third and early fourth century CE, each holding the articulated remains of a dog, and either one or two wickerwork baskets containing an infant; in several of the shafts there was also a pair of shoes, quite obviously too large for the child. The shafts were aligned with what has been identified as an earlier first-century shrine with deposits such as a dog and a bull's head.[47] Given the ritual nature of the site, a dedication to a fertility deity is hard to dismiss.

But not all offerings were so directed. Health and healing were as important in Celtic religion as they were in other religions in the Mediterranean and the Near East, and numerous shrines to healing deities are found across the Celtic lands. Watery sites seemed to be especially associated with such deities, particularly when curative springs were involved – one of the best known being that at Bath, at the temple of Sulis-Minerva. The source of rivers was important to the ancients: The Younger Pliny (*Ep.* 8.8) writes with gentle irony of the reverence afforded the source of the

---

[45] Cunliffe, *Celtic World*, 92–4.
[46] Ross and Feacham, *"Ritual Rubbish,"* 229–37.
[47] Anon., "Cambridge Shrine."

Celtic Religion in Western and Central Europe

Clitumnus in Italy, and the shrine at the source of the Seine near Dijon is still a place of peace and reflection for visitors. Many ex-votos, especially in oak wood, have been found at such sites, perhaps representing the goddess herself (for these deities were mainly female). Other items might be identified with the donor, such as hair or dress pins; and still others from the Romano-Celtic period represented the part of the body which required healing (Greg. Tours *Vita Patr.* c.6). Model legs, arms, eyes, genitalia, and even model breasts attest the types of treatments sought. At Lydney, in Gloucestershire, a water shrine dedicated to Nodens yielded a model hand with concave fingernails, a condition known as koilonychia, the result of iron deficiency. Close by was an iron-rich spring, and it has been proposed that drinking the water in small quantities would have improved the red blood cell count.[48]

Offerings to deities might be made at other places that are not now immediately recognizable as sacred. For example, a huge Late Iron Age hoard, mainly of coins of the Corieltauvi tribe, has recently been reported from Market Harborough in Britain. It included not only over three thousand gold and silver coins but also a silver-gilt clad iron cavalry helmet and was found in fifteen separate caches buried near the entrance of what has been interpreted as a sacred enclosure on a hilltop.[49] The entrance was of great importance in a Celtic shrine.[50] This site is similar to the *Viereckschanzen* often found in Germany and parts of France, rectangular enclosures that sometimes included votive shafts. However, treasure could also be hidden in water. In Gaul, the Roman general Caepio is said to have looted 15,000 talents of gold[51] from sacred enclosures and lakes at Toulouse. When the Romans completed the conquest of Gaul, such lakes and their contents were sold off to the highest bidder (Strab. 4.1.13).

SHRINES AND TEMPLES

Buildings specifically constructed as temples or shrines were often similarly used as repositories of great wealth. Diodorus Siculus (5.27) says, "In temples and sanctuaries throughout the country (Gaul), large amounts of gold are openly displayed as dedications to the gods. No one dares to touch these sacred depositions." They were also where the spoils of war

---

[48] Wells, "Human Burials," 135–202.
[49] Priest et al., "Gold," 358–60.
[50] Brunaux, *Celtic Gauls,* 27.
[51] The figure varies in the ancient sources, but that of Posidonius is probably closest to reality.

were displayed as offerings to the gods (Livy 23.24). But sometimes the "treasure" had little intrinsic worth: At Witham, in Essex, a Late Iron Age ritual site with a modest deposit of Palaeolithic hand axes was probably dedicated to the Celtic sky/thunder deity of a Taranis type.[52]

There were both elaborate and simple shrines and sanctuaries throughout the Celtic world. Close to the Mediterranean, shrines were built with stone columns and adorned with sculptured cult figures. In Central Europe and in Britain, most were fairly basic rectangular timber structures. With the Roman conquest, they lost their wholly native identity, as Romans saw the gods to be similar or identical to their own. There was a change in the type of shrine built as the Romano-Celtic temple emerged; the greatest concentration of these was in Britain, France, around the Moselle, and in Switzerland.[53] The adoption of stone foundations, then stone structures, for the most common "square-within-a-square" buildings was confirmation of Roman influence; in France particularly large temples of this style are known – impressive remains still stand at Autun and Périgueux.[54] However, by the third century CE there was a decline in these structures, as Roman culture came to dominate Gaul.[55] In Britain, the decline was not as great; even in the Christian fourth century, temples continued to be used and others to be refurbished.[56]

Variations on the concentric squares plan occurred, especially as round or polygonal temples, and there were many more simple single-celled buildings, some of which will not have been recognized as having a religious function. A notable feature was that temples were often erected over earlier sacred buildings or sites. In France, a sanctuary near a spring at Gournay-sur-Aronde saw cult buildings built and rebuilt over a period of eight centuries.[57] In Britain, the circular Romano-Celtic temple at Hayling Island was erected over the remains of a circular Iron Age shrine, and the temple at Maiden Castle directly over a site that had not had obvious cult activity for two to three hundred years.[58] The focus at Uley may have been a sacred tree, a standing stone, or post in the shrine that preceded a Romano-Celtic building. Uley also appears to have had a Christian phase from the fifth to the seventh century CE.[59] Thus the

[52] Green, "Religion," 255–57.
[53] Lewis, *Temples*, 9.
[54] King, "Romano-Celtic Religion," 220–41.
[55] Horne, "Temples," 1–6.
[56] Watts, *Religion*, fig. 4.
[57] Brunaux, *Celtic Gauls*, 13–16.
[58] Drury, "Religious Buildings," 48, 64, 68.
[59] Woodward and Leach, *Uley*.

"tradition of sanctity"[60] lived on – of twelve Romano-British temples that had Iron Age origins, religious activity in at least ten continued beyond the Roman occupation.[61]

BURIALS

A similar continuity did not apply to burials through the period of identifiable Celtic culture. Funerary practices changed according to fashion and outside influences, and frequently no one method was preferred to the exclusion of others. In fact, Pausanias (10.21) says that the Gauls did not care whether their warriors killed in battle were buried or not, because they had "no natural pity for the dead." This may have been a general attitude and would fit well with a belief in the indestructibility of the soul. It is unfortunate that a comparative study of burials across the Celtic world is not possible, owing to deficiencies in archaeological records at present. There are several reasons for this. The first is that burial in the Iron Age in Europe was not necessarily organized on a community basis, and thus cemeteries or designated burial grounds were not the norm. The alternative to a communal burying place was discrete single burials in caves, pits, rivers, or convenient hollows in the ground. If the remains of a person were not placed in some kind of container such as a coffin or, in the case of cremation, a vessel, they would in time become archaeologically invisible. Moreover, those spectacular but statistically few burials involving mounds, wagons, chariots, and treasure that are mentioned by most modern writers on the Celts have tended to reduce interest in the graves of the majority, which, because of an absence of wealthy grave goods, have received scant attention in any publications.

Methods of disposal of the dead could be by inhumation, cremation, or excarnation. If cremation or excarnation was practiced, it depended on the customs of a community whether the remains were then gathered up and given some formal burial. However, it is difficult to determine, even when burial does take place, whether any beliefs in an afterlife are present in the minds of those interring the remains. It is only with the addition of grave goods/furniture that such beliefs can be presumed. Even then there can be traps for the anthropologist or social historian: Ucko[62] warns of the dangers of such an assumption among, for instance, certain tribes in

---

[60] Lewis, *Temples*, 50.
[61] Watts, *Religion*, fig. 6.
[62] Ucko, "Ethnography," 262–77.

Africa, where a buried object representing a living person's soul was kept in the grave to prevent that person from dying (the Nankanse of Ghana), or where the object merely indicated the status or occupation of the deceased (the Lugbara of Uganda). It is with such problems in mind that Celtic burial practices should be approached.

The burial material from the Late Hallstatt period (ca.650–450 BCE) does not present a coherent picture. In the major cemetery at Hallstatt itself, about 55 percent were inhumations, and the remainder cremations. Inhumations were accorded careful burial in stone-lined graves. Grave furnishings including food suggest a belief in an afterlife where material possessions and sustenance were important. In Switzerland, the Helveti people of the Late Hallstatt period were also well organized, with regular cemeteries. Inhumation was practiced, and burial mounds were part of the landscape. There is some evidence that women had social status: At Subingen the burial mounds of women were exceptionally high; and at Ins there was an elite cemetery with two wagon burials, both male, and females with gold jewelry. Changes occurred in the La Tène period. Mounds were rare, and grave goods tended to decrease in number and quality, although the occasional rich burial – weapons for males, jewelry for women – was still found. There was a move from inhumation to cremation, undoubtedly owing to Roman influence.[63] Evidence from a group of burials in central Belgium differs yet again. In these cemeteries there was a long-standing practice of cremation, from Hallstatt B to La Tène (ca.700–400 BCE), but the grave furniture was poor in comparison with other parts of Europe.[64]

Some very wealthy burials have come from Late Hallstatt Europe, particularly barrows containing four-wheeled vehicles. Two of the best known examples are the tomb at the hill fort of Mont Lassois in France of a woman known as "the Lady of Vix," whose grave furniture included a dismantled four-wheeled vehicle and a 1.64 meter bronze *krater* decorated in archaic Greek style, and a similarly rich male burial at Hochdorf ("the Hochdorf Prince") about ten kilometers from the Hohenasperg hillfort, near Stuttgart. Wagon burials, which had begun in the Urnfields period, are a feature of the Late Hallstatt, and almost 250 have been found in Central Europe extending from the Loire Valley to Hungary.[65]

They were replaced by two-wheeled "chariot" or "cart" burials as society became more warlike. Introduced in Europe in the Late Hallstatt, the

---

[63] Müller and Lüscher, *Kelten.*
[64] Guillaume, "Nécropoles."
[65] Pare, *Wagons,* I, 7–II, 231–3, 247–9.

Celtic Religion in Western and Central Europe 383

practice seems to have arrived in La Tène Britain a century later. Around twenty chariot burials have been discovered, mostly in Yorkshire near the village of Arras, but one or possibly two in Scotland.[66] East Yorkshire was the location of the Parisi tribe, and it is supposed that these were descendants of members of the Gallic tribe who had migrated to Britain, bringing with them burial customs from the continent. Three of the chariot burials were known to be of women, indicating the status of at least some Iron Age women in Britain. Occasional prestige grave goods and weapons were found, and frequently a joint of a pig was placed on the body. Other "warrior"-type burials in the same general area yielded just one or two items of military equipment, but some were found with several weapons apparently thrust into the grave after the bodies had been interred. These "speared corpse" burials were in other respects similar to the rest of the cemetery population; the strange ritual cannot be satisfactorily explained.[67]

Most of the "Arras" chariot burials are from the Middle La Tène period. The one from Ferrybridge in West Yorkshire may be earlier and is thought to be similar in many respects to La Tène chariot burials in northeastern France, or even to some Late Hallstatt examples in Switzerland. It differed from those of East Yorkshire in that the chariot had not been dismantled and that, some five hundred years after the original burial, the bones of about three hundred cattle were piled into the ditch around the mound, apparently the remains of commemorative feasting.[68] The find gives a rare insight into burial practices of the Celtic elite for the period in Britain, and the spread of La Tène culture.

Grave goods of such elites have been mentioned in general terms. They might include furniture, weapons, large vessels for holding wine, cups for drinking wine, pottery dishes and platters, and items of personal adornment and toilet equipment, as found in many archaeological contexts. Such wealth must have been needed in an afterlife. Caesar (*B. Gall.* 6.19) says that the Celts so believed in a material Otherworld that they had all their possessions thrown into the funerary fire, in order to have the use of them in the afterlife; and Diodorus Siculus (5.28) embellishes this story by saying that some cast letters into the fire for the dead to read them – an unlikely tale as the Celts were mostly illiterate. There was, however, a widespread view among the ancient writers that the Celts believed in the immortality of the soul and its metempsychosis.

---

[66] A possible chariot burial in Moray, noted but dismissed as unlikely by Greenwell, "Iron Age," 290–1, might be added to the discovery at Newbridge.

[67] Stead, *Cemeteries*, 29–122.

[68] Boyle, "Riding."

384   *Dorothy Watts*

Such belief must have transferred to the ordinary folk, about whom generally very little is known. However, an analysis of the grave goods in pre-Roman Britain shows that, as contact with Rome increased, imported items like pottery were the prestige pieces. Apart from the dress brooch or pin that presumably held the burial clothes together, the most common grave goods were cooking pots and animal bones, especially pig, and sheep or goat.[69] It seems that these burials of the lower class reflected in their own way the practices of their social superiors and, presumably, also their beliefs.

With the coming of Rome, Celtic burial changed as did all aspects of Celtic religion. Cremation became the usual form of disposal of the dead in dedicated cemeteries outside of town limits and flanking main roads into the towns. Grave goods, particularly imported items, had less status and declined in number and value; and prestige burials in cemeteries were marked by Roman-style mausolea. Ireland alone avoided direct influence; once again geography had an effect on Celtic religious practice. Any exotic grave goods there are seen to be indicative of the burials of foreigners.[70]

CONCLUSION

The transformation of Celtic to Roman religion was thus almost complete by the end of the first century CE. Druids lost their exalted status; rituals involving human sacrifice and head-hunting gradually disappeared; gods were given a Roman identity and form; emperors were worshipped instead of trees; new hybrid temples marked old sacred places; and the Celtic dead shared their final resting place with legionaries, magistrates, and other Roman citizens. Pockets of resistance to Roman religious dominance remained only in the more distant areas where Celtic peoples retained remnants of their old culture and religion, such as the Cisalpine region of northern Italy in the Val de Non, and in Normandy and the Loire and Seine valleys in northern Gaul. But these Celts, like those in Ireland, would find that remote geographic location, up till now sufficient to resist the force of Rome, could not isolate them from the spread of Christianity and the conversion of Europe.

BIBLIOGRAPHY

Anon. "The Cambridge Shrine." *Current Archaeology* 61 (1978): 58–60.
Birkhan, Helmut. *Celts: Images of their Culture.* German-English ed. (Vienna, 1999).

[69] Watts, *Boudicca,* 19–20.
[70] Raftery, *Pagan Ireland,* 189.

Boyle, Angela. "Riding into History." *British Archaeology* 76 (2004): 22–7.

Brunaux, Jean L. *The Celtic Gauls: Gods, Rites and Sanctuaries*, trans. Daphne Nash (London, 1988).

Carr, Gillian, and Simon K. F. Stoddart. *Celts from Antiquity* (Cambridge, 2002).

Chadwick, Nora K. *The Druids*. 2nd ed. (Cardiff, 1997).

Collis, John. *The Celts: Origins, Myths and Reinventions* (Stroud, 2003).

Cunliffe, Barry W. *The Celtic World* (London, 1979).

The Ancient Celts (Oxford, 1997).

Derks, T. *Gods, Temples and Ritual Practices. The Transformation of Religious Ideas and Values in Roman Gaul* (Amsterdam, 1998).

Drury, Paul J. "Non-classical Religious Buildings in Iron Age and Roman Britain: A Review." In *Temples, Churches and Religion in Roman Britain*, ed. Warwick Rodwell (Oxford, 1980): 45–78.

Green, Miranda J. *The Gods of the Celts* (Stroud, 1986).

Exploring the World of the Druids (London, 1997).

"Religion and Deities." In *Excavations of an Iron Age Settlement and Roman Religion Complex at Ivy Chimneys, Witham, Essex 1978–83*. East Anglian Archaeology Report 88, ed. Robin Turner (Chelmsford, 1999): 255–7.

Greenwell, William. "Early Iron Age Burials in Yorkshire." *Archaeologia* 60 (1906): 251–324.

Guillaume, Alain. "Les Nécropoles hallstattiennes de Wallonie (Belgique): Donneés Rituelles." In *The Iron Age in Europe*, Acts of XIVth UISPP Congress, University of Liège, Belgium, 2–8 September 2001 (Oxford, 2005): 9–24.

Haywood, John. *The Historical Atlas of the Celtic World* (London, 2001).

Horne, Peter D. "Romano-Celtic Temples in the Third Century." In *The Roman West in the Third Century*, ed. Anthony King and Martin Henig (Oxford, 1981): 21–6.

James, Simon. *The Atlantic Celts: Ancient People or Modern Invention?* (Madison, Wis., 1999).

Kennedy, Maev. "Senua, Britain's Unknown Goddess Unearthed." *The Guardian*, 1 September 2003.

King, Anthony. "The Emergence of Romano-Celtic Religion." In *The Early Roman Empire in the West*, ed. Anthony King and Martin Henig (Oxford, 1990): 220–41.

Lewis, Michael J. T. *Temples in Roman Britain* (Cambridge, 1966).

MacCulloch, John A. *The Religion of the Ancient Celts* (Edinburgh, 1911; repr. London, 1991).

Maier, Bernhard. *Dictionary of Celtic Religion and Culture*, trans. C. Edwards (Woodbridge, 1997).

Menghin, Wilfried, ed. *Hallstattzeit: Die Altertümer im Museum für Vor- und Frühgeschichte* (Mainz, 1999).

Müller, Felix, and Geneviève Lüscher. *Die Kelten in der Schweiz* (Stuttgart, 2004).

Owen, James. "Murdered 'Bog Man' Found with Hair Gel, Manicured Nails." *National Geographic News*, 17 January 2006.

Pare, Christopher F. E. *Wagons and Wagon Graves of the Early Iron Age in Central Europe* (Oxford, 1992).

Potrebica, Hrvoje. "Greek Elements in the Religious Phenomena of the Eastern Hallstatt Circle." In *The Iron Age in Europe* Acts of XIVth UISPP Congress, University of Liège, Belgium, 2–8 September 2001 (Oxford, 2005): 29–35.

Priest, Vicki, Patrick Clay, and Jeremy D. Hill. "Iron Age Gold from Leicestershire." *Current Archaeology* 188 (2003): 358–60.

Raftery, Barry. *Pagan Celtic Ireland: The Enigma of the Irish Iron Age* (London, 1994).

Ross, Anne. *Pagan Celtic Britain*. Rev. ed. (London, 1992).

——— . *Druids* (Stroud, 1999).

Ross, Anne, and Richard Feacham. "Ritual Rubbish? The Newstead Pits." In *To Illustrate the Monuments*, ed. J. Vincent Megaw (London, 1976): 229–37.

Saragoza, Florence. "Le Pilier des Nautes: Redécouverte d'une Oeuvre." *Archéologia* 398 (2003): 15–27.

Stead, Ian M. *Iron Age Cemeteries in East Yorkshire* (London, 1991).

Tierney, James J. "The Celtic Ethnography of Posidonius." *Proceedings of the Royal Irish Academy* 60 C (1960): 189–275.

Tomlin, Roger S. O. *Tabellae Sulis: Roman Inscribed Tablets of Tin and Lead from the Sacred Spring at Bath* (Oxford, 1988).

Ucko, Peter J. "Ethnography and Archaeological Interpretation of Funerary Remains." *World Archaeology* 1 (1969–70): 262–77.

Watson, Alasdair. *Religious Acculturation and Assimilation in Belgic Gaul and Aquitania from the Roman Conquest until the End of the Second Century CE* (Oxford, 2007).

Watts, Dorothy J. *Religion in Late Roman Britain: Forces of Change* (London, 1998).

——— . *Boudicca's Heirs: Women in Early Britain* (London, 2005).

Weiss, Rainer-Maria. "Die Hallstattzeit in Europa." In *Hallstattzeit: Die Altertümer im Museum für Vor- und Frühgeschichte*, ed. Wilfried Menghin (Mainz, 1999): 7–22.

Wells, Calvin. "The Human Burials." In *Romano-British Cemeteries at Cirencester*, ed. Alan McWhirr, Linda Viner, and Calvin Wells (Cirencester U.K., 1982): 135–202.

Woodward, Ann, and Peter Leach. *The Uley Shrines: Excavation of a Ritual Complex on West Hill, Uley, Gloucestershire: 1977–9* (London, 1993).

SUGGESTIONS FOR FURTHER READING

CHAPTER 1: SUMERIAN RELIGION

The Electronic Text Corpus of Sumerian Literature (http://etcsl.orinst.ox.ac.uk/).
The Diachronic Corpus of Sumerian Literature (http://dcsl.orinst.ox.ac.uk/).

CHAPTER 2: ASSYRIAN AND BABYLONIAN RELIGIONS

Black, J., and A. Green. *Gods, Demons, and Symbols of Ancient Mesopotamia: An Illustrated Dictionary* (Austin, 1992).
Bottero, J. *Mesopotamia: Writing, Reasoning, and the Gods* (Chicago, 1992; originally published 1987).
  Religion in Ancient Mesopotamia, trans. T. L. Fagan (Chicago, 2001).
Jacobsen, T. *The Treasures of Darkness: A History of Mesopotamian Religion* (New Haven, 1976).
Nijhowne, J. *Politics, Religion, and Cylinder Seals: A Study of Mesopotamian Symbolism in the Second Millennium B.C.* (Oxford, 1999).
Wiggerman, F. A. M. *Mesopotamian Protective Spirits: The Ritual Texts* (Groningen, 1992).

CHAPTER 3: HITTITE RELIGION

Beckman, G. "Temple Building among the Hittites." In *From the Foundations to the Crenelations: Essays on Temple Building in the Ancient Near East and Hebrew Bible*, ed. M. J. Boda and J. Novotny (Münster, 2010): 71–89.
Collins, B. J. "Hittite Religion and the West." In *Pax Hethitica: Studies on the Hittites and Their Neighbours in Honour of Itamar Singer*, ed. Y. Cohen, A. Gilan, and J. Miller (Wiesbaden, 2010): 54–66.
Haas, V. *Materia Magica et Medica Hethitica* (Berlin, 2003).
  Hethitische Orakel, Vorzeichen und Abwehrstrategien (Berlin, 2008).
Hoffner, H. A. "The Royal Cult in Hatti." In *Text, Artifact, and Image: Revealing Ancient Israelite Religion*, ed. G. Beckman and T. J. Lewis (Providence, 2006): 132–51.
Strauss, R. *Reinigungsrituale aus Kizzuwatna* (Berlin, 2006).

388   *Suggestions for Further Reading*

Taggar-Cohen, A. *Hittite Priesthood* (Heidelberg, 2006).
Taracha, P. *Religions of Second Millennium Anatolia* (Wiesbaden, 2009).

CHAPTER 4: ZOROASTRIANISM

Briant, P. *From Cyrus to Alexander: A History of the Persian Empire*, trans. P. T. Daniels (Winona Lake, Ind., 2002).
Kellens, J. *Essays on Zarathustra and Zoroastrianism*, trans. and ed. Prods Oktor Skjærvø (Costa Mesa, Calif., 2000).
Kent, R. G. *Old Persian Grammar, Texts, Lexicon.* 2nd rev. ed. (New Haven, 1953).
Shaked, S., trans. *The Wisdom of the Sasanian Sages* (Dēnkard VI) (Boulder, 1979).
Wiesehöfer, J. *Ancient Persia from 550 BC to 650 AD* (London, 1996).
Williams, A. V. *The Pahlavi Rivāyat Accompanying the Dādestān ī Dēnīg.* 2 vols. (Copenhagen, 1990).

CHAPTER 5: SYRO-CANAANITE RELIGIONS

Ahituv, S. *Echoes from the Past: Hebrew and Cognate Inscriptions from the Biblical Period* (Jerusalem, 2008).
Fleming, D. E. *The Installation of Baal's High Priestess at Emar: A Window on Ancient Syrian Religion.* Harvard Semitic Studies 42 (Cambridge, Mass., 1992).
Lipiński, E. *The Aramaeans: Their Ancient History, Culture, Religion.* Orientalia Lovaniensia Analecta 100 (Leuven, 2000).
Smith, M. S., and W. T. Pitard. *The Ugaritic Baal Cycle. Volume II: Introduction with Text, Translation and Commentary of KTU/CAT 1.3–1.4.* Vetus Testamentum Supplement 114 (Leiden, 2008).

CHAPTER 6: ISRAELITE AND JUDEAN RELIGIONS

Alberz, R. *A History of Israelite Religion in the Old Testament Period.* 2 vols. (Louisville, 1994).
Amihai, M. *Archaeology of the Land of the Bible, 10,000–586 B.C.E.* (New York, 1990).
Miller, P. D. *The Religion of Ancient Israel* (Louisville, 2000).
Smith, M. S. *The Origins of Biblical Monotheism: Israel's Polytheistic Background and the Ugaritic Texts* (New York, 2001).
Zevit, Z. *The Religions of Ancient Israel: A Synthesis of Parallactic Approaches* (London, 2001).

CHAPTER 7: EGYPTIAN RELIGION

Allen, J. P., et al. *Religion and Philosophy in Ancient Egypt* (New Haven, 1989).
Englund, G., ed. *The Religion of the Ancient Egyptians: Cognitive Structures and Popular Expressions* (Uppsala, 1989).
Forman, W., and S. Quirke. *Hieroglyphs and the Afterlife in Ancient Egypt* (Norman, Okla., 1996).
Hornung, E. *Conceptions of God in Ancient Egypt: The One and the Many* (Ithaca, 1981).
Meeks, D., and C. Favard-Meeks. *Daily Life of the Egyptian Gods* (Ithaca, 1996).
Tobin, V. A. *Theological Principles of Egyptian Religion* (New York, 1989).

Suggestions for Further Reading

CHAPTER 8: PHOENICIAN-PUNIC RELIGION

Aubet, M. E. *The Phoenician Cemetery of Tyre al-Bass: Excavations 1997–1999*. BAAL Hors Série 1 (Beirut, 2004).

"The Phoenician Cemetery of Tyre." *Near Eastern Archaeology* 73 (2010): 144–55.

Dussaud, R. *Carthage: Approche d'un civilisation* (Tunis, 1993).

López-Ruiz, C. *When the Gods Were Born: Greek Cosmogonies and the Near East* (Cambridge, Mass., 2010).

Markoe, G. E. *Phoenicians. Peoples of the Past* (Berkeley, 2000).

Schmitz, P. C. "Deity and Royalty in Dedicatory Formulae: The Ekron Store-Jar Inscription Viewed in the Light of Judg 7:18, 20 and the Inscribed Gold Medallion from the Douïmès Necropolis at Carthage (*KAI* 73)." *Maarav* 15.2 (2008): 165–73.

CHAPTER 9: MINOAN RELIGION

d'Agata, A. L., and A. van de Moortel. *Archaeologies of Cult*. Hesperia Suppl. 42. American School of Classical Studies (Athens, 2009).

Dickinson, O. T. P. K. "Comments on a Popular Model of Minoan Religion." *OJA* 13 (1994): 173–84.

Goodison, L., and C. Morris. *Ancient Goddesses: The Myths and the Evidence* (London, 1998).

Kyriakidis, E. "Unidentified Objects on Minoan Seals." *AJA* 109 (2005): 137–54.

Laffineur, R., and R. Hägg. *POTNIA. Deities and Religion in the Aegean Bronze Age.* Aegaeum 22 (Liège, 2001).

Marinatos, N. *Minoan Kingship and the Solar Goddess* (Urbana, 2010).

Nissinen, M., ed. *Prophets and Prophecy in the Ancient Near East*. Writings from the Ancient World 12 (Atlanta, 2003).

Renfrew, C. *The Archaeology of Cult: The Sanctuary at Phylakopi* (London, 1985).

CHAPTER 10: MYCENAEAN RELIGION

Chadwick, J. *The Mycenaean World* (Cambridge, 1976).

Laffineur, R., and R. Hägg, eds. *POTNIA. Deities and Religion in the Aegean Bronze Age.* Aegaeum 22 (Liège, 2001).

Palaima, T. G. "Mycenaean Religion." In *The Cambridge Companion to the Aegean Bronze Age*, ed. C. W. Shelmerdine (Cambridge, 2008): 342–61.

CHAPTER 11: ARCHAIC AND CLASSICAL GREEK RELIGION

Bremmer, J. *Greek Religion* (Oxford, 1999; reissue of 1994 ed. with addenda = *G&R*, New Surveys in the Classics 24).

Bremmer, J. N., and A. Erskine, eds. *The Gods of Ancient Greece: Identities and Transformations*. Leventis Studies 5 (Edinburgh, 2010).

Bruit Zaidman, L., and P. Schmitt Pantel. *Religion in the Ancient Greek City* (Cambridge, 1992; French original 1989).

Detienne, M. *Dionysos Slain* (Baltimore, 1979; French original 1977).

Ferguson, J. *Among the Gods: An Archaeological Exploration of Ancient Greek Religion* (London, 1989).

390 *Suggestions for Further Reading*

Gernet, L., and A. Boulanger. *Le génie grec dans la religion* (Paris, 1932).
Graf, F. *Greek Mythology: An Introduction* (Baltimore, 1993; German original 1991).
Harrison, T. *Divinity and History: The Religion of Herodotus* (Oxford, 2000).
Kearns, E. "Order, Interaction, Authority: Ways of Looking at Greek Religion." In *The Greek World*, ed. A. Powell (London, 1995).
Ancient Greek Religion: A Sourcebook (Malden, Mass. 2010).
Kirk, G. S. *The Nature of Greek Myths* (Harmondsworth, 1974).
Lexicon Iconographicum Mythologiae Classicae (= *LIMC*), 8 vols. (Zurich, 1981–1997).
Lupu, E. *Greek Sacred Law. A Collection of New Documents (NGSL)*. Religions in the Graeco-Roman World 152 (Leiden, 2005).
Mikalson, J. D. *Ancient Greek Religion* (Malden, Mass., 2005).
Ogden, D., ed. *A Companion to Greek Religion* (Malden, Mass. 2007).
Parker, R. *Athenian Religion: A History* (Oxford, 1996).
Price, S. *Religions of the Ancient Greeks* (Cambridge, 1999).
Pulleyn, S. *Prayer in Greek Religion* (Oxford, 1997).
Sourvinou-Inwood, C. "Further Aspects of Polis Religion." In *Annali dell'Istituto Universitario Orientale di Napoli (Archeologia e Storia Antica)* 10 (1988): 259–74 (= *Oxford Readings in Greek Religion*, ed. R. Buxton [Oxford, 2000]: 38–55).
Versnel, H. S. *Coping with the Gods: Wayward Readings in Greek Theology* (Leiden, 2011).
ed. *Faith, Hope, and Worship: Aspects of Religious Mentality in the Ancient World* (Leiden, 1981).
Vidal-Naquet, P. *The Black Hunter: Forms of Thought and Forms of Society in the Ancient World* (Baltimore, 1986; French original 1981).
West, M. L. *The East Face of Helicon: West Asiatic Elements in Greek Poetry and Myth* (Oxford, 1999).

CHAPTER 12: ETRUSCAN RELIGION

De Grummond, N. T., and I. Edlund-Berry, eds. *The Archaeology of Sanctuaries and Ritual in Etruria*. JRA Supplementary Series 81 (2011).
De Grummond, N. T., and E. Simon, eds. *The Religion of the Etruscans* (Austin, 2006).
Edlund, I. *The Gods and the Place: Location and Function of Sanctuaries in the Countryside of Etruria and Magna Graecia (700–400 B.C.)* (Stockholm, 1987).
Jannot, J.-R. *Religion in Ancient Etruria* (Madison, Wisc., 2005).
Maras, D. *Il dono votivo, Gli dei e il sacro nelle iscrizioni etrusche di culto* (Pisa, 2009).
Van der Meer, L. Bouke, ed. *Material Aspects of Etruscan Religion* (Leuven, 2010).
Warden, G. P. "The Tomb: The Etruscan Way of Death." In *From the Temple and the Tomb: Etruscan Treasures from Tuscany* (Dallas, 2008): 95–112.

CHAPTER 13: ROMAN RELIGION THROUGH THE EARLY REPUBLIC

Ando, C., ed. *Roman Religion*. Edinburgh Readings on the Ancient World (Edinburgh, 2004).
Bispham, E., and C. Smith, eds. *Religion in Archaic and Republican Rome and Italy: Evidence and Experience* (Edinburgh, 2000).
Orlin, E. *Temples, Religion, and Politics in the Roman Republic* (Leiden, 1997).

Rüpke, J., ed. *A Companion to Roman Religion* (Oxford, 2007).
Scheid, J. *An Introduction to Roman Religion* (Bloomington, 2003).
Schultz, C. *Women's Religious Activity in the Roman Republic* (Chapel Hill, 2006).

CHAPTER 14: CELTIC RELIGION IN WESTERN AND CENTRAL EUROPE

Kruta, V. *Celts: History and Civilization* (London, 2004).
Rankin, D. *Celts in the Classical World* (London, 1996).
Wait, G. A. *Ritual and Religion in Iron Age Britain* (Oxford, 1986).

GENERAL INDEX

Aaron, brother of Moses, first chief priest, 161
at the parting of the Red Sea, 169
see also Israelite and Judean religions
Abraham, patriarch, 155–7
Abram. *See* Abraham, 155, 162
Abu, Syro-Canaanite month, 146
Abu Salabikh, capital of Sumerian city-state, 44, 47
deity list from, 44, 46, 68
Abydos, Egyptian cult center, 182, 190, 192–3, 200
Achaemenes, Persian ancestor of Darius and Cyrus, 103
Achaemenid,
Empire, 103
religion,
gods and goddesses
Ahura Mazdā, 104–22, 124, 126
Ashi, 114, 121
Great God, 121
Humban, 121
KI, the Earth, 121
Mizhdushī, 121
Naryasanga, 121
Spentā Ārmaiti, 107, 121.
See also Humility
ritual, 104
baga-dauçiya, "libation ritual for the god(s)," 121
dauça (dauçiya), "libation service," 121
lan, principal ritual, 121
priests in: *ātru-wakhsha*, priest in charge of fire, 121; *magush*, 121; *shaten*, main priest, 121
see also Zoroastrianism

Acherontic Books, Etruscan books on death and life, 320
Achvizr, male and female Etruscan deity, 319
acrobatics
in Minoan Crete, 248
Acropolis Treasure at Mycenae, 259
acroterion statue of Apollo, 353
Adad, Babylonian weather god, 67–8, 121
Adad-guppi, mother of Babylonian king Nabonidus
tomb inscription of, 59
Adad-nirari II, Assyrian ruler (921–891 BCE), 60
Adad-nirari III, Assyrian ruler, 58
'ădōnāy, "my Lord," 153. *See also* Israelite and Judean religions
Adonis
cult of, 210–115
festival, 211–13, 215
myth, 210
see also Etruscan Atunis, Melqart-Adonis
aedes Vestae, "House of Vesta." *See* Roman religion
Aegean,
religious *koine* of, 246
sea, 239–40
world, 242
Aeschylus, Greek playwright (525–456 BCE),
Agamemnon, 376
Suppliants, 259
Aesculapius, cult of,
at Epidaurus, 13
at Pergamun, 13
see also Asklepios
Afghanistan, 102
afterlife,
in Assyrian and Babylonian religions, 61

393

General Index

afterlife (*cont.*)
 in Celtic religion, 381–4
 in Egyptian religion, 177, 184, 195, 197–202
 in Etruscan religion, 321, 329, 331–2
 in Hittite religion, 96
 in Mycenaean religion, 269
 in Punic religion, 223, 227
 in Syro-Canaanite religion, 145–8
Africa,
 Caelestis, deity of, 5
 North, 7, 19, 24, 181, 205–8, 213, 215, 222
 Punic, 7, 19, 205–8, 222
 Roman, 215
Agade, capital of the Akkadian empire, 38, 39, 50
Agamemnon, Greek hero,
 sacrifice of his daughter Iphigenia, 376
Aglauros, Greek heroine, 295
Agramer Mumienbinden (*liber linteus*),
 Etruscan sacrificial calendar, 348
Agum-kakrime, Kassite ruler, 62
Ahaz, king of Judah, 171
Ahhiyawa, 256, 263, 270
Ahmose, founder of the Egyptian eighteenth dynasty (1550–1525 BCE), 191.
 See also mortuary complex
Ahmose Nefertari, "god's wife," wife of Ahmose, 191
ahu, existences or worlds. *See* Zoroastrianism
Ahuna Vairiya, one of four holy prayers.
 See Zoroastrianism
ahura, Lord/Ruler, 107
Ahura Mazdā (Ahuramazdā) (All-knowing Lord/Ruler), good Zoroastrian deity, 104–22, 124, 126
Airyaman, "heavenly fire," Zoroastrian god of peace and healing, 105, 107–8, 111–12, 114, 118
Airyaman Ishiya, one of four holy prayers.
 See Zoroastrianism
Aita, Etruscan god of the underworld, 331.
 See also Hades
aiviyānghana, girdle. *See* Zoroastrianism coming-of-age ceremonies
Akhenaten ("One who is effective for the Aten"), Egyptian king (1352–1336 BCE), 183, 193–5. *See also* monotheism
Akhetaten ("Horizon of the Aten"), modern Amarna, 194

akītu, Babylonian New Year's Festival, 77.
 See also festivals, religious; Assyrian and Babylonian religions
Akkad, area in northern Mesopotamia, 36, 38
Akkadian. *See* languages, Semitic. *See also* Sumer
akkant, spirits of the dead, 95
Akrotiri, site at Thera (modern Santorini), 246
Alaksandus, Luvian king of Wilusa,
 treaty with Hittites, 271
al-Bass, necropolis of Tyre. *See* Carthage, religion of
Aleppo, Syrian city, 88
Alexander the Great,
 conquest of the Near East by, 23–4, 26
 fall of the Achaemenid empire and, 103
 Hellenization and, 23
 reign of, 5, 6, 18, 24, 280
Algiers, modern city in N. Africa, 207
alieni, as a term applied to Christians, 18
allies,
 of Rome, 212, 336, 347–8
Allobrogi, Gallic tribe, 371
Alpan, Etruscan deity of goodwill and gladness, 319
alphabetic period. *See* Mycenaean/Minoan religion. *See also* Greek religion
altars,
 in Greek religion,
  at sanctuaries, 292–3
  burning God's portions on, 293
  Poseidon's, 294
  processions and animal sacrifice, 291–3
 in Etruscan religion,
  at the Portonaccio sanctuary, Veii, 325
  at the "Sacral-Institutional Complex," Pian di Civita, 323–4
  human sacrifice at, 320, 324
  in cemeteries, 330
  representations in art of, 314, 320
 in Minoan religion,
  in Cretan caves, 247
  portable, 246
 in Mycenaean religion,
  circular, at the "House of Frescoes," 264
 in ancient Israelite and Judean religions,
  dedication of, 162
  at the Jerusalem Temple, 160, 162
 in Zoroastrianism,
  fire, 122
 see also rituals, sacrifice
Althiburus, Punic inscription from, 212, 219–20

General Index

Alwanzatar, black magic. *See* Hittite religion

Amarna, modern name for Akhetaten,
  letters, by rulers of Canaanite city-states to
    their Egyptian overlords, 155
  workers' village, as site of archaeological
    evidence, 194
  see also Egyptian religion

Amar-Utu ("Calf of Utu"). *See* Marduk.
  See also Sumerian religion

Amduat ("what is in the afterlife"). *See* Egyptian
  religion

Amen, god of Thebes, 178, 192, 194

Amenhotep III, Egyptian New Kingdom ruler
  (1390–1352 BCE), 183

Amenhotep IV. *See* Akhenaten

Amen-Ra, preeminent god of Egypt during the
  New Kingdom, 178–9, 186, 192

amertatāt ("non-dyingness"), term connected
  with sacrifice in Zoroastrianism, 107

amesha spenta, Life-giving Immortals, 107,
  113–14, 126
  see also Zoroastrianism

Amman Citadel Inscription. *See* Syro-Canaanite
  religion

Ammattalla, palace woman. *See* Hittite religion,
  divination

Amnisos (Amnissos), Cretan cave,
  Minoan worship at, 247

Amon, Judean king (642–640 BCE), father of
  Josiah,
  assassination of, 167

Amorites, rulers of Sumer in the second
  millennium BCE, 38, 56

Amos, non-priestly Judean prophet and
  agriculturalist, 170

Amphiaraos, Greek healing sanctuary
  (Amphiareion) at Oropos, 298.
  See also incubation, sacrifice

Amphiareion. *See* Amphiaraos

Amran, Levite, father of Aaron, 161

amulets,
  Egyptian, 179, 194–5, 197
  Etruscan, 328
  in Syro-Canaanite religion, 131, 145

Amun, Egyptian deity, 179

An, "The heavens," Sumerian deity, 34, 52

analogy,
  in Egyptian religion,
    of solar god to scarab, 184
  in Syro-Canaanite religion,
    for production of knowledge, 129

in sacrifice, 139
  to explain association of deities with
    natural phenomena, 132
  from human social organization, 138
  see also metaphor

Anat, west Semitic goddess of violence,
  in Syro-Canaanite religion,
  Baal's ally and sister, 133
  in Aqhat story, 136
  in Baal Cycle, 136. *See also* Anath

Anath,
  in Egyptian texts, 10. *See also* Anat

Anatolia, Asia Minor,
  Hittites in, 62, 84, 88
  Hurrian deities in, 88

Anatolian. *See* languages, Indo-European

Andescociuoucus, Celtic god, 371

a-ne-mo ("winds"), Mycenaean god at Knossos,
  260

Anglesey, island,
  massacre of Druids by Romans at, 375

animal worship. *See* Egyptian religion

annals, Assyrian, 67, 74

Anna Perenna, cult of, 351

Ankara, Turkish capital, Asia Minor, 84

ankh, Egyptian sign for life,
  adaptation to represent Phoenician betyl, 221

Anquetil-Duperron, A. H., Orientalist,
  translator of languages of modern
    Zoroastrians, 123

antae, projecting walls,
  in Etruscan sacred architecture, 324

anthropomorphism,
  in Assyrian and Babylonian religions, 75
  in Celtic religion, 366, 370, 372
  in Egyptian religion, 179
    rejection of, by king Akhenaten, 193
  in Etruscan religion, 325
  in Hittite religion, 87
  in Sumerian religion, 31, 44
  of Syro-Canaanite gods, 135–7

anthroponym,
  used to infer a theonym, 260

anthropopathic imagining,
  of Syro-Canaanite gods, 135

Anubis, Egyptian funerary god, 179, 200.
  See also jackal

a-pa-i-ti-jo, Mycenaean Haphaistios, 260

Apām Napāt ("Scion of the Waters"),
  Zoroastrian deity, 114

Apaosha, Zoroastrian demon of drought, 114

General Index

Apellon. *See* Apollon
aperta, Etruscan week-like period,
  influence on Roman structuring of the
    months, 357
  see also išveita, celuta, tiniana
Aphaia, goddess from Aegina, 267
Aphrodite, Greek goddess of love and beauty,
  on Etruscan mirrors, 211
  of Paphos, 213
  sanctuaries of, 213
  temples of,
    at Byblos, 213
  see also Carthage, religion of; Greek religion
Aphrodite Ourania (heavenly Aphrodite),
  cult of, 213, 283
  Phoenician influence, 213
Aphrodite Pontia,
  cult of, 213
  Phoenician influence, 213
Apis, Egyptian deity,
  cult of, 179
Aplu, Apulu, Etruscan deity, 319. *See also* Apollo
Apollo, Greek sun god, 260, 271, 283, 296, 353,
    369, 371
  see also Celtic religion, Mycenaean religion,
    Roman religion, theonyms
Apollo Agyieus (Apollo "of the streets"), 283
Apollo-Cunomaglos,
  inscription to, 372
Apollo Epikourios,
  sanctuary of, 296
Apollo-Grannus,
  inscription to, 372
Apollo Maleatas. *See* Mt. Kynortion
Apollo-Maponus,
  inscription to, 372
Apollo Patroös, guarantor of phratry
    membership in Athens, 287
Apollon. *See* Apollo
Apophis, serpent. *See* Egyptian religion
appeasement,
  of Babylon by Assyrians. *See* Esarhaddon
  of gods. *See* Celtic religion
Apsu, male/father waters,
  in Babylonian creation stories, 63
  see also enuma elish
Aqhat,
  famine caused by murder of, 133
  son of patriarch Daniel, 139
  story of. *See* Syro-Canaanite religion
    Baal Cycle
Arad, Judean sanctuary at, 157, 168–9

Aram,
  attack on Judah, 171
  influence on Judean religion, 171
  rule by David, 158
Arameans,
  in Babylon, 57–8
  religion of,
    storm deity Hadad, 155. *See* Assyrian religion
Aramaic,
  language. *See* languages, Semitic
  letters from Elephantine, 120
  texts,
    Tell Fekherye Inscription, 132, 143, 145
    Panammu I Inscription, 131, 146
    Sefire Inscriptions, 131, 145
    Zakir Inscription, 131, 144
    see also Zoroastrianism
Araunah, hill, site of Jerusalem Temple, 159
Arcadia, Greece,
  deities of, 282–3
  sanctuaries at, 296
Archaic period,
  Etruscan (600–450 BCE), 310, 314, 326, 331–2
Archedamos of Thera. *See* Greek religion
archdruid, leader of druids. *See* Celtic religion
archon, Athenian magistrate,
  in Greek religion, 286–7
Ardwī Sūrā Anāhitā, Heavenly River, 112, 115, 117
A-re, Mycenaean deity worshipped at Knossos,
    260
Areion, Greek deity worshipped in Arcadia, 282
Arezzo, Etruscan altars at, 326
Argos,
  Greek sanctuaries at, 296
Arinna, Sun-goddess of. *See* Hittite religion
Aristotle, Greek philosopher (384–322 BCE), 287
  nn 17–18
  as teacher of Theophrastos, 288
Aritimi (Artumes), Etruscan goddess Artemis,
    319
Arjad-aspa, 117
arkuwar, "plaidoyer" in Hittite religion, 92
Armenia,
  Manichaeism and Zoroastrianism in, 8
Arnobius, Christian apologist (third-fourth
    centuries CE),
  Adversus Nationes (Against the Heathen), 310,
    319–20
Arras, village in England,
  chariot burials at, 383
Arslan Tash,
  amulets found at. *See* Syro-Canaanite religion

General Index

Artaxerxes II, Achaemenid king, follower of
Zoroastrianism, 120
Artaxerxes III, Achaemenid king, 120
Artemis, Greek goddess, Apollo's sister,
sanctuaries of, 295–6. *See* theonyms
Artemis Brauronia,
sanctuary of, 295
artisan-production,
in Sumerian religion,
as part of temple's economic role, 37
Artumes. *See* Aritimi
Arušna, Hittite deity of, 93. *See also* divination
Arval brethren, Roman religious group, 355
Aryans,
enemies of Frangrasyan and the Turanians,
116
A-sag ("Arm-beating") demon. *See* Sumerian
religion
'āšām, "Guilt Offering." *See* Israelite and Judean
religions
A-sa-sa-ra, Minoan Solar goddess, 250
Ashem Vohū, "Order is the best good [reward],"
one of four holy prayers. *See Gāthā*s
Asherah. *See* Ashertu
Asherata. *See* Ashertu
Ashertu (Asherah, Athirat),
fertility goddess, Baal's wife, 134
goddess and palm tree in Israelite cult, 250
see also Israelite and Judean religions,
Syro-Canaanite religion
Ashi, Zoroastrian goddess,
hymn to, 117
offerings to, 121
Ashtoreth. *See* Astarte
Ashurnasirpal II, Assyrian ruler, grandson of
Adad-nirari II, 60
Asia Minor,
religions in, 7–8, 20
worship of Roman emperor in, 11
Asine,
statues. *See* Greek religion
Asklepios. *See* Aesculapios
assimilation,
in ancient religions, 14
Assmann, J., twentieth-century scholar,
Solar Religion in the New Kingdom, 178
Assur,
Assyrian city,
inscriptions from, 59
Assyrian god, 60, 64, 69, 71–2
Assurbanipal, last major Assyrian ruler,
library and museum of, 61

Assur-uballit, Assyrian ruler (1365–1330), first to
use title "king," 60
Assur-uballit II, Assyria's last ruler (614–609
BCE), 61
Assyria,
army of, 60
kings of, 57–8, 67
religion of. *See* Assyrian and Babylonian
religions
Assyrian and Babylonian religions,
Afterlife, 61
"Babylonian Theodicy," acrostic poem, 73
cult statues,
of Marduk, 62, 72
divination,
extispicy, 76
hepatoscopy, 76
leconomancy, 76
libanomancy, 76
Epic of Gilgamesh, 70
festivals, religious, 59, 62, 72, 77–8
akītu, New Year's Festival, 77–8
gods and goddesses,
Adad, weather god, 67
An, sky god, 63, 68, 71
Apsu, male/father god, 63
Assur, 64, 71–3
Damkina, 63
Dumuzi/Tammuz, 66
Ea, god of the subterranean freshwater
ocean, 63, 66
Enlil, king of the gods, 68–9, 71–2
Ereshkigal, queen of the netherworld, 65
Ishtar, goddess of love and war, 65–6,
68–70
Mami, 65
Marduk, patron deity of Babylon, 56–8,
62–4, 68–9, 71–3, 78
patron deities, 71, 74–5
personal, 72–3
Qingu, Babylonian god, 63
Shamash, Assyrian and Babylonian sun
god, 67
Sin, moon god of Haran, 59
Tiamat, female/mother goddess, 63
magic and magicians, 76. *See also heka*, rituals
marriage,
sacred, 70
myths,
Atrahasis, 8, 64–5
Descent of Ishtar to the Netherworld, 70
creation,

General Index

Assyrian and Babylonian religions (*cont.*)
  enuma elish, 57, 61–2, 71, 74, 78
  netherworld, 65–6, 70
  omens, 73, 76
  personnel, sacred,
    diviners, 76
    nadītu, women dedicated to serve a
      god, 77
    portents, 73
    prophecy, prophets, 77
    seals,
      cylinder and stamp, 67
    Shurpu, collection of spells and rituals, 76
    temples, 73–5
    wisdom literature, 73
    Man and His God, A, 73
Assyro-Babylonian. *See* languages, Semitic
ast, (human) bones. *See* Zoroastrianism
Aštart of Battle. *See maš ʾartu*
Astarte, Syrian goddess, 5, 134–5, 138, 210–11,
    213, 215, 221, 225, 314, 319, 341.
    See also Anat-Astarte, Aphrodite, Uni
Astō-widātu, "Bone-untier," 115
asuras, superhuman beings in Greek religion,
    282
Atalanta. *See* Atlenta
A-ta-na po-ti-ni-ja. See Mycenaean religion.
    See also theonyms
Atenism. *See* Ahkenaten
āter-wakhsh. See ātru-wakhsha
Athanaspotnia, Mycenaean war goddess,
    on frescoes, 262
Athena, Greek goddess of wisdom, 281–2,
    294–5, 341
Athena Ergane,
    sanctuary of, 282
Athena Nike,
    temple of, 295
Athena Polias, Athena "of the city,"
    sanctuary of, 282
Athena Pronaia, Athena "in front of the
      temple,"
    sanctuary of, 294
Athena Skiras,
    ritual of, 296
Athena Soteira, Athena "savior,"
    sanctuary of, 282
Athene. *See* Athena
Athens,
    officials/magistrates in
      archon, 286
      basileus, 286

exēgētai, 286
hieromnēmones, 286
hierophylakes, 286
hieropoioi, 286
polemarchos, 286
Athirat. *See* Ashertu
athletes,
  in Hittite cult, 94
Athrpa, Etruscanized Greek fate goddess
    Atropos, 320
a-ti-mi-ti, Mycenaean deity of Pylos,
    260
Atlenta, Etruscanized Greek Atalanta,
    320
atonement. *See npy*
Atonement, Day of. *See* Yom Kippur
Atrahasis, myth of. *See* Assyrian and Babylonian
    religions
atrium Vestae, "House of the Vestals,"
    339
Atropos, Greek fate goddess, sister of Clotho
    and Lechesis, 320
ātru-wakhsha, priest in charge of fire in Elamite
    ritual, 121
Attica,
  cult of Daeira in, 282
  festivals of, 296
  sacrifices in, 286
  see also Greek religion
Atum, Lower Egypt's creator god, 177, 181, 183.
    See also Ptah, Ra
Atunis. *See* Adonis
augur, 3, 321–2, 331, 348, 355–7
augur maximus, eldest member of augural
    college, 356
augural college. *See* augury
augury, observation of flight and behavior of
    birds. *See* divination
Augustine, fourth-fifth century North African
    Christian theologian, 1–2
Augustus, Roman emperor (27 BCE – 14 BCE),
    ban of druidic practices by, 369
Aura Jorro, F., twentieth-century scholar,
    DMic = Diccionario micénico, xi, 257,
    266
auspices, 3, 323, 348, 355
autobiographies,
  sources of Egyptian religion, 179
Autun,
  Celtic temples in, 380
Aventine, hill in Rome,
  temples on, 351

General Index
399

Avesta, Zoroastrian sacred texts, 102–3, 120,
   122–3
  Old Avesta, 103–4, 107, 111, 116, 119, 126
  Gāthās, "songs," 103–5, 107, 109, 111,
    113–14, 117–18, 123–7
  Yasna Haptanghāiti, 103–4, 107, 109
  Young Avesta, 1–7, 103–4, 109, 111–12, 114–17,
    119, 123–4
    Khorda Avesta, 103
    Videvdad (Vi-daēwa-dāta), 103, 111–12,
     114, 117, 119–20, 123
    yashts, "hymns," 103–4, 111–20
    Yasna, 103–11, 113–19, 123, 126
Avile Vipiiennas (Vipenas),
  dedication at Veii by, 327
  see also Etruscans, religions of
Avl Tarchunus, 316
  haruspication
  see also Etruscans, religions of
Ayia Irini (island of Ceos),
  Mycenaean sanctuary at, 264
Azatiwada, Anatolian ruler,
  inscriptions of, 132
  see also Syro-Canaanite religion
Azhi Dahāka, giant dragon, 116

ba, mobile spirit,
  need to appease it, 195
  portrayal as human-headed bird, 195
  see also Egyptian religion
Baal ("Lord"), Canaanite storm god, 7, 131,
   133–5, 138–41, 143, 145, 147–8
  see also Hadda
Baalat ("Lady" of Byblos), head of pantheon at
  Byblos. *See* Syro-Canaanite religion
Baal-Hammon (Baal Ḥamon), chief god at
  Carthage, 222
  association with child sacrifice, 224–5
  inscription commemorating vow to, 212
  priests of, 213
Baal *krntryš,* Syro-Anatolian deity,
  sacrifice to, 219
Baal Saphon,
  temple of, in Carthage,
    sacrificial tariff from, 216
Baal-Shamayn. *See* Zakir Inscription
Baal-Shamem, head of pantheon, with Baalat, at
  Byblos, 138
Baal's Cycle, myths. *See* Syro-Canaanite religion
Babili. *See* Babylon
Babylon,
  Amorite rulers of, 62

Kassite rulers of, 57
Marduk, patron deity of, 56–7, 62–3, 69,
  71–2, 78
sack of, 56–7, 62
Babylonia,
  conquest by Assyrians, 57
  Nebuchadnezzar, 57–8
  see also Hammurabi
Babylonian,
  chronicles, 58
  language, 56–7
  literature, 57–8
"Babylonian Theodicy," acrostic poem, 73
Bactria, kingdom of Semiramis, 122
Bactrian-Margiana Archeological Complex,
  Central Asia, 102
baga-dauçiya, "libation ritual for the god(s),"
  121
Balaam, "seer of the gods." *See* Deir 'Allah text.
  See also Syro-Canaanite religion
Baldock, England, Celtic inscriptions from,
  to Senua, goddess, 372
bard. *See* archdruid
Barré, M. L., twentieth-century scholar,
  210
barsman (barsom), ritual grass.
  See Zoroastrianism
Bartholomae, C., nineteenth-century scholar,
  Avestan dictionary, 124, 126
basileus, Athenian magistrate,
  role in Greek religious festivals, 286
Bassai, Arcadia,
  sanctuary of Apollo Epikourios at, 296
Bath, England,
  hot springs at,
    Sulis, Celtic goddess of, 370
  see also Minerva
battle
  Baal's,
    with death and sea, 133
    see also Syro-Canaanite religion
  gods of,
    Inana, Sumerian goddess, 50–1
    Ishtar, Assyro-Babylonian goddess, 70
'bd mlqrt, "servants of Melqart,"
  on Althiburus inscription, 212
Beautiful Festival of the Valley, 192
Beer Sheba, temple at, 157, 168
Bel and the Dragon (Greek Daniel), 140
Belenus, god of Noricum, 5
Belgium,
  burial sites in. *See* Celtic religion

General Index

Belisama, Celtic goddess, 367, 372.
    See also Brigit, Minerva
Bell, C., twentieth-century scholar, 303
Bendall, L., twentieth-century scholar of the
    Mycenaeans, 257
Beor, father of Balaam. *See* Deir 'Allah text
Bes, apotropaic god, 194, 196
Beth El,
    appearance of God at, 162
    sanctuary at, 7, 157, 162, 167–71
    see Israelite and Judean religions
Bible, Hebrew, 131–3, 137, 141, 146, 151, 156, 161,
    167–8
Bir Bou Rekba, Tunisia,
    stelae from, 222
birth,
    goddesses of, 319, 370
Bisenzio urn. *See* Etruscan religion
bny bnwt ("creator of creatures"), 134
Boaz, bronze pillar of Solomon's Temple, 159
Boğazköy/Hattuša, Hittite metropolis,
    cuneiform tablets from, 84
bog men, 376. *See also* Celtic religion,
    offerings
Book of the Dead. *See* Egyptian religion
Book of Gates. *See* Egyptian religion
Book of Two Ways. *See* Egyptian religion
Books of the Afterlife. *See* Egyptian religion
Books of Heaven and Earth. *See* Egyptian
    religion
Bordj Djedid, Punic excavations at, 209
Boyce, M., twentieth-century scholar of
    Zoroastrianism, 126
Branchidai, Greek shrine, 285
Brigit, Irish goddess of knowledge, 372
building of Nin-Girsu's temple, The, 47
bullae,
    Etruscan religion,
        amuletic, 328
    Hittite religion,
        images of gods on, 86
bull-leaping, in Minoan religious festivals, 249
Bunnens, G., twentieth-century scholar,
    L'expansion phénicienne en Méditerranée, 208
burial. *See also,* cremation, excarnation,
    inhumation
Burkert, W., twentieth-century scholar,
    Greek Religion, 302
    Homo necans, 301
Byblos, Lady of. *See* Baalat
Býčí-Skála cave at Blansko, Czech Republic, 368
Byrsa (St Louis), Carthaginian cemetery, 209

Cadiz. *See* Gadir
Caecina, Aulus, Roman writer (first century
    BCE),
    *De etrusca disciplina (On the Etruscan
    discipline),* 315, 332
Caelestis, worship of, 5
Caesar, Julius, Roman politician (100–44 BCE),
    de Bello Gallico (Gallic War), 366–7, 369,
    371–2, 374, 376–7, 383
Calah, modern Nimrud, Assyrian capital, 60, 72
Calaurian Amphictiony, 267
calendars,
    cultic, 77
    festival, 163, 192, 225, 299, 353, 376
    liturgical, 314
    lunar, 141, 163, 316, 357
    sacrificial, 283, 287, 348
    solar, 163, 348
    see also fasti, Capua Tile
Calendar, Brontoscopic. *See* Etruscans,
    religion of
Calendar, Coligni. *See* Celtic religion
Calf, Golden, 166, 168
Cambridge Ritualists. *See* Greek religion
Campus Martius,
    altar to Roman god Mars in, 351
Canaan,
    land of, 151, 155, 166
    religion,
        Israelite and Judean. *See* Israelite and
            Judean religions
        Syro-Canaanite, 9, 132, 139
candelabra, 160
cannibalism,
    in Ireland, 365
Cannicella,
    Etruscan Necropolis, 330
Canutes, Gallic tribe, 374
Capitoline,
    hill,
        temples on, 321, 353
    Triad, 344, 351
    see also Roman religion
Capua Tile, calendar. *See* Etruscans, religion of
Carmentae. *See* Roman religion
Carthage,
    alliance with Rome, 208
    Althiburus inscription from, 212, 219–20
    Bir Bou Rekba, Tunisia,
        stelae from, 222
    Bordj Djedid,
        excavations at, 209

General Index

Byrsa (St Louis),
  cemetery at, 209
Douïmès, necropolis at, 220
funerary practices at,
  cremation, 226–7
  inhumation, 227
Junon, cemetery at, 209
Milkpilles,
  Punic epitaph at, 223
Pyrgi,
inscriptions from, 215, 227
religion of,
  afterlife, 223, 227
  Astarte. *See rbtn*
  Baal-Hammon (Baal Ḥamon), chief god at
    Carthage,
    association with child sacrifice, 222–3
    inscription commemorating vow to, 212
    priests of, 213
  Baal Saphon,
    temple of: sacrificial tariff from, 216
  festivals, religious, 205, 211–13, 215, 225
  khn, khnm, priest, priests, 213, 216
  'lm, Punic deity, 211
    see also Melqart
  maledictions, 223–4
Marseilles, France,
  Tariff. *See* sacrifice
mnḥt. See also offerings
mqdš, Punic temple, 212–13
rbtn, "our Lady," 222
ritual,
  sacrifice 209, 211, 213, 216, 219–20, 223–4
sĩĩĩw't. See ritual sacrifice
Tanit. *See tnt*
tariffs, 213, 216, 219–20
temples,
  of Ba'al Saphon, 216
Tinnit-Ashtarte, Punic deity, 221. *See also tnt
  'štrt*
  Tinnit Phane Ba'al, Punic deity, 223
  tnt, Punic goddess, 221–2. *See also* Tanit,
    Tinnit
  tnt 'štrt. See Tinnit-Ashtarte
tophet of Carthage,
  burials at, 224
  excavations at, 209
  inscriptions, 209, 222
  sacrifice at, 209, 224–5
Tharros. *See tophet*
Tipasa, cemetery at, 207
urns from, 225

Yahimilk,
  inscriptions, 132
Yehawmilk,
  inscriptions, 132, 135
Carthaginians, Phoenician people, 210, 341
cartouches,
  Egyptian writing on, 193
Castor,
  cult of, 351
  sanctuary of, 351
catastrophe, natural, Syro-Canaanite religious
    rites to alleviate, 144
Catha, consort of Śuri, Etruscan deity, 318, 323,
    328
caves,
  Blansko, 368
  burials in, 369, 381
Cretan, 247
  Pan's, 283
  Nymphs', 283, 291–2
  sanctuaries in, 13, 243
  see also geography, sacred
Cel Ati, Etruscan Mother Earth,
  dedications to, 316, 328
Celius, Etruscan month of September, 316
cella, chamber or ritual enclosure.
    See sanctuaries, shrines, temples
Celtic. *See* languages, Indo-European
Celts,
  cannibalism by, in Ireland, 365
  Calendar, Coligny, inscription, 364
  defixiones, at the temple of Minerva-Sulis, 374
  divination, 374
  funerary practices,
    chariot burials, 383
    cremation, 381–2, 384
    excarnation, 381
    Hochdorf Prince, Late Hallstatt Celtic
      burial, 382
    inhumation, 381–2
    Ins, cemetery at, 382
    Lady of Vix, 382
    Subingen, burials at, 382
  language of. *See* Celtic
  monuments,
    Pilier des Nautes (*Nautae Parisiaci*), 373,
      377
  myths,
    Finn saga, 373
  religion of,
    afterlife, 381–3
    appeasement of gods, 377

General Index

Celts (*cont.*)
augury. *See* divination
cult,
of the Head, 367
festivals, religious, 376
gods and goddesses, Andescociuoucus, 371
Belisama, 367. *See also* Brigit, Minerva
Brigit, Irish goddess of knowledge, 372
Cernunnus, hunter deity, 370.
See also Gundestrup cauldron
Clota, goddess of the Clyde, 370
Danuvius, god of the Danube, 370
Deae Matres, triple mother goddesses, 370
Dis Pater, 371
Earth Mother, 366, 378
Epona, Gallic goddess, 370
Esus,
sacrifice to, 373
Genii loci, "spirits of place," 373
Lenus, healing god, 372. *See also* Mars
Lugh ("shining light"), 370
Minerva Medica, 367, 372, 374.
See also Sulis
Moccus, boar god, 373
Nodens, healing god, 372–3, 379
Senua, inscriptions to,
from Baldock, England, 372
Sequana, goddess at the source of the
Seine, 370
Sinann, goddess linked to the Shannon,
370
Smer[trius], 373
Sulis, temple of: at Bath, England, 370,
374, 378. *See also defixiones*, Minerva
Taranis, god of thunder, 370–1, 377, 380
Tarvos Trigaranus, "bull with three
cranes," 373, 377
Teutates, 377
magic and magicians, 375–6.
See also defixiones, rituals
offerings, at Dellingen, 368
at Farchant, 368
at Holzhausen, Bavaria, 378
at Market Harborough, 379
at Newstead, Scotland, 378
at Osterstein, Bavaria, 368
at Witham, 371, 373. *See also* bog men
priests,
archdruid, leader of druids, 374
bard. *See* archdruid
Druids, priestly group,

ban by Tiberius of, 375
rituals of, 374–5
δρῦς, oak. *See* Druid
temples and shrines,
at Entremont, 367
at Hayling Island, 380
at Hockwold, 376
at Libenice, 368
at Maiden Castle, 380
at Périgueux, 380
at Roquepertuse, 367
at the source of the Seine, 370, 379
at Uley, 380
nemeto, Celtic sacred grove, 370
underworld. *See* afterlife
Viereckschanzen, enclosures, 379
celuta, Etruscan week-like period, 357.
See also iśveita, tiniana, aperta
cenotaph,
of Seti I, 193
Censorinus, Roman writer (fl. third century CE),
De die natali (*On the Birthday*), 316
centralization, religious. *See* Roman religion
Ceos, island, Mycenaean sanctuaries on, 264
cepen, Etruscan priest, 322–3, 354
Ceres, Roman deity, part of the "plebeian triad,"
351
Cernunnus, Celtic hunter deity, 370
Cerveteri, city, site of Etruscan sanctuary,
tombs at, 325, 327, 329–31
Cetamura del Chianti, Etruscan sanctuary at,
offerings, 318, 321, 326
Chabot, J. B., early twentieth-century scholar of
the Carthaginians, 216
Chaldeans,
in Babylonia, 58
Chamalières and Larzac Tablets. *See* Celtic
religion
chaos,
in Egyptian religion, 186
in Minoan religion, 252
in Israelite and Judean religions, 156
in Zoroastrianism, 105–6, 108, 110
chapels,
Egyptian, 199, 200
Minoan, 249
chariot burials. *See* Celtic religion
chariot races,
in Rome,
Equirria, Consualia, and *Equus October*,
358
in Zoroastrianism, 117, 125

General Index

charis, reciprocity in relations between Greek Gods and humans, 290–1

Charites,
 sanctuary of, 295

Charu, Etruscan hammer-god, 321, 331

Cheshire, England. *See* bog men

Chios, Greek sanctuary in, 292

Chiusi,
 Etruscan reliefs at, 326
 Etruscan tombs at, 353

chōra Tuscan, boundary of. *See* Althiburus.
 See also pagus Thusca

Christian sects. *See* heresies

Christianity,
 Pauline, 14
 Roman state's support of, 19

chronicle, Babylonian, 58

Cicero, Roman orator (106–43 BCE),
 de Legibus (*On the Laws*), 356
 de Natura Deorum (*On the Nature of the Gods*), 2–3, 343
 Oratio pro Fonteio (*Oration for Marcus Fonteius*), 369

Cintas, P., excavator of the *tophet,* 209

cinwatō pertu, "Ford of the Accountant," 106, 110, 115

circus,
 games, 354
 valley, sanctuaries in, 351

citadel, Mycenae,
 Phylakopi, 256, 259, 264

Cities list. See Sumerian religion

city-state,
 Canaanite, 155
 gods of, 45–6, 52
 Phoenician, 205, 216
 Sumerian, 7, 10, 35, 38, 49
 see also polis

civilization,
 Anatolian, 86
 Etruscan, 310, 326
 Greek, 256, 369
 Iron-Age, 368
 Minoan, 237
 Phoenician, 207
 Sumerian, 31

Claudius, Roman emperor (41–54 CE),
 ban of Druidic practices by, 375

clay tablets, 33

Cleisthenic tribes,
 cults of, 11

Clota, Celtic goddess of the Clyde, 370

Clotho, Greek fate goddess, sister of Atropos and Lechesis, 320

Coffin Texts, 181, 200–1

coins, as offerings to deities, 328, 379

collegia, collegium of priests. *See* Etruscan religion

combat, gladiatorial,
 in Etruria, 330, 354

coming-of-age ceremonies. *See* Zoroastrianism

comitia calata, Roman assembly of the *curiae,* 356

comitia centuriata, Roman assembly, 356
 see also centralization, religious

Comitium, assembly area in Rome
 shrine in, 339

Consualia. See chariot races

Consus, Roman deity,
 altar to, 351

Corieltauvi, Celtic tribe, 379

Cortona, Italian city,
 Etruscan offerings at, 328
 Etruscan tomb at, 330

cosmogony,
 in Egyptian religion, 180–1
  Heliopolitan, 181
 in Zoroastrianism, 111

cosmology,
 in Egyptian religion, 180–1, 186
 in Sumerian religion, 52

cosmos,
 in Egyptian religion, 177, 181–2
 in Etruscan religion, 317, 319
 in Hittite religion, 84, 88, 90, 92, 96
 in Sumerian religion, 34, 37, 52
 in Zoroastrianism, 105, 108–10, 115, 121, 125

Coulanges, F. de, nineteenth-century French historian, 302. *See also* Greek religion

Covenant,
 Ark of the, chest that symbolized YHWH's presence, 157–8, 160–2, 165, 168, 171
 Code, 165–6
 see also Israelite and Judean religions

cow goddesses, 180, 250, 260

Cow, prototype of human beings, in Zoroastrianism, 114

Creation,
 gods of, 68, 104, 134, 156, 159, 194
 myths. *See* creation narratives

creation narratives, 34. *See also enuma elish, En-ki and Nin-mah*

cremation,
 Celtic, 381–2, 384

404 *General Index*

cremation (*cont.*)
  Etruscan, 330
  Punic, 226–7
  Roman, 349
Crete,
  historical periods of, 239
  palaces of, 242
  scripts of, 240
  see also Minoan religion
Ctesias of Cnidus, Greek historian,
  History of the Persians, 122
Culsans, Etruscan god, 328
cult,
  private, 7, 12, 195, 221, 246, 292, 346, 355–6
  public, 2, 10–12, 332, 355
  state, 12–13, 76, 84, 86, 89, 93, 350
  statues, 62, 67, 75, 179, 188, 191–3, 284, 293–4,
    324–5, 331
Cult of the Head. *See* Celtic religion
cultus ("cult"), 343. *See also* Cult
cuneiform, script,
  Hittite, 84, 86
  Sumerian, 40
  see also clay tablets
Cunliffe, B. W., twentieth-century scholar of the
    Celts, 366
Curia "Hostilia," meeting structure for Roman
    senate. *See comitia calata*
curses,
  in Syro-Canaanite religion, 145–6
  see also defixiones
Cursing of Agade, The, 39. *See also* Sumerian
    religion
Cybele, Phrygian "Mountain Mother," 14
Cyprus, island, Phoenician inscriptions at, 213,
    225
Cyrus, Persian king (c 600–529 BCE), 59, 103, 121
Cythera. *See* syncretism

da-da-re-jo/daidaleon, Mycenaean sanctuary in
    Knossos, 263
dadwāh, the "establisher" (Ahura Mazdā), 111.
    See also dātar
Daeira, Greek Attic goddess, 282
daēnā, "vision soul," in Zoroastrianism, 109–10,
    115. *See also dayanā*
daēwa, evil god in Zoroastrianism, 103, 108,
    112–14, 117–18, 120
Dagan, Syro-Canaanite god, 131, 141–2
daimon, Greek spirit, 210
Dan, Israelite sanctuary at, 157
daiva. *See daēwa*
Damkina. *See* Marduk

damos. *See demos*
Danae. *See da-nwa*
Daniel. *See* Syro-Canaanite religion.
    See also Aqhat
Danuvius, Celtic god of the Danube, 370
da-nwa, Mycenaean deity, 260
da-pu₂-ri-to-jo po-ti-ni-ja, "lady of the
    Labyrinth," 260–1
dātar. *See dadwāh*
dauça, "libation service." *See* Zoroastrianism
dauçiya. *See dauça*
David, king of Judah, 158, 250
dayanā. *See daēnā*
Deae Matres, triple mother goddesses, 370
Death of Gilgamesh, The, 49
debate between hoe and plough, The, 51
dĕbîr, "inner sanctum." *See* Holy of Holies
Deborah, prophet and judge, 169
defixiones, at the temple of Minerva-Sulis, 374
Deir 'Alla, text from, 132, 144, 170
Deir el-Bahri, temple at. *See* Hatshepsut
deity,
  lists, 44, 46
  see also deities by name, gods, goddessess,
    goddess, patron
Delattre, A. L. *See* Carthage, religion of
Dellingen, Germany, Celtic offerings at, 368
Delos, island,
  sanctuaries at, 213
Delphi,
  games of, 284
  oracles at, 286, 297
  sanctuaries at, 285, 294
deme, basis of Attic local government, 287.
    See also dēmos
Demeter, Greek goddess, 213, 228, 261, 271, 283.
    See also Astarte
demons, 49, 64, 73, 84, 86, 114, 250, 252, 321,
    331–2. *See also* demons by name
dēmos, people, 268
Dendera, sanctuaries at, 192
Denmark. *See* Gundestrup cauldron
Derrida, Jacques, twentieth-century
    deconstructionist, 239
Descent of Ishtar to the Netherworld, 70
Despoina, Greek Arcadian deity, 282
devas, Greek superhuman beings, 282
Diana, Roman goddess of the hunt, 351
Diaspora, 8, 14
Dii Involuti, Roman "Shrouded Gods," 319
Dikte, Mt, Crete. *See* Mycenaean religion.
    See also theonyms
Di Manes, "good gods," 349

General Index

Diodorus Siculus, Greek writer (first century BCE),
  Bibliotheca historica (*Historical Library*), 365, 377, 379, 383
Dionysius of Halicarnassus, Greek writer of the Roman Augustan age, 343, 346, 352, 354
Diòs, Greek divine name. *See* Baal Hammon
Dioscuri, temple of, 341. *See also* Dioskouroi
Dioskouroi,
  cult of, 319. *See also* Dioscuri
Dius Fidius (Semo Sancus), Roman sanctuary of, 351
di-pi-si-jo, 258, 269. *See also* theonym
dipsia-festival. *See di-pi-si-jo*
di-pte-ra-po-ro, Mycenaean religious official, 267
di-ri-mi-o, Mycenaean deity, 260
disk,
  in Egyptian religion, 180, 184, 190, 193
  in Hittite religion, 87
  in Syro-Canaanite religion, 137
  in Zoroastrianism, 122
Dis Pater, Celtic god of the Underworld and death, 371
di-u-ja. *See* Diwia
di-u-jo, sanctuary of Zeus. *See* Mycenaean religion
divination,
  in Celtic religion, 374
  in Etruscan religion, 310, 325, 332
  in Roman religion, 343, 348, 355
  in Syro-Canaanite religion, 143–4
diviners,
  in Assyrian and Babylonian religion, 76
  in Israelite and Judean religions, 170
  in Syro-Canaanite religion, 142.
    See also personnel, sacred
di-we, Mycenaean Zeus, 260
Diweus, 263, 272. *See also di-we*
Diwia. *See Diweus*
Di-wi Di-ka-ta-i-o, Mycenaean Zeus Diktaios, 270
di-wo-nu-so, Mycenaean Dionysus, 260
Djer, Egyptian king from the first dynasty, tomb of, 192
Djoser, Egyptian king from the third dynasty, tomb of, 198
Dodona, oracular shrine in northern Greece, 285, 297–8
do-e-ra, female slave of a god. *See* Mycenaean religion

do-e-ro, male slave of a god. *See* Mycenaean religion
Dog Star,
  in Punic religion, 225
  in Young Avestan pantheon, 112
do-po-ta, "lord of the house," Mycenaean deity, 261
double axe, symbol of Minoan great goddess, 249
Douïmès, Carthaginian necropolis at, 220
doule. *See doulos*
doulos, slave, 268
dragon,
  in Minoan religion, 253
  in Syro-Canaanite religion, 140
  in Zoroastrianism, 116
drauga, Lie, 108–9
dreams,
  in Greek religion, 283, 298–9
  in Hittite religion, 92
  in Sumerian religion, 47
  in Syro-Canaanite religion, 133, 143–4
  see also divination
Drimios, Mycenaean deity,
  sanctuary for, 262
Drioton, E., twentieth-century Egyptologist, 178
drug. *See drauga*
Druids, Celtic priestly group,
  ban by Tiberius of, 375
  rituals of, 369, 374
δρῦς, oak. *See* Druid
Duamutef, Egyptian funerary god, 179
Duat, Egyptian underworld, 183, 201
Dumézil, Georges, twentieth-century French scholar of Roman religion, 345
Dumuzi, husband of Ishtar, 66.
    See also Tammuz
Dumu-zid and En-ki-imdu, 51
Dursares, god of Arabia, 5

Ea, Babylonian deity, 63, 66
Earhart, B., twentieth-century scholar, definition of religion, 5
Early Dynastic period,
  of Egyptian history, 178–9, 192, 198
  of Mesopotamian history, 38–40, 44–8, 50
Early Minoan, historical period of Crete, 239.
    See also Middle Minoan, Late Minoan
Earth Mother, 366, 378
Ebla, ancient city,
  texts from, 130
ecstasy. *See* ecstatic rites

General Index

ecstatic rites, 247
Edfu, site of Horus sanctuary, 192
Edom, ancient nation. *See* Israelite and Judean
  religions
Egypt,
  religion of. *See* Egyptian religion
Egyptian religion,
  Akhenaten (Amenhotep IV), primacy of Sun
    god during reign of,
    rejection of anthropomorphic
      representations by, 193
  amulets,
    animals identified with gods, 197
    as grave goods, 197
    to facilitate prowess in hunting, 195
    to promote strength, fertility, and love, 195
    to protect against everyday dangers, 195
    to ward off enemies, 195
    used by magical/medical practitioners, 197
  animal cult in, 179
  ankh, sign for life, 221
  ba, mobile spirit, 185, 195
  concepts,
    afterlife, 177, 181, 184, 195, 197–201.
      See also Duat, underworld
    Amduat ("what is in the afterlife"), 201
      derived from the Book of Two Ways, 201
    chaos, 186
    Duat, underworld, 182–3, 200
    ka, life force, 195
    maat, order, 202
    Nun, limitless expanse of impenetrably
      dark water, 183
    rebirth, 181, 183, 197
    resurrection, 194, 201
  cosmogony,
    Heliopolitan, 181
  cosmology, 180–1, 186
  festivals, religious,
    Beautiful Festival of the Valley, 192
    of Osiris, 193
    Opet, 192
  funerary practices,
    mastabas. *See* tombs
    mortuary complex of Senwosret III, 193
    tombs,
      at Hieraconpolis, 197
      of Djoser, third-dynasty king, at
        Saqqara, 198–9
      of Ramesses VI, 182
      Osireion, ceremonial tomb of Osiris, 193
    ushabti, Egyptian funerary servant, 200

  see also texts
  gods and goddesses,
    Amen, god of Thebes, consort of Mut, 178,
      192, 194
    Amen-Ra, preeminent god during the New
      Kingdom, 178–9, 186, 192
    Amun, 179
    Anubis, funerary god, 179, 200
    Apis,
      cult of, 179
    Aten, 193–4
    Atum, Lower Egypt's creator god, 177, 181,
      183. *See also* Ptah, Ra
    Bes, apotropaic god, 194, 196
    Duamutef, funerary god, 179
    Geb, earth, 181, 183
    Harsaphes, 180
    Hathor, 192
    Heliopolitan Ennead, nine primeval
      deities, 181, 186
    Heqet, frog-goddess of fertility, 196
    Horus, son of Osiris, personification of
      divine kingship, 180, 182–3, 186, 193,
      197
    Isis, sister and wife of Osiris, mother of
      Horus, 181–2, 201
    Khentiamentiu, funerary god, 179
    Khnum, associated with source of the Nile,
      177, 180, 196
    Khonsu, son of Amen and Mut, 192
    Mut, Amen's consort, 192
    Nephthys, 181, 201
    Nut, sky goddess, 181, 183
    Osiris, 179, 181–2, 184, 193, 198, 200–1
    patron deities, 177
    Ptah, 177, 179
    Ra, sun-god, 178, 180, 183, 198, 201
    Ra-Horakhty, "Horus of the horizon," 183
    Renenutet, serpent goddess, 197
    Seth, storm god, 182, 186, 193
    Shu, 181, 183
    Taweret, fertility goddess, 194, 196
    Tefnut, 181
    Thoth, 179, 194
    Wepwawet, funerary god, 179
  "Litany of Ra," 183
  magic and magicians,
    heka, "magic," 195
    pekheret. *See* medico-magical papyri
    see also incantations and spells, rituals
  noute, "god," 178
  papyri,

General Index

funerary, 183–4
medico-magical,
   ruu, 197
   shesau, 197
personnel, sacred,
   God's Wives of Amun, 191
   High Priests of Amun, 191
   hem-netjer, "god's servant," priestly title,
      188, 191
   kheri-hebet, lector priests, 191
   wab ("pure") priests, 191
prophecy, prophets, 186
rituals and ceremonies,
   Opening of the Mouth ceremony, 179
temples and sanctuaries,
   at Deir el-Bahri, 186
   at Hieraconpolis, 187
   at Karnak, 192
   hut-netjer, "house of god," 188
   of Hathor, at Dendera, 192
   of Horus, at Edfu, 192
   of Ramesses II, 193
   of Seti I, 193
texts,
   Book of the Dead, 181, 201–2
   Book of Gates, 201
   Book of Two Ways, 200–1
   Books of the Afterlife, 181, 184
   Books of Heaven and Earth, 201
Egyptian Report of Wen-Amon.
      See Syro-Canaanite religion
Egyptian slavery, 163
Egyptians, ancient, religion of. *See* Egyptian
   religion
Egyptologist, 177
e-ke-ra₂-wo, Mycenaean ruler, 268
El, Syro-Canaanite god, 131, 133–4, 136–8, 144–5,
   147, 155–6. *See also* Baal Cycle
Elam, ancient Near Eastern state, 69
Elamites,
   deities of the, 121
Eleazer, Levite priest, 161
El Elyon, "God Most High." *See* Israelite and
   Judean religions. *See also* Abram
Elephantine, Egypt,
   letters from, 120
   ostracon from, 142
Eleusis,
   cultic center at. *See* Mycenaean religion
   Mysteries of. *See* Greek religion
Elijah, prophet, 154, 170
Elkurnisa, 134

El Shaddai. *See* YHWH
e-ma-a₂, Mycenaean god. *See also* Hermes
Emar, texts from. *See also* Syro-Canaanite
   religion
empire,
   Achaemenid, 103, 122, 171
   Assyrian, 58, 151, 157, 171
   Babylonian, 152, 171
   Hellenistic, 7
   Hittite, 3, 89, 241
   Persian, 167, 171, 336
   regional, 7, 10–11
   Roman, 11, 18–19, 315
   Ur, 39
endogamy, 226
e-ne-si-da-o-ne, Mycenaean Ennosidas, 260
En-hedu-ana,
   first accredited author of hymns, 50
En-ki (Enki), creator god, 32, 34, 37, 44–5, 48–9,
   50, 52
En-ki and Nin-mah, 34, 49. *See also* creation
   narratives
En-ki and the world order, 34, 49
Enlightenment, Age of, 148
En-lil (Enlil), "Lord Wind," 34, 43–5, 49, 52
Entremont, France,
   Celtic shrine at, 367
enuma elish, creation narrative, 57, 61–5, 68,
   71, 74
e-nu-wa-ri-jo, Mycenaean Enualios, 260
Ephraim,
   son of Joseph, 157
   tribe, 157
   see also Israelite and Judean religions
Epic of Creation, *enuma elish*, 8, 57, 61–2,
   64–5, 68, 71, 74, 78. *See also* creation
   narratives, myths
Epic of Gilgamesh, 70
Epidauros,
   Aesculapius sanctuary at, 13, 264
Epona, Gallic goddess, 370
Equirria, Roman chariot races, 358
Equus October, "October horse," Roman chariot
   races, 358
e-ra, Mycenaean Hera, 260
Erechtheion, Greek sanctuary, 295
Erechtheus, Greek hero, 295
Erichthonios, Greek hero, 295
Ereshkigal, queen of the netherworld, 65
e-re-u-ti-ja, Mycenaean Eleithia, 260
Eridu, Mesopotamian city,
   temple at, 74

General Index

e-ri-nu, Mycenaean Erinus ("Fury"), 260
Eritha, a Mycenaean priestess, 267
Esarhaddon, Assyrian king, 58
Esau, Jacob's brother, 155
Eshmun, Phoenician god, 134, 138, 221
Esquiline, hill,
    Roman sanctuaries on, 351
Esus, Celtic deity, 373, 377
Etruscans,
    religion of,
        Acherontic Books, books on death and life,
            320. *See also* afterlife
        afterlife, 329, 331–2. *See also* underworld
        altars,
            at Cortona, 330
            at Fiesole, 326
            at the sanctuary of Fontanile di
                Legnisina, 328
            at the Grotta Porcina, 330
            at Marzabotto, 326
             at Orvieto, 330
            at Pieva a Socana, 326
            at the Portonaccio sanctuary, Veii, 325
            at Pyrgi, 326
            at the "Sacral-Institutional Complex,"
                Pian di Civita, 323–4
        bulla, amuletic, 328
        calendar,
            Agramer Mumienbinden (*liber linteus*),
                314
            Brontoscopic, 314
            Capua Tile (*Tabula Capuana*),
                314
        divination,
            augury, 323, 331
            auspices, 323
            haruspication, 309, 316, 331–2.
                See also Avl Tarchunus
            liver, model of. *See* Piacenza liver
            omens, 318, 322
            Piacenza liver, 311–12, 317
            sortes, lots, 332
        etrusca disciplina, religious precepts and
            practices, 315, 329
        funerary practices,
            Cerveteri: tombs at, 325, 329–31
            Chiusi: tombs at, 326, 353
            combat, gladiatorial, 330
            cremation, 330
            François Tomb, tomb of Vel Saties, 323
            inhumation, 329
            L(a)ris Pulenas: tomb of, 323

Melone del Sodo II, in Cortona, tomb
    at, 330
Regolini-Galassi, tomb, 330
Tarquinia, tombs at, 330–1
Tomb of the Augurs, 330. *See also* ritual
Tomb of the Blue Demons, 331.
    See also afterlife
Tomb of the Reliefs, 329–30
Tomba della Scimmia, 353. *See also* ritual
Tomba delle Bighe, 353. *See also* ritual
gods and goddesses,
    Achvizr, male and female deity, 319
    Aita, god of the underworld, 331
    Alpan, deity of goodwill and gladness,
        319
    Aphrodite, Greek goddess of love and
        beauty: on Etruscan mirrors, 320
    Aplu, Apulu, Etruscan deity, 319, 325.
        See also Apollo
    Aritimi (Artumes), Etruscan goddess
        Artemis, 319, 328
    Athrpa, Etruscanized Greek fate goddess
        Atropos, 320
    Atlenta, Etruscanized Greek Atalanta,
        320
    Atunis, Etruscanized Adonis, 320
    Catha, consort of Śuri, 318, 323, 328
    Cel Ati, Etruscan Mother Earth, 316, 328
    Charu(n), 321, 331
    Culsans, 328
    Dii Involuti, "Shrouded Gods," 319
    Dioskouroi, 319
    Evan, 319
    Favores Opertanei, "Secret Gods of
        Favor," 319
    Fufluns, 318–19
    Hercle, 318–19, 328. *See also* Herakles
    Janitores Terrestres, "Doorkeepers of the
        Earth," 318–19
    Laran, god of lightning and thunder,
        317. *See also* Mars
    Lasa, flying spirit, 319
    Leinth, deity of fate and fortune, 318–19
    Letham, 318
    Lur, deity of fate and fortune, 318
    Lynsa Silvestris, 318
    Mariś, Etruscan deity appearing as
        triplets, 319
    Meleager. *See* Meliacr
    Meliacr, 320
    Menrva, 317, 319. *See also* Minerva
    Nethuns, 317–18

General Index

Neverita, 318
Nortia, 321
Pacha, 323
Phersipnei, deity of the underworld, 331.
  See also Persephone
Satre, 317
Selvans, 318, 328. *See also* Silvanus
Sethlans, 317. *See also* Vulcan
Silvanus. *See* Selvans
Soranus, epiclesis of Apollo, 318.
  See also Śuri
Śuri, 318
Tec Sans, 318
Thalna, Etruscan spirit, 319
Thuflthas, 318
Tinia, chief deity, 315, 317–18, 328
Turan, 316, 328. *See also* Aphrodite
Turms, 319, 327
Uni, consort of Tinia, 314, 317–19, 327.
  See also Astarte, Juno
Vanth, winged goddess, 331
Vecuvia, 315, 331. *See also* prophecy,
  Vegoia
Vei, 328
Veltune (Vertumnus), 318
mirrors,
  from Volterra, 326
  of Pava Tarchies (*puer Tages*), 313, 316,
    318, 321
personnel, sacred,
  cepen, Etruscan priest, 322
  collegia, collegium of priests, 322
  haruspex, 318, 321
  haruspex fulguriator, "reader of entrails"
    or "reader of lightning," 322
  hatrencu, priestess, 322
  Larth Cafates, priest: inscription of,
    322
  maruχva, association of priests, 322
prophecy, prophets,
  Tages, 315
  see also etrusca disciplina
ritual,
  sacrifice, 324, 326–7, 330.
    See also Agramer Mumienbinden
temples and sanctuaries,
  at Cerveteri, 314, 325, 329
  at Cetamura del Chianti, 321, 326–7
  at Fiesole, 326
  at Graviscae, 329
  at Marzabotto, 325
  at Orvieto, 325, 329–30

at Pian di Civita, 323–4, 327
at Piazza d'Armi, 324
at Poggio Casetta, 324
at Pyrgi, 325–7
at Rusellae, 324
Sacral-Institutional Complex, 323–4.
  See also altars
at Tarquinia, 320, 323, 325
at Veii, 325
at Volterra, 320, 326
at Vulci, 325, 328
underworld, 331–2. *See also* afterlife
votives,
  anatomical, 311, 328, 332
  see also Etruria
etrusca disciplina, Etruscan religious precepts
  and practices, 315, 329. *See also* Cicero
Euphrates, river, 36, 46, 57, 130–1, 142
Europe,
  Central, 364, 367–8, 380, 382
  Western, 19, 24, 336, 364
Eusebius, Christian writer (263–339 CE),
  *Praeparatio evangelica (Preparation for the
    Gospel)*, 209
Evan, Etruscan deity, 319
Evans, Sir Arthur, excavator of Knossos
  (1851–1941), 237–9, 241, 244, 246–9,
  252, 254
Eve, 169
evidence,
  archaeological, 8, 37, 167, 177, 188, 266,
    309–10, 338, 364, 372
  material, 7–8, 367
  textual, 3, 6, 33, 35, 39, 44, 155, 180, 202, 257,
    266, 268, 309
evil in Zoroastrianism, 103, 105, 108–21, 124,
  127
excarnation,
  in Celtic funerary practices, 381
exēgētai, "explicators," Athenian officials, 285
exta, entrails. *See* Syro-Canaanite religion
ex-voto, offering, 379
extispicy. *See* divination
Ezekiel, Zadokite priest and prophet, 160, 171
  see also Bible
Ezra, 162

façades,
  of palaces, 186
  of temples, 179
falcon in Egyptian religion, 179–80, 183–4, 186,
  188, 197. *See also* Ra

410 *General Index*

Fara, ancient Shuruppak, 68
Farchant, Celtic offerings at, 368
Fashioner of the Cow, Zoroastrian divine being, 108, 110
fasti, calendars
Fasti, Praenestini, 356
Fate, 49, 95, 309, 318, 320–1. *See also* Fate deities by name
Favores Opertanei, "Secret Gods of Favor," 319
feasts. *See* rituals
Ferrybridge, England, Celtic chariot burials at, 383
Fertility, 135, 137, 155–6, 169, 194, 197, 328, 366. *See also* fertility deities by name
festivals, religious,
    in Assyrian and Babylonian religions, 59, 62, 72, 77–8
    in Celtic religion, 376
    in Egyptian religion, 187–8, 192–4, 202
    in Greek religion, 284, 286, 288–9, 292, 294, 296, 299, 301
    in Hittite religion, 93–4
    in Israelite and Judean religions, 160, 162–4, 166, 168–9
    in Minoan religion, 241–2, 246, 248
    in Mycenaean religion, 257–8, 265–6
    in Punic religion, 205, 211–13, 215, 225
    in Roman religion, 353, 356
    in Sumerian religion, 33, 46–7
    in Syro-Canaanite religion 131, 141–2
    see also calendars
Festus, Sextus Pompeius, second-century-CE Roman writer,
    De verborum significatu (On the Meaning of Words), 354–5
Février, J. G., twentieth-century French scholar of the Carthaginians, 216, 230
Ficana, Italy, Roman burials at, 349
Fiesole, Italy, Etruscan temples at, 326
Figulus, Nigidius, Romanized Etruscan writer (98–45 BCE), 314, 332
Finn saga, Celtic myth, 373
Flamen Dialis, Roman priest of Jupiter, 357
flamines. See personnel, sacred, priests
    flamines maiores, major flamens, priests of Jupiter, Mars, and Quirinus, 344
flood stories, 49, 64
Fontanile di Legnisina, Italy, sanctuary at, 328
Ford of the Accountant., 106, 110, 115
Fors Fortuna, Roman temple of, 351
Forum, Roman, temples in, 338–9, 351
Forum Boarium, Cattle Market, temples in, 351

France, modern, 95, 216, 364, 367–8, 378, 380, 382–3. *See also* Gaul
François Tomb, Etruscan tomb, 323
Frangrasyan, enemy of Aryans, 116
frawashi, "pre-existing soul." *See* Zoroastrianism
frescoes, Mycenaean, 259, 261–5, 269–71
Fufluns, Etruscan deity, 318–19

Gadir, modern Cadiz,
    Phoenician and Punic settlements at, 206–7
Garbini, G., twentieth-century scholar of Phoenician history, 221
garō.nmāna, Ahura Mazdā's House of Songs, 115
Gaul,
    religion in. *See* Celtic religion
gaya, "life" in Zoroastrianism, 114
Gaya Martān, prototype of living beings, 114
Geb, earth. *See* Egyptian religion
Geertz, C., twentieth-century anthropologist, 129
Genii loci, "spirits of a place," 373
gentes, Roman social structures, 357
geography,
    importance of, for study of ancient religions, 13–14, 19
    sacred, 13
Gerard-Rousseau, M., twentieth-century French scholar, 257
Gershom, son of Moses, 162
Gershonites, Levitical family, 162
ghost,
    of humans, 146
gifts. *See* offerings
gift-exchange, 105, 125, 290
Gilgal,
    Passover at, 162
    temples at, 157, 168
    see also Israelite and Judean religions
Gilgamesh, 49, 70, 250. *See also* Assyrian and Babylonian religions, *Epic of Gilgamesh*; Sumerian religion
Death of Gilgamesh, the (as a source)
Girsu,
    Sumerian texts found at, 46–7
    see also Nin-Girsu (patron deity of Girsu)
gnāh, Ahura Mazdā's "women," 108
god, gods. *See* individual gods by name
Godart, L. and A. Sacconi, twentieth-century French scholars of Mycenaean history, 267
goddess. *See* individual goddesses by name

General Index 411

God's Wives of Amun, 191
Göttingen bronzes, 321
Gracious One, epithet of El, 146
Grave Circle A, Mycenaean burials, 269
grave goods, 197–8, 227, 358, 381–4
Graviscae, Etruscan sanctuary at, 329
Great God, Zoroastrian deity, 121
Great Goddess, Minoan deity, 238, 248–50, 252
Greater Greece, Greek settlements in southern
    Italy or Sicily, 347
Great Mother, Minoan goddess, 237
Greece,
    Archaic, 10–11, 272
    Mycenaean, 19, 240–1, 256–7, 265, 270, 373
    religion of. *See* Greeks, religion of
    worship of Roman emperor in, 11
Greeks, religion of,
    altars,
        burning God's portions on, 293
        leading animals to, 291
        of Poseidon, 294
    divination,
        dreams, 298–9
        omens, 297
        mantikē technē, art of prophecy, 297
        seers (*manteis*), 285
        see also oracles
    festivals, religious,
        Panathenaia, 294
        Pyanopsia, 296
        games,
            at Delphi, 284
            at Olympia, 284
            of Isthmus, 284
            of Nemea, 284
        in Attica, 296
        roles of Athenian magistrates in,
            archon, 286
            basileus, 286
            polemarchos, 286
    gods and goddesses,
        Aesculapius. *See* Asklepios
        Aphrodite, goddess of love and beauty, 283
        Aphrodite Ourania (heavenly Aphrodite),
            283
        Apollo, sun god, 283, 296. *See also* Apollon
        Apollo Agyieus (Apollo "of the streets"),
            283
        Apollo Epikourios, 296
        Apollo Patroös, guarantor of phratry
            membership, 287
        Areion, deity of Arcadia, 282

Artemis, Apollo's sister, 283, 296
Artemis Brauronia, 295
Asklepios, Greek god of healing, 298
Athena (Athene), Greek goddess of
    wisdom, 281, 283, 295
Athena Ergane, 282
Athena Nike, 295
Athena Polias, Athena "of the city," 282
Athena Pronaia, Athena "in front of the
    temple," 294
Athena Skiras, 296
Athena Soteira, Athena "savior," 282
Daeira, Attic goddess, 282
Demeter, 283
Despoina, Arcadian deity, 282
Dionysus, 281, 296
Hephaestus (Hephaistos), smith-god, 281
Hera, 281
Hermes, 295
Hestia, goddess of the hearth, 282
Koios, 282
Kourotrophos, "nurturer of children," 282
Kronos, god of time, 282
Olympians, 282
Ouranos, 282
Pan, 283
Persephone, 283
Phoibe, 282
Poseidon, 283, 295
Rhea, ancient mother of Zeus and Hestia,
    282
Tritopatores, 282
Zeus, Greek "father of the gods," 14, 122,
    210, 252, 254, 260, 263, 271, 281–3
Zeus Herkeios, Zeus "of the enclosure" or
    "of the household," 287
Zeus Meilichios, "the kindly one," 283
Zeus Polieus, 295
heroes and heroines,
    Agamemnon, 283
    Aglauros, 295
    Erechtheus, 295
    Erichthonios, 295
    Herakles (Heracles, Hercules), 283
    Neoptolemos, 293
    Pandrosos, 295
incubation, 298. *See also* dreams
Mysteries, 298–9
oracles,
    Amphiareion at Oropos, 286
    at Branchidai, 285
    at Delphi, 285–6, 297. *See also* Pythia

General Index

Greeks, religion of (*cont.*)

  at Didyma, 285

  at Dodona, 285, 297–8

  of Trophonios, 297. *See also* divination

personnel, sacred,

  priest, 285–6, 288, 292–3, 297

  priestess, 285, 292–3

Pythia, 286, 297

rituals,

  mystēria. See Mysteries

  Oschophoria, 296

  role of Athenian magistrates in,

    exēgētai, "explicators," 285

    hieromnēmones, "rememberers" of sacred

      rites, 286

    hierophylakes, "guardians" of sacred

      rites, 286

    hieropoioi, "sacred/ritual doers," 286

sacrifice,

  in Attica, 286

  mageiros, butcher-cook, 291

  roles of Athenian magistrates in,

    archon, 286

superhuman beings and spirits,

  asuras, superhuman beings, 282

  devas, superhuman beings, 282

  nymphs, 283

  Titans, 282

temples and sanctuaries,

  Amphiaraos, healing sanctuary

    (Amphiareion) at Oropos, 292, 298.

    See also incubation

  at Chios, 292

  at Olympia, 294

  Erechtheion, 295

  Heraia,

    of Argos, 296

    of Samos, 296

  of Apollo, at Delphi, 294

  of Apollo Epikourios, 296

  of Artemis Brauronia, 295

  of Athena Ergane, 282

  of Athena Nike, 295

  of Athena Polias, 282

  of Athena Pronaia, 294

  of Athena Soteira, 282

  of the Charites, 295

  of Hekate Epipyrgidia, 295

  of Hermes, 295

  of Zeus, 262–3, 341

  of Zeus Polieus, 295

  Parthenon, on the Athenian Acropolis, 295

  underworld, 283, 293

Green, M. J., twentieth-century scholar of

  Celtic religion, 367

Gregory of Tours, Gallo-Roman historian

  (538–594 CE),

  Vitae Patrum (Lives of the Fathers), 379

Grotta Porcina, Etruscan altar at, 330

Gsell, S., twentieth-century French scholar of

  North Africa, 208

Gu-dea, "the chosen one," Sumerian ruler, 47

guest-friends, guest-friendship, 105, 125

Gulšeš, Hittite Fate Deities, 95

Gundestrup cauldron, 370

Gwowia, Mycenaean cow-goddess, 260, 262.

  See also qo-wi-ja

Habakkuk,

  Psalm of, 155

  see also Bible

Hadad (Hadda). *See* Baal

Hades. *See* Aita

Hadrumetum, modern Sousse, Tunisia, 222

Hagia Triada, Minoan sarcophagus from, 246

hāiti, each of the seventeen sections into which

  the *Gāthā*s are subdivided, 103

Hallstatt culture,

  artifacts, 369, 371

  see also Celtic religion

Hammurabi,

  Code of, 71, 166

  Dynasty, 56, 59, 69

  see Assyrian and Babylonian religions

Handsome (one). *See* Adonis

haoma, divine plant. *See* Zoroastrianism

Haphaistios, Mycenaean anthroponym.

  See Hephaestus

harioli, "charlatans," 355

Harsaphes, Egyptian god, 180

haruspex, Etruscan priest, 318, 321

haruspex fulguriator, "reader of entrails" or

  "reader of lightning," 322

haruspication, Etruscan science,

  practice of, 309, 316, 331–2

Hašauwaš, "the one of birth," Hittite female

  magicians, 95

haššēm, "the Name," 153

Hathor, Egyptian deity,

  sanctuary of, 192. *See also* Isis

hatrencu, Etruscan priestess, 322

Hatshepsut, Egyptian New Kingdom female

  pharaoh (1473–1458 BCE), 186

Hatti. *See* Hittite religion

Hattuša. *See* Boğazköy/Hattuša
Hattušili III, Hittite ruler,
  "Apology" of, 91
Haug, M., nineteenth-century German scholar
  of Zoroastrianism, 123
Hayling Island, England, Romano-Celtic temple
  at, 380
Healer. *See* Baal
heaven, 10, 34, 39, 48, 50, 68, 105, 109–10, 113–
  14, 120, 122, 171, 201, 250. *See also* hell
Heavenly River, 112, 115, 117
Hebat, Sun-goddess of Arinna, 88–9.
  See also Aleppo
Hebrew,
  Bible. *See* Bible, Hebrew
  see also languages, Semitic
Hebron, Judean area, 155, 157, 169
hegemony,
  Assyrian, 58
  Persian, 103
  Roman, 342, 347–8
  Sumerian, 69
heka, "magic." *See* Egyptian religion
hêkal, "palace" or "great hall" of Solomon's
  Temple, 159–60
Hekate Epipyrgidia, sanctuary of, 295
Heliopolis, Egypt, center of solar cult, 181
Heliopolitan Cosmogony. *See* Cosmogony,
  Heliopolitan
Heliopolitan Ennead, nine primeval deities,
  181, 186
hell, 106, 109, 113, 115, 118. *See also* heaven
Hellene, used by Christian apologists and
  polemicists for non-Christians, 17
Hellenistic,
  age, 11, 18–20, 23, 331
  kingdoms, 18. *See also* Alexander the Great
Hellenization, 23–4
Helveti, people of the late Hallstatt period, 382
hem-netjer, "god's servant," Egyptian priestly
  title, 188, 191
Henchir Medeine. *See* Althiburus
Henning, W. B., twentieth-century scholar of
  Iranian religion, 126
hepatoscopy. *See* divination
Hephaestus (Hephaistos), Greek smith-god, 281
Heqet, personified birth brick, frog-goddess, 196
Hera, Greek goddess, 210, 254, 260, 262, 271,
  281, 341. *See also* e-ra
Heraclitus, Greek philosopher (535–475 BCE),
  294
Heraia, sanctuary,

  of Argos, 296
  of Samos, 296
Herakles (Hercules), Greek hero, 210, 283, 318,
  340, 351
Hērbedestān, Zoroastrian manual, 103. *See also*
  Etruscans, religions of
Hercle. *See* Herakles
Hercules. *See* Herakles
heresies,
  Christian, 19
  Zoroastrian,
    Zurvanism, 124
Hermes, Greek god, 295. *See also* e-ma-a₂,
  theonyms
heroes, heroines,
  Celtic, 365, 369
  Greek, 7, 283–4, 293–6
  in Zoroastrianism, 106, 116–17
Herodotus, Greek historian (fifth century
  BCE),
  Histories, 103, 122, 179, 228, 281, 286
Hesiod, Greek poet (eighth-seventh century
  BCE),
  Theogony, 281
  Works and Days, 299
Hestia, Greek goddess of the hearth, 282
Hezekiah, Judean king, 162, 166–7
ḥḥ aṭ ḥ tā't, "Sin Offering" in Israelite and
  Judean religions, 164
ḥḥ êq hā'āresh, "the bosom of the earth" in
  Israelite and Judean religions, 160
Hieraconpolis, ancient Nekhen, modern Kom
  el-Ahmar,
  Egyptian temple at, 187
  tomb at, 197
hierarchy,
  of gods, 147, 370
  social, 187
hiereus, priest, 267. *See also* i-je-re-u, and Greek
  religion, personnel, sacred
hierodules, slaves of the god. *See* Mycenaean
  religion. *See also* slaves
hierogamia, sacred marriage, 111
hieroglyph, 178, 189
Hieroglyphic A and B, Minoan scripts, 237
hieromnēmones, "rememberers" of sacred rites,
  Athenian officials, 286
hieron, sanctuary, 263. *See also* i-je-ro
hierophylakes, "guardians" of sacred rites,
  Athenian officials, 286
hieropoioi, "sacred/ritual doers," Athenian
  officials, 286

414   *General Index*

hierourgos, doer of ritual, 267. *See also i-je-*
    ro-wo-ko, and Etruscans, religions of
High Priests of Amun, 191
Hittites,
  Boğazköy/Hattuša, metropolis of,
    tablets from, 84. *See also* Hattuša
  empire of, 89
  Kuşaklı/Šarišša, Hittite provincial center, 84.
    See also tablets
  language of, *See* languages, Indo-European
  religion of,
    afterlife, 96
    akkant, spirits of the dead, 95
    arkuwar, "plaidoyer," 92
    bullae,
      images of gods on, 86
    cosmos, 84, 90, 96
    cult, athletes in, 94
    divination,
      augury, 93
      dreams, 92
      extispicy, 93
      incubation, 93
      omens, 92
      oracles, 92–3
    festivals, religious, 93–4
    gods and goddesses of,
      Arinna, Sun-goddess of, 89, 92
      Arušna, deity of, 93. *See also* divination
      DINGIR.MAH^MEŠ/HI.A, mother
        goddess, 95
      Gulšeš, fate deities, 95
      Hebat, Sun-goddess of Arinna, 88–9
      Iyaya, goddess, 87
      patron deities, 89
      Protective Deity. *See* patron deities
      Šapinuwa, Storm god of, 89
      Šaušga, 87, 91. *See also* patron deities
      Tazzuwašši, 89
      Teššub, storm god, 88–9
      Thousand Gods, 90
      Yazılıkaya, 87
      Zaliyanu, 89
      Zašhapuna, 89
      Zawalli, 96
      Zippalanda, storm god of, 89
    huwaši, god's ineffable essence located in
      an image, 87
    impurity. *See papratar*
    "Instructions to Temple Officials," Hittite
      text. *See* sacrifice
    magic and magicians,

    alwanzatar, black magic, 94
    hašauwaš, "the one of birth," Hittite
      female magicians, 95
    incantations, 95
    papratar, impurity, 94–5
    parā handandatar, "prior arrangement" or
      "providence," 91
    prophecy, prophets,
      šiunaš antuhšaš, "man of god" or
        prophet, 92
    sacrifice, 91, 93
    temples,
      šiunaš per, "house of the god," 85
      Yazılıkaya, temple of, 87
    underworld, 95. *See also* afterlife
    seals,
      cylinder and stamp, 86
    writing of,
      cuneiform, script, 86
hmhh šbm'š ln, "our comptrollers," on Punic
    inscriptions, 219
Hochdorf Prince, Late Hallstatt Celtic burial,
    382
Hockwold, Romano-British temple at, 376
Hoffmann, K., twentieth-century German
    scholar of Zoroastrianism, 125
holocaust. *See* offerings, *See also* sacrifice
Holy of Holies, "inner sanctum." *See* Jerusalem
    temple. *See also dḥ bîr*
Holy One. *See* YHWH
Homer, ninth/eighth-century BCE Greek epic
    poet,
    Iliad, 205, 258, 294
    Odyssey, 205, 261
Horden, P. and N. Purcell, twentieth-century
    scholars,
    The Corrupting Sea, 13–14. *See also* geography
Horon, Syro-Canaanite deity, 145
Hornung, E., twentieth-century scholar,
    Conceptions of God in Ancient Egypt, 178
Horus, Egyptian god, son of Osiris,
    personification of divine kingship,
      180, 182–3, 186, 192–3, 197.
    See also falcon
"house of god." *See hut-netjer*
House of the Frescoes. *See* Mycenaean religion
House of the Idols. *See* Mycenaean religion
Huldah, female prophet in southern Judah,
    170
humans,
  domain of, 31, 34, 39, 48, 52
  life of, 23, 49, 119, 146

General Index

relationships, with other humans or gods, 2, 50, 73, 84, 179, 288, 290, 352, 359
Humbach, H., twentieth-century German scholar of Zoroastrianism, 125–6
Humban, Elamite deity, 121
Humility, 106–7, 109, 111, 114
Hurrians, 60, 67
hut-netjer, "house of god," 188
huwaši. *See* Hittite gods worship
hybridity, as a term of analysis of religion, 16
Hyde, T., seventeenth-century English orientalist, 123
Hygieia, Apollo's granddaughter, 372
hymns,
  in Egyptian religion, 183, 187, 194–5
  in Zoroastrianism, 103, 105–6, 112–13, 116–18, 125
  see also, En-hedu-ana, *Khorda Avesta, yashts*

Iba 'lt, Syro-Cannanite month, 143
ibis. *See* Thoth
Icard, F., French excavator of Carthage, 209
iconography,
  Assyrian, 61, 68, 77
  Egyptian, 186, 194
  Minoan, 242, 254
  Mycenaean, 271
  Punic, 221
  Syro-Canaanite, 137
Ides. *See* calendars
idols, 179, 246, 259, 264
Idrimi, inscription of, 131, 144
i-je-re-u. *See* hiereus
i-je-ro. *See* hieron
i-je-ro-wo-ko. *See* hierourgos
Illahun, Egyptian town, 187
Iluma-ilum, Babylonian ruler, 57
images. *See* statues
Immortals, Life-giving. *See* amesha spenta
impiety, 147
Inana, goddess of the Venus star, 34–5, 40–1, 43–5, 49–51, 66, 69–70.
  See also Sumerian religion
Inana and An, 50
Inana and En-ki, 35, 49
Inana's descent to the netherworld, 50
incantations,
  in Assyrian and Babylonian religions, 76
  in Egyptian religion, 197
  in Hittite religion, 95
  in Sumerian religion, 48–9

in Syro-Canaanite religion, 131, 144
incubation, 93, 298
Indara, evil god in Zoroastrianism, 114
Indic. *See* languages, Indo-European
Indo-Aryans,
  language of, 102
Indo-European. *See* languages
Indo-Iranian. *See* languages, Indo-European
inner sanctum. *See* Holy of Holies
infanticide. *See* Carthage, religion of
inhumation,
  Celtic, 381–2
  Etruscan, 329
  Punic, 227
  Roman, 349
initiations, 268, 270, 298–9, 346. *See also* rituals, *teletai*
Ins, Celtic cemetery at, 382
inscriptions,
  Achaemenid, 104, 120
  Assyrian, 59
  Celtic, 364–5, 370–2, 374
  Egyptian, 8, 177, 180–1, 186, 200
  Etruscan, 309, 314, 318, 322–3, 328
  Greek, 287, 291–2, 302
  Judean, 169–70
  Minoan, 250
  Phoenician and Punic, 209–13, 215–16, 219–20, 222, 226, 228
  Roman, 337, 370
  Sumerian, 33, 45–7, 50–1
  Syro-Canaanite, 131–2, 140, 142, 144–6.
    See also individual inscriptions by name
Insler, S., twentieth-century linguist, 126
instructions of Shuruppak, The, 49–50
"Instructions to Temple Officials," Hittite text, 139
interpretatio (interpretation),
  of other religions, 14
Iphigenia, Agamemnon's daughter, 376
i-qe-ja po-ti-ni-ja, Mycenaean deity, 261.
  See also theonyms
Iran,
  religion of. *See* Zoroastrianism
Iranian. *See* languages, Indo-Aryan
Iranian Plateau, 19, 102
Ireland, Celtic, 365, 367, 370, 372, 375–6, 384
Isaac, patriarch, 155, 157
Isad-wāstar, Zarathustra's son, 118
Ischia (Pithecoussai), island, Phoenician settlement on, 206

416 *General Index*

Ishbi-Irra, Amorite ruler, 69
Ishkur. *See* Adad
Ishtar, goddess of love and war, 65–6, 68–70.
    See also Inana
Isin, Sumerian city, 38–9, 50
Isis, Egyptian goddess, sister and wife of Osiris,
    mother of Horus, 181–2, 197, 201, 213,
    223, 225, 228
    see also Astarte, Hathor
Israel,
  ancient,
    destruction of northern kingdom, 151, 157
    origins of, 155
    religion of. *See* Israelite and Judean
      religions
    twelve tribes of, 156–7
Israelite and Judean religions,
  Asherah (Asherata), goddess, 134, 156, 169,
    250. *See also* Syro-Canaanite religion
  El Elyon, "God Most High,"
    veneration by Abram, 155, 162
    see also El
  El Shaddai, YHWH, as known to Abraham,
    Isaac, and Jacob, 155. *See also* El
  festivals,
    pesaḥḥ, "Passover," beginning of grain
      harvest and Exodus from Egyptian
      slavery, 163. *See also* Matzot, "Unleavened
      Bread"
    šābûʿôt (Shavuot), "Weeks (Pentecost),"
      conclusion of the grain harvest, and
      commemoration of the revelation of
      Torah, 163
    Sukkôt (Sukkot), "Booths" or
      "Tabernacles," conclusion of the fruit
      harvest and beginning of the rainy
      season, 163
  first collections of Israelite law,
    Covenant Code, 165–6
    Ten Commandments, 165–6
  Golden Calf,
    cultic apostasy with, 166, 168
  hymns,
    in Book of Psalms, 164
  judges,
    Deborah, 169
    Othniel, first judge of Judah, 157
    šōpēṭḥ, "judge," 157
  Kenites, descendants of Cain, early
    worshipers of YHWH, 154
  Jethro, priest of Midian, father-in-law of
    Moses, 154

Rechabites, Bedouin group devoted to
    YHWH, 154
offerings,
  ʾāšām, "Guilt Offering," 164
  ḥḥaṭṭāʾt, "Sin Offering," 164
patriarchs,
  Abraham, 155–7. *See also* Abram
  Isaac, father of Esau and Jacob, 155, 157
  Jacob, grandson of Abraham, brother of
    Esau, ancestor of Israel, 155, 157, 162
priestly roles,
  instruction of the people in the Torah
    (*tôrâ*), 161
  liturgies, 161
  sacrifices, 161–2
priests,
  Kenites,
    Jethro, 154
  Levites,
    Aaron, brother of Moses, first chief
      priest of Israel, 161, 169
    Eleazer, ancestor of the Zadokites, 161
    Gershonites, Levitical line founded by
      Gershom, son of Moses, 162
    Ithamar, ancestor of the subsidiary
      priestly line of Abiathar, 161–2
    Kohathites, Levitical family, 161
    Jeremiah, 170–1
    Merarites, Levitical family, 162
    Moses (Moshe), 153, 157, 161, 165–7,
      169–70
  Zadokites,
    Ezekiel, 170
prophets,
  Amos, non-priestly Judean prophet, 170
  Deborah, 169
  Elijah, 154, 170
  Ezekiel, 170
  Huldah, 170
  Isaiah, non-priestly prophet, 170
  Micah, non-priestly prophet, 170
  Miriam, sister of Moses and Aaron, 169
  Second Isaiah, 171
  Zechariah, 170
rōʾš haššanâ, New Year, beginning of liturgical
    year, 163
sacrifices,
  ʿōlâ, "whole burnt offering," 164
    see also holocaust
  zebaḥḥ šĕlāmîm, "Sacrifice of Well-being,"
    164
Scriptures

General Index

Bible, Hebrew, 151, 154, 156–7, 161–2,
  167–8, 170
  Old Testament, 151
  Tanakh, 151
temples,
  at Arad, 157, 168
  massetbot (*mashshēbôt*), uninscribed
    cultic pillars at, 169
  at Beer Sheba, 157, 168
  at Beth El, 157, 162, 167–8, 170
  massetbot at, 7, 169
  at Dan, 157, 167–8
  at Gibeon, 168
  at Gilgal, 157, 168
  at Megiddo, 168
  at Shechem, 168
  at Shiloh, 157, 168
  Ark of the Covenant at, 157
  Jerusalem (of Solomon),
    altar of, 160, 162
    Boaz, bronze pillar of, 159
    candelabra at, 160
    'ûlām, portico of, 159
    dĕbîr, "inner sanctum," Holy of Holies
      at: Ark of the Covenant in, 160–1
    Jachin, bronze pillar of, 159
    Joshua ben Jehozadak, high priest of
      Second Temple, 161
    hêkal, "palace" or "great hall" of, 159–60
    liturgy at, 159–60. *See also* Yom Kippur
  theophoric names,
    forms of Hezekiah, 153
    hḥizqîyâ, 153
    hḥizqîyāhû, 153
    yḥ hḥizqîyāhû, 153
  women, liturgical roles of,
    Deborah, 169
    Miriam, 169
  worship,
    celebration of Passover (*pesahh*), 162–3
    celebration of Sukkot, 162, 168
    prayers, 162
    psalms, 162, 169–70
    sacrifices, 160–4, 166, 168–9
  YHWH (*Yahweh, Yh, Yhw, Y-hw-h, Yw*),
    ineffable name of the deity
    worshiped in
    ancient Israel and Judah, 151, 153–71
    creation of the world by, 156
    Sabbath (*Šabbāt*), day of rest, at the end
      of, 156, 163
    origins of the name in Edom and Midian,

153, 155
  see also '*ădōnāy*, "my Lord"; *haššēm*, "the
    Name"; *šĕmā'*, "the Name"
yôm kippûr (Yom Kippur), Day of
  Atonement, annual fast day, 153,
  164. *See also* Canaan, religion of,
  Israel, religion of; Jews and Judaism;
  in ancient Israel and Judah; Judah,
  religion of; Palestine, Judaism in
Isthmus, Greek games of, 184
iśveita, Etruscan week-like period, 357.
  See also aperta, celuta, tiniana
Italic. *See* languages, Indo-European
Italy,
  Christian communities in, 8, 20
  Jewish communities in, 8, 20
Ithamar, son of Aaron, 161–2
itus. See Ides
Iuppiter Lapis, "Jupiter the Stone." *See* Roman
  religion
Iyaya, Hittite goddess, 87
iyerowworgos. See hierourgos

Jachin, bronze pillar in Solomon's Temple, 159
Jackson, A. V. W., nineteenth-century scholar,
  Zoroaster the Prophet of Ancient Iran, 124
Jacob, patriarch, grandson of Abraham, brother
  of Esau, 155, 157, 162
Janitores Terrestres, "Doorkeepers of the Earth,"
  Etruscan deities, 318–19
Jehovah, 153
Jeremiah, Levitical priest, 170–1
Jeroboam,
  establishment of sanctuaries, 168
  offerings, 162
  see also Israelite and Judean religions
Jerusalem,
  city, 58, 155, 158
  Temple, 153, 158–60, 162, 164–9, 171
Jethro, Kenite priest, father-in-law of Moses,
  154
Jews and Judaism,
  in ancient Israel and Judea. *See* Israelite and
    Judean religions
Jochebed, Aaron's mother, 161
Josephus, Titus Flavius, Jewish historian
  (37–100 CE),
  Against Apion (Contra Apionem), 209
  Antiquities of the Jews (Antiquitates judaicae),
    209
Joshua, 157, 162
Joshua ben Jehozadak, high priest, 161

418   *General Index*

Josiah, Judean king, son of Amon,
   religious reform by, 167
Judah,
   kingdom of, 151, 157–8, 171
   religion of. *See* Israelite and Judean religions
   tribe, 158
Judaism,
   in diaspora communities, 8, 14
   in Palestine, 8, 20
   see also Israelite and Judean religions
Judea,
   religion of. *See* Israelite and Judean
     religions
judges, 157, 169
Juno, Roman goddess, wife and sister of Jupiter,
   317, 341, 351, 357
   see also Capitoline Triad
Juno Lacinia,
   temple of, 210
Juno Lucina,
   sanctuary of, 351
Juno Moneta,
   sanctuary of, 351
Juno Regina,
   sanctuary of, 351
Juno Sospita,
   statue of, 353
Junon, Carthaginian cemetery at, 209
Jupiter, Roman king of the gods, 315, 317, 319,
   357, 371
   priests of, 344, 357
   temple of, 341, 351
   see also Capitoline Triad, Roman religion
Jupiter Feretrius,
   sanctuary of, 351
Jupiter Optimus Maximus. *See* Jupiter
Justi, F., nineteenth-century scholar of
   Zoroastrianism, 123

ka, life force, 195
Kabkab, Semitic astral deity, 133–4
Kalapodi, temple at. *See* Mycenaean religion
Kalends, first day of Roman month, 356
   see also calendars
Kamish, Moabite chief god, 132
   see also Kemosh
ka-ra-wi-po-ro. *See kleidoukhos*
Karnak, temple at. *See* Egyptian religion
karpan, evil sacrificer, 105
ka-ru-ke. *See kerux*
Kashtiliash IV, Babylonian Kassite king, 72
Kassites, 57, 62, 69, 72, 74. *See also* Assyrian and
   Babylonian religions

kawi, evil sacrificer, 105
Kawi Wishtāspa, Aryan hero in Zoroastrianism,
   117
Keftiu, Cretans, 239
Kellens, J., and E. Pirart, twentieth-century
   scholars of Zoroastrianism, 126
Kelsey, F. W., twentieth-century scholar of the
   Carthaginians, 209
Keltoi, Celts, 364
Kemosh. *See* Kamish
Kenites, descendants of Cain, 154
ke-re-ta. *See khrestes*
kerp, sunlit heavenly spaces, "form" of Ahura
   Mazdā, 108–9
Kersāspa, dragon slayer, 116
kerux (karux), "herald," 267. *See also ka-ru-ke*
Kesh, city, 43
   gods of, 43
   temples at, 43, 48
   see also Sumerian religion
Kesh temple hymn, The, 48
Khasekhemwy, Egyptian king of the second
   dynasty (2676–2649 BCE), 198
Khentiamentiu, Egyptian funerary god, 179
   see also jackal
Khepri ("one who comes into being)," scarab.
   See Egyptian religion
kheri-hebet, Egyptian lector priests, 191
khn, priest. *See khnm*
khnm, priests,
   of Carthage. *See* Carthage, religion of
   of Ugarit. *See* Syro-Canaanite religion
Khnum, Egyptian god, 177, 180, 196
Khonsu, son of Amen and Mut, 192
   see also Egyptian religion
khrafstra, harmful being, 114
khratu, "guiding thought." *See saoshyant*
khrestes, "prophet," 267
KI, Earth in Achaemenid religion, 121
king list,
   Assyrian, 59
   Sumerian, 37, 39, 59
   Tyrian, 209, 220
kingship,
   divine, 182, 193
   Egyptian, 182, 186, 193
   Hittite, 96
   Minoan, 240, 253
   Roman, 342
   Sumerian, 10, 39, 69
kings,
   and religious roles,
     Gu-dea (Sumerian kingship), 47

General Index

ki-ri-te-wi-ja, Mycenaean female ritual
  specialist, 267. *See also kritheuia*
Kirk, G., twentieth-century scholar of Greek
  myth, 302
Kirta,
  story, 134, 136, 138, 140, 146–7
  text, 145, 147
  see also Syro-Canaanite religion
kleidoukhos, "key-bearer," 267. *See also*
  ka-ra-wi-po-ro
Knossos,
  gods and goddesses of, 247–50, 252–4
  kings of, 241–2, 253
  palace of, 240, 242, 244, 246, 248–9
  tablets, 254
  see also Mycenaean religion
Kohathites, Levitical family of priests, 161.
  See also Ark of the Covenant
kôhēn, priest, 213
koine,
  religious, 12, 241, 246
  social, 13
Koios, Greek deity, 282
Komawenteia, Mycenaean deity, 262
ko-ma-we-te-ja, Mycenaean deity, 261
Konsolaki-Yannopoulou, E., twentieth-century
  scholar of the Aegean Bronze Age,
  266
Kontorli-Papadopoulou, L., twentieth-century
  scholar of Aegean frescoes, 260
Kotharat, Syro-Canaanite birth goddesses, 139
Kothar-wa-Hasis, Syro-Canaanite craftsman
  god, 139
Kourotrophos, "nurturer of children," Greek
  deity, 282
Krahmalkov, C. R., twentieth-century scholar of
  the Phoenicians and Carthaginians,
  221
krithewia. See ki-ri-te-wi-ja
Kronos, Greek god of time, 282
krr, Phoenician month, 225
Kuntillet 'Ajrud, YHWH inscriptions at, 169
Kuşakli/Šarišša, Hittite provincial center, 84.
  See also tablets, clay
Kuttamuwa, inscription. *See* Syro-Canaanite
  religion
Kynortion, mountain, Mycenaean sanctuary
  at, 264

Lactantius, second/third-century-CE Christian
  writer,
  Institutiones divinae (divine Institutes), 1
Lady of Vix, 382

Lagash, Sumerian state, 46–7
lan, principal Elamite ritual, 121
languages,
  Babylonian, 57
  Indo-Aryan,
  Sanskrit, 102
  Indo-European,
  Anatolian, 10
  Celtic, 10, 368
  Indo-Iranian, 10
  Italic, 10
  Hellenic, 10
  Hittite, 86, 131
  Latin, 337
  Luwian, 86
  Palaic, 86
  Iranian, 102
  Semitic,
  Akkadian, 10, 35–6, 131
  Aramaic, 10, 132
  Assyro-Babylonian, 10
  Hebrew, 10, 223
  Palaeo-Syrian, 10
  Phoenician, 10, 132, 205
  Sumerian, 31
Lapeyre, G. G., twentieth-century French
  scholar of Carthage, 209, 216, 222
Laran, Etruscan god of lightning and thunder,
  317. *See also* Mars
L(a)ris Pulenas,
  tomb of, 323
larnakes, 269
Larsa, Sumerian city, 38, 43, 75
Larth Cafates, 322
Lasa, Etruscan flying spirit, 319
Late Helladic period. *See* Mycenaean religion
Late Minoan, historical period of Crete, 239.
  See also Early Minoan, Middle
  Minoan
La Tène culture. *See* Celtic religion
Late Period (760–332 BCE). *See* Egyptian
  religion
Latins, people of Italy, 337, 376
Latium, Italy, 349
  Etruscan, 310
  non-Etruscan, 328
law,
  codes of, 165–7, 342
  divine, 216
  of kings, 121
lawagetas, Mycenaean official, 268
Lazpa, Mycenaean deity of, 263. *See also* Lesbos
Lebadeia. *See* Trophonios

General Index

Lechesis, Greek fate goddess, sister of Clotho and Atropos, 320

leconomancy. *See* divination, *See also* Assyrian and Babylonian religions

lectisternium. See lekhe-stro-terion

Leinth, Etruscan deity, 318–19

lekhe-stro-terion, "spreading the couches," 266. *See also lectisternium, re-ke-e-to-te-ri-jo*

Lenus, Celtic healing god, 372. *See also* Mars

Lesbos. *See* Lazpa

Letham, Etruscan deity, 318

Levi, tribe, 161. *See also* Israelite and Judean religions

Leviathan, Yahweh's enemy, 137, 253. *See also* Litan

Levites, priests, 161–2, 169–70

lex Hortensia, Roman law of 287 BCE accepting the binding force of plebiscites, 342

lex Ogulnia, third-century-BCE Roman law opening priesthoods to plebeians, 342, 348, 357

libanomancy. *See* divination. *See also* Assyrian and Babylonian religions

Libenice, Czech Republic, Celtic sanctuary at, 368

Liber, Roman deity, part of the "plebeian triad," 351

Libera, Roman deity, part of the "plebeian triad," 351

liber linteus, Etruscan sacrificial calendar, 314. *See also* Agramer Mumienbinden

Lie, principle of chaos, 108–9

life,
  eternal, 49, 137
  human, 23, 49, 119
  political, 4, 7, 12, 322, 331
  religious, 12, 24, 54, 68, 84, 269
  social, 7, 12

Life-Giving Immortals, 107, 113–14, 126. *See also* Zoroastrianism

lightning, 68, 93, 135, 155, 160, 310, 317–18, 320, 322, 348

Lindos, sanctuary of Aphrodite at, 213

Lindow Man. *See* bog men

Linear A, script of ancient Crete, 270

Linear B, script of ancient Crete, 256–7, 260, 263, 265–6, 281

Lipiński, E., twentieth-century scholar of the Phoenicians and Carthaginians, 221

lists,
  deity, 44, 46

Litan. *See* Leviathan

"Litany of Ra," 183

literature,
  Babylonian, 57–8
  biblical, 161
  devotional 48–50
  Egyptian, 194
  Greek, 208
  omen literature, 73
  prophetic, 164
  Mesopotamian, 61
  Sumerian, 31–2, 39, 47–8
  Ugaritic, 134
  wisdom, 73, 202

liturgy,
  in Israelite and Judean religions, 153, 159–60
  in Syro-Canaanite religion, 143, 146–7

liver, model of, 311–12, 317. *See also* divination, Piacenza liver

Lixus, Punic city, 208

Livy, Titus, Roman historian (59 BCE-17 CE),
  Ab Urbe Condita (From the Founding of the City), 210, 315, 343–4, 346, 348, 354, 369, 376–7, 380

'lm, Punic deity, 211. *See also* Melqart

Lommel, H., twentieth-century scholar of Zoroastrianism, 125–6

Lord. *See 'ădōnāy. See also* Baal, El

'lt, Punic sacrifice. *See* holocaust

Lucan, Roman writer (39–65 CE),
  Pharsalia, 371, 377

Lucian of Samosata, Greco-Roman writer (125–180 CE),
  De syria dea (The Syrian Goddess), 132, 213

ludi, Roman games, 357–8
  Capitolini, 358
  Plebeian Games, 358
  votivi, victory games, 358
  see also chariot races, festivals

Lugal-banda, Sumerian "Junior king," 50

Lugal-banda and Nin-sumuna, Sumerian religious literature, 50

Lugh ("shining light"), Celtic deity, 370

Lupercal, Roman sanctuary on the Palatine, 351

Lur, Etruscan deity, 318

Luwian. *See* languages, Indo-European

Lydus, Johannes, sixth-century-CE Byantine writer, 315

Lynsa Silvestris, Etruscan deity, 318

maat, order, 183. *See also* Egyptian religion
MacCulloch, John A., twentieth-century scholar
  of Celtic religion, 366
Macrobius, fifth-century-CE Roman writer,
  Saturnalia, 356
maga, exchange of gifts, 106
mageiros, butcher-cook, 291
Magi. *See* Zoroaster
magic and magicians,
  in Assyrian and Babylonian religions, 77
  in Celtic religion, 375–6
  in Egyptian religion, 182, 195, 197, 200, 228
  in Etruscan religion, 310
  in Hittite religion, 85, 94–5
  see also heka, rituals
magistrates,
  religious functions of,
    Athenian, 285–6
    Etruscan, 322
Magna Mater, Cybele, 14. *See also* Mountain
  Mother
magoi. See magic and magicians
magush, Elamite priests, 121
Maiden Castle, Celtic temple at, 380
Malaka, Spain, Punic settlement, 207
Málaga. *See* Malaka
maledictions. *See* Carthage, religion of
Mami. *See* Assyrian and Babylonian religions
  Atrahasis
Man and His God, A, 73
manah, "thought" in Old Avestan
  Zoroastrianism, 109
ma-na-sa, Mycenaean deity, 261
Manasseh,
  son of Jacob, 157
  tribe, 157
  see also Menasheh
Manichaeism,
  in Iran and Armenia, 8
manteis, seers, 285
manthra, Zoroastrian poems, 108
manthra spenta, Life-giving Poetic Thought, 112
mantikē technē, art of prophecy, 297
Marcii, seers, 355
  see also divination
Marduk,
  cult statue of, 62, 72
  see also Assyrian and Babylonian religions
Mariś, Etruscan deity appearing as triplets, 319
Market Harborough, England,
  Celtic offerings at, 379
marriage,

next-of-kin, 111, 120
sacred,
  in Assyrian and Babylonian religions, 70
Mars, Roman deity of war, 317, 344, 351, 355–6,
  371. *See also* Laran, *tubilustrium*
Marseilles (France),
  Tariff. *See* Carthage, religion of
martān, "that which contains something dead,"
  114
Martianus Capella, fifth-century-CE Roman
  writer,
  *De nuptiis Philologiae et Mercurii (On the
    marriage of Philology and Mercury)*,
  317–18
maruχva, Etruscan association of priests, 322
Marzabotto, Etruscan temple at, 325
marzeah, ritual feast, 142, 147
maš 'artu, Syro-Canaanite priestess, 142
Maşat Höyük/Tapikka, Hittite provincial
  center, 84
mashshēbôt, cultic pillars, 169. *See also massetbot*
Maspero, G., nineteenth/twentieth-century
  French Egyptologist, 178
massetbot. See mashshēbôt
Massilia (modern Marseilles, France), Greek
  settlement at, 368
mastabas, tombs. *See* Egyptian religion
Master of Animals, 198
ma-te-re te-i-ja (Mater Thehia), Mycenaean
  deity, 260
Mater Matuta, 339, 341, 344, 351
matrons. *See* women, roles of
Matzot, "Unleavened Bread," 163.
  See also Israelite and Judean religions
  festivals
mazdā, "all-knowing." *See* Ahura Mazdā
Mazdaism. *See* Zoroastrianism
Mazza, F., S. Ribichini, and P. Xella,
  twentieth-century Italian scholars,
  Fonti classiche per la civiltà fenicia e punica,
  209
medicine. *See* Apollo*See also* magic and
  magicians
Mediterranean,
  Sea, 9–11, 14, 30, 206, 221, 336, 341
  world, 1, 12, 14, 23–4, 26, 171, 228, 240
    as the birthplace of Judaism, Christianity,
      and Islam, 25
megaron, ceremonial hall, 262, 264
Megiddo, Judean temple at, 168
Meleager. *See* Meliacr
Meliacr, 320

422   *General Index*

Melone del Sodo II, Etruscan tomb at, 330
Melqart, Syro-Canaanite deity, 138, 211–13, 215,
    225–6. *See also* Adonis, Baal
Memphis, Egypt,
  gods of, 177, 179
  temple at, 228
men,
  religious roles of, 8
me-na, Mycenaean deity, 260
Menander, Greek dramatist (342–291 BCE),
  Dyskolos (Grouch), 283
Menander of Ephesus, second-century-BCE
    Greek writer, 209, 220
Menasheh. *See* Manasseh
Menrva. *See* Minerva
Merarites, Levitical family, 162. *See also* Levites
mercenaries,
  Carthaginian, 208
  Celtic, 369
  David's, 158
Mercuriales, Roman religious group, 355
Mercury, Roman god, 319, 371, 377
  temples of, 351, 371
  see also Turms
Mesha, Canaanite king,
  inscription of, 132, 144, 154
Meskhenet, personified birth brick, 197.
    See also Egyptian religion
Mesopotamia,
  calendar of, 62, 77
  literature of, 61, 72
  lower, 36–8
  upper, 36–7
metaphor. *See* analogy
me-tu-wo ne-wo, Mycenaean festival, 265
Meuli, K., twentieth-century Swiss philologist,
  301
Mezzula, grandchild of the Storm-god of Hatti,
  89
Middle Kingdom, historical period of Egypt
    (ca.2140–1640 BCE), 181, 186, 192–3,
    196, 199–201. *See also* New Kingdom
Middle Minoan, historical period of Crete, 239.
    See also Early Minoan, Late Minoan
Midian, region, 153–5. *See also* Israelite and
    Judean religions
Milkpilles, Punic epitaph at, 223
Minerva, Roman goddess, 317, 340–1, 351, 371–2,
  374, 378
Minerva Medica, 351, 367. *See also* Sulis
Minoan religion. *See* Minoans, religion of
Minoans,

acrobatics, 248
divination,
  ecstatic, 245, 249
Hagia Triada, sarcophagus from, 246
Hieroglyphic A and B, Minoan hieroglyphic
    scripts, 237
kingship, 240, 253
Linear A, script of ancient Crete, 270
Linear B, script of ancient Crete, 256–7, 260,
    263, 265–6, 281
murals of, 246, 248–9
Poros,
  ring in a tomb at, 244–5
religion of,
  altars, 244
    in Cretan caves, Amnisos (Amnissos),
      worship at, 247
    portable, 246
  bull-leaping. *See* festivals
  double axe, symbol of Great Goddess, 249
    representations on rings and seals, 249
  festivals, religious, 241–3, 246, 248
  gods,
    A-sa-sa-ra, Solar goddess, 250
    Drimios,
      shrine of, 262
    Great Goddess, 238, 248–50, 252
    Great Mother, 237
    patron goddess, 247
  house of god. *See* sanctuaries and shrines
  mythology, 237
  offerings, 246–7
    at Amnissos, 247
    at Psychro, 247
    at Skoteino, 247
  sanctuaries and shrines, 243–4, 246
  underworld, 247
  see also Cretans, Crete, historical periods of,
    palaces of, scripts of
Miriam, prophet, 169
mirrors, Etruscan, 211, 316, 318, 320–2, 326
Mithra, Zoroastrian deity, 112–13, 119–20, 126.
    See also ritual
Mizhdushī, Zoroastrian goddess "who grants
    rewards," 121
mnḥt. See Carthage, religion of
Moab, ancient nation. *See* Moabites
Moabite Stone, stele. *See* YHWH
Moabites, Canaanite ethnic subgroup,
  gods of, 132
  kings of, 141, 144, 154
Moccus, Celtic boar god, 373

General Index

Mochus, Phoenician writer, 209
Mogador, Punic settlement on, 222
Molé, M., twentieth-century French scholar of
    Zoroastrianism, 125
monarchy,
    Israelite, 151
    Judean, 157
    Roman, 342, 355–6
monotheism,
    Egyptian, 178, 194
monsters, 137, 156, 252, 323
monuments,
    non-royal, 183
    religious, 193–4, 339–40, 373
    royal, 121, 186, 198
moon,
    god of,
        in Babylonian religion, 59
        in Sumerian religion, 39–40, 43, 50, 70
        in Syro-Canaanite religion, 132, 134
    see also moon deities by name
mortuary complex. *See* Egyptian religion
Moscati, S., twentieth-century Italian scholar of
    the Phoenicians and Carthaginians,
    208
Moses, Levitical priest, 153, 157, 161, 165–7,
    169–70. *See also* Moshe
Moshe. *See* Moses
Mot, "Death." *See* Baal cycle.
    See also Syro-Canaanite religion
Mountain Mother (*Meter Oreia*), Phrygian
    goddess, 14. *See also* Cybele
Movers, F. C., nineteenth-century German
    scholar,
    Die Phönizier, 208
mqdš, Punic temple, 212–13
mummification, 198, 201
murals, Minoan, 246–9
Muršili II, Hittite ruler, 91
museum,
    Allard Pierson, Amsterdam, 225
    Assurbanipal's, 61
    Bardo, Tunis, 209
    Berlin
    British, 183
    Carthage, 209
    Villa Giulia, Rome, 353
    Zagreb, 314
music and musicians, 76, 143, 170, 191, 330
Mut, Amen's consort, 192
Mycenae, kingdom of,
    burials at,

Grave Circle A, 269
    palaces at, 257, 259, 263–4, 266, 268, 272
    see also Crete
Mycenaean religion,
    altars,
        circular, 264
    cult centers, independent,
        House of the Frescoes, 264
        House of the Idols (Temple Complex),
        259, 264
        Megaron, 262, 264
        Tsountas' House, 259, 262, 264
    divination,
        omens, 258
    Eleusis,
        cultic center at, 264
    festivals, religious, 257, 265–6
        dipsia-festival (*di-pi-si-jo-i*), 258
        lekhe-stro-terion, Mycenaean *lectisternium*
        (?) ("spreading the couches"), 266
        see also re-ke-e-to-te-ri-jo
        me-tu-wo ne-wo, 265
        po-re-no-tu-te-ri-a, 265
        po-re-no-zo-te-ri-ja, 265
        to-no-e-ke-ter-i-jo, 265
    figurines, female (*phi, psi*, and *tau*), 259
    gods and goddesses,
        a-ne-mo ("winds"), deity worshipped at
        Knossos, 260
        A-re, deity worshipped at Knossos, 260
        A-ta-na po-ti-ni-ja, Mycenaean war
        goddess Athanaspotnia, 261
        a-ti-mi-ti, Mycenaean deity of Pylos, 260
        da-nwa, 260
        da-pu₂-ri-to-jo po-ti-ni-ja, "lady of the
        Labyrinth," 260–1
        Dionysus, 262
        di-pi-si-jo-i ("thirsty ones"?), 258, 269
        di-ri-mi-o, 260
        di-we (Diweus), Mycenaean Zeus, 260, 272
        Diwia, 260, 262, 272
        Di-wi Di-ka-ta-i-o, Mycenaean Zeus
        Diktaios, 270
        di-wo-nu-so, Mycenaean Dionysus, 260
        Dopotas, 262
        Drimios, 262
        e-ma-a₂ (Hermes), 260
        e-ne-si-da-o-ne, Mycenaean Ennosidas, 260
        e-nu-wa-ri-jo, Mycenaean Enualios, 260
        e-ra, Mycenaean Hera, 260
        e-ri-nu, Mycenaean Erinus, 260
        Gwowia (qo-wi-ja), cow-goddess, 260, 262

424 General Index

Mycenaean religion (*cont.*)
Haphaistios, Mycenaean Hephaestus, 260
Hera, 262
Hermes, 262
i-pe-me-de-ja, (Iphimedeia), 260, 262
i-qe-ja po-ti-ni-ja, 261
Komawenteia, 262
ko-ma-we-te-ja, "she of the hairy one"(?), 261
ma-te-re te-i-ja (Mater Thehia), 260
me-na, 260
pa-ja-wo-ne, Mycenaean Paian (Paiaon), 260
pe-re-*82, 258, 262
pi-pi-tu-na, 260
po-si-da-e-ja, 260
po-si-da-o, Mycenaean Poseidon, 260
po-ti-ni-ja A-si-wi-ja, "mistress of Asia" (?), goddess, 261, 271. *See also potnia Aswias*
Potnia, 262
qo-wi-ja, 262
si-to-po-ti-ni-ja, "lady of the grain," 261
s-mi-te-u, Mycenaean Apollo Smitheus, 260
ti-ri-se-ro, Mycenaean Triseros ("Thrice-hero"), 261–2, 269
u-po-jo po-ti-ni-ja, 261
Zeus, 262–3. *See also* Greek religion, gods
ideology of death,
larnakes, 269
offerings, 265–7
o-te-mi, 266
qe-te-jo, "payment" or "fine," 265
personnel, sacred
di-pte-ra-po-ro, religious official, 267
i-je-ro-wo-ko, doer of ritual, 267
ka-ra-wi-po-ro, Mycenaean *kleidoukhos* ("key-bearer"), 267. see also *klawiphoros*
ka-ru-ke (karux), 267
ke-re-ta, 267
ki-ri-te-wi-ja (krithewia), female ritual specialist, 267
pu-ko-wo (purkowos), "fire-priest," 267
wo-ro-ki-jo-ne-jo, 267
po-ti-ni-ja, title for Mycenaean goddesses, 260. see also *potnia, po-tni-ja*
ritual,
i-je-ro-wo-ko, Mycenaean *hierourgos* ("doer of ritual"), 267. *See also iyeroworgos*

te-o-po-ri-a, Greek *theophoria,* 265
sacrifice, 264–5
sa-pa-ka-te-ri-ja (sphakteria or "animals to be sacrificed"?), 265
slaves of a god (hierodules),
do-e-ra, female, 268
do-e-ro, male, 268
temples and sanctuaries,
at Ayia Irini (Ceos), 264
at Kalapodi, 239
at Mt Kynortion, 264
at Phylakopi, 239
da-da-re-jo/daidaleon, sanctuary in Knossos, 263
di-u-jo, sanctuary of Zeus, 263
on Mt Oros, 264
pa-ki-ja-ne, sanctuary at Pylos, 262
po-si-da-i-jo, sanctuary of Posidaon, 262
sa-ra-pe-da, sanctuary in Pylos, 263
theonyms, 258, 260–2, 270–2
Mycenaeans, religion of. *See* Mycenaean religion
mystēria. See Mysteries
Mysteries, ritual in Greek religion, 298–9. *See also* mystēria
mythology,
Assyrian and Babylonian, 55, 61, 77–8
Greek, 250, 282, 284, 299, 301, 342

Nabonassar, Babylonian king, 58
Nabonidus, Babylonian king, 58
Nabopolassar, Babylonian king, 58
nadītu, women dedicated to serve a god, 77
Nairyasangha, "divine messenger," 114
Namtar ("Fate") demon, 49
Nānghaithyā, evil being in Zoroastrianism, 114
Nanna (Nannar), Sumerian moon-god, 39, 43–4, 50, 70
naos, temple, 263, 271, 293. *See also* Greek religion, Mycenaean religion
Naqada II, period in Egyptian history (ca 3650–3300 BCE), 197
Naqsh-e Rostam, site of Achaemenid kings' tombs, 121–2
nar spenta, "life-giving man" in Zoroastrianism, 110
Nāsatyā twins, evil beings in Zoroastrianism, 114
Nasu ("carrion"), demon in Zoroastrianism, 114
Navius, Attus, Roman augur, 355
na-wi-jo. See naos
Nebuchadnezzar I, Babylonian king, 57
Nebuchadnezzar, Babylonian king, 58
necropolis,

General Index 425

Etruscan, 330
Punic, 220–1, 226
Nefertiti, Egyptian queen, Akhenaten's wife, 193
negative confessions, in Egyptian religion, 202
Nemea, games of, 284
nemeto, Celtic sacred grove, 370
Neoptolemos, Greek hero, 293
Neo-Punic, Punic script, 212, 222
Nephthys, Egyptian goddess, 181, 201
Neptune. *See* Nethuns
netjer, "god," 178–9. *See also noute*
netherworld,
  in Assyrian and Babylonian religions, 65–6, 70
  in Syro-Canaanite religion, 136, 146
Nethuns, Etruscan deity, 317–18
netśvis trutnvt frontac. See haruspex fulguriator
Neverita, Etruscan deity, 318
New Kingdom, historical period of Egypt (ca.1550–1070 BCE), 178–9, 181–4, 186, 188–9, 191, 195, 199, 201. *See also* Middle Kingdom
Newstead, Scotland, Celtic offerings at, 378
New Year,
  celebration. *See* Egyptian religion, ceremony. *See* Zoroastrianism, *See also akitu, rō'š haššanâ*
Nile, river in Egypt, 177, 181, 192, 202
Nilsson, Martin Persson, twentieth-century Swedish scholar,
  Minoan Mycenaean Religion, 238–9, 246, 252, 256
Nimrud. *See* Calah
Nin-ana ("Lady of heaven"), 34
NIN.DINGIR, priestess of the Storm god, 142
Nin-dub, "Lord Tablet," Sumerian deity, 47
Nineveh, Assyrian city, 72
Nin-Girsu (Ningirsu), warrior god, patron deity of Girsu, 46–7, 250
Nin-hursaga, "Lady of (the) foothills," Sumerian mother-goddess, 32, 43, 45, 48–9
Nin-lil, "Lady Wind," Sumerian goddess, En-lil's wife, 44, 49
Nin-mah, Sumerian mother-goddess, 34, 49
Nin-sumuna, "Lady of the wild cows," Sumerian goddess, 50
Ninsun, cow goddess in Gilgamesh, 250
Nin-urta, "Lord of the (arable surface of the) earth," Sumerian warrior-god, 44
Nin-urta's exploits, 49
Nippur, city in Sumer, 45, 52
Niqmaddu, king of Ugarit, 146

Nīrangestān, Zoroastrian manual, 103
Nisaba, Sumerian goddess of writing, 47
Nodens, Celtic healing god, 372–3, 379
Noricum (in Austria and Slovenia). *See* Belenus
Nortia, Etruscan goddess, 321
noute, "god," 178
npy, "atonement" or "well-being," 140
Numa, legendary king of Rome (753–673 BCE), 343, 353, 355
Nun, limitless expanse of impenetrably dark water, 183
Nut, Egyptian sky goddess, 181, 183
nympholēptos, "possessed by the nymphs," 291
nymph, 283, 291. *See also* Greek religion

offerings, 37–8, 41, 44–7, 89, 91, 105, 121, 131, 140, 143, 146, 159, 161, 163–4, 166, 168, 179, 187, 190–1, 194–5, 199, 205, 212, 219–20, 225–7, 246, 258, 260, 265–6, 268–70, 283, 289, 291, 294, 298–9, 311, 317, 321, 323–4, 327–9, 350, 367–8, 371, 376, 378–80. *See also* ritual
oikos, Greek household or dwelling place, 263, 287. *See also wo-ko*
oinochoe, wine jug, 300
'ôlâ, "whole burnt offering." *See* Israelite and Judean religions,*See also* holocaust
Old Kingdom, period in Egyptian history (ca. 2649–2150 BCE), 184, 186, 192, 195, 198, 202
Old Testament, 151
Olympia,
  games of, 284
  sanctuaries at, 294, 341
  see also festivals
Olympians, Greek gods, 282
omens,
  in Assyrian and Babylonian religions, 73, 76
  in Etruscan religion, 318, 322
  in Greek religion, 297
  in Hittite religion, 92
  in Mycenaean religion, 258
  in Syro-Canaanite religion, 131, 143–4
  see also divination
Omri, house of. *See* Omride
Omride, northern Israelite dynasty, 154, 156. *See also* Omri
Opening of the Mouth ceremony in Egyptian religion, 179
Opet, Egyptian religious festival, 192

426

General Index

Oppenheim, A. Leo, twentieth-century scholar
of Mesopotamia, 54
oracles,
in Greek religion,
Amphiareion, 286
at Branchidai, 285
at Delphi, 285–6, 297
at Didyma, 285
at Dodona, 285, 297–8
of Trophonios, 297
in Hittite religion, 92–3
in Israelite and Judean religions, 170.
See also divination
Order,
in Egyptian religion, 187. *See also maat*
in Sumerian religion, 31. *See also En-ki and
the world order*
in Zoroastrianism, 104–15, 120–2
Orientalizing period of Etruscan history, 330
Oros, mountain on Aegina, Mycenaean
sanctuary at, 264
Orphic gold leaves, Greek texts, 302.
See also Orphism
Orphism, 302. *See also* Greek religion
orthopraxy, in ancient religion, 5–6, 289
Orvieto, Italy,
Etruscan temples at, 325, 329–30
Oschophoria, Greek religious ritual, 296
Osco-Umbrians, people of Italy, 337
dialect of, 337
Osireion, ceremonial tomb of Osiris, 193
Osiris, Egyptian funerary god, 179, 181–2, 184,
193, 198, 200–1
festival of, 193
Osterstein, Germany, Celtic offerings at, 368
ostraca, ostracon, 142, 221–2
o-te-mi. See Mycenaean religion, offerings
Othniel, first judge of Judah, 157
Ovid, Roman poet (43 BCE-18 CE),
Fasti (Festivals), 356
Metamorphoses (Transformations), 318

Pacha, cult of, 323
pagan, paganism,
as religious terms, 17–18
see also Hellene, *pagani*, polytheism
pagani. See pagan, paganism
pagus Thusca (chōra Tuscan), 212
Pahlavi, Middle Persian, 104
Paian (Paiaon). *See pa-ja-wo-ne*
pa-ja-wo-ne, Mycenaean deity, 260
pa-ki-ja-ne, sanctuary at Pylos, 262

palaces,
Achaemenid, 121
Egyptian, 186
Minoan, 240, 242, 244, 246–9
Mycenaean, 257, 259, 263–4, 266, 268, 272
Sumerian, 46
Syro-Canaanite, 142
Palaeo-Syrian. *See* languages, Semitic
Palaic. *See* languages, Indo-European
Palatine, hill, Roman temples on, 351
Palestine, Judaism in, 8, 20
Palladion. *See* Tsountas' House. *See
also* Mycenaean religion
Pallottino, M., twentieth-century Italian scholar
of the Etruscans, 318
Panammu I, inscription, 131, 146
Panathenaia, Greek festival, 294
Pandrosos, Greek heroine, 295
pantheon, 12, 31, 34, 39, 44, 50, 52, 62, 66–9, 72,
78, 88–90, 112, 131, 133, 135, 138, 177,
210, 220, 222, 238, 249, 260–2, 271–2,
281–2, 284–5, 301, 315, 317–18, 371–2
papratar, impurity, 94–5
papyri, Egyptian,
funerary, 183–4
medico-magical, 197
parā handandatar, "prior arrangement" or
"providence" in Hittite religion, 91
Parisi, Celtic tribe, 383
Paris school. *See* Greek religion
Parker, R., twentieth-century scholar of the
Greeks, 299
Parsis, Zoroastrians, 123
Parthenon, Greek temple on the Athenian
Acropolis, 295
Pasargadae, tomb of Cyrus de Great at, 121
pa-si-te-o-i, "to all the gods." *See* Mycenaean
religion, theonyms
Passover, 162–3. *See also pesahh*
pataikoi, Ptah-images of the Phoenicians, 228
patron deities,
in Assyrian and Babylonian religions, 71, 74–5
in Egyptian religion, 177
in Hittite religion, 89, 91
in Israelite and Judean religions, 158, 171
in Minoan religion, 242, 247
in Sumerian religion, 35, 39, 41, 43, 46
Pausanias, Greek geographer (second
century CE),
Graeciae description (Description of Greece),
381
Pava Tarchies, mirror of, 313, 316, 318, 321

General Index

Peckham, J. B., twentieth-century scholar of the Phoenicians, 220
Peiraieus, sanctuary of Athena at, 282
pekheret. See papyri, Egyptian
Peloponnesians, 281
Pentateuch. *See* Israelite and Judean religions
Pentecost. *See šābû'ôt*
Pergamun, sanctuary of Aesculapius at, 13
Périgueux, Celtic temple at, 380
Persephone. *See* Phersipnei
Persepolis, Achaemenid capital, 121–2
Persians,
   religion of. *See* Zoroastrianism
personnel, sacred,
   augurs, 3, 321–2, 331, 348, 355–7
   diviners, 3, 76, 142, 170
   priests, 11, 14, 72, 76, 78, 87–8, 92, 94, 106,
      121–2, 142, 145, 153–4, 157, 160–2, 165,
      168–71, 186–8, 190–1, 213, 216, 219,
      240–1, 265, 267, 285–8, 292–3, 297,
      310–11, 314, 317, 321–2, 325, 332, 344,
      348, 354–5, 357–8, 374–5
   priestesses, 50, 70, 142, 244, 250, 267, 285,
      292–3, 321–2
   soothsayers, 3
Persson, A. W., twentieth-century scholar of
   Greek religion, 252
pesahḥ. See Passover
Phaleron. *See* Oschophoria
pharaoh, 154, 186
Pheidias, Greek sculptor, 284
Phersipnei, Etruscan Persephone, deity of the
   underworld, 331
phi, female figurine. *See* Mycenaean religion
Philo of Biblos, first/second century CE writer,
   History of the Phoenicians, 132, 138, 209
philosophers and philosophy, 2, 17, 123, 125,
   294, 343
Phoenician. *See* languages, Semitic
Phoenicians, 19, 156, 206, 208–9, 213, 227, 341
Phoenician-Punic Religion, *See* Carthage,
   religion of
phoinīkes, origin of word Phoenicians, 205
phratria. See phratry
phratry, a division of Greek population, 287.
   See also phratria
Phylakopi, Mycenaean sanctuary at, 239
phylē, "tribe," a division of Greek population,
   287
Piacenza liver, 311–12, 317
Pian di Civita, Italy, Etruscan sanctuaries at,
   323–4

Piazza d'Armi, Italy, Etruscan temple at, 324
pietas, piety in Roman religion, 343
Pieva a Socana, Etruscan altar at, 326
Pilier des Nautes (*Nautae Parisiaci*), Celtic
   monument, 373, 377
pillars, cultic. *See massetbot*
pi-pi-tu-na, Mycenaean deity, 260
plague. *See* Resheph, Syro-Canaanite god of
Plato, Greek philosopher (fifth-fourth centuries
   BCE),
   Laws, 290
   Statesman (*Politicus*), 285, 288
   Republic, 299
Platon, N., twentieth-century Greek scholar of
   the Minoans, 240
Plebeian Games, 358
Pliny the Elder, Roman writer (23–79 CE),
   Natural History (*Naturalis historia*), 341, 354,
   374–5
Pliny the Younger, Roman writer (61–112 CE),
   Letters (*Epistulae*), 378
Plutarch, Greco-Roman writer (46–120 CE),
   Lives, 316, 377
pn b'l, "face of Baal," 222. *See also* Carthage,
   religion of
Poeni, Phoenicians, 205
poets and poetry,
   Greek, 259, 281–2, 284, 294
   Sumerian, 48
   Roman, 371, 377
   in Zoroastrianism, 104–10, 116
Poggio Casetta, Etruscan sanctuary, 324
Poinssot, L. and R. Lantier, twentieth-century
   scholars of the Carthaginians, 209
polemarchos, Athenian magistrate, 286
Polybius, Greek historian (200–118 CE),
   Histories, 209–10, 341, 343
polis, Greek city-state, 6, 10, 280, 285–8
polis-religion model of interpretation of ancient
   religious traditions, 11–12, 280, 288,
   302
pollution in Zoroastrianism, 114, 119
polytheism, 17, 19, 31, 88, 124–5, 178, 253,
   260, 369. *See also* pagan, paganism;
   polytheist
polytheist. *See* polytheism
pontifex maximus (supreme pontiff), 339, 346,
   356
porena (porenes), "sacrificial victims"?
   See Mycenaean religion
po-re-no-tu-te-ri-a, Mycenaean festival, 265
po-re-no-zo-te-ri-ja, Mycenaean festival, 265

428   *General Index*

Poros, tomb at, 244
portent,
   in Assyrian and Babylonian religions, 73
   in Hittite religion, 92
   in Roman religion, 3
Portonaccio, Etruscan temple at Veii, 325
Poseidon, Greek god, 283, 295
   altar of, 294. *See also po-si-da-o*
Posidaeia (*po-si-da-e-ja*), Mycenaean deity, 260, 262
po-si-da-i-jo, sanctuary of Posidaon, 263
po-si-da-o, Mycenaean god, 260, 262–3.
        See also Poseidon
Posidonius, Greek philosopher and historian
     (second-first centuries BCE), 374
po-ti-ni-ja, title for Mycenaean goddesses, 260.
        See also potnia, po-tni-ja, theonyms
po-ti-ni-ja A-si-wi-ja, Mycenaean goddess, 261,
    271. *See also potnia Aswias*
po-ti-ni-ja-we-jo, "belonging to potnia."
        See Mycenaean religion
potnia. See po-ti-ni-ja
potnia Aswias. See po-ti-ni-ja A-si-wi-ja
potniaweios. See po-ti-ni-ja-we-jo
po-tni-ja. See po-ti-ni-ja
Potrebica, H., twentieth-century scholar of
     Hallstatt cultures, 369
Praeneste, Latin city, burials at, 349
Praxiteles, Greek sculptor, 284
priest. *See* personnel, sacred
priestess. *See* personnel, sacred
primitivism, approach toward Roman religion,
    345–6
private/domestic religion, 7, 12
processions. *See* festivals
prodigies, 3. *See also* portents
Promised Land, of the Hebrews, 163, 165, 170
Propertius, Roman poet (50–15 CE),
    Elegies (Elegiae), 318
prophecy, prophets,
   in Assyrian and Babylonian religions, 77
   in Celtic religion, 374–5
   in Egyptian religion, 186
   in Etruscan religion, 315
   in Hittite religion, 92
   in Israelite and Judean religions, 160, 169–71
   in Syro-Canaanite religion, 132, 143–4
   in Zoroastrianism, 124
Protective Deity. *See* patron deities.
        See also Hittite religion
Psychro, 247
Ptah, Egyptian deity, 177, 179. *See also* Atum

Puduhepa, Hittite queen, 89
puer Tages. See Pava Tarchies
pu-ko-wo (purkowos), "fire-priest" in Mycenaean
    religion, 267. *See also* personnel,
    sacred
Punic,
   language. *See* languages, Indo-European
   religion. *See* Carthage, religion of
   settlements, 206–8, 227
Punicus. See Poeni
purification, 49, 103, 118–19, 123, 164, 227, 294,
    328
   see also rituals
purity. *See* purification
purkoos. See pu-ko-wo
putto Graziani, Etruscan bronze, 328
   see also statues
Pyanopsia, Greek festival, 296
Pylos,
   cult places at, 257, 262–3
   deities of, 258, 260, 262
   festivals at, 265
   offerings from, 258, 266, 269
   sacrifice at, 265
   see also Mycenaean religion
Pyramid Texts, 181, 183, 198, 200
pyramids, Egyptian, 198
Pyrgi,
   Punic inscriptions from, 227
Pythia, at Delphi, 286, 297

Qadesh, Syro-Canaanite goddess, 135.
        See also Astarte
qe-ra-si-ja. See Mycenaean religion
qe-te-jo, "payment" or "fine." *See* Mycenaean
    religion
   see also offerings
Qingu, Babylonian god, 63. *See also enuma elish*
*qny' rs, "creator/possessor of the earth," 134.
        See also El, Syro-Canaanite religion
qo-wi-ja. See Gwowia
Quirinal, hill, Roman sanctuaries on, 351
Quirinus, Roman god, 344, 347, 351

Ra, Egyptian sun-god, 180, 183, 198, 201
   Litany of, 183. *See also* Atum, ram, falcon
Ra-Horakhty, "Horus of the horizon."
    See Horus
Ramesses II, Egyptian pharaoh (ca 1279–1213
    BCE),
   temple of, 180, 193
Ramesses VI,

General Index

tomb of, 182

rapa 'ūma, "ghosts of King," 146

Ras Shamra, ancient Ugarit, 131

ratu, "models," 106, 110

rb khnm, chief priest of Ugarit, 142

rbtn, "our Lady," Astarate, 222. *See also* Astarte

rebirth, in Egyptian religion, 181, 183, 197

Rechabites, Kenite Bedoun group, 154

reciprocity, hierarchical,
  in Sumerian religion, 40–1, 52

Red Sea,
  crossing of, 133, 160
  parting of, 155, 162, 169
  see also Israelite and Judean religions

Regia, "Royal Palace," 339

regina sacrorum. *See rex sacrorum*

Regolini-Galassi, Etruscan tomb, 330

re-ke-e-to-te-ri-jo. *See lekhe-stro-terion*

reliefs, 121, 289, 326, 330–1, 350, 353

religio. *See* religion

religion,
  as an analytical category, 2, 4
  Assyrian and Babylonian. *See* Assyrian and Babylonian religions
  Celtic. *See* Celts, religion of
  Egyptian. *See* Egyptian religion
  Etruscan. *See* Etruscans, religion of
  Greek. *See* Greeks, religion of
  Hittite. *See* Hittites, religion of
  Israelite and Judean. *See* Israelite and Judean religions
  Minoan. *See* Minoans, religion of
  Mycenaean. *See* Mycenaean religion
  Persian. *See* Zoroastrianism
  Punic. *See* Carthage, religion of
  religio, 1–3
  Roman. *See* Roman religion
  Sumerian. *See* Sumerian religion
  Syro-Canaanite. *See* Syro-Canaanite religion
  see also Christianity

religions, ancient,
  analogy, and the study of, 9
  and geography, the influence of, 13–14
  comparative study of, 24, 26
  see also assimilation, *interpretatio*

religious personnel, *See* personnel, sacred

Renenutet, Egyptian serpent goddess, 197

Renfrew, C., twentieth-century scholar,
  Archaeology of Cult, 239

rĕpā'îm, dead or shades in Syro-Canaanite religion, 146

Resheph, Syro-Canaanite god of plague and

illness, 134

resurrection,
  in Egyptian religion, 194, 201

resuscitation,
  in Syro-Canaanite religion, 133

Reusch, H., twentieth-century German scholar of the Minoans, 242

rex sacrorum, 339, 357. *See also regina sacrorum*, calendars

Rhea, ancient mother of Zeus and Hestia, 282

rings, representations on. *See* Minoan religion*See also* Mycenaean religion

rites. *See* ritual

rites de passage, rites of passage, 94, 247.
  See also ritual

ritual, 1–7, 9–15, 17–18, 31, 34, 37, 46–7, 50–2, 55, 61–3, 65, 70, 75–8, 85, 87–8, 90, 92, 94–6, 103–10, 113, 117–23, 125–6, 131, 139–44, 146–8, 169, 179, 190–1, 198, 210–11, 213, 219–20, 224–7, 237, 242, 246–7, 257, 259, 262–8, 270–1, 281, 285–9, 296, 298–9, 301, 309–10, 314–15, 317, 320, 322–6, 328, 330, 332, 343–6, 348–50, 352–4, 356–8, 367, 369, 373–6, 378, 380, 383–4

Rives, J. B., twentieth-century scholar of Roman religion, 3

Roman religion,
  altars,
    of the Carmentae, 351
    to Consus, 351
    to Mars, in the Campus Martius, 351
  atrium Vestae, "House of the Vestals," 339
  Arval brethren, Roman religious group, 355
  calendars,
    Fasti Praenestini, 356
    Ides (*Idus*) on, 357
    Kalends (*Kalendae*) on, 357
    Nones (*Nonae*) on, 357
    regina sacrorum, 357
    rex sacrorum, 357
  centralization, religious, *See comitia centuriata*, Roman assembly
  divination,
    augurs and augury, 348, 356–7
    auspices, 3, 348, 355
    Navius, Attus, Roman augur, 355
    Numa, legendary king of Rome (753–673 BCE), role in augury, 355
  festivals,
    Equus October, "October horse," 358

430 *General Index*

Roman religion (*cont.*)
  Tubilustrium, festival to Mars, 356. *See also*
    ludi
  funerary practices,
    cremation, 349
    inhumation, 349
  games. *See ludi*
  gods and goddesses,
    Anna Perenna, 351
    Capitoline Triad,
      Juno, wife and sister of Jupiter, 317,
        341, 351
      Jupiter, king of the gods, 317, 341, 344,
        351, 357
      Minerva, 317, 340–1, 351, 371–2, 374, 378
    Diana, goddess of the hunt, 351
    Dii Involuti, Roman "Shrouded Gods,"
      319
    Di Manes, "good gods," 349
    Dius Fidius (Semo Sancus), 351
    Iuppiter Lapis, "Jupiter the Stone," 345
    Juno Lacinia, 210
    Juno Lucina, 351
    Juno Moneta, 351
    Juno Regina, 351
    Juno Sospita,
      statue of, 353
    Jupiter Optimus Maximus. *See* Jupiter
    Mars, god of war, 317, 344, 351, 355–6,
      371. *See also tubilustrium*
    Mater Matuta, 339, 341, 344, 351
    Mercury, 351, 371
    Plebeian triad,
      Ceres, 351
      Liber, 351
      Libera, 351
    Quirinus, 344, 347, 351
    Saturn, 317, 351
    Vesta, 351, 355, 377. *See also* Vestal
      Virgins
    Vulcan, 317, 339, 351
  ludi,
    Capitolini, 358
    chariot races,
      Consualia, 358
      Equirria, 358
      Equus October, 358
    Plebeian Games, 358
    votivi, victory games, 358
  matrons. *See* women, religious roles of
  Mercuriales, religious group, 355
  personnel, sacred,

augur, 348, 355
augur maximus, eldest member of augural
  college, 356
Flamen Dialis, priest of Jupiter, 357
flamen, flamines, priest(s), 321, 345, 355–6
flamines maiores, major flamens, priests of
  Jupiter, Mars, and Quirinus, 344
pontifex maximus (supreme pontiff), 339,
  346, 356
regina sacrorum, 357
rex sacrorum, 339, 357. *See also* ritual,
  calendars
sacerdotes, priests, 343
sacerdotes publici, public priests, 355
Salian priests, 321, 355
pietas, piety, 343
sacra, rituals,
  role of *Flamen Dialis*, 357
  role of *rex* and *regina sacrorum*, 357
  role of *Tubicines*, trumpeters, 357
sodales Titii, religious group, 355
temples and sanctuaries,
  aedes Vestae, "House of Vesta," 346
  at Fontanile di Legnisina, 328
  Lupercal, on the Palatine, 351
  of the Capitoline triad, 351
  of Castor, 351
  of Diana, on the Aventine, 351
  of Dius Fidius, 351
  of Fors Fortuna, in Trastevere, 351
  of Fortuna and Mater Matuta, 351
  of Juno Lucina, on the Esquiline, 351
  of Juno Moneta, on the Arx, 351
  of Juno Regina, on the Aventine, 351
  of Jupiter Feretrius, 351
  of Mars, 351
  of Mercury, 351
  of Minerva, on the Aventine, 351
  of Minerva Medica, on the Esquiline, 351
  of the Plebeian triad, 351
  of Quirinus, 351
  of Saturn, 351
  of Vesta, 351
  Volcanal, for Vulcan, 339
votives, anatomical, 350
Romanization, process of acculturation, 346,
  348, 374
Rome,
  alliance with Carthage, 208, 341
  city of, 336, 338, 341, 347, 350
  kings of, 342–3, 346, 354
  Orientalizing period of, 338, 349

General Index

origins of, 336

religion of. *See* Roman religion

rule by Etruscans, 342, 354

sack of, 342

Romulus Augustulus, last western Roman emperor in 476 CE, 19

Room of the Frescoes. *See* Mycenaean religion

Roquepertuse, Celtic sanctuary at, 367

rō'š haššanâ, New Year. *See* Israelite and Judean religions

Ross, A., twentieth-century scholar of the Celts, 367, 376

Rüpke, J., twentieth-century German scholar of the Romans, 2

Rusellae, Etruscan sanctuary at, 324

ruu. *See* Egyptian papyri

Šabbāt (Sabbath), day of rest. *See* Israelite and Judean religions

Sabellian. *See* Osco-Umbrian

Sabines, people of Italy, 347

šābû'ôt, Pentecost. *See* Israelite and Judean religions

sacerdotes, priests, 343

sacerdotes publici, public priests, 355

sacra, rituals. *See* Roman religion

Sacral-Institutional Complex. *See* Etruscan religion

saeculum, saecula, "age," "generation," "lifetime," 316

sacrifice,

   animal, 91, 119, 122, 141, 162, 164, 219, 246, 265, 291, 322, 352, 376

   as a central religious rite in antiquity, 9

Sader, H., twentieth-century scholar, 221

Salian priests, 321, 355

Samaria, temple of Baal in, 219

Samos, Greek sanctuary at, 296

Samsu-ilum, Hammurabi's son, 57

Sanchuniathon, Phoenician writer, 209

sanctity, 45, 161, 165–6, 224, 381

sanctuaries, sanctuary, 12

   Assyrian and Babylonian, 74

   Celtic, 367–8, 379–80

   Egyptian, 187–8, 190–2, 194

   Etruscan, 310, 314, 318, 321, 323–30

   Greek, 13, 281–2, 286, 289–90, 292–9, 302

   Hittite, 92

   Israelite and Judean, 7, 157, 162–3, 167–9

   Minoan, 240, 242–4, 246

   Mycenaean, 257, 262–6

   Phoenician and Punic, 212–13

Roman, 339, 341, 343–4, 350–2

Sumerian, 43

Syro-Canaanite, 143

see also shrines, temples

San Omobono, Roman temple of Fortuna and Mater Matuta at, 351

Sanskrit. *See* languages, Indo-Aryan

Santorini, island, 246. *See also* Thera

saoshyant, revitalizer, sacrficer in Zoroastrianism, 106, 110, 113, 118, 125

sa-pa-ka-te-ri-ja, animals to be sacrificed in Mycenaean, 265

Sapanu, mountain, 141

Saphon, mountain. *See* Sapanu, mountain

Šapinuwa, Hittite town,

   Storm god of, 89

Saqqara, tomb of Egyptian ruler Djoser at, 198

sa-ra-pe-da, Mycenaean sanctuary in Pylos, 263

sarcophagus, 246, 323

Sardinia, Phoenician settlements on, 206

Sargon. *See* Sharru-kin

Šarrumma. *See* Zippalanda

Satre, Etruscan deity, 317. *See also* Saturn

Saturn, Roman temple of, 351

Saul, first king of unified Israel, 158

Saurwa, evil god in Zoroastrianism, 114

Šaušga, Hittite goddess of Šamuha, patron deity of Hattušili III, 91

scarab in Egyptian religion, 184, 201.

   See also Khepri

scribes, 41, 72, 86, 94. *See also* writing

Sealand Dynasty, Babylonian dynasty, 57

seals,

   cylinder and stamp,

     Assyrian and Babylonian, 67

     Hittite, 85–6

     Sumerian, 37, 40

   Minoan, 237, 246–7, 249

   Mycenaean, 258, 260, 266–7

Second Isaiah, prophet, 171

Second Palace Period, in Minoan history, 240

seers. *See manteis*

Sefire Inscriptions, 131, 145.

   See also Syro-Canaanite religion

Seine, river, Celtic shrine at the source of, 370, 379

Selvans, Etruscan deity, 318, 328.

   See also Silvanus

šĕmā', 153

Semiramis, queen of Babylon and Bactria, 122

Semo Sancus. *See* Dius Fidius

Senate. *See* senators

432 *General Index*

senators,
Roman, 4, 339
Seneca, Roman philosopher (4 BCE-65 CE),
Quaestiones Naturales, 317, 319
Sennacherib, destroyer of Babylon, 58
Senua, Celtic deity, 372
Senwosret III, Egyptian king (ca. 1878–1841
BCE),
mortuary complex of, 193
Sequana, Celtic goddess at the source of the
Seine, 370
Seth, Egyptian storm god, 182, 186, 193
Sethlans, Etruscan deity, 317. See also Vulcan
Seti I, Egyptian king (ca 1294–1279 BCE),
temple of, 193
Shalmaneser III, Assyrian king (858–824 BCE),
60
Shamash, Assyrian and Babylonian sun god,
67–8, 70
Shamshi-Adad, Assyrian king, 59
Shamshi-Adad V, Assyrian king, 60
Shapsh (Shapash), Syro-Canaanite sun goddess,
133–4
Sharru-kin, Sumerian king, 38
Sharuma, son of Hittite sun goddess Hepat, 250
Sharva. See Saurwa
Shataqat, female healing being in
Syro-Canaanite religion, 134
shaten, main Elamite priest, 121
Shavuot. See *šābûʿōt*
Shechem, sanctuary at, 168
shesau. See Egyptian religion, papyri
Shiloh, Israelite temple at, 157, 168. See also Ark
of the Covenant
shrines
Assyrian and Babylonian, 75
Celtic, 367, 378–80
Egyptian, 184, 188, 190, 193
Etruscan, 324
Greek, 285, 294, 298
Hittite, 85, 87
Israelite and Judean, 158
Minoan, 243, 246
Mycenaean, 259, 262, 264, 269
Roman, 339, 352
Sumerian, 43–4
Syro-Canaanite, 141
see also sanctuaries, temples
Shu, Egyptian god, 181, 183
Shurpu, collection of spells and rituals, 76
Shuruppak,
place, 44, 46–7, 49, 64, 68

ruler, 49
see also Assyrian and Babylonian religions,
Sumerian religion
Sicily, settlements in,
Greek, 347
Phoenician, 206, 208, 222, 341
sîtîwʿt. See Carthage, religion of, ritual
sacrifice
Silvanus. See Selvans
Sin, moon god of Haran, 59. See also Assyrian
and Babylonian religions
sin,
in Israelite and Judean religions, 153, 164
in Syro-Canaanite religion, 140
Sinai, mountain, 163, 165
Sinann, Celtic goddess linked to the Shannon,
370
Sirius, 211, 226. See also Dog Star
si-to-po-ti-ni-ja, "lady of the grain," Mycenaean
goddess, 261. See also theonyms
šiunaš antuhšaš, "man of god" or prophet in
Hittite religion, 92
šiunaš per, "house of the god," Hittite temple, 85
sky, 40, 68, 107–8, 119, 181, 183, 247, 317–18, 325,
331, 371, 377, 380. See also sky deities
by name
slavery and slaves, 163, 166, 268.
See also hierodules
Smer[trius], Celtic deity, 373
Smintheus. See *s-mi-te-u*
s-mi-te-u, 260. See also Apollo, Smitheus
Smith, C., twentieth-century historian of
Roman religion, 343
sodales Titii, Roman religious group, 355
solar disc,
in Egyptian religion, 180, 184, 190, 193
see also Aten
Solomon,
Temple of, 159–62
song of the hoe, The, 49
soothsayers, 3
Soranus, epiclesis of Apollo, 318. See also Šuri
sortes, lots, 332
soul, 105–6, 109–11, 113, 115, 117, 121, 146, 223,
269, 320, 367, 381–3
Sourvinou-Inwood, C., twentieth-century
scholar of ancient religions, 239
Sousse, Tunisia, ancient Hadrumetum, 222
Sphagianes. See *pa-ki-ja-ne*
Spain, Phoenician settlements in, 207, 222
spells,
in Assyria and Babylonia, 76

General Index

in Egypt, 177, 195, 197–8, 200

spenta, "holy" or "endowed with swelling (power)." *See* Zoroastrianism

Spentā Ārmaiti, "(life-giving) Humility," Ahura Mazdā's daughter, 106–7, 109, 111, 114, 121

sphakteria. See sa-pa-ka-te-ri-ja

Spiegel, F., nineteenth-century scholar of Iran, 123

spirits, 108, 112, 184, 203, 227, 237, 319–20, 367
cosmic, 108
evil, 112–19, 124
holy, 125
of the dead, 84, 95, 170, 202
of nature, 366

Sraosha, "readiness to listen," Zoroastrian divine being, 108, 113, 118, 125

statues, 48, 87, 132, 140, 146, 179, 189, 199, 211, 249, 259, 261, 265, 289, 294, 314, 321, 325, 328–9, 331, 350, 352–3, 358, 371, 378
cult, 56–7, 62, 67, 72, 75, 179, 188, 191–3, 284, 293–4, 324–5, 331, 350
see also statuettes

statuette. *See* statues

stela (stelae, stele),
Egyptian, 183, 193–4, 199, 202
Hittite, 87
Moabite, 154
Punic, 209, 221–3, 226–7
Syro-Canaanite, 135, 140, 144

sti, "temporal existence" in Zoroastrianism, 111

storm, 49, 87–9, 92, 132–3, 135, 142, 146, 155, 182, 242, 250, 252–3. *See also* storm deities by name

Strabo, Greek geographer (64 BCE–24 CE), *Geography*, 365, 379

Subingen, Celtic burials at, 382

Sucharski, R. and K. Witczak, twentieth-century scholars of the Mycenaeans, 261

Suen, Sumerian moon-god, 40

Suetonius, first/second-century-CE Roman historian,
Divus Claudius (*Claudius*), 375

Suinu, Syro-Canaanite moon-god, 132

Sukkot, festival of, 162–3, 168

Sulis, Celtic goddess,
temple of, 370, 374, 378
see also defixiones, Minerva

Sumer,
religion of. *See* Sumerian religion*See also* Ur

Sumerian,
language, 32, 35–6, 40, 46
see also clay tablets
religion,
cosmos, 34, 37, 52
creation narratives, 34
En-ki and Nin-mah, 34, 49
Death of Gilgamesh, the (as a source), 49
deity lists, 33, 44, 46
demons,
A-Sag ("Arm-beating"), 49
Namtar ("Fate"), 49
devotional literature, 48–9
divination, 47
festivals,
religious, 33, 46–7
gods and goddesses,
An ("The heavens"), 34, 43–4, 52
En-ki (Enki) ("Lord of the earth"), creator god, 32, 34, 37, 44–5, 48–9, 50, 52
En-lil (Enlil) ("Lord wind"), 34, 43–5, 49, 52
Inana, goddess of the Venus star, 34, 41, 43–5, 50, 66; as goddess of physical love and battle, 51. *See also Inana and En-ki*, *See also* Nin-ana
Ishkur, 67
Marduk, 39
Moon-god, 39, 40. *See also* Nanna, Suen
Nanna, 39, 43–4, 50
Nin-ana, 34
Nin-dub ("Lord tablet"), 47
Nin-Girsu ("Lord of Girsu"), warrior god, 46–7
Nin-hursaga, "Lady of (the) foothills," 32, 43, 45, 48–9
Nin-lil ("Lady wind"), 44, 49
Nin-mah ("Majestic lady"), mother-goddess, 34, 49
Nin-urta ("Lord of the [arable surface of the] earth"), 44
Nin-sumuna ("Lady of the wild cows"), 50
Nisaba, goddess of writing, 47
offerings to, 41, 44, 46–7
pantheon of, 31, 44, 50, 52
patron gods, 35, 41, 43, 52
Suen, 40
Utu, sun-god, 39, 43–4
hymns of praise (*zame*), 48, 50

434   *General Index*

Sumerian (*cont.*)
    The Kesh temple hymn, to Nin-hursaga's
       temple, 48
    incantations, 48–9
    rituals,
       for the beginning of the agricultural
         year, 51
       see also The debate between hoe and
        plough
    temples, 31, 37, 40–1, 45–6, 47, 51–2
       hymns to, 48, 50
       ziggurat, 38
       theology, 45, 49
Sumerian King List, The, 37, 39
Sumu-la-el, first Amorite ruler of Babylon
    (1936–1901), 62
sun, 39, 43, 67, 70, 74, 88–9, 92, 122, 133–4, 137,
    155, 180, 183–4, 186, 189, 194, 198, 250,
    369. *See also* sun deities by name
Šuri. *See* Soranus
syncretism, term of analysis of ancient religions,
    16
Syria,
    deities of. *See* Syro-Canaanite religion
Syro-Cannanite religion,
    afterlife, 145–6
       rapa'ūma, 146
    altar, 140
    amulets,
       texts, 145
       to avert evil, 145
    curses, 145
    deity lists, 131
    divination and diviners, 144
       dreams, 143–4
       omens, 131, 143–4
       *lú*HAL, diviner, 142
    festivals,
       religious, 131, 141–2
    gods and goddesses,
       Anat, west Semitic goddess of violence,
         Baal's ally and sister, 133, 136, 138,
         146–7
         see also Anath
       Ashertu (Asherah, Athirat), fertility
         goddess, Baal's wife, 134, 136–8, 140,
         147
       Astarte, 134, 138. *See also* Anat, Ashtoreth
       Baal ("Lord"), Canaanite storm god,
         brother of Anat, husband of Ashertu,
         131, 133–6, 138–9, 141, 143, 145, 147–8.
         See also Hadda

       Baalat ("Lady" of Byblos), head of
         pantheon, with Baal-Shamem, at
         Byblos, 136–9
       Baal-Shamem, head of pantheon, with
         Baalat, at Byblos, 138
       Dagan, 131
       El, 131, 133–4, 136–9, 143–4, 147
       Eshmun, 138
       Hadda (Hadad) ("The Thunderer"),
         storm-god, 131–3, 138, 146.
         See also Baal
       Horon, 145
       Kabkab, 133–4
       Kotharat, birth goddesses, 139
       Kothar-wa-Hasis, craftsman god, 139
       Melqart, 138
       Mot ("Death"), 133, 136–7
       pantheon of, 131
       Qadesh, 135. *See also* Anat, Astarte
       Resheph, god of plague and illness, 134
       Shapsh (Shapash), sun goddess, 133–4
       Shataqat, female healing being, 134
       Suinu, moon-god, 132
       ^dUTU, sun-god, 132, 134
       Yam, 136–7
       Yarih, 134
    incantations, 131, 144–5
    myths, 131, 141, 147
       Aqhat story, 133, 136, 147
       Baal Cycle, 133–4, 136, 139, 141, 147–8
    offerings, 130, 140, 143
    personnel, sacred,
       diviners, 142
       khn, priest. *See* khnm
       khnm, priests of Ugarit, 142
       maš 'artu, priestess, 142
       NIN.DINGIR, priestess of the Storm
         god, 142
       rb khnm, chief priest of Ugarit, 142
       'rbm, "those who enter (the temple),"
         142
       tnnm "guards"(?), 142
    prophecy, prophets, 132, 143–4
       Balaam, "seer of the gods," 132, 144
    rites and rituals, 131, 139, 143, 147
       marzeah, ritual feast, 142, 147
       sacrifice, 140–1
       to alleviate natural catastrophe, 144
       zukru, seven-day rite for the god Dagan,
         142
       see also festivals, religious
    temples, 139, 141–2, 145

General Index — 435

of Baal, 141
of Dagan, 141
underworld. *See* afterlife
see also Canaan, religion of; Ugarit, religion of

Tabernacles. *See sukkôt*
tablets, 33, 40, 62, 64, 84, 86, 120, 130, 314, 341, 364
  administrative, 33, 130, 258
  curse. *See defixiones*
  religious, 131, 142
  school texts, 33
Tabula Capuana, Etruscan calendar, 314
Tacitus, Roman historian (56–117 CE),
  Annals (Annales), 355, 375
  Germany (Germania), 14, 371
  Histories (Historiae), 355
Tages, Etruscan prophet, 315. *See also etrusca disciplina*
Tammuz. *See* Dumuzi
Tangier (Tingis), Punic settlements at, 206
Tanipiya, Hittite town,
  deities of, 89
Tanit. *See tnt*
Taranis, Celtic god of thunder, 370–1, 377, 380
Tarchon, founder of Tarquinia, 315–16
Tarquinia,
  sanctuaries at, 323, 329
  sarcophagi from, 320, 322–3
  tombs from, 330–1, 353
  see also etrusca disciplina
Tarquins, Etruscan kings of Rome, 354
Tarvos Trigaranus, "bull with three cranes," Celtic deity, 373, 377
Taweret, Egyptian fertility goddess, 194, 196
Tazzuwašši, Hittite deity, 89
Tec Sans, Etruscan deity, 318
Tefnut, Egyptian goddess, 181
teletai, initiations. *See* Greeks religion of
Tell Fekherye Inscription, 132, 143, 145
Tell Mardikh, excavations at. *See* Syro-Canaanite religion
temenos, sacred precinct. *See* Mycenaean religion
temples, 8
  Assyrian and Babylonian, 8, 55, 73–8
  Celtic, 371, 373, 375–6, 378–81, 384
  Egyptian, 179, 181, 186–94, 198, 201
  Etruscan, 310, 314, 321, 323–8, 331–2
  Greek, 281, 293–5, 297
  Hittite, 85–9, 94–5
  Israelite and Judean, 153, 157–71
  Minoan, 243–4

Mycenaean, 257, 263–4, 268, 270–1
Punic, 210–13, 215–6, 219, 221, 223, 228
Roman, 339–41, 343–4, 347–8, 350–1, 353, 358–9
Sumerian, 9, 31, 33–4, 37, 40–1, 43–8, 50–2
Syro-Canaanite, 133, 139–43, 145, 147
see also sanctuaries, shrines
templum, inaugurated space, 4, 325
Ten Commandments, 165–6
te-o, Mycenaean term for god, 260. *See also theos*
te-o-po-ri-a, Mycenaean religious ritual, 259. *See also theophoria*
Tertullian, Christian writer (160–225 CE),
  Apologeticus, 5
Teššub, Hurrian storm god, 88–9
Teutates, Celtic deity, 377
texts, 61, 66, 68, 70, 72, 86, 111, 114, 121, 123, 131, 134, 136, 138, 145, 147, 151, 153, 156, 179, 195, 197, 199, 209, 212, 216, 219, 221, 223, 227, 239, 242, 244, 247, 254, 257, 260, 262, 267, 271, 280, 302, 309, 316, 339, 341, 343, 353, 364, 367
  funerary, 177, 183, 201–2
  prophetic, 77
  ritual, 6, 62, 75, 103–4, 106, 125–6, 131, 140, 142–3, 146, 237, 314, 356
  sacred, 3, 102, 191
  see also tablets, clay
Thalna, Etruscan spirit, 319
Tharros. *See tophet*
Thebes,
  Egyptian, 178, 183, 191–2, 194, 201
  Greek and Mycenaean, 256–7, 260, 262–3, 265–7, 320
Thefarie Velianas (Thefarie Vel[i]unas), Etruscan ruler, 327
theology, Sumerian, 45, 49
theonyms. *See* Mycenaean religion
theophoria. See te-o-po-ri-a
Theophrastos, Greek philosopher (371–287 BCE), 288–9
theos, god, 178, 260, 271
Thera. *See* Santorini
thorno-helkterion. See to-no-e-ke-ter-i-jo
Thoth, Egyptian deity, 179, 194. *See also* ibis
Thousand Gods, Hittite gods, 90
Thraêtaona, dragon slayer, 116
Thucydides, Greek historian (460–395 BCE),
  History of the Peloponnesian War, 288
Thuflthas, Etruscan deity, 318
thvāsha, firmament in Zoroastrianism, 111

General Index

Tiamat, female waters. *See enuma elish*

Tiglath-pileser I, Assyrian king (1115–1077 BCE), 67

Tiglath-pileser III, Assyrian king (745–727 BCE), 60

Tigris, river, 36

Timaeus of Tauromenion, Greek writer (350–260 BCE), 342

Tingis. *See* Tangier

Tinia, chief Etruscan deity, 315, 317–18, 328

tiniana, Etruscan week-like period, 357. *See also iśveita, celuta, aperta*

Tinnit-Ashtarte, Punic deity, 221. *See also tnt 'štrt*

Tinnit Phane Ba'al, Punic deity, 223

Tipasa, Punic cemetery at, 207

ti-ri-se-ro-e, "Thrice-hero," Mycenaean deity, 261–2, 269

Tiryns. *See* Minoan religion

Tishtriya, Dog-star, Zoroastrian deity, 112, 114

Titans, 282

Tnnm, 142

tnt, Punic goddess, 221–2. *See also* Tanit, Tinnit

tnt 'štrt. See Tinnit-Ashtarte

tombs, 8, 59, 121–2, 169, 180, 182–4, 187, 192–5, 197–203, 220, 226, 239, 244, 252, 284, 294, 320, 322–3, 325, 329–31, 349, 353, 382

Tomb of the Augurs, 330

Tomb of the Blue Demons, 331

Tomb of the Reliefs, 329–30

Tomba della Scimmia, 353

Tomba delle Bighe, 353

to-no-e-ke-ter-i-jo, Mycenaean festival, 265

tophet, Carthaginian, 209

burials at, 209, 224, 226

excavations at, 209, 222, 224

sacrifice, 209, 224–5

see also Carthage, religion of

tôrâ. See Torah

Torah, "instruction," 161–7. *See also tôrâ*

Toscanos, Phoenician settlement, 207

trade and traders, 14, 41, 46, 205–7, 368–9, 371

Traneus, Etruscan month, 316

Trastevere, temple of Fors Fortuna in, 351

treaties, treaty, 25, 89–90, 145, 209–10, 271, 341

tribute, 25, 160, 170, 247

Tritopatores, Greek deities, 282

Trophonios, Greek oracle of, 297

Troy, ancient city, 122, 294, 320, 347, 376

Tsountas' House. *See* Mycenaean religion, cultcenters

tubicines, trumpeters, 357

Tubilustrium, festival to the Roman god Mars, 356

week-like period, 357. *See also* Etruscan *celuta*

Tudhaliya IV, Hittite king, 90

Tukulti-Ninurta I, Assyrian king, 57, 72

Tunisia, ancient Carthage, excavations at, 209

Turan, Etruscan goddess, 316, 328

Turanians, enemies of the Aryans, 116

Turms. *See* Mercury

Tuscania, Italy, 316

Twelve Tables, codification of Roman laws (450 BCE), 342, 357

Tylor, E. B., nineteenth/twentieth-century English anthropologist, 237

Tyre, Phoenician city, 138, 159, 220–1, 226–8

Uchitel, A., twentieth-century scholar, 78

Ucko, P. J., twentieth-century scholar, 381

Ugarit, modern Ras Shamra, Syria, Baal Cycle from, 133–4

myths from, 136, 147

religion of. *See* Syro-Canaanite religion

temples at, 140–1

texts from, 130–1, 134, 140–2, 145, 239, 247

Ugaritic, dialect, 131

'ûlām, portico of Solomon's Temple, 159

Uley, England, Celtic shrines at, 380

Unas, Egyptian king (ca. 2353–2323 BCE), 181, 198

Uni, Etruscan deity, consort of Tinia, 314, 317–19, 327. *See also* Astarte, Juno

underworld, Celtic, 371, 376, 378

Egyptian, 182, 184. *See also Duat*

Etruscan, 317–19, 331–2

Greek, 283, 293

Hittite, 95

Minoan, 247

Sumerian, 50

Syro-Canaanite, 133–4, 136

see also afterlife

universe, 31, 34–5, 63–4, 68, 69, 73, 90, 96, 105–7, 181, 250, 252–3, 315

u-po-jo po-ti-ni-ja, Mycenaean deity, 261. *See also* theonyms

Ur, first city of Sumer, 5, 38–40, 44. *See also* patron gods

Ur III period, period of Sumerian history, 39

Urhi-Teššub, Hittite king, 91

urns, 224–5, 227, 320, 323, 330–1, 337
Urnfields period of Celtic culture, 367, 369,
    373, 382
Uruk, city in Sumer, 35, 38–41, 43–4, 50
    alabaster vase from, 41–2, 50–1
Uruk period,
    of the history of Sumer, 38, 40–1, 44
Urum, Sumerian city, 40
urwan, "breath-soul," 109, 115
ushabti, Egyptian funerary servant, 200.
        See also afterlife
ushtāna, "life-breath." *See* Zoroastrianism
Utu, Sumerian sun god, 39, 43–4

vahma, "orderly poem," 110
vairiya, "well-deserved," 108
Valerius Maximus, first-century-CE Roman
        writer, *memorable Doings and Sayings*
        (*Facta et dicta memorabilia*), 354
Valley of the Kings, Egypt, 183, 201
Vanth, Etruscan winged goddess, 331
Varro, Marcus Terentus, Roman polymath
        (116–27 BCE),
        On the Latin Language (*De lingua latina*),
        315, 318, 339
Vāyu, Zoroastrian god, 112–13
Vecuvia, Etruscan deity, 315, 331.
        See also prophecy, Vegoia
Vegoia. *See* Vecuvia
Vei, Etruscan deity, 328
Veii, Etruscan town, temple at, 325
Vel Saties, tomb of, 323
Veltune, Etruscan deity, 318. *See also* Vertumnus
Vendidad. See Videvdad
Venus,
    planet, 34, 70, 74
    see also Inana
Verthraghna, warrior god, 114
Vertumnus. *See* Veltune
Vesta, Roman goddess, 351, 355, 377
Vestal Virgins (Vestals), 322, 346–7, 355–6, 376–7
Victory,
    as a goddess, 4
Videvdad, Young Avestan text, 103, 111–12, 114,
        117, 119–20, 123. *See also Vendidad*
videvdad sade, purification ritual, 119
Viereckschanzen, Celtic enclosures, 379
Villanovan period,
    of Etruscan religion, 310, 321, 330, 337
Virgil, Roman poet (70–19 BCE),
    Aeneid, 221
vision-soul. *See daēnā*

visions, 143–4, 171, 247, 298
Vitruvian plan. *See* Vitruvius. *See also* temple
Vitruvius, first-century-BCE Roman architect,
        On Architecture (*De Architectura*), 324
vohu/vahishta manah, "good/best thought."
        See Zoroastrianism
Volcanal, shrine for Roman god Vulcan, 339
Volterra, Etruscan city,
    mirrors from, 326
    temple at, 326
votives. *See* offerings
votives, anatomical. *See* Etruscan
        religion*See also* Roman religion
vows,
    in Etruscan religion, 328
    in Greek religion, 289
    in Punic religion, 212
    in Syro-Canaanite religion, 134, 143
Vulcan. *See* Volcanal
Vulci, Etruscan city, 322
    temple at, 325, 328
    tomb at, 323

wab priests, "pure priests," 191. *See also* Egyptian
        religion
Wagenvoort, Hendrik, twentieth-century
        scholar, 345–6
wanax, Mycenaean king, 259, 263, 268, 270
war and warriors, 44, 46, 48–50, 63–5, 70–1, 75,
        87–9, 94, 114, 116–17, 187, 198, 207–9,
        221, 239, 250, 252, 254, 260, 262,
        282, 342–4, 347–8, 351, 357–8, 365–6,
        369, 371–2, 375–7, 379, 381, 383.
        See also war-gods by name
Warka. *See* Uruk vase
weapons. *See* offerings
Wepwawet, Egyptian funerary god, 179.
        See also jackal
West, M., twentieth-century English scholar,
        302
"Westcar Papyrus, " 186
Westergaard, N. L., nineteenth-century scholar
        of Zoroastrianism, 123
wilderness, 154–5, 163, 165–6
Wilson, J., nineteenth-century writer, 123
wisdom literature,
    Babylonian, 73
    Egyptian, 202
Wishtāspa, Zarathustra's patron, 117, 125–6
Wissowa, G., nineteenth/twentieth-century
        German philologist, 344
Witham, Celtic offerings at, 371, 373

438   *General Index*

wo-ko, Mycenaean sanctuary, 263. *See also oikos*
women,
  religious roles of,
    Roman matrons, 347
    see also individual religions, prophets;
      personnel, sacred; priestesses
world,
  creation of. *See* creation narratives
wo-ro-ki-jo-ne-jo, "ritual intentors," 267
wo-ro-ki-jo-ne-jo ka-ma, 268
worship, 1–2, 5, 7, 11, 13, 17, 73, 86–7, 89, 93–4,
    113, 125, 142, 148, 151, 153–4, 162, 165,
    167–9, 171, 179, 188, 194, 199, 239,
    244, 246–7, 281–3, 285, 287–9, 291–2,
    294, 296, 314, 326, 345, 369
Wrath, dark night sky, 108–9, 113–14
writing,
  cuneiform script in Sumer, 40
  see also scribes

Xanthus of Lydia, Greek fifth-century-BCE
    historian, 122
Xenophon, Greek historian (430–354 BCE),
    Cyropaedia, 122
    Hellenica, 369
Xerxes, Persian king (519–465 BCE), 103, 120, 122
xwaētuwadatha, next-of-kin marriage in
    Zoroastrianism, 111

Yahimilk,
  inscriptions of, 132
Yahweh. *See* YHWH
Yam, "Sea," 136–7
yasht, hymn to an individual deity in
    Zoroastrianism, 103–4, 111–20
yashtā, sacrificer, 121
yasna, sacrifice, 103–4, 113, 118
Yarih, Syro-Canaanite moon, 134
yazata, "deserving of sacrifices."
    See Zoroastrianism
Yazılıkaya, Hittite deity,
  temple of, 87
year, Sothic, 211
Yehawmilk,
  inscriptions of, 132, 135
Yenghyē Hātām, one of four holy prayers in
    Zoroastrianism, 105
Yh. *See* YHWH
Yhw. *See* YHWH
Y-hw-h. *See* YHWH
YHWH, deity of ancient Israel and Judah, 151,
    153–71. *See also* Israelite and Judean

    religions, Yahweh, Yh, Yhw,
    Y-hw-h, Yw
Yima, ruler of the golden age, 116, 127
Yom Kippur, "Day of Atonement," 153, 164
Yunis, H., twentieth-century scholar of the
    Greeks, 290
Yw. *See* YHWH

Zabala, Sumerian city, shrines at, 43
Zadokites, line of priests, 170
Zagreb mummy, 314
Zakir, king of Hamath,
  inscription of, 131, 144
  see also Syro-Canaanite religion
Zaliyanu, Hittite deity, 89
zame, hymns. *See* Sumerian religion
zaothra. *See dauça*
Zarathustra, poet and sacrifice, author of the
    Gāthās, 104–5, 110–13, 116–18, 122–7
  see also Zoroaster, Zoroastrianism
Zašhapuna, Hittite deity, 89
Zawalli, Hittite deity, 96
zebaḥḥ šĕlāmîm, "Sacrifice of Well-being,"
    164
Zechariah, prophet and temple priest, 170
Zeus, Greek "father of the gods," 14, 122, 210,
    252, 254, 260, 263, 271, 281–3
  sanctuaries of, 262–3, 341
  statue of,
    at Olympia, 294
  see also Greek religion, Mycenaean religion,
    di-we, theonyms
Zeus Diktaios. *See Di-wi Di-ka-ta-i-o*
Zeus Herkeios, Zeus "of the enclosure" or "of
    the household," 287
Zeus Meilichios, "the kindly one,"
  cult of, 382
Zeus Polieus,
  sanctuary of, 295
ziggurat, 38
zilc, Etruscan magistrate, 323
Zimri-Lim, king of the Sumerian city of Mari,
    239
Zintuhi, grandchild of the Storm-god of Hatti,
    89
Zippalanda, Hittite town,
  storm god of, 89
Zi-ud-sura ("Life of distant days"), ruler of
    Shuruppak, 49
Zoroastrianism
  altars,
    fire, 122

General Index 439

Ardwī Sūrā Anāhitā, Heavenly River, 112,
115, 117
hymn to, 117
cosmogony,
Young Avestan, 111
cosmos,
and order, 105
sustainer of, 108
chaos, agents of: *daēwa*s (evil gods), 103,
108, 112–14, 117–18, 120; Lie (*drug*),
108–9; Wrath, 108–9, 113–14
death,
Astō-widātu, "Bone-untier," remover of
human consciousness (*baodah*) at, 115
frawashi "pre(-existing)-soul," 105, 109, 111,
115, 117, 121, 125
demons,
Apaosha, demon of drought, 114
Nasu ("carrion"), main cause of pollution,
114
Gods, goddesses, and divine beings,
Ahura Mazdā or Ahuramazdā (All-knowing
Lord/Ruler), good deity, *dātar*
(dadwāh), creator or "establisher" of
ordered cosmos, 104–22, 124, 126
dwelling of, *See* House of Songs
amesha spenta, Life-giving Immortals, 107,
113–14, 126
Anāhitā, protector of Artaxerxes II and
Artaxerxes III, 120
Apām Napāt ("Scion of the Waters"), 114
Ardwī Sūrā Anāhitā, Heavenly River, 112,
115, 117
Airyaman, "heavenly fire," god of peace
and healing, 105, 107–8, 111–12, 114,
118
Ashi, 108, 114, 117, 121
*daēwa*s, evil beings, 103, 108, 112–14,
117–18, 120
Indara, 114
Nānghaithyā, 114
Nāsatyā twins, 114
Saurwa, 114
Sharva, 114
see also daiva
Fashioner of the Cow, 108, 110
Great God, 121
Humility, Ahura Mazdā's daughter and
spouse, 106–7, 109, 111, 114
*khrafstra*s, harmful beings, 114
Life-Giving Immortals (*amesha spenta*),
107, 113–14, 126

Mithra, protector of Artaxerxes II and
Artaxerxes III, 120
Mizhdushī, Zoroastrian goddess "who
grants rewards," 121
Nairyasangha, "divine messenger,"
114
sraosha, "readiness to listen," 108, 113, 118,
125
Tishtriya, Dog-star, Zoroastrian deity,
112, 114
Vāyu, 112–13
Verthraghna ("obstruction-smashing
force"), warrior god, 114.
See also Achaemenid religion, hymns
to deities, *yashts*
heresies,
Zurvanism, 124
House of Songs (*garō.nmāna*), destination of
the good soul (*urwan*), 115
in Iran and Armenia, 8
Isad-wāstar, son of Zarathustra, 118
manthra spenta, Life-giving Poetic Thought,
112
myth of Zarathustra,
in Young Avesta, 116–18
dragon-slayers, 116
Kersāspa, 116
Thraētaona, 116
dragons,
Azhi Dahāka, 116
Kawi Wishtāspa's war,
against Arjad-aspa and his Khiyonians,
117
kawis' war,
against, Frangrasyan and the Turanians,
Aryans' archenemies, 116
Yima (ruler of golden age), 116, 127
prayers, holy, 104
Ahuna Vairiya (*Yathā ahū vairiyō*), 104–6,
117
Airyaman Ishiya, 105, 107
Ashem Vohū, 105, 117
Yenghyē Hātām, 105
prototypes of living beings,
Cow, 114
Gaya Martān, 114
rituals,
coming-of-age ceremony,
tying on the girdle (*aiviyānghana*) in,
119
haoma, divine plant used in, 118
morning (*yasna*), 118

440 *General Index*

Zoroastrianism (*cont.*)
  use of sacrificial grass (*barsman, barsom*)
    in, 119
  to Mithra, 119
  videvdad sade, purification ritual, 119
  see also, libations, Achaemenid religion,
    zaothra
  sacred texts,
    Avesta, 102–3, 120, 122–3
      Old Avesta, ritual text, 103–4, 107, 111,
        116, 119, 126
      *Gāthā*s, "songs," 103–5, 107, 109, 111,
        113–14, 117–18, 123–7
      Yasna Haptanghāiti, sacrifice in seven
        sections, 103–4, 107, 109
      Young Avesta, 1–7, 103–4, 109, 111–12,
        114–17, 119, 123–4
      Khorda Avesta, short hymns and other
        ritual texts, 103
      Videvdad (*Vi-daēwa-dāta, Vendidad*),
        collection of texts
        concerned with purification rituals,
        103, 111–12, 114, 117, 119–20, 123
      yashts, hymn to individual deities,
        103–4, 111–20
      Yasna, text accompanying the *yasna*
        ritual, 103–11, 113–19, 123, 126
      Hērbedestān, manual of priestly schooling
        and performance of rituals, 103
      Nīrangestān, manual of priestly
        schooling and performance of rituals,
        103
  sacrifice,
    animal, 119
    gift-giving,
      of "pre-souls" (*frawashi*s), 105
    evil sacrificers,
      *karpan*s, 105
      *kawi*s, 105

"Ford of the Accountant" (*cinwatō pertu*),
  where soul's thoughts and deeds were
  Weighed, 106, 110, 115
khratu (guiding thoughts) of sacrificers,
  106
maga, exchange of gifts, 106
  to Airyaman, 112
  to Life-giving Poetic Thought (*manthra
    spenta*), 112
yashtā, sacrificer, 121
  becoming *saoshyant*, "revitalizer," 107,
    110, 113, 118, 125
  fee of (*mizhda*), 107
yasna, sacrifice, 103–4, 113, 118
theonyms,
  Ārmati-dāta, "(child) given by Life-giving
    Ārmaiti," 121
  Hauma-dāta, "(child) given by Hauma,"
    121
  Mazda-yazna, "who sacrifices to (Ahura)
    Mazdā," 121
  Mithra-dāta, "(child) given by Mithra," 121
  Mithra-pāta, "protected by Mithra," 121
  Mithra-yazna, "who sacrifices to Mithra,"
    121
  Spanta-dāta, "(child) given by Life-giving
    Ārmaiti," 121
Wishtāspa, Zarathustra's princely patron, 117,
  125–6
xwaētuwadatha, next-of-kin marriage,
  of Zarathustra and his daughter after
  sacrifice, 111
Zarathustra, poet and sacrifice, author of the
  Old Avesta, 104–5, 110–13, 116–18,
  122–7. *See also* Persians, religion of;
  Zoroaster
zukru, seven-day rite for the god Dagan, 142
Zurvanism, Zoroastrian heresy, 124
zurwan, "time," in Zoroastrianism, 111

INDEX OF CITATIONS

Textual and Material Sources

Aesch. *Ag.* — Aeschylus, *Agamemnon*
198–217 — 376

Aesch. *Supp.* — Aeschylus, *Suppliants*
890 — 259

Agramer Mumienbinden (*liber linteus*) — 348

Althiburus inscription (*KAI* 159) — 212
159.2–4 — 212
4 — 212
5 — 212–13
7 — 213
8 — 212–13, 219–20
8–9 — 212
9 — 212

Amarna letters — 155

Amman Citadel Inscription (*COS* 2.24) — 144

Amphiareion regulations (*LSCG*, 69) — 292, 293 n 35

An-Anum text list — 62

ANET — *Ancient Near Eastern Texts Relating to the Old Testament*
xi

App. *Pun.* — Appian, *Punica*
59 — 212

Aristotle, *Constitution of the Athenians* — 287 nn 17–18

Arn. *Adv. nat.* — Arnobius, *Adversus Nationes*
2.62 — 320
3.40 — 319
7.26 — 310

Archedamos of Thera inscription — 291 n 29

Aristophanes, *Clouds* 506–8 — 297 n 46

Arnth Churcles epitaph (Rix *ET* AT 1.171) — 323

Arslan Tash amulets — 145

Assyrian king list — 59

Atunis mirror — 211

augur statuette (Louvre) — 321

Aug. *Civ.* 10.1 — Augustine, *De civitate Dei*
2 n 4

Aulus Caecina — *De etrusca disciplina*
315

Aul. Gell. — Aulus Gellius, *Noctes Atticae*
356 n 53

Avesta — 102–3, 120, 122–3

Old *Avesta*, — 103–4, 107, 111, 116, 119, 126

*Gāthā*s — 103–5, 107, 109, 111, 113–14, 117–18, 123–7

Yasna Haptanghāiti — 103–4, 107, 109

441

Index of Citations

Avesta (cont.)

Young Avesta,	1–7, 103–4, 109, 111–12, 114–17, 119, 123–4
Khorda Avesta,	103
Videvdad (Vi-daēwa-dāta)	103, 111–12, 114, 117, 119–20, 123
yashts	103–4, 111–20
Yasna,	103–11, 113–19, 123, 126

Azatiwada inscription
(KAI 26) — 132

"Babylonian Theodicy"	73
Bisenzio urn	323
BM	British Museum
Book of the Dead (Book of Going forth by Day in the Afterlife)	181, 201–2
Book of Gates	201
Book of Two Ways	200–1
Books of the Afterlife, (Books of the Underworld)	181, 184
Books of Heaven and Earth	201
Brontoscopic calendar	314
bronze and lead weight	327
building of Nin-Girsu's temple, The (ETCSL 2.1.7)	47

Caecina	315, 332
Caes. B. Gall.	Caesar, Bellum Gallicum
1.2–5	369
6.13–16	374
6.14	367 n 13
6.16	376–7
6.17	371–2
6.19	383
7.55	369
Capua Tile (Rix ETTC)	314
Carthage Tariff (KAI 74)	132, 140
CAT	The Cuneiform Alphabetic Texts from Ugarit, Ras Ibn Hani and Other Places
	xi

cenotaph of Seti I	182
Censor. D. N.	Censorinus, De die natali
17.5–6	316
Chamalières and Larzac Tablets	364
Cic. Font.	Oratio pro Fonteio
33	369
Cic. Leg.	Cicero, De legibus
2.48	356
Cic. Nat. deor.	Cicero, de Natura Deorum (On the Nature of the Gods)
1.3	343
1.117	343
3.2.4	3
3.5	343
cippus (ILLRP 3)	339
CIS	Corpus Inscriptionum Semiticarum
	xi
I 165	216
I 167	216
I 168	216
I 170	216
I 3915–3917	216
I 3922–5275	222
I 4937.3–5	223
I 5511	223
I 5632.6–7	223
cities list, The,	41
CMS	Corpus der minoischen and mykenischen Siegel
	xi
I, n 17	259
Code of Hammurabi	71, 166
Coffin Texts	181, 200–1
Coligny Calendar	364
COS	The Context of Scripture
	xi
1.55	134
Covenant Code	165–6
Ctesias of Cnidus, History of the Persians	
	122

Textual and Material Sources

443

cursing of Agade, The
(ETCSL 2.1.5) — 39

DCSL — Diachronic Corpus of Sumerian Literature — 32

death of Gilga-mesh, The
(ETCSL 1.8.1.3) — 49

debate between hoe and plough, The
(ETCSL 5.3.1–5.3.7) — 51

Deir 'Allah Inscription — 132, 144, 170

Demosthenes

18.258–260 — 299 n 52

Descent of Ishtar to the Netherworld (Epic of Gilgamesh, Tablet VI, obv. col. i-iii.) — 70

Diodorus Siculus, Bibliotheca historica

5.27 — 379
5.28 — 383
5.29 — 367 n 11
5.32 — 365, 377

Dion. Hal. — Dionysius of Halicarnassus — 343

1.68.2 — 352
4.74.4 — 346
7.72–3 — 354

Dumu-zid and En-ki-imdu
(ETCSL 4.08.33) — 51

Egyptian Report of Wen-Amon — 144
Elamite tablets — 120–1

En-ki and Nin-mah
(ETCSL 1.1.2) — 34, 49

En-ki and the world order
(ETCSL 1.1.3) — 34, 49

enuma elish, — 57, 61–5, 68, 71, 74

Epic of Gilgamesh, — 70

Eshmun ostraca (KAI 283.13, 284b e) — 221

ETCSL — Electronic Text Corpus of Sumerian Literature

— 32

Etruscan linen book
(Rix ET LL) — 314

Euripides — 290

Eusebius, Praeparatio evangelica
8 — 209

Fast. Praen. — Fasti Praenestini — 356

Fest. — Festus, De verborum significatu

340–2 L — 354
439.18–22 L — 355

First Botorrita Inscription — 364

flood story, The (ETCSL 1.7.4) — 49

François Tomb — 323

Göttingen bronzes — 321

"Great Hymns to the Aten" — 194

Greg. Tours Vita Patr. — Gregory of Tours, Vitae Patrum

c.6 — 379

Gundestrup cauldron — 370

Hattušili III's "Apology" — 91

Heraclitus, Fr — 5, 294 n 38

Hērbedestān — 103

Herodotus, Histories, — 103, 179

1.46–9 — 286
1.131 — 122
1.140 — 122
2.53.2 — 281
3.37.2 — 228

Hesiod, Theogony, — 281

Hesiod, Works and Days

334–40 — 299

Hieraconpolis tomb — 197

Homer, Il. — Homer, Iliad

6.302–3 — 294
21.470 — 258
23.744 — 205

Homer, Od. — Homer, Odyssey

4.43 — 261
6.305 — 261

Index of Citations

Homer, *Od.* (*cont.*)

13.272	205
14.288	205
15.415	205
15.419	205
15.473	205
Horace, *Ep.*	Q. Horatius Flaccus, *Epistulae*
2.1.156–7	16
Idrimi stela (*ANET* 557)	144
Ikhernofret's stela	193
ILLRP	*Inscriptiones Latinae Liberae Rei Publicae*
Inana and An (*ETCSL* 1.3.5)	50
Inana and En-ki (*ETCSL* 1.3.1)	35, 49
Inana's descent to the netherworld (*ETCSL* 1.4.1)	50
instructions of Shuruppak, The (*ETCSL* 5.6.1)	49–50
"Instructions to Temple Officials" (*KUB* 13 i 21–26)	139
Isis temple in Carthage (*CIS* 1 6000bis.8)	228
Johannes Lydus	315
Josephus, Titus Flavus *C. Ap.*	*Against Apion*
1.116–19	209
121–25	209
156–58	209
AJ	*Antiquities of the Jews*
8.144–49	209, 324
9.284–87	209
Justin	
24.4–8	369
25.2.9	369
KAI	*Kanaanäische und aramäische Inschriften* xi
4	138
4:1–4	138

5	138, 140
6	138, 140
7	138, 140
10	138
10:2	139
13	138, 142
14	138, 142, 145
17	140
25	140
26 A ii 19–iii 1	219
26 A iii 18	134
26 iii 2–6	143
38	140
43	140
61 A, B	141
66	134
74	216
79.10–11	223
175.2	222
176.1–2	222
201	140
225	145
277.9	226
303.7	219
6916, 60:1	142
Kesh temple hymn, The (*ETCSL* 4.80.2)	48
Khirbet el-Kom tomb inscriptions	169
KUB	*Keilschrifturkunden aus Boghazköi* xii
14.10 iv	9–13, 92
21.27 i	3–6, 89
22.70 i	7–11, 93
24.2 rev. 12D-16D	91
24.3 ii 4D-17D	91
25.6 iv 5–24	94
29.1 i 17–19	92
29.4 i 1–12	87
38.1 iv 1–7	88
41.8 iv 29–32	95
Kuntillet 'Ajrud inscriptions	169
Kuttamuwa inscription	146
Lactantius, *Inst.* 4.29	Lactantius, *Divinarum institutionum* 1

Textual and Material Sources

Larth Cafates inscription
(Rix *ET* Um 1.7) 322
Lex Hortensia, 342
Lex Ogulnia, 342, 348, 357
Linear B tablets
KN C 941.B 265
KN Fp 1 267
KN Gg702 258
KN V 52 270
KN V 280 258, 266
K-P70 264
K-P72 264
K-P72a 261
K-P74a 262, 264, 269
K-P74b 262, 264
K-P76 264
K-P78 262
K-P79 264
K-P80 262, 264
K-P88 262
K-P96 265
K-P106 265
K-P108 262
PY Cn 1287.6 267
PY Ea59 262
PY Ep74 267
PY Fr 1206 271
PY Jn829 263
PY Tn 316 258, 262, 265–6, 268–9
PY Un2 268
PY Un718 263, 268
PY Un718.11 267
TH Av 106 [+] 91, 267
TH Of 26.3 265
"Litany of Ra" 326
Liv. Livy, *Ab Urbe Condita*
343
1.35.7–9 354
2.2.1 346
5.1.6 315
5.33–35 369
5.35–49 369
6.41 348
7.2.1–12 354
8.6 376
10.26 367 n 11
22.57 377
23.11.7 210
23.24 380

24.12.4 210
26.11.4 210
28.46.15–16 210
33.27.4 344
Lucan. *Phars.* Lucan, *Pharsalia*
1.444–446 371, 377
1.455–8 367 n 13
Lucian, *Syr. d.* Lucian, *De Syria dea*
6 132, 213
Lugal-banda and Nin-sumuna (DCSL) 50
Lydus, Johannes 315

Macr. *Sat.* Macrobius, *Saturnalia*
1.15.9–12 356
Man and His God, A, 73
Marseilles Tariff (*KAI* 69) 132, 140, 216–17
1–2 216
3–12 216
3–15 213
13 216
14 216
15 216
16–17 216
17 220
18–19 216
20–21 216
Mart. Cap. *Nupt.* Martianus Capella, *De nuptiis Mercurii et Philologiae*
I. 45–61 317–18
Menander, *Dyskolos*
412 283 n 6
Mesha inscription (*KAI* 181:14) 132, 144, 154
Milkpilles epitaph (*CIS* I 6000bis.3b-4)
223
Mochus *FGrH* Mochus, *Fragmente der griechischen Historiker*
87 F67 209
784 F6 209

Nigidius Figulus 314, 332

Index of Citations

Nin-urta's exploits (*ETCSL*
    1.6.2) — 49
Nirangestān, — 103

"Orator" bronze
    (Florence) — 328
Ov. *Fast.* — Ovid, *Fasti*
    2.21–2 — 356
Ovid *Metamorphoses*
    14.623–771 — 318

"Palladion" from Tsountas'
    House (*CMS* 1,
    n. 17)
    259 — 262
Panammu I Inscription
    (*KAI* 214) — 131, 140, 146
Pausanias
    10.21 — 381
Pava Tarchies mirror — 316, 318, 321
Pesaro inscription
    (Rix *ET* Um 1.7) — 322
phanēbalos coin — 222
Philo of Byblos, *History of
    the Phoenicians* — 132, 138, 209
Philostratus, *Ant.* — Philostratus,
    *Antiquities
    of the Jews*
    (Josephus)
    10.228 — 209
Philostratus, *Ag. Ap.* — Philostratus,
    Against Apion
    (Josephus)
    1.143–44 — 209
Philostratus, *FGrH* — Philostratus,
    "Fragmente der
    griechischen
    Historiker"
    789 F1a-b — 209
Piacenza Liver (Rix *ET*
    Pa 4.2) — 311, 317
Pilier des Nautes (*Nautae
    Parisiaci*) — 373, 377
Plato, *Laws,*
    10 885b — 290 n 28
    10 909d–910d — 285 n 13
Plato, *Politicus*
    290c — 288 n 21
Plato *Republic*

364b-65a — 299 n 52
Plin. *NH* — Pliny the Elder,
    *Naturalis
    historia*
    8.65 — 354
    16.95 — 374
    30.3 — 375, 377 n 42
    30.4 — 374–5
    35.157 — 341
Pliny, *Ep.* — Pliny the
    Younger,
    Epistulae
    8.8 — 378
Plut. *Fab. Max.* — Plutarch, *Fabius
    Maximus*
    18 — 377
Plutarch, *Life of Sulla*
    7.3–6 — 316
Polyb. — Polybius,
    Histories
    341, 343
    7.9 — 209
    7.9.2.-3 — 210
    7.9.3 — 210
Pomponius Mela — 367 n 13
Propertius — Propertius,
    Elegiae
    4.2 — 318
Punic plaque (*KAI* 302) — 223–4
    1 — 223
    4–5 — 223
    6–7 — 226
putto Graziani — 328
Pyramid Texts — 181, 183, 198,
    200
Pyrgi inscription (*KAI*
    277)
    277.4–5 — 211
    277.9 — 211
    277.9–11 — 212
    277.9b-11 — 211
Pyrgi tablets (Rix *CR*
    4.3–4.5) — 314, 327, 341

Regulation pertaining to a
    king (*ILLRP* 3)
    339
RIB — *The Roman
    Inscriptions of
    Britain*
    xii

Textual and Material Sources

213 372
219 377
Rix *ET* Helmut Rix,
Etruskische
Texte, Editio
Minor
xii
AT 1.161, 1.96 322
Um 1.7 354

Sarepta ivory plaque
(*KAI* 285.304) 221
Sefire Inscriptions
(*KAI* 222–224) 131, 145
Seneca, *Quaest. nat.* Seneca,
Quaestiones
naturales
2.32.2 317
2.41 319
song of the hoe, The
(*ETCSL* 5.5.4) 49
Strab. *Geog.* Strabo,
Geography
4.1.13 379
4.4.4 367 n 13
4.4.5 367 n 11, 377
4.5.4 365
Suet. *Claud.* Suetonius,
Divus
Claudius
25 375
Sumerian king list, The
(*ETCSL* 2.1.1) 37, 39, 59
Suti and Hor's stele
(BM 826) 183

Tabula Capuana 356
Tac. *Ann.* Tacitus,
Annales
1.54 355
14.29–30 375
Tac. *Germ.* Tacitus,
Germania
43 371
Tac. *Hist.* Tacitus,
Historiae
2.95 355
Tell Fekherye
Inscription 132, 140, 143, 145
temple hymns, The
(*ETCSL* 4.80.1) 50

terracotta Atunis figure
(Gregorian Etruscan
Museum, Vatican
14147) 212
Tertullian, *Apol.* Tertullian,
Apologeticus
24.7 5
Theophrastos, *Fr.* Theophrastos,
Fragmenta
12 288–9
Thucydides, *History of the*
Peloponnesian War
2.38 288
Timaeus 342
Tomb of the Augurs 330
Tomb of the Blue Demons 331
Tomb of Ramesses VI 182
Twelve Tables 342, 357

Ugaritic Texts
CAT 1.1–1.2 133
CAT 1.1 iii 24 138
CAT 1.2 I 10 138
CAT 1.2 iv 136
CAT 1.3 i 2–17 139
CAT 1.3 i 2–27 148
CAT 1.3 v 19–25 136
CAT 1.4 ii 11 134
CAT 1.4 iii 32 134
CAT 1.4 iv 38–39 136
CAT 1.4 vi 40–59 139
CAT 1.5–1.6 133
CAT 1.5 i 1–3 137
CAT 1.5 ii 2–4 137
CAT 1.5 vi 12–19 136
CAT 1.5 vi 18–22 137
CAT 1.6 i 40 138
CAT 1.6 ii 13 138
CAT 1.6 iii 14–21 133
CAT 1.10 137
CAT 1.14 ii 24–25 138
CAT 1.14 iii 52–54 143
CAT 1.14 iv 34–43 140
CAT 1.15 ii 16–20 136
CAT 1.15 iii 25–30 134
CAT 1.16 i 20–23 139, 146
CAT 1.16 v 24-vi 9 134
CAT 1.17 i 2–15 139
CAT 1.17 i 34–43 136
CAT 1.17 ii 26–42 139
CAT 1.17 v 3–33 139

448 — Index of Citations

Ugaritic Texts (*cont.*)

CAT 1.17 vi	137
CAT 1.18 i 6–14	136
CAT 1.18 iv	137
CAT 1.19 i 40–46	133
CAT 1.19 ii 21–25	145
CAT 1.19 iii 42–45	145
CAT 1.19 iv 24–25	140
CAT 1.23	143, 147
CAT 1.23:7	142
CAT 1.23: 34–37	136
CAT 1.24	139, 143
CAT 1.39	146
CAT 1.40	140
CAT 1.41/87	141
CAT 1.48	146
CAT 1.63	144
CAT 1.78	144
CAT 1.86	144
CAT 1.100	145, 147
CAT 1.101 rev. 1–6	143
CAT 1.103	144
CAT 1.105	146
CAT 1.106	141, 146
CAT 1.107	145, 147
CAT 1.108	143, 146
CAT 1.112	141
CAT 1.114 136	142, 147
CAT 1.119	141, 143
CAT 1.124	145, 147
CAT 1.126	141
CAT 1.127	144
CAT 1.140	144
CAT 1.141–144	144
CAT 1.155	144
CAT 1.161	146
CAT 1.169	144
Uruk (Warka) vase	41–2

Val. Max.	Valerius Maximus, *Facta et dicta memorabilia*
2.4.7	354
Varro, *ling.*	Varro, *De lingua latina*
5.143	315
5.46	318
5.155	339
Vercelli Inscription	364
Verg. *Aen.*	Vergil, *Aeneid*
1.738	221
Vitruvius, *De architectura*	
IV.7	324
"Westcar Papyrus"	186
Xanthus of Lydia	122
Xenophon, *Cyropaedia,*	
8.3.24	122
Xen. *Hell.*	Xenophon, *Hellenica*
7.1.20	369
Yahimilk Inscriptions	
(*KAI* 4)	132
Yehawmilk Inscriptions	
(*KAI* 10)	132
yd'mlk pendant (*KAI* 73)	220
Zakir Inscription	
(*KAI* 202)	131, 144
Zoroastrianism's Four Holy Prayers	104
Ahuna Vairiya	104–6, 117
Airyaman Ishiya,	105, 107
Ashem Vohū	105, 117
Yenghyē Hātām	105

Scriptural Sources

Amos	
9	156
1 Chronicles	
16	162
2 Chronicles	
2:7	158
5–7	162
20:12	223

29:25	170
30	162
35	162
35:15	170
Deuteronomy	
5	166
12	167
12:3	222

Scriptural Sources

14	164	25:27–34	155
16	163	27	155
16–17	165	28	157, 162, 169
17:14–20	165	32	157, 164
28–30	156	35	157, 162
33 (Song of Moses)	155		
33:2	154	**Habakkuk**	
		3 (Psalm of Habakkuk)	155, 164
Exodus		3:3	154
3	154	3:7	154
3:14	153	3:8	133
14–15	155, 162	**Hosea**	
15	164	4	156
15:8–10	133		
18	154	**Isaiah**	
19	160	6:8–10	138
19–40	165	11	156
20–24	165	12	164
20:19–23	160	14	134
22:17	170	24	156
23	163	25:8	133
25–30	166	27:1	133, 137
32	137	28	170
33–34	170		
34	163	**Jeremiah**	
28–29	162	35	154
34	166	**Job**	
34:19–20	169	38	156
35–40	166	41:1	137
40	160	**Joshua**	
Ezekiel		4–5	157
1	160	5	155, 162
8	169	22:23	220
20:29	244	24	157
43:14	160	**Judges**	
45:25 220		1:16	154
47–48	156	4–5	169–70
Ezra		5 (Song of Deborah)	155, 164
3	162	5:4	154
3–6	161	11	169
6	162	13	139
		18:30	157
Genesis		21	157, 162
1	159	**1 Kings**	
1:1–2:3	156	2	162
3	169	3	165
4	154	5–8	158
9	164	8	162
14	155, 162	12	168
18	139	12:25–33	137
21	169	13	162
25–35	155	16	169

Index of Citations

1 Kings (cont.)

17	154
17–18	156
18	162
19	154
22:19–23	138

2 Kings

3	169–70
3:26–27	141
9–10	154, 156
10:24	219
10:25	219
21	169
22	170
24–25	56

Leviticus

1	164
1:14–17	220
1–16	166
2	164
3	164
4–5	164
5:10	220
8	162
10	161
10:10–11	161
16	160, 164
17–26	166
23	163
23:37	220

Malachi

1:8	139

Nehemiah

8–10	162, 167

Numbers

3–4	169
3–8	161
3:40–51	161
4	162
8	162, 169
8:23–26	162
9	168

17–18	161
22–24	170
26:59	161
28–29	163

Proverbs

8	156
30	156

Psalms

2	164
6	164
7	164
8	164
18	160
30	164
34	164
46	164
48	164
68	155, 160
74	156
74:12–17	133
74:14	137
76	164
77:16–20	133
89	146, 164
96–99	164
104	155
105	164
106	164
110	164
114:2–6	133
118	164
120–134	164

1 Samuel

1	162, 169
1–2	169
1–4	157
28	170
31	158

2 Samuel

6	162
7	158
7:14	139
12	165
24	159

Lightning Source UK Ltd.
Milton Keynes UK
UKHW022157151218
334096UK00018B/276/P